T0295786

QUANTITATIVE EQUITY PORTFOLIO MANAGEMENT

QUANTITATIVE EQUITY PORTFOLIO MANAGEMENT

SECOND EDITION

AN ACTIVE APPROACH TO PORTFOLIO CONSTRUCTION AND MANAGEMENT

LUDWIG B. CHINCARINI & DAEHWAN KIM

NEW YORK   CHICAGO   SAN FRANCISCO   ATHENS   LONDON
MADRID   MEXICO CITY   MILAN   NEW DELHI
SINGAPORE   SYDNEY   TORONTO

1 2 3 4 5 6 7 8 9   LCR   27 26 25 24 23 22

ISBN   978-1-264-26892-4
MHID   1-264-26892-0

e-ISBN 978-1-264-26893-1
e-MHID   1-264-26893-9

This publication is designed to provide accurate and authoritative information in regard to the subject matter covered. It is sold with the understanding that the publisher is not engaged in rendering legal, accounting, or other professional service. If legal advice or other experts assistance is required, the services of a competent professional person should be sought.

—From a declaration of principles jointly adopted by a committee of the American Bar Association and a committee of publishers.

McGraw Hill books are available at special quantity discounts to use as premiums and sales promotions or for use in corporate training programs. To contact a representative, please visit the Contact Us pages at www.mhprofessional.com.

McGraw Hill is committed to making our products accessible to all learners. To learn more about the available support and accommodations we offer, please contact us at accessibility@mheducation.com. We also participate in the Access Text Network (www.accesstext.org), and ATN members may submit requests through ATN.

CONTENTS

FOREWORD

$\mathbf{T}$his is an ambitious book that both develops the broad range of artillery employed in quantitative equity investment management and also provides the reader with a host of relevant practical examples. While the authors firmly take the view that active management can be rewarded, their book offers a solid practitioner's guide to quantitative passive management in the efficient-market/index-fund world on the one hand and to active managers on the other. Far too often quantitative management is equated with passive management, and active quantitative management is thought to be an oxymoron. The authors' rigorous dispelling of this tired canard opens the way for the traditional active manager to make use of quantitative tools. Readers of this book soon learn that quantitative management is a technology that they can use to hone their evaluation of their fundamental ideals, implement them successfully, and finally, control the risk of the portfolios they manage while doing so.

Often investment ideas are anomalies that fit uncomfortably, if at all, with neoclassical efficient-market theories. Typically, such anomalies are observations formed from studying historical stock market returns. This book surveys the rich collection of anomalies that form the basis for much of what is current practice in the active quantitative arena. The student of portfolio management who is interested in learning what academics and empiricists have discovered will find this of particular interest. What about the small-firm effect or momentum? This book is an excellent place to introduce the manager to these important anomalies.

But where this book excels is in melding theory with practice. Issues of liquidity, leverage, market neutrality, transactions costs, and the pitfalls and virtues of backtesting that are so often skirted in other treatments take center stage here. So, too, there is an extensive analysis of optimal after-tax portfolio management, a topic often not even mentioned in other books. Throughout this book, the authors expend much useful effort on ridding their analysis of naive reliance on mathematics at the expense of practicality.

While the mathematics can at times be demanding, it is about at the level of the CFA requirements and should be well within the command of the analytic abilities of most portfolio managers.

Helpfully, the prose is lively and far removed from the usual pedantry that surrounds mathematics in finance. Extensive questions test the reader's understanding and make this book perfectly suited to the needs of an advanced course in investment management at the MBA or PhD level.

Stephen A. Ross
The late Franco Modigliani Professor of
Finance and Economics
Massachusetts Institute of Technology

PREFACE TO THE FIRST EDITION

The world of active portfolio management has been changing over the last few years to become more quantitative in nature. This trend is inspiring because it lends itself to a more controlled approach to asset management, which ultimately benefits individual and institutional investors. In some ways quantitative asset management is an old field, but in many ways it's a very new field that has bundled together lots of old concepts. It is a vast and diverse field because quantitative managers use a variety of different techniques to manage their portfolios. Despite this diversity, though, there are central themes that remain at the core of the work of most quantitative asset management firms.

When we were first introduced to the field of quantitative portfolio management, we sensed that a lot of the issues it covered were unclear not only to us but also to our colleagues. In fact, there was no formal, authoritative source on the topic. Naturally, through our years at Seoul National University, UC Berkeley, Harvard, and MIT, we learned many of the concepts related to quantitative portfolio management, such as statistics and basic financial theory. And through our years working for portfolio management companies, we learned some of the real-world aspects of the trade. Still, we never really had a comprehensive reference to turn to for an understanding of the nuts and bolts of quantitative equity portfolio management. We also would sometimes see practitioners approach this kind of management with holes in their analytics or listen to academics speak about the theory with no attention to the details of real-world portfolio management. We began teaching the concepts to students at our respective universities and realized that it would be useful to write a book on the subject that attempted to cover the whole spectrum of quantitative equity portfolio management, including the theoretical side and the practical side.

Since the field of quantitative equity portfolio management (QEPM) is vast, we chose to focus on its core concepts. We chose to write a book that goes step by step through the entire process of building a quantitative equity portfolio. At times we explain concepts in much detail for those who are new to the field, yet we use mathematical rigor and develop new concepts for those already quite proficient in the field. Our main goal was to write a book that would be useful as a reference to professional money managers but also very useful for teaching an advanced investments course to undergraduate, MBA, or PhD students. Although our topic is QEPM, parts of this book can be used to teach the fundamental concepts of most advanced financial economics programs. We also wrote some parts of the book in such a way that other departments within a portfolio management operation can understand the main drivers of QEPM. Thus, marketing, business development, and salespeople should feel comfortable using this book.

We would like to thank Emilie Striker, a graduate of Georgetown University, for doing an excellent job of editing our writing. She pursued her work on this book with an enthusiasm and effort that is rare among people today. Not only did she improve the prose, but she also did a thorough job of catching errors and made a number of substantial improvements. We thank Joe Abboud, Stela Hristova, and Mariya Mitova for excellent research assistance. Furthermore, we would like to thank Steve Ross, Dan diBartolomeo, Mark Holowesko, and William Seale for extensive comments and suggestions, as well as Eric Rosenfeld, David Blitzer, Lawrence Pohlman, Prem Jain, Laurens Leerink, Ron Kahn, Wayne Wagner, Wolfgang Chincarini, Neer Asherie, Kevin Garrow, Mark Schroeder, and Mark Esposito for their comments. We thank David Bieri for supplying us with macroeconomic data and KLD for supplying us with social-responsibility data.

We would also like to thank everyone at McGraw-Hill who made this book possible, including James K. Madru, Cheryl Hudson, and especially Stephen Isaacs and Daina Penikas.

We are delighted with the positive response to our book. Since publication, we have received many comments and suggestions from readers, quantitative practitioners, and professors. We wish to thank all of you; including Ravi Agarwal, Mark Bradshaw, Yuan Chumming, Levon Goukasian, Allen Huang, Gergana Jostova, Doug Martin, Natalie Michelson, Masaka Mori, Marco Navone, Merav Ozair, Angel Samaniego, Lucio Sarno, Robert Schumaker, Felipe Vargas, Michael Verhofen, Bovorn Vichiansin, Russ Wermers, Chun Xia, Arthur Young, Giovanna Zanotti, Guofu Zhou, and the students of quantitative investment management at the University of San Francisco. If you are using this book in the classroom, we would appreciate hearing from you. Please contact us so that we can include your name in our acknowledgments. Additional teaching materials for the book are available at www.ludwigbc.com.

Ludwig Chincarini would like to thank the undergraduate students of Georgetown who patiently sat through his derivatives, investment, and global financial markets courses (in particular an anonymous student who wrote, "Write the book, man!") and the MBA students of 2005, 2006 and 2007 who took his course on investment analysis and special topics in investments. Thanks as well to Mellissa Cobb, Emma Curtis, John Carpenter, Juanita Arrington, David Walker, Keith Ord, Rohan Williamson, George Daly, Lee Pinkowitz, Gary Blemaster, and Reena Aggarwal and others of the faculty and staff of Georgetown University for making his life at Georgetown more enjoyable. Ludwig also would like to thank James Angel, William Droms, Joseph Mazzola, and Georgetown University for their initial encouragement for him to come back to teaching. Without that encouragement, this book may never have been written. Finally, he thanks the late Fischer Black and the late Rudiger Dornbusch for the inspirational influence they had on him.

Ludwig would like to dedicate this book to his family: to his brother, for being his best friend and always encouraging him; to his mother, for her love and encouragement, for wanting the best for him, and for opening a window for him when the door would close, in particular for giving him the opportunity to attend a top-rated university; to his father, for showing him, by example, the importance of thinking and of questioning; to his sister, the promise of tomorrow; and to everyone in his family, for allowing him the freedom to think or say anything, however outrageous, yet making him realize that it was he who would bear the burden of any rational or irrational thoughts.

Daehwan Kim would like to thank the American University in Bulgaria and Korea University, which provided a stable cash flow while the book was being written. Students in the two universities were the source of constant inspiration, whether they were taking a finance class or something else. Taeyoon Sung, a colleague at KAIST Graduate School of Management, provided various supports to the book writing. Daehwan also would like to thank his lovely wife, Ksenia Chizhova. Not only did she dutifully perform the traditional role of a book writer's wife (i.e., spending weekend after weekend without her husband at home), but she also was an excellent student of languages and literature who undertook the difficult task of trying to improve his writing style.

In the movie *Wall Street*, Gordon Gekko gives a famous speech about greed, a speech that is based on one given by Ivan Boesky years earlier at a University of California commencement. In his speech, Gekko states that "Greed—for lack of a better word—is good. Greed is right. Greed works. Greed clarifies, cuts through, and captures the essence of the evolutionary spirit . . . and has marked the upward surge of mankind." Unfortunately, both Gekko and Boesky got it wrong. There is a better word than greed, and it is *truth*. It is the search for truth that clarifies, works, and marks the upward surge of humankind. Speaking the truth eliminates inefficiency in all its forms; seeking the truth leads to great discoveries; passing the truth between loved ones provides strength over oceans, over time, and over death. Honesty would have prevented the corporate disasters that occurred in the last several years, and the truth is finally bringing the guilty, who were motivated by greed, to justice. Truth is indeed the highest summit we can achieve, whether we are managing a portfolio, managing a corporation, involved in a relationship, or taking part in any other aspect of everyday life.

If you would like to send us suggestions or comments on this book, please send them to our e-mail addresses with the subject line "Book comments."

Ludwig Chincarini, CFA, PhD
chincarinil@hotmail.com

Daehwan Kim, PhD
kimdaewan@hotmail.com

May 19, 2006
Tysons Corner, Virginia and Blagoevgrad, Bulgaria

PREFACE TO THE SECOND EDITION

When we wrote the first edition of *Quantitative Equity Portfolio Management* in 2006, quantitative equity portfolio management was still a new field mainly reserved for elite hedge funds. Since the publication of our book, the world of quantitative management has exploded. The most revolutionary changes have been smart beta and the launch by mutual funds, ETFs, and many companies of their own quantitative factor indices. In fact, the amount of assets under management following quantitative strategies has increased from approximately $238 billion when we published the first edition of *QEPM* to $2.3 trillion in 2020.[1] There are now all kinds of companies providing smart beta or factor indices, including Charles Schwab, Vanguard, BlackRock's iShares, Invesco, Goldman Sachs, and many others. In fact, the enormous growth in quantitative strategies has raised concerns among investors that there may be too much crowding in factor strategies, crowding that might be linked to crises like the quant crisis of 2007 [Chincarini (2012)]. Despite the concern about crowding and the efforts to understand it, we are extremely excited about the growth of this form of portfolio management.

Our book was also among the earliest to discuss the use of socially responsible factors in quantitative portfolio management, factors that have since become more commonly called ESG (environmental, social, and governance) factors. Since the first edition

---

[1] *Source*: Morgan Stanley and author's interpolation.

of our book was published, the amount of funds managed by ESG factors has increased from \$2.5 billion to \$249 billion worldwide.[2] Although we do not advocate for or against the use of ESG factors for portfolio construction, we are still amazed by the growth in this quantifiable rule-based method of socially responsible investing.

For the first edition of *QEPM*, we were fortunate enough to have Professor Stephen Ross of MIT write the Foreword to our book. He was one of the big thinkers in finance, being widely credited with the invention of the APT, the binomial option pricing formula, and agency theory.[3] Stephen Ross was not only successful in his career but also generous in writing the Foreword to our book and helping two young, talented researchers get a push. In the words of Anton Ego in the movie *Ratatouille*, "But there are times when a critic truly risks something, and that is in the discovery and defense of the new. The world is often unkind to new talent, new creations. The new needs friends." In 2018, Stephen Ross suddenly died. Although he is no longer here to dazzle us, he remains in our thoughts and in our prayers. Thank you, Steve.

In this new edition of *QEPM*, we have added some additional anomalies, a new list of behavioral explanations for some of the anomalies, new discoveries in transactions costs optimization, and new techniques for optimizing market-neutral portfolios. In addition, we present the backtests for many factors so that readers can get a peek at all of them. We also update all the data in the book through the end of 2020. Finally, we provide, on the book's website, teaching materials for instructors and practice materials for practitioners, including solutions to all the end-of-the-chapter questions, a folder with additional appendices for each chapter, a folder with general appendices (Appendices A—E), a folder with programs for every chapter written in MATLAB, R, and Stata for learning or for classroom labs, a folder with PowerPoint slides for every chapter, a folder with sample stock data, and a downloadable file of historical factor returns for 164 factors.[4] We hope you enjoy the website. If you are an instructor using our book, let us know, and we will thank you in subsequent printings of the book.

---

[2] *Source*: Morningstar's Passive Sustainable Funds: Global Landscape 2020.

[3] See Chincarini and Fabozzi (2018) for a detailed description of his contributions.

[4] Available at www.ludwigbc.com. Once you reach the website, choose Books, then Quantitative Equity Portfolio Management, then QEPM Exclusive Content. Or just go to this link https://ludwigbc.com/books/qepm/ exclusive_qepm_content_2020/ The password is qepm2020rig179.

Along the road to writing this new edition, we benefited from the generous help of many people. We would especially like to thank Steve Glass, Michael Chigirinsky, Richard Sloan, Scott Esser, Rob Arnott, Fabio Moneta, Dan diBartolomeo, Snehil Misha, Brandon Lee Gipper, Jeffrey Pontiff, Lubos Pastor, Pete Kyle, Jim Angel, Andrei Bolshakov, Jeff Silk, Ryan Losson, Susan Leake, Fernando Comiran, Michael Scanlon, Chris Murray, Natasha Grasso, Jamie Comer, Phil Ellis, and William Ding. Daehwan would like to thank Martin Brückner, Tobias Klein, Walter Levy and other colleagues at First Private, Lewis Chan at Maunakai Capital, and Taegyeong Han, Yunho Heo, and Hyunjai Shin at Samsung Hedge for sharing their perspectives on quantitative investing with him and keeping him interested in this field in the years after publication of the first edition. At McGraw Hill, we thank Judith Newlin, Stephen Isaacs, Jim "Hawk Eyes" Madru, and the man who makes the magic happen Peter Mccurdy.

It's never easy to write a book or even modify a book. It takes hours of endless patience and solitude. During my rewriting (Ludwig), my wife was pregnant with our second child, and we had our beautiful two-year-old daughter causing us all kinds of chaos, while I was diagnosed with two types of cancer. I strongly encourage all people to inform themselves about the important checkups all men and women should be scheduling with their doctors and to insist that your doctors perform those tests yearly. For example, all of us should check our skin every year, women should check for breast cancer, and men should do a PSA test every year. I also remind people to stop and enjoy the beautiful things in life and worry less about the rat race. With help from my mother and my in-laws, and the touch of God, somehow this new edition was created. I pray every day that I can continue to enjoy this beautiful life as my body is now on the mend. I would like to dedicate this new edition of the book to the most important people in my life: my wife, Gina, my daughter, Gemma, and my son, Angelo Ludovico. They make everything worthwhile. I am also eager to watch Angelo and Gemma achieve much more than I have—I only hope that the first steps that I build for them launch them onto a path of happiness, success, and fulfillment.

In the Preface to the first edition of QEPM, we wrote that truth is one of the purest objectives we can pursue as humans. In recent times, while free speech and freedom to disagree with the crowd are seemingly under attack, we often wake up feeling as though it is

"Opposite Day." The danger is that these social fads seemingly designed to conceal the truth may ultimately lead to inefficiency and unhappiness for everyone. Keep fighting for liberty, my friends!

If you would like to send us suggestions or comments on the book, please send them to our email addresses with the subject line "Book Comments."

Ludwig Chincarini, CFA, PhD
chincarinil@hotmail.com

Daehwan Kim, PhD
kimdaewan@hotmail.com

June 1, 2022
San Francisco and Seoul

NOTATIONS AND ABBREVIATIONS

MATHEMATICAL SYMBOLS

$d_{i,t}$	the dividend paid by stock i during period t
$f_{k,t}$	the premium of factor k for period t
$\mathbf{f}_t$	the premium vector of many factors for period t
F_t	the price of futures contracts
$\mathbf{I}$	the identity matrix
$I_{t,t+k}$	the gross interest of a cash position whose portions may be paid differing interest
l	the net leverage rate
m_f	the required margin for futures contracts
N_f	the number of futures contracts
N_o	the number of call options
$p_{i,t}$	the price of stock i at the end of period t
q	the futures contract multiplier
q_s	the single-stock-futures contract multiplier
$r_{i,t}$	the return of stock i for period t
$r_{B,t}$	the benchmark return for period t
$r_{P,t}$	the portfolio return for period t
R^2	the goodness-of-fit from a regression
$\bar{R}^2$	the adjusted goodness-of-fit from a regression
s_i	the number of shares of stock i holding
S_t	the value of the equity index

V_t	the dollar value of a portfolio at time t
w_i^B	the benchmark weight of stock i
$\mathbf{w}^B$	the benchmark weight vector
w_i^P	the portfolio weight of stock i
$\mathbf{w}^P$	the portfolio weight vector
x_t	the portfolio return in excess of the benchmark at time t $(= r_{P,t} - r_{B,t})$
$x_{i,t}$	the contribution of stock return i to the portfolio excess return at time t $[= r_{i,t}(w_{i,t}^P - w_{i,t}^B)]$
$z_{i,k,t}$	the Z-score of stock i to factor k for period t
$\mathbf{z}_{i,t}$	the Z-score vector of stock i to many factors for period t
$\bar{z}_{i,t}$	the aggregate Z-score of stock i at time t
α_i^B	the benchmark alpha of stock i
α_i^{CAPM}	the CAPM alpha of stock i
α_i^{MF}	the multifactor alpha of stock i
$\beta_{i,j,t}$	the exposure of stock i to factor j for period t
$\boldsymbol{\beta}_{i,t}$	the exposure vector of stock i to many factors for period t
Δ	the delta of an option
ϵ_i	the residual return of stock i
ι	the vector of 1
μ_B	the expected return of the benchmark
μ_i	the expected return of stock i
μ_P	the expected return of the portfolio
$\boldsymbol{\mu}$	the expected return vector of stocks
ξ	the percentage of equity capital invested in cash
$\rho_{i,j}$	the correlation of the returns of stock i and stock j
σ_B	the standard deviation of the benchmark return
σ_i	the standard deviation of the return on stock i
σ_P	the standard deviation of the portfolio return
σ_x	the standard deviation of the portfolio excess return over the benchmark
Σ	the variance-covariance matrix of stock returns
τ	the tax rate
ω_i	the residual risk of stock i
ω_i^2	the residual variance of stock i

MATHEMATICAL FUNCTIONS

$C(\cdot)$	the covariance function
$E(\cdot)$	the expectation function (returns the mean of a random variable)
$I(\cdot)$	the indicator function (1 if true and 0 otherwise)
$M(\cdot)$	the median function
$P(\cdot)$	the probability function
$p(\cdot)$	the probability density function
$S(\cdot)$	the standard deviation function
$V(\cdot)$	the variance function
$\phi(\cdot)$	the standard normal probability density function
$\Phi(\cdot)$	the standard normal cumulative distribution function
$\rho(\cdot)$	the correlation function

ABBREVIATIONS

ADTV	the average daily trading volume
ADDTV	the average daily dollar trading volume
AE	the allocation effect
APT	arbitrage pricing theory
BR	breadth
CAPM	the capital asset pricing model
DVOL	the dollar trading volume
GLS	the generalized least squares method
IC	the information coefficient
IL	information loss
IR	the information ratio
MAD	the minium absolute deviations method
MVO	mean variance optimization
OLS	the ordinary least squares method
QEPM	quantitative equity portfolio management
SD	standard deviation
SR	the Sharpe ratio
SSE	the security selection effect
SVOL	the share trading volume
TC	transactions costs

TE	tracking error
TWR	time-weighted return
VAR	vector autoregression
VaR	value-at-risk

ABBREVIATION OF FACTOR NAMES

ADR	the advance–decline ratio
AILIQ	the Amihud illiquidity
ARMD	the median change in analyst ratings
ARMR	the median analyst rating
ARMS	the Arms index
ARPB	the percent of analyst buy recommendations
ARPD	the percent of analyst recommendation downgrades
ARPS	the percent of analyst sell recommendations
ARPU	the percent of analyst recommendation upgrades
ARSD	the standard deviation in analyst ratings
BB	the Bollinger band
BBBS	the BBB spread
BBBSD	the change in BBB spread
BCG	the growth rate of the business confidence index
BETA	the beta premium
B/P	the book-to-price ratio
CACC	the current accruals
CB	the channel breakout
CC	the community contribution index
CCC	the cash conversion cycle
CCCD	the change in the cash conversion cycle
CCCX	the cash conversion cycle in excess of the industry average
CCG	the growth rate of the consumer confidence index
CCX	the community contribution index in excess of the industry average
CE	the natural log of common equity
CEG	the growth rate in the natural log of common equity
CFOR	the cash-flow-from-operations ratio
CFORD	the change in the cash-flow-from-operations ratio

CF/P	the cash-flow-to-price
CF/TA	the cash-flow-to-total assets
CF/TS	the cash-flow-to-total sales
CG	the corporate governance index
CGX	the corporate governance index in excess of the industry average
CIG	the growth rate of the commodity price index
CMI	the cost management index
CMID	the change in the cost management index
CMIX	the cost management index in excess of the industry average
CPG	the gross profit growth
CPIG	the growth rate of the consumer price index (i.e., inflation)
CR	the cash ratio
CRD	the change in cash ratio
CROWDA	the crowding measure based on analysts
CROWDV	the crowding measure based on valuation
CSG	the growth rate of the consumer sentiment index
CUR	the current ratio
CURD	the change in current ratio
DE (D/E)	the debt-to-equity ratio
DED	the change in debt-to-equity ratio
DEX	the debt-to-equity ratio in excess of the industry average
DIV	the diversity index
DIVX	the diversity index in excess of the industry average
DY (D/P)	the dividend yield
E	the environment index
EBIT	earnings before interest and taxes
EBITDA	earnings before interest, taxes, depreciation, and amortization
EBITDA/EV (EBITIDAEV)	earnings before interest, taxes, depreciation, and amortization divided by enterprise value
EBITDA/P (EBITDAP)	earnings before interest, taxes, depreciation, and amortization divided by stock price

E/P	earnings-to-price ratio
EPS	earnings-per-share
EPSFPD	the percent of downward revisions in earnings-per-share forecasts
EPSFPU	the percent of upward revisions in earnings-per-share forecasts
EPSFSD	the standard deviation of earnings-per-share forecasts
EPSSD	the earnings-per-share forecasts divided by the standard deviation of analyst forecasts
ER	the employee relation index
ERX	the employee relation index in excess of the industry average
ET	equity turnover
ETD	the change in equity turnover
ETX	equity turnover in excess of the industry average
EV/EBITDA (EVEBITDA)	enterprise value divided by earnings before interest, taxes, depreciation, and amortization
EX	the environment index in excess of the industry average
FAT	fixed-asset turnover
FATD	change in fixed-asset turnover
FATX	fixed-asset turnover in excess of the industry average
FLR	financial leverage ratio
FLRD	change in financial leverage ratio
FLRX	financial leverage ratio in excess of the industry average
GDPR	the revision in forecast of gross domestic product
GDPS	the surprise in forecast of gross domestic product
GDPG	the growth rate of real gross domestic product
GPG	gross profit growth
GPM	the gross profit margin
GPMD	the change in gross profit margin
GPTA	gross profits to total assets
HR	the human rights index

HRX	the human rights index in excess of the industry average
ICFCR	the inverse cash-flow coverage ratio
ICFCRD	the change in the inverse cash-flow coverage ratio
ICFCRX	the inverse cash-flow coverage ratio in excess of the industry average
ICR	the interest coverage ratio
IICR	the inverse interest coverage ratio
IICRD	the change in the inverse interest coverage ratio
IICRX	the inverse interest coverage ratio in excess of the industry avareage
INVIL	the invariance illiquidity measure
IPEGF	the earnings-to-price ratio multiplied by forecasted earnings growth
IPEGH	the earnings-to-price ratio multiplied by historical earnings growth
IPEGY	the earnings-to-price ratio multiplied by earnings growth plus dividend yield
IPG	the growth rate of industrial production
IPR	the revision in industrial production
IT	inventory turnover
ITD	the change in inventory turnover
ITX	the inventory turnover in excess of the industry average
LGPG	long-term gross profit growth
LNPG	long-term net profit growth
LOGCE	log of common equity
LOGCEG	equity growth
LLOGCEG	long-term equity growth
LOGSIZE	log of market capitalization
LOGTA	log of total assets
LOGTAG	total asset growth
LLOGTAG	long-term total asset growth
LOPG	long-term operating profit growth
M12M	12-month momentum
M1M	one-month momentum

M3M	three-month momentum
M6M	six-month momentum
M9M	ninth-month momentum
M9ML1	nine-month momentum lagged one month
MA	the moving-average indicator
MACD	the moving-average convergence divergence indicator
MAILIQ	the modified Amihud illiquidity measure
NPG	net profit growth
NPM	the net profit margin
NPMD	the change in net profit margin
NPTA	net profit to total assets
OBV	on-balance volume
OLBI	the odd-lot balance index
OPG	operating profit growth
OPM	the operating profit margin
OPMD	the change in operating profit margin
OPTA	operating profit to total assets
P	the price of the stock
P/B	the price-to-book ratio
P/CF	the price-to-cash-flow ratio
P/E	the price-to-earnings ratio
P/EBITDA	the price divided by the earnings before interest, taxes, depreciation, and amortization
P/S	the price-to-sales ratio
PCG	the growth rate of personal consumption
PCR	the revision in personal consumption growth
PEG	the price-to-earnings-to-growth ratio
PEGF	the forecasted price-to-earnings growth ratio
PEGH	the historical price-to-earnings-growth ratio
PEGY	the price-to-earnings-to-growth-to-dividend-yield ratio
PRO	the product index
PROX	the product index in excess of the industry average
PSL	the Pastor and Stambaugh liquidity measure

QR	the quick ratio
QRD	the change in quick ratio
RNDS	the research-and-development-to-sales ratio
RNDSD	the change in the research-and-development-to-sales ratio
ROA	the return on assets
ROCE	the return on common equity
ROE	the return on owner's equity
ROTC	the return on total capital
RSI	the relative strengh index
RT	receivables turnover
RTD	the change in receivables turnover
RTX	the receivables turnover in excess of the industry average
SB	stock buybacks
SIR	the short interest ratio
SIRX	the short interest ratio minus its one-year average
SIZE	the market capitalization of a company
S/P	the sales-to-price ratio
SR	the support and resistance indicator
SS	the swap spread
SSD	the change in the swap spread
SUE	standardized unanticipated earnings
TACC	the total accruals
TAT	total asset turnover
TATD	the change in total asset turnover
TATX	the total asset turnover in excess of the industry average
TDR	the total debt ratio
TDRD	the change in the total debt ratio
TDRX	the total debt ratio in excess of the industry average
TP2Y	the term premium (10-year rate over 2-year rate)
TP3M	the term premium (10-year rate over 3-month rate)
TT	trading turnover
UDR	the upside–downside ratio

UDV	the upside–downside volume
UR	the unemployment rate
URD	the change in the unemployment rate
VL	the volume lead indicator
VOL	the volatility of a stock

PART I

An Overview of QEPM

Modern financial theory has long described the stock market as a place that rewards investors who take calculated risks over the long run. Today's understanding of the market, however, argues for a different kind of approach to risk-taking from the kind that was popular just a couple of decades ago. The conventional wisdom at that time was that stock returns related only to stocks' correlations with the total market and that the best investment strategy was simply to follow the market. More recent insights show that other sources of risk fuel stock returns and that the market rewards investors who seek them.

More specifically, recent work in finance finds that stock returns, over time periods of a year or more, are fairly predictable with certain groups of factors. Prices no longer seem to zigzag randomly in Brownian motion. Rather, when viewed through the right prism of risk factors, they follow decipherable patterns. These additional insights in financial theory not only reveal the possibility of profiting from active investment strategies, but they also make the case for a specifically quantitative approach. If it takes multiple factors to predict stock returns most accurately, then quantitative models of stock returns are needed to identify and combine factors efficiently. If returns are somewhat predictable over the long run, then stable quantitative models should work more reliably than picking individual stocks intermittently on qualitative information. The current state of technology, which supports data-heavy quantitative research and complex trading strategies, makes it possible to put these ideas into practice.

Quantitative equity portfolio management (QEPM) is what we call the approach to portfolio management that takes full advantage of today's better understanding of the markets and greater technological capacity for sophisticated investing. QEPM is a broad and flexible umbrella that encompasses as many individual strategies as managers can develop with the set of quantitative methods that we explain in this book. The commonality of all the various QEPM applications is the discipline and accuracy that mathematics lend to the pursuit of returns and the control of risk. In the first three chapters we will introduce you to QEPM, why and how it works, and the essential framework on which it operates.

CHAPTER 1

The Power of QEPM

The first duty of intelligent men is the restatement of the obvious.

—George Orwell

1.1 INTRODUCTION

Personal investors place their savings in the hands of professional money managers in the belief that the professionals, with their specialized skills, will make the best investment decisions for them. In fact, more than 106 million Americans, the equivalent of about half of all U.S. households, entrust their money to mutual funds. They and other investors are the reason why there are more than 11,000 U.S. stock mutual funds and exchange-traded funds (ETFs) managing $24.9 trillion and more than 3,000 U.S. hedge funds.[1] Yet, while assets in these types of investment funds stand in the trillions of dollars, many people have begun to question whether the professionals really do have an edge on amateur investors. There is evidence that only 14% of equity mutual funds managed to beat the

---

[1] In 2021, there were approximately 11,323 stock mutual funds and 3,508 U.S. hedge funds. There were also about 126,457 open-end funds in the world managing $63.1 trillion in assets and 8,042 hedge funds worldwide managing $3.6 trillion. In 2021, there were also approximately 1,974 quantitative hedge funds in the world managing $1.004 trillion. *Source:* Collins et al. (2021) and Hedge Fund Research (www.hfr.com) .

Standard and Poor's (S&P) 1500 from 2000 to 2020.[2] Despite poor performance by some funds, however, we firmly believe that professional managers *do* invest better than the average investor when they use certain tools available to them to quantify and truly understand the risks they are taking. Superior portfolio returns are possible through *quantitative equity portfolio management* (QEPM).

In this book, we use *QEPM* to refer mostly to an active, quantitative style of equity portfolio management, although the quantitative tools we describe can be applied easily to passive management strategies. Broadly speaking, equity portfolio management styles can be defined in two dimensions: *passive* versus *active* and *qualitative* versus *quantitative*. The passive-versus-active dimension reflects whether the portfolio is being managed simply to match the return of the benchmark or exceed the return of the benchmark. Passive management, also referred to as *indexing*, involves following and trying to match the returns of an equity index (e.g., the S&P 500) or other benchmark as closely as possible. The "passive" portfolio manager only initiates trades in order to mimic changes in the composition of the index, to reinvest dividends, to deal with the portfolio's cash inflows and outflows, or to respond to corporate actions that affect stocks that make up the index. Index portfolio managers typically are rewarded for their ability to replicate the index. In the U.S., passive management grew from 8.69% in 2000 to 40% in 2020 of all managed mutual funds and ETFs, primarily owing to the poor performance of many active fund managers versus standard equity indices. Passive management implicitly assumes that portfolio managers cannot beat the market.

Active management takes the view that it is possible to choose stocks that will outperform an equity index or other benchmark. "Active" managers also sometimes aim for some absolute level of performance without any reference to an index or benchmark. Trading takes place when the manager wants to buy stocks expected to have superior returns, when there are dividends to reinvest, or when cash flows into or out of the portfolio. In many cases, actively managed portfolios have higher turnover than passively managed ones because active portfolio managers tend to trade

---

[2] See Liu and Sinha (2021). In addition, over this 20-year period, only 6% of large-cap funds beat the S&P 500, 12% of mid-cap funds beat the S&P 400, and 12% of small-cap funds beat the S&P 600.

more frequently than passive managers do. Active managers usually are rewarded for the portfolio's absolute return or risk-adjusted return over a benchmark.

The second way to define portfolio management styles is to look at whether the manager bases decisions mainly on qualitative or quantitative analysis. Of the two general styles, perhaps the easiest for the average investor to understand is *qualitative management*, which is sometimes called *fundamental management* (although that term can be misleading because quantitative managers look at stock fundamentals as well). What makes the style qualitative is the fact that the research focuses on intangibles and generally does not involve using mathematics or computer programs specifically to identify "good" and "bad" stocks. Qualitative management is almost always a kind of active management because qualitative managers handpick stocks that they expect to outperform the market. Their selections are based on information from income statements and balance sheets, financial ratios, phone interviews with company personnel, research reports, and ad hoc methods of analysis. They also rely on their own gut reactions. For the most part, qualitative managers use their own judgment and informal calculations to filter the information that they and their analysts gather.

Peter Lynch, who led the Fidelity Magellan Fund to a compounded return of more than 2,700% during his tenure as fund manager from 1977 to 1990, is one of the best-known practitioners of the qualitative style. One of Lynch's largest holdings at Magellan was inspired by his wife's enthusiasm for L'eggs, Hanes Corporation's brand of women's hosiery packaged in egg-shaped containers and sold at local drugstores and supermarkets. Magellan's position in Hanes prospered when L'eggs became a huge hit with consumers. Subsequently, a competitor of Hanes, the Kayser-Roth Corporation, tried to copy the success of L'eggs by selling its own brand of panty hose. Concerned about possible erosion of Hanes' market share, Lynch undertook what he has termed "fundamental research" on the matter. He bought 48 pairs of Kayser-Roth's No Nonsense panty hose and asked a group of female coworkers to try them for a few weeks. Based on their assessment that the No Nonsense product was not nearly as good as L'eggs, Lynch decided to hold onto Hanes' stock. He was richly rewarded for his (somewhat unconventional) qualitative methods when Hanes' stock continued to rise, and the company eventually was acquired by what is currently known as the Sara Lee Corporation.[3]

Quantitative management, unlike the rather intuitive process of qualitative management, is rooted in mathematics and statistics and less concerned with intangibles. Quantitative portfolio managers use any numerical data or quantifiable information relevant to the investment decision. This could include stock fundamentals from the income statement and balance sheet, technical data (e.g., stock prices and trading volumes), macroeconomic data, survey data, analyst recommendations, and any other data collected and stored in a database. Quantitative managers, unlike their counterparts in the qualitative tradition, use their data to build quantitative models of security returns. These models, along with advanced statistics, mathematics, and computer software, are used to identify "good" and "bad" stocks. Essentially, quantitative managers filter information mathematically rather than intuitively.

The particular field of quantitative management that we refer to as QEPM is, like most forms of qualitative management, an active approach to investing. With QEPM, the manager aims for returns that exceed a benchmark or market index. QEPM's tools for measuring and controlling risk do allow for highly accurate passive management. QEPM can accomplish much more than pure indexing, though, so our focus is on exploiting quantitative methods for outperformance.

Quantitative management is associated less with great individuals than with great institutions, and many successful mutual funds practice QEPM. There is a strong quantitative management presence at Acadian Asset Management, AQR Capital, Blackrock, Goldman Sachs Asset Management, Parametric Portfolio Associates, Putnam Investments, Quantitative Management Associates, State Street Global Advisors, and Two Sigma, among others. Many hedge funds' portfolios are based on QEPM as well. And even many enhanced index managers (more passive style) who manage portfolios with respect to a benchmark with the goal of modest excess performances also practice QEPM.

Over the years, quantitative management gradually has gained prevalence as even self-described qualitative managers have adopted some quantitative methods. A number of forces have

---

[3] See "Interview with Peter Lynch," https://www.pbs.org/wgbh/pages/frontline/shows/betting/pros/lynch.html. Warren Buffett is also another well-known qualitative-style manager.

propelled this shift toward the quantitative, the first being the advancement of technology since the 1990s. Complicated computer models of stock returns that once took days to run are now generated in a matter of minutes. Computing speed also allows computer programs to dig through great amounts of data in order to uncover buried treasures. The internet, meanwhile, makes it easier to access a wealth of data to analyze. With so much information at their fingertips, though, investors sometimes can become overconfident and make poor investment choices. The near glut of data only increases the need for quantitative analysis, which imposes discipline on the decision-making process.

In some ways, quantitative approaches also fare better in the post-Enron regulatory environment than qualitative styles do. Now that companies are required to give *fair disclosure* of events, portfolio managers and analysts can no longer get company news ahead of the rest of the market by chatting with the CFO, for instance. Fair disclosure means that all information must be uniformly distributed and available through public data resources—a boon for quantitative managers, who typically use software programs to access large quantities of data, but a blow to qualitative managers, who traditionally have gathered a great deal of their information through informal, one-on-one conversations with company executives.

Quantitative methods help managers to respond to calls for greater transparency as well. Average folks are becoming savvier investors and demanding more information from the people who manage their money. Employees want to know exactly how pension funds are investing their retirement savings. When questioned about their investment strategies, quantitative fund managers can point to clear, objective methods as the basis for their decisions.

Finally, the stability of quantitatively managed portfolios is becoming a selling point with investors. Quantitative strategies can control risk precisely. Precise risk control helps the portfolio avoid large swings in value and instead earn reliable, if modest, returns, which are what many investors seek. Although there have been a number of star managers who have consistently figured out how to beat the market, many qualitative managers have failed to beat the S&P 500 on average over time. Their portfolios have sporadically earned extremely high returns only to sink subsequently into years of underperformance. Portfolios that employ the quantitative risk controls that keep volatility low offer an attractive alternative to such roller-coaster rides.

1.2 THE ADVANTAGES OF QEPM

Quantitative equity portfolio managers gain numerous advantages over their traditional, qualitatively oriented counterparts by organizing and filtering great amounts of data with advanced statistics and mathematics. The disadvantages of QEPM mainly have to do with the possibility of relying the wrong way on quantitative models and historical data. Table 1.1 lists QEPM's advantages and disadvantages in comparison with qualitative management.

One of the greatest advantages of QEPM is that when a model of stock returns is in place, construction of the portfolio is a highly objective process. The quantitative manager creates quantitative models of returns from underlying financial and other data, and these models tell the manager how to construct an optimal portfolio of stocks. The actual buy and sell decisions of the quantitative portfolio manager come directly from the model. This significantly lessens the impact of one person's biases on the portfolio. In contrast, a qualitative manager's buy and sell decisions often are based solely on the manager's opinion and thus are relatively more susceptible to the influence of behavioral biases. The objectivity of QEPM boosts the portfolio's returns and also supports management

TABLE 1.1

The Advantages and Disadvantages of QEPM versus
Qualitative Management

Criteria	Advantages	
	QEPM	**Qualitative**
Objectivity	High	Low
Breadth	High	Low
Behavioral errors	Low	High
Replicability	High	Low
Costs	Low	High
Controlled risk	High	Low
Disadvantages		
Qualitative inputs	Low	High
Historical data reliance	High	Low
Data mining	High	Low
Reactivity	Low	High

transparency. There is a clearly defined process for selecting stocks that can be presented to investors.

Another major advantage of QEPM is that computerized quantitative models can analyze large amounts of data and a large volume of stocks in a short amount of time. We call this the *advantage of breadth*. The same breadth is practically impossible with qualitative management because, to use Peter Lynch's metaphor, there are simply too many rocks to turn over one by one.[4] In the course of analyzing literally thousands of stocks with computer programs, the quantitative manager may unearth some diamonds in the rough that the qualitative manager would never find. Some qualitative portfolio managers do use stock screens and elements of quantitative management to help them sort through the stock universe. Ultimately, though, a total QEPM approach is a more complete analysis of the entire stock universe than this sort of mixed analysis.

As we mentioned earlier, QEPM inoculates the portfolio, to some extent, against behavioral biases and errors. The area of behavioral finance has grown in recent years as economists have identified the types of impulses that lead to irrational investment decisions. Portfolio managers may be better than the average investor at controlling these impulses, but they have them just the same. One such impulse is the *disposition effect*, the desire to hold onto "loser," or poorly performing, stocks too long. Investors often hope that losers will rebound despite all evidence to the contrary. Strict adherence to QEPM procedures helps to prevent a portfolio manager from trading on this sort of wishful thinking because it takes the final decision out of the manager's hands to some extent. If the quantitative model of stock returns recognizes a "bad" stock, that is the trigger for selling the stock. (It is easy for the model to make the tough calls about selling; after all, it lacks any emotional attachment to the stocks.) *Overconfidence*, another common behavioral bias, leads to too much trading, raising transactions costs. QEPM curbs overconfidence because the optimization model specifically controls trading costs. *Confirmation bias* leads some investors to block out relevant bad news on stocks they like. Again, with QEPM, the quantitative model processes all relevant information objectively.

QEPM strategies also have the benefit of being replicable. Portfolio managers can pass their models on to their successors when they leave a firm. The firm is not completely dependent,

---

[4] See Morgenson (1997).

therefore, on the presence of a star manager. Replicability also makes it possible to backtest investment strategies on historical data over different time periods, in different markets, and with alternative specifications. Unlike quantitative methods, qualitative interpretations of market events are largely in the eye of the beholder, making them difficult to replicate in the absence of the manager who comes up with them, difficult to backtest, and difficult to articulate to investors as a methodology.

The cost of portfolio management is generally lower with QEPM than it is with qualitative management. The Ph.D.'s and other "quants" who must be hired to build the stock models generally demand high salaries, but, after the models are implemented, computers do a big share of the work. This keeps the QEPM department's head count relatively low compared with departments that delve into extensive qualitative research.

One of the most important advantages of QEPM is that it provides precise measurements of risk. A good understanding of stocks' exposure to risk factors is essential to the entire construction of the portfolio. More specifically, the ability to measure the risk of the portfolio versus a benchmark has opened the gate for controlled enhanced index management. By quantifying the tracking error of the portfolio, managers can select stocks that both earn high returns and keep the risk of the portfolio within very specific boundaries. This is difficult to do without using quantitative risk-control mechanisms.

There are some minor disadvantages to QEPM, the most prominent being the problem of translating qualitative inputs into quantitative data for use in a quantitative model. Despite the problems inherent in investing in subjective perceptions, there are valuable insights to be gained from, for instance, visiting a store and evaluating its level of customer service. Incorporating this sort of evaluation into QEPM is not simple. Numerical customer satisfaction ratings of the store might be a useful stand-in for a manager's first-hand observations, but such information probably would be difficult to obtain. Even if it were available, how should it be added to a model already built on other data? Later in this book we will show how qualitative inputs from fundamental analysts can be translated into data suitable for quantitative models.[5]

---

[5] Chapter 14 explains how Bayesian statistics serve as a powerful method for converting qualitative data into quantitative data.

QEPM's heavy reliance on historical data has drawbacks. Historical relationships may not continue in the future, throwing off stock-return forecasts. New types of companies and new market environments, such as the internet bubble of the late nineties, diminish the relevance of inferences and expectations based on past patterns. QEPM is not unique in its reliance on historical information, however, and the statistical tests that quantitative managers apply to a set of data may help them to determine what portion of it is no longer useful. Statistical tests resolve some, but not all, questions about the continuity of trends in the data.

There is the potential for misuse of statistical tests. Data mining, a highly inappropriate practice, involves testing many statistical relationships in historical data and picking the one that apparently explains past stock returns most accurately.[6] The "mined" strategy will have almost no relation to current market conditions and therefore very little ability to predict future stock returns.[7] Unfortunately, many quantitative managers and analysts nonetheless are tempted to do data mining because it is so easy to keep testing and discarding models until finding one that works well on historical data. It takes integrity and discipline to resist the temptation.[8] Qualitative managers are susceptible to a form of data mining known as *data snooping*,[9] so the misapplication of historical relationships is endemic to active portfolio management as a whole.

The last disadvantage we associate with QEPM is its reaction time.[10] QEPM strategies may be slow to react to a shift in the economic paradigm or a change in the investment environment because they are drawn from historical data. Advanced statistical

---

[6] In general, QEPM requires a good understanding of statistics. Not using statistical methods appropriately may create a number of problems. Data mining is just one of them. Not accounting for parameter uncertainty and overinterpreting the estimation from a small sample are other serious problems. We discuss some of these issues in Chapter 2. Nonetheless, the abuse and misunderstanding of statistics, not QEPM itself, are mainly to be blamed.

[7] We discuss the issue of data mining in more detail in Chapter 2.

[8] We have noticed that data mining occurs with particular frequency in investment departments dominated by office politics.

[9] See Chapter 2 for an explanation of this concept as well.

[10] This is not the same as *skid,* a term used in the industry to describe a movement in price that occurs in the time between the recognition of an idea and its implementation in the portfolio. Skid is also a problem for portfolio managers because a price movement may eliminate an investment opportunity.

analysis, research, and ingenuity can improve the reaction time. Delayed reaction to new conditions is a problem shared, though to a lesser extent, by qualitative managers. Qualitative strategies can be modified quickly in the face of changing conditions. How well the modifications work depends, of course, on how accurately the manager and analysts interpret events.

Overall, we believe that QEPM's advantages far outdistance its disadvantages. Many of the disadvantages of QEPM are common to all types of active portfolio management. Its particular benefits, however, make it especially well suited to this age of information overload and ever-growing competition among investment funds to find good, unexploited opportunities.

1.3 QUANTITATIVE AND QUALITATIVE APPROACHES TO SIMILAR INVESTMENT SITUATIONS

We have spoken in general about the advantages of QEPM, but you may be wondering how a quantitative manager's response to specific market conditions differs from a qualitative manager's. In this section we discuss quantitative versus qualitative strategies for real-world investment problems.[11]

The Federal Reserve of the United States sets interest rates through the Fed funds target rate, which is typically announced at Federal Open Market Committee (FOMC) meetings. At its meeting on March 15, 2020, at the outbreak of the Covid-19 pandemic, for instance, the Fed lowered the Fed funds target rate to a range between 0% and 0.25%. Such changes in the target rate reverberate throughout the bond and equity markets, so investors try to anticipate them and also gauge what the rest of the market expects them to be. The market trades on these expectations via Fed futures that are based on the effective Fed funds rate, the daily average of the Fed funds rate over the previous month.

With an FOMC meeting on the horizon, a qualitative manager might say, "It's highly likely that Fed Chairman Powell will raise rates by 25 basis points. We should reduce the β exposure of the portfolio." This assessment may be right on the nose, especially

---

[11] On a lighter note, in Appendix E found at www.ludwigbc.com under QEPM Exclusive Content, we also hypothesize about how a quantitative manager and a qualitative manager might differ in their approaches to the game of craps.

given the qualitative manager's years of experience watching the markets. A quantitative manager, however, is more likely to use market data, such as Fed fund futures prices, to specify exactly the implied probability that the Fed will raise rates. In this way, the quantitative manager can state with confidence, "The market has already priced in a 98% probability of a 25 basis point raise in rates." The quantitative manager also has the tools to quantify the effect of a rise in rates on various types of equities, including cases in which the market expects the increase.[12] This is a much more precise analysis, for investment purposes, than the qualitative manager's gut-feeling approach.

Recently, the government of a major country, certain that interest rates were on the rise, wanted to invest in a portfolio of stocks inversely related to interest rates. There are many types of fixed-income investments that would have been appropriate for protecting against a rise in interest rates, but the government wanted an all-equity portfolio. A qualitative analyst might have begun constructing the portfolio using some rule of thumb, such as screening for companies with low debt-to-equity ratios or for companies in the utilities industry, which is known to hold up well in the face of high interest rates. The screen would have yielded a list of stocks that ought to do well in the upcoming high-rate environment.

By contrast, a quantitative analyst probably would have started work on this portfolio by creating an economic factor model that explicitly modeled stock returns in relation to the macroeconomic factor of concern, interest rates.[13] From the results of the model, the analyst then would have constructed a portfolio of equities with low or negative exposures to interest rates. As opposed to the merely directional prediction of the qualitative manager's rule of thumb, the quantitative model would have shown *how much* individual stocks and the entire portfolio likely would react to higher interest rates, with an estimate of the degree of uncertainty of the expected behaviors. Being able to anticipate not only the direction but also the amount and uncertainty of movement in stock prices, the quantitative manager would have formulated a more precise interest-rate hedge.

---

[12] For more details, the reader is referred to Bieri and Chincarini (2005).

[13] We introduce economic factor models in Chapter 3 and discuss them in greater detail in Chapter 7.

Sometimes companies are provided with windfall revenue streams, such as when another company or the government awards them a contract. This happened during the Covid-19 pandemic to AstraZeneca when it won a contract with the U.S. government for its Covid-19 product AZD7442. On October 9, 2020, the U.S. government announced that it would provide AstraZeneca with approximately $486 million for two phase 3 clinical trials and related development activities. A qualitative manager might have seen this announcement and said, "The stock has only gone up about 62 cents per share. I have a feeling this deal is worth a lot more than that. Let's make it a short-term buy." This intuition may have merit, but it is not very precise. Given the available information, it would have been possible to do a much more precise analysis quantitatively.

The manager could have used a modified discounted cash-flow model to evaluate the impact of this deal on the stock price of the company. The manager then could have observed the actual change in the stock price, compared it with the predicted change in the stock price from the model, and made an informed decision about whether to go long or short the stock as a short-term trade.[14]

Performance attribution is another type of analysis that benefits from quantitative techniques. With classic performance attribution, a quantitative performance analyst can split the portfolio's excess returns over the benchmark into their underlying sources, making it easier to pinpoint the investment decisions that augmented or diminished the portfolio's performance. Calculations of risk-adjusted performance tell the analyst whether a portfolio's excess performance was due to extra risk (pseudo-outperformance) or to additional return without additional risk (true outperformance). For analyzing the performance of a competitor's portfolio, techniques such as style analysis help the analyst to get an idea of the competitor's investment strategy even if the individual securities in the portfolio are unknown. QEPM approaches to performance measurement analyze performance rigorously and provide a great deal of information and feedback to portfolio managers and investment committees.

Ultimately, investors care about the after-tax returns of their portfolios. Both qualitative and quantitative managers try various

---

[14] In Appendix B at www.ludwigbc.com under QEPM Exclusive Content, we discuss additional realistic uses of discounted cash-flow models.

ways to reduce the tax burden. Qualitative managers use some very good rules of thumb, such as selling the oldest tax lots first and selling the tax lots with the lowest gains. They also take futures positions that can be traded in the short term with relatively little tax burden. Quantitative methods incorporate these techniques and also generate many more tax-reduction strategies. Moreover, it is possible to integrate tax considerations directly into a quantitative investment model.[15] With QEPM, the manager can look at the tax effects of a transaction before deciding whether to buy or sell. QEPM also offers a solution to instances in which trades made to reduce the tax burden end up disturbing the balance of stocks in the portfolio. For instance, selling poorly performing stocks at year end to generate capital losses that offset capital gains may make the portfolio less than optimal versus the benchmark or increase its tracking error. A method known as *characteristic matching* can be used to find stocks similar to those that were sold to generate capital losses. Purchasing the matching stocks restores some of the overall characteristics of the portfolio even though some of the original stocks were sold temporarily for tax purposes. Such quantitative tax management strategies protect and often significantly increase after-tax returns.

The financial markets often stray from efficiency. For example, when companies report higher-than-expected earnings, their stocks often earn higher-than-normal returns during the few weeks following the report. Qualitative managers may or may not trade on this sort of market anomaly. If they do—for instance, by purchasing stocks with higher-than-expected earnings announcements—it is often in an ad hoc fashion. QEPM equips quantitative managers to study anomalies in detail and exploit them in a calculated fashion. Quantitative methods help to determine the underlying source of an anomaly, which (if any) time period or industry it is specific to, and the expected excess return of a strategy that centers on it. Quantifying the risks, the gains, and the idiosyncrasies of the anomaly makes for a well-informed trading decision.

Managing a portfolio involves buying and selling stocks repeatedly. Buying and selling generates transactions costs in the form of commissions, price impact, and delay. Studies of equity mutual funds show that most mutual fund managers fail to beat the S&P 500 after accounting for transactions costs.[16] Qualitative

---

[15] See Chapter 11 on tax management.
[16] See Bogle (1999).

managers typically only consider transactions costs implicitly. Quantitative managers can use optimization algorithms to focus directly on the effect of transactions costs on the portfolio's return. Now that some commercial research vendors gather detailed data on the costs of trading, including commissions, price impact, and delay, it is possible to determine the effect of the costs on returns quite precisely. Some investment funds also do their own in-house estimates of transactions costs. From either in-house or vendor-provided data, the quantitative manager can find out whether certain transactions are worthwhile and can avoid *churning*, or excessive turnover.[17]

Many equity portfolio managers use leverage to increase the returns of their portfolio. The typical way to leverage the portfolio—through index futures such as the S&P 500 futures—achieves levered exposure to the overall market but is not always the optimal route because it dilutes a manager's excess performance. Qualitative managers, for the most part, ignore the dilution effect and leverage with index futures. QEPM makes it possible to design a plan that does not dilute the performance. Single-stock futures or equity-swap baskets lever the excess returns of the portfolio in addition to its market exposure, thereby multiplying the excess return rather than diminishing it. To the extent that a manager is able to generate excess returns, the quantitative approach to leverage produces better results.[18]

The QEPM method of *factor tilting* highlights another difference between qualitative and quantitative approaches. Qualitative managers typically purchase stocks that they believe will outperform, accepting all risks associated with each stock. Although this is not necessarily a bad decision, and quantitative managers sometimes do the same, it is possible, using factor tilting, to calibrate the portfolio's exposures to different types of risks. Suppose that a manager is very good at forecasting the future value premiums of stocks but very bad at forecasting the other variables that compromise his or her stock-return model. Factor tilting lets the manager create a portfolio with zero exposure, relative to the benchmark, to all variables except the future-value factor. The result is a model that is relatively more exposed to the factor that the manager is fairly capable of forecasting and relatively less exposed to the ones

---

[17] We discuss transactions costs further in Chapter 10.
[18] For more on leverage, see Chapter 12.

that he or she cannot forecast well. Factor tilting can be a very effective way of managing an equity portfolio and is one of the many powerful tools of QEPM.

These are only a sample of the types of decisions that might differentiate portfolio managers who use QEPM from those who do not avail themselves of quantitative methods. Clearly, responses to specific investment situations vary from manager to manager. Along the spectrum of management styles, some qualitative managers use quantitative methods frequently, and some quantitative managers draw significantly on qualitative information. As we see it, the more consistently a manager uses quantitative methods, the more consistent and precise are the portfolio's results. QEPM structures the decision-making process, and it is a structure adaptable to practically all types of investment scenarios.

1.4 A TOUR OF THE BOOK

The field of QEPM is vast, and there are literally thousands of ways to go about building quantitative models to select stocks for a portfolio. In this book we focus on the most prevalent QEPM methods. Our goal is to cover the entire QEPM process, from modeling stock returns, to building the actual portfolio, to assessing the performance of the portfolio.

The book is divided into five parts. Part I introduces the concept of quantitative equity portfolio management. Chapter 2 discusses the fundamental principles of QEPM, as well as the concept of market efficiency and why QEPM works in mostly efficient markets. Chapter 3 describes the typical QEPM process and introduces the most common models of stock returns.

Part II of the book is about portfolio construction and maintenance. The first step in building a model of stock returns is to choose a mix of explanatory variables for the model. Chapter 4 defines the most commonly used factors and provides simple methods for selecting ones for the model. Factors also can be used for preliminary stock screening and ranking. Chapter 5 explains the basics of stock screening and introduces the aggregate Z-score model, a simple model for ranking stocks. We also describe the investment philosophies of famous portfolio managers and suggest stock screens that emulate their strategies.

Chapters 6 and 7 discuss in detail how to build fundamental and economic factor models, the two types of models that quantitative managers use to estimate and explain stock returns and volatility. Chapter 8 discusses how to forecast future factor premiums, which, in the framework of the factor models, can be used to forecast future stock returns and risks. The forecasts are the basis for including or excluding stocks from the portfolio.

Chapter 9 ties together Chapters 4 through 8 by showing how to use stock-return models and concepts from optimization theory to determine the optimal weights for the stocks in the portfolio while abiding by any investment constraints.

Chapters 10 and 11 discuss refinements to the basic construction and maintenance process. Chapter 10 explains ways to improve the performance of the portfolio by paying particular attention to transactions costs. Managers can avoid excessively high turnover and high transactions costs by incorporating the costs explicitly into the model of stock returns. Chapter 11 discusses ways to improve performance by managing the effect of taxes. By taking taxes into account in the model itself, the manager can be clever about the timing and composition of trades.

In Part III of the book we step outside the core set of QEPM procedures to explore methods for increasing the portfolio's performance that are not related to actual stock picking. We refer to these methods collectively as α *mojo* ("alpha mojo") because they boost α, which is the portion of a portfolio's returns that goes above and beyond the return of the benchmark or reference portfolio.

Chapter 12 looks at the first form of α mojo, leverage. Leverage is used by many portfolio managers to increase the exposure of the portfolio to the market. The chapter shows various methods for leveraging an equity portfolio to boost its excess returns.

Chapter 13 discusses creation of the market-neutral portfolio. Market-neutral and long-short portfolios are widely used structures for quantitative portfolios, especially among hedge funds. They eliminate or reduce market exposure and increase α, improving the risk-return profile of the portfolio. A market-neutral portfolio is ideal for a quantitative equity portfolio manager who wants to focus on his or her specialty of picking good stocks.

In Chapter 14 we use some advanced statistical concepts, known collectively as *Bayesian analysis*, to show how a quantitative portfolio manager can take advantage of qualitative insights. We also show how scenario analysis fits into the quantitative stock-return model.

Part IV of the book brings the portfolio management cycle to its last stage, performance analysis. Though often neglected, the cultivation of an excellent performance measurement department is one of the keys to an investment firm's success. Chapter 15 discuses various standard practices, as well as some new concepts related to quantitative performance measurement and attribution.

Part V implements all the ideas in the first four parts of the book. With an example of the practical application of QEPM, we discuss everything related to building a quantitative portfolio, including data issues, estimation problems, portfolio construction with real data, transactions costs, tax issues, leverage, and performance analysis.

Five appendices can be found online.[19] Appendix A is a history of financial theory for readers who need a quick overview of the subject. Appendix B explains three well-known models of stock returns: the dividend discount model (DDM), the capital asset pricing model (CAPM), and the arbitrage pricing theory (APT) model. Appendix C provides a basic review of mathematical and statistical concepts useful to readers of this book. Appendix D includes a discussion of organizational considerations for investment research departments, followed by a summary of commercial databases and software modeling programs useful for QEPM. Finally, Appendix E looks at the game of craps as an entertaining example of the importance of using quantitative techniques.

1.5 CONCLUSION

Quantitative equity portfolio management (QEPM) is growing in popularity among professional portfolio managers. This style of management offers plenty of advantages over traditional qualitative portfolio management. A combination of advanced statistics,

---

[19] Go to the website www.ludwigbc.com. Once you reach the website, choose Books, then Quantitative Equity Portfolio Management, then QEPM Exclusive Content. The password is qepm2020rig179. You will find a folder with all the solutions to the end-of-chapter questions in the book, a folder with additional appendices for each chapter, a folder with General Appendices (Appendices A–E), a folder with programs and examples written in MATLAB, R, and Stata for learning and for classroom labs, a folder with PowerPoint slides for every chapter, a folder with sample stock data, and a downloadable file of historical factor returns.

mathematics, and a disciplined approach, QEPM makes it possible to quantify stocks' expected returns and risks with a good degree of precision, as well as quantify the uncertainty of the forecasts themselves. To begin the book, we described what we see as the major advantages of QEPM over qualitative approaches to asset management, and we gave examples of typical differences between the two styles of management in the face of specific investment decisions. In the rest of the book we will attempt to guide you through the very broad field of QEPM. We will take you step by step through every aspect of the QEPM process, from stock-return forecasting, to portfolio building, to performance measurement.

QUESTIONS

1.1. Name three advantages of QEPM versus qualitative equity management.

1.2. Name three disadvantages of QEPM versus qualitative equity management.

1.3. Name four realistic investment situations in which a quantitative portfolio manager differs from a qualitative portfolio manager in his or her approach.

1.4. In some ways, a qualitative portfolio manager could never really be an index portfolio manager, whereas a quantitative portfolio manager could be. Explain why.

1.5. What is factor tilting? What type of portfolio manager engages in it?

1.6. Fed fund futures are actively traded instruments on the Chicago Board of Trade. The contract is cash settled to the simple average of the daily effective Fed funds rate for the delivery month. Although the daily effective Fed funds rate is not perfectly equal to the Fed funds target rate, it is very close. Market practitioners use the Fed fund futures rate to gauge the market's assessment that the Fed will change the Fed fund's rate. Suppose that there will be an FOMC meeting 10 days into the current month. Use the following variables, i_t^f as the Fed fund futures rate, i_t^{pre} as the target rate prevailing before the FOMC meeting, i_t^{post} as the target rate expected to prevail *after* the FOMC meeting, p as the probability of a target rate change, d_1 as the number of days between previous month end and the FOMC meeting, d_2 as the number of days between the FOMC meeting at the current month end, and B as the number of days in the month. (*Note*: In practice, the Fed attempts to achieve a certain target rate or target range, but it varies from day to day. For i_t^{pre} you can think of it as the midpoint of the previous target range or use the average Fed funds effective rate of the prior month. For i_t^{post} you can use the midpoint of the next jump in the target range [e.g., 25 basis points] or some other value of your choice.)

(a)   Write down a general formula for the probability of an FOMC target-rate change.

(b)   Given that the current target rate is 3.5%, the expected rate after the meeting is 3.75%, the Fed futures implied rate is 3.60%, there are 30 days in the month, and the FOMC meeting will take place on the tenth day of the month, what is the probability implied by the market prices that the Federal Reserve will raise interest rates?

CHAPTER 2

The Fundamentals of QEPM

Some people recognize beauty before others have recognized it, some people see beauty that no one else can see, and some people see no beauty.

2.1 INTRODUCTION

Quantitative equity portfolio managers cannot simply go through the motions of quantitative analysis. Implementing quantitative equity portfolio management (QEPM) the right way requires a firm grasp of the underlying concepts that make the analysis work. Since quantitative equity portfolio managers generally aim to outperform a benchmark or index, we start our conceptual discussion with alpha (α), the measurement of a portfolio's risk-adjusted returns over and above a reference instrument. There are a number of variations of alpha, but no matter what type of alpha a manager strives for, his or her work should be guided by the seven tenets of QEPM. The seven tenets encompass ideas necessary to the very existence of QEPM. One of these essential ideas is that financial markets do not operate entirely efficiently. Neither QEPM nor any other form of active management would succeed in a perfectly efficient market. We examine the evidence for market inefficiency, which is found mainly in studies of market anomalies, and we explore possible explanations for these anomalies. The seven tenets of QEPM also lay down important principles for the practice of QEPM, including the efficient use of information in quantitative models. We discuss the popular but frequently misinterpreted fundamental law of active management as an important framework for understanding and achieving efficiency. Finally, the seven tenets demand the consideration of statistical issues that have direct bearing on the statistics-intensive methods of QEPM. We reflect on these issues, which include data mining, parameter instability, and parameter uncertainty, at the end of the chapter.

2.2 QEPM α

The word *alpha* is constantly bandied about in the world of active portfolio management. Active managers use the term in many contexts, and sometimes it is not clear exactly what they are referring to when they use it. The simplest, colloquial meaning of α is outperformance. You might hear a portfolio manager say, "I'm trying to generate positive α." He or she probably means that he or she wants the portfolio to outperform some other instrument. In general, α represents the excess return of the portfolio over the return of a reference instrument. There are different ways to define *excess performance*, though. In QEPM, α is a measure of the *risk-adjusted* excess return, which is the portfolio's performance after accounting for its risk relative to the reference instrument. Increasing the α therefore means increasing the portfolio's return without increasing its direct exposure risk to the reference instrument. When the reference instrument is the portfolio manager's benchmark, we will refer to α as the *benchmark* α or α^B.[1] When the reference instrument is a series of multifactor benchmarks, we will refer to α as *multifactor* α or α^{MF}. When the reference instrument is the market portfolio, we will refer to α as the *CAPM* α or α^{CAPM}.[2]

Given the returns of the reference instrument, it is possible to use statistical techniques to decompose the portfolio's return into two parts—one that is related to the reference instrument and one

---

[1] In practice, many quantitative managers simply refer to benchmark α as α because ultimately they measure their success or failure against a benchmark. The portfolio manager does typically increase his or her residual risk when pursuing α. Theoretically, a portfolio manager could increase his or her α with zero incremental risk, but practically this is rare.

[2] CAPM α is also sometimes referred to as *Jensen's* α.

that is not. The related part is typically called *expected return* or *consensus return*, and the second part is known as *residual return* or *the return not explained by the model*. For each of the three types of α, there is a slightly different method for separating these two components of the portfolio's return.

2.2.1 Benchmark α

Given the portfolio return r_P and the benchmark return r_B, we can estimate the following equation[3]:

$$r_P = \alpha + \beta r_B + \epsilon \qquad (2.1)$$

In this equation, βr_B is the expected or consensus return, which is the part of the portfolio's return related to the benchmark. The remaining $\alpha + \epsilon$ is the residual return.[4]

The residual return is all that matters to the quantitative portfolio manager, because his or her goal is to increase the risk-adjusted return. If the benchmark return is positive, it is easy enough to generate higher returns simply by increasing the portfolio's exposure to the benchmark, but the portfolio manager has not added value. The part of the portfolio return that represents an increase in return independent of increased direct benchmark exposure is the residual return. Benchmark α is the expected value of the residual return, and the second component of the residual return, ϵ, is the deviation of the residual return from its mean. Equation (2.1) is constructed so that ϵ averages zero. The benchmark α, also known as α^B, therefore has special significance: It is the risk-adjusted excess return over the benchmark.

2.2.2 CAPM α

Given the portfolio return r_P and the market return r_M, we can estimate the following equation:

$$r_P = \alpha + \beta r_M + \epsilon \qquad (2.2)$$

---

[3] The reader can think of these returns in these regressions as the returns minus the risk-free rate.

[4] Note that this usage of residual is somewhat different from the standard usage in econometrics. In econometrics, the residual refers to the realization of ϵ and does not include α. Unfortunately, the use by practitioners does not always coincide with the use by academics.

In this equation, βr_M is the expected or consensus return, which is the part of the portfolio's return related to the market. The remaining $\alpha + \epsilon$ is the residual return.

The reader will notice that this version of α is very similar to the one created using the benchmark return. In fact, since the market return is typically the Standard and Poor's (S&P) 500 return, if the benchmark is the S&P 500, then those two measures of α are the same. In this equation, however, α is called the *CAPM α* because this decomposition of a portfolio's returns follows from the capital asset pricing model (CAPM).[5] The equation says that the returns of all portfolios are related to the market portfolio. According to CAPM theory, the CAPM α should equal zero. When it is significantly positive, the portfolio manager is providing excess risk-adjusted returns. The CAPM α, or α^{CAPM}, is the risk-adjusted excess return over the market.

2.2.3 Multifactor α

Given the portfolio return r_p and a series of factor returns $f_1, \ldots, f_K$, we can estimate the following equation:

$$r_p = \alpha + \beta_1 f_1 + \cdots + \beta_K f_K + \epsilon \qquad (2.3)$$

where $\beta_1 f_1 + \cdots + \beta_K f_K$ is the expected or consensus return from a multifactor model of stock returns (i.e., the part of the portfolio's return related to the underlying risk factors in the economy). The remaining $\alpha + \epsilon$ is the residual return, as before.

Note that this version of α is created using a model with many factors that influence stock returns. There will be more discussion of this framework in subsequent chapters. The α in this model is called the *multifactor α*, or α^{MF}, and it is a measurement of risk-adjusted excess return given multiple explanatory variables.

2.2.4 A Variety of α's

The α's in Eqs. (2.1), (2.2), and (2.3) are interrelated. In special cases, they are equivalent to each other.

---

[5] For those unfamiliar with the CAPM, see a brief discussion of the fundamental models of stock return in Appendix B at www.ludwigbc.com under QEPM Exclusive Content.

1. The multifactor α of a stock or a portfolio is the same as the CAPM α if the market return is the only factor in the model.

2. The benchmark α of a stock or a portfolio is the same as the CAPM α if the market portfolio is the benchmark.

3. The multifactor α and the benchmark α of a stock or portfolio are the same if the market return is the only factor in the model and is also the benchmark.

In other cases, the three α's are not equivalent. Suppose that the manager uses an inefficient benchmark, which is evidenced by the fact that the α of the benchmark against the market return is negative. As a result, the benchmark α of the portfolio will be higher than the market α of the portfolio. To use our notation, $\alpha^B > \alpha^{\text{CAPM}}$. Using an inefficient benchmark therefore will make the portfolio's performance look better than it would if it were measured against the entire market.[6]

Many practitioners and academics may ask whether or not positive benchmark α is consistent with the arbitrage pricing theory (APT).[7] In fact, the answer is yes. Although it is practically difficult to test the APT because the theory does not specify the underlying factors of security returns, let's assume for a moment that we know the true factors of stock returns. Suppose that the portfolio's return is determined according to APT and can be expressed as

$$r_P = \alpha + \beta_1 f_1 + \cdots + \beta_K f_K + \epsilon \qquad (2.4)$$

Let us also suppose that the first factor, f_1, is the benchmark (e.g., S&P 500). What would the benchmark α be in this case? Could it be positive?

Recall that the benchmark α is the part of the average return that is not related to the benchmark. If all the other factors in the APT model are uncorrelated with the first factor (the benchmark), then the benchmark α is given by

$$\alpha^B = E(\alpha + \beta_2 f_2 + \cdots + \beta_K f_K) \qquad (2.5)$$

---

[6] Suppose that we postulate the following models of stock returns: $r_P = \alpha' + \beta' r_B + \epsilon'$, $r_P = \alpha'' + \beta'' r_M + \epsilon''$, and $r_B = \alpha + \beta r_M + \epsilon$. By substitution of variables, we see that $r_P = \alpha' + \beta' \alpha + \beta' \beta r_M + \beta' \epsilon + \epsilon'$. From this relationship we can see that $\alpha'' = \alpha' + \beta' \alpha$. Thus, for a positive β', $\alpha'' < \alpha'$ when $\alpha < 0$, and vice versa.

[7] For those unfamiliar with the APT, see a brief discussion of the three fundamental models of stock returns in Appendix B at www.ludwigbc.com under QEPM Exclusive Content.

The benchmark α includes the effect of all the other factors. Thus it is quite likely that the benchmark α is positive. In general, if we allow the benchmark to be correlated with all other factors, the benchmark α is given by

$$\alpha^B = E(\alpha + \beta_2 f_2 + \cdots + \beta_K f_K) - (\beta_2 \gamma_2 + \cdots + \beta_K \gamma_K)E(f_1) \qquad (2.6)$$

where γ_j is the coefficient in the regression of f_j on f_1 [i.e., $C(f_1, f_j)/V(f_1)$]. While the formula is somewhat more complicated, the conclusion is the same. The benchmark α includes the effect of all factors aside from the benchmark, so it is very possible that the benchmark α is positive.

This analysis shows that when measuring the performance of a manager with benchmark α, benchmark α can be positive even if multifactor α equals zero. Although multifactor α equals zero, benchmark α still can be positive if the portfolio manager loads his or her portfolio with positive exposures to factors that have positive premiums according to the APT. A positive benchmark α therefore is consistent with the APT model, in which managers are rewarded for statistical arbitrages.

2.2.5 Ex-Ante and Ex-Post α

Whichever type of α we use, there is usually a difference between the value we expect it to reach in the future and the value that it ultimately realizes. The *ex-ante* α is the expected α, whereas the *ex-post* α is the realized one. The ex-ante α is of interest to the quantitative portfolio manager when he or she is constructing his or her portfolio. Clearly, he or she sets out trying to achieve the highest possible α when he or she builds the portfolio subject to the portfolio constraints. Once the portfolio has been active for some period of time, the ex-post α shows whether the actual risk-adjusted performance lived up to expectations. The manager's bonus is based on the ex-post α.[8] The best a manager can realistically hope for is that the ex-post and ex-ante α's will be highly correlated.

2.2.6 Ex-Ante and Ex-Post Information Ratio

Though α by itself is the primary measure of a portfolio's excess return, there is also a key metric, the *information ratio*, that adjusts

---

[8] In golf, there is a saying that goes, "Drive for show, putt for dough." In QEPM, it would be "Ex-ante α for show, ex-post α for dough."

α for the portfolio's residual risk. As with α, there are ex-ante and ex-post information ratios. We will discuss only the ex-ante information ratio at this stage because the ex-post information ratio is discussed in detail in Chapter 15 on performance measurement. The information ratio is directly related to the benchmark α, α^B. The ex-ante information ratio (IR) is given by

$$IR = \frac{\alpha^B}{\omega} \qquad (2.7)$$

where α^B is the expected or predicted α of the portfolio manager, and ω is the predicted standard deviation of the residual [i.e., $S(\epsilon)$]. The ex-ante information ratio measures the expected excess return over the benchmark per unit of excess risk over the benchmark. The higher the ex-ante information ratio, the better we expect the portfolio to perform. All else equal, a higher forecasted ratio is better.

2.3 THE SEVEN TENETS OF QEPM

A quantitative equity portfolio manager aims for the twin goal-posts of a high alpha and a high information ratio, and getting there requires knowing the rules of the game. QEPM is organized around certain principles. We call these principles the *seven tenets of QEPM*.

Tenet 1: *Markets are mostly efficient.*

Tenet 2: *Pure arbitrage opportunities do not exist.*

Tenet 3: *Quantitative analysis creates statistical arbitrage opportunities.*

Tenet 4: *Quantitative analysis combines all the available information in an efficient way.*

Tenet 5: *Quantitative models should be based on sound economic theories.*

Tenet 6: *Quantitative models should reflect persistent and stable patterns.*

Tenet 7: *Deviations of a portfolio from the benchmark are justified only if the uncertainty is small enough.*

Tenets 1 and 2 set boundaries on QEPM's reach. Markets are mostly efficient, which means that it is not possible to make profits without taking risk. Risk-free opportunities, or pure arbitrage opportunities, do not exist. Still, the markets are not perfectly efficient. There is room to make profits by taking relatively small amounts of additional risk. QEPM is the process of searching for such "statistical arbitrage opportunities," as stated in tenet 3. Statistical arbitrage opportunities exist because stock prices do not always properly reflect all the available information. QEPM provides statistical methods for identifying information that the market has overlooked. As tenet 4 says, the quantitative manager must combine all the available information into an efficient model in order to identify the pieces that are key to earning higher returns.

Tenets 5, 6, and 7 establish standards for applying econometric techniques to choices involving the portfolio. Tenet 5 is absolutely fundamental to creating quantitative models of stock returns. All models used to pick stocks should be based on sound economic theory. Data mining violates this tenet. Factors dredged up from the data through data mining may seem to relate to stock returns on their surface, but they are unlikely to reveal real opportunities for statistical arbitrage. The manager has to have a good reason for choosing each factor that he or she includes in the model. There should be reason to believe that stock prices do not yet, but eventually will, reflect the information contained in each factor or in the group of factors as combined in the model. The model is not meaningful without a strong theoretical underpinning.

Likewise, the relationship between the factors and stock returns needs to be one that holds up over time. As tenet 6 says, the model should only make use of data patterns that are persistent and stable. Parameter stability is essential to the generation of precise estimates and reliable forecasts with the model.

Tenet 7 cautions that QEPM does not always involve differentiating the portfolio from the benchmark. Many quantitative portfolio managers mistakenly believe that deviations from the benchmark are necessary in QEPM. In fact, a deviation from the benchmark portfolio is justified only if the portfolio's estimation error (a measure of uncertainty) is small enough. Quantitative managers always should take parameter uncertainty into account before steering the portfolio away from the benchmark onto another path dictated by the model.[9]

---

[9] Parameter uncertainty depends, among other things, on sample size. If the sample size is small, the parameter uncertainty will be large. By properly accounting for the parameter uncertainty, portfolio managers can avoid the common mistake of exaggerating the estimation from small sample sizes.

In the following sections we discuss the seven tenets of QEPM in greater detail. We start with the concept of market efficiency and its implications for QEPM. Then we discuss how to use information efficiently, adopting the framework of the fundamental law of active management. Finally, we examine issues arising from the application of econometric techniques to QEPM.

2.4 TENETS 1 AND 2: MARKET EFFICIENCY AND QEPM

Tenets 1 and 2 of QEPM are based on the belief that markets are mostly, but not completely, efficient. If markets were completely efficient, QEPM would be a futile exercise. An active portfolio manager has to believe that there are inefficiencies in the market that he or she can exploit. In this section we discuss what it means for the market to be efficient and what the evidence is for some degree of market inefficiency.

2.4.1 The Efficient-Market Hypothesis

There are those who say that financial markets are efficient and those who say they are not, but what are people really talking about? In general terms, an efficient market is a market in which all information is reflected in current stock prices. For instance, in an efficient market, an investor could not earn excess returns by buying a stock on a tip that the company has a new CEO who is expected to improve operations. The price of the stock already would reflect this news and any other relevant information. In a perfectly efficient market, investors cannot earn excess returns without bearing extra risk, and portfolio managers, therefore, cannot create α.[10]

In an efficient market, stock prices move randomly. If we looked at the historical prices of any stock in an efficient market, the

---

[10] If the market were perfectly efficient, would it have been possible for Warren Buffett to earn an average annual return of 20% between 1965 and 2020, beating the S&P 500 by 9.8% per year? (*Source*: Berkshire Hathaway 2021 Annual Report, Chairman's Letter to Shareholders, p. 2.) Even in a perfectly efficient market, a few investors would indeed earn very high returns because there would still be some outliers in the distribution of returns. In a truly efficient market, however, Buffett's returns would have come at the price of extra risk rather than generating α. Also, his performance would have been simply good fortune rather than an ability to find companies selling below their intrinsic values.

day-to-day changes would show no discernible pattern. When stock prices do move in some predetermined fashion, then presumably an investor can make money by trading around the pattern, which means that there is an inefficiency in the market.

Not even *near-arbitrage* opportunities exist in a perfectly efficient market. For example, if a publicly traded company traded at a price of $100, a subsidiary in which it owned a 95% stake could not trade at $200. If it did, an investor could buy the main company's stock at $100 per share and short sell the subsidiary's stock at $200 per share, making a profit when the two prices eventually aligned. When PALM was spun off from 3COM on March 1, 2000, the two companies' stock prices displayed a similar imbalance, leading some to seriously doubt the efficiency of the stock market.

Asset bubbles are also signs of inefficient markets. In early 2000, the NASDAQ was overvalued by almost any measure of valuation. Internet startups traded at market capitalizations many multiples of the market caps of established brick-and-mortar companies in similar lines of business. From March 2000 to January 2003, however, the NASDAQ fell by 71%. A $100 million portfolio invested in the new technology revolution in 2000 would have been reduced to a mere $29 million in less than three years. The internet bubble was a huge, unsustainable deviation from market efficiency.

Perhaps one of the greatest dislocations of prices from fundamentals occurred during the housing bubble of 2008, also known as the Great Recession. In the period from 2003 to 2008, easy liquidity and lack of accountability caused housing prices and the stock market to soar. In 2008, the housing market came crashing down along with the stock market. The S&P 500 declined by 38% in 2008, and the national housing price index declined by 11.88%, with some cities experiencing even larger declines in housing prices. This perplexing inefficiency may have been caused by an immensely crowded investment space and pointed to the potential inefficiencies of markets.[11]

In the 1970s, Eugene Fama, a professor at the University of Chicago, decided to establish testable criteria for market efficiency. Fama recognized that the market's level of efficiency has to do with the degree to which security prices reflect information relevant to the investment decision. The nature of investment-relevant information is a continuum that spans from the most obvious public

---

[11] See Chincarini (2012) for a detailed account of crowding and the financial crisis of 2008.

information to the most private insider information. In Fama's criteria, market efficiency is directly related to how much of the continuum is incorporated in market prices.

Fama described three increasing levels of efficiency—*weak form*, *semistrong form*, and *strong form*—at which market prices reflect increasingly more of the information continuum. (Table 2.1 provides a quick overview of the three definitions of efficiency.) At the lowest level of efficiency, weak-form efficiency, *security prices reflect the information available in previous security prices.* This means that past prices of stocks give an investor no actionable information. For portfolio managers, it means that *technical analysis* does not work.

Technical analysis is popular with many investors, especially traders. A classic text written by John Murphy defines technical analysis as the study of market action through the application of charts and/or statistical techniques to forecast future price trends.[12] Whereas the fundamental analyst looks for the causes of market movements in the form of economic or operating data, the technical analyst is more concerned with patterns in the market movements themselves. Technicians look for patterns in data directly obtainable from securities, such as past prices, volume, and open interest. Like fundamental analysts, technicians believe that prices

TABLE 2.1

Definitions of Market Efficiency

Type of Efficiency	Definition	Practical Implication
Weak form	Security prices reflect the information available in previous security prices.	You should not expect technical analysis to aid you in picking stocks.
Semistrong form	Security prices reflect all information that is publicly available.	You should not expect models built from macroeconomic, fundamental, analyst, or any other publicly available information to aid you in picking stocks.
Strong form	Security prices reflect all information that is publicly or privately held.	You should not expect inside information or proprietary information to aid you in picking stocks.

---

[12] See Murphy (1999).

adjust slowly to their proper levels when new information reaches the marketplace because not all investors have equal access to information. The time it takes for information to percolate through the hierarchy of professional traders down to the general investing public creates a window of opportunity for technicians to trade on the patterns that they have identified in the data.

One of the simplest patterns identified by technicians is *momentum*. The idea is that if a stock had a positive return in the period prior to this one (e.g., last week), then there is a good chance that the stock will have a positive return in the subsequent period (e.g., this week). If this pattern holds, the market is not weak-form efficient because past prices, which indicate the past returns, help you to invest for the future. In a weak-form efficient market, current prices incorporate all the information contained in past prices.

The next level of efficiency covers more of the public-to-private continuum of information. In the semistrong form of market efficiency, *security prices reflect all information that is publicly available.* This means that quantitative portfolio managers and other investors cannot use any publicly available information to pick stocks and earn risk-adjusted excess returns. Semistrong-form efficiency is bad news for QEPM. Most quantitative portfolio managers use some form of macroeconomic or fundamental data to choose superior stocks. If markets were semistrong efficient, these methods would not work. For example, some portfolio managers buy stocks with low price-to-book (P/B) ratios on the belief that such stocks are probably undervalued. This would not work in a semistrong-form efficient market because P/B ratios are public information, so stock prices already would correctly reflect low P/B ratios. Active management succeeds only by finding niches of the market that are not semistrong-form efficient, perhaps owing to the slow diffusion of information, or by developing proprietary investment strategies, which become themselves nonpublic information. In the semistrong form of efficiency, market prices do not incorporate nonpublic information.

At the highest level of market efficiency, strong-form efficiency, *security prices reflect all information that is publicly or privately held.* In a strong-form efficient market, even private information gives an investor no consistent advantage in picking stocks that will outperform the rest. Strong-form efficiency is the hardest form of efficiency to test because testing requires a precise definition of private information, yet the boundary between public and private information fluctuates. Many years ago (November 4, 1998), the Bureau

of Labor Statistics (BLS) accidentally posted its weekly unemployment report on its Web site two days before the report was supposed to be published. Some investors found the number, acted on
it, and made abnormal profits. Since no one expected the report to
be released until two days later, what was supposed to be released
as public information ended up available ahead of time to a small
group of lucky, or particularly diligent, investors. Private information often transforms into public information, but as the bureau's
slip-up demonstrates, information also can pass from the private
domain into an in-between space not universally accessible. The
law does at least draw one bright line between public and private
by prohibiting trading on *inside information*. Company insiders and
those who receive information from them are not allowed to take
advantage of privileged knowledge. If the law is effective in bar-
ring people from trading on this sort of private information, then
the market cannot be strong-form efficient.

The entire premise of active management, including QEPM, is
that there are market inefficiencies prevalent and predictable
enough to exploit consistently for high returns. Semistrong-form
efficiency and strong-form efficiency would make active management nearly impossible. After all, a portfolio manager cannot
depend on fluke opportunities such as the BLS's early unemployment data release, much less on illegal insider stock tips. The fact
that some active managers consistently outperform the market or a
benchmark is enough to convince some people that the market is
not wholly efficient. More rigorous evidence against strong-form
and even semistrong-form efficiency comes from researchers who
have documented signs of inefficiency in market prices.

2.4.2 Anomalies

Investment professionals and academics have observed patterns
in historical financial data that contradict the theory of efficient
markets.[13] Table 2.2 lists some of these so-called anomalies, along
with references to studies on each of them.

---

[13] A test of the efficient-market theory requires an asset pricing model (e.g., CAPM) for the
purpose of calculating risk-adjusted returns. Thus the rejection of efficient-market
theory, or the discovery of an anomaly, may indicate the failure of the chosen asset
pricing model rather than the failure of the efficient-market theory. This ambiguity
regarding the nature of an anomaly is known as the *joint hypothesis problem*. In this
chapter, for the purpose of simple exposition, we describe an anomaly as
representing the failure of efficient-market theory.

TABLE 2.2

Well-Known Anomalies

Anomaly	Associated Factor	Research Papers
1. Value effect. Low price-to-earnings ratio stocks outperform high price-to-earnings ratio stocks. Similar results for price-to-book ratio, price-to-sales ratio, and price-to-dividend ratio.	Price-to-earnings ratio, price-to-book ratio, price-to-sales ratio, and price-to-dividend ratio.	Ball (1978), Barberis and Schleifer (2003), Basu (1977, 1983), Bhanderi (1988), Conrad et al. (2003), Daniel and Titman (1997), Cook et al. (1984), Fama and French (1992, 1993), Goodman et al. (1986), Reinganum (1981, 1988), Rosenberg et al. (1985), and Senschak et al. (1987).
2. Size effect. Small-cap stocks outperform large-cap stocks.	Market capitalization (size).	Banz (1981), Fama and French (1992, 1993), Ferson and Harvey (1999), Kim and Moon (2002), and Reinganum (1997).
3. January effect. Small-cap stocks and last year's poorly performing stocks tend to outperform in January.	Low market capitalization, low returns in the previous year.	Blume and Stambaugh (1983), Constantinides (1984), Ferris et al. (2001), Givoly (1983), Haugen and Jorion (1996), Keim (1983, 1985, 1986), Lakonishik (1984,1986), Reinganum (1983), Ritter (1988), Roll (1983), Schultz (1985), and Thaler (1987).
4. Other calender effects (not including January)	Day of the week, Halloween, weather, daylight savings, and other calender events.	Ariel (1987), Bouman and Jacobsen (1997), Cross (1973), Harris (1986a, 1986b), Hensel and Ziemba (1996), Hirshleifer and Shumway (2001), Jaffe and Westerfield (1985), Kamstra et al. (2000, 2003), Rogalski (1984), Smirlock (1986), Sullivan et al. (2001), Thaler (1987), and Wang et al. (1997).
5. Neglected firm effect. Stocks with low analyst coverage tend to have risk-adjusted excess returns.	Number of analysts following the stock.	Arbel (1985), Arbel and Strabel (1982, 1983), Arbel et al. (1983), Dowen and Bauman (1984, 1986), Beard and Sias (1997), and Merton (1987).
6. Price-to-earnings-growth ratio effect. There is an inverse relationship between the price-to-earnings-growth ratio of a stock and its performance.	Price-to-earnings-growth ratio.	Peters (1991) and Reilly and Marshall (1999).

Anomaly	Associated Factor	Research Papers
7. IPO effect. IPOs tend to underperform on a risk-adjusted basis in the first 3–5 years.	Dummy variable indicating whether the stock recently had an IPO.	Carter et al. (1998), Dharan and Ikenberry (1995), Loughran and Ritter (1995), and Carter and Ritter (1991).
8. Index change effect. The stocks to be included in the index will have significantly positive returns, while the stocks to be dropped from the index will have significantly negative returns. (Every year the Russell 1000, 2000, and 3000 are rebalanced. The S&P 500 is also rebalanced at the discretion of the S&P Index Committee.)	Dummy variable indicating whether the stock is going to be included in or dropped from an index.	Jain (1987) and Harris and Gurel (1986).
9. Momentum. Stocks that perform well during one investment period will continue to do well in the subsequent investment horizon.	Return of stock in prior investment period.	Chan et al. (1996), Chan et al. (2000), Grundy and Martin (2001), Hong and Stein (2000), Jegadeesh (1990), Jegadeesh and Titman (1993, 2001), Moskowitz and Grinblatt (1999), O'Neal (2000), Richards (1997), Rouwenhorst (1999), and Swinkels (2002).
10. Other technical effects (other than momentum). Certain technical indicators have been shown to provide excess returns.	Various technical indicators, including volume, reversals, relative strength index, Bollinger bands, moving average, and others.	Brock et al. (1992).
11. Wall Street analyst forecasts. Stocks with buy ratings have been shown to outperform, but this effect has subsided in recent years. Changes in analyst ratings have been shown to be predictive of security returns, and earnings surprises in which reported earnings exceed the consensus estimate have been shown to produce excess returns.	Analyst recommendations on stocks.	Alexander and Ang (1998), Arnott (1985), Barron and Stuerke (1998), Bartov et al. (2000), Bauman et al. (1995), Brown and Chen (1990, 1991), Brown and Rozeff (1978, 1980), Chopra (1998), Clement (1999), Cornell (1989), Dowen (1990), Dreman and Berry (1995), Givoly and Lakonishok (1980), Jones et al. (1984), Kim and Kim (2003), LaPorta (1996), Latane and Jones (1977), Mendhall (2004), Peters (1993), and Womack (1996).

TABLE 2.2 *(Continued)*

Anomaly	Associated Factor	Research Papers
12. Insider trading. Stocks that insiders have recently bought produce excess returns. Stocks that insiders have recently sold produce negative returns.	Net purchases or sales by insiders.	Fishe and Roby (2004), Givoly and Palmon (1985), Jaffe (1974), and Seyhun (1986, 1988).
13. Overreaction. It has been found that investors overreact to news events, bad and good. One basic result is that previous "loser" stocks tend to outperform previous "winner" stocks over a 3- to 5-year period.	Past returns of stocks conditional or unconditional on certain news events.	Chincarini and Llorente (1999), Chopra et al. (1992), Conrad and Kaul (1993), Daniel et al. (1998), Debondt and Thaler (1985, 1987), Hong and Stein (1999), Lo and MacKinlay (1990), and Veronesi (1999).
14. Stock buybacks. When a company buys back its stock, the stock subsequently has positive risk-adjusted returns.	Change in treasury stock.	Choi and Chen (1997) and Ikenberry et al. (1995).
15. Stock splits and reverse splits effect. Stock splits are followed by positive returns.	Signals of a stock split.	Desai and Jain (1997), Doran (1994), Dowen (1990), Ikenberry et al. (1996), and Ye (1999).
16. Spin-offs effect. A parent company has excess returns after the spin-off of a subsidiary.	Signals of a spin-off.	Cusatis et al. (1993) and Desai and Jain (1999).
17. Accruals. It has been documented that stocks that have low accruals perform better in the subsequent investment horizon than companies with high accruals. Accrual accounting measures a company's performance by recognizing economic events regardless of when cash transactions occur.	Accrual of company in prior period. Accruals are defined as revenues earned or expenses incurred that impact a company's net income on the income statement, even though cash related to the transaction has not yet changed hands. Accruals can also affect the balance sheet, as they involve non-cash assets and liabilities.	Sloan (1996), Bradshaw, Richardson, and Sloan (2001), Lev and Nissam (2006), Ali et al. (2008), Richardson et al. (2005), Thomas and Zhang (2002), Xie (2001), Shi and Zhang (2011), Allen et al. (2010), Richardson et al. (2006), Bhorraj and Swaminathan (2008), and Liepold and Llore (2012).
18. Low volatility. It has been documented that stocks with low historical volatility outperform stocks with high historical volatility.	Historical volatility in prior period. Different researchers have used different methods to compute the historical volatility of each stock.	Thomas and Scapiro (2009), Clarke et al. (2006), Ang et al. (2006), Blitz and Van Vliet (2007), and Baker et al. (2011),

Anomaly	Associated Factor	Research Papers
19. Low beta. It has been documented that stocks with low historical measured beta outperform stocks with a high historical measured beta on a risk-adjusted basis.	Historical beta of stock in prior period. Different researchers use different methods to measure historical beta.	Black et al. (1972), Black (1993), Frazzini and Pederson (2014), and Baker et al. (2011),
20. Liquidity. There is research that shows that less liquid stocks provide higher average returns than more liquid stocks. Despite lots of evidence, there are also researchers who doubt that this is a true anomaly.	There are various measures of liquidity. Share turnover, which is volume of shares traded divided by shares outstanding. Also called *trading turnover* when done in dollars. Amihud liquidity, which is the return of stock for the day divided by dollar volume for the day. The Modified Amihud measure, which is the same but measures the daily return using open-to-close prices. Pastor and Stambaugh use regressions on daily stock returns to assess how volume causes reversal in stock returns due to liquidity. Invariance is also used, which is related to the standard deviation of returns and average volume.	Chincarini and Llorente (1999), Chincarini and Kim (2006), Amihud (2002), Amihud and Mendelson (1986), Pastor and Stambaugh (2003), Brown, Crocker, and Foerster (2009), Chrodia et al. (2001), Liu (2006), Acharya and Pederson (2005), Fama and French (2008), Drienki et al. (2017), Hoe et al. (2017), Li et. al (2017), Barardehi et al. (2019, 2020), Kyle and Obizhaeva (2016), and Ibbottson et al. (2013).
21. Crowding. There is evidence that stocks that are disproportionately invested in by money managers underperform stocks that are less saturated by money managers.	The measure of crowding in an investment space. There are various measures of crowding, including return-based measures and holding-based measures. An example of a holding-based measure is the percentage of holdings by active managers relative to average turnover. An example of a return-based measure is to look at how the returns or residual returns of grouped stocks are correlated over time.	Chincarini (1998, 2012, 2017), Chincarini et al. (2018), Cahan and Luo (2013), Yan (2014), Chue (2015), Zhong et al. (2016), Baltas (2019), Brown et al. (2019), and Volpati et al. (2020).
22. Profitability	The profitability of a company. There are various measures of profitability that seem to generate excess returns.	Chincarini and Kim (2006), Novy-Marx (2013), Ball et al. (2015), Wahal (2018), Linnainma and Roberts (2018), Fama and French (2015, 2018), Chen et al. (2018), Cacecki et al. (2020), Bouchaud et al. (2019), Wahal (2019), and Asness et al. (2019).

Anomalies pose a significant challenge to the theory that markets are perfectly efficient. Proponents of efficiency might dismiss certain price irregularities as one-time aberrations in a generally efficient market. Anomalies cannot be dismissed so easily because they are patterns of recurrent irregularities. An anomaly suggests that investors habitually fail to consider and correctly interpret all the information relevant to the investment decision, or that institutional barriers prevent them from acting on certain information, or that, even with all the relevant information staring them in the face, they persist in making irrational choices. There are anomalies that contradict each definition of market efficiency from weak form to strong form.

Weak-Form Anomalies

Typical tests of weak-form market efficiency try to determine whether past prices can be used to predict future prices of individual stocks. For example, researchers may test whether there is significant autocorrelation in a stock's returns. *Autocorrelation* is the statistical term for correlation between returns from period to period. If stock returns are positively autocorrelated over time, a positive return in one period suggests a positive return in the next. An investor could profit from this pattern, which technical analysts call *momentum*, by buying stocks that performed well in the last period.

Researchers have found that there is autocorrelation in stock indices over a daily, weekly, and monthly horizon. One study found that between July 1962 and December 1994, the autocorrelation in a certain stock index was about 35%. Individual securities exhibited a slightly negative autocorrelation, but this autocorrelation was economically and statistically insignificant.[14] Other studies found significant positive autocorrelation in quarterly stock returns over horizons of less than one year.[15] However, for horizons of one week or one month, individual monthly stock returns seem to be negatively autocorrelated.[16] There is also evidence that industry returns may exhibit positive autocorrelation.[17]

There is mixed evidence on other technical indicators. Traders believe that they work, but tests of technical rules do not clearly confirm that belief. The standards for testing technical rules have

---

[14] See Lo, MacKinlay, and Campbell (1997), p. 66.
[15] See Conrad and Kaul (1988) and Jegadeesh and Titman (1993, 2001).
[16] See Jegadeesh (1990). Also see the list in Table 2.2.
[17] See Moskowitz and Grinblatt (1999).

been inconsistent. Many practitioners fail to include transactions costs in their tests, making excess returns appear greater than they actually would have been. Tests are also usually done on closing prices, which may be the best and most complete data available but are not necessarily the prices at which trades would have been placed. In general, tests cannot easily replicate a trader's discretion in applying technical strategies. A trader might have thought that a technical rule applied during one period but not during another. Technical trading is also not necessarily comparable with portfolio management. Some trading rules might work on intraday data, but they will not serve as portfolio strategies, which are supposed to work for months or years. Taking these limitations into account, the results of the tests of technical rules tend to fall on the side of weak-form efficiency because most technical rules do not seem to work consistently over time.

Semistrong-Form Anomalies

If technical data fail to provide reliable investment strategies, what about other publicly available information? There is a host of anomalies that provide evidence that market prices do not reflect all public information and that therefore the market is not semi-strong-form efficient.

One well-known anomaly is the *earnings surprise anomaly*. Stocks that report higher-than-expected earnings tend to have excess risk-adjusted returns in the weeks following the announcement. What do we mean by *higher-than-expected earnings*? Wall Street stock analysts typically forecast the earnings they expect a company to report each quarter. The average of all analysts' earnings forecasts is known as the *consensus estimate* of earnings for that company. When a company's earnings clear the hurdle of the consensus estimate, they are higher than expected. The earnings surprise anomaly violates semistrong-form efficiency because some stocks continue to earn excess returns for weeks after earnings are reported to the public. A semistrong-form efficient market would incorporate the earnings report into the stock price immediately, but the real market responds more slowly. Studies show that stocks actually provide excess returns for 13 to 26 weeks after positive earnings surprises.

Another old and well-known anomaly is the *January effect*.[18] Small-cap stocks and the previous year's poor performers tend to

---

[18] The January effect is often attributed to Sidney Wachtel [see Wachtel (1942)].

do very well in January, especially in the first week. There are some logistical reasons for this phenomenon. One is that tax-loss harvesting by institutional and private investors involves selling poorly performing stocks in December to generate capital losses that offset capital gains and, to a lesser extent, income taxes.[19] The December sell-off depresses those stocks to prices below their actual nontax values, so investors might repurchase them once the new year rolls around.[20] The January effect is stronger when more investors engage in this tax-sensitive strategy.

Aside from tax harvesting, mutual fund managers also sell losing stocks at year end before they report their holdings to the Securities and Exchange Commission (SEC), in compliance with the required quarterly reporting. By selling a loser stock, the mutual fund manager does not have to report it as a holding and be scrutinized by investors who notice it on the SEC report. This tactic is known as *window dressing*. In the SEC report, investors will be able to see a mutual fund's overall low return, but window dressing prevents them from seeing each of the manager's bad picks.

It is also possible that the January effect occurs because many mutual fund managers "bet the house" early in the year. The annual bonus system at most funds might give managers an incentive to take big risks in January. They might think that if they lock in good returns at the beginning of the year, they will have gained a head start toward their bonuses; at the same time, if they lose a lot early on, they will have the rest of the year to grind their way back to a decent return.[21] Whatever the reasons for January buying, it is interesting to note that it is possible to see the forces of market efficiency at work on this anomaly. The January effect is gradually shifting backward as arbitrageurs and quantitative managers try to take advantage of it by placing trades ahead of time in December.

Other calendar effects exist as well. Mondays and the onset of daylight savings are among the calendar events associated with

---

[19] The law currently only allows up to $3,000 to be used to offset income taxes.

[20] There is a wash-sale rule that prohibits repurchasing before 30 days after the sale, so that adds some delay to the repurchasing by sellers.

[21] In general, some portfolio managers may take big bets regardless of the month because they figure that the worst that will happen to them personally is to miss a bonus. There are no income penalties for poor performance, generally. Of course, after too many years of poor returns, a manager is likely to lose his or her job, not just his or her bonus. For more information on mutual fund incentives at other times of the year, see Brown et al. (1996), Busse (2001), and Taylor (2003).

trading patterns. The *Monday effect* is that the market tends to drop slightly on Mondays. The *daylight savings effect* is that the market tends to drop slightly on the first trading day after the beginning of daylight savings, supposedly because the disruption of traders' circadian rhythms increases their aversion to risk.

There are many anomalies associated with fundamental data, which are the data obtained from a firm's income statements, balance sheets, and cash-flow statements. Several studies have shown that a portfolio of stocks with a low P/B ratio or a low price-to-earnings (P/E) ratio will earn high risk-adjusted returns. If a simple strategy of purchasing stocks based on publicly available P/B or P/E ratios can lead to excess returns, then the market is clearly not semistrong-form efficient. Small-cap stocks also have tended to earn higher risk-adjusted returns than large-cap stocks over long periods, even though large-caps might outperform small-caps in any given time period. Is there any rationale for this behavior? Some people argue that small-cap stocks are actually inherently riskier than large-caps because there is less information on them, and standard measurements of risk do not capture this discrepancy in the amount of available information. Small-cap out-performance may, however, be an instance of the *neglected-firm effect*, in which firms with low analyst coverage or low institution-al ownership tend to have higher risk-adjusted returns. Whatever the explanation for it, the fact that small-caps do especially well over the long run seems to imply that the difference between the amount of public information on small-caps and large-caps is a kind of information itself, and this sort of second-degree informa-tion is not efficiently factored into stock prices.

In recent years, some new anomalies have been documented and some old anomalies have become in vogue again. In particular, the low volatility and low beta anomalies have become popular again. These anomalies find that stocks with low measured his-torical volatility outperform stocks with high measured historical volatility. Similarly, stocks with low beta tend to outperform stocks with high beta. More recently, factors regarding liquidity and crowding have surfaced. *Crowding* is a recently identified risk in investing that might occur when multiple market participants begin to follow the same trade in such concentration that liquidity becomes fragile, altering the risk and return dynamics of the trade. Research has found that there are excess returns to purchasing less crowded stocks.

There are many studies that point to additional violations of semistrong-form efficiency (see Table 2.2). Some academics still believe that these sorts of anomalies are not a sufficient basis for successful portfolio strategies. Professor Richard Roll of UCLA once wrote that "[i]t's extremely difficult to profit from the slightest deviation from market efficiency."[22] Quite a few active managers, however, make a living doing exactly that.

Strong-Form Anomalies

The strong form of market efficiency is probably the hardest kind to believe in because it means that market prices already reflect *all* information, both public and private. It is also hard to test for strong-form efficiency. Some clever tests have been done, though.

One test is known as the *insider-traders test*. Company executives and other insiders have, *ceteris paribus*, a better understanding of a company's operations and financial health than an outsider does.[23] Executives are required by the SEC to report their own purchases and sales of their companies' securities. Researchers have obtained these reports and asked the following question: If an outsider purchased a stock when insiders purchased it and sold it when insiders did, would the outsider have earned risk-adjusted excess returns? The answer is oftentimes yes. Insider information is not immediately priced into stocks, as it would be if the market were strong-form efficient.[24]

In the past, researchers were able to perform a test of the profits from specialists on the exchange. Stock exchange specialists were supposed to maintain an orderly market and manage their limit-order books. Access to the limit-order book was equivalent to having private information, because it contained the prices at which prospective buyers and sellers were prepared to buy or sell

[22] Let us mention that Professor Roll used to have a money management shop with the late Professor Stephen Ross of MIT. In addition, Fuller-Thaler Asset Management, named after Nobel prize–winning behavioral economist Richard Thaler, manages around $11 billion to exploit behavorial biases.

[23] As Gekko says in the movie *Wall Street*, "If you're not inside, you're way outside."

[24] It is illegal to trade on "material, nonpublic" information. However, to a certain degree, insiders have greater information about a company than outsiders. Some of this information can be traded on legally, leading them to profit from the trades they place on their companies' stock. According to the SEC's Rule 10b5–1, an executive's trade is not considered "insider trading" if a detailed contract planning the trade was established before the executive gained the "material, nonpublic" information in question and the contract was executed exactly as written.

a stock. One could imagine that a specialist might be able to use this knowledge to his or her advantage, and, indeed, historically, specialist profits have been extraordinary. Was this due to the contrarian nature of their trades, which must balance the order flow, or was it due to the fact that they could make use of private information? If it was the latter, the specialists' profits of the past were another sign that markets were not strong-form efficient.[25]

Behavioral Explanations for the Anomalies

Traditional theories of investor behavior have a difficult time explaining market anomalies. Staunch believers in the efficiency of the market usually argue that any strategies that yield excess returns must be a great deal riskier than other strategies. Another argument for market efficiency is that any statistical arbitrage opportunities that do exist are extremely small, not scalable, fleeting, and very costly to discover.[26] These arguments are hard to reconcile with the many studies that describe long-term strategies that produce risk-adjusted excess returns. The seemingly small eddies of inefficiency in the market sometimes create major opportunities for statistical arbitrage. The risk involved in statistical arbitrage, including the possibility of misjudging how long an anomaly will persist, does not always negate the return. It may be necessary to turn from the CAPM to a multifactor model of stock returns in order to completely understand a less-than-efficient market.

Additional explanations for the existence of anomalies can be found in a field of economics known as *behavioral finance theory*. Researchers cannot fully explain the presence of anomalies with theories that presume that investors behave rationally. Behavioral finance theory attempts to account for anomalies with a study of the effect of psychology and irrational behaviors on investment decisions. Behavioral biases, like the ones listed in Table 2.3, contribute to the kind of buying and selling that leads to mispriced securities.[27]

---

[25] This test was known as the *specialist's* test, but it is no longer useful because the structure of securities markets has dramatically changed and specialists are now known as *designated market makers* (DMMs). Electronic limit-order books and high-frequency trading have dramatically reduced the importance of specialists on the exchange.

[26] See Ross (2002).

[27] Some investors believe anomalies exist due to institutional constraints. That is, institutions may have constraints on their ability to buy or sell that create arbitrage opportunities for less constrained investors.

TABLE 2.3

Common Behavioral Biases

Name	Description	Example
Anchoring	Anchoring bias is the tendency to rely too heavily on, or to anchor to, a past reference or single piece of information when making a decision. Anchoring bias can occur, for example, when investors base their future decisions on an initial set of information they began with—as when investors make future trade allocations based on their initial wealth many years ago. This allocation is no longer the correct allocation since their wealth is much greater now.	Anchoring bias can also occur when investors find a target price for buying a stock. The stock passes this price and the investor doesn't reevaluate the target price, thus never buying a possible long-term winner— missing out on the investment due to anchoring around their initial estimate.
Ambiguity aversion	An avoidance of unfamiliar stocks and a preference for familiar ones, even if some unfamiliar stocks are *great buys*.	Most investors invest the bulk of their money in their home countries, even though diversification would require owning more foreign stocks. In defined-contribution plans, many employees place much of their money in the stock of their own companies, which is terrible for diversification. Some studies have shown that investors place more money in stocks headlined in the newspaper, possibly because of their familiarity (this could also be due to the saliency effect).
Availability bias	The tendency to judge a future event more likely if there is a memory of a similar event, even though the memory may be distorted.	A trader may think that the stock market rallies every time a war starts, even though he has only experienced this once.
Confirmation bias	The tendency to give greater weight to information that confirms one's original beliefs and less weight to information that contradicts those beliefs.	Analysts who originally recommended a stock might be more likely to upgrade it on good news than to downgrade it on bad news. Wall Street analysts often follow stocks that they like, and confirmation bias may explain why the majority of stock ratings by Wall Street analysts are typically quite positive (either "buys" or "strong buys").

Name	Description	Example
Disposition effect	Holding on to *losers* (stocks with negative returns) too long and selling *winners* too soon. The psychological explanation is that humans fear losses more than they value gains. Holding on to a poor stock lets an investor avoid realizing paper losses and makes it easier to pretend that the stock was not a bad pick.	A foreign exchange trader one of the authors knew used to call the disposition effect, "Hope, Mope, and Dope." Basically, you make a stock purchase and, when it falls, you first hope it will go back up. Then you mope around as it continues going south. Finally, when it really goes down, you've become the dope. Although different from disposition, investors also have inertia bias, which prevents them from taking appropriate actions.
Endowment effect	The idea that people will demand more to give up an object than they would be willing to pay to acquire it.	This could lead to investors preferring stocks that they already own above and beyond the reasonable price, which leads to other attractive stocks remaining at prices below their reasonable value. Eventually, these mispricings will adjust as the inertia is overcome. Can also lead to less efficient after-tax returns by investors who avoid tax harvesting because of their reluctance to sell stocks they already have.
Escalation bias	The tendency to put more money in an investment even when the original decision to buy it was based on bad analysis, thus compounding any potential losses. Also known as *commitment bias*.	Suppose an investor purchases a stock at $40 and tells everyone what a great buy it is. The stock then falls to $30. There are two ways to look at the situation. One reaction is, "I made a poor decision." The other is, "If it's a buy at 40, it's a steal at 30!" Usually you run into the second kind of thinking. The investor therefore purchases more of the stock, which was a bad investment to begin with.
Herding mentality	The idea that people like to follow what others are doing. This applies to many aspects of life but also to investing.	Herding may lead to asset prices deviating from fundamental values. For example, the inelastic market hypothesis predicts that flows into an asset class can lead to a much larger move in valuation than might be justified. Herding can also lead to a

TABLE 2.3 *(Continued)*

Name	Description	Example
		phenomenon known as *crowding*. Crowding occurs when lots of investors have similar trades or de facto similar trades that are squeezing the liquidity of a space. This lack of liquidity can lead to a dramatic collapse in prices and mismeasurement of the risk of an investment.
Illusion of knowledge	The assumption that having more data on a stock automatically means having a better understanding of the stock.	This may be one reason why studies have found that investors who trade online trade more often. The massive amounts of information provided by brokerage firms to investors feed an illusion of certainty. Or take the example of the game of roulette. A player chooses a number to bet on the roulette wheel. Suppose you then give the player a piece of paper with the results of the last 1,000 spins of the roulette wheel. His number has shown up frequently in recent spins, and this makes him more confident about his bet. This is only an illusion of knowledge, though, since every outcome is independent and his chance of winning is the same no matter what.
Narrow framing	Considering individual gambles or investments in isolation from other, related investments. Also sometimes referred to as mental *accounting* or as individuals having different *mental pockets.*	An investor might shy away from stocks that experience big short-term fluctuations even though those stocks could, if they are negatively correlated with the rest of the investor's portfolio, reduce the overall portfolio's long-term level of volatility.
Overconfidence	Humans tend to be overconfident. Researchers have documented that the average investor is overconfident in his own ability, causing him to trade too often, incur more transactions costs, and cut into returns. Overconfidence may come from *self-attribution bias*, which is the tendency to attribute one's successes to one's own talent but	One example of overconfidence is demonstrated in many classrooms. The professor asks the class, "How many people believe they are better at driving than the average driver in this room?" Typically, more than 50% of the students will raise their hand, which is a clear impossibility. Only 50% can be better than the average in the

Name	Description	Example
	consider one's failures the fault of other people or circumstances. Overconfidence may also relate to *hindsight bias*, which is what persuades people that they knew in advance how a decision was going to turn out.	room. Self-attribution bias probably had a hand in the internet bubble. In the late 1990s, investors believed they were genius stock pickers as they watched their stocks soar. After the bubble burst, they blamed their losses on a terrible economy or a world that had gone mad.
Probability distortion	Individuals' perceived probabilities might differ from actual objective probabilities. This is because, as psychologists observe, individuals exhibit diminishing sensitivity to actual probabilities. As individuals move away from so-called reference points, such as sure bets (i.e., probability equals 1) and sure losses (i.e., probability equals 0), they are less sensitive to changes in this probability. For example, an individual reacts to a change in probability of 1 to 0.95 much more than a reduction in probability from 0.55 to 0.50. In addition to this, psychological experiments found that individuals tend to overweight low-probability events and underweight high-probability events.	This probability distortion might lead to overestimating a bad situation. For example, from March 2 to March 23, 2020, the S&P 500 declined by 28%, only to rebound strongly throughout the remainder of the year. This may have been rational due to extreme uncertainty over the Covid-19 virus, but some of it may also have been investors' overweighting the probability of a really bad scenario versus the actual likelihood of a bad scenario. In general, this may lead to bouts of overreaction to bad news, which could present a profitable investment opportunity.
Recency effect	Investors might be overly influenced by recent events.	For example, if there has been a huge drop in the stock market as in 2000 or 2008, certain investors may shy away from the market for a while. As the market slowly does better, a slow trend of these investors returning eventually adds to the momentum. This might also be called the *snake-bite effect* when the recent experiences are negative. It might also lead to positive momentum effects when recent experience is positive.
Regret aversion	Regret aversion or regret theory is related to an anticipated regret that an individual may consider when facing a decision. Individuals might	There are many potential examples of regret aversion in the financial markets. One example is the investor who buys an overvalued stock because he

TABLE 2.3 *(Continued)*

Name	Description	Example
	anticipate regret and incorporate in their choices their desire to eliminate or reduce this possibility. Regret is a negative emotion with a powerful social and reputational component. Researchers have shown that it might explain rationally various behaviors of humans.	does not want to later be upset with himself for not buying a winner like Tesla or Amazon. This could push the stock even higher. Another example is investors who have recently witnessed a market downturn and are very reluctant to invest newly acquired cash; as a result, they hold off, thus missing years of gains in the market.
Representativeness	Oversimplification of investment decisions using rules of thumb. Investors try to come up with easy tests for *good* and *bad* stocks. Most of the time, rules of thumb are helpful in summarizing a lot of complicated information, but taken by themselves, they can also lead to irrational decisions.	Investors might pour money into stocks that have recently had good earnings announcements simply because that is said to be the sign of a good company. However, consideration should also be given to whether the market expected the earnings, in which case the stocks' prices should already reflect the news. This may be the cause of an overreaction of stock prices to recent earnings announcements.
Saliency	Salience refers to any aspect of a stimulus that, for any of many reasons, stands out from the rest. Investors might thus give more attention to higher-stimulus items, while neglecting lower-stimulus items. Also related to *vividness* in the psychological literature.	For example, investors might be more attracted to attention-grabbing stocks (e.g., stocks in the news). This could lead to an overvaluation of stocks that are grabbing everyone's attention, leaving opportunities for less glamorous stocks.

Note: Although there are many papers on these particular behavioral biases, we try to cite just the early studies in these areas. Anchoring [Kahneman and Tversky (1981)], ambiguity aversion [Ellsberg (1961)], availability bias [Kahneman and Tversky (1973)], confirmation bias [Bacon (1620), Wason (1960), Lord et al. (1979)], disposition effect [Shefrin and Statman (1985)], endowment effect [Kahneman and Tversky (1979), Thaler (1980)], escalation bias [Staw (1976)], herding mentality [Keynes (1936), Asch (1955)], crowding [Chincarini (1998, 2012)], [Stein (2009)], Illusion of Knowledge [Oskamp (1965)], narrow framing [Kahneman and Tversky (1981)], overconfidence [Marks (1951), Irwin (1953), Oskamp (1965), Fischoff and Slovic (1978), Odean (1998)] and for the subset of hindsight bias [Miller and Ross (1975) and Fischoff (1977)], probability distortion [Preston and Barrata (1948)], recency effect [Ebbinghaus (1902), Crowder (1976), and Roediger and Crowder (1976)], regret aversion [Loones and Sugden (1982) and Bell (1982)], representativeness [Kahneman and Tversky (1973)], and saliency [Kanouse (1972), Taylor and Fiske (1975), Nisbett et al. (1977), Nisbett and Ross (1980), and Bordalo et al. (2012)]. There is disagreement on whether the endowment effect truly exists or not and whether the phenomenon reflects patterns of decision mistakes that go away with experience and careful analysis [Plott and Zeiler (2007)]. In a survey of behavioral biases that plague investment advisors in 2020, recency bias and loss aversion seemed to affect people the most [Smith (2020)].

2.4.3 Market Efficiency and QEPM

Anomalies and behavioral biases give fairly strong evidence that markets may not be much more than weak-form or only sporadically semistrong-form efficient. Summarizing the evidence, here are our top 10 reasons why markets are not perfectly efficient and why active portfolio management such as QEPM is a worthwhile endeavor:

1. Obtaining information is costly. Not everyone is able or willing to pay for information.
2. Information, even public information, travels somewhat slowly through the market.
3. Not every investor has the ability to process a large amount of information, especially quantitative information.
4. By filtering public information, some people may create what amounts to private information.
5. Some investors base their investment decisions on sentiment rather than on the logical interpretation of information.
6. Some attempts to exploit others' presumed irrationality actually creates more inefficiency.
7. Economic conditions, especially the state of technology, change all the time, and it takes time for people to adapt to these changes.
8. Transactions costs create gaps between economic models and reality.
9. Taxes cause distortions in the markets.
10. Government regulation of financial markets creates gaps between economic models and reality.

Efficiency means that the market incorporates all relevant information into security prices, and this happens only when all investors have all the information relevant to investment decisions. In reality, investors operate with varying sets of information partly because accessing it is costly. Portfolio managers have access to extensive market databases paid for by their firms. Even with the introduction of low-cost databases tailored for individual investors, the majority of them simply cannot replicate the volume and functionality of commercial databases that contain historical and up-to-the-minute data.

Since people's access and exposure to information vary, information moves through the market slowly and unevenly. Private information obviously stays within a fairly small radius, but even public information travels slowly and stops before reaching everyone. Many people rarely come in personal contact with the markets, do not keep track of market news, and never receive some information. Also, private information usually becomes public eventually, but often in a delayed and uneven fashion. This is especially the case with bad corporate news, which companies sometimes release in bits and pieces in order to avoid dropping bombs on their own stock prices.

Once information is publicly accessible, quantitative portfolio managers are in the best position to make use of it. They are alerted to news almost immediately via electronic data services, whereas average investors may not learn about it until later from the TV or newspaper headlines. Compared with other professional managers with access to data services, quantitative managers also have a great advantage because they make use of software and quantitative methods that sort through large data areas relatively quickly, and their stock-return models can be updated accordingly. The quantitative model of stock returns will warn the manager in as little time as it takes for the computer to run the program whether any news warrants selling stock.

By filtering public information with quantitative analysis and proprietary models, quantitative portfolio managers gain insights and uncover strategies that are essentially private information derived from public inputs. Since most investors cannot uncover the same things, this information is not yet priced into securities, and there is the potential for statistical arbitrage. Even if a number of portfolio managers use similar models, they still can earn excess returns as long as they are relatively few compared with the entire population of investors.

Investors' biases also create statistical arbitrage opportunities because they cause mispricings. People inevitably let irrational hopes and fears creep into investment decisions, which causes them to ignore or misjudge certain relevant information. Quantitative equity portfolio managers are in a good position to both avoid and exploit irrational decisions. Quantitative models of stock returns help the manager to take his or her own emotions out of the investment decision while also uncovering irrational price movements that are vulnerable to statistical arbitrage.

Statistical arbitrage usually helps to return security prices to their efficient levels. Sometimes, though, it actually exacerbates market inefficiencies. For example, during the internet bubble of the late 1990s, many stocks were overvalued. Amazon (AMZN) was in the same line of business as Barnes & Noble (BKS), but it traded at a much higher multiple. If someone assumed that the higher multiple was a symptom of a short-lived overvaluation, then one could have gone long BKS and short AMZN. In contrast, if one assumed that the internet bubble was going to get bigger, one could have gone long AMZN and short BKS, thereby compounding the overvaluation.[28]

The internet bubble also was a case in which the market did not appreciate or understand a change in economic conditions. Sometimes information is not priced into securities because it is not yet understood or even recognized. It takes time for even the best analysts, economists, and strategists to understand the real significance of changes in the economic environment. During the learning period, markets most likely will not factor the changes into securities prices correctly. During the late 1990s, for instance, investors' zeal over the prospects of new e-commerce business models outstripped the actual growth potential of many startups.

The process of buying and selling in the market is itself a source of inefficiency. Transactions costs divert money away from its most efficient use. While an economic model may say what prices should be in equilibrium, actual prices may be quite different because of transactions costs. These costs can take the form of *broker commissions, price impact,* and *delay.* Mispricings due to transactions costs may not be exploitable by any investors, or they may be exploitable only by those who can keep their own transactions costs low. For instance, commissions and delays prevent many small investors from trading as frequently as professional traders do and from pursuing strategies of scale that require large funds.

---

[28] At the end of 1999, Amazon was trading at a large multiple to Barnes & Noble. A short position in AMZN and a long position in BKS would have made a return of 74% on the AMZN position and a 28% return on the BKS position as the price of Amazon collapsed while Barnes & Noble's price rose. In the long run, however, it turned out that Amazon was much more than a bookseller, and an investment in Amazon turned out to be spectacular. From 2000 to 2019, a long position in Amazon yielded around 7,500%, while Barnes & Noble lost about 14%. This brings to mind another conundrum: is efficiency intrinsically related to the investment horizon?

Taxes are another significant cost and source of inefficiency in investing. Investors are ultimately concerned with after-tax returns, so tax consequences weigh on investment decisions. The distribution of investors' tax rates, as well as any changes in that distribution as a result of changes in the tax laws, affects the relative prices of securities. If even a few large institutions buy or sell stock for tax reasons, prices can shift away from their true nontax values. At times, the price shifts create exploitable market inefficiencies.

Market inefficiencies can be the by-products of other government regulations as well. Some countries with fixed exchange rates have experienced fluctuations in which the exchange rate suddenly dropped by as much as 40% of its value in a matter of hours. The drastic rate corrections have cost foreign investors enormous amounts of money. Clearly, such fixed exchange rates did not price the currencies according to all the information available in the marketplace. Government-imposed systems also create less dramatic distortions. In the case of equities, numerous government regulations alter the flow of investment, including restrictions on short selling, rules related to tick increments (i.e., decimal pricing), and rules related to stock ownership.[29] Although the intent of the regulations is presumably to ensure some public good, they still cause distortions that may be exploited for excess returns.

These are the essential reasons why markets are not perfectly efficient, which is to the benefit of quantitative equity portfolio managers. Why haven't QEPM managers and other arbitrageurs already eliminated inefficiencies from the market? There are two simple answers to this question. The first is that inefficiencies lead not to pure arbitrage opportunities but rather to statistical arbitrage opportunities that are low but not zero risk (as stated in tenets 2 and 3). The second answer is that there are simply not enough arbitrageurs in the marketplace, with enough investing power relative to the rest of the investing public, to trade away every inefficiency. The markets remain an abundant source of potentially profitable mispricings for the active manager.

---

[29] For example, Regulation T of the Federal Reserve permits borrowing of stocks up to only 50% of their investment. Thus, borrowing, in reality, is not unlimited. Markowitz (2005) has reiterated that in the absence of unlimited borrowing and lending, the market portfolio will not be efficient.

2.5 TENETS 3 AND 4: THE FUNDAMENTAL LAW, THE INFORMATION CRITERION, AND QEPM

The portfolio manager has to apply good quantitative analysis to market data to find and exploit the opportunities for excess return that are hidden in market inefficiencies. Tenets 3 and 4 of QEPM state that quantitative analysis opens up the possibility of statistical arbitrage so long as the methods and models that are used combine all the available information efficiently. These two tenets are best illustrated within the framework of the *fundamental law of active management*.[30] The fundamental law has gained popularity among portfolio managers. Through a simple formulation, it shows the portfolio manager's contribution to the portfolio management process. We know from Section 2.2.6 that a high information ratio is one of the goals of QEPM, and the fundamental law helps us to understand how to achieve it through the application of statistics and the efficient, full use of information.

The fundamental law states that the *information ratio* (*IR*) is the product of the *information coefficient* (*IC*) and the square root of *breadth* (*BR*), that is,

$$IR = IC \cdot \sqrt{BR} \tag{2.8}$$

Given the definition of the information ratio in Eq. (2.7),

$$\frac{\alpha^B}{\omega} = IC \cdot \sqrt{BR} \tag{2.9}$$

This equation shows that a higher information ratio can be achieved by increasing the information coefficient or by increasing the breadth. For quantitative managers who build stock-return models, the *IC* can be increased by finding factors that are more significant than the ones already in the model, and the *BR* can be increased by finding more factors that are relatively uncorrelated with the ones already in the model.

The fundamental law was first introduced as a way to gain insights into the quantitative portfolio management process, but its nature and use are sometimes misunderstood. We use the results of standard econometrics to accurately quantify and make clear statements about the components of the law, which will be especially useful to quantitative managers who use linear stock-return models

---

[30] See Grinold and Kahn (1995).

to build their portfolios. We stress, however, that the fundamental law is for *understanding* QEPM, not for *doing* QEPM. A quantitative portfolio manager does not use the law to actually create portfolios. Rather, the law provides the manager with a useful conceptual framework for analyzing the QEPM process.

2.5.1 The Truth about the Fundamental Law

One of the essential tasks of QEPM is to predict future stock returns by estimating a model that specifies a relationship between the stock return and a list of explanatory variables (a.k.a. *factors*). Suppose that the model specifies that the return of stock i at time t, r_{it}, is a linear function of the value of K factor premiums at time t, that is, $f_{1t}, \ldots, f_{Kt}$:

$$r_{it} = \alpha_i + \beta_{i1} f_{1t} + \cdots + \beta_{iK} f_{Kt} + \epsilon_{it} \qquad (2.10)$$

where $\alpha_i, \beta_{i1}, \ldots, \beta_{iK}$ are parameters to be estimated, and ϵ_{it} is the random-error term (i.e., the deviation of the stock return from its expected value). Assume that the portfolio manager estimates the preceding equation using data from time 1 to T, that is, $t = 1, \ldots, T$.

The fundamental law assesses how well Eq. (2.10) explains the stock-return process, and it expresses the equation's goodness of fit as the product of the *number of explanatory variables* and each variable's *average contribution*. Depending on what portfolio managers do after estimating Eq. (2.10), the fundamental law may be expressed in different ways, but several truths always hold[31]:

1. IR^2 approximately equals the goodness of fit (R^2) of the return forecasting equations.[32]
2. The breadth is the number of explanatory variables in the return forecasting equations.[33]

---

[31] Since the mathematics involved is rather heavy, we have placed the derivations of these truths in Appendix 2A, which can be found at www.ludwigbc.com under QEPM Exclusive Content.

[32] One may notice that the range of values R^2 can take is bounded, whereas that is not the case for IR^2. This discrepancy results from a number of approximations introduced in the fundamental law. If IR^2 has a high value, the approximations that the fundamental law introduces create a huge approximation error.

[33] In theory, the breadth can be much larger than the number of explanatory variables if one counts the number of distinctive signals. We show in Appendix 2A, which can be found at www.ludwigbc.com under QEPM Exclusive Content, that this way of determining the breadth has limited practicality.

3. IC^2 is the average contribution of each explanatory variable in increasing R^2.
4. The fundamental law decomposes the goodness of fit into the number of explanatory variables and their average contribution.
5. When the benchmark is ignored and the risk-free rate is subtracted from the portfolio returns, IR is essentially the maximum Sharpe ratio one can achieve, and the fundamental law decomposes the maximum Sharpe ratio into the number of explanatory variables and their average contribution.

2.5.2 The Information Criterion

One misconception about the fundamental law is that it applies to all active portfolio management. *The fundamental law applies only when the portfolio manager creates the optimal portfolio.* While it may be surprising, many portfolio managers unknowingly create suboptimal portfolios often because they do not use all the available information in the most efficient way (thereby violating tenet 4). When constructing the portfolio, a manager should use all the information gathered from the estimation of Eq. (2.10). This important point has not been emphasized enough by proponents of the fundamental law, so we want to state it as a general principle.

LEMMA 1 (THE INFORMATION CRITERION). *The fundamental law of active portfolio management as expressed in Eq. (2.8) is valid only if the portfolio manager combines all the available information in the most efficient way.*

An example helps to illustrate the preceding criterion. A portfolio manager may follow the analyst-revision strategy: Construct an equal-weighted portfolio of stocks whose analyst ratings improved in the last month. We can consider "inclusion in the portfolio" a variable. That is, we may define a variable β_{it} that has a value of 1 if stock i's rating improved at time t and a value of 0 otherwise. The manager estimates the following equation from historical data:

$$r_{i,t+1} = \alpha + \beta_{it}f + \epsilon_{i,t+1} \qquad (2.11)$$

where $r_{i,t+1}$ is the return to stock i at time $t+1$, α and f are the parameters to be estimated, and $\epsilon_{i,t+1}$ is the error (the part of the return that is not explained by the model). If the value of f is positive, the equation suggests that those stocks with $\beta_{it} = 1$ will have higher future returns. Thus the portfolio manager constructs an equal-weighted portfolio of stocks for which $\beta_{it} = 1$, indicating that their ratings improved in the last month.

In doing this, however, the portfolio manager is not using all the available information. Equation (2.11) not only says that those stocks with $\beta_{it} = 1$ have a higher expected return, but it also identifies which stocks have higher risk (volatility). Stocks with higher volatility should have smaller weights in the eventual portfolio. Since the portfolio manager did not use this piece of information, the information criterion is not satisfied.

We believe that some of the current industry practices do not pass the information criterion. We will encounter such examples in the following chapters, and we will discuss exactly what aspects of the practices violate the information criterion in each case. The bottom line is that if the portfolio construction strategy does not satisfy the information criterion, then there must be a better way to construct the portfolio.[34]

2.5.3 Information Loss

The loss that results from not using all information can be quantified easily within the framework of the fundamental law. The fundamental law suggests that the contribution of the portfolio manager (and, by implication, of the information that the portfolio manager uses to increase the portfolio's return) is summarized by the information ratio. Similarly, the lack of contribution of the portfolio manager is also reflected in the information ratio. By comparing the information ratio that the portfolio manager could have achieved using all available information with the information ratio that he or she actually obtained using only a subset of the available information, we can quantify the amount of information he or she lost, known simply as the *information loss* (IL). Thus

$$IL = \text{maximum } IR - \text{actual } IR \qquad (2.12)$$

To the extent that the information ratio is similar to the maximum Sharpe ratio, the information ratio can be understood as the reward-to-risk ratio. If the information ratio is 0.5, this means that

---

[34] See Chincarini and Kim (2007).

taking on 10% more risk will result in 5% extra return. On the flip side, the information loss shows the reduction in the reward-to-risk ratio. If the information loss is 0.1, then the portfolio manager is missing out on 1% of potential extra return for every 10% of risk he or she takes.

2.6 TENETS 5, 6, AND 7: STATISTICAL ISSUES IN QEPM

Tenets 5, 6, and 7 of QEPM concern issues arising from the application of statistical techniques to the portfolio-choice problem. In this section we discuss the three issues that a portfolio manager cannot neglect: *data mining, parameter stability,* and *parameter uncertainty.*

2.6.1 Data Mining

One of the biggest challenges for quantitative portfolio managers is to avoid the problem of data mining. Data mining violates tenet 5, which requires that quantitative models be based on sound economic theory. In some quantitative analyses, the use of data mining is quite obvious, but in other cases it is harder to detect.

Data mining is the practice of running regressions of historical stock returns on so many combinations of factors that one is virtually guaranteed of finding a model or handful of factors that seem significantly correlated with stock returns but are in fact not particularly meaningful. Suppose that there are 99 potential factors $f_1, ..., f_{99}$ that may explain a stock's return. Let $f_{1t}, ..., f_{99t}$ and r_t be the values of the factors and the stock's return for month t. Suppose that we observe the value of these factors and the stock's return for 100 months, and then we regress the stock return on all 99 factors. That is, we estimate the following equation:

$$r_t = \alpha + \beta_1 f_{1t} + \cdots + \beta_{99} f_{99t} + \epsilon_t \qquad t = 1, ..., 100 \qquad (2.13)$$

What will we find out from the estimation? In this case, the goodness of fit (R^2) of the regression will be 100% because there will be no error in the regression (i.e., $\epsilon_t = 0$). With this equation, we superficially "explain" the stock return completely.[35] In truth,

---

[35] We have 100 unknown parameters and 100 observations. Thus 100 unknown parameters are determined from a system of 100 equations. As long as the 100 equations are not linearly dependent, there will be a unique solution, and ϵ_t will not have any role.

though, the R^2 of 100% simply reflects the fact that we included too many variables in the regression. From this regression, we cannot make any statistical inference about whether the model is valid or not. Even if we had made up the values of factors for the 100 months using a random-number generator, the regression still would have assigned coefficients so that R^2 would equal exactly 100%. In fact, when there are 100 observations and more than 99 explanatory variables, the R^2 always will be 100%. Basic statistics tells us not to include 99 variables when there are 100 observations.

Sometimes the problem is not so obvious. Suppose that we do a so-called stepwise regression. That is, we deliberately find the most significant variable out of 100 variables. Can we make statistical inferences from such a regression? No. Imagine again that we made up the value of factors using a random-number generator. If we deliberately look for the most significant of the 100 variables, we are guaranteed to get a significant variable because we have such a large pool of variables from which to choose. We set up the regression so that it would generate a significant variable, knowing in advance that whatever variable we eventually selected would be significant. The statistical significance of the variable is therefore no real indication that the variable explains stock returns well.

To illustrate the concept, Fig. 2.1 shows the frequency distribution of the absolute value of t-statistics when we deliberately choose the most significant variable out of 100 randomly generated variables. For each simulation, 100 observations of the dependent variable and 100 explanatory variables were generated from the standard normal distribution independently. Given 100 explanatory variables, we selected the most significant explanatory variable by running regressions of the dependent variable on the selected explanatory variable and a constant. The simulation was repeated 1,000 times.

As can be seen from the figure, in most cases the absolute value of the t-statistic is greater than 2. The standard interpretation of this high t-statistic is that the selected variable is significant. But we know from the design of the simulation that the selected explanatory variable does not have anything to do with the dependent variable. The R^2 of the regression will be high simply because the t-statistic is high, so the R^2 also will be meaningless. For each simulation just described, we selected the 10 most significant explanatory variables and ran a regression of the dependent

FIGURE 2.1

Frequency distribution of the absolute values of t-statistics from 1,000 simulations.

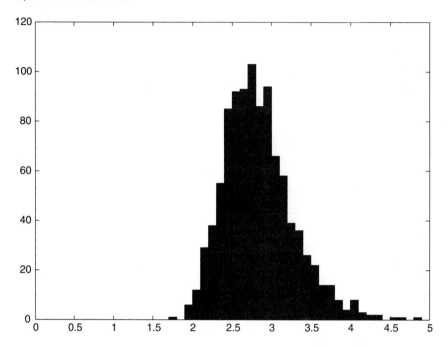

variable on the selected variables and a constant. The frequency distribution of the resulting R^2 is plotted in Fig. 2.2. R^2 is mostly around 30% and 40%, quite high values, but again, the high R^2 does not suggest true statistical significance. The outcomes of stepwise regressions are, in a sense, rigged, and this is not the kind of research a portfolio manager ought to perform.

Even avoiding stepwise regression in one's own analysis, statistical conclusions still may be tainted indirectly by data mining. Even when an individual researcher does not select variables deliberately, the community of researchers may be doing a stepwise regression collectively. For example, in the 1970s, an MBA student in the business school of the University of Chicago found that the size (i.e., market capitalization) of a stock explained its return. Let's say that the student came to this conclusion through valid statistical methods. We know, however, that there must have been thousands of other MBA students (not to mention hundreds of academics and practitioners) who have tried to explain stock

FIGURE 2.2

Frequency distribution of R^2 from 1,000 simulations.

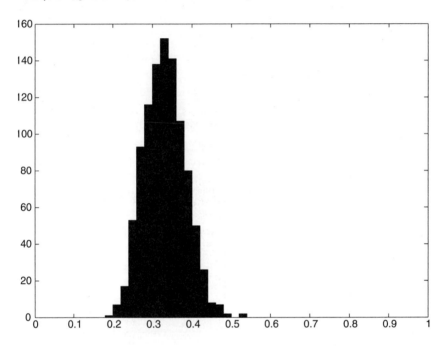

returns with other variables. The fact that one student's conclusion about stock size gained widespread acceptance, whereas the
conclusions of other studies did not, suggests that the community
of financial researchers as a whole probably has been engaging in
a kind of collective data mining referred to as *data snooping*. One
therefore cannot accept in full faith the finding that the size of the
stock is a significant explanatory variable.

We cannot completely avoid data mining or data snooping
when we test a factor unless we use data that have never before
been used to test that particular factor. When we test a factor with
the same data that many other people have already used to test
it, our conclusions may be influenced by their conclusions. For
instance, authors of numerous investment textbooks have written
about tests that they and others performed using U.S. stock data
from the S&P Compustat database. In fact, many of these tests analyzed the same factors with the same stock data over the same time
period. The P/E ratio in particular was one of the factors studied
quite extensively. Thus, when we read in some textbooks that the
P/E ratio explains stock returns well, we know, even before actually running any of our own regressions, that the P/E ratio will be

a good explanatory variable for much of the available data on U.S. stock returns. We cannot make any statistical inference from our own regression of returns on the P/E ratio unless we use data that have not already been extensively tested.

These problems suggest that careful empirical study is not enough to avoid the data-mining problem. The best way to generate meaningful statistics is to follow tenet 5 and make sure that the model is based on sound economic theory and common sense. Empirical evidence alone is not a sufficient basis for good practical decisions. A model will work only if there is a good reason to think that its factors explain stock returns and that the relationship between those factors and stock prices has not been exploited already by other investors.

In addition to letting theory guide the portfolio manager and using out-of-sample data, there are other methods to mitigate the data-mining problem.[36] In particular, portfolio managers, guided by the past research that has been done on factor anomalies, should attempt to control for data snooping through one of two methods: using statistical techniques like a Bayesian adjustment about a factor or investment strategy or adjusting the p-values or t-statistics of the significance of tests by the number of tests they are performing—and even the number of tests that may have occurred prior to their own testing and that might have influenced their beliefs. In the case of the Bayesian methods, they should adjust the significance of the empirical tests by their a priori belief about the importance of the factor (that is, theory leading). In the case of the p-value or t-statistic adjustments, the methods increase the critical values by which a factor should be accepted due to the repeated testing of many factors.[37]

---

[36] Since the publication of the first edition of this book in 2006, there has been an explosion of factor research and a movement to address the data-mining problem that we emphasized in the first edition of this book. See Arnott et al. (2019), Harvey et al. (2016), and Harvey (2017).

[37] These methods include the Bonferroni test, the Hommel test, the Holm test, the Hochberg test, the Dubey-Armitage-Parnar test, and the Tukey-Ciminera-Heyse test. See Sankoh et al. (1997), Hochberg (1988), Holm (1979), Hommel (1988), Armitage and Parmar (1986), Dubey (1985), Shi et al. (2012), and Tukey et al. (1985). The simplest method, the Bonferroni method, was named after Italian mathematician Carlo Emilio Bonferroni. A simple example may help. Suppose a researcher wants to test some data on whether 160 factors are significant with 60 months of data. The typical 5% error threshold for each factor would imply a t-statistic of 2 or greater. A Bonferroni adjustment would require a t-statistic of 3.83 for each factor. This assumes that factors are independent. One can adjust Bonferroni for correlations in a multiple of ways. One of the simplest would reduce the critical t-statistic for each factor to 3.66 with an average correlation of 0.4 amongst factors. See Appendix 4B for more information on these techniques.

2.6.2 Parameter Stability

To make forecasts based on past data, we have to assume that history repeats itself. If the historical average of the stock return is around 1%, then we may assume that the stock return will be around 1% next month. If the standard deviation of the stock return is historically around 10%, then we may expect it to be around 10% next month.

Unfortunately, the constant flux of the market often interrupts the historical patterns that we might count on continuing. CEOs, employees, products, market conditions, and regulations change. As companies change, the properties of stocks also change. When the properties of stocks change, the parameters of stock-return models change. Thus, if we estimate β from the CAPM for, say, General Electric, then we have to ask ourselves, "Is the β of General Electric going to be the same next month? Next quarter? Next year?" If we estimate a more complicated model, we have to determine whether the estimation will be stable over time.

Consideration of parameter stability plays an important role in determining data sample size. For example, if we believe that β is generally not constant for more than five years, we should not estimate it from a sample that includes data covering more than five years. Or knowing that Daimler and Chrysler merged, we should not create a sample that includes both premerger data and postmerger data. Understanding parameter stability is crucial to QEPM. In Chapter 16 we will discuss some simple ways to ensure parameter stability.

In the last decade, the threat to factor return stability has increased, and the risks associated with quantitative investing have also increased. The reason is partly due to the phenomenon of crowding.[38] Crowding is a recently identified risk in investing that can occur when multiple market participants begin to follow the same trade in such concentration that liquidity becomes fragile, altering the risk and return dynamics of the trade. That is, as portfolio managers and investors discover a new factor, the popularity

---

[38] See the work of Chincarini (2012), as well as Chincarini (1998, 2017), Chincarini et al. (2018), Cahan and Luo (2013), Yan (2014), Chue (2015), Zhong et al. (2016), Baltas (2019), Brown et al. (2019), and Volpati et al. (2020). For the problems related to copycat trading amongst quantitative funds, see Chincarini (1998), Rothman (2007, 2008), Goldman Sachs (2007a, 2007b), and Khandani and Lo (2008). There are also more references for crowding in some of the presentations at https://ludwigbc.com/presentations/slides/.

of the strategy can actually reduce the future performance of the strategy. When quantitative strategies or factor strategies become public through publication or through the launch of an investment product, the future risk-adjusted returns of that strategy decrease by a large magnitude. Thus, the measured performance might not be a stable estimate of the future performance.[39] In order to assess future strategy performance, portfolio managers should make sure historical backtesting is realistic (i.e., consider trading costs), be aware of crowding, and be aware of how the nature of the factors themselves is changing over time.

2.6.3 Parameter Uncertainty

Having extra information never hurts and is often helpful. However, extra information should not necessarily alter the portfolio composition. A portfolio manager may be able to construct a portfolio that is expected to outperform the benchmark. Does this mean that he or she should automatically choose the active portfolio instead of an indexed one? No. The active portfolio may have too much risk compared with the gain in expected return. Whether the risk is "too much" depends on an individual portfolio manager's attitude, but the amount of risk can be checked in principle.

Even if the active portfolio does not look too risky on its surface, it could have a high degree of parameter uncertainty, which is a component of risk. Standard statistics overlooks this important point. Parameter uncertainty exists in all statistical estimations of stock-return models because all estimations contain some degree of estimation error, as measured by the standard error. Mean-variance optimizations therefore should take standard error into account as one aspect of a portfolio's risk. When the standard error is considered, it may become apparent that a supposedly superior active portfolio's risk-adjusted return is, in fact, no better than the benchmark's.

The standard error, which measures the error of the estimation, depends on two things: the variance of the error in the model and the variance of the explanatory variables.[40] The variance of the

---

[39] See Arnott et al. (2016), Calluzzo et al. (2019), McLean and Pontiff (2016), Jacobs and Muller (2020), and Hou et al. (2020).

[40] Readers who are not familiar with these concepts may consult Appendix C at www. ludwigbc.com under QEPM Exclusive Content.

error shows how precise the model is. If the model is 100% precise, the error always will be zero. The variance of the explanatory variables shows how informative the data are. If the variables do not change at all, their variance is zero, and the standard error will be infinite. Therefore, to reduce the standard error, the model and the explanatory variables should be selected carefully.

In general, the portfolio manager should consider not only the estimated value but also the standard error of the estimates. If the standard error is large, then that should be considered part of the portfolio's risk. This is one of the fundamental implications of Bayesian econometrics for portfolio selection. Bayesian econometrics is gaining acceptance by industry practitioners, and we will discuss the Bayesian approach in Chapter 14.

2.7 CONCLUSION

We started this chapter with a discussion of α and the information ratio, the concepts of risk-adjusted excess return, because the goal of QEPM is to create portfolios with high levels of return for risk. We then looked in detail at the seven tenets of QEPM that all quantitative equity portfolio managers should follow. The seven tenets deal with concepts of market efficiency, the fundamental law of active management, and statistical issues. As a form of active management, QEPM is based on the belief that markets, despite functioning efficiently in general, contain many patterns of inefficiency that open up opportunities for statistical arbitrage. An understanding of the information criterion and the concept of information loss from the fundamental law helps portfolio managers to exploit these opportunities to the fullest. Successful QEPM also depends on managers being vigilant about data mining, parameter uncertainty, and parameter stability.

Now that we have a firm grasp of QEPM concepts, we turn to the key piece of QEPM, the quantitative model of stock returns, which brings together theory and observation into one tool for selecting stocks for the portfolio.

QUESTIONS

2.1. (a) What are the three types of α used in QEPM, and how are they different?

   (b) What is another type of α commonly used by the general investing public, and why is it less relevant to QEPM?

2.2. (a) When does $\alpha^B = \alpha^{CAPM}$?

   (b) Can α^{MF} ever be the same as the other types of α?

2.3. (a) What distinguishes ex-ante α from ex-post α?

   (b) Ideally, what relationship would a portfolio manager want between them?

2.4. (a) Define the information ratio.

   (b) Why is it important in QEPM?

2.5. Name the seven tenets of QEPM.

2.6. Explain the difference between a pure arbitrage and a statistical arbitrage.

2.7. Name the three types of market efficiency.

2.8. Define weak-form market efficiency.

2.9. Define semistrong-form market efficiency.

2.10. Define strong-form market efficiency.

2.11. Give an example of a type of quantitative analysis that would not work for each of the types of market efficiency.

2.12. Name three documented anomalies. Can you think of a theoretical or behavioral justification for these anomalies? If so, explain.

2.13. Name the three anomalies that are most likely to be subject to data mining or data snooping. Explain.

2.14. What is ambiguity aversion? Give an investment example.

2.15. What is the disposition effect?

2.16. It has been documented that trading volume decreases during bear markets. Can you explain this phenomenon with common behavioral biases?

2.17. Give three reasons why practitioners of QEPM might believe that markets are inefficient.

2.18. A special case of the fundamental law is related to the idea that independent forecasts with informational value can improve the power of the overall forecasts. Suppose that you and your QEPM department decided to forecast the equity markets every month. The choices are market up, market down, or market flat. You collected the forecasts of every participant and then constructed the QEPM department's consensus forecast as follows. The aggregate forecast is the majority. Thus, if there are more than $n/2$ "long" signals, the combined forecast goes "long"; if there are fewer than $n/2$, the combined forecast goes "short"; and if there are exactly $n/2$, the combined forecast is determined by a coin flip. Suppose furthermore that you make the assumption that everyone's opinions are independent of each other.

(a) Under what conditions would the QEPM department's consensus forecast be better than any individual forecast?

(b) Suppose that everyone had the same probability of being right, p. Consider the following individual probabilities: 0.5, 0.53, 0.60, 0.65, 0.70, and 0.75. What would be the corresponding probabilities of the QEPM department's consensus being right, assuming that there are 22 participants in the consensus?

2.19. The fundamental law makes a number of approximations. One of them is

$$\frac{R^2}{1-R^2} \approx R^2$$

(a) Calculate the error from the preceding approximation when the value of R^2 is 10%, 20%, 50%, and 80%.

(b) Express the approximation error as a function of R^2. Is the approximation error bounded?

(c) We have claimed in this chapter that IR^2 is approximately equal to R^2. However, while the value of R^2 is bounded $(0 \le R^2 \le 1)$, the value of IR^2 is not. Can you explain this discrepancy?

2.20. That IR^2 is approximately R^2 can be verified by a very simple situation. Suppose that we estimated the following equation for stock XYZ:

$$r_{t+1} = \alpha + \beta_1 f_{1t} + \cdots + \beta_K f_{Kt} + \epsilon_{t+1} \quad t = 1, ..., T-1$$

where $f_{1t}, ..., f_{Kt}$ are forecasting factors. Using this equation, we predict the return for $T+1$.

(a) What is the expected return of stock XYZ for $T+1$? What is the standard deviation of stock return for $T+1$? Express the Sharpe ratio of stock XYZ for $T+1$ in terms of data and estimates.

(b) Express R^2 and $R^2/(1-R^2)$ in terms of data and estimates.

(c) Show that the squared Sharpe ratio of stock XYZ can be approximated by R^2. When would the approximation create a large error?

(d) Show that IR^2 can be approximated by R^2 if the portfolio is made only of stock XYZ and the benchmark is the cash return.

2.21. Suppose that a portfolio manager predicts the return of MSFT and GE from earnings forecasts of 10 analysts. Let r_{MSFT} and r_{GE} be the return of MSFT and GE and $E_{MSFT,1}, \ldots, E_{MSFT,10}$ and $E_{GE,1}, \ldots, E_{GE,10}$ be the forecasts of 10 analysts.

(a) Using the historical data, the portfolio manager may estimate the following equations:

$$r_{MSFT,t} = \alpha + f_1 E_{MSFT,1,t} + \cdots + f_{10} E_{MSFT,10,t} + \epsilon_{MSFT,t}$$

$$r_{GE,t} = \alpha + f_1 E_{GE,1,t} + \cdots + f_{10} E_{GE,10,t} + \epsilon_{GE,t}$$

If the portfolio manager predicts return based on this model, what would be the breadth?

(b) Quite often in reality the portfolio manager has access only to the consensus forecasts (i.e., the average earnings forecasts). Then the portfolio's return prediction may be based on the following equations:

$$r_{MSFT,t} = \alpha + f \frac{1}{10} \sum_{j=1}^{10} E_{MSFT,j,t} + \epsilon_{MSFT,t}$$

$$r_{GE,t} = \alpha + f \frac{1}{10} \sum_{j=1}^{10} E_{GE,j,t} + \epsilon_{GE,t}$$

What would be the breadth?

(c) An alternative definition of the breadth is the number of "distinct signals." If we adopt this alternative definition of the breadth, do your answers to (a) and (b) change?

(d) One disadvantage of defining the breadth as the number of distinct signals is that the two preceding models will have the same breadth. Discuss why this is a disadvantage.

2.22. Suppose that a portfolio manager predicts the return of MSFT and GE from earnings forecasts of 10 analysts. Five analysts provide earnings forecasts for MSFT, and five analysts provide earnings forecasts for GE. Let r_{MSFT} and r_{GE} be the return of MSFT and GE and $E_{MSFT,1}, \dots, E_{MSFT,5}$ and $E_{GE,6}, \dots, E_{GE,10}$ be the forecasts. Using the consensus earnings forecasts (i.e., average forecasts), the portfolio manager may estimate the following equations:

$$r_{MSFT,t} = \alpha + f \frac{1}{5} \sum_{j=1}^{5} E_{MSFT,j,t} + \epsilon_{MSFT,t}$$

$$r_{GE,t} = \alpha + f \frac{1}{5} \sum_{j=6}^{10} E_{GE,j,t} + \epsilon_{GE,t}$$

(a) If the portfolio manager predicts return based on this model, what would be the breadth?
(b) If the portfolio manager applies the models to GM stock as well as MSFT and GE, would your answer to (a) change?
(c) If we define the breadth as the number of "distinct signals," would your answer to (b) change? Explain why it is not practical to define the breadth as the number of distinct signals.

2.23. The information loss is defined as the difference between the maximum information ratio and the actual information ratio.
(a) What does it mean to have an information loss of 0.1?
(b) What is the value of the information loss when the information criterion is satisfied?
(c) What is the minimum possible value of the information ratio? Is there a maximum possible value of the information ratio?

2.24. A portfolio manager believes that the expected returns of stocks A, B, C, D, and E are as follows:

$$E(r_A) = 10\% \quad E(r_B) = 20\% \quad E(r_C) = 30\%$$
$$E(r_D) = 40\% \quad E(r_E) = 50\%$$

She also found out that the risk (standard deviation) of each stock is 25% and that the five stocks are independent from one another. After examining this information, the portfolio manager created an equal-weighted portfolio of stocks C, D, and E.

(a) Is the information criterion satisfied?
(b) Calculate the expected return and the standard deviation of the portfolio.

(c) What is the best portfolio one can create out of five stocks? Calculate the expected return and the standard deviation of the best portfolio.

(d) Calculate the information loss.

2.25. (a) What are data mining and data snooping?

(b) Is it possible for a quantitative portfolio manager to avoid them? Explain.

2.26. What does it mean for parameters to change? What might cause parameters to change? Why might a quantitative portfolio manager be worried about parameter stability?

CHAPTER 3

Basic QEPM Models

The greatest work is inside man.

—Pope John Paul II

3.1 INTRODUCTION

The central, unifying element of quantitative equity portfolio management (QEPM) is the quantitative model that relates stock movements to other market data. Quantitative equity portfolio managers create such models to predict stock returns and volatility, and these predictions, in turn, form the basis for selecting stocks for the portfolio.

Some readers may wonder whether it is necessary to know how to make quantitative models from scratch when there are so many excellent commercial software packages with prepackaged models. When a portfolio manager relies completely on commercial software, he or she may not be able to use all the information available to him or her. Different models make use of different types of information, and any given software program likely ignores some relevant information. If the portfolio manager tries to be "creative" and combine his or her own calculations with a prepackaged model, the resulting hybrid most likely will violate the information criterion. Some dependence on commercial software may be unavoidable,[1] but with an understanding of the modeling process,

---

[1] One advantage of commercial software packages is that the companies that produce them tend to do a lot of data cleaning, which makes them a good source of polished data.

the manager will know how to get the most out of the software, what to do with it, and what not to do with it.

We begin this chapter by discussing the two basic models of QEPM. As we discuss these models, we consider how they fit into the entire construction of the portfolio, from picking factors to determining the portfolio weights. It turns out that the basic models of QEPM share many properties and produce similar portfolios in certain circumstances. We explain the equivalence of the models in Section 3.3. Portfolio managers often combine one of the basic models with some ad hoc model of stock returns. In Section 3.5 we discuss how these combinations are attempted and why they are not advisable in light of the information criterion. Section 3.6 weighs the basic models' strengths and weaknesses and discusses reasons for using one rather than the other.

3.2 BASIC QEPM MODELS AND PORTFOLIO CONSTRUCTION PROCEDURES

The central idea of modern financial economics is that the average return of a stock is the payoff to the shareholder for taking on risk. Factor models express this risk-reward relationship. *Factors* are explanatory variables that represent different types of risk. A factor model shows that the average stock return is proportional to the stock's exposure to the risk that the factor represents (the *factor exposure*) and to the payoff for each unit of exposure to the risk (the *factor premium*).

There are two generic factor models in QEPM that are used to determine how stock returns and risks vary with factors. They are the *fundamental factor model* and the *economic factor model*. The models take their names from the types of factors typically associated with them. The fundamental factor model uses fundamental factors, which are stock characteristics such as the P/E ratio and market capitalization. The economic factor model was developed originally for macroeconomic variables such as gross domestic product (GDP) and inflation, but it is general enough to handle other types of factors as well. While the models are distinguished in name by the types of factors that go into them, it is important to understand that, in addition, *the fundamental factor model and the economic factor model employ different techniques for modeling stock returns.*

Both the fundamental factor model and the economic factor model are based on the principle that the average stock return is determined by the product of the *factor premium* and the *factor exposure*. The factor premium measures how much investors are willing to pay for each factor, whereas the factor exposure measures how sensitive the stock return is to a factor. The factor premium and factor exposure operate differently in the fundamental and economic factor models. Factor exposures are directly observable for the fundamental factor model but not directly observable for the economic factor model. For the fundamental factor model, the exposures of fundamental factors can be read straight from companies' financial statements and other data sources. For the economic factor model, each stock's exposure to economic (or other) factors is not observable and instead must be estimated from the historical relationship between stock returns and factor premiums.

The factor premium functions in almost the opposite manner in the two basic models. In principle, the factor premium is not observable and must be estimated. This is the case in the fundamental factor model, for which the factor premium must be estimated from the historical relationship between stock returns and the factor exposures. In the economic factor model, however, the factor premium can be determined up to a proportionality without a statistical estimation in certain cases. In other cases, it is determined by constructing *zero-investment portfolios* or through a mathematical method called *principal-component analysis*. We will explain these methods a little later.

Table 3.1 summarizes the different ways that the basic QEPM models estimate the expected returns and risks of stocks. The specific steps involved in constructing a portfolio depend partly on which model is used. In the remainder of this section we summarize the procedures of portfolio construction from A to Z, beginning with the factor choice and ending with the assignment of portfolio weights. The procedures outlined in this overview will be discussed in detail in subsequent chapters.

3.2.1 Factor Choice

The first step toward building a quantitative portfolio is choosing factors that seem to drive stock returns. Good factors are really the secret sauce of QEPM. All quantitative portfolio managers are at

TABLE 3.1

How Expected Return and Risk Are Determined in Basic
QEPM Models

	Fundamental Factor Model	Economic Factor Model
Factor exposure (β)	Directly observed	From time-series regression
Factor premium (f)	From cross-sectional regression	Directly observed*
Expected return	Factor exposure × factor premium	Factor exposure × factor premium
Risk	Factor exposure × risk of factor premium + specific risk	Factor exposure × risk of factor premium + specific risk

*Up to a proportionality. Depending on the factors used, the factor premium may be determined by constructing zero-investment portfolios or by principal-component analysis.

least reasonably proficient at using the various types of quantitative models. What distinguishes one manager from another is the particular set of factors that he or she uses in his or her model. Managers use a wide variety of factors to explain stock returns, but not all factors can be used in all models. The fundamental factor model restricts factor choice somewhat because it typically takes only fundamental factors. The economic factor model is more flexible, allowing for both economic factors and all fundamental factors. We catalog many factors and discuss how to choose them in Chapter 4, so for the rest of this chapter's discussion on portfolio construction we shall assume that we have already completed the first step of portfolio construction and chosen K factors to represent the behavior of stock returns.

3.2.2 The Data Decision

The data set for the model is determined with a type of factor model and a set of factors in mind. A data set has two dimensions: the *cross-sectional dimension* and the *time-series dimension*. The cross-sectional dimension defines a data set by the characteristics of the stocks it includes. One may decide to gather data on stocks in a specific industry, stocks in the Standard and Poor's (S&P) 500, or all stocks traded on the New York Stock Exchange (NYSE). The cross-sectional dimension of data matters because the attributes of the data set will affect the attributes of the ultimate portfolio and because the number of stocks included in the data set will affect the ease of estimation. The time-series dimension concerns the *periodicity* of the data (i.e., the time intervals at which data points were recorded) and the time *period* of the entire data set. The data could have been recorded daily, weekly, monthly, quarterly, or annually. The entire set of data could cover a few years or just one. The periodicity and the period of the data may affect parameter stability and parameter uncertainty.[2]

Given the model and the data set, the portfolio manager may have to make a few more decisions. If the portfolio manager measures his or her performance against a benchmark, which is typically the case, there is the question of whether to include the benchmark itself as a factor in the model. Also, the portfolio manager should decide whether to use the gross return or the logarithm of the return and whether to use the return in excess of a risk-free rate.

3.2.3 Factor Exposure

Once the portfolio manager has chosen the factors and defined the data set, it is possible to determine the factor exposure and factor premium. We begin with the factor exposure, also referred to as *factor loading*. In the fundamental factor model, determining the factor exposure is fairly straightforward. For example, if the factor is the P/B ratio, the factor exposure of stock i is the latest observed value of the P/B ratio for stock i. (The factor also could be something more complicated, such as an average of the P/B ratio or a forecast of the P/B ratio.)

We will now introduce some mathematical symbols to represent the factor exposure. Suppose that there are K factors chosen for the model. We denote the K factor exposures of stock i by $\beta_{i1}, \ldots, \beta_{iK}$. If the first factor in the model is the P/B ratio, then β_{i1} is the P/B ratio of stock i.[3]

---

[2] We will discuss these issues further in Chapters 6 and 7.

[3] The convention in statistics is to use Greek letters for unobservable quantities and Latin letters for observable quantities. In the economic factor model, the factor exposure is unobservable, so it makes sense to use Greek letters for factor exposure. In the fundamental factor model, although the factor exposure is observable, it is still represented by the Greek letter β so that the notation is consistent in both types of factor models.

In the economic factor model, because the factor exposure is not directly observable, the factor premiums must be determined first (we explain how in the next section). Then the factor exposure can be estimated from the relationship between returns and factor premiums. We denote the factor premium of K factors as $f_1, \ldots, f_K$. Given the factor premium, the following equation for the return of stock i, r_i, can be estimated:

$$r_i = \alpha_i + \beta_{i1} f_1 + \cdots + \beta_{iK} f_K + \epsilon_i \qquad (3.1)$$

where $\beta_{i1}, \ldots, \beta_{iK}$ are the factor exposures of stock i, whereas α_i is the constant term of the equation. The last term, ϵ_i, is the error, which reflects the random nature of returns. The equation is typically estimated by a time-series regression using observations made at various time periods. That is, the portfolio manager takes factor premiums, which are the variables of interest that affect stock returns, and regresses stock i's returns at every time interval in the data period on the corresponding factor premiums. The estimate from this regression becomes the factor exposure. For example, the factor premium f_j might be real GDP growth. The factor exposure β_{ij} found by estimating the regression shows how sensitive stock returns are to real GDP growth.

3.2.4 Factor Premium

The quantitative portfolio manager also must know the factor premium, which is essentially the premium that the market places on exposure to whatever risk a factor represents. If we know that a stock has a high exposure to the P/B ratio factor, for instance, we need to know what kind of return the P/B ratio provides. These two pieces of information together will allow us to predict the return of the stock.

In the fundamental factor model, the factor premium is estimated from the historical relationship between the stock return and the factor exposure. The equations representing the fundamental and economic factor models are identical to Eq. (3.1), but whereas in the economic factor model the factor exposures $\beta_{i1}, \ldots, \beta_{iK}$ need to be estimated, in the fundamental factor model the factor premiums $f_1, \ldots, f_K$ must be estimated. The factor premium for the fundamental factor model is estimated by means of either cross-sectional regression, which involves using observations for various stocks at a single point in time, or panel regression, which entails using observations for various stocks at many points in time.

In the economic factor model, the factor premium is determined first and in various ways depending on the nature of factors. For macroeconomic factors, the values of the variables themselves are taken as factor premiums. For example, if the inflation rate is 3% this month, then the premium for the inflation factor is 3%. This value is not exactly the premium; it does not mean that investors are willing to pay exactly 3% for a unit of stock exposure to inflation. However, the exact premium is proportional to the inflation rate, so for the purpose of forecasting the stock return, the rate itself can be called the factor premium. More generally, the factor premium is calculated by constructing zero-investment portfolios. A *zero-investment portfolio* is a theoretical construct in which the hypothetical investor does not have to invest any capital. For example, if an investor shorts $100 of one stock, theoretically he or she can use the $100 in short-sale receipts to buy $100 of another stock. In the real world, margin requirements prevent such a neat transfer of funds, but for theoretical exercises, it is helpful to imagine such a zero-investment portfolio. We can determine the factor premium by calculating the return on a zero-investment portfolio of investments that exhibit the factor in question. Suppose that size is one of the factors in a model. A zero-investment portfolio could be created for the size factor by going long a small-cap subportfolio and shorting an equivalent amount of a large-cap subportfolio. The factor premium on size would be the difference between the return of the small-cap subportfolio and the return of the large-cap subportfolio.

3.2.5 Expected Return

Whichever factor model is used, estimation of the model provides important information about a stock's expected returns. The estimation essentially allows us to determine the expected returns of stocks based on their factor exposures and the factor premiums.

3.2.6 Risk

The estimation of the model also provides important information about stock risks. The estimation essentially decomposes the risk of stocks into two components: nondiversifiable risk and diversifiable risk. *Nondiversifiable risk* is the primary concern for investors because it comes from a stock's exposure to risks in the market that cannot be removed from the portfolio. Nondiversifiable risk is represented by $\alpha_i + \beta_{i1}f_1 + \cdots + \beta_{iK}f_K$ in Eq. (3.1). *Diversifiable risk*, on the other hand, can be removed from the portfolio by diversifying holdings. It is captured by ϵ_i. Diversifiable risk is often called the *stock-specific risk*. By calculating the variance or the standard deviation of each component of risk, we can estimate the stock's total risk.

3.2.7 Forecasting

Expected stock returns are simply the product of the factor premiums and the factor exposures. Once the stocks' risk levels have been determined, the portfolio manager has gathered all the information needed to construct a portfolio. But he or she does not have all the information to construct an optimal portfolio. The factor premiums and factor exposures in the model are determined from past data. The relationships among return, exposure, and premium are likely to change in the future. The portfolio manager wants to know *future* values, not historical values. In all likelihood, the factor exposure will not change in the immediate future, but the factor premium *is* likely to change in a very short amount of time. Thus it is usually necessary to forecast the factor premium. We explain how to forecast it in Chapter 8.

3.2.8 Security Weighting

With the estimates of stock returns and risks based on the new forecasts, the portfolio manager can use optimization techniques to select the stocks for the portfolio and assign them their respective weights. The weighting of stocks in the portfolio can be set to maximize the portfolio's overall return, minimize its risk, and satisfy other constraints such as diversification requirements and specific investment style requirements. Alternatively, the portfolio manager may decide to minimize the tracking error between the portfolio and the benchmark. This issue is explored fully in Chapter 9.

3.3 THE EQUIVALENCE OF THE BASIC MODELS

The fundamental factor model and the economic factor model are built on the same principle: The expected stock return can be expressed as the product of the factor exposure and the factor premium. Therefore, it is not surprising that the two models produce identical portfolios when certain assumptions are satisfied. The equivalence of the factor models can be established starting with the following proposition:

LEMMA 1 (THE EQUIVALENCE OF FACTOR MODELS) *The fundamental factor model and the economic factor model are equivalent to each other if the expected stock return is a linear function of the fundamental factor exposure.*

If the fundamental factor model is a correct model, then the economic factor model is also a correct one.[4] The proof of this claim proceeds in the following way: First, we assume that expected stock returns are a linear function of fundamental factor premiums, as described by the fundamental factor model. Then, under this assumption, we show that the expected stock return can be expressed as a linear function of the factor exposure, as described by the economic factor model.

Let us first express the stock return using the fundamental factor model. If there are K factors, then the return of stock i, r_i, is

$$r_i = c_i + \pi_1 x_{i1} + \cdots + \pi_K x_{iK} + \omega_i \qquad (3.2)$$

where $x_{i1}, \ldots, x_{iK}$ are the factor exposures of stock i, $\pi_1, \ldots, \pi_K$ are the factor premiums, and c_i is the constant term of the equation. For this section only, we have deliberately changed the notation to distinguish the fundamental factor model from the economic factor model.

What happens if we use the same K factors but in the economic factor model? Does the economic factor model correctly describe stock returns? The answer is yes. All we need to show is that the expected stock return can be expressed as a linear function

---

[4] The reverse relationship cannot be established in general. That is, even if the economic factor model is a correct description of reality, the fundamental factor model still may not be correct.

of the factor premium, as described by the economic factor model. We provide the proof for the case in which the factor exposures are independent of one another.[5] In the economic factor model, the factor premium is determined by constructing the zero-investment portfolio. To determine the premium of factor k, one could distribute all stocks into two or three groups based on the value x_{ik}. Suppose that each stock is assigned to one of three groups: a high group (if $x_{ik} > \bar{x}_k$), a low group (if $x_{ik} < \underline{x}_k$), and a middle group (with the cutoff values $\bar{x}_k$ and $\underline{x}_k$). The factor premium f_k is the expected return to the zero-investment position that puts \$1 into the high group and shorts \$1 in the low group,[6] that is,

$$f_k = E(r \,|\, x_k > \bar{x}_k) - E(r \,|\, x_k < \underline{x}_k) \tag{3.3}$$

If factor exposures are independent, then, using Eq. (3.2), we can rewrite the equation as

$$f_k = \pi_k d_k \tag{3.4}$$

where d_k is a constant defined as

$$d_k \equiv [E(x_k \,|\, x_k > \bar{x}_k) - E(x_k \,|\, x_k < \underline{x}_k)] \tag{3.5}$$

Using Eq. (3.4), we can rewrite Eq. (3.2) in the following way:

$$r_i = c_i + \left(\frac{f_1}{d_1}\right)x_{i1} + \cdots + \left(\frac{f_K}{d_K}\right)x_{iK} + \omega_i \tag{3.6}$$

This equation shows that the expected stock return can be written as a linear function of the factor premiums. In fact, it shows the exact relationship between the fundamental factor model and the economic factor model. The constant term in the economic factor model (α_i) is identical to the constant term in the fundamental factor model (c_i). The factor exposure in the economic factor model (β_{ik}) is proportional to the factor exposure of the fundamental factor model (x_{ik}/d_k).

For practitioners, the equivalence of the factor models means that to the extent that the fundamental factor model is a correct model, it does not really matter whether one use the fundamental factor model or the economic factor model. The two models produce essentially identical results. The only catch is that if the fundamental factor model is not correct, then it is best to use the

---

[5] This proof can be modified easily for the more general case.
[6] Note that the expectation is taken across stocks. It is the cross-sectional average of the expected stock return.

economic factor model because it has a stronger theoretical basis than the fundamental factor model does.

3.4 THE SCREENING AND RANKING OF STOCKS WITH THE Z-SCORE

Many portfolio managers screen and rank stocks using *Z-scores*. Sometimes stock screens and rankings supplement the use of a factor model in determining the mix of stocks for the portfolio. More often they are used as alternatives to the factor model. Since screening and ranking are widespread practices among managers, we discuss them more fully in Chapter 5.

In the context of stock screening and ranking, a Z-score is a stock's standardized exposure to a fundamental factor. To calculate the Z-scores for the stocks in some investment universe, we need to know the factor exposures of every stock. Then, for each stock, we subtract the universe's mean factor exposure from the stock's individual factor exposure and divide that difference by the standard deviation of factor exposures for the universe. What comes out of this standardization is a set of Z-scores, factor exposures with a mean of 0 and a standard deviation of 1.

For example, suppose that we want to calculate Z-scores for exposure to the P/B ratio. If $\beta_1, \ldots, \beta_N$ are the P/B ratios of stocks $1, \ldots, N$, then the Z-score of stock i is defined as

$$z_i = \frac{\beta_i - \mu}{\sigma} \tag{3.7}$$

where μ and σ are the average and standard deviation of $\beta_1, \ldots, \beta_N$. The standardization allows us to interpret the Z-score in the following way: If z_i is 2, then the P/B ratio of stock i is 2 standard deviations away from the average.

Given the Z-score of one factor—or, more commonly, of many factors—portfolio managers can develop a number of screening and ranking strategies. We look at a simple example in the next section and more realistic examples in Chapter 5.

3.5 HYBRIDS OF THE MODELS AND THE INFORMATION CRITERION

Practitioners often try to add extra inputs to the basic QEPM models by combining them with ad hoc models. The resulting hybrid models are sometimes reasonable descriptions of stock returns, but in many cases they have a number of undesirable effects. The most critical problem with hybrids is that they frequently violate the information criterion.

Recall that in order to uphold tenet 4 of QEPM and satisfy the information criterion, a portfolio manager must use all available information in the most efficient way. A hybrid model combining two models that are based on different information may violate the information criterion by combining the two original sets of information inefficiently. If a hybrid model is based on two models that use the same information, the hybrid may violate the information criterion by incorrectly "double counting" the information. Consider the following hypothetical situation: Adam, a portfolio manager, creates a fundamental factor model but decides to combine it with a Z-score analysis. Specifically, Adam calculates the expected return based on the Z-score method and adds this expected return to the fundamental factor model as a constant. Adam uses portfolio management software that implements the fundamental factor model automatically and allows the user to add a constant [i.e., α in Eq. (3.1)].

Is Adam using all the available information in the most efficient way? Not if he created the Z-score model and the fundamental factor model from the same data. The addition of the Z-score analysis not only presents no gain, but it in fact also introduces distortion in the model, which will lead to a less-than-optimal portfolio. Even if Adam used different sets of information to create the Z-score model and the fundamental factor model, the two sets of information are still not being combined in the most efficient way. In either case, the hybrid does not satisfy the information criterion. With data on his models and portfolio, we can find out exactly how inefficient Adam's hybrid is by calculating the information loss. The following numerical example illustrates the problem with patching together two models.

3.5.1 The Setup

Imagine that there are only two stocks in the world, stock A and stock B. Suppose that current stock returns r are determined by the price-to-earnings (P/E) ratios at the end of the previous period. Specifically, we assume[7]

---

[7] In reality, we never know the true return-generating process, so the example may seem unrealistic. The fact that we are assuming certainty in the return-generating process, though, does not affect the lesson of the example that combining two models creates distortion.

$$r_{A,t+1} = 0.1 \left(\frac{P}{E}\right)_{A,t} + \epsilon_{A,t+1} \quad \epsilon_{A,t+1} \sim N(0,20) \tag{3.8}$$

$$r_{B,t+1} = 0.1 \left(\frac{P}{E}\right)_{B,t} + \epsilon_{B,t+1} \quad \epsilon_{B,t+1} \sim N(0,10) \tag{3.9}$$

where ϵ is the random component of the stock return and is assumed to have a normal distribution with a variance of 10 or 20.[8] We also assume that the covariance between the two random errors is zero. Suppose that for the last period T, the P/E ratio of stock A is 20 and of stock B is 10. Therefore, the average P/E ratio is 15 [$=(20 + 10)/2$], the variance is 25 {$= [(20 - 15)^2 + (10 - 15)^2]/2$}, and the standard deviation is 5 ($=\sqrt{25}$). Suppose further that the average and the variance are constant over time and across stocks. Table 3.2 summarizes this assumption and the corresponding calculations of the Z-score.

3.5.2 The Z-Score Model

The Z-score is the normalized factor exposure. To calculate one stock's Z-score, we subtract the mean factor exposure of all stocks from the individual stock's factor exposure and then divide that difference by the cross-sectional standard deviation of the factor exposures of all stocks. The Z-score for stocks A and B are reported in Table 3.2. Once the Z-score is calculated, it is possible to estimate the following equation to predict the expected stock return:

$$r_{i,t+1} = a_i + bz_{it} + v_{i,t+1} \quad i = A,B; t = 1, \dots, T - 1 \tag{3.10}$$

TABLE 3.2

Price-to-Earnings Ratio and the Z-Score

	Stock A	Stock B	Mean	Variance	SD
$\left(\frac{P}{E}\right)_T$	20	10	15	25	5
z_T	1	-1	0	1	1

---

[8] When we typically estimate these factor models, we use information at time t to predict returns at time $t + 1$. This is to avoid any look-ahead bias. Sometimes in this book, for convenience, we write the equation with time subscript t everywhere. It should still be interpreted as using information at time t to predict returns at time $t + 1$. Sometimes we will refer to this as having beginning-of-month or equivalently end-of-the-previous-month factor exposures with this month's returns.

where z_{it} is the Z-score of stock i at time t, a_i is a constant, and $v_{i,t+1}$ is the error. From the numbers given in Table 3.2, the values of a_A, a_B, and b are as follows[9]:

$$b = \frac{1}{2}\frac{C(r_A, z_A)}{V(z_A)} + \frac{1}{2}\frac{C(r_B, z_B)}{V(z_B)}$$

$$= \frac{1}{2}\sqrt{V\left[\left(\frac{P}{E}\right)_A\right]}\frac{C\left[r_{A'}\left(\frac{P}{E}\right)_A\right]}{V\left[\left(\frac{P}{E}\right)_A\right]} + \frac{1}{2}\sqrt{V\left[\left(\frac{P}{E}\right)_B\right]}\frac{C\left[r_{B'}\left(\frac{P}{E}\right)_B\right]}{V\left[\left(\frac{P}{E}\right)_B\right]} \quad (3.11)$$

$$= \frac{1}{2}\cdot 5\cdot 0.1 + \frac{1}{2}\cdot 5\cdot 0.1 = 0.5$$

$$\begin{aligned} a_A &= E(r_A) - bE(z_A) \\ &= 1.5 - 0.5\cdot 0 = 1.5 \end{aligned} \quad (3.12)$$

and

$$\begin{aligned} a_B &= E(r_B) - bE(z_B) \\ &= 1.5 - 0.5\cdot 0 = 1.5 \end{aligned} \quad (3.13)$$

Given the time T value of the Z-score, the preceding estimates imply the following expected returns for stock A and stock B:

$$E(r_{A,T+1}) = a_A + bz_{A,T} = 1.5 + 0.5\cdot 1 = 2 \quad (3.14)$$

$$E(r_{B,T+1}) = a_B + bz_{B,T} = 1.5 + 0.5\cdot(-1) = 1 \quad (3.15)$$

Note that the expected returns of stock A and stock B are correct. The Z-score model itself does not create any problem with the efficient use of information. The problem arises when the Z-score model is combined incorrectly with other models, as illustrated below.

3.5.3 A Hybrid of the Z-Score Model and a Fundamental Factor Model

Adam first estimated the fundamental factor model, i.e., Eq. (3.1). Then he did the Z-score analysis. Now he creates his hybrid model by setting the term α in the fundamental factor model according to the expected return from the Z-score model. Specifically he adjusts α of stock A to be 1 and α of stock B to be -1 so that the sum of

---

[9] The formula can be obtained by demeaning (i.e., subtracting the mean from) both sides of the equation and applying the standard ordinary least squares (OLS) formula.

the α's remains equal to 0. For time $T + 1$, he incorrectly modifies Eqs. (3.8) and (3.9) into the following:

$$r_{A,T+1} = 1 + 0.1 \left(\frac{P}{E}\right)_{A,T} + \epsilon_{A,T+1} \quad \epsilon_{A,T+1} \sim N(0,20) \qquad (3.16)$$

$$r_{B,T+1} = -1 + 0.1 \left(\frac{P}{E}\right)_{B,T} + \epsilon_{B,T+1} \quad \epsilon_{B,T+1} \sim N(0,10) \qquad (3.17)$$

Given time T's P/E ratio, Adam is going to construct a portfolio at time $T + 1$ based on the following numbers:

$$E(r_{A,T+1}) = 1 + 0.1 \cdot 20 = 3 \qquad (3.18)$$

$$E(r_{B,T+1}) = -1 + 0.1 \cdot 10 = 0 \qquad (3.19)$$

$$V(r_{A,T+1}) = V(\epsilon_{A,T+1}) = 20 \qquad (3.20)$$

$$V(r_{B,T+1}) = V(\epsilon_{B,T+1}) = 10 \qquad (3.21)$$

$$C(r_{A,T+1}, r_{B,T+1}) = C(\epsilon_{A,T+1}, \epsilon_{B,T+1}) = 0 \qquad (3.22)$$

If the weight of stock A in the portfolio is w, then the expected return and the variance of the portfolio (according to Adam's calculations) are

$$\mu_p = 3w + 0(1 - w) \qquad (3.23)$$

$$\sigma_p^2 = 20w^2 + 2 \cdot 0 \cdot w(1 - w) + 10(1 - w)^2 \qquad (3.24)$$

To construct his optimal tangent portfolio, Adam finds the value of w that maximizes μ_p/σ_p. This value is $w = 1$. Thus 100% of Adam's portfolio will go into stock A and 0% into stock B.

3.5.4 Information Loss

Adam thinks that he has created the optimal portfolio, but he is actually not achieving the maximum Sharpe ratio because his estimates of the expected return are not correct. The information loss reveals exactly how much potential Sharpe ratio Adam is losing by combining two models. Let us first determine the maximum Sharpe ratio Adam could have achieved if he had not combined the Z-score analysis with the fundamental factor model. By not combining the models, we obtain the true expected returns of stock A and stock B:

$$E(r_{A,T+1}) = 2 \qquad (3.25)$$

$$E(r_{B,T+1}) = 1 \qquad (3.26)$$

We should emphasize the fact that the loss of potential returns does not arise from choosing one model over the other. Adam would have found the correct expected return whether he used the Z-score model or the fundamental factor model. It was the combination of the two that muddied the analysis. Given the correct expected return of the individual stocks, the expected return and variance of Adam's current portfolio (invested 100% in stock A and 0% in stock B) are

$$\mu_P = 2w + (1 - w) = 2 \tag{3.27}$$

$$\sigma_P^2 = 20w^2 + 10(1 - w)^2 = 20 \tag{3.28}$$

Thus Adam's portfolio's actual Sharpe ratio (SR) (ignoring the risk-free rate) is

$$\text{Actual } SR = \frac{\mu_P}{\sqrt{\sigma_P^2}} = 0.4472 \tag{3.29}$$

Adam's current portfolio weights are not optimal. The maximum Sharpe ratio is achieved when $w = 0.5$. When $w = 0.5$, the expected return and the variance of the portfolio are

$$\mu_P = 2w + (1 - w) = 1.5 \tag{3.30}$$

$$\sigma_P^2 = 20w^2 + 10(1 - w)^2 = 7.5 \tag{3.31}$$

If the portfolio had been constructed optimally, Adam could have attained a maximum Sharpe ratio of

$$\text{Maximum } SR = \frac{\mu_P}{\sqrt{\sigma_P^2}} = 0.5477 \tag{3.32}$$

Given the actual Sharpe ratio and the maximum Sharpe ratio, the information loss (IL) is the difference between the two:

$$IL = \text{maximum } SR - \text{actual } SR = 0.1005 \tag{3.33}$$

The information loss of 0.1005 means that when Adam takes 1% extra risk, his reward for taking that extra risk is 0.1% lower than it could have been. Since Adam is currently taking 4.5% risk, he earns 0.45% less than he could have. He loses 0.45%, or 45 basis points, in expected return by incorrectly combining two models. The moral of the story is clear. The best thing to do is to choose one model and stick with it. Combining basic models is hard to justify in terms of the information criterion. Another practical implication of this example is that there are benefits to building one's own model at the outset. Many managers want to model information in a specific way, but prepackaged programs are not flexible to modifications. It does no good to tack an ad hoc model onto the one that the software generates, so designing an entire custom model may be the best course of action.

3.6 CHOOSING THE RIGHT MODEL

It is clearly best to choose just one model of stock returns in order to create the portfolio, but which one of the two general factor models is the right one to use in a given situation? As we noted earlier, the economic factor model handles a different range of factors and operates differently from the fundamental factor model. Here we discuss some criteria for choosing one type of model over the other (see Table 3.3 for a summary).

3.6.1 Consistency with Economic Theory

Tenet 5 of QEPM states that quantitative models should be based on sound economic theory. The economic factor model upholds tenet 5 better than the fundamental factor does. Economic theory suggests that high expected returns are justified only as the payoff for bearing extra risk. Small-cap and value stocks might produce extra returns not because there is anything especially good about being small cap and value but because being small cap and value increases the stocks' risk. If this were the case, a fundamental factor model using those two variables would not give us meaningful information about the sources of risk and how they affect stock prices. It would be better to use a model that gets to the underlying risk of the stocks directly rather than looking at size and value. An economic factor model can measure the sensitivity of stocks to various economic risk factors.

Of course, if the relationship between the stock return and the fundamental factor exposure is linear, then the fundamental factor model is equivalent to the economic factor model, as we showed earlier. If the relationship is not linear, however, the fundamental factor model not only lacks theoretical backing, but it also lacks econometric justification because the cross-sectional regression becomes misspecified. In other words, we are estimating the wrong equation.[10]

---

[10] Another assumption typically adopted in implementing the fundamental factor model is that the factor premium is stable for some time. Similarly, in implementing the economic factor model, the assumption is often that the factor exposure is stable for some time. Whether these assumptions make sense or not can be another criterion for choosing a model. However, as we explain in Chapter 8 on forecasting, neither of these assumptions has to be adopted.

3.6.2 Ability to Combine Different Types of Factors

Not all factors can be used in both the economic and fundamental factor models. Both models can handle fundamental factors, such as the P/B ratio, the P/E ratio, and size. They also can use technical factors, such as momentum and trading volume. There are some factors, however, that only the economic factor model can handle. These include macroeconomic factors, such as GDP and inflation. If a portfolio manager wants to use a mix of all types of factors, the economic factor model is the necessary choice.

3.6.3 Ease of Implementation

In terms of ease of implementation, however, the fundamental factor model is preferable to the economic factor model. For the fundamental factor model, only factor premiums need to be estimated. For the economic factor models, factor exposures of individual stocks need to be estimated, and forecasts of factor premiums are usually needed as well. A manager should remember, though, that the ease of implementing the fundamental factor model comes at the cost of restrictions on the types of factors that can be used.

3.6.4 Data Requirement

The fundamental factor model can be estimated without a large amount of historical data.[11] On the other hand, to estimate the economic factor model, portfolio managers have to gather a relatively large period of historical returns because the estimation of factor exposures requires a time-series analysis of returns.

In terms of the cross-sectional dimension, the data requirement for the economic factor model may be lower than the data requirement for the fundamental factor model. The economic factor model

---

[11] To estimate the variance of each stock return requires the variance of the error terms of each stock and the variance-covariance matrix of the factor premiums. It is possible to obtain the variance-covariance matrix of the factor premiums from (the estimation error of) a single cross-sectional regression. Thus a historical time series may improve the estimation but is not necessary. However, to be able to estimate the variance of the error of each stock, we do need some historical data because in a cross-sectional regression the variance of the error is assumed to be the same across stocks. The importance of estimating the error, however, is somewhat less than other estimations. Thus the fundamental factor model requires some historical data to be able to estimate the variance of individual stock returns, which is ultimately required to build optimized portfolios. However, the data required are still less than what are required in the economic factor model.

is estimated for each stock separately, and in the extreme case, it may be estimated for just one stock. To estimate the fundamental factor model, however, one needs a significant number of stocks (typically a few hundred).

However, this difference should not be exaggerated. When the economic factor model is estimated for a small number of stocks, the estimation error in the factor exposure may remain significant *after* the portfolio is constructed. If the portfolio is composed of a large number of stocks, the estimation error in the factor exposure of one stock is likely to be canceled out by the estimation error of another stock. This sort of canceling out is not likely to happen in a portfolio composed of very few stocks. Thus, in practice, the economic factor model also requires data on many stocks in order to be useful in the portfolio construction process.[12]

3.6.5 Intuitive Appeal

The intuitive appeal of a model goes beyond whether it can be explained with economic theory. The best model is the one that makes common sense and is easy enough to explain in plain language. Portfolio managers always should understand the models they are using. Even an excellent model is dangerous in uneducated hands. In terms of gaining familiarity and becoming comfortable with quantitative models, reading this book carefully is a step in the right direction.

TABLE 3.3

Criteria for Selecting the Right Model

Criterion	Fundamental Factor Model	Economic Factor Model
Theoretical basis		Better
Factor accommodation		Better
Ease of implementation	Better	
Data requirement	Better	
Intuitive appeal	Depends	Depends

---

[12] It also means that since the fundamental factor model is affected by the errors of factor returns and not of factor exposures, the fundamental factor model's estimation errors will be similar regardless of the diversification of a portfolio. Thus one might believe that fundamental factor models would work better for very undiversified or concentrated portfolios.

3.7 CONCLUSION

In this chapter we introduced the basic models that quantitative equity portfolio managers use to predict stock returns. The main models of QEPM are the fundamental factor model and the economic factor model. The fundamental factor model is used primarily to explain stock returns with stock fundamentals, whereas the economic factor model can be used to explain returns with almost any type of factor. The fundamental and economic factor models work somewhat differently but follow a common formula: the average stock return equals the product of factor exposures and factor premiums. We demonstrated that the two types of models produce identical results under certain conditions, but we also looked at reasons for choosing one type over the other.

Many managers use stock screening and ranking methods in addition to or instead of factor models. Although the Z-score analysis involved in screening and ranking stocks works fine by itself to estimate stock returns, it is best not to combine it with factor models. The resulting hybrid models fail the information criterion, and the resulting portfolios miss out on potential returns.

In this chapter we described how quantitative models fit into the seven steps of portfolio construction (factor choice, data preparation, estimation of factor exposures, estimation of factor premiums, determination of risk, forecasting of factor premiums, and, finally, security weighting). We will examine the fundamental and economic factor models in greater detail in Chapters 6 and 7, again in the context of the overall portfolio construction process, which is the subject of Part II of this book.

QUESTIONS

3.1. What are the two most frequently used models of stock return in QEPM?
   (a) How do you obtain the factor exposure for each model?
   (b) How do you obtain the factor premium for each model?
   (c) How do you obtain expected returns for each stock from each model?
   (d) How do you measure the risk of each stock with each model?

3.2. What are the steps in the general portfolio construction process of QEPM? Describe each one briefly.

3.3. What is the difference between a cross-sectional data set and a time-series data set?

3.4. Below is a series of statements by a quantitative portfolio manager. Decide whether each statement relates more to a fundamental factor model or to an economic factor model.
   (a) The average P/B ratio of our portfolio is very high.
   (b) Our portfolio will be quite resilient if oil prices rise to our negative exposures.
   (c) Our philosophy at the Financial Artists Hedge Fund is that economics drives stock returns; thus we use economic data to predict individual stock returns.
   (d) The factor exposure of every stock is known and publicly available.
   (e) Analyst forecasts drive stock returns.
   (f) Our investment department is very good at predicting presidential elections. We choose stocks accordingly.

3.5. Macroeconomic variables cannot be used in stock return models because they are the same for all stocks. True or false. Explain.

3.6. How do you obtain the factor premium for an economic factor model and a fundamental factor model? Give an example of each.

3.7. How useful is the annual inflation rate of the United States as a factor premium?

3.8. Why is forecasting factor premiums necessary? Why doesn't this same logic apply to factor exposures? Please answer with respect to both types of QEPM stock return models.

3.9. In this chapter we proved the equivalence of factor models under the assumption that the factor exposures are independent of one another. Prove the equivalence of factor models without this assumption.

3.10. In this chapter we proved that if the fundamental factor model is correct, then the economic factor model is also correct. However, the reverse is not true. Consider the following example. Suppose that the expected stock return is proportional to the squared firm size and that the stock return can be written as

$$r_i = \alpha + \pi x_i^2 + \epsilon_i$$

where x_i is the size of stock i.

(a) Show that it is possible that the economic factor model is correct; i.e., the expected stock return is a linear function of the factor premium f defined as

$$f = E(r \mid x > \mu_x) - E(r \mid x < \mu_x)$$

where μ is the average of the firm size.

(b) Explain why the fundamental factor model may not be consistent with the preceding setup.

(c) Given this one-way relationship, which model would you prefer in practice?

3.11. What is a common standardization that portfolio managers use before screening stocks?

3.12. Why might it be dangerous for a quantitative equity portfolio manager to combine the Z-score model with a commercial risk model to build an optimized portfolio?

3.13. In the example of Section 3.5 we assumed that the true return-generating process is

$$r_{A,t+1} = 0.1\left(\frac{P}{E}\right)_{A,t} + \epsilon_{A,t+1} \quad \epsilon_{A,t+1} \sim N(0, 20)$$

$$r_{B,t+1} = 0.1\left(\frac{P}{E}\right)_{B,t} + \epsilon_{B,t+1} \quad \epsilon_{B,t+1} \sim N(0, 10)$$

That is, we assumed that α is zero. Suppose that α is not zero. Instead, assume that the true return-generating process is

$$r_{A,t+1} = 1 + 0.1\left(\frac{P}{E}\right)_{A,t} + \epsilon_{A,t+1} \quad \epsilon_{A,t+1} \sim N(0, 20)$$

$$r_{B,t+1} = 0.1\left(\frac{P}{E}\right)_{B,t} + \epsilon_{B,t+1} \quad \epsilon_{B,t+1} \sim N(0, 10)$$

(a) If Adam estimates the Z-score model, what would be the estimated expected return of stock A and stock B? Are the estimates correct?

(b) If Adam uses the estimated expected return from the Z-score model as α in the fundamental factor model, what would be the estimated expected returns of stock A and stock B? Are the estimates correct?

(c) Explain why the information criterion is not satisfied regardless of whether the true α is zero or not.

(d) Calculate the information loss.

3.14. A portfolio manager estimated the expected stock return from a Z-score model of the price-to-earnings ratio and used it as α in the fundamental factor model, as discussed in Section 3.5. This time, however, instead of estimating the fundamental factor model with the price-to-earnings ratio, the portfolio manager estimated the fundamental factor model with the size. Thus the portfolio manager is not double counting any information. Is the information criterion satisfied now?

3.15. Below we list some criteria for selecting a stock return model. Indicate which factor model (fundamental or economic) best meets each criterion.

(a) Theoretical reasoning
(b) Factor accommodation
(c) Ease of implementation
(d) Data requirements
(e) Intuitive appeal

3.16. Economic and fundamental factors are both used in practice.

(a) Which type of factor is more theoretically justified?
(b) Give one reason why this is so.
(c) Eugene Fama might be heard saying the following: "I still would rather not use the type of factor in part (a) because it does not perform well out of sample." What does he mean? Is he right?

Portfolio Construction and Maintenance

The next eight chapters are a user's manual for QEPM. We will lay out the nuts and bolts of constructing and maintaining the optimal portfolio for the manager's objectives. What is the job of a portfolio manager, after all, but to assemble and run a portfolio of securities that consistently outperforms the market? Intuitive and purely qualitative investment strategies can be hit or miss. QEPM helps the manager to identify the strategies that are most likely to earn high returns consistently. It is also a systematic, concrete way to make daily decisions about the portfolio.

The factor model of stock returns, the central element of QEPM, subjects investment strategies to the rigors of the scientific method. In so doing it fulfills principles embodied in several of the seven tenets of QEPM. Ideas for the model must be formed as hypotheses based on sound economic theory (satisfying tenet 5); statistical analyses used in creating the model identify which hypotheses reflect persistent, stable patterns (satisfying tenet 6); and the resulting model combines all the available information in the most efficient way (satisfying tenet 4).

QEPM guides the manager in both the initial selection of securities and in the ongoing work of maintaining the optimal mix of holdings. With QEPM, the manager even can maximize the portfolio return after transactions costs and taxes, whose corrosive effects on the accumulation of portfolio wealth are sometimes not fully appreciated by personal investors or professional managers.

CHAPTER 4

Factors and Factor Choice

Not everything that can be counted counts, and not everything that counts can be counted.

—Albert Einstein

4.1 INTRODUCTION

Factors are the ingredients of quantitative equity portfolio management (QEPM) models. Just as high-quality ingredients make for excellent cuisine, carefully selected factors can, in the right combination, create models for outperformance. Factors come in many varieties: fundamental, technical, economic, and alternative. How does a portfolio manager select the right ones for a model? QEPM tenets 4 and 5 advise the manager to build quantitative models that reflect sound economic theories and persistent, stable patterns. Good factors therefore exhibit relationships with stock returns that not only are stable and persistent but also can be explained by economic theory. As we discussed in Chapter 2, the likelihood of finding high-quality factors depends on how one goes about looking for them. Data mining produces factors that appear to be highly correlated with stock returns, but the relationships between those factors and returns are only superficial. The way to find good factors is to apply solid, well-reasoned quantitative techniques to the search. This chapter describes the main types of factors and some methods of choosing them.

4.2 FUNDAMENTAL FACTORS

A *factor* is any variable that can predict stock returns. Perhaps the most obvious influence on stock performance is the financial condition of the firm. *Fundamental* factors describe a firm's financial condition. The most common fundamental factors are ratios calculated directly from the income statement, balance sheet, and statement of cash flows. Innumerable financial ratios and combinations of financial statement variables potentially could be constructed from the financial statements and used to forecast stock returns. Since many of these possible fundamental factors are correlated with each other, we can boil the list down to some essential ones that every portfolio manager should know.

We group the fundamental factors into seven subcategories: valuation factors, size factors, operational efficiency factors, operating profitability factors, solvency factors, financial risk factors, and corporate activity factors. Valuation factors, such as the price-to-book (P/B) ratio and the price-to-earnings (P/E) ratio, attempt to measure whether stocks are relatively cheap or expensive. Size factors, such as market capitalization, attempt to classify companies by their size and measure whether size has effects on stock return behavior. Operating efficiency factors, such as inventory turnover, and operating profitability factors, such as gross profit margin, tell us how well management is running the company. Solvency factors attempt to measure a company's ability to meet future short-term obligations. Indicators in this subcategory include the current ratio and the cash ratio. Financial risk factors measure financial health in ratios such as debt-to-equity and interest coverage. Finally, corporate activity measures factors that are related to corporate executive decisions or do not necessarily fall into any of the other categories. Tables 4A.1 through 4A.7 in Appendix 4A provide complete lists of the fundamental factors for QEPM models.

4.2.1 Valuation Factors

Table 4.1 shows the values of popular valuation factors for selected stocks. Legions of managers have based investment strategies on the P/E ratio, and, as we saw in Chapter 2, many studies have documented a P/E ratio effect.[1] Low P/E ratio stocks tend to

---
[1] See Table 2.2.

outperform high P/E ratio stocks on a risk-adjusted basis.[2] One possible explanation for this effect is that the market generally overreacts to bad news, leaving the prices of some stocks excessively deflated. Portfolio managers can purchase the "unpopular" stocks at bargain prices and eventually earn outsized returns as the rest of the market realizes that the stocks are underpriced. Since the P/E ratio is such a popular factor, it is important not to fall into the trap of including it in a model by default. There always should be a clear reason for including it based on sound economic theory. When considering P/E ratio or any other factor to add to a model, it is also important to anticipate how it will fit with the rest of the factors in the model.

The P/E ratios of the companies listed in Table 4.1 vary substantially. Tesla, one of the world's leading electric auto companies, carries a P/E ratio of approximately 1,203, whereas megabank J.P. Morgan has a mere 15.18 P/E ratio.[3] This quick cross-industry comparison does not tell us the whole story, though. A company's P/E ratio—and other financial metrics—needs to be viewed in the context of the company's industry. In 2020, J.P. Morgan's P/E ratio was roughly in line with a banking-industry multiple of about 17 times. Tesla's P/E ratio of 1,203, on the other hand, was very high compared with the automobile industry's average of about 317. Sometimes, though, a stock's P/E ratio may exceed the overall market P/E ratio but fall a bit below its industry's average P/E ratio. PayPal, the digital payment company, provides a prime example of undervaluation within its industry. Paypal's P/E ratio of 87 (as of December 2020) is above the current 78.70 P/E ratio of the S&P 500.

---

[2] In this chapter, when we characterize a ratio as "high," we generally mean that it falls within the top quartile or top decile of the investment universe. When we describe a ratio as being "low," we generally mean that it falls within the bottom quartile or decile of the universe.

[3] For those readers who replicate the calculations, some notes about our calculations will help. First, we use quarterly data and lag the data to avoid look-ahead bias, as discussed in Chapters 6 and 16. Thus, for December 2020, we use firm financial data from September 2020, with the exception of market data like prices. Second, when we discuss the S&P 500 averages, we remove companies that do not have a share code of 10, 11, or 12 in CRSP. This effectively removes REITs from our S&P 500 index. Thus, our averages might differ from the actual S&P 500. For industry and sector averages, we use the GICS code of the respective industry for only stocks in our S&P 500. Third, it must be remembered that many of the average statistics of the indices are weighted averages by the float-weighted capitalization, which is different than a straight average.

TABLE 4.1

Valuation Factors for the Top 10 Standard and Poor's (S&P) 500 Companies

Ticker	Dividend Yield (DY)	Price-to- Book Ratio (P/B)	Price-to-Cash-Flow Ratio (P/CF)	Price-to-Earnings Ratio (P/E)	Price-to-Earnings-to-Growth Ratio (PEG)	Price-to-Earnings-to-Growth-plus-Yield Ratio (PEGY)	Price-to-Sales Ratio (P/S)
AAPL	0.61	34.53	27.96	39.30	3.24	3.08	8.22
MSFT	0.92	13.63	25.40	35.41	2.45	2.30	11.43
AMZN	0.00	19.74	29.56	94.04	2.59	2.59	4.70
GOOGL	0.00	5.19	19.43	30.94	1.87	1.87	6.43
TSLA	0.00	41.73	153.81	1,203.07	2.95	2.95	23.74
FB	0.00	5.58	19.43	25.98	1.57	1.57	8.31
BRK.B	0.00	1.31	13.16	15.17	N/A	N/A	1.95
JNJ	2.47	6.43	19.19	24.39	5.66	3.60	5.12
WMT	1.48	5.42	12.35	22.79	3.38	2.77	0.75
JPM	2.86	1.61	12.40	15.18	N/A	N/A	2.91

Note: DY is in percentage terms. Ticker symbols are for the following companies: Apple Inc. (AAPL), Microsoft Corporation (MSFT), Amazon (AMZN), Alphabet Inc. or Google (GOOGL), Tesla Inc. (TSLA), Facebook Inc. (FB), Berkshire Hathaway (BRK.B), Johnson & Johnson (JNJ), Walmart Inc. (WMT), and J.P. Morgan Chase & Co. (JPM). Some of these companies have multiple share listings that would have made the top 10 largest companies of the S&P 500 at the end of 2020; however, we excluded these so as to have a distinct set of different companies. PEG ratios were computed using one-year growth rates if positive. Data are for end of 2020.

Yet PayPal falls short of the average P/E ratio of 274 that the information technology sector commands as a whole.

Dividend yield (DY), P/B ratio, price-to-sales (P/S) ratio, price-to-cash-flow (P/CF) ratio, and price-to-EBITDA (P/EBITDA) ratio all attempt to capture the value of a stock. These variables are highly correlated with each other, so a manager can pick one according to his or her preference.[4] Some portfolio managers prefer to use P/B ratio rather than P/E ratio because P/E ratio cannot be calculated for firms with negative earnings.[5] Some portfolio managers also prefer the P/B ratio because of its prevalence in academic studies. Some quantitative portfolio managers instead use the P/CF ratio because they view cash-flow measures as less susceptible to manipulation by a company's management. All these ratios have been linked to the same trend, though. It has been documented that companies with high dividend yields and low P/B, P/S, P/CF, and P/EBITDA ratios tend to outperform stocks for which the reverse is true. There are many potential explanations for this trend. One explanation is that stocks with low values of these variables have experienced a serious price decline, which could lead many investors to shy away from them or demand a higher risk premium for holding them.

Stocks with high P/B ratios generally are referred to as *growth stocks*, and stocks with low P/B ratios are referred to as *value stocks*. In 2020, retail behemoth Walmart (WMT) had a P/B ratio of 5.42, whereas technology giant Apple had a P/B ratio of 34.53. Judging from the P/B ratios, Apple is more of a growth stock and Walmart more of a value play. As with the P/E ratio, though, we need to put the stocks in industry context to get the full story. In comparison with the 2020 retailing industry P/B ratio of about 13.21 or the subindustry of general merchandise stores' P/B ratio of 5.92, Walmart is undervalued. On the other hand, if a P/B ratio is too low, it could be evidence that management has failed to generate sufficient returns to its shareholders and that the stock price has slid in response. P/S and P/CF ratios reveal similar information and also may help to expose incidences of manipulation of earnings because sales and cash-flow numbers are generally

---

[4] In the Practical Application section of this book (Part V; see Chapters 16 and 17), we give some idea of the correlation and relationships between many common factors.

[5] Some portfolio managers also use the inverse of P/E for evaluating stocks since it allows for the consideration of negative-earnings companies. In footnote 2 of Chapter 5 we expand on the reasons for choosing the inverse of certain ratios.

more transparent than book values. While Walmart's P/B ratio was well below Apple's P/B ratio, its P/CF ratio, at 12.35, was closer to Apple's 27.96 P/CF ratio.

The price-to-earnings-to-growth (PEG) ratio is another valuation measure typically used to identify good growth companies. The idea behind the PEG ratio is that a high P/E ratio is justified if a company's earnings are expected to grow a lot in the next few years. From the P/E ratio alone, a stock might appear overvalued, but if the stock has a low PEG ratio, the high P/E ratio could be reasonable given the company's expected earnings growth. Consider data on Microsoft (MSFT), one of the world's leaders in software and technology, and the giant drug manufacturer Johnson & Johnson (JNJ). In 2020, Microsoft had a P/E ratio of 35, and Johnson & Johnson had a P/E ratio of about 24. From the P/E ratios, we might hasten to conclude that Johnson & Johnson was undervalued relative to Microsoft. However, as of December 2020, given the median analyst-forecasted earnings-per-share (EPS) growth rates of 14.45% and 4.31% for Microsoft and Johnson & Johnson, respectively, we can calculate the PEG ratio. Microsoft's PEG ratio is 2.45, and Johnson & Johnson's is 5.66. Owing to Microsoft's superior earnings growth outlook, Johnson & Johnson now appears to be slightly overvalued with respect to Microsoft. Microsoft's greater rate of forecasted earnings growth more than compensates for its higher price multiple. Although we used the stock analysts' consensus forecasts of earnings growth to compute the PEG ratio, some investors prefer to use historical earnings growth instead since they are unaffected by overly optimistic analyst forecasts.

The P/E ratio can be adjusted one step further by dividing it by the sum of the company's expected growth rate and its dividend yield. The resulting ratio, the price-to-earnings-to-growth-plus-yield (PEGY) ratio, indicates how attractive the stock's valuation is, given both its expected growth rate and its dividend yield.[6] For example, Apple and Walmart have PEG ratios that are roughly equivalent at 3.24 and 3.38, respectively. However, when we take into account Apple's dividend yield of 0.61% and Walmart's 2.77% yield, we end up with different PEGY ratios of 3.08 and 2.77, respectively. A relatively low PEGY ratio makes Walmart look more attractive than Apple on a pure valuation basis.

---

[6] Another way of calculating this ratio is to divide the PEG ratio by the stock's dividend yield.

The dividend yield also can serve as an invaluable aid in determining a company's maturity and growth prospects. Stable, mature businesses tend to generate sufficient cash flow and offer relatively high dividend yields. Many of these companies find that they have limited opportunities to undertake highly lucrative growth projects, so they return discretionary cash to shareholders in the form of dividends rather than squandering it on low-return investments. Of the 10 companies in Table 4.1, J.P. Morgan Chase and Johnson & Johnson, the two oldest and most mature businesses on the list, have the highest dividend yields, 2.86% and 2.47% respectively. On the opposite end of the spectrum, Amazon, Google, Facebook, and Tesla do not even issue a dividend and instead reinvest all their earnings to fund future growth. Observations of the dividend yield will provide insights into a company's prospects for growth, whether organic or through mergers and acquisitions.

4.2.2 Size Factors

Table 4.2 shows the values of size factors for selected stocks. The market capitalization of a company, which is usually called its *size*, is another popular fundamental factor. It has been documented that small-cap stocks outperform large-cap stocks in the long run.

TABLE 4.2

Size Factors for the Top 10 S&P 500 Companies

Ticker	Common Equity (CE)	Market Capitalization (SIZE)	Total Assets (TA)
AAPL	65.34	2,255.97	323.89
MSFT	123.39	1,681.61	301.00
AMZN	82.77	1,634.17	282.18
GOOGL	212.92	1,104.81	299.24
TSLA	16.03	668.91	45.69
FB	117.73	656.67	146.44
BRK.B	415.15	543.61	829.95
JNJ	64.47	414.31	170.69
WMT	75.31	407.84	237.38
JPM	241.05	387.34	3,246.07

Note: Data are for end of 2020. For the company names, see the note to Table 4.1. Numbers are in billions.

Although this may not be the case during a single investment period, there are several reasons why it might occur over the long term. Some people believe small-cap companies pose greater risks than large, established companies and that they therefore merit an additional risk premium. The information story is that small-cap stocks receive less analyst coverage or less attention in general, so it takes longer for information about them to diffuse through the market. Ambiguity aversion might also explain why investors require a risk premium on small-cap companies, which tend not to be household names. Other size factors include the common equity of a firm and the total assets of a firm.

4.2.3 Operating Efficiency Factors

In Table 4.3 we list the values of popular operating efficiency factors for selected stocks. Operating efficiency factors attempt to describe how efficiently a firm operates over both the short and the long term. An analysis of short-term efficiency would involve the inventory turnover (IT) ratio. The IT ratio is the cost of goods sold divided by average inventory, which represents the rate at which products move from inventory to sale. A high IT ratio generally is a good sign that a company's products are selling at a fast clip.

TABLE 4.3

Operating Efficiency Factors for the Top 10 S&P 500 Companies

Ticker	Equity Turnover (ET)	Fixed Asset Turnover (FAT)	Inventory Turnover (IT)	Total Asset Turnover (TAT)
AAPL	3.52	6.64	38.82	0.85
MSFT	1.28	2.85	12.84	0.49
AMZN	5.00	3.09	8.67	1.23
GOOGL	0.84	1.98	59.42	0.57
TSLA	2.37	1.35	5.07	0.62
FB	0.75	1.71	N/A	0.54
BRK.B	0.68	1.58	10.55	0.34
JNJ	1.32	4.51	2.18	0.47
WMT	6.85	4.36	9.32	2.28
JPM	0.50	5.14	4.09	0.04

Note: Data are for end of 2020. For the company names, see the note to Table 4.1.

Accounting standards and inventory conditions affect this ratio, so in making comparisons between companies, it is important to adjust the ratios for accounting discrepancies and to focus on companies in similar industries. For a test of a company's long-term efficiency, the total asset turnover (TAT) ratio, which is net sales divided by average total assets, attempts to measure how much revenue the company gets out of its assets. A very high ratio suggests that the company is making the most of its assets. Equity turnover (ET) and fixed-asset turnover (FAT) ratios show how well the company converts those particular classes of assets into sales revenue.

Although a high IT ratio generally is a good thing, keep in mind that extremely rapid turnover increases the risk of failing to meet customer demand owing to a shortage of inventory on hand. Of course, this is often preferable to an extremely sluggish turnover, which means that the company either cannot sell its products or it ties up too much money by overordering supplies (which will hurt profits). The "normal" turnover for a particular line of business depends on marketplace competition and demands and industry practices and requirements. Taking a look at the consumer staples sector, of which Walmart is considered part, we find an average industry turnover rate of about 6.17 times. Walmart's IT ratio is about 9.32, so it seems to be selling its products well by the standards of its industry. The trend in turnover also matters as much as the most recent numbers. It is an encouraging sign that Walmart has maintained an average inventory turnover of approximately 8.10 times (also greater than the industry average) since 2016 and has shown an increase in turnover from 8.78 times a year ago. Walmart's turnover ratio is, by casual observation, strong for its industry and stable, which suggests that the company manages its supply chain well.[7]

The ET, FAT, and TAT ratios, like the IT ratio, vary substantially across industries. Table 4.4 lists the ET, FAT, and TAT ratios of S&P 500 companies in the semiconductor industry. We have calculated the average turnover ratios for the industry as a whole as well. Nvidia's ET ratio of 1.08 and its TAT ratio of 0.52 are lower than the industry levels of 1.50 and 0.60, respectively. These TAT

---

[7] The consumer staples sector of the S&P 500 has about 30 companies in it. If one compares Walmart to the smaller industry set of food and staple retailing, which includes companies like Walgreens and Costco, then Walmart's inventory turnover ratio is slightly lower than the industry average of 11.78.

TABLE 4.4

Semiconductor Industry in 2020

Ticker	Equity Turnover (ET)	Fixed-Asset Turnover (FAT)	Total Asset Turnover (TAT)
NVDA	1.08	5.58	0.52
INTC	1.05	1.38	0.54
AVGO	1.03	8.02	0.29
QCOM	3.96	5.99	0.61
TXN	1.59	4.00	0.75
AMD	2.86	11.78	1.23
MU	0.57	0.72	0.40
AMAT	1.84	9.87	0.77
LRCX	2.13	9.75	0.73
ADI	0.47	4.24	0.26
KLAC	2.18	9.55	0.64
MCHP	0.97	5.53	0.31
XLNX	1.15	7.18	0.53
SWKS	0.81	2.56	0.66
MXIM	1.30	3.71	0.62
TER	1.74	7.49	0.88
QRVO	0.81	2.71	0.45
Industry average	1.50	5.89	0.60

Note: Ticker symbols are for the following companies: Nvidia Corp. (NVDA), Intel Corp. (INTC), Broadcom Inc. (AVGO), Qualcomm Inc. (QCOM), Texas Instruments Inc. (TXN), Advanced Micro Devices Inc. (AMD), Micron Technology, Inc. (MU), Applied Materials Inc. (AMAT), Lam Research Corporation (LRCX), Analog Devices Inc. (ADI), KLA Corporation (KLAC), Microchip Technology Inc. (MCHP), and Xilinx Inc. (XLNX), Skyworks Solutions Inc. (SWKS), Maxim Integrated Products Inc. (MXIM), Teradyne Inc. (TER), and Qorvo, Inc. (QRVO).

ratios of roughly 1.0 or less are relatively normal for capital-intensive industries such as the semiconductor industry. We would expect higher levels of turnover for industries that maintain large levels of inventory and current assets, such as retail. The FAT ratio varies widely among the semiconductor companies as well, with Nvidia operating at 5.58 times turnover, Micron Technology at 0.72, and Applied Materials at nearly 10 times turnover.

4.2.4 Operating Profitability Factors

In Table 4.5 we list the values of popular operating profitability factors for selected stocks. One or more of these operating profitability factors (or transformations of these factors) appears in most

TABLE 4.5

Operating Profitability Factors for the Top 10 S&P 500 Companies

Ticker	Gross Profit Margin (GPM)	Net Profit Margin (NPM)	Operating Profit Margin (OPM)	Return on Assets (ROA)	Return on Common Equity (ROCE)	Return on Total Capital (ROTC)
AAPL	42.26	20.91	28.17	20.47	87.87	35.33
MSFT	76.75	32.29	46.64	18.65	38.49	27.18
AMZN	47.06	4.99	12.70	7.23	20.99	11.40
GOOGL	61.31	20.80	28.00	11.64	16.77	14.49
TSLA	29.89	1.97	14.87	4.28	3.47	6.10
FB	89.23	32.01	44.60	19.64	21.47	22.31
BRK.B	25.73	12.84	25.73	7.41	8.63	11.67
JNJ	74.65	21.01	33.80	11.85	26.35	19.78
WMT	26.71	3.30	6.65	10.51	23.76	16.55
JPM	73.54	19.17	43.87	1.53	9.93	5.95

Note: Data are for end of 2020. For the company names, see the note to Table 4.1. Numbers are in percent.

QEPM models. After all, highly profitable companies are the ones to own. All the variables in the table are standard measures of profitability. Quantitative managers look not only for profits but also for some percentage growth in profits. They typically look at year-on-year growth in the gross profit margin (GPM), the operating profit margin (OPM), or the net profit margin (NPM).[8] Other common profitability factors include the return on total capital (ROTC) and the return on common equity (ROCE). Portfolio managers compare these ratios both within and across industries.

Let's take a look at Microsoft's profitability factors. Microsoft has a GPM of 76.75%, an OPM of 46.64%, and an NPM of 32.29%. It is always important to examine these three ratios along several dimensions: within an industry, in relation to the market as a whole, and over time. Each dimension will provide different insights. At the moment, we shall focus on the trend over time. Table 4.6 shows that Microsoft had a very high GPM of 77% in

---

[8] A strand of literature has noticed that while the market may treat all earnings the same, there is a difference between the accrual and cash-flow components of earnings, and it has an impact on future stock returns. In particular, the higher the accrual component of earnings, the lower are the future stock returns. For more information, see Sloan (1996).

TABLE 4.6

Microsoft Trend Analysis

Year	Gross Profit Margin (GPM)	Net Profit Margin (NPM)	Operating Profit Margin (OPM)
2016	69.56	20.22	33.60
2017	74.56	26.62	40.11
2018	74.43	16.38	41.69
2019	75.66	31.66	44.30
2020	76.75	32.29	46.64

Note: Numbers are in percent.

2020 and that the margin has been increasing since 2016. The OPM simultaneously had risen from about 34% in 2016 to 47% in 2020. The 14% increase in OPM is larger than the 7% increase in GPM. Since operating profit is simply gross profit less sales, general, and administrative expenses, it appears that Microsoft has been able to control sales, general, and administrative expenses somewhat better than the cost of goods sold.

We can dissect Microsoft's profitability even further. The ROTC measures the profitability of the company's overall capital resources, whereas return-on-assets (ROA) and ROCE focus solely on the profitability of those types of resources. (These ratios also should be compared with the ratios of other firms within the industry to measure the capability of management to generate returns.) Microsoft has an ROA of 18.65%, an ROCE of 38.49%, and an ROTC of 27.18%. If these returns were below those of other rates available in the marketplace at a similar level of risk, then it would be better for the company to be broken up and have the assets reinvested where they would be more productive. For Microsoft, not surprisingly, these ratios only confirm that the company enjoys relatively high profitability.

4.2.5 Solvency Factors

In Table 4.7 we list the values of popular solvency factors for selected stocks. The cash-flow-from-operations ratio (CFOR), the cash ratio (CR), the current ratio (CUR), and the quick ratio (QR) are all measures of a company's ability to cover liabilities with varying amounts of liquid cash. Companies with high solvency

TABLE 4.7

Solvency Factors for the Top 10 S&P 500 Companies

Ticker	Cash-Flow-from-Operations Ratio (CFOR)	Cash Ratio (CR)	Current Ratio (CUR)	Quick Ratio (QR)
AAPL	0.77	0.86	1.36	1.22
MSFT	0.94	1.97	2.53	2.30
AMZN	0.54	0.67	1.11	0.84
GOOGL	1.18	2.75	3.41	3.28
TSLA	0.33	1.11	1.63	1.24
FB	2.83	4.68	5.51	5.35
BRK.B	N/A	N/A	N/A	N/A
JNJ	0.56	0.79	1.48	1.17
WMT	0.40	0.21	0.79	0.27
JPM	N/A	N/A	N/A	N/A

Note: Data are for end of 2020. For the company names, see the note to Table 4.1.

factor values are more liquid or solvent and less likely to be forced into bankruptcy by payments owed on debt and other liabilities. Many portfolio managers use one or more of these variables as a screen for financially sound stocks.

CUR and QR are very industry sensitive, but a general rule of thumb in assessing these ratios is that the more liquid the current assets are, the less crucial it is that those assets exceed the current liabilities by a wide margin. CUR, which divides current assets by current liabilities, gives a general sense of the company's liquidity versus its liabilities; QR refines the assessment by narrowing current assets down to cash, marketable securities, and accounts receivable. A high CUR generally indicates adequate short-term liquidity, but it should be examined alongside other ratios such as the inventory turnover (IT) ratio and return on assets (ROA) to ensure that there is not an inefficient use of cash or other marketable equivalents. Large inventories inflate CUR but may be a sign that the company's products are not selling and are even becoming obsolete. QR is a better measure of liquidity in relation to liabilities for companies that rely on large inventories.

Microsoft's CUR of 2.53 and QR of 2.30 contain several important facts about the company's liquidity situation. Microsoft is adequately funded on a short-term basis. The QR is only slightly less than the CUR as a result of excluding inventories from current assets, which indicates that the bulk of Microsoft's current assets are in the form of cash and marketable securities rather than shelf upon shelf of inventory. By contrast, Walmart has a CUR of 0.79 and a QR of 0.27. The significant difference, percentagewise, between CUR and QR reveals that most of Walmart's current assets are tied up in inventory, and the company may be suffering from inadequate liquidity. Although QR by itself raises a red flag, we should analyze other factors in conjunction with this, such as Walmart's debt-to-equity and profitability ratios, which we also discuss in this chapter.

4.4.6 Financial Risk Factors

Table 4.8 lists the values of popular financial risk factors for selected stocks.[9] By controlling for signs of financial risk, portfolio managers can identify which companies are not well equipped to weather the storm if sales temporarily slow down or if the economy hits a slump. A company with a high level debt-to-equity (D/E) ratio

TABLE 4.8

Financial Risk Factors for the Top 10 S&P 500 Companies

Ticker	Cash-Flow Coverage Ratio (CFCR)	Debt-to-Equity Ratio (D/E)	Interest Coverage Ratio (ICR)	Total Debt Ratio (TDR)
AAPL	0.66	3.96	23.35	0.38
MSFT	0.80	1.44	22.21	0.28
AMZN	0.58	2.41	12.12	0.34
GOOGL	2.06	0.41	127.29	0.09
TSLA	0.29	1.67	1.33	0.33
FB	3.03	0.24	N/A	0.08
BRK.B	0.38	0.98	11.72	0.13
JNJ	0.57	1.65	95.82	0.22
WMT	0.48	1.92	9.50	0.29
JPM	0.06	10.97	N/A	0.17

Note: Data are for end of 2020. For the company names, see the note to Table 4.1.

[9] The work of researchers such as Professor Edward Altman of New York University's Stern School of Business, who used financial ratios to predict bankruptcies, has encouraged the QEPM community to look closely at financial risk factors. Financial risk factors are closely related to solvency factors. See Altman (2019).

relative to other companies is more susceptible to bankruptcy even if its core business is solid. A high D/E ratio in conjunction with a low interest coverage ratio (ICR), which equals earnings before interest and taxes over interest expense, is cause for further concern because it means that the firm's current earnings will not cover many interest payments.

A high D/E ratio alone does not automatically spell financial danger. Higher levels of debt generally lead to greater earnings volatility and a higher risk of financial distress or possibly bankruptcy. However, businesses that generate large, stable cash flows can handle relatively large amounts of debt because they can finance the interest payments on the debt. They are therefore more likely to have higher D/E ratio values than companies that are short on cash. In 2020, Apple's D/E ratio equaled 3.96, compared with an industry average D/E ratio of 3.34. Apple's capital structure included a greater-than-average portion of debt, but its interest coverage of 23.35 times was also greater than the industry average. Its earning power covered its debt burden.

The best possible position to be in is to have little debt and plenty of cash on hand to cover the interest payments on it. Google's D/E ratio is a mere 0.41, and its interest coverage ratio is 127 times. The fact that the company is capable of taking on much more debt gives it room to start new projects. Low financial risk does not just avert disaster; it is a big plus for expansion and new investment.

4.2.7 Corporate Activity Factors

The final category of fundamental factors is a category that concerns corporate activity like stock buybacks, insider purchases, and decisions on research and development (R&D) expenditure, as well as other factors that do not neatly fit in the other factor categories. Although stock buybacks are public information, quantitative portfolio managers sift through the data better than the average investor, and this ability is an informational advantage that creates near-arbitrage opportunities. Stock buybacks could reveal that management is upbeat about the future of the company. Some people refer to the shareholder yield as dividends plus net buybacks of stocks. Buybacks have the additional advantage that they are not taxed as much as dividends. Insider purchases could also represent good news about a stock that is not yet public or could simply reflect management's confidence in the company. Either way, studies have shown positive excess returns from stocks experiencing insider purchases and lower returns for stocks experiencing insider selling.[10] R&D expenditures reveal that management is actively betting on the future, which could be an indication of beneficial corporate activity.

4.3 TECHNICAL FACTORS

Most technical factors are constructed from past price and volume data (usually, open prices, high prices, low prices, closing prices, volume, open interest, and bid and ask prices) and other readily available financial information. One of the great advantages of technical factors is that they constantly update themselves. New fundamental data are available only quarterly at most, when a company files its financial statements with the Securities and Exchange Commission (SEC). Up-to-date technical indicators, on the other hand, are available as often as every few seconds— although most portfolio managers are happy with daily or monthly technical data. Portfolio managers typically use technical factors to capture very short-term changes in the relative value of stocks.

We group the technical factors into four subcategories: liquidity risk factors, price-based factors, volume-based factors, and overall market movement factors. Liquidity risk factors are used to understand the consequences and effects of trading a stock. Price-based factors are factors that are generated mainly from stock prices or stock returns and are used as indicators of potential future price movements in the stocks. Volume-based factors are generated principally from information in past trading or volume that might signal the intentions and changing behavior of market participants. Overall market movement factors are aggregate technical indicators that might help decipher overall stock market movements and their implications for the near future. Tables 4A.8 through 4A.11 in Appendix 4A provide complete lists of some of the most important technical factors for QEPM models.[11]

---

[10] See Table 2.2.

[11] There are thousands of potential technical factors. For good descriptions of many technical indicators and how to use them, we recommend Achelis (2001).

4.3.1 Liquidity Risk Factors

Table 4.9 shows the values of some important liquidity factors—trading turnover (TT), Amihud illiquidity, and invariance illiquidity—for selected stocks. Liquidity factors gauge whether a stock's liquidity matches trading demand. One of the easiest and most common liquidity factors is TT. TT, which is calculated as the average daily dollar trading volume (ADDTV) divided by market capitalization, measures the percentage of outstanding shares traded in a day on average. It gives an indication of how easy or difficult it is to trade the stock. Other proxies for liquidity include market capitalization and float capitalization, the portion of the market capitalization available for public trading. Floating shares and total shares traded are typically highly correlated, but some stocks have a very small float. The number of shareholders also indicates the ease with which an investor can enter and exit a position in a stock.[12] Amihud illiquidity (AILIQ) is a measure of illiquidity based on the ratio of the daily return of the stock to the daily volume. The idea is that the higher the daily return for a given volume, the less liquid is the stock due to price impact.

TABLE 4.9

Selected Technical Liquidity Measures for the Top 10 S&P 500 Companies

Ticker	Amihud Illiquidity (AILIQ)	Invariance Illiquidity (INVIL)	Trading Turnover (TT)
AAPL	0.14	0.83	0.61
MSFT	0.24	1.02	0.36
AMZN	0.13	0.76	0.87
GOOGL	0.57	1.27	0.48
TSLA	0.25	1.16	3.52
FB	0.38	1.16	0.77
BRK.B	1.00	1.55	0.35
JNJ	0.91	1.45	0.25
WMT	1.00	1.49	0.24
JPM	1.01	1.80	0.42

Note: Data are for end of 2020. For the company names, see the note to Table 4.1. Trading turnover is in percentage terms.

[12] This type of data is not easily available.

A more recently discovered measure of liquidity, or lack thereof, is invariance illiquidity (INVIL), which measures illiquidity based on a theoretical model. This measure is related to the average dollar volume of the stock and its volatility. As we can see from the table, TT, AILIQ, and INVIL vary even among relatively large, well-known stocks. In 2020, Amazon's measured trading turnover was 0.87% compared to Walmart's 0.24%. This says that Amazon is more liquid than Walmart in that much more trading occurs given Amazon's market capitalization. More precisely, on average, about 1% of Amazon's shares are being traded daily compared to one quarter of 1% for Walmart's shares. Similar conclusions are drawn by using Amihud illiquidity and invariance illiquidity. For these measures, higher values mean that the stock is less liquid. Amazon's AILIQ value is 0.13 compared to Walmart's 1, suggesting Walmart is even less liquid than was implied by TT. Finally, Amazon's INVIL is 0.76 compared to Walmart's 1.49. Thus, all of these measures suggest, to varying degrees, that Amazon stock is more liquid that Walmart's stock. Generally, these liquidity factors are correlated with each other.

All these liquidity factors matter only in relation to the size of the manager's portfolio and the value of the trades he or she wants to place. Trading liquidity mainly becomes a concern when a manager wants to buy more than the available number of shares or sell more than the market will take. Some portfolio managers build liquidity factors into portfolio models as transactions costs, whereas others leave it to the trading desk to sort out the costs of the trades in light of liquidity constraints.

4.3.2 Price-Based Factors

Table 4.10 shows the values of some prevalent price-based factors for selected stocks.[13] These factors attempt to capture short-term movements in stock prices or measures related to stock prices that might indicate something about future stock returns. Momentum is a very popular short-term indicator of future performance. Various academic studies have found positive auto-correlation in stock returns, meaning that positive returns in one period tend to lead to positive returns in the next period.[14]

---

[13] For an expanded list, see Table 4A.9 and Chapter 16.
[14] See Table 2.2.

TABLE 4.10

Selected Technical Price-Based Factors for the Top 10 S&P 500 Companies

Ticker	Beta (BETA)	Bollinger Band (BB)	Twelve-Month Momentum (M12M)	Relative Strength Index (RSI)
AAPL	1.28	1.00	82.31	66.88
MSFT	0.82	1.00	42.53	56.43
AMZN	1.19	1.00	76.26	60.18
GOOGL	0.98	0.00	31.03	48.96
TSLA	2.18	1.00	743.44	47.44
FB	1.18	0.00	33.09	45.65
BRK.B	0.84	1.00	2.37	46.49
JNJ	0.70	1.00	10.85	50.56
WMT	0.42	−1.00	23.34	50.74
JPM	1.23	1.00	−5.52	66.29

Note: Data are for end of 2020. For the company names, see the note to Table 4.1.

There is also evidence of negative autocorrelation in individual stock returns over periods of one week and one month.[15] Some portfolio managers measure momentum as the stock return over the last year, some measure it as the stock return over the last month, and others use more complicated variations. The same idea prevails: stocks that have performed well recently tend to continue performing well in the near future. You might argue that momentum cannot last because no stock can continue to rise forever. The technician would tell you that a positive stock return in the last period contains useful information that may not be fully distributed throughout the investing population. It could represent insider buying by company executives who anticipate profit growth, or it could represent buying by some knowledgeable investors who have deduced some as yet unreleased piece of good news that will help the stock in the near future. Tesla's momentum (i.e., stock return for 2020) was 743%, while J.P. Morgan's was −5.5%. To the extent that momentum works, it would tell you to buy stocks like Tesla, Apple, Amazon, and Google and avoid the smaller-momentum stocks.

---

[15] See Jegadeesh (1990).

Portfolio managers use various moving averages to capture information traveling through a stock's price. The relative strength index is a popular indicator that attempts to pinpoint when a stock is a buy and when it is a sell. Bollinger bands, which delineate limits around the mean price for buying and selling, improve on simple moving-average models. When a stock hits the top band above the mean, it is a signal to sell; when it hits the bottom band below the mean, it is a signal to buy. Both moving averages and Bollinger bands may be useful for identifying short-term changes in the relative attractiveness of stocks. At the end of 2020, the Bollinger band signals for Apple and Microsoft are 1.00, meaning that there is positive movement in these stocks and they are a buy, while the signal is neutral on stocks like Google and Facebook and bearish on Walmart.[16]

Beta is not conventionally thought of as a technical factor, since it's based on the capital asset pricing model (CAPM) of finance. Beta is also different from other factors in that each stock's beta exposure is estimated by a regression. Nevertheless, research dating back to the early 1970s shows that beta might be useful in predicting future stock returns. In fact, in recent years, this strategy has become so popular, it's part of many QEPM portfolio models and tailored investment strategies for retail investors.[17] Contrary to theory, people have found that low-beta stocks have higher risk-adjusted returns than high-beta stocks. As of December 2020, the beta of Apple was 1.28, while the beta of Johnson & Johnson was 0.70. Theory would predict that Johnson & Johnson would be less volatile in relation to the stock market than Apple. However, recent empirical evidence might indicate that a portfolio of low-beta stocks will outperform a portfolio of high-beta stocks on a risk-adjusted basis.

4.3.3 Volume-Based Factors

Table 4.11 shows the values of a very important factor—the short interest ratio—for selected stocks.[18] Some people use a high degree of short interest as a contrarian signal. That is, when many

---

[16] The reader should remember that many technical signals, like the Bollinger band, can be computed on various time horizons but also that these signals are for the very short term and must be updated frequently. For more details on how we computed this indicator, see the formulas in Chapter 16.

[17] Also known as the *low-beta strategy* or *betting against beta*.

[18] For an expanded list of volume factors, see Table 4A.10 and Chapter 16.

TABLE 4.11

Selected Technical Volume-Based Factors for the Top 10
S&P 500 Companies

Ticker	Short Interest Ratio (SIR)	SRI Minus One Year Average (SIRX)
AAPL	1.32	−3.02
MSFT	2.15	0.12
AMZN	1.26	0.13
GOOGL	1.73	−0.73
TSLA	1.97	−5.11
FB	2.08	0.17
BRK.B	2.94	−0.76
JNJ	2.76	−0.24
WMT	2.86	−0.07
JPM	2.08	−0.10

Note: Data are for end of 2020. For the company names, see the note to Table 4.1.

investors are shorting a stock, if the stock continues to rise due to buying pressure, it may force the very investors who shorted the stock to buy it back—causing the stock to rally even further. This factor was much in the news in 2021 as many retail traders targeted stocks with large amounts of short interest.[19] Consider data on Walmart, with a relatively small short interest ratio of 2.86%, and Tesla, which has a ratio of 1.97% but whose value declined significantly in 2020. In December 2015, Tesla's short interest was 64 and in December 2019 it was 23 as people strongly believed the company was overvalued. Since that time, the stock is up 18-fold. Amongst companies in the S&P 500 not in the table, insurance broker AON and specialty chemical company IFF both have short interest ratios around 20%.

4.3.4 Overall Market Movement Factors

Table 4A.11 lists the technical factors that are not computed for individual stocks but are rather computed for the overall market and are usually indicators of where the overall market is headed.

---

[19] In 2021, a group of social network–connected amateur traders made millions targeting high-short-interest stocks to buy, including Gamestop (GME), AMC Entertainment (AMC), and others. As they bought the highly shorted stocks, these stocks soared in price.

These are appropriately called *overall market movement factors*. In order to compute the exposures of individual stocks, you must estimate regressions of individual stock returns on these market-wide factors. In Chapters 16 and 17 we actually compute these factors and their returns.

4.4 ECONOMIC FACTORS

The first arbitrage pricing models were based on economic indicators, and the popularity of economic factors endures in QEPM models.[20] Table 4A.12 gives a list of the most common economic factors used in QEPM models.

For macroeconomic models of stock returns, the portfolio manager should choose factors that affect all stock returns to some degree. GDP growth, the yield-curve slope, unemployment, and inflation are popular factors because they influence almost every corner of the market. Although each of these variables can be defined in different ways, there are some standard definitions. A common way of calculating inflation, for instance, is to take the latest monthly inflation number and annualize it. Quantitative managers must be careful to use the right data when calculating macroeconomic figures. There are significant delays between the measurement and release of macroeconomic data. The most current monthly inflation data are usually data on the conditions one month prior. Other macro variables are reported at different delays. The portfolio manager should create a table of data release months and adjust models to account for the lag in information.[21]

---

[20] Arbitrage pricing theory (APT) was invented by the late Stephen Ross of MIT, and his suggested factors include macroeconomic factors such as monthly growth in industrial production, inflation and expected inflation, real interest rates, risk premiums (measured as the spread in returns between Baa bonds and government bonds), and the term structure or difference in returns between long-maturity government bonds and short-term Treasury bills. See Chen, Roll, and Ross (1986).

[21] The original arbitrage pricing models assumed that the factor premiums should be unanticipated variables because it is only unanticipated changes that should affect returns. For macroeconomic variables, this usually means constructing derivatives of the variables that are unanticipated or have an average of zero. Most economic variables do not have an average of zero. This does not necessarily create a problem, however. We can simply interpret the economic factors as something that is proportional to the true factor premiums. We also could attempt to construct economic factors that are more like innovations, such as constructing unexpected inflation variables.

4.5 ALTERNATIVE FACTORS

We group the remaining factors into a category called *alternative factors* for lack of a better name. There are three subcategories of alternative factors: analyst factors, captivus factors, and social responsibility factors. Tables 4A.13 and 4A.14 in Appendix 4A list the most common alternative factors used in QEPM models.

4.5.1 Analyst Factors

Analysts on Wall Street and elsewhere spend a lot of time researching individual companies. Wall Street analysts' earnings forecasts, buy–sell recommendations, and related information can be valuable in forecasting stock returns.[22] There have been hundreds of studies documenting the success of analyst recommendations in predicting stock returns.[23] The beauty of an analyst recommendation is that it condenses hours and hours of research into a single directive, buy or sell. A portfolio manager can transform recommendations into factors that work in a quantitative model.

Some studies show that a portfolio of analyst-rated "strong buys" outperforms a portfolio of analyst-rated "strong sells." Since the analyst recommendations are public information, one might wonder how portfolio managers could use them for statistical arbitrage. One argument is that quantitative managers have an advantage in filtering the vast amount of analyst data for useful recommendations. In mere seconds they can access newly released analyst ratings and use software to create or update a portfolio of the top-rated stocks. The average investor may not hear about ratings changes until the end of the trading day, and even then he or she probably does not own the kind of software that can quickly sort through hundreds of ratings.[24]

---

[22] IBES is the main provider of analyst data, although Bloomberg and other data providers provide similar information. IBES is owned by Refinitiv, which was purchased by the London Stock Exchange Group in 2019.

[23] For a list of some of those studies, see Table 2.2.

[24] StarMine, which is now owned by Refinitiv, has made a name for itself by building models that weight analyst recommendations according to analysts' historical ability to predict stock returns, taking into account preannouncements and using changes in recommendations to filter the information efficiently. The company finds that its models improve on the basic earnings revision model and have much higher information coefficients than the basic model. For more information, see https://www.refinitiv.com/en.

TABLE 4.12

Selected Analyst Factors for the Top 10 S&P 500 Companies

Ticker	Median Rating (ARMR)	Percent Buys (ARPB)	Percent Sells (ARPS)	SD of Rating (ARSD)	Number of Analysts (EPSFN)
AAPL	2.00	75.00	5.00	0.90	29.00
MSFT	2.00	91.43	0.00	0.64	27.00
AMZN	2.00	94.00	0.00	0.58	40.00
GOOGL	2.00	92.31	0.00	0.65	29.00
TSLA	3.00	37.14	31.43	1.32	15.00
FB	2.00	88.24	3.92	0.76	40.00
BRK.B	2.50	50.00	0.00	0.96	3.00
JNJ	2.00	72.22	0.00	0.80	14.00
WMT	2.00	79.41	2.94	0.81	28.00
JPM	2.00	62.96	7.41	0.74	22.00

Note: Data are for end of 2020. For the company names, see the note to Table 4.1. Each analyst rating is ranked 1–5. 1 = strong buy, 2 = buy, 3 = hold, 4 = sell, and 5 = strong sell.

A strategy of purchasing stocks that have been upgraded by analysts in the last month has been shown to outperform on a risk-adjusted basis. Similarly, selling downgraded stocks outperforms on a risk-adjusted basis. One would expect even better results from a strategy of shorting the firms that were downgraded by analysts of their own underwriter. Other analyst-related strategies seem to produce strong returns as well. It also has been documented that purchasing a group of stocks with recent upward earnings revisions by analysts outperforms on a risk-adjusted basis. The degree of dispersion in analyst ratings also may create opportunities to outperform.

Table 4.12 shows the values of several analyst factors for selected stocks, including the median recommendation, the percentage of buy and sell recommendations for each stock, and the standard deviation of the analyst ratings. Analyst recommendations are given as numbers from 1 to 5, such that 1 is for "strong buy," 2 is for "buy," 3 is for "hold" or "neutral," 4 is for "sell," and 5 is for "strong sell." Tesla has the lowest median analyst rating at 3 (i.e., neither a buy nor a sell, but a hold). The highest median rating of a buy (i.e., 2) is shared by many companies. The most bullish sentiment from analysts is for Amazon, with 94% of analysts suggesting a buy or strong buy. The most bearish sentiment is for Tesla, with 37% of analysts recommending a buy or strong buy and 31% recommending a sell or strong sell. Finally, the greatest disagreement amongst analysts concerns Tesla and Berkshire Hathaway, judging by the standard deviation of analyst ratings.

If analyst coverage provides useful information for models of stock return, what should be done about stocks that receive little or no analyst coverage? For example, Amazon has about 40 analysts researching the company, Tesla has about 15, but at the bottom of the S&P 500 there are companies with no analyst coverage or just a few, such as one analyst for Under Armour and three for NRG Energy. Lack of analyst coverage may in fact be an advantage unto itself. There is a neglected-firm effect in which stocks followed by few analysts or owned by few institutions tend to have relatively higher long-run risk-adjusted returns than heavily covered stocks. There could be an informational story for this effect. If it takes time for good information to seep through the marketplace, then information about a stock that is not covered will spread more slowly than information that is publicized by analyst comments and recommendations. When there is good news about a neglected stock, the stock's price adjusts to the news more slowly than a well-known stock's price would, which gives investors more time to buy before the gain. The neglected-firm effect suggests a strategy of purchasing neglected firms on good news and selling them on bad news. In reality, many quants look for good neglected stocks using a multifactor model that examines fundamental characteristics and assigns a bonus point to neglected status. Given two stocks with identical fundamentals, the model would rate the neglected one more highly than the well-known one.

4.5.2 Captivus Factors

With the advent of the internet and the explosion of technology into everyday life in the form of personal computers, smart phones, satellites, cameras, and social networks, everyone from police to investors has realized that capturing this information can be very valuable. As of 2020, about 45% of asset managers use some form of captivus data.[25] This type of data is often called *alternative data* or *big data*, but we prefer to call it *captivus* data,

---

[25] See Thornton et al. (2020).

which is the Latin word for "captured." Whether it's GPS or satellite data, social media data, or news feeds, the data are essentially captured by sophisticated programs. Some of the data is collected by specialized companies for resale and some is captured by portfolio managers for proprietary usage. One of the benefits of captivus data over other data used in QEPM is their usually higher frequency: captivus data are obtained earlier than typical fundamental data. Another advantage is that captivus data usually supplement or are complementary to more traditional data sources. The most popular method of obtaining captivus data is through *web scraping*. Web scraping is the process of locating web pages and extracting data from them, whether they are company sites, consumer sites, or social media sites. For example, a program that captures the posts of a group of Twitter and Instagram users and stores the data is web scraping. This data set is already large and growing. As of 2019, there were 5.5 billion mobile users worldwide, 4 billion internet users, and 3 billion users on social networks.

Since there is such a vast array of captivus data and these data are typically either proprietary to an institution or very expensive to purchase, we do not use them in this book directly. However, any serious investor could purchase the data from existing providers or hire a team to scrape the data themselves.[26] We can, however, provide some examples of how the data might be used. When attempting to predict the sales of a business in advance of earnings releases, you might use geolocation, foot traffic, and app usage data to predict the number of customers frequenting a particular store or stores. For example, as the 2020 Covid-19 pandemic unfolded, data on foot traffic from mobile phones and geolocation could be used to understand which cities were rebounding and which were not. For those interested in workout companies, you might use Instagram and Twitter posts to model trends in buying home workout equipment and other personal trends that are related to public companies. For earnings calls, rather than read and/or listen to every transcript, you could use machine learning and textual analysis to determine if there are any key language patterns that might be undetectable to the average person that hint at potential future company health. You might use data on air traffic and other transportation resources to

---

[26] See Thornton et al. (2020) for a list of some companies that sell these types of data.

gauge the behavior of economies long before the actual GDP numbers are released.[27] And, of course, consumer trends can be analyzed for a host of retail companies through web traffic, Google Trends, and social media applications.

Captivus data are more varied than traditional data and are oftentimes expensive and more difficult to obtain. However, captivus data can offer many advantages to the quantitative manager, including higher frequency of information, earlier understanding of important metrics for a company, and significantly more accurate information for understanding a specific issue. Captivus data will continue to be an important part of the QEPM data tool kit in the future.

4.5.3 Social Responsibility Factors

Many investors believe that in order to maximize the return on their portfolios, they must separate financial decisions from social concerns. Some socially responsible business practices may in fact do nothing for a company's bottom line over the short term. Yet, contrary to the view that socially responsible investing necessarily sacrifices profits in the name of doing good, many studies show that factoring social concerns into investment decisions does not reduce the return of a portfolio.[28] Regardless of one's philosophical stance on socially responsible investing, data on what we might call "social responsibility" factors may offer useful information for portfolio managers.[29] Probably the most useful factor in this arena is the employee relations factor. Quantifying the state of management's relations with employees is admittedly not as

---

[27] For example, using FlightRadar24 (https://www.flightradar24.com/) or something similar.

[28] See Hamilton (1993), Cohen (1995), Diltz (1995), Kurtz and DiBartolomeo (1996), Guerard (1997), Guerard et al. (2002), Derwall et al. (2005), and Whelan et al. (2020).

[29] Since the writing of the first edition of this book, new terminology has gained vogue, using the acronym ESG for environmental, social, and governance factors. Incorporating ESG factors is also called *sustainable investing* or *impact investing*. In addition, many more studies on this topic have been written, including Madhavan et al. (2020), Amel-Zadeh and Serafeim (2018), Briere et al. (2017), Pastor et al. (2021), Munoz et al. (2014), Berg et al. (2020), and Ezeokoli et al. (2017). Also, many of the leading investment banks are regularly publishing pieces on ESG, including J.P. Morgan, Sanford Bernstein, Bank of America Merrill Lynch, and others. One must also remember that investors can trade either side of these factors. For example, those who don't agree with diversity can reduce the number of diversity-proponent companies in their portfolios, while those who agree with diversity can increase the number of these companies in their portfolios.

straightforward as calculating the P/E ratio, and the quality of the measurement will affect the model.[30]

This factor adds depth to a strictly financial model, though, because it contains information that may not be obvious from the most recent financials and yet may indicate a burgeoning operational problem (or, conversely, the seed of a future competitive advantage).

Table 4.13 shows the values of some prevalent socially responsible, or ESG, factors for selected stocks. For each category, we measure each company's percentage of strengths in that category minus their percentage of weaknesses.[31] Many of the companies on the list are weak on corporate governance, which includes items such as exposure to bribery and fraud, controversial investment practices, and governance structure issues. Diversity includes elements such as the diversity of the board and discrimination practices. On the extreme positive side is Microsoft, with a 100% net positive reading, and on the negative side is Amazon with a −50% reading. Employee relations covers areas such as the health and safety of the workforce, as well as whether or not the firm engages in profit sharing with employees and human capital development and growth. By this score, Johnson & Johnson is on the positive side with a score of 44%, and Tesla is on the negative with a score of −22%. As for the environment and human rights, most firms are neutral to positive. QEPM's ultimate goal is portfolio outperformance. Thus, QEPM should focus on using these factors to find signals of future good and bad stock performance. Some readers

---

[30] MSCI ESG KLD STATS is a database that classifies companies according to social criteria. The MSCI ESG database provides in-depth profiles of more than 3,000 U.S. corporations, including every company in the S&P 500, most of the Russell 3000, and all of KLD's Domini 400 Social Index. The profiles present analyses on a range of issues that reflect a company's overall social record and include social ratings that highlight a company's strengths and weaknesses. The following issues are covered: community relations, employee and union relations, environmental liabilities, corporate governance, human rights, environmental impact, diversity, product quality and safety, environmental policies and practices, and company involvement in businesses related to abortion, contraceptives, military weapons, adult entertainment, firearms, nuclear power, alcohol, gambling, and tobacco. This database is maintained by MSCI after it bought KLD and its competitor, the Investor Responsibility Research Center (IRRC). There are other providers of social responsibility data, including Bloomberg, Sustainalytics, Vigeo Eiris, RobecoSAM, and Eikon. More information on all of these data providers can be found at https://www.msci.com/, https://www.bloomberg.com/, https://www.sustainalytics.com/, https://vigeo-eiris.com/, https://www.robeco.com/, and https://www.refinitiv.com/, respectively.

[31] For more details on the measures, the reader should see Table 4A.14 and Chapter 16.

TABLE 4.13

Selected Socially Responsible Factors for the Top 10 S&P 500 Companies

Ticker	Community Contribution (CC)	Corporate Governance (CG)	Diversity (DIV)	Employee Relations (ER)	Environment (E)	Human Rights (HR)	Product (PRO)
AAPL	0.00	-25.00	50.00	0.00	14.29	0.00	-23.33
MSFT	0.00	25.00	100.00	5.56	35.71	50.00	10.00
AMZN	0.00	-25.00	-50.00	-16.67	0.00	0.00	-66.67
GOOGL	0.00	25.00	0.00	33.33	14.29	0.00	-23.33
TSLA	0.00	-50.00	0.00	-22.22	7.14	0.00	-16.67
FB	0.00	-25.00	50.00	0.00	0.00	50.00	-6.67
BRK.B	0.00	-25.00	0.00	0.00	7.14	0.00	0.00
JNJ	0.00	-25.00	0.00	44.44	14.29	0.00	-40.00
WMT	0.00	-25.00	-50.00	-16.67	14.29	0.00	-33.33
JPM	0.00	25.00	0.00	33.33	14.29	0.00	-16.67

Note: Data are for end of 2020. For the company names, see the note to Table 4.1. These factors are also known as environmental, social, and governance (ESG) factors. More details on these factors are supplied in Table 4A.14 of Appendix 4A.

might be skeptical about the validity of certain social responsibility variables, but they may help capture aspects of investor sentiment not captured by other variables. Therefore, we list them in Table 4A.14 for those interested in this area of analysis.[32]

4.6 FACTOR CHOICE

Earlier in this chapter we compared QEPM factors with cooking ingredients. Building an investment model, like creating a meal, is a mix of science and art, and many managers build models very intuitively, adding factors according to taste. When it comes to building most quantitative models, though, the cooking comparison only goes so far. The chef may not need to know chemistry, but the quantitative portfolio manager must understand financial and economic theory in order to choose and combine factors appropriately, always keeping in mind the seven tenets of QEPM.[33] The manager has to ask himself or herself why the market has not already identified the arbitrage opportunity that he or she sees. He or she needs to consider whether factors that worked in backtests using historical data will continue to work in the future. In this section we suggest several techniques of factor choice supported by theory. As we discussed in Chapter 3, there are two basic types of quantitative stock return models: the fundamental factor model and the economic factor model. To choose factors for the fundamental factor model, we suggest using the univariate and multiple regression techniques. To choose factors for the economic factor model, we suggest using the unidimensional and multidimensional zero-investment portfolio techniques.[34] In addition to these techniques, we also suggest using a simple correlation statistic or

---

[32] In recent years, it has been popular to consider socially responsible, or ESG, factors regardless of the future returns of stocks. Even when these factors are used in this fashion, the investor must be extremely cautious in interpreting the data. First, many providers of socially responsible data differ on their analyses of the same companies [Berg et al. (2020)]. Second, when investors choose criteria for their particular social concern, the screen brings up companies or sectors that would not even have this issue as part of their business—which begs the question of whether one is really doing anything like impact investing. Third, it is not always clear if social screening criteria are really Pareto improving. That is, while investing based on that view may be positive from a particular investor's point of view, it might be detrimental to an entire other class of investors.

[33] See Chapter 2.

[34] For an additional discussion on testing the out-of-sample predictability of factors, see Chapter 9 of Campbell et al. (1997).

Kendall's rank-correlation statistic to determine the correlation among factor choices. These techniques aid in combining and grouping factors.

4.6.1 Univariate Regression Tests

Many portfolio managers simplify the process of searching for relevant factors by performing a series of simple regressions of factors.[35] That is, they begin by first identifying a group of factors that they can theoretically justify explaining stock returns. They then run panel regressions on each factor versus the stock returns in the universe. Thus

$$r_{i,t} = \alpha + f\beta_{i,t} + \epsilon_{i,t} \qquad (4.1)$$

where $\beta_{i,t}$ is the factor exposure of stock i at time t, and the estimate of f from this panel regression will show the relationship between the factor and stock returns. If a factor has a significant value of f, then the factor is useful in explaining stock returns.[36]

The drawback of univariate regressions is that the portfolio manager may find many variables that are significant in explaining stock returns but are surrogates for each other. For instance, he or she may find that both the P/E and P/B ratios explain stock returns but that they represent the same idea. Thus, only one of them may be needed in the model. Ideally, one would like to find factors that help in explaining stock returns but are not highly correlated with each other. In terms of the fundamental law discussed in Chapter 2, we know that the more factors that we find to explain stock returns, the higher will be our information ratio, *provided* that the average contribution of each factor *does not decrease*. Thus, if we add a factor that is highly correlated with an existing factor, we probably will decrease the contribution of each factor, which will not improve the model. In that case, why use simple regressions for factor searching

---

[35] Simple regression is a regression of one variable on another. Multiple regression is a regression of one variable on many other variables.

[36] When we typically estimate these factor models, we use information at time t to predict returns at time $t + 1$. Sometimes, in this book, for convenience, we write the equation with time subscript t everywhere, as we do here. The factor exposure and the returns are at time t. It should still be interpreted as using information at t to predict returns at time $t + 1$. In other words, the factor exposure at time t is really the factor exposure value as of the end of the previous period, $t - 1$, which we may refer to sometimes as the beginning of month exposure for time t.

at all? First, they are very simple to perform. Second, they are a way to get an early idea of what might be relevant and what might not be relevant. If there are too many potential factors, the simple regression can be used to make the first round of cuts.

4.6.2 Multiple Regression Tests

The multiple regression is more sophisticated for determining which factors to include because it considers the relationship among factors while estimating the impact on return. The greatest danger with this method is that if the portfolio manager includes too many factors in the regression, there is a chance of *misspecification bias*, which leads to misleading statistical inference.

If the portfolio manager has limited the number of explanatory factors to something reasonable, say, fewer than 10 factors, then a multivariate panel regression can be estimated, that is,

$$r_{i,t} = \alpha + f_1 \beta_{i,1,t} + \cdots + f_K \beta_{i,K,t} + \epsilon_{i,t} \qquad (4.2)$$

where K is the number of factors to investigate, and $\beta_{i,k,t}$ is the exposure for stock i to factor k at time t. Once this regression is estimated, all insignificant factors are dropped. The significant factors go into the factor model.[37]

One of the biggest dangers here is data mining, of course. Data mining is the process of taking historical data on stock returns and factors and testing a variety of models until the portfolio manager finds the model that best predicts or explains past stock returns. There are many ways to do data mining, and we discourage all of them for two reasons. First, by searching in a set of historical data for the factors that best explain stock returns, the portfolio manager is guaranteed to find a group of factors that would have worked historically, but this provides absolutely no guarantee that these factors will work in the future. The t-statistics or significance of these factors historically also is misleading because the manager did not take into account every factor he or she tested. If these were taken into account, the actual t-statistics would be much lower (see Chapter 2 for more details on problems related to data mining). Second, by only finding the factors that explain stock returns statistically in the past, the portfolio manager has clearly failed to provide any

---

[37] Appendix C describes some of the potential problems with including too few or too many factors in a factor model. Appendix C can be found at www.ludwigbc.com under QEPM Exclusive Content.

theoretical explanation of why those factors were chosen. This is very bad practice for any serious quantitative portfolio manager. Data mining can be a serious problem when one uses the *stepwise regression* technique.[38] This method involves starting with a collection of factors and then running a regression on every possible combination of the factors and picking the set of factors with the largest $\bar{R}^2$. It's dangerous because, by searching for the best fit in a set of historical data, one might find a model that fits the past data very well but has no bearing on the underlying stock return generation and has a high likelihood of failing in predicting future stock returns.

A related technique is the sequential specification search. The portfolio manager begins with a list of factors that he believes explains stock returns, and, for this set of factors, he looks at the estimated coefficients. He may then decide to drop one factor because of insignificance and add another factor based on theory. The manager may do this a few times until he obtains a desired level of significance at explaining stock returns. This also leads to exaggerated statistical significance. Usually, the portfolio manager will not report the failed model attempts, which makes it very difficult for the investment committee to evaluate the truth or significance of the final stock return model.

The best advice for choosing factors is to begin with a strong explanation, grounded in theory, of why a model with certain factors will work. A manager might even start with a few potential models. She then should test the models on the data but be wary of adding and dropping variables. She should test the model over a variety of time periods for model robustness.

4.6.3 Unidimensional Zero-Investment Portfolio

Portfolio managers may construct zero-investment portfolios based on a factor and study the characteristics of the portfolio. Typically, a manager will split the universe of stocks conditional on a particular factor exposure into thirds, quintiles, or deciles. Of course, any other division of the stocks is acceptable. Usually, a portfolio is created from the first division, and another portfolio is created from the last division. The returns of the top division are

---

[38] Unfortunately, we have met many portfolio managers who do this without understanding its implications. Most econometric software packages actually have procedures that do this very easily. Even if one understands the pitfalls of stepwise regression, it may be difficult to avoid stepwise regression completely. The point that we want to make is that one should be cautious interpreting the reported statistical significance.

subtracted from those of the last division. These are the returns to a hypothetical zero-investment portfolio in which the top-division portfolio is bought and the last-division portfolio is shorted. It is called *zero investment* because, theoretically, no capital needs to be used to create the portfolio. The returns of this portfolio measure the benefits from using this factor to pick stocks.

We shall do an example with quintiles. Suppose that the factor of interest is the P/B ratio. The first task is to rank the universe of stocks by their P/B ratio exposure in each historical period. There are a variety of methods to do this. The stocks can be ranked monthly, quarterly, or yearly. The stocks should be ranked for every month for some historical period, say, 5 to 10 years of historical data to the present. The next step is to create an equal-weighted portfolio of stocks in the first quintile and an equal-weighted portfolio of stocks in the fifth quintile. The first quintile is just the 20% of stocks ranked highest according to the factor, which in this case is the P/B ratio. The fifth quintile is the bottom 20% of stocks ranked according to the P/B ratio. The next step is to compute the returns of the two portfolios for each monthly period. Of course, these portfolios will change over time on a monthly, quarterly, or yearly basis depending on the QEPM's choice of rebalancing period. The final step is to calculate statistics on the historical returns of the first-quintile portfolio minus the fifth-quintile portfolio. This procedure should be repeated for every factor that the manager is interested in using as a predictor of stock returns.[39]

After the zero-investment portfolio returns have been calculated, one can do a statistical test of whether the average portfolio return is significantly different from zero. Suppose that we calculated portfolio returns for T periods and obtained $r_1, \ldots, r_T$. Then the t statistics can be calculated as follows:

$$\hat{t} = \frac{\bar{r}}{\hat{S}(\bar{r})} = \frac{\bar{r}\sqrt{T}}{\sqrt{\frac{1}{T-1}\sum_{s=1}^{T}(r_s - \bar{r})^2}} \qquad (4.3)$$

where $\bar{r}$ is the sample average, i.e., $\bar{r} = \frac{1}{T}\sum_{s=1}^{T} r_s$, and $\hat{S}(\bar{r})$ is the standard error of the mean. The value of the t-statistic should be

---

[39] We provide programs in R, MATLAB, and Stata that actually create these portfolios with real data. See https://ludwigbc.com/books/qepm/exclusive_qepm_content_2020/. We also discuss this topic more in Chapter 16.

compared with the t distribution with $T - 1$ degrees of freedom. Although one should look at a t-statistics table for the actual critical values of the t-statistic to determine significance, a good rule of thumb is that if the absolute value of the t-statistic is greater than 2, the average portfolio return is significantly different from zero, and the factor is statistically significant.[40]

4.6.4 Multidimensional Zero-Investment Portfolio

Zero-investment portfolios also can be created by considering many factors simultaneously. This approach is more rigorous than the unidimensional approach because we can examine the joint significance of factors. Construction of the zero-investment portfolio proceeds almost in the same way as before. The portfolio manager ranks all stocks by each factor of interest. If there are two factors, say, size and P/B ratio, then each stock will be assigned two rankings, one by size and the other by P/B ratio. Based on these rankings, the portfolio manager can group stocks into a number of joint quintiles or deciles. If the portfolio manager wants to create 10 groups out of each factor, then there will be 100 groups eventually. From the size factor, there will be 10 portfolios starting from the smallest to the largest. From the P/B ratio, there also will be 10 portfolios from the lowest to the highest. By taking intersections of these portfolios, one can obtain 100 portfolios.

Given 100 portfolios, the method to create the zero-investment portfolios depends on what the portfolio manager is interested in. If he or she is interested in whether small size and low P/B ratio together influence stock returns, he or she could create the zero-investment portfolio by taking a long position on a small–low portfolio and a short position on a large–high portfolio. Once the zero-investment portfolio is constructed, t-statistics can be calculated to determine whether the joint effect of the factors is significant, as explained in the preceding subsection.

Alternatively, one may apply a multiple regression analysis. For each of the factors that we consider, we may define an indicator variable that takes the value of 1 if the stock belongs to the top division (e.g., quintile), a value of -1 if the stock belongs to the

---

[40] When considering the testing of many factors, researchers may wish to adjust the t-statistics as explained earlier. Some suggestions for how to do this are contained in Appendix 4B.

bottom division, and a value of 0 otherwise. If we run a regression of stock returns on the indicator variables, the estimated coefficients can be interpreted as the returns to suitably constructed zero-investment portfolios. Thus, the significance of the multiple regression can be taken as an indicator of the joint significance of selected factors.

4.6.5 Techniques to Reduce the Number of Factors

There are several methods to determine the correlation among factors. A quantitative portfolio manager could use these methods to determine whether certain factors are highly similar to one another either for the grouping of factors or to aid in reducing the number of factors in one's stock return model. We discuss two types of statistics here, one based on simple correlation and the other based on rank correlation.

In general, a perfect correlation (i.e., a correlation of 1) indicates that the two factors are almost identical, whereas a correlation of 0 would indicate that the factors are quite independent. In the extreme cases of perfect positive or negative correlation, the two factors are more likely to be redundant. In the in-between cases, the quantitative analyst would have to have a cutoff criterion.

The first statistic we discuss is called the *within-correlation coefficient*. It is the correlation coefficient adjusted for the panel structure of the data. We first subtract the mean from each variable for each period and then calculate the correlation coefficient. The adjustment is necessary to make sure that we are examining the contemporaneous correlation amongst variables. Specifically, given two variables X and Y, the within-correlation coefficient is calculated as

$$\hat{\rho}\left(X_{i,t}, Y_{i,t}\right) = \frac{\hat{C}(X_{i,t} - \bar{X}_t, Y_{i,t} - \bar{Y}_t)}{\hat{S}(X_{i,t} - \bar{X}_t)\hat{S}(Y_{i,t} - \bar{Y}_t)} \qquad (4.4)$$

where $\hat{C}$ and $\hat{S}$ are sample covariance and standard deviation, and $\bar{X}_t$ and $\bar{Y}_t$ are the sample means of X and Y for period t, respectively.

The second statistic we discuss is based on Kendall's τ. Kendall's τ shows the rank correlation (i.e., whether the ranking by one variable is related to the ranking by another variable).

Conceptually, Kendall's τ answers the following question: "Suppose that you choose a pair of observations. You rank these two observations based on the value of one variable. Then you rank the observations based on the value of another variable. Then what is the probability that the ranking by one variable is identical to the ranking by another variable?" Thus, if Kendall's τ is 100%, then for every pair of observations, the ranking by one variable is always identical to the ranking by another variable. If Kendall's τ is negative 100%, then for every pair of observations, the rankings by two variables are opposite. If Kendall's τ is 0, half the time the rankings by two variables are the same, and the other half of the time the rankings are opposite.

Kendall's τ needs to be adjusted for the panel structure of the data as well. We calculate the numerator (the number of pairs for which the rankings by two variables are the same minus the number of pairs for which the rankings by two variables are the opposite of each other) and the denominator (the total number of pairs) for each period and then aggregate over time. These techniques can be used to group factors or to reduce the number of significant factors in a model.[41]

4.7 CONCLUSION

In this chapter we went through a wide range of factors for QEPM models. Portfolio managers should have a good understanding of why each factor may or may not be helpful in predicting stock returns. As we have reiterated several times, what distinguishes a portfolio manager from the crowd is the combination of factors he or she chooses for stock return models. There is no automatic way to select the best factors. We presented a number of statistical methods to aid the selection process, but they do not substitute for human judgment. Theoretical justification for including a factor in a model is as important as statistical proof. Finally, factor choice sometimes comes down to a matter of preference. Great managers, just like great chefs, often add things "to taste." In Chapter 5 we will examine the signature stock screens of some well-known managers who combined factors according to their individual investment styles.

---

[41] Other techniques for reducing factors are also discussed in Chapter 6 of Campbell et al. (1997), Bai and Ng (2003), and Barillas and Shanken (2018).

APPENDIX 4A

Factor Definition Tables

TABLE 4A.1

Fundamental Valuation Factors

Factor	Description
Dividend yield (DY)	The dividend per share of a company divided by its stock price. High dividend yield stocks are also known as *dogs*. High dividend-yielding stocks have been shown to outperform over the long run.
Enterprise-value-to-earnings-before-interest-taxes-depreciation-and-amortization ratio (EV/EBITDA)	Also known as the *enterprise multiple*. Looks at a firm from a buyer's perspective because it takes debt into account; it is used to find attractive takeover targets. Low ratios may indicate an undervalued company. Also good for comparisons of companies in different countries because it ignores tax effects.
Price-to-book ratio (P/B)	The price of the stock divided by book value of common equity per share. Low P/B ratio stocks are commonly referred to as *value stocks* and high P/B ratio stocks as *growth stocks*. Low P/B ratio stocks have been found to outperform high P/B ratio stocks over the long run.
Price-to-cash-flow ratio (P/CF)	The price of a stock divided by its cash flow per share (various measures of cash flow). Lower P/CF ratio companies have been found to outperform high P/CF ratio firms. Although P/CF ratio is correlated with P/E and P/B ratios, some portfolio managers use it because cash flow is less vulnerable to accounting manipulation.
Price-to-earnings ratio (P/E)	Price of a stock divided by the earnings per share. Low P/E ratio stocks are known as value stocks. High P/E ratio stocks are known as growth stocks. It has been found that low P/E ratio stocks outperform stocks with higher P/E ratios over the long run.

Factor	Description
Price-to-earnings-before-interest-taxes-depreciation-and-amortization ratio (P/EBITDA)	The price of a stock divided by its earnings before interest, taxes, depreciation, and amortization. It is computed by adding depreciation and amortization to the earnings before interest and taxes. Lower P/EBITDA ratio companies have been found to outperform high P/EBITDA ratio firms. It is used because it is a proxy for cash flow; however, it suffers some problems, including variations in accounting methods, cash required for valuation purposes, debt service and other fixed-charge requirements, and the need to maintain productive capacity.
Price-to-earnings-to-growth ratio (PEG)	Price-to-earnings ratio divided by earnings growth rate. Historical earnings growth rates or forecasted consensus analyst growth rates are usually used. It incorporates anticipated growth rates of a company to adjust P/E ratios for different potential earnings' growth rates. EV/EBITDA, P/EBITDA, and P/E neglect a company's growth rate, which can be vastly different across companies.
Price-to-earnings-to-growth-to-dividend-yield ratio (PEGY)	The price-to-earnings-growth ratio divided by the dividend yield of the stock. Some analysts use P/E ratio divided by earnings growth plus dividend yield.
Price-to-sales ratio (P/S)	The price of a stock divided by its sales per share. This ratio is very industry sensitive. Low P/S ratio stocks have been found to outperform high P/S ratio stocks.

Note: Oftentimes, in quantitative research, in order to have a richer dataset, the inverse of many of these ratios is used (e.g., EBIDTA/EV, B/P, CF/P, E/P, EBITDA/P, 1/PEG, 1/PEGY). For example, a company with zero earnings or negative earnings would make the relative comparison of P/E ratios confusing.

TABLE 4A.2

Fundamental Size Factors

Factor	Description
Common equity (CE)	Common equity, or book value of equity, is a measure of the size of a company.
Market capitalization (SIZE)	The market capitalization of the shares outstanding, which is the price of a share multiplied by the number of shares outstanding. Commonly referred to as *size*. Smaller size stocks have been found to outperform larger size stocks over the long run.
Total assets (TA)	Total assets represent the short- and long-term assets of a company. This includes cash, marketable securities, inventory, fixed assets like buildings, and more.

Note: Oftentimes, in quantitative research, due to the skewness of these variables, $\log_e(CE)$, $\log_e(SIZE)$, or $\log_e(TA)$ is used.

TABLE 4A.3

Fundamental Operating Efficiency Factors

Factor	Description
Cash conversion cycle (CCC)	Accounts receivable turnover in days plus inventory turnover in days minus accounts payable turnover in days. It is the time between outlay of cash and cash recovery. A company may have a negative cash conversion cycle because it is able to get money from customers quicker than it has to pay its creditors. This can be a sign of strong power in the industry.
Cost management index (CMI)*	Cost of goods sold plus selling and administrative fees divided by operating revenue.
Equity turnover (ET)	This is defined as net sales divided by average shareholders' equity.
Fixed asset turnover (FAT)	This is defined as net sales divided by average fixed assets. This reflects the level of sales from investments in productive capacity. For a variety of reasons, it can be rather erratic, including the discreteness of fixed-asset investment, the particular stage in a company's development, depreciation, and the timing of fixed-investment purchases.
Inventory turnover (IT)	This is equal to the cost of goods sold divided by average inventory. This is a measure of the efficiency of inventory management. A higher ratio indicates that inventory turns over rapidly from the time of acquisition to sale. This ratio is affected by the choice of accounting method, and, thus, when comparing companies, the analyst should make sure that the accounting methods are similar.
Receivables turnover (RT)	This is defined as net sales divided by average receivables. The calculation method may differ depending on the analyst, but an analyst may use the last 2 years (or more or less data) of receivables and average them. This measures the effectiveness of credit policies of the firm. It also is an indication of the level of investment necessary to maintain the firm's sales level.
Total asset turnover (TAT)	This is defined as net sales divided by average total assets.

*When dealing with banking or financial firms, an alternative measure of cost management might be used. The cost management index for banks is defined as noninterest expense divided by net interest income (interest income minus interest expense) plus noninterest income.

TABLE 4A.4

Fundamental Operating Profitability Factors

Factor	Description
Accruals (ACC)	Accruals are revenues earned or expenses incurred that impact a company's net income on the income statement, although cash related to the transaction has not yet changed hands. It has been documented that buying stocks with low accruals and selling stocks with high accruals produce excess returns.

Factor	Description
Cash flow to total assets (CFTA)	This is defined as operating cash flow divided by total assets.
Cash flow to sales (CFTS)	This is defined as operating cash flow divided by total sales.
Gross profit margin (GPM)	This is defined as net sales minus the cost of goods sold divided by net sales. This measures how profitable a firm is. This is a historical measure. Portfolio managers implicitly assume that some form of this measure will continue into the future.
Gross profits to total assets (GPTA)	This is defined as gross profits divided by total assets.
Net profit margin (NPM)	This is defined as net income divided by net sales. It is known as the "bottom line." This represents the true income of the firm. A very important measure of profitability for companies.
Net profit to total assets (NPTA)	This is defined as net income divided by total assets.
Operating profit margin (OPM)	This is defined as operating profit (net sales minus the cost of goods sold and the sales and general administrative expenses) divided by net sales.
Operating profits to total assets (OPTA)	This is defined as operating profit (net sales minus the cost of goods sold and the sales and general administrative expense) divided by total assets.
Return on assets (ROA)	This is defined as net income plus after-tax interest cost divided by average total assets. Or it is defined as earnings before interest and taxes divided by average total assets. This measures management's ability and efficiency in using the firm's assets to generate profits.
Return on common equity (ROCE)	This is defined as net income minus preferred dividends divided by average common equity. This is a measure of return directly related to common equity holders.
Return on owner's equity (ROE)	This is defined as net income divided by average total equity. It measures the return to common and preferred shareholders.
Return on total capital (ROTC)	This is defined as net income plus gross interest expense divided by average total capital. This measures the total return to investors on their investment with the firm. It includes both debt and equity capital. Thus it's a return to all investors in the proportion of their contribution.

Note: Although we do not directly analyze them in this book, there are two additional measures that can help with company assessment. One is the return on net financial assets (RONA). This is computed as net financial income divided by average net financial assets. Net financial income (after tax) is interest income minus interest expense multiplied by one minus the tax rate, and average net financial assets is financial assets minus financial liabilities. This is the complement to the return on net operating assets. The other is the return on net operating assets (RNOA). This is computed as net operating income divided by average net operating assets. Net operating income (after tax) is net income minus net financial income, and average net operating assets is net assets minus net financial assets. Financial assets are cash and marketable securities, while financial liabilities are notes payable, short-term debt, current portion of long-term debt, long-term debt, and preferred stock. This measure is useful for nonfinancial companies in understanding that the returns to the business of the firm are independent of its financial activities. The actual way of computing these variables can vary by analyst.

TABLE 4A.5

Fundamental Solvency Factors

Factor	Description
Cash-flow-from-operations ratio (CFOR)	This equals cash flow from operations divided by current liabilities. Measures liquidity by looking at actual cash flows instead of current and potential cash resources.
Cash ratio (CR)	This is equal to the sum of cash and marketable securities divided by current liabilities. If inventories and/or accounts receivable are not liquid, then this is a bettermeasure of solvency.
Current ratio (CUR)	Current assets of the firm divided by current liabilities. If accounts receivables and inventories are relatively liquid, then this ratio is a good measure of solvency. Firms that are more solvent have less likelihood of going into bankruptcy and thus can withstand paying their current liabilities.
Quick ratio (QR)	This is equal to the sum of cash, marketable securities, and accounts receivable divided by current liabilities. This measure is also known as the "acid test." It's a better measure of liquidity or solvency, especially when inventories are not that liquid. It is essentially the current ratio minus the ratio of inventories to current liabilities.

TABLE 4A.6

Fundamental Financial Risk Factors

Factor	Description
Cash-flow coverage ratio (CFCR)	This is defined as the cash flow from operations divided by the total debt of the firm. It measures the ability of cash flows to cover debt obligations.
Debt-to-equity ratio (D/E)	The long-term debt of a company divided by its common equity. This is a very common measure of the financial risk of a firm. Many portfolio managers view a high D/E ratio relative to the universe as a bad thing, all else equal.
Financial leverage ratio (FLR)	This is measured as the total assets of the firm divided by the total common equity.
Interest coverage ratio (ICR)	This is defined as the earnings before interest and taxes divided by the interest expense. Also known as the *times interest earned*. It gives an investor an idea of financial risk because it indicates how well interest payments are covered by the current earnings of the firm before taxes and, obviously, interest. It gives an indication of how capable the firm will be in making interest payments. A high ratio is comforting because even if the company struggles but is ultimately a good company, it will unlikely default on an interest payment, causing even more problems.
Total debt ratio (TDR)	This is defined as the total debt (short- and long-term debt) of the firm divided by the total capital (total liabilities plus total equity).

TABLE 4A.7

Fundamental Corporate Activity Factors

Factor	Description
Insider purchases (IP)	This factor is the number of insiders making purchases on stocks. The more insiders purchasing the stock is a positive signal for the stock return. The more insiders selling the stock is a negative signal for purchasing the stock. It has been documented that if a stock is bought when there is insider buying, this leads to abnormal returns. Similarly, selling a stock when there is insider selling leads to abnormal returns.
Research-and-development-to-sales ratio (RNDS)	Measured as the dollar amount spent by the company on research and development divided by the dollar value of sales revenue for the company. A high value relative to the industry might indicate a company that is poised for strong future growth owing to the investment in research and development.
Stock buybacks (SB)	This factor looks at companies that are buying back their stock. One proxy for this is the change in Treasury securities for a company. It has been documented that companies that buy back their shares tend to have subsequent abnormal returns.

TABLE 4A.8

Technical Liquidity Risk Factors

Factor	Description
Amihud illiquidity (AILIQ)	A measure of illiquidity based on the ratio of the daily return of the stock to the daily volume. The idea is that the higher the daily return for a given volume, the less liquid is the stock due to price impact.
Crowding (CROWD)	Crowding is a recently identified risk in investing that might occur when multiple market participants begin to follow the same trade in such a concentration that liquidity becomes fragile and it alters the risk and return dynamics of the trade. There is no one definitive measure of crowding, but rather many proxies.
Invariance illiquidity (INVIL)	Invariance is a measure of illiquidity based on a theoretical model. This measure relates the illiquidity of a stock to a constant multiplied by the ratio of the volatility of a stock to its average dollar volume.
Modified Amihud illiquidity (MAILIQ)	A measure of illiquidity that is exactly the same as the Amihud measure, but rather than using close-to-close prices to measure daily returns, uses open-to-close prices.
Pastor and Stambaugh liquidity (PSL)*	A measure of liquidity through an empirical regression of volume on daily stock returns. It has been documented that this may be a risk factor in the financial markets.

TABLE 4A.8 *(Continued)*

Factor	Description
Trading turnover (TT)	The percentage of outstanding shares of the security traded during a given period. A common measure is the average daily trading volume figure divided by the market capitalization of the company. The average daily trading volume is usually measured as an average of the last 90 days' trading volume. This measure allows a gauge of liquidity. For larger funds, it also places limits on how much of a certain stock can be traded in the portfolio.

Note: Although we do not directly analyze them in this book, floating shares is another measure of liquidity. This measure of liquidity considers only the shares available to the public for trading. It is the number of floated shares multiplied by the price per share. It is highly correlated with market capitalization, but not always, and this is the more relevant measure since it represents the amount of shares that can be traded by the public. In fact, many indices, including the S&P 500, switched from market capitalization–weighted to float-weighted during the 2000s. Another factor that can be useful is the number of security owners. This represents the number of investors who own the stock. This can be important for liquidity. For most securities, it is not a concern since securities are so widely held. However, for some securities it can be very important since if a few institutional shareholders own the majority of the security, then buying/selling the security may prove difficult and make the security less attractive for portfolio management strategies. Compustat does provide a variable from 10K reports of companies, CSHR, which is supposed to be the number of common shareholders. CSHR can be very misleading as it usually but not always fails to include the number of shareholders who hold the shares in "street name" at their brokers.
*This factor could also be considered an "economic" factor because we must estimate each stock's exposure from the factor via regression.

TABLE 4A.9

Technical Price-Based Factors

Factor	Description
Beta (BETA)/Market (MKT)*	The historical beta of a stock. There are numerous ways to compute the beta of a stock. This factor is known amongst practitioners as *low beta*, reflecting the belief that low beta is associated with a higher risk-adjusted return. Because the beta of a stock is derived from regressing returns against the market factor, we also share this space with the market factor (i.e., the return of the market minus the risk-free rate).
Bollinger bands (BB)	A moving average of the stock price with two bands around it, one below and one above, representing some number of standard deviations away from the mean. The mean over k days is given by $\bar{P} = \frac{\sum_{i=1}^{k} P_i}{k}$. The upper band is given by: $\bar{P} + l\sqrt{\frac{\sum_{i=1}^{k}(P_i - \bar{P})^2}{k}}$, where l is the number of standard deviations from the mean, and k is the number of historical days used in the Bollinger band. The lower band has the same formula, but the second term is subtracted. This concept is named after its inventor, John Bollinger. The idea is that one should not just buy or sell a stock when its price crosses its moving average but rather when its price moves away from its moving average by a sufficient amount (e.g., 1 standard deviation).

Factor	Description
Channel breakouts (CB)	Channel breakouts are defined as conditions where a channel is breached. The channel is formed when the high price over the last n days is within $x\%$ of the low price for the same period. When a channel is followed by a new high level, $y\%$ above the old high, it signals a buy. If the opposite occurs, it signals a sell.
Momentum (MOM)	A positive return of a stock over a specified time horizon. There are numerous ways to compute momentum. One of the simplest ways is just the k-month total return. Studies have documented that stocks with high relative momentum have subsequent high relative returns.
Moving average (MA)	An average of the stock's price over a specific window in the past. For example, if you want a 60-day moving average, simply average the stock price over the last 60 days. Doing this every day creates a history of 60-day moving averages for the stock. The moving average can be weighted in various ways. Investors usually use the moving average as follows: When the actual stock price today rises above the moving average, this is a buy signal. When it falls below the moving average, this is a sell signal.
Moving-average convergence–divergence indicator (MACD)	Originally defined as a 26-day exponential moving average minus a 12-day exponential moving average. This trend following the momentum indicator shows the relationship between two moving averages. It was developed originally by Gerald Appel. There are many ways to interpret this indicator. One method is to buy when it goes above the zero line and sell when it goes below the zero line. It also can be used as an overbought/oversold indicator when it rises or falls very rapidly.
Price (P)	Some evidence has been found that stocks with low prices have high returns. One argument is that small investors feel that these stocks get them more. It's a psychological affordability. If stock price increments are limited to a certain movement, one might think that this could partially be responsible for these results. This factor is known amongst practitioners as *low price*.
Relative strength index (RSI)	The RSI is a measure of the strength of a security. This is an indicator that takes on values between 0 and 100. Generally, when the RSI is above 70, this is an overbought market, and one should sell the stock. An RSI reading of less than 30 indicates an oversold market, and one should buy the stock. This index was first introduced by Welles Wilder in an issue of *Commodities* magazine in June 1978. There are various ways to measure the RSI.
Support resistance (SR)	This measure looks for prices of stocks that are establishing new highs or lows. Generally, the investor constructs a look-back window, say, 30 days. If the price of the stock exceeds the previous high for the last 30 days, this is a buy signal. If the price of the stock falls below a previous low, this is a sell signal.
Volatility (VOL)	The historical volatility of a stock. There are numerous ways to compute the historical volatility of a stock. One of the simplest ways is to choose a look-back period and compute the standard deviation of returns. This factor is known amongst practitioners as *low vol*, reflecting the belief that low volatility is associated with a high rate of return.

*The beta factor is really like an "economic" factor in the sense that we must estimate regression equations of the returns of stocks on the market returns in order to obtain each stock's exposure, or beta. We left it in the technical category, since to compute it involves technical data and also so as not to confuse the reader by placing it in another category of data.

TABLE 4A.10

Technical Volume-Based Factors

Factor	Description
Odd-lot balance (OLBI)	This is a measure of the ratio of odd-lot sales to odd-lot purchases. Odd lots are transactions in a stock that are fewer than 100 shares. The idea is that small-investor money is "dumb" money. Thus, when the OLBI is high, this means that small investors are selling more than buying, and it's a signal to buy. When the OLBI is very low, it's a signal to sell. Some practitioners take a moving average of the OLBI.
On-balance volume (OBV)	If the security moves down, all the volume is considered down volume. The formula is $OBV_t = OBV_{t-1} + V_t$ if $P_t > P_{t-1}$, and $OBV_t = OBV_{t-1} - V_t$ if $P_t < P_{t-1}$. For zero price movements, the OBV remains the same. The investor should take an action when the OBV breaks out or changes trend. Thus, if the OBV were falling and it suddenly begins rising, this would be a buy signal.
Short interest ratio (SIR)	This measures the amount of short selling on a particular stock. Some people use a high degree of short interest as a contrarian signal. That is, when short interest is high, then a slight increase in the stock price might force the short sellers to buy the stock back, causing the price to increase even further. This is called a *short squeeze*. A general guide is to look at a stock's short interest versus its historical average.
Volume lead (VL)	Volume is used in many technical indicators. One simple rule is that if the stock has a return on larger than average volume, it is overreactive and may reverse itself. If the stock has a return on lower than average volume, it is informative and may lead to subsequent returns in the same direction.

TABLE 4A.11

Technical Overall Market Movement Factors

Factor	Description
Advance–decline ratio (ADR)	This technical indicator measures the participation in market rallies. It is the ratio of the number of advancing issues (i.e., stocks whose stock price has increased) to the number of declining issues (i.e., stocks whose price has declined). Some investors smooth this ratio by taking a moving average of it. If the indicator is very high, this indicates an overbought situation and a sell signal. If the indicator is very low, this indicates an oversold condition and a buy signal.
Arms index (ARMS)	This indicator measure is a combination of two other well-known indicators and attempts to measure the flow of volume into stocks that are going either up in price or down in price. That is, it is computed by dividing the advance–decline ratio by the upside–downside ratio. It shows whether volume is flowing into advancing or declining stocks. A ratio below 1 indicates a buying opportunity, whereas a ratio above 1 indicates a selling opportunity. Many practitioners take a moving average of this variable and use that as their indicator. It is named after its developer, Richard W. Arms.

Factor	Description
Upside–downside ratio (UDR)	This measure compares the volume of stocks that have upward price movements with the volume of stocks that have downward price movements. It is computed by dividing the daily volume of advancing stocks by the daily volume of declining stocks.
Upside–downside volume (UDV)	This measure compares the volume of stocks that have upward price movements with the volume of stocks that have downward price movements. It is computed by subtracting the total volume of stocks that increase from the total volume of stocks that decrease. Typically, the investor can look at the historical average of this variable. When the UDV is very positive, this is a buy signal. When it is very negative, this is a sell signal.

TABLE 4A.12

Economic Factors

Factor	Description
Consumption growth (PCG)	This measures the growth in real personal consumption in the economy based on the breakdown of GDP numbers.
Change in commodity prices (CIG)	This measures the change in oil or commodity prices in the economy. Typically, the percentage change in oil prices is used or the return on some commodity index is used.
Corporate bond spread [e.g., BBB spread (BBBS)]	This attempts to measure the risk premium in the economy as derived from corporate bond spreads. It can be defined as the spread between lower-grade corporate bonds (BBB or lower) and U.S. Treasury bonds. The higher the spread, the greater is the risk premium being paid in the marketplace for riskier securities. It can also be measured as the return of lower-grade bonds minus the return of U.S. Treasury bonds of a similar duration. Sometimes swap spreads, the lending rate of banks on collateralized loans versus the U.S. government interest rates, are used as well.
Industrial production (IPG)	This attempts to measure the growth rate of the economy. Usually, the change in industrial production or the growth in industrial production is used as the economic factor. The industrial production number is released monthly and therefore perhaps is more useful than GDP growth, which is released quarterly. Presumably, different stocks will have different exposures to different stages in the business cycle as measured by the growth in industrial production.
Inflation (CPIG)	This measures the monthly inflation rate in the economy. Typically, either the consumer price index (CPI) or the producer price index (PPI) is used to measure inflation. Some use the actual inflation rate as the economic factor, and some attempt to build a series of unexpected inflation rates and use this as the economic factor. Presumably, different stocks behave differently during different inflation cycles.

TABLE 4A.12 *(Continued)*

Factor	Description
Real GDP growth (GDPG)	This measures the growth in real GDP from quarter to quarter. Some people also use the survey of economic forecasts to compute the innovation or surprise growth in real GDP.
Slope of yield curve (e.g., 10 year rate minus 2 year rate (TP2Y))	This measures the slope of the yield curve. Usually it is measured as the 10-year yield minus the 2-year yield or the 10-year yield minus the 3-month Treasury bill yield, although other variations are possible. The yield-curve slope is a proxy for measuring expected changes in the future state of the economy according to bond market participants.
Unemployment rate (UR)	This measures the unemployment rate in the economy. Some practitioners also may use the change in the unemployment rate.

TABLE 4A.13

Alternative Analyst Factors

Factor	Description
Analyst rating—median rating (ARMR)	A median rating of all analysts on a particular stock. Each analyst rating is ranked 1–5. 1 = strong buy, 2 = buy, 3 = hold, 4 = sell, and 5 = strong sell.
Analyst rating—percent buys (ARPB)	This represent the percentage of analysts that recommend a buy or better on the stock.
Analyst rating—percent sells (ARPS)	This represents the percentage of analysts who recommend a sell on the stock.
Analyst rating—SD of ratings (ARSD)	This is the statistical measure of standard deviation of all analyst recommendations in a cross section. It indicates the degree of heterogeneity in the analysts' forecasts.
Analyst rating—percent downgrades (ARPD)	This represents the percentage of analysts whose ratings on the stock have decreased in the last month.
Analyst rating—percent upgrades (ARPU)	This represents the percentage of analysts whose ratings on the stock have increased in the last month.
EPS forecast—normalized SD (EPSSD)	This factor represents the median EPS estimate by all analysts covering the stock divided by the statistical standard deviation of all EPS estimates for the stock. Since EPS estimates will vary by type of company, this measure normalizes the measure for interpretation.
EPS revision—percent downward (EPSFPD)	This factor represents the percentage of analysts who have decreased their EPS estimates on the stock over the last month.

Factor	Description
EPS revision—percent upward (EPSFPU)	This factor represents the percentage of analysts who have increased their EPS estimates on the stock over the last month.
Number of analysts (EPSFN)	Also called the *indicator of neglected firms*. The factor is the number of analysts covering a firm. The idea is to choose firms with less analyst coverage. It has been documented that firms with low analyst coverage or low institutional ownership tend to have higher risk-adjusted returns. There is some controversy over whether this is a small-cap effect or something else.
Standardized unanticipated earnings (SUE)	$SUE = \dfrac{EPS^a - \overline{EPS}}{S(EPS)}$, where $\overline{EPS}$ is the mean earnings-per-share estimates by analysts prior to the earnings announcements, $S(EPS)$ represents the standard deviation of analyst earnings-per-share estimates, and EPS^a is the actual earnings per share reported. It has been documented that companies that exhibit positive earnings surprises continue to perform well over the next 13 to 26 weeks; similarly, companies that exhibit negative earnings surprises continue to underperform into the future.

Note: Although we do not directly analyze them in this book, when detailed analyst information is available, it can also provide additional valuable information. High EPS and low EPS forecasts represent the highest and lowest analyst estimates for the EPS of a company. High and low recommendations represent the highest and lowest analyst recommendations for the company. In addition to these simple statistics, other statistics related to individual analyst data can also be valuable.

TABLE 4A.14

Alternative Social Responsibility Factors

Factor	Description
Community contribution (CC)	This factor measures how much the company contributes to charitable giving and other such causes.
Corporate governance (CG)	This factor measures how much the company compensates executives. Higher compensation is seen as a bad indicator.
Diversity (DIV)	This factor measures how much the company promotes women and minorities.
Employee relations (ER)	This factor measures whether the company shares profits with employees, promotes safety and the health of employees, and has a strong retirement program and strong union relations.
Environment (E)	This factor measures how much the company is involved in activities that attempt to reduce pollution or benefit the environment.
Human rights (HR)	This factor measures how well the company considers human rights.
Product (PRO)	This factor measures how much the company promotes the quality of its products, whether it's a leader in R&D for innovative products in the market, and whether the products have notable social benefits.

On Data Mining and Techniques to Adjust the Significance of Factors

One way to describe the danger of data mining is as follows: If we determine a factor to be statistically significant whenever the absolute value of the t-statistic associated with the factor is greater than 1.96, we are most likely overstating the statistical evidence. In many real-life situations, we do not test a factor in isolation but consider many factors jointly. A particular factor that we like may have been selected because of its large t-statistic in comparison with the conventional critical value of 1.96. This may not be the appropriate critical value. Such a comparison will lead us frequently to declare a factor to be significant even when the factor is in reality not significant. The probability of false discovery will be much higher than our intended target of 5% (i.e., our selected significance level).

One straightforward solution is to choose a higher critical value so that the probability of false discovery declines to 5% even when we focus on one factor out of many due to its sample t-statistic. While this sounds straightforward in principle, applying this idea in practice is not so easy. The biggest challenge is that, quite often, we are not able to determine the total number of factors under consideration. If another portfolio manager conducted the analysis and only reported a factor with a large t-value, we cannot know the total number of factors that he or she tested. Even if we conducted the analysis ourselves, our choice of candidate factors may have been influenced by our reading of others' research reports, and it is not easy to decide how many factors were considered in the numerous research reports that we may have read over the years.

Despite these difficulties, we briefly describe two approaches to data mining that have been discussed in the academic literature. These approaches will not shield us from the danger of data mining completely, but may help us have a better sense of the magnitude of potential problems. The first approach, which we refer to as the *Bonferroni-type adjustment*, is based on the traditional, frequentist statistical theory in which the calculated *t*-statistic is compared to the distribution of all the *t*-statistics that we could have obtained assuming the truth about the null hypothesis. The second approach is based on Bayesian statistical theory in which our subjective probability of the null hypothesis being true is derived from the data and our personal beliefs.

4B.1 THE BONFERRONI-TYPE ADJUSTMENT

In the Bonferroni adjustment, the critical value for the *t*-test is determined by the total number of factors tested. The critical values are shown in Table 4B.1. These values are computed in the following way. Let M be the number of factors tested. Let α be the significance level that we choose (e.g., 0.05). Then the critical *p*-value in the Bonferroni adjustment is calculated as α/M. From this critical *p*-value, we can recover the critical *t*-value as $t^* = \Phi^{-1}(1 - p^*/2)$, where p^* is the critical *p*-value, Φ is the standard normal distribution function.

The Holm adjustment, a variation of the Bonferroni adjustment, proceeds in a slightly different way. When M factors are considered, we may order these factors from the one with the highest absolute *t*-value to the one with the lowest absolute *t*-value. Thus, we may denote these *t*-values by $t_1 \geq \cdots \geq t_M$. If we denote the *p*-values of these M factors, $p_1 \leq \cdots \leq p_M$. To proceed with the Holm adjustment, we first need to determine the index j such that $p_1 \leq \cdots \leq p_j \leq \alpha/(M - j) < p_{j+1} \leq p_M$. Once we determine j, we may conclude that the first j factors are significant. Note that the critical *p*-value, $\alpha/(M - j)$, is a function of the entire set of *p*-values and that it is not possible to convert this into a generic critical *t*-value. What we show in Table 4B.1 instead is the *t*-value corresponding to $\alpha/(M - j)$ assuming $j = 0.05M$.

As mentioned earlier, the most difficult part of implementing the Bonferroni or Holm adjustment is the choice of the number of factors tested. Some researchers have suggested using the total number of published and unpublished research articles since 1967 for this purpose. By some counts, this is about 313 articles (or 316 factors) through 2012. The Bonferroni critical t-value corresponding to the previously discovered factors is 3.78. If the rate of research articles produced continues at this same rate, the Bonferroni critical t-value will be 4.00 by 2032.[1]

4B.2 A BAYESIAN ADJUSTMENT

Consistently applying the Bayes rule to assess the subjective probability of a null hypothesis may alleviate the problems associated with data mining. In the Bayesian approach, the posterior probability of a null hypothesis being true is determined as the product of the prior probability of the null hypothesis being true and its likelihood (i.e., the probability of the observed data being generated when the null hypothesis is true). The same can be said about the posterior probability of an alternative hypothesis. Combining these two ideas leads to this statement: the posterior odds ratio (the posterior probability of the null hypothesis being true divided by the posterior probability of the alternative hypothesis being true) is the product of the prior odds ratio and the likelihood ratio. Among these three concepts—the posterior odds ratio, the prior odds ratio, and the likelihood ratio—the likelihood ratio can be calculated without reference to a particular individual's beliefs. Thus, this is a good starting point to construct a test statistic.

One potential choice to guide the portfolio manager is the minimum possible value of the likelihood ratio, determined by considering all the possible alternative hypotheses. This ratio might be called the *minimum Bayes factor* (MBF).[2] Once the value of MBF is determined, a new critical value of the t-test can be determined. At the significance level of 5%, a critical value of t is the one corresponding to the 95% posterior probability of the null hypothesis being true. Table 4B.2 presents the critical t-values for different prior odds ratios. The prior odds ratio of 0.01 indicates that the null hypothesis is highly likely with 99:1 odds. The prior odds ratio of 0.50 indicates that the null hypothesis is as likely as the alternative hypothesis. In other words, the higher the odds ratio, the more the analyst or portfolio manager is convinced that the factor is important in predicting stock returns. A value of 0.99 or 99% would mean that he or she is almost certain of it.

---

[1] See Harvey et al. (2016).
[2] See Harvey (2017).

TABLE 4B.1

Critical *t*-Values for Bonferroni and Holm Adjustments

Number of Factors Tested	Bonferroni Critical *t*	Holm Critical *t*
10	2.81	2.81
20	3.02	3.02
30	3.14	3.13
40	3.23	3.22
50	3.29	3.28
60	3.34	3.33
70	3.38	3.37
80	3.42	3.41
90	3.45	3.44
100	3.48	3.47
200	3.66	3.65
300	3.76	3.75
400	3.84	3.82
500	3.89	3.88
600	3.93	3.92
700	3.97	3.96
800	4.00	3.99
900	4.03	4.02
1,000	4.06	4.04

Note: For the Bonferroni adjustment, you may simply use the reported critical values for each factor under consideration. For the Holm adjustment, you need to order all the factors from the one with the highest absolute *t*-value to the one with the lowest absolute *t*-value and then choose the *j*th factor such that $p_1 \leq \ldots \leq p_j \leq \alpha/(M-j) < p_{j+1} \leq \ldots \leq p_M$, where $p_1, \ldots, p_M$ are the *p*-values for the *M* factors. The critical *t*-values reported correspond to the *p*-value of $\alpha/(M-j)$ assuming $j = 0.05M$.

TABLE 4B.2

Critical *t*-Values for a Type of Bayesian Adjustment

Prior Odds Ratio	MBF Critical *t*	SD-MBF Critical *t*
0.01	3.88	4.29
0.02	3.70	4.11
0.04	3.50	3.93
0.05	3.43	3.86
0.20	2.94	3.41
0.50	2.43	2.93

Note: The prior odds ratio is the prior probability of the null hypothesis being correct divided by the prior probability of the alternative hypothesis being correct. The minimum Bayes factor (MBF) critical *t* is relevant when there is no information about the appropriate alternative hypothesis; the symmetric, descending minimum Bayes factor (SD-MBF) critical *t* is relevant when one believes that the prior probability density for alternatives should be symmetric and descending around the null hypothesis.

QUESTIONS

4.1. What is a factor, and why is it important in QEPM?

4.2. What are the four basic categories of factors in QEPM?

4.3. What are some common fundamental valuation factors?

4.4. Suppose that there is a group of stocks, group A, with an average P/B ratio that is lower than the industry average, and another group of stocks, group B, that has a P/B ratio that is higher than the industry average. Which group would a growth portfolio manager choose? A value manager?

4.5. What would be more appropriate for a P/E ratio factor, a trailing P/E ratio or a forward P/E ratio? Explain.

4.6. Using concepts from Appendix B, at www.ludwigbc.com under QEPM Exclusive Content, about the dividend discount model, combined with the discussion in this chapter, answer the following questions:

    (a) Derive an expression for the P/E ratio in terms of the payout ratio k, the required rate of return on equity r_{ce}, and the growth rate of earnings g.

    (b) Rearrange this expression so as to obtain the implicit growth rate of earnings implied by the actual P/E ratio of the stock and other parameters.

4.7. Why would fundamental solvency factors be included in a stock return model?

4.8. What might you expect to be more effective at explaining stock returns, gross profit margin or the change in gross profit margin? Explain.

4.9. All else equal, would you prefer a low D/E ratio or a high D/E ratio company in your portfolio? What are some other measures of fundamental financial risk?

4.10. (a) Why might fundamental liquidity factors be important for QEPM?

    (b) What do you think is more relevant in this regard, average daily trading volume, market capitalization, or float-weighted capitalization? Explain.

4.11. Technical factors are being used increasingly in QEPM.

    (a) What is the main reason for using technical factors?

    (b) Name four types of technical factors.

    (c) Which type of quantitative portfolio manager is likely to use a technical indicator as a factor, one who rebalances monthly or one who rebalances quarterly?

4.12. Given the data in the following table on the stock AALC, please do the following:

(a) Compute the mean, upper, and lower bands of a Bollinger band with two standard deviations (i.e., $l = 2$) and a 10-day rolling window (i.e., $k = 10$) for the dates July 26, 2020–July 29, 2020.

(b) Suppose that the quantitative portfolio manager is a contrarian. Thus she believes that markets overreact to information. Should she buy or sell or do nothing on each of those days according to the Bollinger band?

(c) Using the same data, compute the relative strength index (RSI) for each of those days, assuming a nine-day Wilder period.

(d) Some technicians would argue that the Bollinger band should not be used in isolation but in conjunction with other indicators, such as the RSI. Given this philosophy, would you buy or sell or do nothing on this stock on July 26, 2020?

Date	Price
7/13/2020	11.31
7/14/2020	11.41
7/15/2020	11.28
7/16/2020	11.57
7/19/2020	11.43
7/20/2020	11.41
7/21/2020	10.92
7/22/2020	10.51
7/23/2020	10.35
7/26/2020	9.35
7/27/2020	9.65
7/28/2020	10.01
7/29/2020	9.67

4.13. (a) What are three of the biggest drawbacks of using macroeconomic factors?

(b) What is one of the biggest benefits of using economic factors in stock return models?

4.14. A quantitative manager is collecting data for use with a stock return model. He finds that there is a positive relationship between this month's inflation and stock returns. What might you be worried about in use of these data?

4.15. Many factors are lumped into an area called *alternative factors*. Please respond to each of the statements below.

(a) Analyst factors are very useful because they incorporate a lot of analysis of a company into one number.

(b) Analyst factors were more useful prior to 2000 than they are today due to the SEC rule known as Reg FD (fair disclosure) that became effective in October 2000.

(c) A change in analyst recommendation describes stock returns better than the recommendation itself (strong buy, buy, sell, etc.) does.

(d) Downgrades of a stock by some analysts probably serve as more useful factors than downgrades of a stock by all analysts.

(e) What are standardized unanticipated earnings (SUE)? Why might this be useful as a factor? (*Hint:* Use the idea of information diffusion in your explanation.)

4.16. Does investing in socially responsible companies hurt portfolio returns?

4.17. What kinds of tests or techniques can an analyst use to choose factors for
(a) a fundamental factor model?
(b) an economic factor model?

4.18. Why might univariate factor tests not be sufficient to determine the factors in a fundamental model?

4.19. True or false? The stepwise regression technique is very powerful in identifying the optimal combination of factors for use in a stock return model. Portfolio managers always should use it.

4.20. What might the Kendall statistic or other rank-correlation statistic be used for?

4.21. From a cross-sectional regression of stock returns on the exposure to factor A, we obtained the slope estimate of 0.5 and the standard error of 0.2.
(a) If you apply the conventional t-test, will you conclude that factor A is a statistically significant factor?
(b) Prior to running the regression, you have read through 100 research reports regarding 100 different factors including factor A and have learned that factor A has the highest t-statistic. In fact, this is why you became interested in factor A. Thus, your regression analysis is likely to be criticized as a data-mining exercise. In response to such criticism, you decided to apply the Bonferroni adjustment described in Appendix 4B. Will you conclude that factor A is a statistically significant factor?
(c) Instead of applying the Bonferroni adjustment, if you adopt the Bayesian adjustment discussed in this chapter, will your answer be different?

CHAPTER 5

Stock Screening and Ranking

Our life is frittered in detail ... simplify, simplify.

—Henry David Thoreau

5.1 INTRODUCTION

The aim of quantitative equity portfolio management (QEPM) is to refine investing to a reliable, repeatable, quantitative method that avoids the biases and errors of purely qualitative stock picking. *Stock screening* is the ranking of stocks within the investment universe such that they are separated easily into those that are more favorable and those that are less favorable according to the views of the portfolio manager. Screening also can be used to narrow the investment universe. There are two kinds of stock screening, sequential and simultaneous. In *sequential* screening, the portfolio manager prioritizes his or her stock-picking criteria. He or she eliminates stocks from the investment universe first based on the most important criterion, then based on the second most important criterion, and so on and so forth until he or she has reduced the investment universe to a list of stocks that meet all his or her criteria. The more advanced version of stock screening is multifactor simultaneous screening. In *simultaneous* screening, the manager applies all the criteria to the investment universe at once. As a result, all the stocks in the universe receive rankings according to their overall scores on the entire set of criteria.

One of the most popular simultaneous screening methods is what we call the *aggregate Z-score approach*. It involves choosing factors that explain stock returns and aggregating the factors into one score with which to rank the stocks in the investment universe. A Z-score ranking either can serve as the basis for a whole model of stock returns or can add information to an existing model. The stand-alone Z-score model relates the return of a stock to its Z-score and is sometimes equivalent to the fundamental factor model that we introduced in Chapter 3. If a manager is already using a fundamental or economic factor model, the Z-score can be added to the model as the constant term α when certain conditions are satisfied.

The stock screening and ranking methods in this chapter are useful starting points for people just beginning to build quantitative portfolios. They are not the most sophisticated tools of portfolio construction, but they are simple to apply because they do not require mastering a great deal of mathematics or statistics. Many practitioners also will find these approaches to be intuitive.

5.2 SEQUENTIAL STOCK SCREENING

Imagine for a moment that a portfolio manager has only one criterion for investing: He or she believes that low P/B ratio stocks provide the highest excess returns. To create his or her portfolio, the manager would compute the P/B ratios of all the stocks in his or her investment universe.[1] He or she then would rank all the stocks from lowest to highest P/B ratio. If the portfolio were to include 60 stocks, then the manager would invest in the 60 lowest P/B ratio stocks on the ranked list. Alternatively, the portfolio manager could have used the inverse of the P/B ratio, that is, the book-to-market ratio (a.k.a., the B/P ratio). Only the criterion for selection would change: the portfolio manager would pick the

---

[1] The investment universe corresponds to the set of stocks that a portfolio manager is allowed to trade in his or her portfolio. For example, a portfolio manager who manages against the Standard & Poor's (S&P) 500 benchmark might only be allowed to purchase the 500 stocks in the S&P 500. His or her *investment universe* would be the 500 stocks that make up the S&P 500. Other managers' investment universes might follow other indices, such as the Russell 1000, or more complicated definitions.

60 highest B/P ratio stocks.[2] This rudimentary process is stock screening in its most basic form.

What are the attributes of a good stock screen? A good stock screen should be easy to automate. In other words, it should be easy to run the screen regularly as stock data change. The screen should be easy to replicate as well. Any analyst who has the screening procedure and the raw stock-specific data should be able to run the screen and come up with the same stock list that another analyst would come up with using the same data.

A good stock screen, of course, should accurately reflect the portfolio manager's preferences. If the goal is to create a *value* portfolio, then the stock screen should use value factors, such as a high B/P ratio.

Finally, in a sequential screen, the factor screens should be run one at a time in order of importance. This means that the first screens should be for the factors that speak most directly to the manager's investment goals. If market cap is the most important factor in the manager's mind, then that should be the very first screen.[3]

Suppose that we would like to invest in the companies that have the highest positive profit margins (which we suppose we can capture by selecting the top 30% of the S&P 500 by net profit margin) and a third of those companies with the highest B/P ratios. We would first screen our investment universe, the S&P 500, by

---

[2] Oftentimes, it is useful to use one version of a factor over another. For example, in Chapter 4, we used the price-to-book (P/B) and price-to-earnings ratio (P/E) because they are familiar to most people. However, we find that using the E/P ratio is more effective. Many companies have negative earnings, which renders a P/E ratio meaningless: it makes no sense to argue that a low P/E ratio company is "cheaper" than a high P/E ratio company when companies with zero or negative earnings are included. However, if we calculate the E/P ratio of companies, we don't have to exclude companies with negative earnings. For example, a company with a very high P/E ratio will have a very small E/P ratio but will still be considered relatively "cheaper" than a company with a negative E/P ratio. The E/P ratio thus gives us a ratio that can be compared across many more companies. Another reason for using the E/P ratio rather than the P/E ratio is that a company's earnings for a particular period could be close to zero. This leads to an enormous value of P/E that isn't really representative of the company. Using the E/P ratio resolves this problem. As with P/E, it is more effective to use the inverse of the P/B ratio, the B/P ratio. In the rest of this book, we shall use both B/P and E/P rather than the more common ratios. In the Practical Application part of this book, Part V, we will use the inverse of many other common ratios for the exact same reason.

[3] Some people argue that the first screens should be the ones that eliminate the most data possible, but we do not agree.

net profit margin and choose the top 150 companies (30% of 500). We would eliminate the other 350 companies from our investment universe. The next step would be to sort the top 150 stocks by the B/P ratio. We would keep the 50 with the highest B/P ratios and eliminate the remaining 100.

We implemented this screen of S&P 500 stocks using data as of December 2020. Table 5.1 shows some of the stocks selected by the screen. First, we chose the 150 stocks with the highest profit margins. It turned out that all 150 had positive net profit margins. The highest (147.9%) belonged to Bio-Rad Laboratories and the lowest (14.7%) to Keysight Technologies. Then we chose the 50 stocks in this group with the highest B/P ratios. Neither Bio-Rad nor Keysight made it through the B/P screen. Among the final 50 stocks, the lowest ratio was 0.23 for American Water Works (which is not included in the table), and the highest was 1.38 for People's United Financial. With this final list of 50 stocks, our hypothetical portfolio would have been complete.[4]

TABLE 5.1

Selected Stocks from a Sequential Stock Screen

Ticker	Book-to-Price Ratio (B/P)	Net Profit Margin (NPM)
PBCT	1.38	21.64
BK	1.07	24.10
FITB	1.06	18.21
AFL	1.04	20.87
KEY	0.99	16.61
CMA	0.96	16.17
TFC	0.96	17.01
BAC	0.94	19.50
MTB	0.91	21.49
STT	0.90	19.63

Note: These represent the preferred stocks according to the sequential stock screen. The ticker symbols are for the following companies: People's United Financial (PBCT), Bank of New York Mellon (BK), Fifth Third Bancorp (FITB), Aflac (AFL), KeyCorp (KEY), Comerica (CMA), Truist Financial (TFC), Bank of America (BAC), M&T Bank (MTB), and State Street (STT). The data are from December 2020.

---

[4] These correspond to P/B ratios of 0.72 and 1.11, respectively.

5.3 SEQUENTIAL SCREENS BASED ON FAMOUS STRATEGIES

The portfolio manager's success lies in his or her ability to identify what it is that leads to superior stock returns. Many managers follow an investment style or philosophy that guides their choices, and they may think that this style or philosophy cannot really be quantified. Yet it is possible to devise quantitative stock screens from a wide range of investment approaches. In this section we examine some of the most successful equity managers' investment strategies—many of them qualitative or fundamental—and translate them into stock screens.[5] The philosophies of each manager and the screens that we built from them are also presented in Tables 5A.1 through 5A.6 in Appendix 5A.

Peter Lynch has come up several times already in this book, and as we have noted, he found success with a fairly qualitative portfolio strategy. However, in his books *One Up on Wall Street* (1989) and *Beating the Street* (1993), Lynch also expounds on certain quantitative methods that can be collected in a valuable screening methodology. The Lynch screen is a combination growth-and-value strategy that seeks a P/E ratio that is less than the industry average but also desires a price-to-earnings-to-growth (PEG) ratio that is less than 1.0. This indicates that the P/E ratio multiple is less than the growth rate in earnings and that the underlying company is generating strong bottom-line growth given its current market valuation. The P/E ratio to dividend yield is limited to stocks with a ratio of less than 4.0, which helps to provide adequate income and downside protection against further market deterioration. By restricting the growth rate in earnings to greater than 0% but less than 50%, we are including stocks with positive earnings momentum and excluding stocks that Lynch would believe to be at risk for failing to meet expectations owing to overly optimistic forecasts. Stocks with higher growth also may be candidates for accounting

---

[5] Our descriptions of these famous portfolio managers and professors and our interpretations of their approaches in the form of quantitative stock screens are based partly on our readings of books written by the managers and on information supplied by the American Association of Individual Investors (AAII). The stock screens we present may not be the actual methods by which these managers select equities. The managers have in no way endorsed the stock screens that we present here.

manipulation. An insider buying-to-selling ratio of greater than 1.5 also may shed light on management's view of the future of the business. Insider selling can occur for a variety of reasons, including a diversification of holdings. However, insider buying generally occurs only when management is optimistic about the future of the company and believes that the share price is undervalued. Further screening criteria include a long-term debt ratio of less than the industry median, a market capitalization of less than $5 billion, and institutional ownership of less than 50%. These criteria increase the possibility that the stocks are undervalued and improperly priced because they lack a large or sophisticated following of investors.

Warren Buffett is perhaps the most widely emulated investor in history. Numerous books have been written about his buy-and-hold strategy. By applying Robert Hagstroms' *The Warren Buffett Way* (1994) and perusing Berkshire Hathaway's annual reports, we were able to construct a simple screen based on Buffett's investment principles. We first decided to limit the screen to the top 30% market capitalization of listed equities on the New York Stock Exchange (NYSE), American Stock Exchange (AMEX), and NASDAQ, which would aid us in excluding small-cap securities. Buffett generally believes in purchasing stocks that have a strong competitive advantage and are capable of outperforming other companies and demanding a premium for their services. Most small-cap firms fail to possess such strong competitive advantages or the economies of scale necessary to compete against large industry titans. They therefore fail to generate the necessary free cash flow to fund expansion and wield pricing power. Buffett is extremely concerned with management's ability to operate efficiently and produce superior returns on equity. High free cash flow indicates management's ability to generate sufficient cash to fund its operations and reward its shareholders for taking on risk. Companies that do not generate sufficient free cash flow may be suffering from liquidity crunches or failing to collect payments on their sales. Hence two screening categories include return on equity (ROE) that is greater than or equal to 15% and free cash flow that ranks in the top 30% of listed securities in the investment database. Net profit margins should exceed industry averages, and the current D/E ratio should be in line with or lower than the industry median. Finally, forecasted free cash flow for the next five years should be greater than the current market price of the stock when discounted back to the present. This may indicate that the stock is undervalued and provides a "margin of safety" for uncertainty over future returns.

The Lakonishok screen is a value screen based on the work of Josef Lakonishok, the William G. Karnes Professor of Finance at the University of Illinois at Urbana-Champaign. Professor Lakonishok is also the CEO and founder of LSV Asset Management and has published widely in many prestigious academic journals. The crux of the Lakonishok screen is that some companies go out of favor with the market owing to overly pessimistic forecasts that depress their share prices. There is a great potential for profit for the patient investor who can identify which companies eventually will rebound from such depressed prices. The screen aims to avoid small companies that may not possess the necessary financial strength or customer base to weather the downturn. Therefore, part of the screen restricts our investment list to companies with market capitalizations in the top 30% of the NYSE, the AMEX, and the NASDAQ. To screen for undervalued stocks, the price-to-earnings (P/E) ratio and the price-to-book (P/B) ratio are set below their respective industry median values. The consensus earnings estimate for the next fiscal year must be greater than the forecasted earnings estimate for the current year. This helps to eliminate companies that are expected to continue on a dismal trajectory. The final step of the Lakonishok screen is to find companies whose stock returns have performed better than the S&P 500 over the last few months. This upward momentum may indicate the beginning of the turnaround, and it will help to filter out companies whose stock prices will continue to languish.

Another value screen similar to the Lakonishok screen but with an increased emphasis on the underlying financial condition of the firm is a screen based on the work of Stanford Professor Joseph Piotroski. Professor Piotroski is a world-renowned expert in financial statement analysis, and the Piotroski screen seeks to uncover undervalued firms with the necessary financial strength to succeed. As in the Lakonishok screen, market capitalization is restricted to the top 30% of the NYSE, AMEX, and NASDAQ. However, this criterion now takes a backseat to other financial ratios. The P/B ratio is restricted to the lowest 30% of listed securities in the database (the investment universe). Return on assets (ROA) must be positive, and both the debt-to-equity (D/E) ratio and the long-term debt-to-equity ratio are evaluated so as to exclude companies with overly burdensome debt obligations and inadequate financing. The current ratio and the cash ratio must be improving from the previous fiscal year to offer adequate liquidity to fund current operations. Finally, the asset turnover must show an improvement on a year-over-year basis, which helps to avoid companies that have failed to manage their assets efficiently and realize adequate top-line growth.

A seasoned money manager, David Dreman was the founder and chairman of Dreman Value Management LLC (the value strategies and funds were purchased by Foundry Partners in 2016). He is the best-selling author of several prominent books on the low P/E ratio contrarian value investment approach, including *Contrarian Investment Strategies: The Next Generation* (1998) and *Psychology and the Stock Market* (1977). The Dreman screen attempts to adopt some of the crucial tenets of Dreman's contrarian philosophy. He favors mid- to large-sized companies because he feels that they have greater visibility in a market rebound, and by being highly scrutinized by a variety of investors, they are less susceptible to accounting manipulation. We therefore have restricted our market capitalization to the top 25% of the S&P 1500. The contrarian strategy seeks out-of-favor stocks, and thus we have limited our investment options to stocks whose P/E ratios are in the lowest 40% of the S&P 1500. This helps to identify undervalued securities. A requirement that the D/E ratio be less than 1 and that the total-liabilities-to-total-assets ratio be less than the industry average ensures that the companies have adequate financial strength. A dividend yield above the S&P 500 dividend yield offers a cushion and provides downside protection to companies in a prolonged downturn. The final major criterion is that earnings growth must continue to outpace the S&P 500 and industry median levels on a current and forecasted basis. All these screening steps attempt to identify firms that may be trading below their historical price levels but still show potential for future development and bottom-line growth that has not yet been priced into the stock.

Another famous investor and one whom Warren Buffett studied extensively in developing his own investment philosophy is the late Philip Fisher. Fisher authored several books on his investment strategy, including *Common Stocks and Uncommon Profits* (1958) and *Conservative Investors Sleep Well* (1975). Fisher believed that the business cycle made annual sales growth inherently unpredictable and failed to convey the proper underlying ability of the business to succeed. Year-over-year metrics could be distorted easily by slight alterations in the business environment and therefore should be judged in light of other, longer-term trends. We therefore have decided to screen for companies whose sales have increased on a year-to-year basis for the last five years and whose three-year compound growth rates in sales are greater than their industries' median sales growth rates over the same period. This helps to smooth out the effects of the business cycle and include only companies that have consistently performed above average in a variety of economic conditions. Fisher also was interested in identifying growth that was a result of a low-cost advantage, strong marketing organization, a strong research and development enterprise, and excellent management depth with the utmost integrity. Growth was important, but only in the context of value, so we confined the PEG ratio to be greater than 0.1 but less than 0.5. This helps to ensure that the stock multiple neither gets ahead of the growth rate in earnings nor falls too far below it. Fisher believed that research and development (R&D) was an important component for maintaining a competitive advantage, but only if it could generate a high level of sales per R&D expense. Hence we have decided to add the criteria that R&D expenses as a percentage of sales be greater than the industry median ratio and that sales growth keep up with or exceed the growth in R&D expenses. Finally, we screen for companies that are not expected to pay a dividend and therefore are likely to reinvest any retained earnings for the future growth of the business.

Bill Miller was the CEO of Legg Mason Capital Management, Inc., a division of the Baltimore financial services firm Legg Mason (purchased by Franklin Templeton Investments in 2020). He managed the Legg Mason Value Trust from 1982 to 2016, beating the S&P 500 in 21 of those 35 years. In 2016, he left Legg Mason and created Miller Value Funds. Miller adheres to a value strategy that aims exclusively for securities that trade below their intrinsic value, as indicated by his multifactor valuation analysis. His strategy differs from that of many value managers in that it focuses on cash earnings rather than on accounting earnings. Many of his holdings, including positions in several "new economy" growth stocks such as internet high fliers Google, Amazon, and Facebook (as of the end of 2020), continue to be controversial among "pure value investors" owing to their speculative and/or growth qualities.

The Miller screen attempts to capture the core principles of his strategy by combining various financial metrics aimed at discovering undervalued companies that possess the necessary competitive advantage to sustain a high level of growth. The first major criterion in the Miller screen is that the current market capitalization of the company cannot exceed three times the total estimated free cash flow for the next five years. This is a value ratio that attempts to eliminate companies whose current market valuation appears overly optimistic and exceeds the amount of discretionary cash the business is expected to generate over the next several years. Free cash flow also should be increasing on a year-to-year basis. This helps to reaffirm Miller's emphasis on cash flows and cash earnings as the impetus behind the dynamics of valuation. The PEG ratio then is restricted to a level of 1.5 or below. A maximum of 1.0 may be too restrictive in this screen because we do not want to eliminate growth companies that may have P/E ratio multiples slightly higher than their growth rates but nevertheless still may possess vast potential that has failed to be discounted properly into the stock price. A skilled management team is highly crucial to success, and therefore, the Miller screen takes into account that gross margins should be increasing and that ROE should exceed the industry median. Finally, the long-term debt ratio should be below industry average levels to prevent future liquidity difficulties or cash-flow shortages.

The late Richard Driehaus was the founder of Chicago-based Driehaus Capital Management. It was one of the top small- to mid-cap money managers. His superior investment performance resulted in his acceptance to the elite *Barron's* All-Century Team of fund managers, whose members include such luminaries as Peter Lynch and Sir John Templeton.

The Driehaus screen is structured around earnings and price momentum. The initial steps focus on year-over-year positive and increasing earnings growth. The next major aspect of the Driehaus screen incorporates earnings surprises. Earnings surprises to the upside are taken as a positive signal of a company's ability to generate income and capitalize on its position in the market. A failure to meet expectations is taken as an indication that the company is failing to execute its strategy and that it may be facing increasing costs or intensified competition. The screen looks for companies that have had positive earnings surprises over the last fiscal year, meaning that the actual rate of earnings growth has exceeded analyst estimates during the most recent time period. The strategy also values surprises in which the range or standard deviation of the estimates is tighter or more significant on subsequent returns. Price momentum then is evaluated to ensure that there is sufficient buyer pressure on the stock price to encourage further demand and maintain an upward trajectory. The screen requires that the current market price be greater than its 200-day moving average, which indicates a long-term uptrend in the stock. The 50-day moving average then is set at greater than the 200-day moving average so that we can eliminate stocks whose momentum has already peaked. The on-balance volume (OBV), a technical indicator that compares price to volume, then is used to determine if the momentum is a net accumulation of shares or a distribution. Finally, the screen requires that the company be followed by fewer than five analysts so that there is a good chance of improper valuation, giving the astute investor an opportunity to purchase neglected securities and profit immensely when the market recognizes their potential.

Several other screens listed in the tables in Appendix 5A include the Neff contrarian screen, the Muhlenkamp screen, the Templeton screen, and the Dogs of the Dow screen. The Neff screen draws on the fundamentals of legendary Vanguard Windsor Fund manager and former *Barron's* Roundtable member John Neff. Neff's value strategy, explained in his book *John Neff on Investing* (1999), targets low P/E ratio stocks with strong sales growth, healthy operating margins, increasing free cash flow per share, and underhyped estimated earnings growth between 7% and 20%. The Muhlenkamp screen is a growth-and-value screen based on Ronald Muhlenkamp's investment strategies and mutual fund performance. It seeks an above-average and stable ROE figure over the last five years. It looks for strong earnings growth, low P/E and P/B ratios, and adequate liquidity, as indicated by the current ratio and others. The O'Shaughnessy value-and-growth screens are named after seasoned investor Jim O'Shaughnessy, who still manages the O'Shaughnessy Funds. Their strategy is to gather data on companies and turn those data into custom factors that can be used to evaluate each stock; these custom factors are then used to build a portfolio with the highest-ranking factor profiles while also managing risk exposures and implementation costs. The Templeton screen has an international focus rooted in the strategies of global pioneer investor Sir John Templeton.[6] It seeks value—through low P/B and P/E ratios, as well as strong forecasted and actual earnings-per-share (EPS) growth—in an entire universe of securities such as the Compustat database.[7] ROE and operating margins for the trailing 12 months should be above average, and financial strength should be strong enough to face a downturn in market conditions. Finally, the Dogs of the Dow screen is a simple strategy of choosing the top 10 highest-yielding stocks in the Dow Jones Industrial Average at the beginning of the year and holding them.

Further information on these screens and others, including background information, a description of the screen, and the actual screening steps, is included in Tables 5A.1 through 5A.6 of Appendix 5A.

5.4 SIMULTANEOUS SCREENING AND THE AGGREGATE Z-SCORE

In the preceding section we discussed the simplest type of screening, sequential stock screening. A more sophisticated way to refine the investment universe is to use multifactor simultaneous screening (a.k.a. *simultaneous screening*). In simultaneous screening, the portfolio manager still picks stocks according to a list of factors, but he or she screens for all the factors at once rather than one at a time. He or she therefore does not need to prioritize the factors in advance of screening. The entire list of factors is taken as a single set of criteria with which to evaluate all stocks in the investment universe.

Since the stocks undergo just one screen rather than multiple rounds, there is no chance of eliminating an otherwise good stock simply because it does not measure up during an early round of screening. For example, suppose that the portfolio manager believes that both the B/P ratio of a stock and its change in gross profit margin are equally important in selecting stocks. With sequential screening, he or she would have to make a choice to screen first for one factor or the other. If he or she screened first for high B/P ratio stocks, he or she might throw out a lot of companies

---

[6] Templeton died in 2008. Prior to that, he requested that a large part of his portfolio be placed in a short strategy, since he was convinced that there was trouble in the markets. In fact, he turned out to be correct, although he died before seeing the entire realization of his prediction.

[7] A low price relative to expected earnings in three to five years is also used as a forward-looking measure of value.

with tremendous profit growth. Simultaneous screening sidesteps this problem by considering stocks for both their B/P ratios and their profit growth concurrently.

Another benefit of simultaneous screening is that the portfolio manager is in no danger of running out of stocks. In sequential screening, the stock list gets smaller and smaller with each successive factor screen. When screening with four or more variables, it is not unusual to end up with a list of fewer than 20 stocks—hardly sufficient for an entire portfolio and probably not diversified in any case. Simultaneous screening preserves all the stocks in the universe and assigns each of them a score based on the whole set of factors.

Once a portfolio manager has chosen the list of factors, how does he or she screen for all of them at once? Unfortunately, since different types of factors are expressed in different units, adding all the factor values together does not work. For a two-factor list of the B/P ratio and size, trying to add a B/P ratio of 0.08 (P/B of 12.5) and a size of $36,026,000,000 would yield a meaningless number. It does not scale the factors, so the size, which is by far the larger factor in terms of absolute value, dominates the stock ranking.

The right way to aggregate factors is to *standardize* or *normalize* them. Standardization or normalization refers to transforming variables so that they are comparable with each other by converting them to a standard unit of measurement. The most commonly used standardization method is known as the *Z-score method*.[8]

5.4.1 The Z-Score

A population of data has a cross-sectional mean and variance. For example, as of December 2020, the average value of the B/P ratio for all stocks in the S&P 500 was 0.3577. The standard deviation of the

---

[8] This term originates from the idea of converting any normal distribution to a standard normal distribution. The new variable created by adjusting the raw data to a standard normal distribution is traditionally called a *Z-score*. The concept of aggregating Z-scores of different variables is loosely linked to the Altman Z-score due to Edward Altman's original model to try to predict stocks that would go bankrupt. The use of the Z-score in QEPM, however, is very different from the use originally proposed by Altman (1968). In Altman's original work, he used a concept known as *multiple discriminant analysis* (MDA) to aggregate financial ratios that would help to predict whether a firm would go bankrupt or not. The weights of the financial ratios were chosen through the statistical optimization of past data. A final Z-score would result for each stock. There was usually a cutoff value below which a stock would be predicted to go bankrupt. Our analysis is slightly different from Altman's, but the growth of these type of models in QEPM is most attributable to his original work.

B/P ratio of all firms in the S&P 500 was 0.3794.[9] We can use this information to standardize any value of B/P ratio for any stock in December of 2020. We obtain the Z-score value of any stock's B/P ratio by taking the difference between the stock's B/P ratio and the mean value of the B/P ratio for the universe of stocks and then dividing the difference by the standard deviation of the B/P ratios of all stocks in the universe. Standardizing the values of factors allows us to make clear statements about how far any particular observation is from the population mean. For example, if we find a company with a B/P ratio Z-score of 2, then we can say that the company's value is 2 standard deviations away from the population mean. The Z-score therefore shows how far a stock is from the norm.

The Z-score also allows us to compare the values of two different factors. Suppose that, as a portfolio manager, you think that companies with high B/P ratios and high profit growth are buys. There is one company whose normalized B/P ratio value is 2 (i.e., the company's B/P ratio is 2 standard deviations from the mean of all the companies' B/P ratios) and whose normalized value of profit growth is also 2. Since the values are normalized (or standardized), you can say that this particular company is as desirable from the perspective of the B/P ratio factor as from the perspective of the profit-growth factor. Also, since both factors are measured in the same units, you will be able to combine these factors into an aggregate Z-score.

In certain situations, standardization is truly normalization, and this is in part why this terminology is used. If the original cross-sectional distribution of the stocks' factor exposures is a

---

[9] The corresponding P/B ratios would be 2.795 for the average and 2.635 for the standard deviation of P/B (just the inverse of the numbers listed in the text). Table 5.2 shows the values for other representative factors for the S&P 500. The numbers for both E/P and B/P may be different than expected for several reasons. First, we are using the inverse of the common ratios. Second, and most important, we are using equal-weighted averages of stocks in the S&P 500 for the Z-score, whereas most published metrics for the S&P 500 are market-capitalization weighted. Third, some published indices eliminate negative P/E or P/B stocks and just average the remaining stocks—or they average the values substituting a value of zero for negative P/E or P/B stocks. Fourth, our data avoid look-ahead bias, since we use the most recent market value of a company and the book or earnings of three months prior, rather than the coincidental values. Fifth, our S&P 500 universe does not include REIT stocks or any stocks that do not have a CRSP share code of 10, 11, or 12. The reason for excluding REITs is that most quant models would not apply to REIT securities. It should be noted that none of these issues alter the basic composition of our S&P 500 universe. Using this S&P 500 universe, we divide the S&P 500 total market value by total earnings or total book value, which results in a P/B of 4.20 and a P/E of 36.82—figures closer to what is more familiar.

normal distribution—and many things in society follow a normal distribution—then we can make clear statements about how probable a particular observation is or how rare it is. For example, a normalized factor score of 2 would mean that the probability of obtaining a stock with a higher value would be less than 2.27%.[10]

Let's look at the mechanics of assigning Z-scores. First of all, a portfolio manager should make sure that the Z-scores match the underlying factor values. That is, if high Z-scores are going to represent good stocks and low Z-scores bad stocks, then the factors themselves must be expressed such that high values are good and low values are bad. For instance, if a high book-to-price (B/P) ratio is considered a good quality in a stock, then the B/P ratio must be used to create the Z-score, not the P/B ratio.[11] Once this issue is resolved, to create a Z-score for a factor, a portfolio manager needs to compute the mean (or average) value of the factor for all stocks in the investment universe.[12] Call this value $\bar{\beta}_k$ for factor k.[13] The next step is to compute the standard deviation of the factor across all stocks in the investment universe. Call this value $S(\beta_k)$ for factor k.[14] Putting these pieces together, the Z-score computation for stock i for factor k is

$$z_{i,k} = \frac{\beta_{i,k} - \bar{\beta}_k}{S(\beta_k)} \tag{5.1}$$

where $z_{i,k}$ represents the Z-score of factor k for stock i, which is the normalized value of the factor value.

---

[10] Standardizing or normalizing the factor values is based on the idea of converting a normal distribution to the standard normal distribution for analysis purposes. The reader can refer to any basic statistics book such as DeGroot (1986). The Z-score concept still works even if the underlying cross-sectional factor distribution is not normal. The Z-score still gives a sense of how far a variable is from the mean of the distribution. If it turns out that the factor distribution is normal, it simply means that you can make statements about the probabilities of factor Z-scores.

[11] The portfolio manager could use the P/B ratio to calculate the Z-scores, but he or she would need to remember to multiply all the Z-score values by -1 so that high Z-scores represented good stocks.

[12] Some portfolio managers who wish to have industry neutrality or believe that their factors are very industry sensitive will create Z-scores for each stock relative to its industry average. They will rank each stock within its industry rather than within the entire investment universe and for the portfolio select the best stocks within each industry.

[13] Most computer programs and software packages compute the mean very easily. The typical formula is $\bar{\beta}_k = (1/N) \Sigma_{i=1}^N \beta_{i,k}$, where N equals the number of stocks in the universe, and $\beta_{i,k}$ represents the factor exposure k for stock i.

[14] Most computer programs and software packages compute the standard deviation very easily. The typical formula is $S(\beta_k) = 1/(N-1) \Sigma_{i=1}^N (\beta_{i,k} - \bar{\beta}_k)^2$, where N equals the number of stocks in the universe, and $\beta_{i,k}$ represents the factor exposure k for stock i.

5.4.2 The Aggregate Z-Score

Multifactor simultaneous screening means screening for more than one factor (hence the name *multifactor*), but since all factors must be screened for simultaneously, they need to be combined into a single screening value for each stock. Once we have calculated a Z-score for every factor of every stock in the investment universe, calculating each stock's aggregate Z-score is fairly straightforward. Since Z-scores are *scale independent*, we can simply add them together. The sum of a stock's Z-scores is its *aggregate Z-score*.

There may be some individual factor or stock aggregate Z-scores with extreme values. Different portfolio managers will deal with these in different ways. If it seems that a Z-score is an *outlier*, then one control mechanism is to round all Z-scores above 3 down to 3 and similarly to round up all Z-scores below -3 to -3.[15] It is also possible to throw out stocks that have extreme Z-score values, but this may result in the loss of good information about potentially very high-return or very low-return stocks. In Appendix 5B, we discuss several methods to deal with outliers.

We can choose how to weight each of the factors within a stock's aggregate Z-score. One option is to weight all the factors equally. The aggregate Z-score with K factors then would equal

$$\bar{z}_i = \left(\frac{1}{K}\right)\left(z_{i,1} + z_{i,2} + z_{i,3} + \cdots + z_{i,K}\right) \qquad (5.2)$$

where $\bar{z}_i$ is the aggregate Z-score for stock i, and $z_{i,k}$ represents the Z-score for factor k and stock i. The equal weighting of Z-score factors is a common method portfolio managers use to compute aggregate Z-scores. Some portfolio managers prefer equal weighting to more sophisticated weighting schemes because it produces relatively more stable results.

5.4.3 Ad Hoc Aggregate Z-Score

There are also a number of ad hoc ways to weight the individual factor Z-scores within the aggregate Z-score. The portfolio manager can weight the factors according to his or her ex-ante beliefs or investing style. If he or she prefers the value factor above all others,

---

[15] An outlier is an observation in a distribution that is very far from the mean and has an extremely small probability of occurring. An outlier looks inconsistent with the rest of the data.

he or she can amplify its importance by assigning it a weight of 80% and dividing the remaining 20% weight among the rest of the factors. Factor Z-scores also can be weighted according to some interpretation of their relative levels of importance in influencing stock returns. It is important not to let this sort of weighting scheme be unduly influenced by past research or past reading, which could amount to "data snooping."[16] In any case, since weighting according to general ideas of factor importance and weighting by preference are not methods of quantitative portfolio management, we do not recommend these methods.

Some portfolio managers weight the factor Z-scores according to the factors' information ratios, obtained by creating decile or quintile portfolios of each factor and computing the factor's historical information ratio.[17] The higher the information ratio, the more important the factor is in predicting stock returns. Factors with high information ratios are weighted more heavily. This ad hoc procedure has more merits than weighting according to general notions of factor importance, although it still neglects the effect of the correlation between factors.

5.4.4 Optimal Aggregate Z-Score

Equally weighting the Z-score factors is a simple procedure. However, it ignores certain information contained in the data. It ignores the importance of each factor Z-score in predicting the returns of stocks. The ad hoc methods of weighting attempt to assign weights that vary with the perceived importance of the factors, but these methods are highly subjective. Both the equal weighting and ad hoc methods also fail to account for the correlation between factors. We can find better ways to weight the factor Z-scores. There are several *optimal weighting* methods.

One very common approach to optimal weighting is to use econometrics to estimate the optimal exposures using a historical sample data set. The portfolio manager takes a series of monthly returns on all the stocks in the universe, combined with the factor Z-score values for each stock at the beginning of the month, and

---

[16] The phenomenon of data snooping, which we discussed in Chapter 2, involves picking factors solely based on past reports of their usefulness without any statistical evidence that they continue to relate significantly to stock returns.

[17] For those unfamiliar with this process, it is discussed in more detail in Chapter 15.

runs a set of cross-sectional regressions over the sample period to find the optimal Z-score weights.[18]

Suppose that we have K factor Z-scores for each of the N stocks in the universe and that we have T periods of return information (e.g., 120 months of sample data). We can use the following econometric techniques to estimate the parameter exposures of each factor. This will tell us the best way to combine Z-scores so as to use the information contained in the variance-covariance matrix of Z-scores and returns. One can estimate the following regression with a sample of historical data:

$$r_{i,t} = \gamma_i + \delta_1 z_{i,1,t-1} + \delta_2 z_{i,2,t-1} + \cdots + \delta_K z_{i,K,t-1} + \epsilon_{i,t} \qquad (5.3)$$

where γ_i represents a constant term, δ_k is the coefficient estimate for the contribution of the factor Z-score k to the stock returns, and ϵ_i is a typical error term.[19] The regression can be estimated as a panel regression. The δ estimates are the optimal combination of the factor Z-scores.[20] The portfolio manager might run this type of regression over various horizons and time periods to check the robustness of the results.

A variation on the optimal weighting scheme is to determine the optimal weights for various economic scenarios. The portfolio manager constructs three or more hypothetical economic environments and calculates a set of optimal Z-score weights for each of

[18] The researcher should be very careful to avoid look-ahead bias, which is sometimes a problem when a portfolio manager uses historical factor data. The data set may contain a factor value for a certain month, but in that month, that piece of data would not have been available. By using data that the market did not have in that month, the quantitative portfolio manager has "looked ahead," potentially causing the model to estimate parameters incorrectly. A typical solution to look-ahead bias is to know the delivery lag of all factors that one is using and place a lag on the factor. For example, if you're using a factor that relates to March but is only reported in April, you may wish to use the $t-1$ value of that factor in any historical estimations. This is discussed in more detail in Chapter 16.

[19] When we typically estimate these factor models, we use information at time t to predict returns at time $t+1$ or similarly use information at time $t-1$ to predict returns at time t. Sometimes, in this book, for convenience, we write the equation with time subscript t everywhere and sometimes we explicitly write the expressions with factor exposure $t-1$ and returns of time t. In all cases, the reader should understand that we are using information at t to predict returns at time $t+1$. In other words, the factor exposure at time $t-1$ is the exposure value as of the end of period $t-1$, which we may refer to sometimes as the beginning of month exposure for time t.

[20] This regression also tells us how Z-scores are related to stock returns. In some cases, like when dealing with returns accounting for transactions costs, it is beneficial to convert Z-scores to returns. In Appendix 5C we suggest a crude way to do this.

them. This method requires the exercise of more subjective judgment than the original method does, but it gives the manager a chance to consider which way the economic winds are blowing and to weight the factors accordingly.

It might be useful to provide a simple example of the aggregate Z-score procedure using real stock data. For simplicity, we took a snapshot of stocks from the S&P 500 as of December 2020. Table 5.2 shows 10 selected stocks from the S&P 500 with their corresponding factor values for E/P, B/P, and D/E ratios, the natural logarithm of market capitalization (SIZE), and the 12-month momentum (M12M), i.e., the average monthly stock return over the previous 12 months.[21] These factors do not necessarily represent some phenomenal α model; they were chosen merely for illustration. One will notice that the table gives the mean and standard deviation of all stocks in the S&P 500 for the month of December 2020. We will need these values to compute the Z-scores.

To compute the Z-score for the B/P ratio factor of the tech company Apple, we need the value for $\beta_{AAPL,B/P} = 0.0290$ for December 2020. The mean for all the S&P 500 stocks is 0.3577 (i.e., $\bar{\beta}_{B/P} = 0.3577$), and the standard deviation is 0.3794 [i.e., $S(\beta_{B/P}) = 0.3794$]. Thus the Z-score for the B/P ratio factor for Apple is -0.866 [$z_{AAPL,B/P} = (0.0290 - 0.3577)/0.3794$]. Although the sign is negative for the Z-score, this does not necessarily imply that it will be a negative contribution to the aggregate Z-score. This will depend on the portfolio manager's ultimate belief regarding this factor. If the portfolio manager believes that a high B/P ratio is a negative for picking stocks based on his or her previous analysis, he or she should multiply this factor Z-score by -1 when computing the aggregate Z-score so that higher Z-scores imply a better stock.

One can continue computing the Z-scores for the other factors for Apple. They are all listed in the table. The aggregate Z-score then will be a combination of the individual Z-scores for each factor. In this example, we assume that the portfolio manager *equal-weights* the individual Z-scores. Thus the aggregate Z-score for Apple in December 2020 is equal to -0.645. It is important that in aggregating the individual Z-scores, the portfolio manager uses the appropriate

---

[21] Using the natural log of market capitalization might also be uncomfortable to some. In order to get the more standard market capitalization, just take the exponential of the value. For example, for Apple, exp (14.6251) = $2,255,991 million or $2.25 trillion.

TABLE 5.2

Selected Factor Exposures and Z-Scores of Selected Stocks

Ticker	Earnings-to-Price Ratio (E/P)	Earnings-to-Book Ratio (B/P)	Debt-to-Equity Ratio (D/E)	Log of Market Capitalization (SIZE)	Momemtum (M12M)	Z-Score of E/P	Z-Score of B/P	Z-Score of D/E	Z-Score of SIZE	Z-Score of M12M	Aggregate Z-Score
AAPL	0.0254	0.0290	3.96	14.6291	82.31	0.117	-0.866	-0.056	3.962	1.431	-0.645
MSFT	0.0282	0.0734	1.44	14.3353	42.53	0.136	-0.749	-0.224	3.688	0.582	-0.699
AMZN	0.0106	0.0507	2.41	14.3066	76.26	0.016	-0.809	-0.159	3.662	1.302	-0.599
GOOGL	0.0323	0.1927	0.41	13.9152	31.03	0.164	-0.435	-0.292	3.297	0.337	-0.588
TSLA	0.0008	0.0240	1.67	13.4134	743.44	-0.051	-0.880	-0.208	2.830	15.535	2.397
FB	0.0385	0.1793	0.24	13.3949	33.09	0.206	-0.470	-0.303	2.813	0.381	-0.479
BRK.B	0.0659	0.7637	0.98	13.2060	2.37	0.393	1.070	-0.254	2.637	-0.274	-0.239
JNJ	0.0410	0.1556	1.65	12.9344	10.85	0.223	-0.533	-0.210	2.384	-0.094	-0.516
WMT	0.0439	0.1847	1.92	12.9186	23.34	0.242	-0.456	-0.191	2.369	0.173	-0.444
JPM	0.0659	0.6223	10.97	12.8670	-5.52	0.392	0.697	0.410	2.321	-0.443	-0.417
S&P 500											
Mean	0.0083	0.3577	4.80	10.3737	15.24	0	0	0	0	0	0
SD	0.1468	0.3794	15.04	1.0741	46.88	1	1	1	1	1	

Note: The Market capitalization is in millions of dollars. Momentum is defined as the monthly cumulative return (in percentage terms) over the past 12 months. The stocks were selected from the S&P 500. Ticker symbols are for the following companies: Apple Inc. (AAPL), Microsoft Corporation (MSFT), Amazon (AMZN) Alphabet Inc. or Google (GOOGL), Tesla Inc. (TSLA), Facebook Inc. (FB), Berkshire Hathaway B shares (BRK.B), Johnson & Johnson (JNJ), Walmart Inc. (WMT), and J.P. Morgan Chase & Co. (JPM). All values were computed as of December 2020. The data were obtained from Compustat.

sign for each individual Z-score according to his or her beliefs. For example, to obtain the aggregate Z-score, we did the following:

$$
\begin{aligned}
z_{AAPL} &= \tfrac{1}{5}[z_{AAPL,E/P} + z_{AAPL,B/P} - z_{AAPL,D/E} - z_{AAPL,SIZE} + z_{AAPL,M12M}] \\
&= \tfrac{1}{5}[(0.117) + (-0.866) - (-0.056) - (3.962) + (1.431)] \\
&= -0.645
\end{aligned}
\tag{5.4}
$$

A negative sign precedes several factors' Z-scores because these factors are considered detrimental to stock returns. All individual factor Z-scores must possess the correct sign. The portfolio manager in this example likes stocks with high E/P and B/P and low D/E ratios, so the negative of the D/E Z-score is added to the total Z-score, while the E/P and B/P Z-scores are added as is. The manager also likes smaller-cap stocks, hence the negative sign in front of the Z-score for the SIZE. He believes that momentum in stock returns is a positive technical indicator, so the momentum Z-score is added to the total Z-score. For a different portfolio manager, the signs might be different. The important thing is consistency. If high exposure to a factor is supposed to boost stock returns, add the factor's Z-score to the total; if high exposure to a factor is supposed to hurt stock returns, subtract its Z-score.

Table 5.2 goes through the computations of Z-scores for nine other stocks from the S&P 500 in December 2020. A portfolio manager would do this for all stocks in his or her investment universe and then rank the stocks by their aggregate Z-scores to determine which stocks are the most and least attractive.

5.4.5 Factor Groups and the Aggregate Z-Score

Some quantitative portfolio managers choose to separate the K factors that they use into M factor groups. For example, suppose that we have a B/P ratio factor, an E/P ratio factor, and a price-to-sales (S/P) ratio factor. A manager might create a composite group known as the *valuation group* and place all three of these factors into the valuation group. He or she may do this for other factors as well.

Although dividing the factors into groups might seem at first like an arbitrary step, it offers several benefits. It organizes the screening process. Rather than having to keep track of a large group of K factors that all represent different attributes of stock returns, the manager will be able to look at the factors in sets of M groups that represent the essential forces that are believed to affect stock returns. This simplifies both modification of the model and presentation of performance results to an investment committee.

Second, a manager might be tempted to use only one factor to represent a category such as value. However, to the extent that there are idiosyncracies in the way individual factors represent the same concept, it might be better to collect more than one factor to represent the concept (e.g., using B/P, S/P, and E/P ratios to represent value rather than just the B/P ratio in isolation).

Third, by creating factor groups that represent fundamental forces on stock returns, a manager can easily change the weights (which represent the relative importance) of factor groups according to changing economic conditions or for other reasons.[21] Although one could change the relative weights of each of the K factors individually, it is easier to change the weights of M factor groups, where $M < K$.

Formally creating composite Z-scores using factor groupings is relatively straightforward. The following steps are very similar to the procedure for aggregate Z-scores discussed in the last section.

1. Determine the number of factor groups M. For example, if $M = 4$, we might have a *valuation composite*, a *profitability composite*, a *financial-soundness composite*, and a *technical composite*. These four composites or groups represent the four main themes that we believe predict stock returns in our investment universe.

2. Decide which factors to include in each factor group. For example, the manager might believe that B/P, E/P, and S/P ratios are all factors that determine value and place those in the valuation composite. He or she then might decide that gross profit margin belongs in the profitability composite. The inverse interest coverage ratio (IICR) and the firm's debt-to-equity ratio then might go in the financial soundness composite. Finally, the manager might put a factor such as momentum in the technical composite.

3. Compute all the factors for every stock in the investment universe. Thus, if there are N stocks in the investment

---

[21] For some procedures related to common tests for structural change, see Chow (1960), Toyoda (1974), Schmidt and Sickles (1977), Toyoda and Ohtani (1986), Ploberger et al. (1989), Banerjee et al. (1992), Stock (1994), Chu et al. (1995), and Hoyo and Llorente (1997). Some of these papers are also useful for parameter stability tests discussed earlier in the book.

universe and K factors, the investor will have to make $N \times K$ computations.

4. Compute the mean and standard deviation of each factor exposure in the cross section of all the stocks in the investment universe. These values should be stored. Label these as $\bar{\beta}_k$ and $S(\beta_k)$, respectively, for each factor k.

5. Compute the Z-scores for every factor and every stock. This is similar to the preceding section, where $z_{i,k} = (\beta_{i,k} - \bar{\beta}_k)/S(\beta_k)$ represents the Z-score of factor k for stock i, which is the normalized value of the factor value.

6. Compute the aggregate Z-score for *every factor group* for every stock. Thus, for each factor group, compute the group Z-score for stock i, that is,

$$\bar{z}_{i,m} = \sum_{k \in S_m} w_k^m z_{i,k} \tag{5.5}$$

where S_m is the set of factors in the mth factor group, w_k^m is the weight of factor k in the mth factor group (so that $\sum_{k \in S_m} w_k^m = 1$), and $z_{i,k}$ represents the Z-score of factor k for stock i. This weighted sum is computed for every factor group to obtain a factor group Z-score for every stock and every factor group.

7. Compute the aggregate Z-score for every stock in the universe. This is the final step for the ranking of the stocks. The final formula is to compute

$$\bar{z}_i = \sum_{m=1}^{M} w_m \bar{z}_{i,m} \tag{5.6}$$

where $\bar{z}_i$ is the aggregate Z-score for stock i, w_m is the weight given to the factor group m, and $\bar{z}_{i,m}$ is the factor group Z-score for group m for stock i.

This procedure is almost identical to the procedure for computing aggregate Z-score. The only real difference between the two is that here we have classified the individual factors into specific factor groups. We have not discussed how to weight the relative factor groups or how to weight the factors within factor groups. The methods available are similar to the ones we described in the preceding section. If the weighting scheme of the factors within groups and across groups is similar to the weighting scheme in the normal Z-score aggregation without groups, this final step should produce results similar to the results of the procedure that does not divide factors into groups.

Let's walk through a simple example of grouping factors. We return to the example from an earlier section that uses data for S&P 500 stocks for December 2020. Following the seven steps of factor grouping, our first step is to choose the number of groups. We choose four factor groups ($M = 4$). The groups are a *valuation composite*, a *profitability composite*, a *financial-soundness composite*, and a *technical composite*.

Our second step is to decide which factors will go in each composite. Suppose we decide on the following factors for our model: E/P, B/P, and S/P ratios; gross profit margin (GPM); IICR and D/E; and M12M.[22] It makes sense to place the first three factors in the valuation composite, the next one in the profitability composite, the next two in the financial-soundness composite, and the last one in the technical composite. See Table 5.3.

The third step is to compute the factor values for all stocks. We have listed these for selected stocks in Table 5.4. The fourth step is to compute the mean and standard deviation of all the factors for the investment universe. In this specific example, the S&P 500 is our investment universe. The mean and standard deviation of each factor are listed in the table as well. The fifth step is to compute the Z-scores for every factor, and the sixth step is to compute the Z-scores for each factor group. We equally weighted the Z-scores of

TABLE 5.3

A Possible Categorization of Factors into Composite Groups

Group Number	Factor Group	Factors
1	Valuation composite	Earnings-to-price ratio (E/P)
		Book-to-price ratio (B/P)
		Sales-to-price ratio (S/P)
2	Profitability composite	Gross profit margin (GPM)
3	Financial-soundness composite	Inverse interest coverage ratio (IICR)
		Debt-to-equity ratio (D/E)
4	Technical composite	12-month momentum (M12M)

---

[22] These acronyms for factors can be found in Abbreviations of Factor Names at the beginning of the book or in Appendix 16A.

each factor within a group to obtain the factor group Z-scores for each stock listed in the table.

The next step is to calculate the factor group Z-scores. As in the aggregate Z-score procedure, the factor Z-scores should be added together (or subtracted from each other) according to the way they are expected to contribute to (or detract from) stock returns. For example, to obtain the valuation Z-score of Microsoft ($z_{MSFT,V}$), we take our three valuation factors of Microsoft and equal-weight them, making sure the signs are correct.[23] Since the portfolio manager believes that higher E/P, B/P, and S/P ratios signal "good" attributes of stocks, each individual Z-score can be added together without multiplying by -1, that is,

$$
\begin{aligned}
z_{MSFT,V} &= \frac{1}{3}\left[z_{MSFT,E/P} + z_{MSFT,B/P} + z_{MSFT,S/P}\right] \\
&= \frac{1}{3}\left[\left(\frac{0.0282-0.0083}{0.1468}\right)+\left(\frac{0.0734-0.3577}{0.3794}\right)+\left(\frac{0.0875-0.6131}{0.9311}\right)\right] \quad (5.7)\\
&= \frac{1}{3}\left[(0.36)+(-0.799)+(-0.564)\right]=-0.393
\end{aligned}
$$

Applying the same process to each factor group, we can calculate other factor group Z-scores for Microsoft as well, including the profitability Z-score ($z_{MSFT,P}$ = 1.273), the financial-soundness Z-score ($z_{MSFT,F}$ = 0.231), and the technical Z-score ($z_{MSFT,T}$ = 0.582). Microsoft receives a poor valuation rating owing in particular to its unusually low B/P and S/P ratios. It scores a very good rating for profitability given its gross profit margin of 76.25% compared to the S&P 500 average of 43.26% and also receives a good rating for financial soundness due to its lower-than-average debt-to-equity ratio and lower-than-average inverse interest coverage ratio. Microsoft also earns decent marks for its technical group, directly due to the factor M12M: relative to the investment universe, its stock price has grown over the last year by 42.5% compared to the S&P 500 average of 15.24%. With an aggregate Z-score of 0.423, Microsoft is overall a mildly attractive stock as of December 2020, according to the set of criteria used in this example (see Table 5.4).

---

[23] Of course, alternative weighting schemes could be used.

TABLE 5.4

Selected Factor Exposures and Group Z-Scores of Selected Stocks

Ticker	Valuation Composite			Profitability Composite	Financial Soundness Composite		Technical Composite	Valuation Composite Z-Score	Profitability Composite Z-Score	Financial Composite Z-Score	Technical Composite Z-Score	Aggregate Z-Score
	E/P	B/P	S/P	GPM	IICR	D/E	M12M					
AAPL	0.0254	0.0290	0.1217	42.26	0.0428	3.96	82.31	−0.426	−0.038	0.148	1.431	0.279
MSFT	0.0282	0.0734	0.0875	76.75	0.0450	1.44	42.53	−0.393	1.273	0.231	0.582	0.423
AMZN	0.0106	0.0507	0.2129	47.06	0.0825	2.41	76.26	−0.408	0.144	0.188	1.302	0.307
GOOGL	0.0323	0.1927	0.1554	61.31	0.0079	0.41	31.03	−0.254	0.686	0.276	0.337	0.261
TSLA	0.0008	0.0240	0.0421	29.89	0.7534	1.67	743.44	−0.515	−0.508	0.016	15.535	3.632
FB	0.0385	0.1793	0.1203	89.23	N/A	0.24	33.09	−0.265	1.747	0.152	0.381	0.504
BRK.B	0.0659	0.7637	0.5136	25.73	0.0853	0.98	2.37	0.452	−0.666	0.234	−0.274	−0.064
JNJ	0.0410	0.1556	0.1952	74.65	0.0104	1.65	10.85	−0.253	1.193	0.234	−0.094	0.270
WMT	0.0439	0.1847	1.3290	26.71	0.1052	1.92	23.34	0.185	−0.629	0.197	0.173	−0.018
JPM	0.0659	0.6223	0.3437	73.54	N/A	10.97	−5.52	0.267	1.151	−0.205	−0.443	0.192
S&P 500												
Mean	0.0083	0.3577	0.6131	43.26	0.4523	4.80	15.24					
SD	0.1468	0.3794	0.9311	26.31	1.7088	15.04	46.88					

Note: For factor and ticker symbols, see Table 5.2. All values are as of December 2020. The data were obtained from Compustat. Some companies, such as J.P. Morgan and Facebook, had a missing value for interest expense for December 2020. We thus gave them a "neutral" Z-score of zero for this particular factor.

5.5 THE AGGREGATE Z-SCORE AND EXPECTED RETURN

5.5.1 Expected Return Implied by the Z-Score

Expected stock returns can be found from aggregate Z-scores by performing a regression of actual stock returns against the aggregate Z-scores. This can be done using a panel series regression of stock returns on the Z-score of the prior periods (e.g., of the previous months). The regression would take the form

$$r_{i,t} = \gamma_i + \delta z_{i,t-1} + \epsilon_{i,t} \tag{5.8}$$

where γ_i represents a constant term,[24] δ is the coefficient that relates the aggregate Z-score to the stock return, and $\epsilon_{i,t}$ is a typical error term. Given the estimates of γ_i and δ, the expected return of stock i for time $T + 1$ can be written as (see Fig. 5.1)

$$E(r_{i,T+1}) = \gamma_i + \delta z_{i,T} \tag{5.9}$$

There are some problems with this methodology. First, Z-scores may not change much from one period to another, but factor premiums may change substantially. Thus one's estimated coefficients may not be stable or reliable. One way to reduce this problem is to run panel regressions on a larger period of historical data rather than just one single cross-sectional regression over one particular period.[25]

The second problem is that there may be a low correlation between the Z-score and the subsequent returns. While we are

FIGURE 5.1

Timeline.

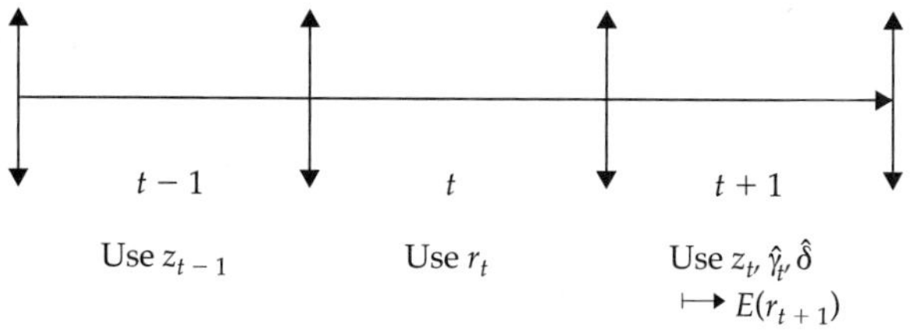

$t-1$ t $t+1$

Use z_{t-1} Use r_t Use z_t, $\hat{\gamma}_i$, $\hat{\delta}$
                                                 $\longmapsto E(r_{t+1})$

---

[24] If a single-period cross-sectional regression were used instead of a panel series regression, then there would not be a γ for each stock; thus γ_i would be replaced by γ.

[25] Panel regressions consist of using a time series of cross-sectional data to estimate the coefficients.

using Z-scores at time t to predict stock returns at time $t+1$, the link might be rather weak because the equation is not based on a rigorous theory.

The third problem with this procedure is that it adds complexity to the process, which is a weakness given that the biggest strength of the aggregate Z-score model is its simplicity.

5.5.2 Forecasting Rule of Thumb

Many portfolio managers are familiar with the *forecasting rule of thumb* and love to talk about it.[26] We personally do not understand what makes this equation so exciting because it is essentially an algebraic manipulation of a simple regression equation. We will make a few comments about it, though, because it may have some limited use in QEPM.

One can manipulate Eq. (5.8) and obtain the following:

$$
\begin{aligned}
E\left(r_{it} \mid z_{i,t-1}\right) - E\left(r_t\right) &= \delta\left[z_{i,t-1} - E\left(z_{t-1}\right)\right] \\
&= \frac{C\left(r_t, z_{t-1}\right)}{V\left(z_{t-1}\right)} z_{i,t-1} \\
&= \rho\left(r_t, z_{t-1}\right) S\left(r_t\right) z_{i,t-1} \\
&\equiv IC \cdot \text{volatility} \cdot \text{score}
\end{aligned}
\tag{5.10}
$$

In this equation, IC is by definition the correlation between the aggregate Z-score or raw signal and the actual security returns, the volatility in this particular case represents the cross-sectional volatility of the returns of the securities, and score refers to the aggregate Z-score.[27]

Although this is a neat formula, the portfolio manager should be sufficiently well versed in econometrics not to need this transformation of variables to make a connection between the raw scores or aggregate Z-score and the actual returns or residual

---

[26] This concept was popularized by Richard Grinold (1989). Significant research discussing and expanding our understanding of this law has been done since it was proposed [see Bolshakov and Chincarini (2020), Buckle (2004), Chincarini and Kim (2007), Clarke and Martin (2002), Ding and Martin (2017), Hallerbach (2014), Van Loon (2018), Ye (2008), and Zhou (2008a, 2008b)].

[27] Because $E(z_{t-1})$ is zero and $S(z_{t-1}) = 1$, we can achieve the second to last part of the derivation. This is so because the Z-score is already normalized.

returns of the security. This equation would be helpful if, for some reason, it were easier to compute IC and volatility than to run a regression. Otherwise, the equation does not add much to the screening process.[28]

5.5.3 The Equivalence between the Z-Score Model and the Fundamental Factor Model

We can show that the Z-score model of Eq. (5.8) produces an expected return identical to that of the fundamental factor model under certain conditions. Specifically, if *the factor premium is inversely proportional to the standard deviation of the factor exposure*, then the aggregate Z-score model produces the same result as the fundamental factor model.

Let us assume that the factor premium is inversely proportional to the standard deviation of the factor exposure. Let β_k be the exposure to the kth factor and f_k be the premium on the kth factor. Then

$$f_k = \frac{c}{\sqrt{V(\beta_k)}} \tag{5.11}$$

where c is a constant. Then the fundamental factor model can be rewritten as

$$
\begin{aligned}
r_i &= \alpha_i + \beta_{i,1} f_1 + \cdots + \beta_{i,K} f_K + \epsilon_i \\
&= \alpha_i + c \frac{\beta_{i1}}{\sqrt{V(\beta_1)}} + \cdots + c \frac{\beta_{iK}}{\sqrt{V(\beta_K)}} + \epsilon_i \\
&= \tilde{\alpha}_i + c z_i + \epsilon_i
\end{aligned}
\tag{5.12}
$$

where $\tilde{\alpha}_i$ is a constant defined as

$$\tilde{\alpha}_i = \left[\alpha_i + c \frac{E(\beta_1)}{\sqrt{V(\beta_1)}} + \cdots + c \frac{E(\beta_N)}{\sqrt{V(\beta_N)}} \right] \tag{5.13}$$

---

[28] The equation we present here differs from Grinold and Kahn's original description because they use actual signals or raw forecasts prior to normalizing the variables. The actual regression of the returns on the raw signals or factors creates this equation where by definition the raw forecasts are normalized. This is why regressions are convenient: You don't have to normalize prior to estimating them. They normalize for you. It is therefore difficult to see the magic in this formula.

Equation (5.12) shows the relationship between the parameters of the aggregate Z-score model and the parameters of the fundamental factor model.

Certain conditions may give rise to an inverse proportionality between the factor premium and the standard deviation of the factor exposure. When the factor exposure variation is large, even a small factor premium can affect the excess return tremendously. Thus, to preserve the overall excess return of the universe, it might make sense to have the factor premium be proportional to the inverse of the standard deviation of the factor exposure. This would imply that a factor with extremely high variation has a low factor premium, thus in some sense preserving the balance of excess return.

5.6 THE AGGREGATE Z-SCORE AND THE MULTIFACTOR α

Ultimately, most portfolio managers will have to optimize their portfolios versus a benchmark and cannot apply ad hoc weightings to the stocks in the portfolio. Typically, many portfolio managers will use commercial software to perform the optimizations versus a benchmark.[29] Commercial software allows the user to supply the multifactor α (i.e., the part of the expected return that a multifactor model cannot explain). Many portfolio managers transform the aggregate Z-score into a multifactor α. In this section we examine three popular methods for doing this, discussing the strengths and weaknesses of each method.

Perhaps the simplest method is a one-to-one transformation that uses the actual Z-scores as α's. Although the aggregate Z-scores clearly do not represent the actual excess returns of the stocks, they do represent the relative ranking of each stock in the manager's mind. Thus, we could just use the Z-score as a surrogate for the α of each stock. One immediate problem with doing this is that if the Z-scores do not really represent returns, they could distort the stock-selection process by favoring stocks with extremely high predicted Z-scores much more than is justified by real excess return

---

[29] Common commercial software platforms include Factset, FTSE BIRR, MSCI Barra, Northfield, and Qontigo's Axioma. For more details, see Appendix D at www.ludwigbc.com under QEPM Exclusive Content. In Chapter 9 we show how a quantitative portfolio manager can build his or her own portfolio optimization models.

potential. Fortunately, though, if the Z-scores are treated for outliers, such as using either windsorization, the IQR method, or the Rank method, the Z-scores will reside within a limited range (e.g., $+3$ to -3). In the extreme case of limiting Z-scores to a range of $+3$ to -3, the highest α a particular stock can have is 3% above its expected return, and the worst it can have is 3% below its expected return, with most values falling somewhere between $+1$ and -1.[30] Therefore, one could add the aggregate Z-score to the expected return of each stock predicted by a risk model. If one uses a standard commercial software package to build the portfolio, then the software will add these aggregate Z-scores to the expected returns of each stock according to the software's risk model. One then performs an optimization to form the portfolio.[31] The basic point is that if the portfolio manager has constructed trimmed aggregate Z-scores, one method to convert aggregate Z-scores to the α of each stock is just to do a one-to-one mapping in which the α of each stock equals the aggregate Z-score of each stock.

The second method is to use the expected excess return from Eq. (5.9) as α. This is a more accurate method since the empirical relationship between the Z-score and actual stock returns is taken into account.

The third method is more complicated. This method attempts to link the Z-score to residual stock returns rather than actual stock returns. The residual stock returns can be computed with respect to a multifactor model or a benchmark. The idea is to obtain all stocks' factor exposures and factor premiums and use them to calculate historical α. Then one can estimate the relationship between α and the aggregate Z-score from the following regression:

$$r_{i,t} - \hat{\beta}_i' f_t = \gamma_i + \delta z_{i,t-1} + \epsilon_{i,t} \tag{5.14}$$

where $r_{i,t}$ is the return of stock i at time t, $\hat{\beta}_i$ is the estimated factor exposures of stock i, f_t represents the realized factor exposures at time t, γ_i represents a constant term, δ is the coefficient that relates the aggregate Z-score to α, and $\epsilon_{i,t}$ is a typical error term.[32] Then the

---

[30] If the factor distribution were truly normal, then 68% of the stocks would fall into this area.
[31] The process of portfolio optimization is discussed in significant detail in Chapter 9.
[32] There are several ways to estimate this equation. For example, one could use a set of data to estimate the factor exposures, $\hat{\beta}_i$, to factor premiums (or benchmark returns) of each stock. In the next sequential period of data, given the stock returns and realized factor premiums (or benchmark returns), the residual returns are regressed against Z-scores to obtain the relationship between Z-score and residual returns.

portfolio manager can use the estimates from this equation to fore-cast the α's of all the stocks for the next period ($t + 1$) given their aggregate Z-scores for time t. Thus, with the estimated coefficients, the portfolio manager can translate aggregate Z-scores into α's. These values eventually will be used with a risk optimizer to create a portfolio of stocks.

There are drawbacks to all three of these methods. It may intro-duce serious distortion if the data behind the Z-score and the data behind the factor model are not sufficiently different. In such a case, the information criterion will be violated.[33] The second and third methods also require more computation, and the improvement in the optimization may not compensate for the added complication. Finally, the third method requires more estimation periods and more stability of estimates through time to be meaningful.

5.7 CONCLUSION

This chapter introduced the aggregate Z-score model of stock selec-tion. We began by discussing the concept of sequential stock screen-ing because it is one of the simplest quantitative methods of picking stocks and easy for most investors to understand. We also discussed some of the investing styles of famous portfolio managers and translated their approaches into sequential stock screens.

While sequential stock screening is a very useful starting point, it is not as efficient or as commonplace in the portfolio management world as multifactor simultaneous stock screening. Using what we call the aggregate Z-score model, we showed how to standardize or normalize all stock return factors in order to perform multifactor simultaneous stock screening. We focused on Z-score standardiza-tion across stocks in the entire universe but also discussed the fact that some portfolio managers might choose to standardize the Z-scores by industry or sector and then select representative sam-ples of stocks from each industry or sector. Finally, we introduced the concept of factor groups as a means of further structuring and clarifying the screening process.

The aggregate Z-score model is helpful in its simplicity, but it has the drawback of ranking stocks relatively instead of directly estimating the stocks' expected returns or α's. The portfolio man-ager who does not manage against a benchmark does not need to

---

[33] We discussed this issue in Chapter 3. Also see Chincarini and Kim (2007).

worry about this because he or she simply can pick the stocks that are most attractive and weight them using any of a variety of methods (e.g., equal weighting the 100 top-ranked stocks). However, for a portfolio manager who manages against a specific benchmark (e.g., the S&P 500), it is necessary to know the expected returns in order to perform a risk optimization versus the benchmark. We have suggested some ways to convert the aggregate Z-scores into the stocks' expected returns or α's. The last step in the portfolio process for portfolio managers who use the aggregate Z-score model is to combine the model with a risk optimizer and create the portfolio of stocks with stock weights.

Stock screening can serve as the basis for a model of stock returns, but in QEPM it is usually just a preliminary step in creating the portfolio. In the next chapters we delve into the core of QEPM, which is the factor model. We introduced factor models in Chapter 3. Now that we are familiar with the various kinds of factors at our disposal, some methods for choosing them, and the option of screening the investment universe, we are ready to take a closer look at how to gather factors into a quantitative model of stock returns. We look first at the fundamental factor model in Chapter 6 and then at the economic factor model in Chapter 7.

A List of Stock Screens Based on Well-Known Strategies

TABLE 5A.1

Well-Known Stock Strategies of Individuals

Screen Name	Background	Description
Buffett	Perhaps the most ubiquitous and famous investor ever, Warren Buffett is currently chairman of Berkshire Hathaway. Berkshire was once a stalwart textile company that Buffett acquired in 1965 and converted into an investment vehicle. Over the period 1965–2020, Buffett earned an average annual rate of return of 20%, pummeling the S&P 500 by 9.8% per year.[1] These extraordinary returns helped propel Berkshire Hathaway to a total annual compounded rate of return of 2,810,526% vis-à-vis the S&P 500's total return of 23,454% over the same period. His "Letter to Shareholders" in Berkshire Hathaway's Annual Reports is one of the most widely read market commentaries on the Street. Buffett's witty stories, common-sense investment approach, and continued success have made him a modern-day legend among investors of all classes.	Known to many as the "buy and hold" approach, this strategy concentrates its efforts on a relentless search for companies selling below their intrinsic values, or what Buffett describes as the "discounted value of the cash that can be taken out of a business during its remaining life."[2] This measure of value is dependent on a variety of conditions that the analyst must forecast, including interest rates, estimates of future cash flows, business prospects, and other valuable competitive advantages. Some measures of value may include a P/E ratio below those of comparable firms, a high book-to-market value, or a high amount of free cash flow to equity. Buffett believes that the more one knows about a particular business, sector, or industry, the better one will be at making assumptions to value it. Therefore, following the Buffett strategy involves purchasing only stocks whose underlying business one truly understands and avoiding all others, even if they possess huge growth potential. With the exception of Apple Computers (in 2016), Buffett generally avoids investing in technology stocks because he does not believe he understands the companies' business models well (even though one of his best friends is Microsoft Chairman Bill Gates!).

Screen Name	Background	Description
Dreman contrarian value	A seasoned money manager, David Dreman was founder and chairman of Dreman Value Management LLC (the value strategies and funds were purchased by Foundry Partners in 2016). He is the author of several prominent books on the low P/E, contrarian value investment approach, including *Contrarian Investment Strategies: The Next Generation* (1998) and *Psychology and the Stock Market* (1977).	This contrarian strategy attempts to pick stocks that have gone out of favor with the public and avoid stocks that are "hot." This usually involves starting with stocks with low P/E ratios relative to the stock universe. Dreman advocated starting with stocks with P/E ratios in the bottom 40% of the universe. Dreman seeks companies with high dividend yields to contribute to total return. He favors large to midsized companies that have good visibility in a market rebound and, due to investor scrutiny, are less susceptible to accounting manipulation. Dreman favors companies of financial fortitude that can endure even when they fall out of favor with investors. Just because it's cheap doesn't mean it's good, so Dreman seeks companies with high earnings growth relative to the S&P 500. Finally, Dreman believes diversification is extremely important. Thus the investor should pick at least 20 to 30 stocks and spread the picks across a variety of industries.
Driehaus growth	Richard Driehaus was the founder of Chicago-based Driehaus Capital Management. It was one of the top small- to mid-cap money managers. He was part of *Barron's* All-Century Team, a group of 25 fund managers that includes such great investors as Peter Lynch and the late John Templeton. His strategies are discussed in *Investment Gurus* (1997) by Peter J. Tanous.	This approach favors companies with momentum in earnings and price. At the core of this strategy are earnings surprises. Companies with positive earnings surprises are buys, and companies with negative earnings surprises are sells. An earnings surprise can be defined many ways. One common definition is actual earnings versus the consensus of all analysts' forecasts. The strategy also values surprises in which the range or standard deviation of estimates is tighter, which has a more significant impact on subsequent returns. Investors also should focus on early earnings announcements that could signal upcoming earnings. In this strategy, one must determine what constitutes a sufficiently large surprise and what is the minimum number of analysts that should follow a stock to consider it valid. These are subjective variables. This strategy looks for companies with positive price momentum over the last four weeks. The strategy also considers how stocks do on a relative strength

TABLE 5A.1 *(Continued)*

Screen Name	Background	Description
		basis versus the S&P 500 and how the stocks' industries do versus the S&P 500. Driehaus preferred small- to mid-cap stocks for this strategy and avoided international stocks, thereby excluding ADRs. The investor also may wish to monitor liquidity in terms of trading volume to make sure the chosen stocks are tradable for the size of the portfolio.
Fisher growth/value	Philip A. Fisher's investment philosophy is described in several books that he wrote, including *Common Stocks and Uncommon Profits* (1958), *Conservative Investors Sleep Well* (1975), and *Developing an Investment Philosophy* (1980). His works have subsequently been published in *Common Stocks and Uncommon Profits and Other Writings by Philip A. Fisher* (1996).	Fisher speaks about relying on recommendations of investment professionals for some screening, so analyst recommendations are a good source of data for a strategy based on his thinking. The Fisher-based strategy involves identifying growth stocks along several dimensions, including excellent management, long-term growth potential due to the company's product line, and a competitive advantage over others in the industry. Fisher sought companies that passed his 15-point system. This system consists of a product that could result in a significant increase in sales in the future, a low-cost advantage in the industry, a strong marketing organization, a strong R&D department, effective cost analysis and accounting, financial strength, management with superior skills, good working relationship among the management team, management with a depth of skills, management that works well together, management with integrity, good labor relations, good and honest investor relations, above-average profitability, and an ability to prevent competitors from entering the company's space in the market. Fisher focused primarily on the manufacturing industry, which he understood best. However, his approach can be applied to other industries. The strategy does not discriminate based on the size of the firm. Fisher believed in limits to diversification and thought that 20 stocks were sufficient in a portfolio. He recommended selling when you realize your analysis is wrong but not out of short-term considerations.
Lakonishok value	Josef Lakonishok is currently the William G. Karnes Professor of Finance at the College	The Lakonishok strategy rests on the belief that certain companies that go out of favor will return to favor if the investor is patient. The idea is to purchase companies with P/B, P/E,

Screen Name	Background	Description
	of Business, University of Illinois at Urbana-Champaign. He is also the CEO and founder of LSV Asset Management. For more information, see Lakonishok et al. (1994).	P/S, and P/CF ratios lower than the industry averages. The strategy could lead the investor to purchase absolute disaster companies. In order to prevent this, Lakonishok advises picking companies that are starting to rebound, either by price return or by analyst revisions.
Lynch growth/value	Peter Lynch is known for his success as the portfolio manager of the Fidelity Magellan Fund from 1977 to his retirement in 1990. His record was impressive. Peter Lynch earned an annual average rate of return of 29.23% compared to the S&P 500 annual return of 15.81%. When Lynch took the helm at Fidelity Magellan, the fund had a mere $20 million in assets. When he retired in 1990, Magellan had grown to a mammoth $14 billion in assets. Lynch is a fundamental portfolio manager, not a quantitative one. He did a lot of research that is hard to model with data (e.g., on Hanes pantyhose). His strategies are detailed in his books *One Up on Wall Street* (1989) and *Beating the Street* (1993).	Lynch's strategy is to know the businesses he invests in very well. A screen based on this sort of strategy is slightly more involved than one based on a quantitative approach. One of the first steps involves computing a modified PEG ratio, which Lynch defines as the P/E ratio divided by the growth rate of earnings plus the dividend yield. A ratio below 1.0 is considered attractive and above 1.0 unattractive. Lynch also seeks stable and consistent earnings. The strategy avoids stocks with enormous, probably unsustainable earnings growth. The target firms are relatively neglected. Thus one might look for stocks with low institutional ownership or analyst coverage. One must observe the size of the firm or its geographic reach, since Lynch thinks that a firm with a small market share has more room to grow than one with a large market share. The Lynch strategy involves finding companies with strong balance sheets and low debt relative to their industries. The strategy considers net cash per share; a high value relative to the industry is best. Finally, Lynch likes to check whether insiders are buying the stock or if the company is buying back shares, either event a potentially positive sign for the company's future.
Miller value	Bill Miller was the CEO of Legg Mason Capital Management Inc., a division of the Baltimore financial services firm Legg Mason (purchased by Franklin Templeton Investments in 2020). He currently manages money at his own firm, Miller	Miller's strategy focuses on identifying securities that are trading below their intrinsic value, as indicated by his multifactor valuation analysis. Miller differs from many value managers in that his approach focuses on cash earnings, not accounting earnings. The strategy seeks to uncover firms that may be undervalued based on the

TABLE 5A.1 *(Continued)*

Screen Name	Background	Description
	Value Funds. During his tenure managing the Legg Mason Value Trust from 1982 to 2016, he beat the S&P 500 in 21 of those 35 years.	present value of future cash flows to the firm and its shareholders. Diversification represents a crucial element in Miller's strategy. However, the strategy aims for diversification among the stocks it incorporates rather than sheer quantity. In fact, Miller's strategy generally has been to hold very few stocks (at the end of 2020, the Miller Opportunity Trust fund had only 42 holdings) while placing a larger emphasis on the research that goes into valuing the companies he does include. Annual turnover generally has been around 20%, which is the equivalent of holding a stock for 5 years. By focusing on companies that are being shunned by the market, this strategy takes on higher risks in hope of higher returns. The value moniker also can be misleading because Miller screens for a wide variety of stocks and has purchased many internet "growth" stocks.[3]
Muhlenkamp growth/value	Ronald Muhlenkamp founded Muhlenkamp & Company in 1977. His firm manages accounts for individuals and institutions. The Muhlenkamp Mutual Fund (MUHLX) was launched in 1988. The Muhlenkamp Fund has underperformed the S&P 500 for the last 15 years (through December 2020).[4]	This strategy involves searching for companies with ROEs above the historical average for all companies. One might also look for ROEs that have remained stable over the last five years. The company should be well priced according to the P/E ratio. The strategy looks for companies with higher earnings growth than that of their industry peers. One also should look at profit and cost control via a factor such as the operating profit margin of the firm relative to its industry. As do many famous strategies, this one looks at financial stability, both through liabilities as a ratio to assets and through the amount of free cash flow of the firm. Muhlenkamp also considers labor relations. Although labor relations are a relatively qualitative dimension, data from MSCI KLD or other firms can be used to assess them. Finally, Mulhenkamp believes no model works for all time periods; thus you must adapt your model to the times. This might require reestimating model parameters on some regular basis.

Screen Name	Background	Description
	John Neff was the portfolio manager of the Vanguard Windsor Fund from 1964 until his retirement in 1995. Neff wrote a book entitled *John Neff on Investing* (1999). For many years prior to his death in 2019, Neff was a member of the distinguished *Barron's* Roundtable.	Neff's strategy involves finding low P/E ratio stocks. A company should have strong earnings growth forecasts, but not so strong that the forecasts might represent investor hype (somewhere between 7% and 20%). The Neff strategy finds companies with high DY ratios. Ultimately, Neff wants to find stocks with the lowest dividend-adjusted PEG ratios, the PEG ratio equaling the P/E ratio divided by the stock's rate of earnings growth. Low PEG ratio stocks fit what he called the "cheapo" profile. The strategy also advocates strong sales growth, free cash flow after paying for capital expenditures, and good operating margin relative to the industry. Neff also strongly encourages looking for little-known stocks.
O'Shaughnessy growth	James O'Shaughnessy, chairman and co-CIO of O'Shaughnessy Asset Management and founder of NetFolio, a basket-trading firm, gives his insights into stock picking in his book *What Works on Wall Street* (1998). O'Shaughnessy believes that consistency beats the market and that many investors fail to be consistent in their investment approaches.	Within the strategies typically used to pick growth stocks, O'Shaughnessy found that earnings growth and relative strength were the key factors of successful portfolios. He found that persistent earnings growth (e.g., over last five years) is key. Stocks with the highest earnings growth are not necessarily the ones to buy. He also found that stocks with the highest relative strength, which he defined as the largest price increase in the previous year, continue to do well for at least one year. This is more commonly known as a *momentum strategy*. The last growth strategy involves picking stocks in the upper half of the market capitalization spectrum. A possible revised earnings screen thus looks for companies with four consecutive years of growth in earnings. To avoid overvaluation, O'Shaughnessy caps the P/S ratio at 1.5 (sales per share of recent 12 months). Finally, the 50 stocks with the highest relative price growth in the last 12 months are chosen for the portfolio.
O'Shaughnessy value	See above.	O'Shaughnessy's value strategy centers on what he terms the "investable universe." This is a stock universe sufficiently liquid for the portfolio managers' trades. The definition of the investable universe is subject to

TABLE 5A.1 *(Continued)*

Screen Name	Background	Description
		interpretation and to the size of the portfolio one is trading, but we limit it to the top 50% of stocks, on the exchange by market capitalization. Next, screen for stocks with the lowest P/E, P/B, P/S, P/CF, and highest DY ratios. (Data mining is a worry with this strategy because O'Shaughnessy tested a vast number of factors and chose the ones that worked.) The next element of the strategy is to choose stocks with more shares outstanding than the average stock in the universe, cash flows per share that exceed the universe average, and total sales 1.5 times the universe average. The final step is to select the 50 stocks with the highest dividend yield, excluding utility companies.
Piotroski value	Joseph D. Piotroski is a professor of accounting at Stanford University. He is an expert on financial statement analysis and researches the impacts of financial information on equity prices and valuation, market expectations, and behavioral investment. For more info, see Piotroski (2000).	The idea of the strategy based on Piotroski's work is to find extremely low P/B ratio stocks that have been ignored by analysts or experienced financial distress and about which the flow of information is inefficient. A nine-point scale of financial condition identifies firms with improving financial health. The firms also must meet a minimum profitability standard. Finally, the firms must have positive ROA growth and meet accounting, financial leverage, liquidity, and operating efficiency criteria.
Templeton growth/value	Sir John Templeton founded the famous Templeton Mutual Fund family. He was a student of Benjamin Graham, and his investment approach was rooted in hunting for bargains. Templeton was also known for his contrarian nature, which led him to buy when the majority was selling and vice versa. In his quest to find bargains anywhere, he purchased stocks both domestically and	The foundation of the Templeton strategy is finding value stocks or stocks with low P/B or similar ratios. However, the strategy goes further in trying to separate "bad" value from "good." This strategy looks for value stocks that have favorable future earnings growth. A company's P/E ratio must sit below its five-year average. One should be wary of companies with abnormally high P/E ratios and perform the standard trimming of outliers (discussed in Appendix 5B). Companies should be selected for positive earnings growth in the last 12 months, as well as the last five years. The strategy also involves choosing firms with positive five-year earnings growth estimates from analysts. In order to capture the competitive advantage idea of Templeton, one might search for stocks that

Screen Name	Background	Description
	internationally. Books on Templeton's investment philosophy include *Lessons from the Legends of Wall Street* (2000) by Nicki Ross and *Money Masters of Our Time* (2000) by John Train.	have higher estimated rates of earnings growth in the next five years than the industry average. The strategy calls for firms with positive operating margins over the last 12 months and a 12-month operating margin greater than the 5-year average. Finally, since financial strength was important to Templeton (as it was to Peter Lynch), one might choose firms whose total-assets-to-total-liabilities ratio is higher than the industry average.

[1]See Buffett (2020).
[2]See Buffett (1996).
[3]See https://millervaluefunds.com/miller-opportunity-trust/.
[4]See https://muhlenkamp.com/.

TABLE 5A.2

Well-Known Rule-Based Stock Strategies

Screen Name	Background	Description
Analyst upgrades	This strategy relies on the belief that markets are not semistrong efficient and that new information is discounted into the stock not immediately but gradually.	This is a strategy of buying stocks that analysts have upgraded and selling stocks that have been downgraded. The theory is that financial analysts are more knowledgeable about the companies they follow than any other outside investors and that they are the best informed to decide when a stock is not properly valued and deserves action. Although the assumption is that a stock will adjust gradually to an analyst's recommendation, an investor pursuing this strategy must act immediately on the recommendation.
Dogs of the Dow	In 1884, Charles Dow created the first market index by choosing 11 of the leading corporations' stocks (which happened to be mostly railroads at the time) and calculating the simple arithmetic mean of their prices. This was the birth of a now broadly used market barometer, the Dow Jones Industrial Average. The Dow is currently a compilation of 30 stocks chosen by the	At the beginning of each year, pick the 10 stocks in the Dow with the highest dividend yield and equally weight them.

TABLE 5A.2 *(Continued)*

Screen Name	Background	Description
	editors of the *Wall Street Journal* to represent a cross section of the largest industrial companies in the economy. The Dow is a price-weighted index unlike the S&P 500's market capitalization weighting. The Dogs of the Dow are a selection of 10 stocks in the Dow.	
Earnings momentum	The theory behind this strategy is that large positive (negative) earnings surprises indicate that a company is more likely to exceed (fall short of) future earnings expectations and hence follow an increasing (decreasing) price trajectory. Chan, Jegadeesh, and Lakonishok (1996) found that, on average, if an earnings surprise occurs in either direction, then the market is likely to be surprised in the same direction over the subsequent two announcements as well.	This strategy involves buying stocks whose earnings exceed expectations and selling stocks that fail to meet earnings targets. Like the analyst upgrades strategy, it depends on the market's failure to rapidly incorporate public information and an investor's ability to take advantage of this sluggishness.
Earnings revisions	Earnings revisions occur when management announces new earnings or target earnings and when financial analysts revise their projections upward or downward (not necessarily in response to such announcements). These earnings revisions mean that the outlook for the business has changed.	The earnings revision strategy is to buy and sell according to the direction of revisions. If projections are revised downward, the stock is probably overvalued. If management revises earnings due to inaccuracies in the company's financial statements, the announcement could trigger a crisis of confidence in the company's management and widespread selling of the stock.
GARP	GARP, or growth at a reasonable price, is a combination of both growth and value methods of investing. Many criticize this approach for trying to combine so many elements of other strategies that it fails to serve as a reliable investment tool of its own.	The strategy focuses on uncovering companies with high earnings growth and projections, strong fundamentals, and low P/E and P/B ratios. The aim is to find firms whose stock values (as measured by P/E, P/B, or some other ratio) are lower than their overall rates of earnings growth.
Neglected firms	Investing in neglected firms may be a way to exploit inefficiencies in the market. Areas of the	The neglected-firms strategy involves seeking out stocks that are covered by few, if any, financial analysts and

Screen Name	Background	Description
	market that attract media attention, public interest, and sophisticated institutional followings are more likely to be properly priced than areas off the beaten investment track.	attempting to discover sources of value that may have been overlooked by other investors. Neglected firms tend to be small, low-profile companies that have not received much media or analyst coverage. It is likely that neglected firms' stock prices do not reflect all the relevant information available and that their prices will react sluggishly to relevant news. This opens a window of time and opportunity for an astute investor to purchase undervalued, neglected stocks and reap the rewards when the market recognizes the stocks' true values.

TABLE 5A.3

Stock Screens Based on Well-Known Strategies of Individuals

Name	Screening Steps
Buffett	Step 1: Market capitalization is in the top 30% of NYSE, AMEX, and NASDAQ listed equities. Step 2: ROE is greater than 15% for each of the past three years. Step 3: The free cash flow per share is in the top 30% of the database. Step 4: NPM is greater than the industry average. Step 5: The forecasted cash flow per share in five years is greater than the current share price. Step 6: The growth rate in the market value is greater than the growth rate in the book value.
Dreman	Step 1: Market capitalization is in the top 80% of the S&P 1500. Step 2: P/E ratio is in the bottom 40% of the S&P 1500. Step 3: D/E ratio is less than 1. Step 4: The ratio of total liabilities to total assets is below the industry median. Step 5: The growth rate of EPS is greater than that of S&P 1500. Step 6: The growth rate of EPS is greater than the industry median. Step 7: The growth rate of EPS this year is greater than that of last year. Step 8: Forecasted growth rate of EPS next year is greater than the forecasted growth rate of EPS this year. Step 9: Dividend yield is greater than the S&P 1500 median. Step 10: The growth rate of net income is greater than 8%.
Driehaus	Step 1: The percentage change in EPS is growing for the past five fiscal years. Step 2: The percentage change in EPS current year is positive. Step 3: Percentage difference between announced earnings and consensus earnings is greater than 10%. Step 4: The percentage change in EPS current year is greater than the industry average. Step 5: Share price is higher than the 200-day moving average. Step 6: The return of the stock's industry is greater than the return of the S&P 500 for the last quarter. Step 7: 20-day on-balance volume is positive. Step 8: The number of analysts following the stock is less than or equal to five. Step 9: Size is in the bottom 85% of all stocks listed in the NYSE, AMEX, and NASDAQ.
Fisher	Step 1: Sales have been growing for the past three years. Step 2: The growth rate of sales over the last three years is greater than the industry median. Step 3: NPM is greater than the industry median for each of the last three fiscal

TABLE 5A.3 *(Continued)*

Name	Screening Steps
	years. Step 4: PEG ratio is in the bottom 10% of the industry. Step 5: Research-and-development-to-sales ratio (RNDS) is greater than the industry median. Step 6: The growth rate in sales is greater than the growth rate in the research and development expenditures. Step 7: The dividend is zero.
Lakonishok	Step 1: Market capitalization is in the top 30% of NYSE, AMEX, and NASDAQ equities. Step 2: P/E ratio is less than the industry median. Step 3: P/B ratio is less than the industry median. Step 4: The forecasted EPS for the next year is greater than the forecasted EPS for the current year. Step 5: The EPS forecasts have been revised upward at least once in the last month, and there have been no downward revisions. Step 6: The return of the stock has been greater than the return of the S&P 500 over the last 6 months.
Lynch	Step 1: P/E ratio is less than the industry average. Step 2: PEG ratio is less than 1. Step 3: The ratio of P/E to DY is less than 4. Step 4: Current P/E ratio is less than the average P/E ratio of the past five years. Step 5: The ratio of long-term debt to equity is less than the industry average. Step 6: The ratio of long-term debt to equity is less than 1. Step 7: The ratio of net cash per share to share price is greater than 0.2. Step 8: The growth rate in EPS is between 0% and 50%. Step 9: The ratio of the current-year insider buying to insider selling is greater than 1.5. Step 10: Institutional ownership is less than 50%. Step 11: The market capitalization is less than $5 billion.
Miller	Step 1: The ratio of market capitalization to free cash flow is less than 3. Step 2: The current-year free cash flow is greater than the previous-year free cash flow. Step 3: PEG ratio is less than 1.5. Step 4: GPM is greater than the industry median. Step 5: ROE is greater than the industry average. Step 6: Sales have been growing for each of the last five years. Step 7: The ratio of the long-term debt to equity is less than the industry average. Step 8: The size is in the top 75% of NYSE, AMEX, and NASDAQ equities.
Muhlenkamp	Step 1: ROE is greater than the industry average. Step 2: The average ROE of the past five years is greater than the industry average. Step 3: P/E ratio is less than the industry average. Step 4: P/B ratio is less than 2. Step 5: The compounded annualized growth rate of EPS over the last five years is greater than 0. Step 6: The compounded annualized percentage growth rate in EPS is greater than the industry average. Step 7: NPM is greater than the industry average. Step 8: The ratio of total liabilities to total assets is less than the industry average. Step 9: The cash ratio is greater than 1. Step 10: Free cash flow is positive.
Neff	Step 1: P/E ratio is less than the industry average. Step 2: The percentage growth rate in EPS is between 7% and 20%. Step 3: PEG ratio is less than 1. Step 4: Sales have been growing for each of the past five years. Step 5: OPM of the current year is greater than OPM of the previous year. Step 6: OPM is greater than the industry average. Step 7: Free cash flow per share has been growing for each of the past three fiscal years.

Name	Screening Steps
O'Shaugnessy growth	Step 1: The market capitalization is in the top 25% of the S&P 1500. Step 2: P/S ratio is less than 1.5. Step 3: The percentage growth in EPS is greater than 0. Step 4: The percentage change in EPS for the past five years is greater than that of the S&P 500. Step 5: P/E ratio is less than the industry average. Step 6: Choose the stocks with the largest one-year momentum (i.e., 12-month return) of the remaining stocks.
O'Shaugnessy value	Step 1: The market capitalization is in top 50% of NYSE, AMEX, and NASDAQ stocks. Step 2: P/E ratio is less than the industry average. Step 3: The ratio of price to cash flow is less than the industry average. Step 4: Sales are greater than 1.5 times the industry average. Step 5: P/S ratio is less than 1.25. Step 6: DY ratio is greater than that of the S&P 500. Step 7: The percentage change in EPS is between 0% and 50%. Step 8: The number of shares outstanding is greater than the average number of shares outstanding of the stocks within the database. Step 9: DY ratio is highest among the remaining stocks excluding utilities.
Piotroski	Step 1: The market capitalization is in the top 30% of NYSE, AMEX, and NASDAQ stocks. Step 2: P/B ratio is in the lowest 30% of NYSE, AMEX, and NASDAQ stocks. Step 3: ROA is positive. Step 4: D/E ratio is less than 1. Step 5: The ratio of long-term debt to equity in the previous year is less than the ratio two years ago. Step 6: NPM of the current year is greater than NPM of the previous year. Step 7: Cash flow from operations is greater than net income. Step 8: The cash ratio of the current year is greater than the cash ratio of the previous year. Step 9: The ratio of cash to current liabilities in the current year is greater than the ratio in the previous year. Step 10: The ratio of sales to total assets is greater than the industry average.
Templeton	Step 1: P/B ratio is in the lowest 40% of the stock database. Step 2: P/E ratio is less than the average P/E ratio of the past five years. Step 3: The percentage changes in earnings over the trailing 12 months and the past 5 years are positive. Step 4: The percentage change in EPS is greater than the industry average. Step 5: OPM is greater than the average OPM of the past five years. Step 6: The ratio of the long-term debt to equity is less than the industry average. Step 7: The ratio of total assets to total liabilities is greater than the industry average. Step 8: ROE is greater than the industry average.

Note: D/E ratio is the debt-to-equity ratio; DY ratio is the dividend yield; EPS is earnings per share, GPM is gross profit margin; NPM is net profit margin; OPM is operating profit margin; P/B ratio is the price-to-book ratio; P/E ratio is the price-to-earnings ratio; PEG ratio is the price-to-earnings-to-growth ratio; ROE is the return on equity; and RSI is the relative strength index.

TABLE 5A.4

Stock Screens Based on Well-Known Rule-Based Strategies

Name	Screening Steps
Analyst upgrades	Step 1: Select the 50 stocks whose average analyst rating has increased the most over the last month.
Dogs of the Dow	Step 1: Exclude all companies not in the Dow Jones Industrial Average. Step 2: DY ratio is in the top 33% of Dow stocks.
Earnings momentum	Step 1: The percentage change in EPS for the past five years is positive. Step 2: The stocks are within the top 20% of the rankings by the percentage change in EPS for the past five years. Step 3: The forecasted percentage change in EPS for the next year is greater than the percentage change in EPS for the past five years.
Earnings revisions	Step 1: Screen for the largest percentage revision in forecasted EPS for the next year during the last two months according to IBES. Step 2: Choose the top 20% in terms of the percentage change in EPS for the past five years. Step 3: The percentage change in EPS is greater than the industry average. Step 4: Choose those with the largest earnings surprises.
GARP	Step 1: PEG ratio is less than or equal to 1. Step 2: The percentage change in EPS for the past five years is greater than that of S&P 500. Step 3: The percentage change in EPS for the past three years is greater than the industry average. Step 4: The ratio of total liabilities to total assets is less than the industry average. Step 5: D/E ratio is less than 1.
Neglected firms	Step 1: Market capitalization is in the top 75% of NYSE, AMEX, and NASDAQ securities. Step 2: The number of analysts following the stock is less than or equal to two. Step 3: The compounded annualized percentage change in EPS is greater than the industry average. Step 4: P/E ratio is greater than the industry average. Step 5: NPM is greater than the industry average. Step 6: P/B ratio is less than or equal to 3. Step 7: The average ROE of the past five years is greater than the industry average.

Note: D/E ratio is the debt-to-equity ratio; DY ratio is the dividend yield; EPS is the earnings per share; NPM is the net profit margin; P/B ratio is the price-to-book ratio; P/E ratio is the price-to-earnings ratio; ROE is the return on equity; and PEG ratio is the price-to-earnings-to-growth ratio.

On Outliers

5B.1 GENERAL CONCEPTS

An *outlier* is an observation in a distribution that is extreme and looks very inconsistent with the rest of the data. These outliers could arise due to data errors by the data supplier or measurement error or could be correct values representing novel phenomena. If they arise due to data errors, it is a good idea for the portfolio manager to remove them entirely. If they are accurate and represent novel phenomena, there is no need to remove them. In practice, however, the portfolio manager may be unable to determine whether he or she is dealing with data errors or with novel phenomena. Thus, the portfolio manager in this case may wish to modify their values to some reasonable values just for safety. The outliers will still be strong signals vis-à-vis other stocks.

Formally speaking, we consider two possibilities. The first possibility (which might be called a *null hypothesis*) is that all the observations are random draws from distribution A. In this case, no outliers exist. The second possibility (which might be called an *alternative hypothesis*) is that most observations are random draws from distribution A, but some observations are from distribution B. Then we might label the observations from distribution B as outliers. In order to apply this categorization of outliers to real data, we need to know or assume the A distribution (of the null hypothesis). If we do not know distribution A or we are very uncertain about it, detecting outliers becomes theoretically difficult, and excluding suspect observations from the analysis might not be justified.

Popular outlier detection techniques assume that the underlying distribution is a normal distribution. Grubb's (1950) test, Dean-Dixon's (1951) test, and Rosner's (1975) test are three examples. There are also procedures applicable to non-normal distributions. Igleewicz and Hoaglin (1993) is a good reference for further discussion.

Dealing with outliers involves two steps. In the first step, we identify certain observations as outliers. This is the *labeling step*. In the second step, we decide what to do with identified outliers. We may remove these observations (*trimming* or *truncation*), replace their values with something less extreme (*winsorization*), or we may use a more creative approach.

5B.2 SPECIFIC PRACTICAL TECHNIQUES

5B.2.1 Utilizing the Z-Score

One method to deal with potential outliers is simply to label stocks with the absolute value of the Z-score greater than 3 as outliers. While easy, this is not a reliable method because the extreme values were used to compute means and standard deviations. A second method is the modified Z-score method, where, rather than using the standard deviation of the factor values, the median is used to compute the modified Z-score. The modified Z-score, $\tilde{z}$, is defined as $\dfrac{(\beta_{i,j} - \bar{\beta}_j)}{M(\beta_{i,j})}$, where $M(\beta_{i,j})$ is the median value of factor j across stocks. All observations with the absolute value of the modified Z-score greater than or equal to 3 are considered outliers. Once the outliers are identified, they can be eliminated or their values can be adjusted.

Winsorization is the process of replacing outliers with other values in order to prevent the outliers from unduly influencing the estimates. One form of winsorization we discussed in the main text is to convert all Z-scores with a value greater than 3 to the value 3 and those with a value less than -3 to -3.

Trimming is the process of removing the n values consisting of $n/2$ of the largest values and $n/2$ of the smallest values. The Z-scores are then recomputed for the remaining data. A version of this is suggested in the text, which is to simply remove all Z-scores whose absolute values are greater than some determined value, such as 3, 4, or 5.

5B.2.2 The Interquartile Method

One effective method to deal with outliers when building QEPM models is the *interquartile method*.[1] To implement the interquartile method, compute for each factor the interquartile range of the factor for the cross section of factors amongst stocks. This will be the value that is a measure of the middle 50% of factor values. This is computed by finding the third-quartile entry of every factor (Q3) and the first-quartile entry of every factor (Q1) and then subtracting them (Q3 − Q1) to find the interquartile range (IQR). At this point, a decision must be made on what deviation from the 75th percentile and 25th percentile constitutes an outlier. This is known as the *IQR coefficient*. For example, if the IQR coefficient is equal to 3, then upper and lower bounds of the factor are computed as[2]

$$UB = Q3 + 3IQR \tag{5B.1}$$

$$LB = Q1 - 3IQR \tag{5B.2}$$

Then consider all stocks with factor values above the upper bound and below the lower bound to be outliers.

For these, set their values to missing and compute the Z-scores for the remaining stocks. For the outlier stocks, fix the Z-scores at the maximum and minimum of the nonoutlier stocks' Z-scores.

A Numerical Example
In December 2020, the raw data for our beta calculations based on excess market returns and company stock returns for the universe of the top 3,000 stocks in the United States by market capitalization ranged from −5.78 to 7.48. These corresponded to the stocks AVGO and IBIO. Based on an IQR coefficient of 3, the values for the IQR procedure were Q3 = 1.7391, Q1 = 0.8721, IQR = 0.8669,

---

[1] See Chincarini (2017, 2018) for more information. This is a better method than simple winsorization, which has a major drawback: after the winsorization method has removed certain stocks and the Z-scores are recomputed, there may be still a group of outliers. The procedure must then be repeated again, leading to an iterative process that takes more time and might be less efficient.

[2] Another common value for the IQR coefficient is 1.5. Other values can be chosen as well.

UB = 4.3398, and LB = -1.7287. This removed 0.83% of all of our cross-sectional data, or 25 observations, but left very stable Z-score values for 99.17% of our stock data. The range of Z-scores was also less extreme. Using the traditional Z-score method, the maximum and minimum Z-scores were 7.46 and -8.75, respectively, compared to 4.10 and -3.97 using the IQR method.

5B.2.3 The Ranking Method

Another reasonable method to remove outliers is to use a ranking method. Rather than use Z-scores for the individual factors, the portfolio manager could use cross-sectional ranks. That is, every evaluation period, order the stocks according to the stock's factor value, and rank the stocks from highest to lowest. Then compute Z-scores on the actual rank, rather than the factor values. This resolves the outlier problem; however, it also loses information contained in the distance between different stocks' factor values, keeping just the relative value of Z-score between stocks. The ranking Z-score value for each stock in a given month is given by

$$Z_{it}^{rank} = \frac{\text{rank}(f_{it}) - \dfrac{\sum_{i=1}^{N} \text{rank}(f_{it})}{N}}{\sigma_{\text{rank}(f_{it})}} \tag{5B.3}$$

where rank is the cross-sectional numerical rank of each stock in the universe from high (better attribute) to low.

A Numerical Example
Using the same example as in Section 5B.2.2 with betas in December 2020 with the rank method, the maximum and minimum rank Z-scores were 1.7312 and -1.7312, respectively.

5B.2.4 The Percentile Ranking Method

A method very similar to the ranking method is the *percentile ranking method*. Once the N stocks are ranked from highest to lowest, the following calculation is made for each stock:

$$Z_{it}^{per} = \frac{N - \text{rank}(f_{it})}{N} \tag{5B.4}$$

Using the same example as in Section 5B.2.2 with betas in December 2020 using the percentile method, the highest-beta stock, AVGO, would have a 100th percentile and the lowest-beta stock, IBIO, would have a 0th percentile. With multiple factors, the factors can be combined by percentile rank—and this can be normalized further to obtain an aggregate percentile rank that ranges from zero to one.

APPENDIX 5C

Converting Z-Scores to Returns

In some instances, it will be useful to convert Z-scores to returns, as we have already mentioned in this chapter. For example, when computing after-tax returns or after transactions costs returns, it will be more pertinent to convert one's Z-scores to returns. There are various ways to do this that are more accurate, which we discussed in Sections 5.5 and 5.6. In this appendix, we will give an example using the second method described in Section 5.6 and based on Eq. (5.10), but it could easily be extended to a method also controlling for other risk factors. In particular, Eq. (5.10) shows that when regressing Z-scores on future stock returns, the expected return of a stock conditional on the Z-score is given by $E[r_{i,t} \,|\, z_{i,t-1}] = E[r_t] + \delta[z_{i,t-1} - E(z_{t-1})] = E[r_t] + \rho(r_t, z_{t-1})S(r_t)z_{i,t-1}$. When estimated as a cross-sectional regression (or a panel regression), the estimates will be the best predictor of the realized return, that is, $\hat{r}_{it} = \hat{\bar{r}}_t + \hat{\rho}(r_t, z_{t-1})\,\hat{S}(r_t)z_{i,t-1}$.

Suppose you are looking forward and have computed the Z-scores for all stocks in period t. You can then use the distribution of stock returns in period t to translate your Z-scores to either α or expected stock returns. If you do not perform estimations and assume that the correlation between stock returns and the Z-score is 1, then the transformation is simple: convert the Z-score distribution and maintain the relative Z-score values between stocks, but convert the distribution to resemble the first two central moments of the cross section of stock returns. Thus, the Z-scores for each stock would be modified as follows:

$$\tilde{Z}_{it}^1 = Z_{it}\sigma_r + \mu_r \qquad (5C.1)$$

where $\tilde{Z}_{it}$ is the adjusted Z-score to be used as the expected return for each stock, and σ_r and μ_r are the cross-sectional standard deviation and mean of stock returns.

However, this is unrealistic and probably exaggerated, since it would be rare for the Z-score and stock returns to be perfectly correlated. If instead a regression had been run or an empirical estimate of the correlation between stock returns and the Z-score had been estimated, then you could transform the Z-scores to the stock return distribution as follows:

$$\tilde{Z}_{it}^2 = \hat{\rho}(r_t, z_{t-1})Z_{it}\sigma_r + \mu_r \qquad (5C.2)$$

where the $\hat{\rho}$ (r_t, z_{t-1}) has been estimated on recent data.[1] This would have the effect of scaling down the distribution to reflect the predictive component of the Z-scores in historical data. Of course, all of these examples involve using past data to extrapolate to the future, which will result in a margin of error. Even when historical correlations are taken into account, if the correlation is low, the result only represents a partial explanation of stock returns. Nevertheless, this is a technique that can aid practitioners in transforming Z-scores to stock returns to be used in optimization models that require assessment of transactions costs or tax costs.

5C.1 A NUMERICAL EXAMPLE

An example of this conversion of Z-scores is shown in Fig. 5C.1 for December 2020. The first graph in Figure 5C.1 shows the distribution of the Z-scores among 3,000 stocks according to a particular Z-score model in December 2020. The second graph shows the distribution of monthly stock returns for the same stocks. The third graph shows the distribution of the modified Z-scores adjusted for the mean and standard deviation of the cross section of stock returns assuming unrealistically a perfect correlation between stock returns and Z-scores. In this particular example, the mean and standard deviation of the cross section of stock returns was 2.98% and 11.07%. The mean of the Z-score was 0 and 1, and the

---

[1] The conversion of Z-scores to returns in Eq. (5C.2) is exactly the same as using the estimated Eq. (5.8) to get the predicted values. That is, $\tilde{Z}_{it}^2 = \hat{\gamma} + \hat{\delta}Z_{it}$.

modified Z-score has the same mean and standard deviation as the stock returns. In the fourth graph, we show the modified distribution of Z-scores using the actual historical correlation between Z-scores and stock returns of 0.0306. One can see that this reduces the return distribution based on Z-scores to something more in line with the Z-score predictive power.

FIGURE 5C.1

Conversion of Z-scores to modified Z-scores using data from December 2020 in a universe of 3,000 stocks. In this figure, $\mu_r = 2.98$, $\sigma_r = 11.07$, $\mu_Z = 0$, $\sigma_Z = 1$, $\hat{\rho}(r_t, z_{t-1}) = 0.0306$, $\mu_{\tilde{Z}} = 2.98$, and $\sigma_{\tilde{Z}} = 11.07$. The means and standard deviations are from a cross section of monthly stock returns.

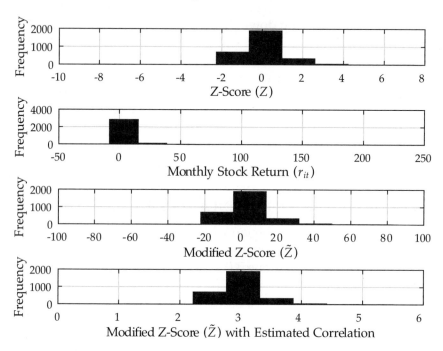

QUESTIONS

5.1. What is stock screening used for in QEPM?

5.2. Compare our Lakonishik-inspired screen with our Piotroski-inspired screen. How are they similar? How are they different?

5.3. How might we screen for management's view of the future of a company?

5.4. There are many ways for a business to increase its earnings. One way is to increase the net profit margin. Another way is to increase the number of stores in operation. How might one measure a company's market saturation?

5.5. What types of factor screening are very common among the famous portfolio managers whom we discuss in this chapter?

5.6. What are the advantages of simultaneous stock screening over sequential stock screening?

5.7. What is the Z-score, and how is it related to simultaneous stock screening?

5.8. (a) What is meant by an ad hoc aggregate Z-score?
(b) What is the danger with using this method of weighting?
(c) Why might some people say that this method is *not really* QEPM?

5.9. What is the optimal aggregate Z-score? How do you come up with it?

5.10. A portfolio manager is building his portfolio of stocks. His benchmark is the S&P 500. He will focus on three factors to build his portfolio of stocks. These factors are P/B ratio, P/E ratio, and 12-month momentum (M12M). He generally believes that high-momentum stocks will continue to perform well in the future. For the other factors, he bases his judgment on the documented anomalies.

Company Name	Ticker	P/E	P/B	M12M	$z_{P/E}$	$z_{P/B}$	z_{M12M}	$\bar{z}$
Eli Lilly	LLY	28.98	33.46	31.06				
AbbVie Inc.	ABBV	25.63	12.39	27.61				
Perrigo Company	PRGO	−110.18	1.05	−11.92				
Gilead Sciences	GILD	57.60	4.19	−6.62				
Mean S&P 500		21.21	7.87	15.24				
SD S&P 500		908.21	64.73	46.88				

(a) In the preceding table, for each stock, compute the Z-scores of each factor ($z_{P/E}$, $z_{P/B}$, z_{M12M}).

(b) The manager believes that momentum is the most important item in determining stock returns. Thus he wishes to assign it a 50% weighting while weighting the other factors equally. In the preceding table, compute the aggregate Z-score for each stock.

(c) If the portfolio manager were to create a long-only port-folio of two stocks weighted by their relative Z-scores, which stocks would go in the portfolio, and what would their weights be?

5.11. Suppose a portfolio manager has created Z-scores for all stocks in the universe for a given factor. What is the probability that a stock with a Z-score of 2 or greater is observed in the population? How is your answer dependent on whether the distribution is normal or non-normal?

5.12. Given the similarity in the signal between the factor group aggregate Z-score and the regular Z-score, why would a quantitative portfolio manager ever use the former?

5.13. A portfolio manager has the data available in the following table. She believes in using a factor group approach to creating aggregate Z-scores. She has decided to construct four groups (i.e., $M = 4$). Group 1 is titled the valuation group (V), group 2 is titled the technical group (T), group 3 is titled the profitability group (P), and group 4 is the alternative group (A). She also has seven factors that she has identified in predicting stock returns. They are the book-to-price (B/P) ratio, the earnings-to-price (E/P) ratio, the cash-flow-to-price (CF/P) ratio, the 12-month past stock return (M12M), standardized unanticipated earnings (SUE), current accruals (CACC), and net profit margin (NPM).

Ticker	B/P	E/P	CF/P	M12M	SUE	CACC	NPM	z_V	z_P	z_T	z_A	$\bar{z}$
CL	0.009	0.037	0.051	27.159	0.500	−0.065	0.167					
KMB	0.007	0.051	0.082	0.999	3.667	−0.089	0.125					
PG	0.140	0.040	0.052	14.150	3.750	−0.039	0.189					
EL	0.074	0.010	0.047	29.777	8.000	−0.043	0.044					
CLX	0.044	0.045	0.065	34.485	2.133	−0.078	0.161					
CHD	0.148	0.036	0.048	25.475	1.000	−0.038	0.164					
Universe												
Mean	0.275	0.041	0.080	9.095	2.067	−0.045	0.108					
SD	0.339	0.026	0.068	17.009	3.017	0.026	0.082					

(a) In which group would each of these factors most likely be placed?

(b) Compute the Z-score of each factor and each stock.

(c) Suppose that factors within each group are equally weighted. Compute the aggregate Z-score for every factor group.

(d) After careful analysis, the portfolio manager has found that the optimal weights of the factor groups are 20%, 30%, 20%, and 30%, respectively, for the four groups. Compute the aggregate Z-score for each stock.

(e) Suppose that the δ in Equation (5.8) is 1. Suppose that the portfolio manager constructs a portfolio with the three stocks with highest Z-scores equally weighted. What would be the difference between the expected return of this portfolio and the return of a portfolio with all six stocks equally weighted?

5.14. Quantitative portfolio managers generally manage their portfolios versus a benchmark. Thus they usually require a set of expected returns and risks to construct a portfolio.

(a) What problem does this requirement pose when using solely the aggregate Z-score to rank favorable stocks?

(b) What are three methods to convert an aggregate Z-score of a stock into an expected return or α for use in portfolio construction?

(c) Describe the strengths and weaknesses of each method.

5.15. Suppose that a portfolio manager is interested in whether an aggregate Z-score is useful in forecasting the return of stocks in the next period. Suppose that he takes a month of stock returns and the aggregate Z-score of the individual stocks and runs the following regression: $r_{i,t} = \gamma + \delta z_{i,t-1} + \epsilon_{i,t}$. What hypothesis should he test?

5.16. Some people express the regression equation $r_{i,t} = \gamma + \delta z_{i,t-1} + \epsilon_{i,t}$ as something called the *forecasting rule of thumb*, which states that the expected return of the stock conditional on the Z-score information minus the unconditional return of the stock is equal to $IC \cdot$ volatility $\cdot$ score.

(a) What does it mean when $IC = 0$, and what does it imply for the conditional excess expected return? What would the regression coefficient $\hat{\delta}$ be equal to if this were true?

(b)   What does it mean when volatility $= 0$, and what does it imply for the conditional excess expected return? What would the regression coefficient $\hat{\delta}$ be equal to if this were true?

(c)   What does it mean when score $= 0$, and what does it imply for the conditional excess expected return? What would the regression coefficient $\hat{\delta}$ be equal to if this were true?

5.17. Suppose that a portfolio manager is examining two sectors of the U.S. economy in which to invest. She constructs Z-scores relative to the sector for each stock. The cross-sectional volatility of stock returns for the latest month is 20% and 40%, and the correlation between the Z-score and returns of stocks is 0.2 and 0.1 for stocks in sectors A and B, respectively.

(a)   In which sector will a Z-score be relatively more important at forecasting returns?

(b)   What are $\hat{\delta}_A$ and $\hat{\delta}_B$ of Eq. (5.8)? Is your conclusion the same as in part (a)?

5.18. When is the Z-score model, as used in Eq. (5.8), equivalent to the fundamental factor model? What does this mean?

5.19. (a)   Why do portfolio managers who use the Z-score typically eliminate Z-scores with absolute values greater than 3?

(b)   What is an alternative way of handling such Z-scores? What is the common name given to this method?

(c)   Name a third way of dealing with these Z-scores that is mentioned in the chapter.

5.20. For each test below, describe what it is used for and to what type of data it applies.

(a)   Rosner's test

(b)   Grubb's test

(c)   Dixon's test

CHAPTER 6

Fundamental Factor Models

In nature there is fundamental unity running through all the diversity we see about us.

—Mohandas Gandhi

6.1 INTRODUCTION

Recall from Chapter 3 the central idea of modern financial economics: *The average return of a stock is the payoff for taking risk.* In a factor model, the factor exposure represents the exposure of a stock to some kind of risk. The factor premium quantifies the payoff to an investor who takes on that risk by buying the stock. The average stock return therefore equals the product of the factor exposure and the factor premium:

$$\text{Average stock return} = \text{factor exposure} \times \text{factor premium} \quad (6.1)$$

In the fundamental factor model, the factor exposure is known. It is some observable fundamental characteristic of the stock, such as its market capitalization or book-to-market ratio. The factor premium, on the other hand, is not known. It is the proportionality between the average stock return and the factor exposure, and it must be estimated empirically.

The formula for the average stock return given above can be extended easily to a more realistic case of multiple factors. When there are K factors, the factor exposures of stock i can be written as

$\beta_{i1}, \dots, \beta_{iK},$ and the factor premium can be written as $f_1, \dots, f_K$.[1] Note that the factor premium does not vary across stocks and therefore does not require the subscript i. The return on stock i, r_i, can be written as

$$r_i = \alpha + \beta_{i1}f_1 + \cdots + \beta_{iK}f_K + \epsilon_i \tag{6.2}$$

where α is the constant term and ϵ_i is the error term (i.e., the part of the stock return that does not depend on the K factors).[2]

The average of ϵ_i is zero, so the average stock return is the cross-sum of the factor exposure and the factor premium[3]:

$$E(r_i) = \underbrace{E(\alpha)}_{\alpha} + \beta_{i1}E(f_1) + \cdots + \beta_{iK}E(f_K) \tag{6.3}$$

For the convenience of exposition, we will define K-dimensional column vectors $\mathbf{f}$ and $\boldsymbol{\beta}_i$ as

$$\mathbf{f} = (f_1, \dots, f_K)' \tag{6.4}$$

$$\boldsymbol{\beta}_i = (\beta_{i1}, \dots, \beta_{iK})' \tag{6.5}$$

Then the preceding equation becomes

$$r_i = \alpha + \boldsymbol{\beta}_i'\mathbf{f} + \epsilon_i \tag{6.6}$$

Using this notation, the average stock return becomes

$$E(r_i) = \alpha + \boldsymbol{\beta}_i'E(\mathbf{f}) \tag{6.7}$$

We can see that the average stock return is simply the product of the factor exposure ($\boldsymbol{\beta}_i$) and the factor premium ($\mathbf{f}$) as before.[4]

---

[1] This notation requires explanation. It is the convention in statistics to use Greek letters for parameters that must be estimated and to use the more familiar Latin letters for variables whose values can be observed. We do not follow the convention here because in other models of stock returns the factor exposure is the unknown variable, whereas the factor premium is directly observable. To remain consistent across all models, we will always call the factor exposure β and the factor premium f.

[2] Even when we estimate the factor premiums using time series of stock returns and factor exposures, one can think of the regressions as pooled regressions, where the intercept term is a constant.

[3] The *expected stock return*, not *the average stock return*, is the correct term to use. We will switch to the technically correct terminology in later chapters.

[4] There is an extra constant term in the formula, but it will be zero if the factor exposure is properly normalized and the risk free rate has already been subtracted from the return. This will be discussed in more detail later.

The average stock return is the payoff for taking risk—but what is this risk exactly? The risk of a stock has two components, diversifiable risk and nondiversifiable risk.

$$\text{Total risk} = \text{nondiversifiable risk} + \text{diversifiable risk} \qquad (6.8)$$

Since investors can eliminate diversifiable risk from their portfolios through diversification, the market only rewards exposure to non-diversifiable risk. Thus we may restate the central idea of modern financial economics as: *The average stock return is the payoff for taking nondiversifiable risk.*

The nondiversifiable risk can be expressed as the product of the factor exposure squared and the risk included in one unit of exposure.[5] We will call the risk of one unit of exposure the *factor risk.* Then we may write

$$\text{Nondiversifiable risk} = \text{factor exposure}^2 \times \text{factor risk} \qquad (6.9)$$

Within the framework of the fundamental factor model, the total risk of a stock (nondiversifiable risk plus diversifiable risk) can be measured by the variance:

$$
\begin{aligned}
V(r_i) &= V(\alpha + \beta_{i1}f_1 + \cdots + \beta_{iK}f_K) + V(\epsilon_i) \\
&= V(\beta_{i1}f_1 + \cdots + \beta_{iK}f_K) + V(\epsilon_i) \qquad (6.10)
\end{aligned}
$$

Using the same vector notation that simplified the formula for the stock return, the variance formula becomes

$$V(r_i) = \beta_i' \, V(\mathbf{f})\beta_i + V(\epsilon_i) \qquad (6.11)$$

where $V(\mathbf{f})$ is a $K \times K$-dimensional variance-covariance matrix. In this model we can see each of the components of the total risk. The nondiversifiable component—the part that the market rewards—is the product of the factor exposure squared ($\beta_i' \cdots \beta_i$) and the factor premium risk [$V(\mathbf{f})$]. The diversifiable component, which an investor can diversify out of his or her portfolio, is the term $V(\epsilon_i)$.

The fundamental factor model can be used to predict both the returns and the risks of stocks, and these predictions can guide a portfolio manager in choosing the best stocks for his or her portfolio. In general, formulating a fundamental factor model involves four broad steps. First, before observing the factor exposure and

---

[5] Risk can be measured either with the variance or the standard deviation. In the formula shown here, risk is defined as the variance.

estimating the factor premium, there is some preliminary work to
do, including deciding on the factors to include in the model, the
treatment of the risk-free rate, the time interval and time period of
the data, and the investment universe. Second, the factor exposures
of individual stocks (β_i) must be determined. The third step is to
estimate the factor premium (f) and the constant α from the factor
exposure and the return. Finally, an assessment of the total risk
should be made by estimating both the factor risk [β_i' $V(f)\beta_i$, a.k.a.
the *nondiversifiable risk*] and the diversifiable risk [$V(\epsilon_i)$]. We explain
these steps in the following sections, and Table 6.1 summarizes the
specifics of the modeling process.

TABLE 6.1

Creating a Fundamental Factor Model

Preliminary work:
1. Choose the factors for the model.
2. Determine the treatment of the risk-free rate.
3. Define the investment universe.
4. Decide on the time interval and time period of the data.

Main steps for modeling total stock return (for nonbenchmark managers):
1. Stock returns are estimated with the following equation: $r_i = \alpha + \beta_{i1}f_1 + \cdots + \beta_{iK}f_K + \epsilon_i$.
2. Collect stock-return and factor exposure data for the time period at each time interval.
3. Estimate the factor premium from a panel regression of the stock return on the factor exposure using either the OLS, MAD, or the GLS method.
4. Check the robustness of the factor premium estimation by splitting the data into subsets and comparing the estimates for each subset. If the estimates are similar across subsets, the estimation is robust.
5. If the estimation is not robust, try a different estimation method.
6. Calculate each stock's average return as the product of the factor premium and the vector containing the stock's factor exposures.
7. Decompose the risk of the stock return into its diversifiable and nondiversifiable components.
8. Calculate the correlation between the returns of the stocks in the investment universe.

Main steps for modeling residual stock return (for benchmark managers):
1. Stock returns are estimated with the following equation: $r_i = \tilde{\alpha}_i + \tilde{\beta}_i r_B + \tilde{\epsilon}_i$.
2. Collect stock return and benchmark return data for the given time period at the given time intervals.
3. After estimating $\tilde{\alpha}$ and $\tilde{\beta}$, calculate the residual return as $\tilde{r}_i \equiv \tilde{\alpha}_i + \tilde{\epsilon}_i$.
4. Estimate residual return with the following equation: $\tilde{r}_i = \alpha + \beta_{i1}f_1 + \cdots + \beta_{iK}f_K + \epsilon_i$.
5. Follow steps 2 through 8 of the main steps for modeling total stock return, substituting the residual return for the total stock return.

6.2 PRELIMINARY WORK

A sound model begins with good planning. The preliminary work of the portfolio manager is to make a series of decisions that will serve as a blueprint for construction of the model. The primary decision is the choice of factors. Other preliminary decisions determine the shape of the data set (including the nature of the stock returns, the time interval between data points, and the overall time horizon of the data) and the scope of stocks to consider for the portfolio. These general decisions come into play in building any factor model.

6.2.1 Choosing Factors

Factors represent risk. There are all kinds of factors, some of which describe stock characteristics and some of which describe conditions in the overall market.[6] Fundamental factors are observable characteristics of the stock itself, and they usually can be read (or easily calculated) from financial statements. Some technical factors and analyst factors also count as fundamental factors. For reference, here are some representative fundamental factors:

1. *Fundamental valuation factors*: dividend yield, book-to-price ratio, earnings-to-price ratio, and the sales-to-price ratio
2. *Fundamental size factors*: log of market capitalization
3. *Fundamental solvency and financial risk factors*: debt-to-equity ratio, current ratio, and the inverse interest coverage ratio
4. *Fundamental operating profitability factors*: net profit growth, return on assets, and the return on common equity
5. *Technical factors*: 12-month momentum, trading volume, and the short interest ratio
6. *Analyst factors*: analyst rating changes and earnings revisions

Note that economic factors [such as gross domestic product (GDP) and inflation] and behavioral factors (such as consumer sentiment) do not fit in the fundamental factor model because neither of these types of factors really can be called a characteristic of the stock itself. Rather, they measure risks in the market that affect all

---

[6] Please refer to Chapter 4 for a comprehensive catalogue of factors.

stocks. Statistical factors, which must be derived from stock-return series, do not belong in the fundamental factor model either.

The astute reader will notice that when listing some of the more common factors, we describe their inverse. This is different than how we used these factors in Chapter 4. For example, most investors refer to the price-to-earnings ratio of a company rather than the earnings-to-price ratio. The reason for using the inverse is very practical. When companies have negative earnings, their P/E ratio doesn't really have any meaning. As a result, it does not make sense to argue that a low P/E ratio company is "cheaper" than a high P/E ratio company when companies with zero or negative earnings are included. However, if we calculate the E/P ratio of companies, we have a ratio that can be compared across companies, which makes a lot more sense. For example, a company with a very high P/E ratio will have a very small E/P ratio but will still be considered relatively "cheaper" than a company with a negative E/P ratio. In practice, some practitioners use P/E and exclude stocks with negative earnings, while others use E/P and have a larger set of stocks to choose from.[7] The key point is that by using the inverse of certain common factors, we are able to analyze many more stocks, which offers a much richer view for stock selection. In the remainder of this book we shall use factors that allow us to evaluate many more stocks, even if the definitions are slightly altered from what the typical investor is accustomed to.

6.2.2 Treatment of the Risk-Free Rate

The factor premium in a fundamental factor model has to be estimated by looking at the relationship between stock returns and factor exposures. The reliability of the model therefore depends greatly on the quality of the stock return data that are used to estimate this relationship. Before gathering stock-return data, the portfolio manager must confront a larger theoretical question: how much of a stock's return comes from the stock itself, and how much could have been earned on any investment? The investor earns a portion of the average stock return for free—not as a reward for taking on risk. The reward for taking on risk by buying a stock is therefore the average stock return in *excess of a risk-free rate*.

---

[7] For major indices or portfolios, some investors calculate the weighted average of the E/P ratio or related ratio and then invert that average so that it appears to investors in the more common form.

In order to focus on the portion of the stock return that actually rewards risk, some portfolio managers subtract a risk-free rate from the stock return before implementing the fundamental factor model. While a theoretically sound move, this is not easy to do in practice. The problem is that it is difficult to identify a truly risk-free asset, the return on which could be considered the risk-free rate. Financial economists tend to use the return on short-term U.S. Treasury bills as the risk-free rate because U.S. Treasury bills are considered a very safe investment. Yet they are not completely risk-free assets. Money market funds (MMFs), another substitute for the theoretical risk-free asset, certainly contain a level of risk as well.[8]

Given the difficulty of identifying the true risk-free rate, subtracting an estimated risk-free rate might seem like an arbitrary practice. We believe, however, that a model that adheres to risk-reward theory by adjusting for the risk-free rate will provide more accurate results than one that does not. Given the return of stock i at time t, r_{it}, and the risk-free rate at time t, r_{ft}, we define the excess return r_{it}^* as

$$r_{it}^* = r_{it} - r_{ft} \tag{6.12}$$

In subsequent calculations, we can replace r_{it} with r_{it}^* to adjust for the risk-free rate.

6.2.3 Choosing the Time Interval and Time Period

Two other interrelated questions also affect the quality of the data set: what time interval should fall between the data points, and what overall time horizon should the data set cover? Ideally, the time interval should reflect the investment horizon (i.e., the rebalancing frequency). If the portfolio is rebalanced every month, a monthly interval should be used. If the portfolio is rebalanced every year, an annual interval should be used. This will make things easier in the later stages of analysis.

However, consideration of the estimation precision may force the portfolio manager to choose a time interval different from the investment horizon. The fundamental factor model assumes that the factor exposure of a stock determines its average return. The

---

[8] It is also important to use a total return risk-free rate index. Sometimes people use the yield of the risk-free rate. Although this might be approximately correct, it's much better to use the actual total return from the chosen risk-free instrument.

statistical estimation of the relationship between the factor exposure and the stock return will be imprecise unless the relationship
is stable over the given time interval. For example, the stock return
could have a stable relationship with the factor exposure for one
month but not for an entire year. In that case, it would hardly make
sense to set the time interval to a year, even if rebalancing occurs
annually. At the same time, if the time interval is too short, the precision of the estimation again may decline because short-term fluctuations in the stock return may be random and unrelated to the
factor exposure. Nonetheless, it is generally best to err on the side
of a shorter time interval rather than a longer one. One can forecast
the results of a longer time interval from the results of a shorter
time interval, but not vice versa.[9] In practice, financial economists
tend to prefer a monthly interval and, to a lesser degree, a weekly
interval. Daily and annual intervals are rather uncommon.

The overall time period that the data cover (in statistical jar-
gon, the *sample period*) should be decided in light of the estimation
precision as well. If the time period is too short, so that the data
encompass only a small number of time intervals, then the estimation precision may suffer. The general rule of estimation precision
is: the larger the sample, the higher is the precision. However, if the
time period covers many years, then the relationship between the
stock return and the factor exposure may change over the course of
the period. It is unlikely that the premium on any given factor will
remain constant for an entire decade, for example. A very long time
period also means that the data will cover more time intervals. The
more time intervals, the more data points there are to collect, and
the bigger will be the problem of finding complete data for a stock.
Financial economists tend to include between 36 and 60 time intervals in their analyses when using a monthly interval (so that the
total time period is three to five years). When using a weekly interval, the number of time intervals tends to be greater than 60 (while
the overall time period tends to be shorter than three years). When
using a quarterly or annual interval, the number of time intervals
tends to be much smaller (while the overall time period is generally longer than five years).

We will use the lowercase letter t to indicate one time interval.
For example, r_{it} represents the return to stock i at time t, whereas
β_{it} denotes the factor exposure of stock i at time t. We will use

---

[9] Chapter 8 discusses this concept in greater detail.

capital letter T to indicate the number of time intervals used in the analysis. Thus t will take an integer value from 1 to T. We write the relationship between the stock return and the factor exposure as

$$r_{it} = \alpha + \boldsymbol{\beta}'_{it}\mathbf{f} + \epsilon_{it} \quad t = 1, \dots, T \qquad (6.13)$$

where, as before, $\boldsymbol{\beta}_{it}$ and $\mathbf{f}$ are K-dimensional column vectors, and r_{it} and ϵ_{it} are scalars.[10]

6.2.4 Choosing the Universe of Stocks

In addition to questions of the nature and time span of the data, the portfolio manager faces the question of how many stocks to consider when applying the model. There already may be external restrictions on the investment universe of the portfolio. The portfolio may be limited, for instance, to technology stocks, value stocks, or stocks of some other stripe. Whether or not that is the case, the portfolio manager may have his or her own preliminary screening strategy that will narrow the list of potential investments. As we discussed in Chapter 5, many well-known portfolio managers put their stamp on a portfolio with a signature stock screen.

In the absence of external restrictions on the investment universe, there is no need (from a technological standpoint) to shrink the investment universe preliminarily. Given the current state of computing technology, the number of stocks is not really an issue. Even a personal computer can handle thousands of stocks without much trouble.

The size of the stock universe does affect some aspects of implementation, though. A very large investment universe provides a large pool of stocks from which to select. The bigger the selection pool, the more likely it is that there are high-return stocks somewhere in the pool. Yet calculation of stock correlations loses precision as the number of stocks in the pool increases, making the model less and less reliable. Thus, even though plenty of good

---

[10] Typically, when we estimate these factor models, we use information at time t to predict returns at time $t + 1$. For convenience, we sometimes write in this book the equation with time subscript t everywhere, as we do here. The factor exposure and the returns are at time t. The equation should still be interpreted as using information at t to predict returns at time $t + 1$. In other words, the factor exposure at time t is really the factor exposure value as of the end of the previous period, $t - 1$, which we may refer to, sometimes, as the beginning-of-month exposure for time t. There is also the issue of when a factor exposure was truly available for the portfolio manager. We discuss that issue later in this chapter.

stocks may be floating around, it is harder to identify them. For this reason, we do not recommend starting with an investment universe of more than a few thousand stocks.

6.3 BENCHMARK AND α

Many portfolio managers have a specific benchmark against which they measure the performance of their portfolios. If the portfolio manager aims to outperform a benchmark while minimizing the portfolio's tracking error, then the benchmark must play a role in the model.

One approach to incorporating the benchmark into the fundamental factor model is to use the model to predict only the residual return rather than the entire stock return. The residual return is the part of the stock return not correlated with the benchmark. To transform the model into one of residual return, we need to run a regression of the stock return on the benchmark.

Given the stock return r_i and the benchmark return r_B, we estimate the following equation:

$$r_i = \tilde{\alpha}_i + \tilde{\beta}_i r_B + \tilde{\epsilon}_i \qquad (6.14)$$

The typical way to estimate this equation is to use a time-series regression. We find the stock return and the benchmark return over many time periods, say, $r_{i1}, \dots, r_{iT}$ and $r_{B1}, \dots, r_{BT}$, where the second subscript refers to time periods. After estimating $\tilde{\alpha}$ and $\tilde{\beta}$, we define the residual return $\tilde{r}_i$ as

$$\tilde{r}_i \equiv \tilde{\alpha}_i + \tilde{\epsilon}_i \qquad (6.15)$$

Once the residual return is defined, the portfolio manager can use the fundamental factor model to predict the value of the residual return. To do so, he or she simply substitutes the residual return for the stock return given in the fundamental factor model in Eq. (6.2).

The portfolio manager's value-added is wrapped up in the term $\tilde{\alpha}$ (also known as α^B). Note that the expected return and the risk of the last term $\tilde{\epsilon}$ are already known from the preceding estimation. The term with flexibility to boost the residual return is $\tilde{\alpha}$. What the portfolio manager does with this fundamental factor model is therefore all about $\tilde{\alpha}$.[11]

---

[11] Be careful not to confuse $\tilde{\alpha}$ with the α of the model for total stock return in Eq. (6.2). The concept of $\tilde{\alpha}$ is so important in the investment world that analysts sometimes refer to it simply as α. Refer to Chapter 2 for a discussion of the various α's of investing and their corresponding models.

An alternative way to account for the benchmark, rather than predicting the residual stock return, is to add the benchmark to the model as one of the factors. This approach fits better with the economic factor model, however, so we will delay discussing it until the next chapter.[12] Accounting for the benchmark at this point in the modeling process, though useful, is not necessary. Some portfolio managers prefer to deal with the benchmark at a later stage in the process by, for instance, controlling for the tracking error in construction of the portfolio. This approach may make the most sense if the composition of the benchmark is known clearly.[13]

6.4 FACTOR EXPOSURE

The factor exposure quantifies the exposure of a stock to risk. In the fundamental factor model, the factor exposure is the value of some observable (or easily calculable) characteristic of the stock. In some cases, the factor exposure shows up right in a company's financial statements or on a price-volume chart. In other cases, a straightforward calculation drawing on figures from financial statements is enough. In other words, once the factors are chosen, determining the factor exposure is rarely a challenging task.

Table 6.2 presents the factor exposures of selected stocks for five commonly used factors. The E/P ratio is the annual earnings per share divided by the share price. The B/P ratio is the value of common equity reported in the company's balance sheet divided by the share price.[14] The D/E ratio is the total value of liabilities divided by the total value of equity reported in the balance sheet. LOGSIZE is the natural log of the market capitalization of the company (in millions of dollars), where market capitalization is defined as the share price multiplied by the number of shares outstanding. Momentum (M12M) is the average monthly return (as a percentage) over the previous 12 months.

---

[12] If we use the benchmark as a factor in the fundamental factor model, we need to estimate the factor exposure of each stock in some way. To estimate the factor exposure, we will need to employ the technique we use for the economic factor model.

[13] See Chapter 9 for an explanation of this method.

[14] As we explained in Chapter 5, there are many advantages to defining certain variables as their inverse. For example, one can analyze many more companies when using the E/P ratio rather than the P/E ratio. One might also notice that unlike in Chapters 4 and 5, we no longer have Tesla in our representative 10 stocks. This is because Tesla was not part of the S&P 500 in November of 2020.

TABLE 6.2

Factor Exposure of Selected Stocks

Ticker	E/P	B/P	D/E	LOGSIZE	M12M
AAPL	0.0289	0.0357	3.3904	14.5206	0.7973
MSFT	0.0274	0.0731	1.5469	14.2970	0.4291
AMZN	0.0083	0.0464	2.5036	14.2790	0.7592
GOOGL	0.0285	0.1871	0.3433	13.9183	0.3493
FB	0.0353	0.1659	0.2648	13.4088	0.3736
BRK.B	0.0414	0.7329	0.9840	13.1935	0.0391
WMT	0.0413	0.1739	1.9235	12.9784	0.3056
JNJ	0.0399	0.1654	1.5148	12.8502	0.0812
JPM	0.0700	0.6523	11.1494	12.7920	−0.0727
V	0.0330	0.0849	1.1924	12.7827	0.1471

Note: Factor exposure is as of the end of November 2020. E/P ratio is the earnings-to-price ratio, B/P ratio is the book-to-price ratio, D/E ratio is the debt-to-equity ratio, LOGSIZE is natural log of market capitalization in millions of dollars, and M12M is the cumulative returns over the past 12 months in decimal form (i.e., 0.79 equals 79%). Ticker symbols are for the following companies: Apple Inc. (AAPL), Microsoft Corporation (MSFT), Amazon (AMZN), Alphabet Inc. or Google (GOOGL), Facebook Inc. (FB), Berkshire Hathaway B shares (BRK.B), Johnson & Johnson (JNJ), Walmart Inc. (WMT), J.P. Morgan Chase & Co. (JPM), and Visa Inc. (V). All values were computed as of December 2020 with appropriate reporting lags. Since many readers are more familiar with P/E and P/B ratios, the P/Es of the companies are 34.60, 36.50, 120.48, 35.09, 28.33, 24.15, 24.21, 25.06, 14.29, and 30.30, respectively, and the P/Bs of the companies are 28.01, 13.68, 21.55, 5.34, 6.03, 1.36, 5.75, 6.05, 1.53, and 11.78, respectively.

From the table we can see that Amazon (AMZN) has a low earnings-to-price ratio of 0.0083 (i.e., a high price-to-earnings ratio of about 120) likely owing to expectations of rapid earnings growth. J.P. Morgan Chase (JPM), on the other hand, has a relatively high earnings-to-price ratio. If the factor premium for the earnings-to-price ratio were negative, then—all other things being equal—we would expect Amazon to have a higher return than J.P. Morgan Chase. Conversely, if the factor premium for the earnings-to-price ratio were positive, we would expect J.P. Morgan Chase to perform better than Amazon.

Looking at another factor, we see that momentum is very high for Apple and Amazon (reflecting their exceptional returns in 2020), whereas it is negative for J.P. Morgan Chase (reflecting its losses in value during the year). We may be able to predict which of these stocks will have the highest return in the following year if we determine the factor premium for momentum. If the factor premium were positive, we would expect Apple and Amazon to perform better than J.P. Morgan Chase.

Factor exposures change over time, and we need to be sure to assign the correct values to the correct dates. For monthly time intervals, it is standard practice to use the factor exposure recorded at the beginning of the month (or, alternatively, the value recorded at the end of the previous month). In calculating the earnings-to-price ratio (E/P), the book-to-price ratio (B/P), and the log of market capitalization (LOGSIZE) for this table (which shows factor exposures at the beginning of December 2020 or, alternatively, at the end of November 2020), we used the closing stock prices and shares outstanding as of November 30, 2020. In calculating momentum, we used the stock returns from December 2019 through November 2020.[15]

Extra care needs to be taken in applying data from a company's financial statements. Companies release their financial statements quarterly but not immediately when the fiscal quarter ends. As of the beginning of December 2020, the most recently released financial statements might represent the second or third quarter of 2020. Since we use quarterly data in calculating the earnings-to-price ratio, we used the earnings for the 12-month period ending in August, July, or June, depending on when a company's fiscal quarter ended. If the fiscal quarter was over in September, the earnings for the July–September quarter might not be known by the beginning of December, so we did not use them to calculate the earning-to-price ratio. For the same reason, we used only figures for fiscal quarters ending in or before August to calculate the book-to-price and debt-to-equity ratios. Generally, it is reasonable to allow two to three months' lag between the end of a fiscal period and the reporting of the variable. Table 6.3 summarizes this timing scheme.

After all the factor exposures are determined, we collect the numbers and save them as a set of vectors $\{(\beta_{11}, \ldots, \beta_{N1}), \ldots, (\beta_{1T}, \ldots, \beta_{NT})\}$ where β_{it} is the factor exposure of stock i for time t. For example, the factor exposure of Apple for December 2020 is (from Table 6.2)

$$\beta_{AAPL,Dec20} = (\beta_{AAPL,E/P,Dec20}, \ldots, \beta_{AAPL,M12M,Dec20})'$$
$$= (0.0289, 0.0357, 3.3904, 14.5206, 0.7973)' \quad (6.16)$$

---

[15] We do this because in our estimations of factor premiums we estimate regressions over time and need to use the latest factor exposure (i.e., end of the month) against the subsequent monthly return of the stocks. Thus, we use end-of-November factor exposures and end-of-December returns to estimate factor premiums.

TABLE 6.3

Assigning the Correct Values to the Correct Time for
December 2020

Data Frequency	If the Fiscal Quarter Ends in:	If the Fiscal Year Ends in:	Use the Data for:
Daily data			End of Nov 2020
Monthly data			Nov 2020
Quarterly data	Mar, Jun, Sep, Dec		Apr 2020–Jun 2020
	Feb, Mar, Aug, Nov		Jun 2020–Aug 2020
	Jan, Apr, Jul, Oct		May 2020–Jul 2020
Annual data		Dec	Jan 2019–Dec 2019
		Nov	Dec 2018–Nov 2019
		Oct	Nov 2018–Oct 2019
		Sept	Oct 2018–Sep 2019
		Aug	Sep 2019–Aug 2020
		⋮	⋮

Note: Factor exposure for month t is calculated from the latest available information as of the beginning of month t (i.e., the end of month $t - 1$). Thus, for December 2020, we use the values known at the end of November 2020. This is what we do for daily and monthly data. For quarterly data, we assume a reporting gap of three months. Thus, if a fiscal quarter ends in March, June, September, or December, then the last fiscal quarter whose information is available as of the end of November 2020 is the fiscal quarter ending in June 2020 (December fiscal quarter information is obviously not yet available, and the September fiscal quarter information does not meet the three-month gap requirement). Similarly, for annual data, we assume a reporting gap of three months. Thus, if a fiscal year ends in December, then the last fiscal year whose information is available as of the end of November 2020 is the fiscal year ending in December 2019.

We can read similar information for other stocks (different i's) and for other time periods (different t's) in a similar way.

6.5 THE FACTOR PREMIUM

The factor premium is the payoff for each unit of factor exposure, or exposure to risk, that the stock possesses. In the fundamental factor model, the factor premium is estimated from the pooled cross-sectional regression (i.e., panel regression) of the stock return on the factor exposure. Estimation of the factor premium with a regression is possible because the premium likely remains constant over several years[16] and across stocks.

Given the returns of N stocks over T time periods, $\{(r_{11}, ..., r_{N1}), ..., (r_{1T}, ..., r_{NT})\}$, and the factor exposures of N stocks over

---

[16] Though, as noted earlier in this chapter, the premium likely changes over the course of an entire decade.

T time periods, $\{(\beta_{11}, ..., \beta_{N1}), ..., (\beta_{1T}, ..., \beta_{NT})\}$, we can estimate the following equation:

$$r_{it} = \alpha + \beta_{it}'f + \epsilon_{it} \qquad (6.17)$$

There are a number of ways to estimate this equation. The simplest is the ordinary least squares (OLS) approach. While the OLS estimator is simple to obtain, it may not be the most reliable estimator. We suggest that portfolio managers do a number of robustness checks on it and then decide whether to use a more sophisticated technique.

6.5.1 OLS Estimator of the Factor Premium

The OLS estimator of the factor premium $\mathbf{f}$ is given as[17]

$$\hat{\mathbf{f}} = \left[\sum_{t=1}^{T}\sum_{i=1}^{N}(\beta_{it}-\bar{\beta})(\beta_{it}-\bar{\beta})'\right]^{-1}\sum_{t=1}^{T}\sum_{i=1}^{N}(\beta_{it}-\bar{\beta})(r_{it}-\bar{r}) \qquad (6.18)$$

where

$$\bar{\beta} = \frac{1}{NT}\sum_{t=1}^{T}\sum_{i=1}^{N}\beta_{it} \qquad (6.19)$$

$$\bar{r} = \frac{1}{NT}\sum_{t=1}^{T}\sum_{i=1}^{N}r_{it} \qquad (6.20)$$

The constant $\hat{\alpha}$ is calculated as $\bar{r}-\bar{\beta}'\hat{\mathbf{f}}$. The standard error for the factor premium is the square root of (the diagonal elements of) the following variance:

$$\hat{V}(\hat{\mathbf{f}}) = \hat{\sigma}^2\left[\sum_{t=1}^{T}\sum_{i=1}^{N}(\beta_{it}-\bar{\beta})(\beta_{it}-\bar{\beta})'\right]^{-1} \qquad (6.21)$$

where $\hat{\sigma}^2$ is the estimated variance of ϵ_{it}, that is,

$$\hat{\sigma}^2 = \frac{1}{NT}\sum_{t=1}^{T}\sum_{i=1}^{N}(r_{it}-\beta_{it}\hat{\mathbf{f}})^2 \qquad (6.22)$$

Table 6.4 presents the factor premium estimates and their standard errors. We made the estimations for Standard & Poors

[17] We present the formulas for consistent estimators. For unbiased estimators, the degree-of-freedom correction is necessary.

TABLE 6.4

The Factor Premium

E/P	B/P	D/E	LOGSIZE	M12M
−3.4248	0.2229	−0.0005	0.0470	−2.4032
(0.4051)	(0.1652)	(0.0008)	(0.0549)	(0.2022)

Note: Estimated for the period from January 2016 to December 2020. Standard errors are inside parentheses. Factors are as in Table 6.2.

(S&P) 500 stocks in the period from January 2016 to December 2020. If we look at the E/P ratio factor premium for a moment, we see that it is −3.425. A negative premium indicates that a high factor exposure hurts stock returns. In the case of the E/P ratio factor, the expected stock return will drop by 3.425% for every unit of exposure. To some, these results may seem counterintuitive, since we are familiar with the value anomaly. However, over a short horizon, as with this period, the realized premium may be different than the long-term premium, and this failure of "value" consumed much of the talk in the quant world from 2016 to 2020.

Standard errors indicate how precise the estimates are. Small standard errors suggest that the estimates are very precise. For the E/P ratio and 12-month momentum, the standard errors are small enough to make the factor premiums "significant" in a statistical sense. For example, we can say with 95% certainty that the "true" value of the E/P ratio premium is approximately between −4.235 and −2.615, whereas the "true" value of the M12M premium is approximately between −2.807 and −1.999.[18]

6.5.2 Robustness Check

A model is not usually an exact description of reality, only a good approximation of it. In statistics, shortcomings in the model are called *specification errors*.[19] Specification errors arise in any regression, and estimation of the factor premium is no exception. Yet we should strive to build models that reflect persistent and stable

---

[18] Refer to Appendix C at www.ludwigbc.com under QEPM Exclusive Content for more on statistical significance, standard errors, and *t*-statistics.
[19] See Appendix C at www.ludwigbc.com under QEPM Exclusive Content for more on specification error.

patterns, as described by tenet 6 of quantitative equity portfolio management (QEPM). With a robustness check, we can gauge whether the factor premium estimates are stable when small details of the estimation change. If the current estimation is not robust, we ought to try an alternative estimation technique.

To check the robustness of the estimation, split the data set into a few subsets and see whether the estimates are very different across the subsets. They should not be too different if the estimation is robust. Subsets can be created along the time dimension. For example, we can estimate the factor premiums for the period from January 2016 to June 2018 and the period from July 2018 to December 2020, as reported in Table 6.5. Subsets also can be divided along the cross-sectional dimension. For example, we can estimate the factor premiums for different sectors, as shown in Table 6.6. These two tables suggest a certain level of stability across time and sectors.[20]

6.5.3 Outliers and MAD Estimator of Factor Premium

The weakness of the OLS method is that in trying to minimize the sum of the squared residuals, it is highly sensitive to outliers. If a robustness check indicates that the OLS estimator is very unstable, it may be necessary to use an alternative estimation procedure that is less sensitive to outliers.

TABLE 6.5

The Factor Premium for Subperiods

Period	E/P	B/P	D/E	LOGSIZE	M12M
Jan 2016–Jun 2018	−2.5101	0.3373	−0.0005	−0.0319	−0.9915
	(0.4041)	(0.1960)	(0.0007)	(0.0628)	(0.2225)
Jul 2018–Dec 2020	−5.1183	−0.2026	−0.0044	0.1601	−4.1142
	(0.7909)	(0.2657)	(0.0047)	(0.0902)	(0.3497)

Note: Standard errors are inside parentheses. Factors are as in Table 6.2.

---

[20] Eugene Fama would say that if you really believe a factor model, then you should not expect to see any sector effect on the estimates because the model already should have accounted for it. Nevertheless, it is industry practice to control for sectors with dummy variables.

TABLE 6.6

The Factor Premium for Various Economic Sectors

Sector	E/P	B/P	D/E	LOGSIZE	M12M
10	−4.8850	2.0557	0.0455	0.1761	−5.6620
	(0.9017)	(0.7182)	(0.1483)	(0.3644)	(1.1626)
15	−10.8167	−0.0625	−0.0157	−0.4396	−3.1329
	(2.0278)	(0.8931)	(0.0828)	(0.3454)	(0.9029)
20	−1.6735	0.7879	−0.0038	−0.0841	−3.0761
	(2.6884)	(0.8404)	(0.0046)	(0.1517)	(0.5620)
25	−4.2285	1.5400	−0.0003	0.3712	−2.4307
	(2.1720)	(0.6386)	(0.0009)	(0.1708)	(0.5544)
30	5.5367	−1.2432	−0.0023	−0.0827	−3.4636
	(2.2242)	(0.6087)	(0.0038)	(0.1641)	(0.7859)
35	5.0186	−1.6256	0.0202	−0.1480	−1.7809
	(3.1616)	(0.6732)	(0.0332)	(0.1437)	(0.4803)
40	−3.2311	0.4321	0.0122	−0.1228	−3.9668
	(3.3614)	(0.3431)	(0.0234)	(0.1343)	(0.6167)
45	−4.5227	−0.7912	0.0023	0.1103	−1.8753
	(2.2509)	(0.6619)	(0.0062)	(0.1250)	(0.4332)
50	−0.4454	0.5284	−0.0977	0.6444	−6.7083
	(3.3899)	(1.1857)	(0.1504)	(0.2827)	(1.6776)
55	−0.6537	0.3741	0.3129	−0.2492	−2.6367
	(0.9968)	(0.9778)	(0.1422)	(0.2326)	(0.8356)

Note: Estimated for the period from January 2016 to December 2020. Standard errors are inside parentheses. Factors are as in Table 6.2. Sector names are based on the Global Industry Classification Standard (GICS), i.e., Energy (10), Materials (15), Industrials (20), Consumer Discretionary (25), Consumer Staples (30), Health Care (35), Financials (40), Information Technology (45), Telecommunication Services (50), and Utilities (55).

The *minimum absolute deviation* (MAD) estimation, also known as *median estimation,* is one such alternative. The MAD minimizes the sum of the absolute value of residuals rather than the squared residuals. Since this approach avoids squaring the residuals, any outliers have a much smaller effect on the estimate than they do in the OLS approach. Standard statistical software supports the MAD approach.

Table 6.7 shows the MAD estimates of the factor premiums in our example. We again performed an estimation using S&P 500 stocks for the period January 2016 to December 2020. Note that the earnings-to-price ratio (E/P) changed its sign from being significantly negative to significantly positive when we shifted from the OLS to the MAD approach. This implies that primarily outliers are driving the E/P ratio estimate here.

TABLE 6.7

The MAD Factor Premium

E/P	B/P	D/E	LOGSIZE	M12M
0.7784	−0.2912	−0.0004	−0.0085	−2.6169
(0.3639)	(0.1484)	(0.0007)	(0.0493)	(0.1817)

Note: Estimated for the period from January 2016 to December 2020. Standard errors are inside parentheses. Factors are as in Table 6.2.

6.5.4 Heteroscedasticity and Autocorrelation-Consistent Estimation of the Standard Error

While OLS estimation often produces a not-so-reliable output, it has been the standard empirical tool for many generations of empirical analysts. Moreover, adopting an alternative estimation technique risks introducing additional errors, since every estimation technique is based on its own set of assumptions—and these assumptions may not be any more realistic than the assumptions driving OLS. Given this consideration, one popular approach is to continue to report the OLS estimates but at the same time to make adjustments for the standard errors so that certain assumptions of the OLS estimation are relaxed. More specifically, when calculating standard error, we may wish to relax two of the OLS assumptions: (1) that all the error terms of different firms have the same variance (the assumption of homoscedastic errors), and, (2) that the error terms of different time periods are independent (the assumption of no autocorrelation). The standard errors that we obtain after relaxing these two assumptions are called *heteroscedasticity- and autocorrelation-consistent standard errors* or, in short, *HAC standard errors*. Even for HAC standard errors, we do maintain certain restrictions regarding the error terms. For example, with HAC, we do not allow error terms of different firms to be correlated (though we allow error terms of one firm for different periods to be correlated). Also, HAC requires error terms of one firm for different periods to have the same variance (though we allow error terms of different firms to have different variances). The maintained assumptions guarantee that the OLS estimates are still consistent (i.e., correct if the sample is large enough), though they may not be the most efficient (i.e., there may be other estimates with greater precision). Under the assumption of heteroscedastic and autocorrelated errors, the variance of the factor premium can be calculated as

$$
\hat{V}\left[\begin{pmatrix} \hat{\alpha} \\ \hat{\mathbf{f}} \end{pmatrix}\right] = \left[\sum_{t=1}^{T}\sum_{i=1}^{N}\begin{pmatrix} 1 \\ \beta_{it} \end{pmatrix}\begin{pmatrix} 1 \\ \beta_{it} \end{pmatrix}'\right]^{-1} \left\{\sum_{i=1}^{N}\left[\sum_{t=1}^{T}\hat{\epsilon}_{it}\begin{pmatrix} 1 \\ \beta_{it} \end{pmatrix}\right]\left[\sum_{t=1}^{T}\hat{\epsilon}_{it}\begin{pmatrix} 1 \\ \beta_{it} \end{pmatrix}\right]'\right\}
$$

$$
\left[\sum_{t=1}^{T}\sum_{i=1}^{N}\begin{pmatrix} 1 \\ \beta_{it} \end{pmatrix}\begin{pmatrix} 1 \\ \beta_{it} \end{pmatrix}'\right]^{-1}
\tag{6.23}
$$

where the residual $\hat{\epsilon}_{it}$ is calculated from the OLS estimate as

$$
\hat{\epsilon}_{it} = r_{it} - \boldsymbol{\beta}_{it}'\hat{\mathbf{f}}
\tag{6.24}
$$

Compared to the simple variance formula in Eq. (6.21), we now have a rather complicated formula. Looking closely, however, one may note that the first and last terms are identical. (For this reason, the formula is sometimes referred to as a "sandwich formula.") The first and last terms represent the variation of factor exposure β_{it} whereas the middle term represents the variance of $\hat{\epsilon}_{it} \beta_{it}$. The HAC standard errors are simply the square root of the diagonal elements of the variance matrix shown above. Table 6.8 shows the HAC standard errors together with the OLS estimates of factor premiums. The earnings-to-price ratio and the book-to-price ratio have noticeably higher standard errors compared to the unadjusted standard errors shown in Table 6.4. That is, the premiums for these two factors are not precisely estimated, and the standard errors shown in Table 6.4 exaggerate the precision for these two premiums.

TABLE 6.8

The HAC Standard Errors along with the OLS Estimates

E/P	B/P	D/E	LOGSIZE	M12M
−3.4248	0.2229	−0.0005	0.0470	−2.4032
(1.1315)	(0.2268)	(0.0003)	(0.0612)	(0.3552)

Note: Estimated for the period from January 2016 to December 2020. Standard errors are inside parentheses. Factors are as in Table 6.2.

6.6 DECOMPOSITION OF RISK

Given the factor exposure β_i, the factor premium estimate $\hat{\mathbf{f}}$, and the constant estimate $\hat{\alpha}$, we can calculate the average stock return as the product of these two plus the constant, $\hat{\alpha} + \hat{\beta}_i'\hat{\mathbf{f}}$. To construct the optimal portfolio, however, we need to know the risk of the stock return. In the fundamental factor model, the risk of the stock return has two components: nondiversifiable risk captured by $\beta_i'\hat{\mathbf{f}}$ and diversifiable risk captured by $\hat{\epsilon}_i$. The total risk of the stock return is simply the sum of these two risks. Let's look at each of these two in turn.

Nondiversifiable risk arises from the randomness of the factor premium. Within the estimation sample, however, both factor exposure β_i and factor premium $\hat{\mathbf{f}}$ vary over time, and it is not necessary to separate these two components. For the purpose of risk decomposition, we carry out a series of cross-sectional regressions, one regression for each month t, rather than a single pooled regression. From the regression for month t, we obtain factor premium and constant estimates $\hat{\mathbf{f}}_t$ and $\hat{\alpha}_t$. By repeating the regressions for all the sample months, we obtain a time series of factor premium and constant estimates, $\hat{\mathbf{f}}_1 \dots \hat{\mathbf{f}}_T$ and $\hat{\alpha}_1 \dots \hat{\alpha}_T$. By multiplying the factor premium by the factor exposure and adding the constant, we also obtain a time series of $\hat{\alpha} + \beta_i'\hat{\mathbf{f}}$, i.e., $\hat{\alpha}_1 + \beta_{i1}'\hat{\mathbf{f}}_1, \dots, \hat{\alpha}_T + \beta_{iT}'\hat{\mathbf{f}}_T$. We can calculate the sample variance from this time series as

$$\frac{1}{T}\sum_{t=1}^{T}\left[\hat{\alpha}_t + \beta_{it}'\hat{\mathbf{f}}_t - \frac{1}{T}\sum_{t'=1}^{T}\left(\hat{\alpha}_{t'} + \beta_{it'}'\hat{\mathbf{f}}_{t'}\right)\right]^2 \tag{6.25}$$

This variance, or the sample standard variation obtained by taking the square root of the variance, is our measure of nondiversifiable risk.

The diversifiable risk represents the part of the variation in the stock return that the variation in the model's factors cannot explain. This part of the stock's variation appears as the error term ϵ_i, that is, σ_i^2. The procedures outlined in the previous paragraph provide an estimate of the variance of the error term:

$$\hat{\sigma}_i^2 = \frac{1}{T}\sum_{t=1}^{T}\left(r_{it} - \hat{\alpha}_t - \beta_{it}'\hat{\mathbf{f}}_t\right)^2 \tag{6.26}$$

This variance is our measure of the diversifiable risk. One can alternatively use the square root of the variance (standard deviation) as a measure of risk. The total risk of stock i is simply the sum of the two risk components:

$$\frac{1}{T}\sum_{t=1}^{T}\left[\hat{\alpha}_t + \hat{\boldsymbol{\beta}}'_{it}\hat{\mathbf{f}}_t - \frac{1}{T}\sum_{t'=1}^{T}\left(\hat{\alpha}_{t'} + \hat{\boldsymbol{\beta}}'_{it'}\hat{\mathbf{f}}_{t'}\right)\right]^2 + \frac{1}{T}\sum_{t=1}^{T}\left(r_{it} - \hat{\alpha}_t - \hat{\boldsymbol{\beta}}'_{it}\hat{\mathbf{f}}_t\right)^2 \quad (6.27)$$

Table 6.9 shows the decomposition of risk for selected stocks estimated from January 2016 to December 2020. We report the risk in terms of the variance and the standard deviation.

When we get to the stage of finding the optimal portfolio, we also need to know the correlations between stock returns. The total risk of a stock is composed of nondiversifiable risk and diversifiable risk. Likewise, the total return on a stock is composed of nondiversifiable and diversifiable components. The correlation between the returns on a pair of stocks consists of the correlation between their nondiversifiable components and the correlation between their diversifiable components. Instead of correlation, we will use covariance; the covariance between r_{it} and r_{jt} is

$$C(r_{it}, r_{jt}) = C\left(\hat{\boldsymbol{\beta}}'_{it}\hat{\mathbf{f}}_t, \hat{\boldsymbol{\beta}}'_{jt}\hat{\mathbf{f}}_t\right) + C(\hat{\epsilon}_{it}, \hat{\epsilon}_{jt}) \quad (6.28)$$

TABLE 6.9

The Risk Decomposition for Selected Stocks

Ticker	Total Risk		Nondiversifiable Risk		Diversifiable Risk	
	V	SD	V	SD	V	SD
AAPL	824.50	28.71	170.47	13.06	654.03	25.57
MSFT	364.38	19.09	149.52	12.23	214.85	14.66
AMZN	667.40	25.83	183.24	13.54	484.17	22.00
GOOGL	438.11	20.93	167.99	12.96	270.12	16.44
FB	682.49	26.12	179.62	13.40	502.86	22.42
BRK.B	368.75	19.20	254.25	15.95	114.51	10.70
JNJ	336.23	18.34	178.93	13.38	157.30	12.54
WMT	450.71	21.23	159.11	12.61	291.60	17.08
JPM	456.13	21.36	272.33	16.50	183.80	13.56
V	275.62	16.60	158.06	12.57	117.55	10.84

Note: Based on the period from January 2016 to December 2020. *V* refers to the variance, and SD refers to the standard deviation. Both variance and standard deviation are annualized and expressed in percentage. Company names for ticker symbols are reported in Table 6.2.

In practice, we estimate only the correlation between the non-diversifiable components of two stocks' returns. As for the diversifiable components, the correlation between them can, in principle, be estimated in a straightforward way using the standard estimation technique. In practice, though, it is rarely done this way. One reason is that there are often simply too many parameters to estimate precisely. If there are N stocks, then $[N(N-1)]/2$ covariances have to be estimated. These covariances cannot be estimated precisely without using a great many time intervals for the estimation. The second reason that the standard estimation technique is hardly used to estimate the diversifiable component of the return is that the diversifiable return, like diversifiable risk, has little bearing on the stock return to the investor (or so says modern financial economic theory). For both these reasons, the convention is to assume that diversifiable risk $C(\epsilon_{it}, \epsilon_{jt})$ equals zero.

6.7 CONCLUSION

In this chapter we explored one of the most common models of stock returns, the fundamental factor model. Factor models relate the return of a stock to the stock's exposure to risks (a.k.a. *factor exposures*) and the market's payoff to investors for taking on those risks (a.k.a. *factor premiums*). We showed how the fundamental factor model can act as a model of overall stock returns or, for managers who track an index, as a model of benchmark α. We explained how to obtain a stock's fundamental observable factor exposures and how to estimate the factor premiums that the market awards them. With the factor exposures and factor premiums in place, the fundamental factor model can predict the expected return and expected risk of any stock in a portfolio manager's investment universe. The model also can decompose the risk of a stock into its diversifiable and nondiversifiable components. The fundamental factor model is one basic tool for constructing a portfolio. In the next chapter we will take a look at an alternative tool, the economic factor model, that the portfolio manager also can use to predict and analyze stock returns and risks.

QUESTIONS

6.1. Describe the main steps in creating and estimating a fundamental factor model.

6.2. Explain why economic factors such as GDP and behavioral factors such as consumer sentiment cannot be included in a fundamental factor model.

6.3. One strength of the fundamental factor model over the economic factor model is that the data requirement is relatively small. What is the minimum data requirement to estimate the fundamental factor model? Is it possible to estimate the fundamental factor model from a single cross section (i.e., the observation of many stocks in one time period)?

6.4. It is possible to derive returns of many periodicities from returns of one periodicity. Suppose that we have estimated the following fundamental factor model using daily data:

$$r_i = \alpha + \beta_i f + \epsilon_i \quad \epsilon_i \sim N(0,\sigma^2)$$

Let us denote the estimates by $\hat{\alpha}$, $\hat{f}$, and $\hat{\sigma}^2$.

(a) What would be the expected daily return and the variance of the daily return?

(b) Assuming that error ϵ_i is serially uncorrelated over time, what would be the expected weekly return and the variance of the weekly return?

(c) Under the same assumption as in part (b), what would be the expected monthly return and the variance of the monthly return?

(d) Is the assumption made in parts (b) and (c) realistic?

6.5. It makes a difference whether one includes the risk-free rate in the model. Consider two versions of a fundamental factor model:

$$r_i = \alpha^{(1)} + \beta_i f^{(1)} + \epsilon_i \quad \epsilon_i \sim N[0, (\sigma^{(1)})^2]$$
$$r_i - r_f = \alpha^{(2)} + \beta_i f^{(2)} + \epsilon_i \quad \epsilon_i \sim N[0, (\sigma^{(2)})^2]$$

where r_f is the risk-free rate.

(a) If r_f is constant for the estimation period, what is the relationship between the estimates of $\alpha^{(1)}$, $f^{(1)}$, and $\sigma^{(1)}$ and those of $\alpha^{(2)}$, $f^{(2)}$, and $\sigma^{(2)}$?

(b) Would your answer to part (a) be different if r_f is not constant but is not correlated with any of the variables in the model?

(c)   Under what conditions does the inclusion of the risk-free rate in the model not change the estimates?

6.6.   Consider a fundamental factor model with many factors:

$$r_i = \alpha + \beta_{i1}f_1 + \cdots + \beta_{iK}f_K + \epsilon_i$$

The goodness of fit of the regression can be measured by the adjusted R^2:

$$\bar{R}^2 = 1 - \frac{\dfrac{N-1}{N-K-1}V(\hat{\epsilon}_i)}{V(r_i)}$$

where N is the number of observations, K is the number of factors, $\hat{\epsilon}_i$ is the residual from the regression (i.e., the part of r_i that was not explained by the regression), and $V(\cdot)$ refers to the sample variance.

(a)   Calculate $\bar{R}^2$ when the number of observations is 100, the number of factors is 2, the sample variance of the return is 5%, and the sample variance of the residual is 3%.

(b)   What will happen to $\bar{R}^2$ if we keep the number of observations constant and increase the number of factors to 4? Assume that the sample variance of the return and the residual did not change.

(c)   What would be the required number of observations to keep $\bar{R}^2$ unchanged when the number of factors increases to 4?

6.7.   Define the residual return. What are the main components of it?

6.8.   Suppose that we estimated a fundamental factor model

$$r_i = \alpha + \beta_i f + \epsilon_i$$

where β_i is the size exposure measured in dollars. Would the estimates of α and f be different if the size exposure were measured in thousand of dollars instead?

6.9.   After estimating a fundamental factor model, we obtained the following estimates:

$$r_i = 1.5 + 0.02\beta_{i1} + 0.3\beta_{i2} + \epsilon_i$$

where β_{i1} is the size exposure of firm i, and β_{i2} is the price-to-earnings ratio exposure.

    (a) What is the expected return of firm A whose size is 100 (million dollars) and that has a price-to-earnings ratio of 20?

    (b) What will happen to the expected return of firm A in part (a) if the firm size grows by 10 (million dollars)?

    (c) Explain why the factor premium can be interpreted as the marginal effect of the factor exposure on the expected return.

6.10. The following is the result of the estimation of a fundamental factor model:

$$r_i = 1.5 + 0.2\beta_i + \epsilon_i \quad \epsilon_i \sim N(0, 400)$$

    (a) If the sample variance of the factor exposure is 100, what would be the standard error of the coefficient estimate?

    (b) What would be the standard error if the factor exposure were almost constant in the sample?

    (c) Can you come up with a criterion to choose a factor based on your calculation in parts (a) and (b)?

6.11. Some portfolio managers remove the outliers from the sample before estimating a model. For example, one may decide to drop observations whose values are more than three standard deviations away from the mean. Considering the properties of ordinary least squares, what would be the consequence? Does it matter whether the outliers are determined based on the values of the stock returns or based on the values of the factor exposure?

6.12. Some portfolio managers may "winsorize" the outliers before using them in the estimation. For example, if the mean of a variable is μ and the standard deviation of the variables is σ, any value that is greater than $\mu + 3\sigma$ or less than $\mu - 3\sigma$ may be replaced with $\mu + 3\sigma$ or $\mu - 3\sigma$. Would the estimate of ordinary least squares still be unbiased (true on average)? Does it matter whether the variable we use for winsorization is the return or a factor exposure?

6.13. One solution to the problem of the outliers is to use the minimum absolute deviation (MAD) estimation instead of the ordinary least squares (OLS) estimation. Under what circumstances do these two estimations produce identical estimates?

6.14. Some researchers believe that small stocks experience higher variability in stock returns than large stocks do. That is, the variance of the error is believed to be greater for small stocks than for large stocks. Discuss the advantages and disadvantages of HAC standard errors in this situation.

6.15. Define diversifiable risk and nondiversifiable risk. In what sense can the risk be diversified?

CHAPTER 7

Economic Factor Models

Beta is the color of an angel's eye.

—Zvi Griliches

7.1 INTRODUCTION

Tenet 4 of quantitative equity portfolio management (QEPM) requires quantitative analysis to efficiently combine all the information relevant to an investment decision. In Chapter 6, we looked at the fundamental factor model as one efficient way to combine relevant information about stocks into a system for determining returns and risks. The economic factor model is the counterpart to the fundamental factor model. It also combines relevant stock information in an efficient way, but with a different twist on the factor model framework.[1]

The structure of the model remains the same as we move from the fundamental factor model to the economic factor model. The model still expresses the central idea that stock returns are the payoff for taking risk. As in the fundamental factor model, stock

---

[1] The material we present in this chapter is based on Chen et al. (1986), Fama and French (1993), Lehmann and Modest (1988), and Connor and Korajczyk (1988), who based their arguments on Ross (1976). Chen et al. developed a model for economic factors, whereas Fama and French developed a model for fundamental factors. Lehmann and Modest (1988) and Connor and Korajczyk (1988) developed models for statistical factors. All these academic studies are based on the arbitrage pricing theory of Ross (1976).

returns are determined by the product of factor exposures (i.e., exposures to risk) and factor premiums (i.e., payoffs for exposure to risk). In the economic factor model, however, the roles of the factor exposure and factor premium are, in a way, reversed. Recall that for the fundamental factor model, the factor exposure is observable in financial statements, whereas the factor premium must be estimated from a cross-sectional regression. In the economic factor model, the factor premium is the known value (or, at least, the value that can be calculated from given data), whereas the factor exposure must be estimated by a regression of stock returns on factor premiums.

Take, for instance, an economic factor model with just one factor, inflation. In this model, the factor premium is the observed rate of inflation (or a rate that corresponds to the inflation rate). The factor exposure is the stock's sensitivity or reactivity to inflation, which is estimated as the relationship between the return on the stock and the rate of inflation. The economic factor model, therefore, takes as a given the premium that the market generally places on exposure to the risk but requires the estimation of a particular stock's exposure to the risk. This type of model especially makes sense for economic factors, which represent external risks in the marketplace that affect all stocks.[2] In this case, the particular type of risk that we are concerned with is inflation. The factor premium therefore shows the amount of reward investors demand when they invest in stocks affected by inflation. This amount of reward demanded most likely will be different from the actual inflation rate for two reasons. The first is that the units are different. The inflation rate is not expressed in risk terms, so we cannot say that the reward for taking 1% inflation rate should be 1% expected return. The second is that not all inflation corresponds to risk. Specifically, the expected component of inflation does not qualify as risk; only the unexpected component of inflation should be considered a risk. So why do we use the actual inflation rate as the factor premium?

The economic factor model does not assume that the amount of reward demanded by investors is the actual inflation rate. What it assumes is that the amount of reward is a linear function of the

---

[2] The economic factor model can process fundamental factors, but it still frames them this way. Since the basic equations of both the economic and fundamental factor models are the same, though, they yield similar results when they use the same factors. Please see Chapter 3 for further explanation of the equivalence of the models.

actual inflation rate. The reward for exposure to an $x\%$ inflation rate may not be $x\%$ expected return, but it may be stated as $a + bx$. This assumption removes the necessity to distinguish between the true factor premium and the observed inflation rate because the estimation of the model will not be affected whether we use the true factor premium or the observed inflation rate. This assumption also takes care of the problem caused by the expected component of inflation. The expected component will be adjusted by the constant a in the formula $a + bx$. For this reason, for the remainder of this chapter we do not distinguish between the true factor premium and the observed values of the economic variables.

Mathematically, the economic factor model defines the return to stock i, r_i, as

$$r_i = \alpha_i + \beta_{i1}f_1 + \cdots + \beta_{iK}f_K + \epsilon_i \qquad (7.1)$$

where $f_1, \ldots, f_K$ are factor premiums (which do not vary across stocks and so do not have the subscript i), and $\beta_{i1}, \ldots, \beta_{iK}$ are factor exposures (which do vary across stocks and have the subscript i). The term α_i is the constant. The term $\beta_{i1}f_1 + \cdots + \beta_{iK}f_K$ represents the nondiversifiable risk of the stock, and ϵ_i, the error, reflects the diversifiable risk of the stock.[3] In terms of the basic equation, there is no difference between the fundamental factor model and the economic factor model.[4]

As with the fundamental factor model, we again define K-dimensional column vector $\mathbf{f}$ and $\boldsymbol{\beta}_i$ as follows:

$$\mathbf{f} = (f_1, \ldots, f_K)' \qquad (7.2)$$

$$\boldsymbol{\beta}_i = (\beta_{i1}, \ldots, \beta_{iK})' \qquad (7.3)$$

Using this notation,

$$r_i = \alpha_i + \boldsymbol{\beta}_i'\mathbf{f} + \epsilon_i \qquad (7.4)$$

As we saw in Chapter 6, the average stock return is the product of the factor exposure and the factor premium plus the constant term,

$$E(r_i) = \alpha_i + \boldsymbol{\beta}_i'E(\mathbf{f}) \qquad (7.5)$$

---

[3] Bear in mind that the only risk that matters to a diversified investor is the nondiversifiable risk.

[4] If you compare Eq. (7.1) to Eq. (6.2) very carefully, you will find one difference: the constant term α does not have subscript i in Eq. (6.2). Subscript i was not necessary in Eq. (6.2) as we presented the simplest version of the fundamental factor model. A more sophisticated version of the fundamental factor model is discussed in Chapter 16, where subscript i is necessary.

whereas the total risk is the sum of the nondiversifiable risk and the diversifiable risk, that is,

$$V(r_i) = \boldsymbol{\beta}_i' \, V(\mathbf{f})\boldsymbol{\beta}_i + V(\epsilon_i) \qquad (7.6)$$

The model also can express the stock return at a particular time interval. We use lowercase letter t to indicate one time interval and the capital letter T to indicate the number of time intervals. Thus the return to stock i at time t, r_{it}, is written as

$$r_{it} = \alpha_i + \boldsymbol{\beta}_i' \mathbf{f}_t + \epsilon_{it} \quad t = 1, \ldots, T \qquad (7.7)$$

where $\boldsymbol{\beta}_i$ is a K-dimensional column vector of the factor exposure of stock i, $\mathbf{f}_t$ is a K-dimensional column vector of the factor premium at time t, and ϵ_{it} is the diversifiable component of the return to stock i at time t.[5] Note that the factor premium has time subscript t because it changes over time. That is, we interpret the factor premium as a random variable that has different values at different times. On the other hand, the factor exposure does not have time subscript t because it is not assumed to change over time. We interpret the factor exposure as an unknown parameter rather than a random variable.

In academia, the economic factor model has long been the only factor model deemed valid, with the fundamental factor model only recently gaining some credence. In fact, the academic literature fails to distinguish between economic and fundamental factor models, using instead the term *multifactor pricing model* to refer generally to the framework of the economic factor model. We choose to distinguish between the two types of models using the terms *economic factor model* and *fundamental factor model* because many practitioners use the former for modeling stock returns against economic indicators and the latter for modeling stock returns against stock fundamentals. Table 7.1 summarizes the process of creating an economic factor model.

---

[5] Typically, when we estimate these factor models, we use information at time t to predict returns at time $t + 1$. For convenience, we sometimes write in this book the equation with time subscript t everywhere, as we do here. The factor exposure and the returns are at time t. The equation should still be interpreted as using information at time t to predict returns at time $t + 1$. In other words, the factor exposure at time t is really the factor exposure value as of the end of the previous period, $t - 1$, which we may refer to, sometimes, as the beginning-of-month exposure for time t.

TABLE 7.1

Creating an Economic Factor Model

Preliminary work:

1. Choose the factors for the model.
2. Determine the treatment of the risk-free rate.
3. Define the investment universe.
4. Decide on the time interval and time period of the data.

Main steps for modeling total stock return (for nonbenchmark managers):

1. Stock returns are estimated with the following equation: $r_i = \alpha_i + \beta_{i1}f_1 + \cdots + \beta_{iK}f_K + \epsilon_i$.
2. Collect stock return and factor premium data for the time period at each time interval. factor premium data are readily available for economic/behavioral/market factors. To calculate factor premiums for fundamental/technical/analyst factors, use the zero-investment portfolio method. To calculate factor premiums for statistical factors, use principal-component analysis.
3. If there are sufficient factor premium data, estimate the factor exposure from a time-series regression of the stock return on the factor premium.
4. If there are insufficient factor premium data to perform a time-series regression, use characteristic matching to identify similar firms that can be used as proxies for the firms lacking data. Collect stock return and factor premium data for the proxies. Using the proxies' data, estimate the factor exposure from a time-series regression of the stock return on the factor premium.
5. Calculate each stock's average return as the product of the factor exposure and the vector containing the stock's factor premiums.
6. Decompose the risk of the stock return into its diversifiable and nondiversifiable components.
7. Calculate the correlation between the returns of the stocks in the investment universe.

Main steps for modeling residual stock return (for benchmark managers):

1. Stock returns are estimated with the following equation: $r_i = \tilde{\alpha}_i + \tilde{\beta}_i r_B + \tilde{\epsilon}_i$.
2. Collect stock return and benchmark return data for the given time period at the given time intervals.
3. After estimating $\tilde{\alpha}$ and $\tilde{\beta}$, calculate the residual return as $\tilde{r}_i \equiv \tilde{\alpha}_i + \tilde{\epsilon}_i$.
4. Estimate residual return with the following equation: $\tilde{r}_i = \alpha_i + \beta_{i1}f_1 + \cdots + \beta_{iK}f_K + \epsilon_i$.
5. Follow steps 2 through 7 of the main steps for modeling total stock return, substituting the residual return for the total stock return.

7.2 PRELIMINARY WORK

As with the fundamental factor model, constructing the economic factor model begins with good planning. The general decisions are the same—the choice of factors, the treatment of the risk-free rate, and the makeup of the sample (in terms of time interval, time period, and stock universe). Since the criteria for deciding how to treat the risk-free rate, for determining the investment universe, and for defining the time interval and period are the same for either type of model, we will just discuss the factor choice here.[6]

The strength of the economic factor model is that it can include practically all kinds of factors. In terms of how the model treats them, there are three categories of factors:

1. *Economic/behavioral/market factors:* Gross domestic product (GDP), inflation, unemployment, interest rates, and other macroeconomic variables; consumer sentiment index, business confidence index, investor sentiment index, or other survey-based indexes; returns on broad market indexes such as the Standard & Poor's (S&P) 500 or returns on other market group/industry indexes

2. *Fundamental/technical/analyst factors:* Log of market capital-ization, book-to-price ratio, earnings-to-price ratio, debt-to-equity ratio, and other firm characteristics available through financial statements; momentum, trading volume, and other information reflected in trading data; analyst rating changes, earnings revisions, or other information provided by analysts

3. *Statistical factors:* Factors obtained from principal-component analysis applied to historical returns

For economic/behavioral/market factors, computation is min-imal. In most cases, relevant information is publicly available or provided by data vendors. On the other hand, for fundamental/technical/analyst factors, computation can be somewhat demand-ing, and even though they may be obtained from an external source, the vendor's methodology should be examined carefully. Some studies suggest, though, that thoroughly vetted fundamental/technical/analyst factors predict stock returns more effectively than other factor groups do.[7] Statistical factors require the highest level of computation.

---

[6] Refer to Chapter 6 for a discussion of the risk-free rate and investment universe decisions.

[7] Chen et al. (1986), Lehmann and Modest (1988), and Connor and Korajczyk (1988), who used nonfundamental factors, report rather limited out-of-sample predictive power of their models. On the other hand, Fama and French (1993) and Daniel and Titman (1997) and others who used fundamental factors generally report higher predictive power. See also Chapter 16.

7.3 BENCHMARK AND α

Many quantitative portfolio managers manage their portfolios against a benchmark. As we mentioned in Chapter 6, it is useful but not necessary to account for the benchmark at the outset of creating a model. Some portfolio managers prefer to account for the benchmark later on—by controlling for the tracking error at the portfolio construction stage, for instance.[8] As a measure of portfolio performance, however, it can be useful to create a model that reflects, or adjusts for, the effects of the benchmark. One way to do this is to remove the benchmark-related return from the stock return before building the model.[9] We first regress stock returns on the benchmark returns and calculate the residual, the part of stock returns that is not correlated with the benchmark return. Then we construct an economic factor model for the residual stock return rather than the total stock return. The resulting model shows the relationship between the factor premium, the factor exposure, and the portion of the stock return that is above and beyond the benchmark return.

Alternatively, we can include the benchmark in the economic factor model explicitly. If the benchmark is the broad-market index, the capital asset pricing model (CAPM) supports its inclusion in the model as a predictor of stock returns. Even if the benchmark is something other than the broad-market index, including it in the model will clarify the relationship between the portfolio and the benchmark.

Let r_B be the benchmark return. If we add the benchmark as the Kth factor in the economic factor model, then the economic factor model becomes

$$r_i = \alpha_i + \beta_{i,1} f_1 + \cdots + \beta_{i,K-1} f_{K-1} + \beta_{i,K} r_B + \epsilon_i \qquad (7.8)$$

Given this formulation, we can interpret the right-hand side of the equation up to the term $\beta_{i,K-1} f_{K-1}$ as the expected return of stock i that is not related to the benchmark. Collectively, these terms represent the benchmark alpha, or α^B, that is,

$$\alpha^B = \alpha_i + \beta_{i,1} f_1 + \cdots + \beta_{i,K-1} f_{K-1} \qquad (7.9)$$

---

[8] See Chapter 9 for a discussion of how to control for the tracking error.
[9] See Section 6.3 of Chapter 6.

The benchmark α shows the contribution of the portfolio manager (and the model he or she creates) to the stock return and is one measure of the portfolio manager's performance.[10]

7.4 THE FACTOR PREMIUM

Recall that to create the fundamental factor model, the portfolio manager collects a data set of many observations of stock return and factor exposure. The factor exposure changes over time (and the factor premium—a single, statistically estimated proportion—remains constant). By contrast, to create the economic factor model, the portfolio manager gathers pairs of stock returns and factor premiums, and the factor premiums change over time. If there are K factors, one needs to find the factor premiums of the K factors at each time interval t, $\mathbf{f}_t = (f_{1t}, ..., f_{Kt})$.

In the economic factor model, the factor premium is the *known* value (as opposed to the factor exposure, which is a regression *estimate*). This does not mean that one can always observe a factor premium directly, though. For economic/behavioral/market factors, the computation is rather trivial. For fundamental/technical/analyst factors, though, the computation is somewhat more demanding, and for statistical factors, it poses quite a bit of a challenge.

7.4.1 Factor Premium for Economic/Behavioral/ Market Factors

Obtaining factor premiums for economic/behavioral/market factors does not involve any computation. All we need to do is simply "copy and paste" the values.[11]

Table 7.2 presents the premiums for three factors: unemployment, consumer sentiment, and overall market return. To find the factor premium for unemployment, we simply take the unemployment rate published by the Bureau of Labor Statistics (BLS). For example, the unemployment rate in December 2019 was 3.6%, so

---

[10] The reader should consult Chapter 2, where we discussed the various types of α's that are used in the portfolio management world.

[11] People sometimes use the variation from the mean as the factor premium to reflect the idea that what matters is the surprise of the variable, not the level of the macro variable. This surprise approach, however, does not improve the model unless the deviation from the mean really reflects the surprise. It is not easy to measure the magnitude of the surprise.

TABLE 7.2

Premium of Unemployment, Consumer Sentiment, and Market Factors

	Unemployment Rate	Consumer Sentiment Growth	Excess Market Return
Jan 2020	3.60	0.50	−0.17
Feb 2020	3.50	1.20	−8.35
Mar 2020	3.50	−11.78	−12.47
Apr 2020	4.40	−19.42	12.82
Apr 2020	14.80	0.70	4.75
Jun 2020	13.30	8.02	1.98
Jul 2020	11.10	−7.17	5.63
Aug 2020	10.20	2.21	7.18
Sep 2020	8.40	8.50	−3.81
Oct 2020	7.80	1.74	−2.67
Nov 2020	6.90	−5.99	10.94
Dec 2020	6.70	4.94	3.83

Note: All numbers are in percent. The specific formulas for each factor can be found in Appendix 16A.

after allowing for a one-month reporting gap, the factor premium for January 2020 is 3.6%. For consumer sentiment, we take the consumer sentiment index compiled by the University of Michigan, which shows the level of consumer sentiment for each month. The factor premium is simply the growth rate of this index from one month to the next month. For example, the consumer sentiment index for December 2019 was 99.3, whereas the index for January 2020 was 99.8. Thus, our consumer sentiment factor premium is 0.50% $[=(\frac{99.8}{99.3}-1)\cdot 100]$. The market factor premium is the S&P 500 total return in excess of the one-month U.S. Treasury bill return.[12] For example, in January 2020, the S&P 500 total return was −0.04%, whereas the one-month U.S. Treasury bill return was 0.13%. Thus, the factor premium for January 2020 was −0.17% (= −0.04 − 0.13).

After we have all the factor premiums for a certain time interval, we may store them in a set of vectors $\{\mathbf{f}_1, ..., \mathbf{f}_T\}$, where $\mathbf{f}_t$ is the

---

[12] We used the one-month Treasury bill return downloaded from the website of Professor Kenneth R. French of Tuck School of Business: https://mba.tuck.dartmouth.edu/pages/faculty/ken.french/data_library.html.

factor premium for time t. In this example, we can write the factor premium for January 2020 as

$$\mathbf{f}_{\text{Jan20}} = (3.6, 0.50, -0.17) \qquad (7.10)$$

The first element of f_t always reflects the existence of the constant term in the return equation.

7.4.2 Factor Premium for Fundamental/ Technical/Analyst Factors

A little more computation is necessary to find the factor premiums for fundamental/technical/analyst factors. The computation involves constructing zero-investment portfolios and calculating their returns. A zero-investment portfolio simultaneously takes a long position in a portfolio of stocks with high factor exposures and a short position in a portfolio of stocks with low factor exposures. Suppose that we want to find the factor premium on value, and suppose that we use the book-to-price (B/P) ratio as a proxy for value. We need to identify a portfolio of stocks with high exposure to the value factor (i.e., high B/P ratio) and a portfolio of stocks with low exposure to the value factor (i.e., low B/P ratio). To be systematic about it, we can start by ranking all the stocks at time t in order of their B/P ratio, with the highest ratio stock ranked first. We can create a high-value portfolio by equally weighting the stocks in the top 33% of the list and a low-value portfolio by equally weighting the stocks in the bottom 33%. The zero-investment portfolio return equals the difference between the return on the high-value portfolio and the return on the low-value portfolio.

The frequency of the zero-investment portfolio construction needs to be carefully selected if the sorting variable is not frequently updated. In the case of the book-to-price ratio, book values are only reported every quarter, while price is updated daily. While it is possible to calculate the book-to-price ratio every day, the daily fluctuation in this ratio would only reflect daily changes in the stock price rather than daily changes in the book value. Therefore, the ratio is likely to have a big jump when the book values are updated. Thus, creating a zero-investment portfolio too frequently may not reflect information an investor needs and, consequently, may not be a wise choice.

It is important to note that a single piece of data can represent more than one type of factor. The same B/P ratio value, for instance, can either be considered high exposure to a value factor or low exposure to a growth factor. There are many instances of this sort of symmetry. We could use market capitalization figures to measure a small-size factor, in which case a large market capitalization would mean low exposure to the small-size factor. Conversely, we could interpret the same large market cap figure as a high exposure to a large-size factor. If we are considering including a momentum factor in the model, a low exposure to the momentum factor means the same thing as a high exposure to the contrarian factor. The same numerical figure can stand in for either factor. In fact, we could use either factor to represent the continuity or change in direction of a stock's return from one year to the next. The sign and name of the factor do not matter as long as we assign consistent meanings (low exposure or high exposure, as the case may be) to high and low values.

In general, these are the steps to calculate the factor premium for fundamental/technical/analyst factors:

1. Rank all the stocks at time 1 in terms of the factor.
2. Create high-exposure and low-exposure portfolios by equally weighting the stocks in the top 33% of the list and in the bottom 33% of the list. (A critical value other than 33% may be justifiable.[13])
3. Calculate the zero-investment portfolio return as the difference between the returns on the high-exposure and low-exposure portfolios. The return on the zero-investment portfolio is the factor premium for time 1.

Repeat these steps for time 2. If lack of data prevents the construction of new portfolios for time 2, calculate the returns as of time 2 on the same portfolios used for time 1. Repeat the procedure for each factor at each time interval. In other words, the total number of iterations of the procedure will equal the number of factors multiplied by the number of time intervals. Table 7.3 presents the premium for the size and value factors.[14]

---

[13] If there are clear breaks elsewhere in the list, then divide the list accordingly. In the absence of other clear breaks, use 33% as the default cutoff value.

[14] For size, we use the log of market capitalization and for value, we use the B/P ratio.

TABLE 7.3

Premium of Market Capitalization and Book-to-Price Factors

	Log of Market Capitalization (LOGSIZE)	Book-to-Price Ratio (B/P)
Jan 2020	3.67	−8.35
Feb 2020	−1.00	−3.34
Mar 2020	6.71	−10.83
Apr 2020	−6.55	2.99
May 2020	1.22	−7.85
Jun 2020	−5.01	−1.67
Jul 2020	2.66	−6.96
Aug 2020	−1.74	1.98
Sep 2020	1.79	−3.81
Oct 2020	−0.83	4.74

Note: The figures are in percent. To create a zero-investment portfolio, we include the stocks with low values (i.e., small market capitalization or low B/P ratio) in the short portfolio and stocks with high values (large market capitalization or high B/P ratio) in the long portfolio. The zero-investment portfolio return is the long portfolio returns minus the short portfolio returns. Thus, a positive number for B/P or value means that value stocks did well in that month and a positive number for market capitalization (also known as SIZE or LOGSIZE) indicates that large companies did better than small companies in that month. In this sense, our LOGSIZE portfolio is different than, for example, the Fama–French SMB, which is the small-cap portfolio minus the large-cap portfolio. In addition, our measure of market capitalization is actually the natural log of the market capitalization of a company.

7.4.3 Factor Premium for Statistical Factors

Obtaining factor premiums for statistical factors involves a rather intensive computation. The computational procedure is known as *principal-component analysis* and is available on standard computer software packages.

The starting point for principal-component analysis is estimating the variance-covariance matrix of stock returns. We will express N stock returns at time t as an N-dimensional column vector; that is, $\mathbf{r}_t = (r_{1t}, \ldots, r_{Nt})'$. We have a total of T such vectors $\{\mathbf{r}_1, \ldots, \mathbf{r}_T\}$. The variance-covariance matrix of returns Σ is estimated as

$$\hat{\Sigma} = \frac{1}{T}\sum_{t=1}^{T}\mathbf{r}_t\mathbf{r}_t' - \bar{\mathbf{r}}\,\bar{\mathbf{r}}' \tag{7.11}$$

where $\bar{\mathbf{r}}$ is the average return vector, that is,

$$\bar{\mathbf{r}} = \frac{1}{T}\sum_{t=1}^{T}\mathbf{r}_t \tag{7.12}$$

Once we have the variance-covariance matrix, we "diagonalize" it by finding an orthogonal matrix $\mathbf{Q}$ (that is, $\mathbf{Q}^{-1} = \mathbf{Q}'$) such that

$$\mathbf{Q}' \hat{\boldsymbol{\Sigma}} \mathbf{Q} = \mathbf{D} \qquad (7.13)$$

where $\mathbf{D}$ is a diagonal matrix whose diagonal elements are eigenvalues (i.e., characteristic values) of $\hat{\boldsymbol{\Sigma}}$. It turns out that each column of $\mathbf{Q}$ is an orthonormal (i.e., of unit length) eigenvector corresponding to eigenvalues of $\hat{\boldsymbol{\Sigma}}$.

To be more specific, let $\lambda_1, \ldots, \lambda_N$ be the eigenvalues of $\hat{\boldsymbol{\Sigma}}$ such that $\lambda_1 \geq \cdots \geq \lambda_N \geq 0$. (Since $\hat{\boldsymbol{\Sigma}}$ is a positive definite matrix, all the eigenvalues are positive.) Then matrix $\mathbf{D}$ is constructed as

$$\mathbf{D} = \begin{pmatrix} \lambda_1 & & 0 \\ & \ddots & \\ 0 & & \lambda_N \end{pmatrix} \qquad (7.14)$$

Let $\mathbf{q}_1, \ldots, \mathbf{q}_N$ be the orthonormal eigenvectors corresponding to $\lambda_1, \ldots, \lambda_N$. Then matrix $\mathbf{Q}$ is

$$\mathbf{Q} = (\mathbf{q}_1, \ldots, \mathbf{q}_N) \qquad (7.15)$$

If we want to find K factors, then we obtain K factor premiums by weighting individual stock returns using the first K columns of $\mathbf{Q}$. That is, factor premiums $f_1, \ldots, f_K$ are defined as

$$f_{1,t} = \mathbf{q}_1' \mathbf{r}_t$$
$$\vdots \qquad\qquad (7.16)$$
$$f_{K,t} = \mathbf{q}_K' \mathbf{r}_t$$

These K factors together have the highest in-sample explanatory power for N stock returns among any set of K explanatory variables constructed from linear combinations of N stock returns.[15]

7.5 FACTOR EXPOSURE

7.5.1 The Standard Approach

In the economic factor model, factor exposures typically are determined from the time-series regression of stock returns on factor premiums. Since the regression coefficients (the factor exposures) measure the sensitivity of the dependent variable (the stock return)

---

[15] For further details, see page 399 of Srivastava (2002).

to the change in the independent variables (the factor premiums), factor exposures sometimes are called *factor sensitivities*. They are also sometimes referred to as *factor loadings*.

Given the returns of stock i and the factor premium for T periods of time, $\{r_{i1}, \ldots, r_{iT}\}$ and $\{\mathbf{f}_1, \ldots, \mathbf{f}_T\}$, we can estimate the following equation[16]:

$$r_{it} = \alpha_i + \boldsymbol{\beta}_i'\mathbf{f}_t + \epsilon_{it} \qquad t = 1, \ldots, T \qquad (7.17)$$

where "coefficient" $\boldsymbol{\beta}_i$ is the factor exposure that we wish to discover, and ϵ_{it} is the error term reflecting the diversifiable risk of stock returns. The ordinary least squares (OLS) estimator of $\boldsymbol{\beta}_i$ is given by

$$\hat{\boldsymbol{\beta}}_i = \left[\sum_{t=1}^{T}(\mathbf{f}_t - \bar{\mathbf{f}})(\mathbf{f}_t - \bar{\mathbf{f}})'\right]^{-1}\left[\sum_{t=1}^{T}(\mathbf{f}_t - \bar{\mathbf{f}})(r_{it} - \bar{r}_i)\right]^{-1} \qquad (7.18)$$

where

$$\bar{\mathbf{f}} = \frac{1}{T}\sum_{t=1}^{T}\mathbf{f}_t \qquad (7.19)$$

and

$$\bar{r}_i = \frac{1}{T}\sum_{t=1}^{T}r_{it} \qquad (7.20)$$

By repeating the regression for each of the N stocks, we will obtain all the factor exposures we need: $\{\hat{\boldsymbol{\beta}}_1, \ldots, \hat{\boldsymbol{\beta}}_N\}$. The standard error of the factor exposure is the square root of (the diagonal elements of) the following variance:

$$\hat{V}(\hat{\boldsymbol{\beta}}_i) = \hat{\sigma}_i^2\left[\sum_{t=1}^{T}(\mathbf{f}_t - \bar{\mathbf{f}})(\mathbf{f}_t - \bar{\mathbf{f}})'\right]^{-1} \qquad (7.21)$$

where $\hat{\sigma}_i^2$ is the estimated variance of ϵ_{it}:

$$\hat{\sigma}_i^2 = \frac{1}{T}\sum_{t=1}^{T}(r_{it} - \hat{\alpha}_i - \hat{\boldsymbol{\beta}}_i'\mathbf{f}_t)^2 \qquad (7.22)$$

Table 7.4 presents the factor exposure estimates and standard errors for selected stocks for a five-factor model. These factor

---

[16] We are assuming that the number of time intervals is constant across stocks. This does not have to be the case in general. If the number of time intervals is different for different stocks, we would indicate the number of time intervals T with the subscript i.

TABLE 7.4

Factor Exposure of Selected Stocks

Ticker	Unemployment Rate (UR)	Consumer Sentiment Growth (CSG)	Excess Market Returns (MKT)	Log of Market Capitalization (LOGSIZE)	Book-to-Market Ratio (B/P)
AAPL	0.215	0.226	1.418	−0.066	−0.647
	(0.411)	(0.191)	(0.218)	(0.354)	(0.310)
MSFT	−0.297	0.127	1.008	0.203	−0.320
	(0.233)	(0.108)	(0.124)	(0.201)	(0.176)
WMT	0.231	−0.302	0.473	0.660	0.244
	(0.280)	(0.130)	(0.148)	(0.241)	(0.211)
JNJ	−0.309	−0.141	0.768	0.191	−0.025
	(0.233)	(0.108)	(0.123)	(0.200)	(0.175)
AMZN	−0.356	−0.181	1.345	−0.088	−0.841
	(0.379)	(0.176)	(0.201)	(0.326)	(0.285)

Note: For the period from January 2016 to December 2020. Standard errors inside the parentheses. Company names for ticker symbols are Apple (AAPL), Microsoft (MSFT), Walmart (WMT), Johnson & Johnson (JNJ), and Amazon (AMZN).

exposures were estimated using monthly data from January 2016 to December 2020. The unemployment factor exposures are negative for Microsoft, Johnson & Johnson, and Amazon but positive for Apple and Walmart. This reflects Apple's and Walmart's positions as business-cycle-defensive stocks: stocks whose values tend to go up when the economy slows down.[17] Although one would expect all five stocks in Table 7.4 to have a positive exposure to the log of market capitalization factor, they do not. That is, Microsoft, Walmart, and Johnson & Johnson have a positive exposure, meaning these stock returns tend to be positive when the portfolio of large-cap companies does better than a portfolio of small-cap companies. However, Amazon and Apple have a slightly negative reading. The value or book-to-price exposures indicate that Walmart is a value stock (with a positive exposure to the value or book-to-price factor), whereas the other companies are growth stocks (with negative exposures to the book-to-price factor).

---

[17] One might not think of Apple as a defensive stock, but it could be that the iPhone has become a staple for individuals and thus has altered the way Apple's stock price behaves.

It is worth noting that while the factor exposure estimates in Eq. (7.4) can be explained with common sense, this does not necessarily imply that they are identical to the factor exposures we used for the fundamental factor model in Chapter 6. For example, the ranking of stocks according to estimated size exposure does not exactly correspond to the ranking of stocks according to actual market capitalization, which was what we used as the size factor exposure in Chapter 6. As a result, here Walmart ranks first in terms of size exposure, whereas it ranks fourth after Apple, Microsoft, Amazon, and Johnson & Johnson in terms of actual market capitalization. Similarly, the ranking of stocks by the estimated B/P ratio or value exposure does not correspond exactly to the ranking of stocks by the observed B/P ratio of each stock.

7.5.2 When the Standard Approach Fails

To run time-series regressions, portfolio managers need to have enough data on stock returns and factor premiums to thoroughly cover a reasonable time period at regular time intervals. Recent initial public offerings (IPOs) and the stocks of recently merged or divested companies lack sufficient data for meaningful regressions. For a stock with insufficient data, we may infer the factor exposures by weighting groups of similar stocks and using the weighted factor exposures as proxies for the original stock's exposures.

When two firms merge, the natural thing to do is to find the weighted average of the factor exposures of the two premerger firms.[18] The appropriate weights would be the market capitalizations of the premerger firms. Suppose that firm A and firm B merged recently. From stock returns of firm A, r_{At}, we can find the factor exposures of firm A, $\hat{\beta}_A$, by regressing factor premiums on stock returns, that is,

$$\hat{\beta}_A = \left[\sum_{t=1}^{T} (\mathbf{f}_t - \bar{\mathbf{f}})(\mathbf{f}_t - \bar{\mathbf{f}})' \right]^{-1} \left[\sum_{t=1}^{T} (\mathbf{f}_t - \bar{\mathbf{f}})(r_{At} - \bar{r}_A)' \right] \qquad (7.23)$$

---

[18] This is one method to approach the problem, especially when running models on a large database of firms. In some cases, the analysis is much more complex, such as when the acquiring firm does so by issuing much more debt.

We can find the factor exposures of firm B, $\hat{\beta}_B$, in a similar way. Then the factor exposures of the merged firm $\hat{\beta}_{AB}$ can be calculated by

$$\hat{\beta}_{AB} = \frac{s_A}{s_A + s_B}\,\hat{\beta}_A + \frac{s_B}{s_A + s_B}\,\hat{\beta}_B \qquad (7.24)$$

where s_A is the premerger market capitalization of firm A, and s_B is the premerger market capitalization of firm B.

For a recent IPO, the only available information about the firm is the observable firm characteristics (i.e., what is reported in financial statements). We can use this information to find similar firms and take the average factor exposures of those similar firms. Suppose that we want to find similar firms using L characteristics. Then we calculate the Z-score for each of the L characteristics of each firm for which we already have factor exposures (see Chapter 5 for Z-score). Let a young firm i's Z-score be $\mathbf{z}_i = (z_{i1}, \ldots, z_{iL})$. To identify similar firms, we can choose a small critical level e and find all firms j such that $(\mathbf{z}_i - \mathbf{z}_j)'(\mathbf{z}_i - \mathbf{z}_j) < e$. We choose a critical level e that will give us more than one similar firm. Once we identify the similar firms, we can take the equal-weighted average of the factor exposures of the similar firms as the factor exposure of firm i. That is, if firms $1, \ldots, M$ are similar to young firm C, then the factor exposure of the young firm C, $\hat{\beta}_C$, is given by

$$\hat{\beta}_C = \frac{1}{M}\left(\hat{\beta}_1 + \cdots + \hat{\beta}_M\right) \qquad (7.25)$$

where $\hat{\beta}_1, \ldots, \hat{\beta}_M$ are the factor exposures of firms $1, \ldots, M$.

This process of identifying similar firms is called *characteristic matching*, and it applies to searching for other characteristics, such as expected stock return, as well.[19] An alternative to characteristic matching is using the industry-average figure. For example, the average factor exposure of the entire pharmaceutical industry can stand in for the factor exposure of one new pharmaceutical company's stock. This approach is used quite often to guess the market "beta" of IPO stocks. Financial economic research suggests, however, that characteristic matching works better than using the industry average.

---

[19] See Chincarini and Kim (2001) for the application.

7.6 DECOMPOSITION OF RISK

7.6.1 The Standard Approach

The total risk of the stock return is the sum of nondiversifiable risk and diversifiable risk. The nondiversifiable risk depends on the factor exposure and the variance of the factor premium, whereas the diversifiable risk equals the variance of the error term, that is,

$$V(r_i) = \beta_i' V(\mathbf{f})\beta_i + V(\epsilon_i) \tag{7.26}$$

We already have the estimate for β_i. Given the factor premium data $\{\mathbf{f}_1, \ldots, \mathbf{f}_T\}$, finding the estimate for $V(\mathbf{f}_t)$ is straightforward:

$$\hat{V}(\mathbf{f}) = \frac{1}{T}\sum_{t=1}^{T}(\mathbf{f}_t - \bar{\mathbf{f}})(\mathbf{f}_t - \bar{\mathbf{f}})' \tag{7.27}$$

The estimate for $V(\epsilon_i)$ is obtained naturally from estimation of the factor exposure if the factor exposure was estimated by the standard approach in Section 7.5.1. However, if the factor exposure was estimated by the approach in Section 7.5.2, we need to use an alternative approach. Given the estimate of the factor exposure and constant $\hat{\beta}_i$ and $\hat{\alpha}_i$, the estimate for $V(\epsilon_i)$ is as follows:

$$\hat{V}(\epsilon_i) = \frac{1}{T}\sum_{t=1}^{T}(r_{it} - \hat{\alpha}_i - \hat{\beta}_i'\mathbf{f}_t)^2 \tag{7.28}$$

Table 7.5 shows the decomposition of risk for selected stocks estimated from January 2016 to December 2020. We show the risk

TABLE 7.5

Risk Decomposition for Selected Stocks

Ticker	Total Risk		Nondiversifiable Risk		Diversifiable Risk	
	V	SD	V	SD	V	SD
AAPL	911.73	30.19	456.93	21.38	454.80	21.33
MSFT	334.74	18.30	188.32	13.72	146.42	12.10
WMT	302.20	17.38	91.42	9.56	210.78	14.52
JNJ	278.29	16.68	133.00	11.53	145.29	12.05
AMZN	823.41	28.70	437.56	20.92	385.85	19.64

Note: Based on the period from January 2016 to December 2020. V refers to the variance, and SD refers to the standard deviation. Both variance and standard deviation are annualized and expressed as percentages. Company names for ticker symbols are reported in Table 7.4.

as measured by the variance and the standard deviation. Note that the relative size of the diversifiable risk varies quite a bit across stocks.

When we get to the stage of finding the optimal portfolio, we also need to know the correlation among stock returns. The correlation between two stocks' returns has two parts: the correlation between the nondiversifiable components and the correlation between the diversifiable components. The covariance between two stock returns r_i and r_j is

$$C(r_i, r_j) = \beta_i' V(\mathbf{f})\, \beta_j + C(\epsilon_i, \epsilon_j) \tag{7.29}$$

The estimate for $C(\epsilon_i, \epsilon_j)$ can be found from estimation of the factor exposure, that is,

$$\hat{C}\left(\epsilon_i, \epsilon_j\right) = \frac{1}{T}\sum_{t=1}^{T}(r_{it} - \hat{\alpha}_i - \hat{\beta}_i'\mathbf{f}_t)\,(r_{jt} - \hat{\alpha}_j - \hat{\beta}_j'\mathbf{f}_t) \tag{7.30}$$

In practice, however, unless T is quite large, it is conventional to assume that $C(\epsilon_i, \epsilon_j)$ is zero. If there are N stocks, then $N(N-1)/2$ covariances should be estimated. Unless T is large, not all these covariances can be estimated precisely. If the model is good, it does not create too much distortion to assume that the covariance is zero. Diversifiable risks, the ϵ terms, can be diversified out of the portfolio and ignored, so their covariance ought to be negligible as well.

7.6.2 When the Standard Approach Fails

If a stock is new and lacks data, then $V(\epsilon_i)$ cannot be estimated in a conventional way. However, even if a stock is new, it usually has at least a short trading history. Thus it may be possible to estimate the variance of the error term at a higher frequency (shorter time interval) and recover the variance of the frequency that we need.

For the purposes of illustration, let us assume that the time interval of the analysis is a month. Suppose that for young stock A the available data cover only a few days. In this situation, we can recover the variance of the monthly error term from the variance of the daily error term. We use letter s to indicate the daily time interval. The data for stock A are available for S days, $s = 1, \dots, S$. Let $\tilde{r}_{As}$ be the return to stock A on day s. Given the factor exposure and constant estimate $\hat{\beta}_A$ and $\hat{\alpha}_A$, we can estimate the variance of the daily error term $\tilde{\epsilon}_{As}$, that is,

$$\hat{V}(\tilde{\epsilon}_A) = \frac{1}{S} \sum_{s=1}^{S} (\tilde{r}_{As} - \hat{\alpha}_A - \hat{\beta}'_A \tilde{\mathbf{f}}_s)^2 \qquad (7.31)$$

where $\tilde{\mathbf{f}}_s$ is the factor premium for day s.[20]

To recover the variance of the monthly error term, first we identify the stocks that are similar to stock A based on the characteristics, as explained in the preceding section. Suppose that stocks $1, \ldots, M$ are such similar stocks. Then we estimate the variance of the daily error term for those similar stocks, $\hat{V}(\tilde{\epsilon}_1), \ldots, \hat{V}(\tilde{\epsilon}_M)$ as well as the variance of the monthly error term for those similar stocks, $\hat{V}(\epsilon_1), \ldots, \hat{V}(\epsilon_M)$. Assuming that the ratio of the monthly variance to the daily variance is similar for similar stocks, we can estimate the monthly variance of stock A as

$$\hat{V}(\epsilon_A) \equiv \hat{V}(\tilde{\epsilon}_A) \frac{1}{M} \left[\frac{\hat{V}(\epsilon_1)}{\hat{V}(\tilde{\epsilon}_1)} + \cdots + \frac{\hat{V}(\epsilon_M)}{\hat{V}(\tilde{\epsilon}_M)} \right] \qquad (7.32)$$

This procedure will allow the estimator to have less extreme values because we are scaling the monthly variance from similar stocks.

7.7 CONCLUSION

In this chapter we turned our attention from one major tool of QEPM—the fundamental factor model—to the other—the economic factor model. The economic factor model, like its counterpart, relates a stock's return to its factor exposures and the factor premiums that the marketplace assigns them, but it emphasizes the fact that stock returns react to changes in the overall economic environment. The economic factor model is one of the most theoretically sound models of stock returns and, at the same time, one of the most flexible in terms of the variety of factors it can handle.

The conceptual distinctions between the economic and fundamental factor models can confuse even the most experienced practitioners. We pointed out that the major difference between the two models is the fact that in the economic factor model the

---

[20] When factor premiums are not available on a daily frequency, we have to make certain approximations, such as calculating a daily premium by dividing the monthly number by the number of trading days in the month.

factor exposure of each stock must be estimated from the data, whereas in the fundamental factor model statistical estimation is instead necessary for the factor premium. For an economic factor model, for instance, we must estimate how much a company's stock reacts to a shift in unemployment or real GDP growth. Another difference between the models is that the economic factor model encapsulates a straightforward, intuitively appealing concept: stocks react to external risks in the marketplace. Even when data are scarce, such as with recent IPOs or recently merged companies, this model can help us to gauge how stocks will respond to the economic environment.

The two factor models achieve similar ends, though. Like the fundamental factor model, the economic factor model can be a model of either overall stock returns or of benchmark α, providing a performance metric for benchmarked portfolios. It can be used to predict the expected return and expected risk of any stock in the portfolio manager's investment universe, as well as decompose the risk of any stock into diversifiable and nondiversifiable components. Both factor models serve as essential tools as we move toward Chapter 9 and strive for the final frontier of portfolio construction, the optimal portfolio. Before we can construct a portfolio, though, we need to gather inputs that are necessary in order to make predictions about future stock returns.

QUESTIONS

7.1. Explain why the capital asset pricing model (CAPM) is a special case of the economic factor model.

7.2. Explain why the economic factor model is typically estimated from time-series data.

7.3. Explain why the factor premium is treated as observable in the economic factor model but not in the fundamental factor model.

7.4. Discuss the strengths and weaknesses of the economic factor model compared with the fundamental factor model.

7.5. If the benchmark is a broad market index, can benchmark α be interpreted as CAPM α?

7.6. Consider a simple economic factor model:

$$r_i = \alpha_i + \beta_i f + \epsilon_i \qquad \epsilon_i \sim N(0, \sigma_i^2)$$

Suppose that the estimation produced $\hat{\alpha}_i = 2$ and $\hat{\beta}_i = 0.5$. The portfolio manager has a benchmark whose return is denoted as r_B.

(a) Calculate the benchmark α when the benchmark return and the factor premium are identical.

(b) Calculate the benchmark α when the benchmark return and the factor premium are perfectly correlated.

(c) Express the benchmark α as a function of the following three quantities: the correlation between r_B and f, the variance of r_B, and the variance of f.

(d) Specify the exact condition under which multifactor α is identical to benchmark α.

7.7. Describe three ways to calculate the factor premium.

7.8. Based on the capital asset pricing model (CAPM), a broad market index is often included as a factor in the economic factor model. Would it be a good idea to use the Dow Jones Industrial Average for this purpose?

7.9. Consider an economic factor model with the following three factors: the size factor (i.e., based on the market capitalization), the return on the S&P 500, and the return on the S&P 600. What problem would you encounter in estimating such a model?

7.10. In the financial economic literature, the factor premium is assumed to have a mean of zero. One way to satisfy this assumption is to write the economic factor model as

$$r_i = \alpha_i + \beta_{i1}[f_1 - E(f_1)] + \cdots + \beta_{iK}[f_K - E(f_K)] + \epsilon_i$$

Would the estimation of this equation result in different estimates of $\beta_{i1}, \ldots, \beta_{iK}$? How about the estimates of α_i?

7.11. Suppose that there is an exact linear relationship between the expected stock return and firm size; that is,

$$E(r_i) = 5 + 0.01x_i$$

where x_i is the size of firm i. Assume that x_i is uniformly distributed between 100 and 900. (That is, every value between 100 and 900 has equal probability of being realized.)

(a) To calculate the size premium, we may sort all the firms by size and create two size-sorted portfolios. That is, we assign the top 50% of the firms to the large-size portfolio and the remaining 50% of the firms to the small-size portfolio. Each portfolio is equal-weighted. The factor premium is defined as the difference between the two portfolios' returns. What would be the expected value of the factor premium?

(b) Instead of making two portfolios, we may create three size-sorted portfolios, each containing 33.3% of firms in the sample. Each portfolio is equal-weighted. The factor premium can be defined as the difference between the first portfolio return and the last portfolio return. What would be the expected value of the factor premium?

(c) Does it matter how many portfolios we create to calculate the factor premium? Do we always get the same expected factor premium?

7.12. Principal-component analysis is used quite often in psychology. For example, a psychologist could have given a test with 100 multiple-choice questions to 1,000 subjects. The answers to each question are treated as a single series, and principal-component analysis can identify a small number of factors that together explain most of the variations in the answers. Then the psychologist is able to interpret each factor by examining the components of each factor (e.g., "This factor represents aversion to the color red," "This factor represents childhood trauma," etc.). In applying principal-component analysis to stock returns, however, portfolio managers cannot easily interpret what each factor really means. Explain why portfolio managers have more difficulty in interpreting factors than psychologists do.

7.13. Discuss whether principal-component analysis is free from the danger of data mining.

7.14. When firm A and firm B merge, we may use the weighted average of the premerger factor exposures of the two firms as the factor exposure for the new merged firm.

(a) Show that the expected return implied by the factor exposure of the merged firm is the weighted average of the premerger expected returns of the two original firms.

(b) If there is synergy from the merger, would the procedure just described be reasonable?

7.15. After estimating an economic factor model for stock A, we obtained the following decomposition of the risk:

Nondiversifiable risk   90

Diversifiable risk   60

The risk is measured in variance.

(a) What is the R^2 of the regression?

(b) Explain the relationship between R^2 and the decomposition of risk.

CHAPTER 8

Forecasting Factor Premiums and Exposures

All things appear and disappear because of the concurrence of causes and conditions. Nothing ever exists entirely alone; everything is in relation to everything else.

—Buddha

8.1 INTRODUCTION

In the two preceding chapters we established the framework for factor models, our main quantitative equity portfolio management (QEPM) tools for assessing stock returns and risk. As we have seen, one idea underlies all factor models: The average stock return equals the product of factor premiums and factor exposures. We have shown how to build both the fundamental factor model and the economic factor model on this idea using past data and estimates based on the data. While the model is built from past data, though, it runs on future values because managers want to predict future stock returns. The predicted future average stock return equals the product of future factor premiums and future factor exposures. Put more formally, the return on stock i at time $T + 1$, $r_{i,T+1}$, is determined by

$$r_{i,T+1} = \alpha_i + \beta'_{i,T+1}\mathbf{f}_{T+1} + \epsilon_{i,T+1} \qquad (8.1)$$

where α_i is the constant term, $\beta_{i,T+1}$ is the K-dimensional vector of the exposure for stock i at time $T + 1$, $\mathbf{f}_{T+1}$ is the K-dimensional vector of the factor premium at time $T + 1$, and $\epsilon_{i,T+1}$ is the deviation of stock i's return from its average.

To generalize the stock return equation here to all types of factor models, we have added a time subscript to both the factor exposure and factor premium terms. Depending on the type of factor model, however, the time subscript can be dropped from one of the variables but kept for the other. In the fundamental factor model that we presented in Chapter 6, for example, only the factor exposure changes over time, and, given stock returns and factor exposures up to time T, we estimated a fixed factor premium through time T.[1] In Chapter 7, on the other hand, we saw that in the economic factor model, only the factor premium changes over time, and, given stock returns and factor premiums up to time T, we estimated a fixed factor exposure through T.

Now we must look beyond the given data to time $T + 1$ and determine the future factor premium ($\mathbf{f}_{T+1}$) and the future factor exposure ($\boldsymbol{\beta}_{i,T+1}$), together with the constant term (α_i) from the information available at time T. In order to do this, we sometimes need to forecast. The term *forecast* takes on a very specific meaning in this chapter. Assuming that a variable follows a normal distribution, forecasting the variable means specifying the variable's distribution (a.k.a. *predictive distribution*) by finding the distribution mean and variance. Once we have found—whether by forecasting or otherwise—the future values of the factor premium and factor exposure, we can forecast future stock returns. Predicting future stock returns, after all, is our goal; if we can predict returns, we can build a high-return portfolio.

---

[1] In Chapter 6, we presented two types of fundamental factors models. One, which we call the simple one, takes the factor exposures of stocks over time along with the stock returns over time and estimates a factor premium over the historical sample period. In this case, there is only one factor premium estimated from the data and one estimate of the factor premium at time $T + 1$, which is simply the historical estimate up to time T. However, in the last part of Chapter 6, and also in Chapter 16, we estimate the fundamental factor model as a series of cross-sectional regressions. That is, for each period or month in our historical data, we use stock returns and factor exposures of stocks to estimate a different factor premium in each period or month. We thus have a series of factor premiums for each time period. In this case, if we choose, we can use a VAR to forecast the period $T + 1$ factor premiums based on the time series of factor premiums through time T. Thus, in the more "complicated" fundamental factor model, both factor premiums and factor exposures change through time. Finally, as a reminder, when we say a fixed factor premium is estimated, we are referring to $\{\mathbf{f}_1, \dots, \mathbf{f}_T\}$, and when we say a fixed factor exposure is estimated, we are referring to $\{\boldsymbol{\beta}_{i,1}, \dots, \boldsymbol{\beta}_{i,T}\}$.

8.2 WHEN IS FORECASTING NECESSARY?

To predict future stock returns, we need future values of the factor premium and factor exposure. In some cases we need to forecast these values; in other cases we can skip the forecasting step. Whether we need to forecast depends largely on the type of factor model we are using.

In fact, if we are using the simple version of the fundamental factor model from Chapter 6, we do not need to forecast anything. We do not need to forecast the explanatory variable, the factor exposure. The fundamental factor model is dynamic in the sense that the explanatory variable is realized before the dependent variable. The explanatory variable (factor exposure β_{it}) is measured at the beginning of time t, whereas the dependent variable (stock return r_{it}) is measured during time t. Thus, at the end of time T, we actually have the value of the factor exposure for time $T + 1$, so we do not need to forecast $\beta_{i,T+1}$ to predict the dependent variable for time $T + 1$, namely, $r_{i,T+1}$.

We do not need to forecast the factor premium either. For any type of factor model, it is conventional to assume that the model estimates will remain constant for a while. Thus, in the fundamental factor model, we can assume that the factor premium $\mathbf{f}$ estimated from time periods 1, ..., T will be valid for time $T + 1$. This assumption follows logically from the way we estimated the factor premium from time 1 to time T; since we assumed that the parameters stay constant from time 1 to time T, we can assume that these parameters stay constant for one more period, time $T + 1$.

Forecasting becomes a necessary step when we are using the economic factor model from Chapter 7. The economic factor model is not dynamic, so we need to forecast the value of the explanatory variable, the factor premium. In the economic factor model, the explanatory variable (factor premium $\mathbf{f}_t$) is known only at the end of time t, as is the dependent variable (stock return r_{it}). Thus, at the end of time T, we do not have the value of the factor premium for time $T + 1$, and we cannot predict the return for time $T + 1$, namely, $r_{i,T+1}$, without forecasting $\mathbf{f}_{T+1}$.

However, since we can always assume that the estimates in a model remain fairly constant, we can avoid forecasting the factor exposure. The factor exposure $\hat{\beta}_i$ estimated from time periods 1, ..., T still should be valid for time $T + 1$.

The principal point is that, regardless of the factor model selected, there is no need to forecast the factor exposure. However,

depending on the factor model selected, one may need to forecast
the factor premium.

8.3 COMBINING EXTERNAL FORECASTS

When reliable external forecasts are available, the portfolio manager
should use them rather than attempt to do forecasts in-house. Factor
premium forecasts can be obtained from economists who publish
their forecasts, from various economic forecasting agencies, and
from research analysts at various firms. This section discusses the
way to combine multiple external forecasts.

Suppose that we obtained the predicted value of the factor
premium $\mathbf{f}_{T+1}$ from J different forecasters. We denote these pre-
dicted values by $\mathbf{f}^{(1)}_{T+1}$, ..., $\mathbf{f}^{(J)}_{T+1}$. Assuming that each forecaster is
equally reliable, the best prediction of $\mathbf{f}_{T+1}$ is the simple average
of the J predictions.[2] This average prediction is our expected value
of $\mathbf{f}_{T+1}$; thus we may write

$$\hat{E}\left(\mathbf{f}_{T+1}\right) = \frac{1}{J}\sum_{j=1}^{J}\mathbf{f}^{(j)}_{T+1} \tag{8.2}$$

Not only should a portfolio manager care about the expected
value of the factor premium from the various forecasts, but he or she
also should care about how reliable it is and how much confidence
he or she can place in it. If the J forecasters more or less agree, we can
be more confident about a prediction than we would be if their predictions were widely divergent. One way to measure the confidence
of the combined forecast, therefore, is to measure the inverse of the
variance of the J predictions. The variance of $\mathbf{f}_{T+1}$ is given by

$$\hat{V}\left(\mathbf{f}_{T+1}\right) = \frac{1}{J}\sum_{j=1}^{J}\mathbf{f}^{(j)}_{T+1}\mathbf{f}^{(j)\prime}_{T+1} - \hat{E}\left(\mathbf{f}_{T+1}\right)\hat{E}\left(\mathbf{f}'_{T+1}\right) \tag{8.3}$$

and the inverse of this variance can be used as a measure of our
confidence. Thus, if the variance of the predictions is large, we
have little confidence, and if it is small, we have more confidence.
If we assume that $\mathbf{f}_{T+1}$ has a normal distribution, the mean and the
variance of $\mathbf{f}_{T+1}$ given above completely specify the distribution
of $\mathbf{f}_{T+1}$, and our task of forecasting the factor premium is done.

---

[2] For combining forecasts from forecasters of differing abilities, we refer the reader to
Chapter 9 of Granger and Newbold (1986).

8.4 MODEL-BASED FORECAST

Forecasting is not usually a portfolio manager's forte. It is a challenging task even for highly quantitatively oriented portfolio managers, and, in any case, it is not the best use of their time. However, there may be an in-house model that seems to forecast a particular factor very well. In this case, the portfolio could benefit from time spent on forecasting. Let us consider a simple example of a model that could be used to forecast the factor premium for an economic factor model that includes a market factor:

$$r_{t+1}^{S\&P500} = a + bLI_t + \epsilon_{t+1} \tag{8.4}$$

where $r_{t+1}^{S\&P500}$ is the next month's return on the Standard and Poor's (S&P) 500, and LI_t is the value of a leading economic indicator. The leading economic indicator can be the actual leading indicator published by the Bureau of Economic Analysis or one component of it, such as average workweek, initial unemployment claims, new orders for consumer goods, plant and equipment orders, sensitive material prices, changes in consumer confidence, changes in gross domestic product (GDP), and so on. Testing whether or not the model can serve as the basis for a forecast is simple. One first estimates the historical relationship that the model describes. If it turns out the estimate for b is significant, then the model can be used to forecast the market factor in the economic factor model. If the economic factor model contains factors besides the market factor, similar regressions can be run to forecast the values of the other factors. Given a leading economic indicator for month T, the return and estimated variance determined from the preceding model can be used to forecast the factor premium for time $T + 1$.

8.5 ECONOMETRIC FORECAST

A portfolio manager might not find external factor premium forecasts satisfactory either because he or she does not believe the forecasters are reliable or because he or she simply cannot find outside forecasts for the particular factors in his or her model. At the same time, there may be no satisfactory in-house forecasting model. In this situation, the manager might consider using some basic econometric or statistical forecasting techniques.[3] We have chosen to focus on the most basic technique, called *vector autoregression* (VAR).[4] Although the VAR procedure is rather mechanical, it has been shown to work well at predicting out of sample in many contexts.

In VAR, we model the factor premiums as a vector autoregressive process. That is, the current factor premiums are a linear function of past factor premiums, that is,

$$\mathbf{f}_t = \boldsymbol{\gamma}_0 + \boldsymbol{\gamma}_1 \mathbf{f}_{t-1} + \cdots + \boldsymbol{\gamma}_L \mathbf{f}_{t-L} + \boldsymbol{\omega}_t \quad t = L + 1, \ldots, T \qquad (8.5)$$

Each of $\boldsymbol{\gamma}_1, \ldots, \boldsymbol{\gamma}_L$ is a $K \times K$ matrix of coefficients, where K is the number of factors (the size of vector $\mathbf{f}_t$). L is the number of past factor premiums relevant for the current factor premium. This model is sometimes denoted as VAR(L) because there are L lags included on the right-hand side.

Given this modeling strategy, the only thing to decide is the number of lags L—in other words, how many past values should enter the equation.[5] Including many past values reduces the potential for misspecification.[6] At the same time, including many past values substantially increases the number of parameters to be estimated. The number of lags therefore should be decided based on the amount of available data. Note that given K factors and L lags, the number of parameters to be estimated is $(KL + 1) \times K$ because $\boldsymbol{\gamma}_0$ has K elements and all other γ's have K^2 elements. For three factors, the number of parameters to be estimated would be 12, 21, and 30 for $L = 1, 2, 3$. For four factors, the number of parameters to be estimated would be 20, 36, and 52. Note also that the number of observations available for estimation declines as the lag size grows. In practical situations, it is not very common to include more than one lagged value. For example, if there are 60 observations,

---

[3] There are many sophisticated econometric techniques to forecast factor premiums. The reader should be warned, though, that more sophisticated models do not necessarily produce better forecasts. Sophisticated models come with an extra set of assumptions, which may or may not apply well to a particular factor model. Unless there is a strong reason for an econometric model, we suggest sticking with a simpler forecasting technique.

[4] Most standard statistical packages can perform VAR estimations and forecasts.

[5] Several selection criteria can be used to determine the number of lags. The two most common are the Akaike information criterion (AIC) and the Schwarz Bayesian information criterion (SIC/BIC/SBIC). Please consult an econometrics textbook on how to use these tools.

[6] Omitting relevant variables creates a problem, whereas including irrelevant variables does not. See Appendix C at www.ludwigbc.com under QEPM Exclusive Content for more details on this matter.

estimating even 12 or 20 parameters is already challenging because the precision of the estimates will be quite low.

By running regressions, we obtain the estimates $\hat{\gamma}_0$, ..., $\hat{\gamma}_L$. We also obtain the variance-covariance matrix estimates of ω. We will call this estimate $\hat{\Sigma}_\omega$. Then the predicted factor premium (i.e., the expected factor premium) for $T + 1$ is

$$\hat{E}(\mathbf{f}_{T+1}) = \hat{\gamma}_0 + \hat{\gamma}_1\, \mathbf{f}_T + \cdots + \hat{\gamma}_L \mathbf{f}_{T-L+1} \tag{8.6}$$

The estimated variance of the factor premiums for $T + 1$ is

$$\hat{V}(\mathbf{f}_{T+1}) = \hat{V}(\omega_{T+1}) = \hat{\Sigma}_\omega \tag{8.7}$$

This completes our task of forecasting factor premiums.

Table 8.1 presents the estimates of VAR(1) for five factor premiums: the premiums of the unemployment rate, consumer sentiment growth, excess market return, the log of market capitalization, and book-to-price ratio. To estimate this model, we used five years of monthly data from January 2016 to December 2020. A VAR(1) means that we chose a lag length of 1; thus L is 1, and T is 59 ($= 60 - 1$). Each column in the table represents an equation

TABLE 8.1

Estimates of the VAR Factor Forecasting Equation

Explanatory Variables	Dependent Variables				
	Unemployment (UR)	Consumer Sentiment Growth (CSG)	Excess Market Return (MKT)	Log of Market Capitalization (LOGSIZE)	Book-to-Price (B/P)
Constant	0.854	−1.543	−1.223	1.778	−1.100
	(0.339)	(1.224)	(1.297)	(0.968)	(1.089)
Unemployment rate ($t-1$)	0.814	0.190	0.588	−0.424	0.164
	(0.066)	(0.239)	(0.253)	(0.189)	(0.212)
Consumer sentiment growth ($t-1$)	−0.169	0.105	−0.339	0.147	−0.011
	(0.031)	(0.112)	(0.119)	(0.089)	(0.100)
Excess market return ($t-1$)	0.041	0.567	−0.261	0.064	−0.129
	(0.035)	(0.127)	(0.134)	(0.100)	(0.113)
Log of market capitalization ($t-1$)	−0.076	0.091	0.045	−0.219	0.374
	(0.058)	(0.207)	(0.220)	(0.164)	(0.185)
B/P ($t-1$)	−0.004	0.226	0.254	−0.103	0.214
	(0.050)	(0.181)	(0.192)	(0.143)	(0.161)

Note: Estimated for the period from January 2016 to December 2020. Standard errors are listed inside parentheses.

for one factor. Since there are five factors, there are five equations. The first row corresponds to γ_0, and each row from the second to the sixth row corresponds to each column in γ_1.

The premium for the unemployment factor is the U.S. unemployment rate of the previous month in percentage terms. The premium for the consumer sentiment growth factor is the percentage change in the University of Michigan Consumer Sentiment Index from the previous month. The premium for the excess market factor is the S&P 500 total return in excess of the one-month Treasury bill return. The premiums for the log of market capitalization factor and the book-to-price factor are calculated by constructing zero-investment portfolios of those factors (see Chapter 7 for more details).

Given the estimates in Table 8.1, we can easily calculate the expected value of the factor premium for January 2020, which is time $T+1$. Using Eq. (8.6), we obtained the expected value reported in Table 8.2. Table 8.3 reports the estimate of the variance-covariance matrix Σ_ω. Since Σ_ω is a symmetric matrix, we report

TABLE 8.2

Predicted Value of Factor Premium from VAR

Unemployment Rate	Consumer Sentiment Growth	Excess Market Return	Log of Market Capitalization	Book-to-Price
5.865	1.964	-0.301	0.664	-1.871

Note: Prediction for January 2021 based on the data from January 2016 to December 2020.

TABLE 8.3

Variance–Covariance of Factor Premium Forecasts from VAR

	Unemployment Rate	Consumer Sentiment Growth	Excess Market Return	Log of Market Capitalization	Book-to-Price
Unemployment rate	1.072				
Consumer sentiment growth	-0.707	13.934			
Excess market return	0.115	-2.907	15.642		
Log of market capitalization	0.248	0.006	-3.846	8.712	
Book-to-price	-0.509	2.711	3.769	-6.042	11.043

Note: Prediction for January 2021 based on the data from January 2016 to December 2020.

only the lower triangular part of the matrix. For example, the unemployment rate variance is 1.072, which is roughly equal to $(1.035)^2$. Thus the standard deviation of the unemployment factor is 1.035% per month.

8.6 PARAMETER UNCERTAINTY

The variance of the factor premiums calculated in the preceding section reflects the uncertainty of the future factor premiums. This uncertainty, like the uncertainty of stock returns themselves, is a component of investment risk and must be recognized as such. Even by recognizing the variance-related risk, though, we still have not fully acknowledged the risk inherent in forecasting until we consider parameter uncertainty. The variance computed above shows the part of the variation in the future factor premiums that cannot be explained by the model. This would be all that mattered if the model were exact and the parameters we estimated ($\hat{\gamma}_0, ..., \hat{\gamma}_L$) were exact, but the parameters we estimated are not exact. All we can say is that the true value of $\gamma_0, ..., \gamma_L$ is likely to be near what we have estimated with the VAR, and our confidence in the estimates is included in the standard error of the estimation. If the standard error of the estimation is large, there is more uncertainty regarding the future factor premiums, and, as a result, the investment risk is higher. To fully account for the parameter uncertainty in the computation of investment risk, we need to include the standard error of $\gamma_0, ..., \gamma_L$ in the calculation of the variance of the future factor premiums. We will examine two approaches to do this. One is an exact method, and the other is an approximate method.

In the exact method, we recognize that the future factor premium has two sources of variation, one coming from the estimation of $\gamma_0, ..., \gamma_L$ and the other coming from the variation allowed in the model. The first component goes in a $K(L+1) \times K(L+1)$-dimensional variance-covariance matrix $V(\hat{\gamma}_0, ..., \hat{\gamma}_L)$, and the second component goes in a $K \times K$-dimensional variance-covariance matrix $\hat{V}(\omega) = \hat{\Sigma}_\omega$. Once we arrive at the VAR estimator, we can compute both these components in a straightforward way. The correct variance of the future factor premium is

$$\hat{V}(\mathbf{f}_{T+1}) = (1+d)\hat{\Sigma}_\omega \qquad (8.8)$$

where d is a constant computed from $\mathbf{f}_T, ..., \mathbf{f}_{T-L}$ (see Appendix 8A).[7]

---

[7] Appendix 8A can be found at www.ludwigbc.com under QEPM Exclusive Content.

PART II: Portfolio Construction and Maintenance

TABLE 8.4

Variance–Covariance of Factor Premium Forecasts, Parameter Uncertainty Considered

	Unemployment Rate	Consumer Sentiment Growth	Excess Market Return	Log of Market Capitalization	Book-to-Price
Unemployment rate	1.152				
Consumer sentiment growth	−0.760	14.973			
Excess market return	0.123	−3.124	16.808		
Log of market capitalization	0.267	0.006	−4.132	9.362	
Book-to-price	−0.547	2.913	4.050	−6.493	11.866

Note: Prediction for January 2021 based on the data from January 2016 to December 2020.

Table 8.4 is a recalculation of the variance-covariance matrix of $\mathbf{f}_{T+1}$ reported in Table 8.3. Note that each diagonal element of Table 8.4 is greater than the corresponding figure in Table 8.3. This shows that as we account for parameter uncertainty, our ignorance (measured by the variance) increases.

If the complexity of the setup increases and the number of parameters increases, this approach may no longer be feasible. The alternative method is known as *bootstrapping*. Given the sample of T observations, we can create T pseudosamples of $T - 1$ observations by dropping one observation at a time. From each pseudosample, we estimate $\gamma_0, \ldots, \gamma_L$ and Σ_ω and obtain T sets of estimates. From each set of estimates, we calculate the predicted value of the future factor premiums and obtain T sets of future factor premiums. These T sets of future factor premiums can be treated as if each were obtained from an independent forecaster (as we discussed at the beginning of this section). That is, the variance of the T sets of future factor premiums includes parameter uncertainty, as well as the variance of the model error.[8]

---

[8] When an observation is dropped in the creation of the pseudosample, the order of the remaining $T - 1$ observations should not change. The time distance among observations should not change either. This reduces the effective sample size by more than one. For example, if $\mathbf{f}_2$ is dropped, we have to ignore not only $\mathbf{f}_2 = \gamma_0 + \gamma_1 \mathbf{f}_1 + \omega_2$ but also $\mathbf{f}_3 = \gamma_0 + \gamma_1 \mathbf{f}_2 + \omega_3$. Thus the effective sample size is reduced by 2. See Appendix 8A at www.ludwigbc.com under QEPM Exclusive Content for a general discussion of bootstrapping.

8.7 FORECASTING THE STOCK RETURN

Up to this point we have discussed ways to forecast the distribution of the factor premium for time $T + 1$, namely, $\mathbf{f}_{T+1}$. As we mentioned earlier, the factor exposure for time $T + 1$, $\boldsymbol{\beta}_{i,T+1}$, is either observable (in the case of the fundamental factor model) or is assumed to be the same as the factor exposure that was estimated from the data through time T (in the case of the economic factor model). Given our forecasts for $\mathbf{f}_{T+1}$ and $\boldsymbol{\beta}_{i,T+1}$, we can now proceed to the forecasting of the stock return. Assuming a normal distribution as usual, the distribution of the stock return is specified by estimating the mean and variance. From the relationship

$$r_{i,T+1} = \alpha_i + \boldsymbol{\beta}'_{i,T+1}\mathbf{f}_{T+1} + \epsilon_{i,T+1} \tag{8.9}$$

the mean and variance of the stock return are

$$E(r_{i,T+1}) = \alpha_i + \boldsymbol{\beta}'_{i,T+1} E(\mathbf{f}_{T+1}) \tag{8.10}$$

$$V(r_{i,T+1}) = \boldsymbol{\beta}'_{i,T+1} V(\mathbf{f}_{T+1})\boldsymbol{\beta}_{i,T+1} + V(\epsilon_{i,T+1}) \tag{8.11}$$

We have the estimates for $E(\mathbf{f}_{T+1})$ and $V(\mathbf{f}_{T+1})$ from the previous sections, and we know the value (or the estimate) of α_i $\boldsymbol{\beta}_{i,T+1}$. $V(\epsilon_{i,T+1})$ was estimated in previous chapters. Thus we simply may substitute the estimates for each component and obtain the estimates for the mean and variance of the stock return, that is,

$$\hat{E}(r_{i,T+1}) = \alpha_i + \boldsymbol{\beta}'_{i,T+1}\hat{E}(\mathbf{f}_{T+1}) \tag{8.12}$$

$$\hat{V}(r_{i,T+1}) = \boldsymbol{\beta}'_{i,T+1}\hat{V}(\mathbf{f}_{T+1})\boldsymbol{\beta}_{i,T+1} + \hat{V}(\epsilon_{i,T+1}) \tag{8.13}$$

If we estimate $\alpha_i + \boldsymbol{\beta}_{i,T+1}$, this expression does not account for the uncertainty regarding the true value of α_i and $\boldsymbol{\beta}_{i,T+1}$. We have to add the estimation error generated in the estimation of α_i and $\boldsymbol{\beta}_{i,T+1}$ to the preceding formula. Note that the estimation error associated with $\boldsymbol{\beta}_{i,T+1}$ is captured by the variance–covariance matrix $\hat{V}(\boldsymbol{\beta}_{i,T+1})$ as presented in the preceding chapter. Similarly, the estimation error associated with α_i is represented by the variance $\hat{V}(\hat{\alpha}_i)$. The only remaining question is how these terms enter into the preceding equation.[9]

Table 8.5 reports the mean and standard deviation estimates of selected stock returns for January 2021, based on the economic factor model of Chapter 7. The last column in the table shows the standard deviation estimate considering parameter uncertainty.

---

[9] We provide the exact formula in Appendix 8A, which can be found at www.ludwigbc. com under QEPM Exclusive Content.

TABLE 8.5

Predictive Return Distribution for Selected Stocks

Ticker	Mean	SD	SD*
AAPL	2.58	8.43	8.65
MSFT	1.71	5.26	5.38
WMT	0.83	5.10	5.27
JNJ	−0.48	4.81	4.93
AMZN	1.31	8.21	8.40

Note: Prediction for January 2021 based on the data from January 2016 to December 2020. SD is the standard deviation, and SD* is the standard deviation considering the parameter uncertainty. All numbers are expressed in percentage terms. Company names for ticker symbols are Apple (AAPL), Microsoft (MSFT), Walmart (WMT), Johnson & Johnson (JNJ), and Amazon (AMZN).

FIGURE 8.1

Predictive return for Walmart stock (January 2021). (Based on the data from January 2016 to December 2020.)

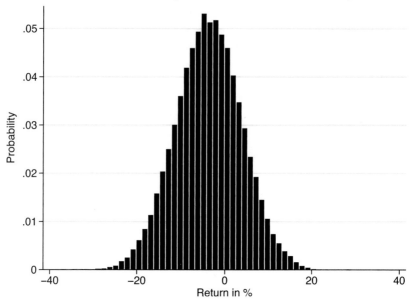

Consideration of parameter uncertainty increases the standard deviation estimate, hence the increase between the third and the last columns.

Once we have estimates of the mean and variance of the stock returns, we can plot the whole distribution of the stock return. Figure 8.1 shows the predictive distribution of the return to ExxonMobil's stock. The figure is based on the variance estimate, not accounting for parameter uncertainty. The height of each bar corresponds to the probability of a particular stock return. For example, there is about an 4.5% chance that the stock return in January 2021 will be around 0% and approximately a 1% chance that the stock return will be around 10%.

8.8 CONCLUSION

We have arrived at the point at which we can set up and run a factor model to generate predictions of stock returns and risk. In Chapters 6 and 7 we had formulated fundamental and economic factor models from past data on stock returns, factor premiums, and factor exposures. In this chapter we showed how the models relate future stock returns to future values of the factor exposure and factor premium. In the case of the simple fundamental factor model, we did not have to worry about forecasting the factor exposure or factor premium because the model uses the existing values of both variables. In the case of the economic factor model, we also could use the existing factor exposure estimate, but we needed a forecast of the future factor premiums. Although we recommend that portfolio managers use outside forecasts whenever possible, we realize that in some cases they want to do forecasts in-house. For this reason, we went through the steps of different forecasting methods and also discussed the need to consider the parameter uncertainty of forecasts. Finally, and most importantly, we showed how to forecast the future returns and risks of stocks regardless of the type of factor model used. Forecasting a stock's return and risk is always the last step of modeling. The goal of this process, after all, is to predict risk-adjusted returns in order to decide which stocks to include in the portfolio. There may be no crystal ball to gaze into for a picture of future stock movements, but a good model may be the closest thing to it. Once we know what a stock might yield and know that we want to include it in the portfolio, we can then decide exactly how much of the portfolio to dedicate to it. Portfolio weighting means building the portfolio, and we start building in the next chapter.

QUESTIONS

8.1. Whether to forecast a factor exposure depends on whether the exposure is likely to change in the near future. Discuss, for each of the following factors, whether the exposure is likely to change in 1 month: size, price-to-earnings (P/E) ratio, dividend yield, and return on equity (ROE).

8.2 Explain why forecasting factor exposures is not necessary in a fundamental factor model if the model is in dynamic form, that is,

$$r_{i,t+1} = \alpha + \beta_{i,t} f_t + \epsilon_{i,t+1}$$

8.3. Consider an economic factor model:

$$r_{it} = \alpha_i + \beta_{i1} f_{1t} + \cdots + \beta_{iK} f_{Kt} + \epsilon_{it}$$

Suppose that we estimated this model using time-series data $(r_{i1}, f_{11}, \ldots, f_{K1}), \ldots, (r_{iT}, f_{1T}, \ldots, f_{KT})$ and obtained the estimates $\hat{\alpha}_i, \hat{\beta}_{i1}, \ldots, \hat{\beta}_{iK}$. Using this model, we would like to predict the future stock return $r_{i,T+1}$, especially its expected value.

(a) Instead of forecasting $f_{1,T+1}, \ldots, f_{K,T+1}$ as discussed in the chapter, if we use the last value of the factor premium $f_{1,T}, \ldots, f_{K,T}$, what would be the expected value of $r_{i,T+1}$?

(b) Instead of forecasting $f_{1,T+1}, \ldots, f_{K,T+1}$ as discussed in the chapter, if we use the sample average of the factor premium $1/T \sum_{t=1}^{T} f_{1t}, \ldots, 1/T \sum_{t=1}^{T} f_{Kt}$, what would be the predicted value of $r_{i,T+1}$?

(c) Explain why forecasting factor premiums is necessary in the economic factor model.

8.4. Suppose that a portfolio manager obtained GDP forecasts $x_1, \ldots, x_{10}$ from 10 independent forecasters.

(a) What would be the expected GDP of the portfolio manager?

(b) If it turns out that the tenth forecaster simply averaged the forecasts of the other nine forecasters, what would be the expected GDP of the portfolio manager?

(c) Suppose that the tenth forecaster made her own forecast x_{10}^*, but instead of reporting her own forecast, she used the formula:

$$x_{10} = \frac{1}{18} (x_1 + \cdots + x_9) + \frac{1}{2} x_{10}^*$$

and reported x_{10}. What would be the expected GDP of the portfolio manager?

(d) Discuss why it is important to obtain independent forecasts.

8.5. What are the strengths and the weaknesses of model-based forecasts compared with econometric forecasts?

8.6. Suppose that the unemployment rate is forecast with the econometric forecasting technique.

(a) Is it reasonable to assume a normal distribution for the error?

(b) Explain how one may obtain a more normal looking distribution by transforming the variable.

8.7. After estimating an AR(1) model for a factor premium, we obtained the following estimates:

$$f_{t+1} = 0.2 + 0.7f_t + \eta_t \quad \eta_t \sim N(0,1)$$

where η_t is an error, and $N(\cdot)$ indicates a normal distribution.

(a) If $f_T = 1.1$, what would be the predicted distribution of f_{T+1}?

(b) If $f_T = 1.1$, what would be the predicted distribution of f_{T+2}?

(c) Find the general formula for the distribution of f_{T+s}.

8.8. Consider an AR(1) model of a factor premium:

$$f_{t+1} = \gamma + \delta f_t + \eta_{t+1} \quad \eta_{t+1} \sim N(0, \sigma^2)$$

Suppose that we estimate this model using T observations $f_1, \dots, f_T$.

(a) Write down the estimates $\hat{\gamma}$ and $\hat{\delta}$ as a function of data $f_1, \dots, f_T$.

(b) Show that $\hat{\gamma}$ and $\hat{\delta}$ are independent of η_{T+1}, the future error.

(c) Show that the predicted variance of f_{T+1} is the sum of the error variance and the parameter uncertainty. Explain why it is important here to have the answer to part (b).

8.9. Describe the strengths and weaknesses of the vector autoregression (VAR) technique.

8.10. In a VAR model, the number of parameters grows very fast as the number of variables K or the number of lags L increases.

(a) If there are five factors and we want to estimate a VAR(2) for these factors, how many parameters do we need to estimate?

(b) If we have 50 observations, what would be the degrees of freedom?

(c) What is the practical implication of having negative degrees of freedom?

8.11. What is parameter uncertainty? Why is it important in QEPM? Explain how the parameter uncertainty can be accounted for in QEPM.

8.12. Consider an economic factor model of the stock return:

$$r_{it} = \alpha_i + \beta_i f_t + \epsilon_{it} \quad \epsilon_{it} \sim N(0, \sigma^2)$$

We estimate this model using T observations $(r_{i1}, f_1), \ldots, (r_{iT}, f_T)$. Using the same data, we also estimate an AR(1) model of the factor premium:

$$f_{t+1} = \gamma + \delta f_t + \eta_{t+1} \quad \eta_{t+1} \sim N(0, \sigma_\eta^2)$$

(a) Express $\hat{\delta}$ in terms of data and errors.

(b) Express $\hat{\beta}_i$ in terms of data and error.

(c) Are $\hat{\delta}$ and $\hat{\beta}_i$ independent of each other conditional on the data? What would happen if they were not independent?

8.13. Consider two random variables A and B whose joint distribution is multivariate standard normal. That is, each variable has a standard normal distribution and is independent of the other variable.

(a) Is the distribution of the product AB still normal?

(b) Explain why the predictive distribution of the stock return may not be normal when considering parameter uncertainty if the factor premium has to be forecasted.

8.14. Consider an economic factor model:

$$r_{it} = \alpha_i + \beta_i f_t + \epsilon_{it} \quad \epsilon_{it} \sim N(0, \sigma^2)$$

where the factor premium is an AR(1) process:

$$f_{t+1} = \gamma + \delta f_t + \eta_{t+1} \quad \eta_{t+1} \sim N(0, \sigma_\eta^2)$$

(a) Show that the stock return is serially correlated as long as $\delta \neq 0$.

(b) Specify the condition under which we may observe momentum profit (i.e., positive serial correlation in the stock return) and contrarian profit (i.e., negative serial correlation in the stock return).

8.15. The bootstrap standard error is often calculated when calculating the exact standard error is too complicated. Let x_t be the data observed in time t. The sample is a collection of observations made at different times. Suppose that our sample is made of observations from $t = 1$ to $t = T$, that is, $(x_1, \ldots, x_T)$. Given the sample of size T, we may create T subsets of the sample, where each subset has $T - 1$ elements. If we index the subsets by j, then subset j is a set of all observations except x_j. We may carry out the estimation using each subset and call the resulting estimate $\theta^{(j)}$. The bootstrap standard error is defined as the sample standard deviation of $\theta^{(1)}, \ldots, \theta^{(T)}$.

(a) Explain the relationship between the bootstrap standard error and the regular standard error.

(b) Under what situation would one prefer the bootstrap standard error to the regular standard error?

(c) What modifications are necessary in order to calculate the bootstrap standard error in a VAR model?

Portfolio Weights

A little caution outflanks a large cavalry.
—Otto von Bismarck

9.1 INTRODUCTION

In Chapters 5 through 8 we discussed how to create models for stock selection.[1] Models serve as essential tools for identifying "good" and "bad" stocks. However, to construct a portfolio, the manager ultimately needs to do more than separate the wheat from the chaff. A good manager does not just throw a bunch of stocks into the same basket. Rather, he or she assigns them relative weights so that they make sense as a single portfolio.

There are many ways to generate stock weights. Some methods are very rudimentary, such as choosing the best stocks in one's universe and weighting them equally. Another simple method is to weight the stocks by market capitalization, as many indices do. A slightly more complicated twist on market-capitalization weighting is to weight by the square root of the market capitalization. The most complex weighting methods draw on ideas from modern portfolio theory and attempt to weight stocks in a way that maximizes the portfolio's expected return and minimizes its overall risk.

For the majority of portfolio managers who manage their portfolios against a benchmark, the weighting possibilities multiply. For

---

[1] The reader may wish to review Chapters 5, 6, 7, and 8 before proceeding with this chapter.

instance, a manager could weight the stocks such that the weighted-average factor exposures of the stocks equal the benchmark's weighted-average factor exposures. Extending the concepts of modern portfolio theory to the weighting decision, the manager could try to maximize the excess expected return while placing a limit on the allowable tracking error of the portfolio versus the benchmark.

In order to weight stocks in a way that minimizes tracking error or risk, the manager needs to know each stock's expected return, each stock's risk or variance, and the covariances among stocks.[2] A manager also may wish to put constraints on the portfolio creation process. He or she may, for instance, prohibit short sales (i.e., not allow negative stock weights) or specify the range of permissible weights for individual stocks (e.g., to uphold mutual fund diversification rules). The manager then puts all these parameters and constraints into a *quadratic optimizer* and solves for the optimal weights of the portfolio.

This chapter discusses the mathematical and statistical concepts of portfolio weighting. For portfolio managers who use commercial software, the discussion will be helpful for understanding the mechanics of combining their preferred stocks with the vendor's risk models to determine the portfolio weights. For those who want to build their own in-house risk models and portfolio optimizers, this chapter will walk you through the important methods.

We begin by discussing the two ways to create a portfolio that is not managed against a benchmark. Ad hoc methods (Section 9.2) use various rules of thumb to weight stocks. The mean-variance optimization method (Section 9.3) minimizes the portfolio's total risk given its expected return.

We then consider the four potential approaches to creating a portfolio that is managed against a specific *benchmark*. The portfolio manager again could use an ad hoc weighting method that only roughly tracks the benchmark. Alternatively, he or she could use a method of sampling known as *stratification*, which involves choosing representative samples of the benchmark. Or he or she could use *factor exposure targeting*, in which the stocks are weighted so that the average factor exposures of the portfolio and the benchmark

---

[2] The choice of how to determine these values is up to the manager. Some managers use models to forecast the expected stock returns (or α) but rely on commercial software to calculate the implicit risks of the portfolio. Other managers build their own risk models.

match. Finally, the manager could follow the most common weighting method of professional money managers—*tracking-error minimization*. The stock weights are chosen so as to achieve the highest possible expected return or α of the portfolio while keeping the tracking error below a specified threshold. Of the four weighting techniques, only the ones that minimize risk have theoretical rigor. They also require, though, a larger skill set, more time, and more effort than do the other less quantitatively precise techniques.

9.2 AD HOC METHODS

Once the portfolio manager decides which stocks to include in his or her portfolio, there are two very easy ways to determine the portfolio weights: equal weighting and value weighting. *Equal weighting* is simply assigning the same weight to every stock. If there are 10 stocks, then each stock will have a weight of 0.1 (= 1/10). If there are 50 stocks, then each stock will have a weight of 0.02 (= 1/50). In general, if there are N stocks, each stock will have the weight of $1/N$. Equal weighting is certainly quick and simple, but it has one major deficiency: It reflects neither the risks nor the expected returns of stocks. Equal weighting makes sense only when the portfolio manager has very poor information about the expected return and the risk of stocks selected.

Value weighting is assigning weights proportional to the stocks' market capitalizations. For example, if the market capitalization of stock A is twice as great as the market capitalization of stock B, then the weight of stock A also should be twice the weight of stock B. In general, if there are N stocks with market capitalizations $x_1, \ldots, x_N$, then the weight of stock i, w_i, is

$$w_i = \frac{x_i}{\sum_{j=1}^{N} x_j} \tag{9.1}$$

Just like equal weighting, value weighting does not reflect the expected returns or the risks of the selected stocks, so it is also not the best method when there is good information about stock returns and risks. In the absence of such information, value weighting may be an improvement on equal weighting. The performance of the value-weighted portfolio is at least guaranteed to match the market average performance because market capitalizations are the weights, so to speak, that the market assigns to stocks.

There are a number of variations on value weighting.[3] Some portfolio managers have gone so far as to weight stocks by the square root of the market capitalization. Using the square root reduces the weighting bias toward stocks with very large market capitalizations. In this scheme, stock i would get a weight of

$$w_i = \frac{\sqrt{x_i}}{\sum_{j=1}^{N}\sqrt{x_j}} \tag{9.2}$$

One could get even more creative and do the cubed root, and so on and so forth.

Instead of equal weighting or value weighting, portfolio managers also can use *price weighting*. In the price-weighting scheme, the manager buys the same number of shares in each stock so that the weights are proportional to the prices of stocks. If the share price of a stock is high, this stock will have relatively more weight in the portfolio. This is the way the Dow Jones Industrial Average and the Nikkei 225 are calculated.

We will discuss a few more ad hoc weighting schemes when we discuss the weighting of benchmarked portfolios.

9.3 STANDARD MEAN-VARIANCE OPTIMIZATION

Given the mean and the variance of future stock returns, we can use the quadratic programming technique to find the portfolio that has the *minimum risk*. That is, we can find the portfolio that has the lowest ex-ante risk among portfolios with identical expected returns. This is known as *mean-variance optimization* or simply, *MVO*.

The underlying idea of this method is the comparison of all the portfolios that potentially could be built given a list of stocks. We theoretically compute each portfolio's ex-ante risk from the variances and covariances of the returns of all stocks and each portfolio's expected return from the mean returns of individual stocks. Then we theoretically compare the ex-ante risks and the expected returns of all the portfolios and choose the one with the lowest risk for a given level of expected return. (Or, conversely, we can choose

---

[3] Many portfolios and indices are also *float-weighted*, which has the same sort of characteristics as value weighting, except stocks are weighted by their floating shares, not their shares outstanding.

the portfolio with the highest expected return for a given level of risk.[4])

Of course, actually calculating the expected return and the risk of every potential portfolio would take forever because there are infinite potential portfolios. Thus we use quadratic programming to find the minimum-risk portfolio without having to explicitly calculate every portfolio's risk and return.

One common objection of MVO is that the selected portfolio often assigns very large weights to certain outlier stocks, including stocks with very low variances or very high means. This in itself should not be a concern. If the stock indeed has a low variance for a given return, then it is smart to overweight it in the portfolio. However, in portfolio construction, we must estimate the means and variances of stocks, so we cannot be sure of their true values. Some outliers could be mismeasurements and throw off our results ("Garbage in, garbage out," as the saying goes). The portfolio manager therefore must do his or her best to account for estimation error.[5] If this is not practical, the manager may include additional portfolio constraints in the quadratic optimization problem that put limitations on the maximum and minimum stock weights. The most common additional portfolio constraints are short-sale constraints, which do not allow for a negative weight on any stock; diversification constraints, which restrict any stock from having more than a certain threshold weighting; and sector constraints, which do not allow the composite weight of any group of stocks in a certain sector of the economy to be beyond a certain level.

The portfolio manager must be careful not to impose so many constraints that some of them begin to contradict each other. As a rather obvious example, not all stocks in a portfolio can weigh less than 5% if the portfolio is limited to 10 stocks; the portfolio will not be fully invested. Typically, portfolio managers impose only the

---

[4] Mathematicians and software programs, however, prefer the formulation in which the objective function is quadratic and the constraint is linear (rather than the other way around). See Appendix 9A and Appendix 9B for the mathematical details of typical quadratic optimization problems.

[5] Chapter 8 discussed methods to measure estimation error. The reader also may be interested in a book that deals with estimation error, such as Michaud (1993). This book is particularly critical of MVO. On page 3, it reads, "MV optimizers function as a chaotic investment decision system. Small changes in input assumptions often imply large changes in the optimized portfolio. The procedure overuses statistically estimated information and magnifies the impact of estimation errors. The result is that the optimized portfolio is 'error maximized.'"

most obvious or needed constraints and let the optimizer do the rest.

9.3.1 No Constraints

Let us first look at how to use MVO without imposing additional constraints. We assume that the portfolio manager already has built a model of expected stock returns and risk either by using one of the models discussed in previous chapters or by using commercial software risk models combined with his or her excess-return models.

The first step is to include all the relevant information about individual stock returns in a vector μ and a matrix Σ. μ is an N-dimensional column vector of expected returns of individual stocks, where N is the number of stocks in the investment universe. Σ is an $N \times N$ matrix of variances and covariances of individual stock returns. That is,

$$\mu = \begin{bmatrix} E(r_1) \\ \vdots \\ E(r_N) \end{bmatrix} \tag{9.3}$$

$$\Sigma = \begin{bmatrix} V(r_1) & C(r_1,r_2) & \cdots & C(r_1,r_N) \\ C(r_2,r_1) & V(r_2) & \cdots & C(r_2,r_N) \\ \vdots & & & \\ C(r_N,r_1) & C(r_N,r_2) & \cdots & V(r_N) \end{bmatrix} \tag{9.4}$$

where $E(r_i)$ is the expected return of stock i, $V(r_i)$ is the variance of stock i's return, and $C(r_i, r_j)$ is the covariance between stock i's return and stock j's return.

A portfolio is specified by a weight vector **w**. **w** is an N-dimensional column vector of stock weights:

$$\mathbf{w} = \begin{bmatrix} w_1 \\ \vdots \\ w_N \end{bmatrix} \tag{9.5}$$

where w_i is the weight of stock i in the portfolio. For **w** to be a valid weight, the sum of all the elements in **w** should be 1. We may define ι as an N-dimensional vector of 1 such that

$$\iota = \begin{bmatrix} 1 \\ \vdots \\ 1 \end{bmatrix} \tag{9.6}$$

The sum of elements in $\mathbf{w}$ is $\Sigma_{i=1}^{N} w_i$ or simply $\mathbf{w}'\iota$, which should be 1. For the portfolio specified by weights $\mathbf{w}$, the expected return of the portfolio is $\Sigma_{i=1}^{N} w_i E(r_i)$ or simply $\mathbf{w}'\boldsymbol{\mu}$, whereas the risk of the portfolio (i.e., the variance of the portfolio return) is $\Sigma_{i=1}^{N} w_i^2\, V(r_i) + 2\Sigma_{i=1}^{N} \Sigma_{j=i+1}^{N} w_i w_j C(r_i, r_j)$ or, in matrix notation, $\mathbf{w}'\boldsymbol{\Sigma}\mathbf{w}$. Thus the portfolio that has the minimum risk with the expected return of μ_P is the solution to the following minimization problem:

$$\min_{\mathbf{w}} \mathbf{w}'\boldsymbol{\Sigma}\mathbf{w} \quad s.t. \quad \mathbf{w}'\boldsymbol{\mu} = \mu_P \quad \text{and} \quad \mathbf{w}'\iota = 1 \tag{9.7}$$

Note that the objective function ($\mathbf{w}'\boldsymbol{\Sigma}\mathbf{w}$) is a quadratic function of $\mathbf{w}$ (i.e., the weight terms are squared), whereas the constraints ($\mathbf{w}'\boldsymbol{\mu} = \mu_P$) are linear in $\mathbf{w}$. Mathematicians call this problem a *quadratic optimization problem* and have developed a way of dealing with this called *quadratic programming*. In fact, mathematicians would prefer to rewrite the constraints in the following way:

$$\mathbf{Aw} = \mathbf{b} \tag{9.8}$$

where

$$\mathbf{A} = \begin{bmatrix} 1 & 1 & \cdots & 1 \\ \mu_1 & \mu_2 & \cdots & \mu_N \end{bmatrix} \tag{9.9}$$

$$\mathbf{b} = \begin{bmatrix} 1 \\ \mu_P \end{bmatrix} \tag{9.10}$$

We show in Appendix 9A that this particular form of the quadratic minimization problem with equality constraints has a closed-form solution. The solution is

$$\mathbf{w} = \boldsymbol{\Sigma}^{-1}\mathbf{A}'\, (\mathbf{A}\boldsymbol{\Sigma}^{-1}\mathbf{A}')^{-1}\mathbf{b} \tag{9.11}$$

Figure 9.1 provides a visual example of the results from a mean-variance optimization. In this particular optimization, we focused on the 32 stocks that comprise the consumer staples sector of the Standard & Poor's (S&P) 500. We created a five-factor model of security returns using the unemployment rate, consumer sentiment growth, excess market returns, log of market capitalization, and book-to-price factor. We estimated the economic factor model

FIGURE 9.1

Efficient frontier for consumer staples sector (January 2021). Based on data from January 2016 to December 2020. Dots indicate the expected returns and the standard deviations of individual stocks. Expected return and standard deviation are annualized and in percent.

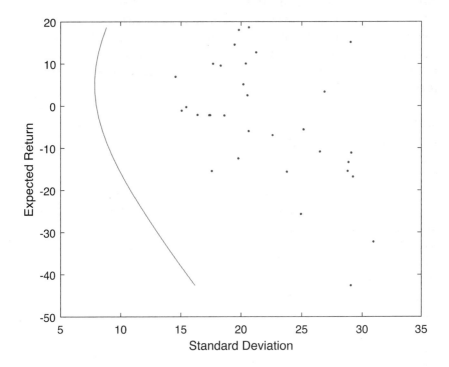

for the period from January 2016 to December 2020,[6] and we produced forecasts for the expected returns and variances of all stocks for January 2021.

After that, we used our mean-variance optimization to create the minimal-risk portfolios for a variety of expected portfolio returns. We first found the stocks with the lowest and highest mean returns. We then began the optimization procedure to minimize risk for a given level of expected return using the expected return of the lowest expected return stock. Storing the optimal portfolio weights that would create this portfolio, we incremented the mean

---

[6] We produce forecasts of the factor premiums using a VAR model as described in Chapter 8. We then use the estimated factor exposures along with the forecasts to calculate expected returns and variances.

return and performed the optimization again, finding the optimal weights for that given mean return. We continued doing this until we reached the expected return of the security with the highest mean return. At this point we stopped running the optimization and plotted all the points in the diagram and connected them. The curve that results from these plotted points is typically called the *efficient frontier* in modern portfolio theory, although, technically, the efficient frontier is only the part of the curve whose gradient is positive (the upper half of the curve). Also, since we forecasted the expected returns and variances, we should call this curve the *predictive efficient frontier*.

Typically, we decide how many intervals of expected return and variance we would like to plot. Smaller intervals necessitate more computation but also result in a smoother plot of the efficient frontier. The interval is usually chosen by taking the highest expected return $\max(\mu)$, subtracting the minimum expected return $\min(\mu)$, and dividing by the number of intervals one desires (that is, $[\max(\mu)-\min(\mu)]$/number of intervals = increment). This value becomes the incremental value to the expected portfolio return in the mean-variance optimization problem. Thus one starts with $\min(\mu)$, computes the optimal portfolio weights, and then recomputes the optimization problem using the portfolio mean of $\min(\mu)$ plus increment. And the process continues until one reaches the maximum expected return.

We also plotted the expected returns and variances of all the individual stocks in the consumer staples sector. (These are represented by dots.) This plot of the efficient frontier completes the process and maps out our portfolio choices. We should decide on the expected-return–expected-risk profile we wish to have and then pick the weights of the stocks corresponding to that profile on the efficient frontier.

Table 9.1 shows the characteristics and composition of selected portfolios along the efficient frontier that we created. We chose to show five portfolios with varying annual expected returns from -5.35% to 18.65%. Every stock in the original universe is included in the portfolios. Stock weights vary from about minus 9.88% to plus 17.64%. Since we did not impose the short-sale restriction, a number of stocks have negative weights. In this table, we show the three largest-weight stocks and the three smallest-weight stocks.

Let's look at portfolio C on the efficient frontier. We expect that portfolio C will generate an annualized expected return of

TABLE 9.1

Selected Efficient Portfolios from the Consumer Staples Sector

Portfolios	A	B	C	D	E
Expected return	−5.35	0.65	6.65	12.65	18.65
SD	8.43	7.95	7.86	8.16	8.82
Market beta	0.38	0.37	0.36	0.35	0.35
Number of stocks	32	32	32	32	32
Max. weight	13.56	13.27	12.99	15.31	17.64
Min. weight	−6.24	−5.75	−5.27	−6.96	−9.88
Selected constituents	HRL	HRL	HRL	PG	PG
(weight)	(13.56)	(13.27)	(12.99)	(15.31)	(17.64)
	PEP	PG	PG	HRL	HRL
	(9.48)	(10.66)	(12.99)	(12.70)	(12.42)
	K	PEP	CLX	CLX	CLX
	(9.28)	(9.26)	(9.90)	(11.03)	(12.15)
	EL	BF.B	KHC	KHC	GIS
	(−4.20)	(−2.12)	(−3.05)	(−4.52	(−5.68)
	COST	COST	TAP	MNST	KHC
	(−4.67)	(−2.71)	(−4.04)	(−4.78)	(−6.00)
	MNST	MNST	MNST	TAP	TAP
	(−6.24)	(−5.75)	(−5.27)	(−6.96)	(−9.88)

Note: The investment universe consists of 32 consumer staples stocks in the S&P 500. The expected returns and risk are estimated from the economic factor model of Chapter 7. The computation is based on data from January 2016 to December 2020. Expected return and standard deviation (SD) are annualized and in percent. Weights are in percent. Ticker symbols are for the following companies: Hormel Foods Corp (HRL), Pepsico Inc. (PEP), Kellogg Co. (K), Estee Lauder Companies Inc. (EL), Costco Wholesale Corp (COST), Monster Beverage Corp (MNST), Procter & Gamble Co. (PG), Brown Forman Corp (BF.B), Clorox Co. (CLX), Kraft Heinz Co. (KHC), Molson Coors Beverage Co. (TAP), and General Mills Inc. (GIS). In the table we show the three largest-weight stocks and the three smallest-weight stocks for each portfolio.

6.65%. The annualized standard deviation is expected to be 7.86%. This optimal portfolio contains 32 stocks. Hormel Foods (HRL) has the highest weighting (12.99%) in this portfolio, and Monster Beverage Corp (MNST) has the lowest weighting (−5.27%). A portfolio manager might like to create a portfolio with a 6.65% annual expected return and a standard deviation of 7.86%, but he or she may not be able to implement the results of this mean-variance optimization. For instance, if he or she is not allowed to short stocks, a 5.27% short of MNST is out of the question. This illustrates why the manager might wish to perform a mean-variance optimization with additional constraints. We discuss some of the most common additional constraints in the next subsections.

9.3.2 Short-Sale and Diversification Constraints

Portfolio managers may face constraints on their investment portfolios for various reasons, such as legal restrictions or prospectus mandates. The main constraint on a long-only portfolio manager is the short-sale restriction that prevents shorting securities. Mathematically, we can represent the short-sale restriction as the condition that

$$\mathbf{w} \geq 0 \qquad (9.12)$$

which indicates that each stock has at least a weight of zero.

This restriction simply can be added to the minimization problem as an additional constraint. This type of constraint, however, is an *inequality constraint*. We show in Appendix 9A that when dealing with inequality constraints, the quadratic optimization problem does not have a simple analytical solution and instead requires numerical methods to solve for the optimal portfolio weighting.

Techniques designed to solve this type of quadratic minimization with inequality constraints are known as *quadratic programming*. Most portfolio managers simply need to formulate the constraints, enter them into the commercial software or quadratic optimizer, and let the software/optimizer do the rest. For readers who are more interested in the mathematics of quadratic programming, we discuss it in Appendix 9A.

Using the same data as before and a quadratic optimization programming tool, we recalculated the set of efficient portfolios with the additional short-sale constraints using the same approach. Figure 9.2 plots the efficient frontier. As before, we focused on the same consumer staples sector of the S&P 500 and used the same time period for estimation, January 2016 to December 2020, and the same model for security returns. We then produced forecasts for the expected returns and variances of all stocks for January 2021.

Compared with Figure 9.1, the efficient frontier has shifted to the right owing to the additional short-sale constraint. This makes sense. By adding an additional constraint to the optimization, the lowest-risk portfolio we can create will have a higher risk than the lowest-risk portfolio we were able to create without the short-sale constraint.

Table 9.2 shows the characteristics and composition of selected portfolios along the efficient frontier. We chose to show three portfolios with target monthly mean returns identical to the

FIGURE 9.2

Efficient frontier for consumer staples sector with short-sale
constraints (January 2021). Based on data from January
2016 to December 2020. Dots indicate the expected returns
and the standard deviations of individual stocks. Expected
return and standard deviation are annualized and in percent.

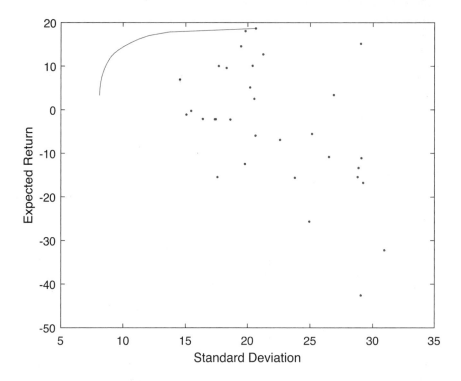

portfolios listed in Table 9.1. We did not include two portfolios
with expected returns of −5.35% and 0.65%. The variances of these
portfolios are higher than the variance of portfolio C, so, in the
strictest sense, they are no longer efficient portfolios. The minimum-
risk portfolio includes fewer stocks to achieve the same expected
return. Its maximum stock weights are also higher than in the
optimization without constraints. In this table, we show the
weights for the five stocks with the largest weights in the optimal
portfolio. Portfolio E is an extreme case in which the entire portfolio
consists of just one stock, CHD.

Let's look again at portfolio C on the efficient frontier. We
expect that portfolio C will generate an annualized expected return
of 6.65%. This is comparable to portfolio C in the unconstrained

TABLE 9.2

Selected Efficient Portfolios from the Consumer Staples Sector with Short-Sale Constraints

Portfolios	C	D	E
Expected return	6.65	12.65	18.65
SD	8.23	9.19	20.65
Market beta	0.41	0.43	0.45
Number of stocks	18	9	1
Max. weight	13.81	16.17	100.00
Selected constituents	HRL	CLX	CHD
(weight)	(13.81)	(16.17)	(100.00)
	PG	MKC	
	(13.61)	(15.23)	
	CLX	CHD	
	(11.71)	(13.07)	
	MKC	PG	
	(7.99)	(12.91)	
	LW	LW	
	(7.40)	(11.61)	

Note: The investment universe consists of 32 consumer staples stocks in the S&P 500. The expected returns and risk are estimated from the economic factor model of Chapter 7. The computation is based on data from January 2016 to December 2020. Expected return and standard deviation (SD) are annualized and in percent. Weights are in percent. Ticker symbols are for the following companies: Hormel Foods Corp (HRL), Procter & Gamble Co. (PG), Clorox Co. (CLX), McCormick & Co. (MKC), Lamb Weston Holdings Inc. (LW), and Church & Dwight Inc. (CHD). In this table, we show the weights for the five stocks with the largest weights in each portfolio.

case reported in Table 9.1. The annualized standard deviation is expected to be 8.23%. Even though this optimal portfolio's expected return is similar to that of portfolio C in Table 9.1, the risk is clearly higher. This optimal portfolio contains 18 stocks compared with the 32 in the unconstrained portfolio, with the highest-weighted stock representing 13.81% of the portfolio. The constraint has removed the extremely negative weighting of MNST, as it should. At first glance, one might be unsatisfied with the results of the mean-variance optimization because this portfolio is not as optimal as the portfolio in the unconstrained case. However, the new portfolio will satisfy the needs of a long-only portfolio manager, demonstrating why it is useful to perform a mean-variance optimization with short-sale constraints.

In addition to short-sale constraints, portfolio managers also may wish to have *diversification constraints*. These are constraints that a mutual fund accepts in compliance with the diversification requirements of the Investment Company Act of 1940.[7] Of course, even if a portfolio manager is not regulated by the Securities and Exchange Commission (SEC), he or she may wish to follow maximum-weight constraints because too much exposure to very few stocks also increases the portfolio's diversifiable risk. Restrictions of this kind generally can be expressed as

$$\underline{\mathbf{w}} \leq \mathbf{w} \leq \overline{\mathbf{w}} \qquad (9.13)$$

where $\underline{\mathbf{w}}$ and $\overline{\mathbf{w}}$ are N-dimensional vectors of maximum and minimum allowed weights. This constraint can be added easily to the optimization problem and satisfies both the short-sale constraint and the diversification constraint simultaneously.

9.3.3 Sector or Industry Constraints

Many portfolio managers—especially those who manage against a benchmark—wish to constrain the sector weightings of the portfolio. Here is a simple modification to the framework to constrain sector weightings:

$$\underline{w}_j \leq w_j \leq \overline{w}_j \qquad (9.14)$$

where w_j represents the weight of sector j in the portfolio.[8]

9.3.4 Trading-Volume Constraint

One of the typical constraints that portfolio managers add to the optimization is the trading-volume constraint. This is particularly relevant when the value of the portfolio is large and the portfolio

---

[7] The Investment Company Act of 1940 specified various rules on investment companies, including Section 12d and Section 5b. Section 12d specifies certain investment constraints for diversified and nondiversified mutual funds. One rule prohibits mutual funds from owning more than 5% of other investment companies, which are firms that derive more than 15% of their revenue from securities-related activity and a maximum of 10% of the investment company's total AUM from such activity. This might be a constraint for any portfolio manager holding any type of banking stocks or investment banking stocks. Section 5b specifies rules for funds that advertise themselves as *diversified*. These funds may not hold more than 5% of their assets in any particular company or hold more than 10% of the voting stock of any company for 75% of the portfolio's assets. Due to this rule, we like to call the restriction on the maximum weight of a stock in the portfolio the *diversification rule*.

[8] Most software packages, such as MATLAB, have a simple way to add upper- and lower-bound constraints to their quadratic optimizer.

manager's transactions have a large price impact.[9] To avoid creating negative price impact, the portfolio manager may restrict the holding of each stock to keep it below some threshold amount, typically a fraction of the average trading volume of each stock.

Suppose that the value of the portfolio is $500 million and that the portfolio manager wants to keep the holding of one stock below 10% of the average daily trading volume of the stock (ADV). If w_i is the portfolio weight of stock i and x_i is the average trading volume of stock i measured in millions of dollars, then the constraint is $500w_i \leq 0.1x_i$ or $w_i \leq (0.1/500)x_i$.

In general, the trading volume constraint can be expressed as

$$\mathbf{w} \leq c\mathbf{x} \tag{9.15}$$

where $\mathbf{x}$ is a vector of average daily trading volume in dollar terms, and c is a constant indicating the threshold.

9.3.5 Risk-Adjusted Return

So far we have formulated the mean-variance optimization problem as a risk minimization. Some portfolio managers may prefer an alternative formulation with expected return maximization. The expected return maximization can be written as

$$\max_{\mathbf{w}} \mathbf{w}'\boldsymbol{\mu} \quad s.t. \quad \mathbf{w}'\boldsymbol{\Sigma}\mathbf{w} = \sigma_P^2 \tag{9.16}$$

and other constraints. The expected return maximization may be more useful if the portfolio manager has a specific target risk level σ_P^2, whereas the risk minimization may be more useful if the portfolio manager has a target expected return.[10]

When the portfolio manager has neither a target risk nor a target expected return, the mean-variance optimization can be expressed in terms of *risk-adjusted* expected return. We can adjust the expected return for the risk by subtracting some multiple of the risk, that is, $\mu_p - A\sigma_P^2$. The multiplier A is called the *risk-aversion parameter* because a high value of A indicates that the portfolio manager considers the risk very costly. If the value of A is 2, it

---

[9] In Appendix 10C, we discuss more direct ways to deal with market impact.

[10] In fact, there is one more practical reason why this formulation may be preferred. In the minimization of the risk with a target expected return, there is a danger that the target expected return may not be feasible given the parameters. Thus the portfolio manager may end up getting a portfolio he or she did not wish to obtain, or, even worse, the optimization may fail altogether.

means that the portfolio manager equates a 1% increase in the variance with a 2% decrease in the expected return. Once the value of the risk-aversion parameter is decided, the mean-variance problem becomes

$$\max_{\mathbf{w}} \mathbf{w}'\boldsymbol{\mu} - A\mathbf{w}'\Sigma\mathbf{w} \qquad (9.17)$$

This formulation turns out to be quite useful in certain applications.[11]

9.4 BENCHMARK

Most portfolio managers manage the portfolio versus a benchmark. Managers who stick very closely to the benchmark sometimes are referred to as *index managers,* but managers who manage very loosely with respect to the benchmark are described more accurately as *active managers* or *enhanced index managers.* The goal of active managers is to produce a portfolio of stocks that is broadly similar to the underlying benchmark but that outperforms the benchmark by some amount. The manager must walk a fine line in order to outperform the benchmark without diverging dramatically from it. Fortunately, when the benchmark itself is not efficient, these two goals do not conflict.[12]

There is a whole set of tools to deal with tracking a benchmark while producing α (outperformance) over the benchmark. We will describe a number of these in the following sections, including ad hoc methods, stratification, factor exposure targeting, and tracking error minimization. The last method is the most popular because, in theory, it provides the tightest control on risk versus the benchmark while still allowing the portfolio manager to select his or her favorite stocks.

---

[11] This formulation has a theoretical appeal as well. The objective function can be interpreted as an investor's utility function, and the optimization can be interpreted as an investor's utility maximization. This is how theory says investors make portfolio decisions. On the other hand, maximizing the information ratio or some ratio of expected return to risk does not have such theoretical appeal.

[12] In practice, the benchmark is rarely efficient. A simple way to see whether the benchmark is efficient is to make a plot similar to the one in Figure 9.1. On the plot, add a dot corresponding to the benchmark. If the dot is close to the efficient frontier, then the benchmark is nearly efficient. If not, then the benchmark is not efficient. This efficiency, sometimes called *mean-variance efficiency,* may not be the only measure of efficiency. Some prefer to define efficiency with respect to the benchmark. In such a case, of course, the benchmark is always efficient. Minimizing tracking errors when the benchmark is inefficient may lead to inefficient portfolios in a variety of cases. For more on this, see Roll (1992).

9.5 AD HOC METHODS AGAIN

One rather simplistic approach to weighting a benchmarked portfolio so that it follows the benchmark closely is to select the largest
holdings of the benchmark for the portfolio. If the portfolio is
going to include 50 stocks, this would amount to choosing the 50
stocks with the largest market capitalization in the benchmark and
then possibly computing the weights of the 50 stocks according to
their relative market capitalizations. A manager could further tilt
the weights slightly toward his or her preferred stocks. There are
a number of ad hoc methods for tilting the weights toward preferred stocks. Let's assume that the portfolio manager has ranked
the stocks by the aggregate Z-score methodology described in
Chapter 5.[13] The portfolio manager should renormalize the aggregate Z-scores so that the sum of the Z-scores of the subset of 50
stocks (or whatever number of stocks he or she chooses) is equal
to 0. The steps to alter the relative market capitalization weighting
are as follows: First, the portfolio manager should decide what is
the maximum percentage deviation in weight he or she is willing
to allow from the market-cap weighting for the maximum absolute Z-score value. Call this η. The second step is to find the maximum absolute Z-score of all the stocks in the universe of 50 stocks.
Thus, take the absolute value of all the individual Z-scores and
find the maximum; call this z^{max}. The third step is to compute the
Z-score multiplier $m = \eta/z^{max}$. The fourth step is to compute the
new weights w_i^* of the portfolio such that $(w_i^* = w_i + mz_i)$, where
w_i is the relative market capitalization weight within the benchmark.[14] The adjusted portfolio is complete.

As a brief example of this method for creating an altered
market-capitalization portfolio to track the benchmark with the top
N stocks by market capitalization, we selected the top 30 S&P 500
stocks and modified the relative market capitalization weights using
the Z-scores methodology used in Table 5.2. The modified weights as
well as the relative weights and the Z-scores are shown in Table 9.3.

---

[13] It is not important for this ad hoc weighting mechanism that the QEPM use the
aggregate Z-score methodology. In fact, the manager can use any relative ranking
method for the stocks. However, so that the ad hoc conversion mechanism we
describe will function properly, the manager should normalize the ranking method
so that the sum of all the ranks equals 0.

[14] One can see that the new weights will add up to 1 as well so long as $\Sigma_{i=1}^{N} z_i = 0$. This is
why it is critical to normalize the aggregate Z-scores or other ranking method
among the subset of benchmark stocks.

TABLE 9.3

Ad Hoc Modified Market-Cap Weights to Reflect Z-Score Model

Ticker	Relative Market-Cap Weight (w_i)	Z-Score	Z-Score-Adjusted Weight (w_i^*)	Change in Weight ($w_i^* - w_i$)
AAPL	0.1498	−1.6817	0.1473	−0.0025
MSFT	0.1117	−1.9532	0.1088	−0.0029
AMZN	0.1085	−1.4515	0.1064	−0.0021
GOOGL	0.0734	−1.3965	0.0713	−0.0021
TSLA	0.0444	13.5251	0.0644	0.0200
FB	0.0436	−0.8509	0.0424	−0.0013
BRK.B	0.0361	0.3480	0.0366	0.0005
JNJ	0.0275	−1.0351	0.0260	−0.0015
WMT	0.0271	−0.6762	0.0261	−0.0010
JPM	0.0257	−0.5420	0.0249	−0.0008
V	0.0246	−1.0393	0.0231	−0.0015
MA	0.0234	−1.3853	0.0214	−0.0020
PG	0.0229	−0.8318	0.0217	−0.0012
UNH	0.0221	−0.4488	0.0214	−0.0007
DIS	0.0218	−0.5556	0.0210	−0.0008
NVDA	0.0215	1.1247	0.0231	0.0017
HD	0.0190	−1.0188	0.0175	−0.0015
PYPL	0.0182	1.1093	0.0199	0.0016
BAC	0.0174	0.6922	0.0184	0.0010
VZ	0.0161	−0.3645	0.0156	−0.0005
ADBE	0.0159	−0.0586	0.0158	−0.0001
CMCSA	0.0159	0.1797	0.0162	0.0003
NFLX	0.0159	0.1099	0.0160	0.0002
KO	0.0157	−1.0718	0.0141	−0.0016
MRK	0.0137	−0.7408	0.0126	−0.0011
PEP	0.0136	−0.9175	0.0123	−0.0014
T	0.0136	0.8621	0.0149	0.0013
PFE	0.0136	−0.2055	0.0133	−0.0003
INTC	0.0136	0.1305	0.0138	0.0002
CRM	0.0135	0.1437	0.0137	0.0002

Note: In this particular example, the maximum absolute Z-score is 13.53 (TSLA), $\eta = 0.02$, and $m = 0.001479$. w_i is the relative market capitalization weights, Z-scores were computed as in Table 5.2, and w^* is based upon the ad hoc method. Finally, the last column represents the change in weights from w_i to w^*. All the data are as of the end of December 2020. The ticker symbols are for the following companies: Apple (AAPL), Microsoft (MSFT), Amazon (AMZN), Alphabet (GOOGL), Tesla (TSLA), Facebook (FB), Berkshire Hathaway (BRK.B), Johnson & Johnson (JNJ), Walmart (WMT), J.P. Morgan Chase & Co. (JPM), Visa (V), Mastercard (MA), Procter & Gamble (PG), United Health Group (UNH), Disney (DIS), Nvidia (NVDA), Home Depot (HD), PayPal (PYPL), Bank of America (BAC), Verizon Communications (VZ), Adobe (ADBE), Comcast (CMCSA), Netflix (NFLX), Coca-Cola (KO), Merck & Co. (MRK), PepsiCo (PEP), AT&T (T), Pfizer (PFE), Intel Corp (INTC), and Salesforce (CRM).

By altering the portfolio in this way, the portfolio manager can continue to track the benchmark relatively closely while still altering the stock weights to take advantage of his or her α model.

Although this is certainly one type of ad hoc method to compute portfolio weights while still tracking the benchmark, it will not be the best solution. For one, there was no attempt to choose the portfolio based on minimum tracking error versus the index. Thus there will be no control of other risk factors or of asset-specific risk in the portfolio. Almost surely it will not be the optimal portfolio. Moreover, the relatively small number of stocks in the portfolio (30 in our example) represent only a fraction of the total market capitalization of the benchmark (less than 50% in our example). Though simple, this is an inefficient way to choose the stocks.

Other ad hoc methods are possible, but a professional portfolio manager will be dissatisfied with them despite their simplicity. Ultimately, a manager wants to quantify his or her risk versus the benchmark, something that simply is not possible with these other, rather amateurish mechanisms.

9.6 STRATIFICATION

Stratification or stratified sampling is another simple way to build portfolios while maintaining a very rudimentary risk control mechanism. Stratified sampling was devised primarily for empirical statisticians who wanted to understand the characteristics of a population but could not afford to gather observations on every member of the population. One method to create a representative sample of the population would be to randomly select members of the universe. While this method converges to the true mean and standard deviation of the population, we can improve on it by first stratifying the sample and then choosing a certain number of observations within each stratum.[15]

We assume that the portfolio manager already has predicted the excess returns of all the stocks in his or her universe. His or her goal is to choose the high-α stocks while controlling risk versus the

---

[15] There really are two types of stratified sampling: proportional and disproportional. The one we describe here is proportional random sampling, in which the same proportion is chosen for the sample as is represented in the population. Disproportional random sampling may overweight certain strata with respect to their size in the population for a variety of reasons that will not be discussed here.

benchmark. The stratification method involves minimizing the exposures of the portfolio along many dimensions of risk. The first stage of stratification is to stratify the universe of stocks by dividing it into J nonoverlapping groups. We might want to stratify, for instance, by dividing the stocks into industry buckets so that each stratum represents a different industry. Call the number of stocks in stratum j, N_j. The total stocks in the universe can be represented by N. Thus $\sum_{j=1}^{J} N_j = N$.

The next step in stratified sampling with one subgroup classification is to select representative stocks from each stratum. At this point the portfolio manager will have to decide how many stocks he or she wants in the portfolio. Let's call this number N_p. The idea of stratification is to select a proportion of stocks from each stratum that is representative of the universe of stocks. Thus, from each stratum, the portfolio manager should choose $N_j N_p / N$ stocks. This value may need to be rounded to the nearest integer. In traditional stratified sampling, an index portfolio manager would select the stocks at random, which is a valid procedure for just replicating the characteristics of the index. Beyond pure mimicry, though, a manager ought to maintain some risk controls while picking the high-α stocks. Thus, before making selections of stocks from each stratum, he or she should rank the stocks in each stratum according to aggregate Z-score, expected return, excess expected return, or α and then choose the stocks with the highest values of the chosen criterion. For example, if the stock universe is divided into sectors and four stocks must be chosen from the transportation sector, those four stocks could be the ones with the highest relative ranking according to future risk-adjusted returns.

Of course, a portfolio manager might wish to create more than one subgroup classification to control risk. This can be accomplished by dividing the universe of N stocks into a group of J categories based on one classification and then dividing each group into subgroups, and so on and so forth. For example, to divide the universe of stocks into two subgroup classifications, we could divide them by industry and then by size.

Figure 9.3 depicts the stratification of the universe of stocks into two subgroup classifications based on 9 industry groups and 3 size groups (large, medium, and small). With the stocks separated into 27 separate groups, or buckets, the manager ranks them according to highest Z-score or some other excess-return criterion.

FIGURE 9.3

The stratified-sample approach.

					Industry				
	1	2	3	4	5	6	7	8	9
Large	•	•	•	•	•	•	•	•	•
Medium	•	•	•	•	•	•	•	•	•
Small	•	•	•	•	•	•	•	•	•

He or she selects stocks from each subgroup based on the formula $N_j N_p/N$ rounded to the nearest integer.

Stratification is an easy way to choose one's preferred stocks while also controlling the risk via broad diversification. A portfolio manager might have an α model that, left to its own devices, tends to select stocks in one particular industry. Stratifying across industries or sectors ensures broad diversification and risk control versus the benchmark. The biggest drawback to stratification is that it is a fairly rudimentary method for controlling risk. Most professional portfolio managers would be averse to using it because it does not precisely quantify ex ante how much risk they are taking. Managers ought to be able to quantify their risks using all the available information. Clearly, stratification lacks a precise, quantitative control mechanism.

9.7 FACTOR EXPOSURE TARGETING

Another way to bring the portfolio in line with the benchmark is to set the benchmark's factor exposures as target factor exposures for the portfolio. Or one may set the portfolio's overall beta with respect to the benchmark equal to (or very close to) 1.[16]

The benchmark beta of any portfolio is simply the weighted average of the benchmark betas of the individual stocks. Let β be

---

[16] This, of course, does not control the asset-specific risk, and thus the tracking error is not bounded. That is, controlling directly for asset-specific risk with similar stocks and similar stock weights will imply a rather tight control of factor risk, but controlling for factor risk will not necessarily imply a tight control on asset-specific risk.

an N-dimensional column vector of the benchmark beta of individual stocks, that is,

$$\beta = \begin{bmatrix} \beta_1 \\ \vdots \\ \beta_N \end{bmatrix} \tag{9.18}$$

where β_i is the beta of stock i with respect to the benchmark. The beta of the portfolio equals $\mathbf{w}'\boldsymbol{\beta}$. We can add the following constraint to the optimization problem:

$$\mathbf{w}'\boldsymbol{\beta} = 1 \tag{9.19}$$

Or we can specify some range for the portfolio β instead:

$$0.75 \leq \mathbf{w}'\boldsymbol{\beta} \leq 1.25 \tag{9.20}$$

Let us return to the consumer staples example. In the example we created the efficient frontier given a short-sale constraint. Now let us add a constraint that requires the β of the portfolio with respect to the benchmark to be no less than 0.85. The benchmark for the portfolio manager in this case is the value-weighted (i.e., market-cap-weighted) return of all stocks in the consumer staples sector. Other than our new constraint, the computation here is based on the same model and the same data as in Tables 9.1 and 9.2.

Table 9.4 shows the selected minimum-risk portfolios created from 32 stocks in the consumer staples sector with the restriction on the benchmark β. Portfolio A (with a mean return of -5.35%) and portfolio B (with a mean return of 0.65%) are not reported because there is no minimum-variance portfolio with either of those mean returns owing to the additional constraint.

We imposed an inequality constraint on the portfolio requiring that the market β be no less than 0.85. In the case of portfolios A and B, since the betas of the portfolios turned out to be exactly 0.85, which hit our minimum requirement, the constraint was binding. Since the constraint was binding, the variances of these portfolios are greater than the variances of the portfolios constructed in Tables 9.1 and 9.2. The compositions of these new portfolios also differ significantly from the compositions of the previous portfolios.

While we began with the simple case of targeting the portfolio's benchmark β to a specified range, we may prefer to stipulate a range for each of the portfolio's other factor exposures as well. This is sometimes referred to as *factor tilting* because we are tilting the portfolio toward greater exposure to certain factors and less

TABLE 9.4

Selected Efficient Portfolios from the Consumer Staples Sector
with Short-Sale and Benchmark β Constraints

Portfolios	C	D	E
Expected return	6.65	12.65	18.65
SD	8.25	9.22	20.65
Benchmark beta	0.85	0.85	0.86
Number of stocks	20	10	1
Max. weight	13.70	15.14	100.00
Selected constituents	PG	MKC	CHD
(weight)	(13.70)	(15.14)	(100.00)
	HRL	CLX	
	(11.82)	(14.71)	
	CLX	PG	
	(11.03)	(14.04)	
	MKC	CHD	
	(8.32)	(12.46)	
	PEP	LW	
	(7.44)	(11.25)	

Note: The investment universe consists of 32 consumer staples stocks in the S&P 500. The benchmark is the market-cap-weighted index of the same 32 stocks. The expected returns and risk are estimated from the economic factor model of Chapter 7. The benchmark β is restricted to be no less than 0.85. The computation is based on data from January 2016 to December 2020. Expected return and standard deviation (SD) are annualized and in percent. Weights are in percent. Ticker symbols are for the following companies: Procter & Gamble Co. (PG), Hormel Foods Corp (HRL), Clorox Co. (CLX), McCormick & Co. (MKC), Pepsico Inc. (PEP), Church & Dwight Inc. (CHD), and Lamb Weston Holdings Inc. (LW). In this table, we show the weights for the five stocks with the largest weights in each portfolio.

exposure to others, according to our view on the factors and upcoming market conditions. If a portfolio manager believes that the market will rally, for instance, he or she may wish to have a higher market β than that of the benchmark while keeping all other factor exposures equal to those of the benchmark. He or she would tilt the portfolio toward the market factor.

The factor exposure of a portfolio is the weighted average of the factor exposures of individual stocks. Let **B** be an $N \times K$ matrix of factor exposures of individual stocks. That is,

$$\mathbf{B} = \begin{bmatrix} \beta_{11} & \beta_{12} & \cdots & \beta_{1K} \\ \beta_{21} & \beta_{22} & \cdots & \beta_{2K} \\ \vdots & & & \\ \beta_{N1} & \beta_{N2} & \cdots & \beta_{NK} \end{bmatrix} \tag{9.21}$$

where K is the number of relevant factors, and β_{ik} is the exposure of stock i to factor k. Then the factor exposure of a portfolio with weight $\mathbf{w}$ is simply $\mathbf{B'w}$. Thus we may add the following general factor exposure constraint:

$$\underline{\beta} \le \mathbf{B'w} \le \bar{\beta} \qquad (9.22)$$

The portfolio manager can exercise his or her particular management style through this sort of constraint. Assigning a minimum exposure (say, 0.9) to the growth factor orients the portfolio toward growth investments. If the first factor is the growth factor, then the manager would set the first element of $\underline{\beta}$ to 0.9.

9.8 TRACKING-ERROR MINIMIZATION

9.8.1 Direct Computation

Most professional portfolio managers with a benchmark use the minimization-of-tracking-error approach to weighting stocks and building a portfolio. There are two ways to formulate the optimization problem using this approach. One way is to minimize the tracking error for a given expected excess return over the benchmark, and the other is to maximize the expected excess return over the benchmark without exceeding a maximum tracking-error constraint. The former approach is explained in this subsection, and the latter approach is explained in Section 9.8.4. We prefer the latter formulation because it is more realistic. In the practical application part of this book (Chapters 16 and 17), we use the latter approach.

Typically, the portfolio manager would like to use all his or her tracking-error constraints so long as he or she is adding to the expected excess return over the benchmark. Tracking-error constraints vary from portfolio to portfolio but can range from as little as 0.5% per annum to 10% per annum. The investment committee of the investment management firm often comes up with the tracking-error constraint, but sometimes portfolio managers choose to be even more conservative than required by the committee's constraint. Fortunately, the quadratic optimization framework we have already discussed is applicable to tracking-error minimization. We need only make slight modifications to the optimization problem.

Tracking error (TE) is defined by most portfolio managers as the standard deviation of portfolio returns minus benchmark returns.[17] Thus

$$TE = S\left(r_P - r_B\right) = \sqrt{V\left(r_P - r_B\right)} \qquad (9.23)$$

where $S(\cdot)$ is the standard deviation function.

The first method for minimizing the tracking error of the portfolio is to minimize it given some expected level of excess returns over the benchmark. Now consider the components of the variance term[18]:

$$V(r_P - r_B) = V(r_P) - 2C(r_P, r_B) + V(r_B) \qquad (9.24)$$

The last term, the variance of the benchmark, is beyond our control. Thus, to find a portfolio that minimizes the tracking error of the portfolio, we minimize $V(r_P) - 2C(r_P, r_B)$.

Given the portfolio weight $\mathbf{w}$, the variance of the portfolio is given as $\mathbf{w'\Sigma w}$. The covariance between the portfolio and the benchmark can be computed from the covariances between individual stock returns and the benchmark return. Let γ be an N-dimensional vector of the covariances between individual stock returns and the benchmark return:

$$\gamma = \begin{bmatrix} C\left(r_1, r_B\right) \\ \vdots \\ C\left(r_N, r_B\right) \end{bmatrix} \qquad (9.25)$$

---

[17] For further details on tracking error, including how to measure it ex post, see Chapter 15. If the standard deviation of the difference between the portfolio return and the benchmark return is zero, but the expected values of the two returns are different, do we have a perfect tracking portfolio? Of course, the answer is no. The tracking error, as defined above, however, would misleadingly equal zero because it ignores the expected difference in returns. A better way of measuring the tracking error is to use the root mean squared error (RMSE). RMSE is defined as

$$\text{RMSE}\left(r_P, r_B\right) = \sqrt{V\left(r_P - r_B\right) + \left[E\left(r_P - r_B\right)\right]^2}$$

RMSE accounts for the expected value of the difference as well as the variation in the difference. The RMSE equals the tracking error as previously defined only if there is no difference between the expected return of the portfolio and the benchmark. Fortunately, however, whether we use RMSE or the standard deviation to measure tracking error, the optimal portfolio selection problem is not affected (see the questions at the end of this chapter). For this reason, and also to follow convention, we use the standard deviation as the measure of the tracking error.

[18] We obtain this by the standard statistical result that $V(a - b) = V(a) + V(b) - 2C(a, b)$.

Then the covariance between the portfolio return and the benchmark return equals $\mathbf{w}'\gamma$.

To find the portfolio that minimizes tracking error, we need to solve the following quadratic minimization problem:

$$\min_{\mathbf{w}} \mathbf{w}'\Sigma\mathbf{w} - 2\mathbf{w}'\gamma \quad s.t. \quad \mathbf{w}'\mu = \mu_p \qquad (9.26)$$

The same quadratic programming routine that was used in the preceding section can solve this problem as well. Typically, the chosen portfolio mean μ_p will be some excess return over the benchmark. Practically, we should think of $\mu_p = \mu_B + \delta$. That is, we should take the expected return of the benchmark and add a small amount to it according to our desire and then run the optimization to find the portfolio weights. Just as in the case of a portfolio with no benchmark, we will see shortly that we can again add various additional constraints, such as the short-sale, diversification, and style constraints.

9.8.2 Tracking by Factor Exposure

There is an alternative but equivalent representation of the tracking-error minimization problem. Recall from Chapters 6 and 7 that the variance of an individual stock i can be estimated as

$$V(r_i) = \beta_i'\, V(\mathbf{f})\beta_i + V(\epsilon_i) \qquad (9.27)$$

Assuming that the covariance between the residuals of the stocks is 0, we can write the variance-covariance matrix of all stock returns as

$$\Sigma = \begin{bmatrix} \beta_{1,1} & \cdots & \beta_{1,K} \\ \vdots & \vdots & \vdots \\ \beta_{N,1} & \cdots & \beta_{N,K} \end{bmatrix} \begin{bmatrix} V(f_1) & \cdots & C(f_1, f_K) \\ \vdots & \vdots & \vdots \\ C(f_K, f_1) & \cdots & V(f_K) \end{bmatrix} \begin{bmatrix} \beta_{1,1} & \cdots & \beta_{N,1} \\ \vdots & \vdots & \vdots \\ \beta_{1,K} & \cdots & \beta_{N,K} \end{bmatrix}$$

$$+ \begin{bmatrix} V(\epsilon_1) & \cdots & 0 \\ \vdots & \vdots & \vdots \\ 0 & \cdots & V(\epsilon_N) \end{bmatrix} \qquad (9.28)$$

$$= BV(\mathbf{f})B' + V(\epsilon)$$

where $\mathbf{B}$ is an $N \times K$ matrix of factor exposures, $V(\mathbf{f})$ is a $K \times K$ matrix of factor premium variances and covariances, and $V(\epsilon)$ is an

$N \times N$ diagonal matrix of error variances. Given this, the squared tracking error is

$$TE^2 = (\mathbf{w}^P - \mathbf{w}^B)'\mathbf{B}V(\mathbf{f})\mathbf{B}'(\mathbf{w}^P - \mathbf{w}^B) +$$
$$(\mathbf{w}^P - \mathbf{w}^B)'V(\epsilon)(\mathbf{w}^P - \mathbf{w}^B) \qquad (9.29)$$

where $\mathbf{w}^P$ is the weight of the portfolio, and $\mathbf{w}^B$ is the weight of the benchmark. Once other relevant constraints are added, this tracking-error minimization problem can be solved using the quadratic optimizer.[19]

Table 9.5 shows the minimum-tracking-error portfolio created from 32 stocks in the consumer staples sector. The table is based on

TABLE 9.5

Selected Portfolios from the Consumer Staples Sector by Minimizing Tracking Error with Short-Sale Constraints

Portfolios	A	B	C	D	E
Expected return	1.36	0.65	6.65	12.65	18.65
SD	10.14	10.17	10.07	10.24	20.65
Tracking error	0.00	0.21	1.79	5.03	19.62
Number of stocks	32	32	26	11	1
Max. weight	17.08	16.80	19.52	21.59	100.00
Selected constituents	WMT	WMT	WMT	WMT	CHD
(weight)	(17.08)	(16.80)	(19.52)	(21.59)	(100.00)
	PG	PG	PG	PG	
	(14.45)	(14.18)	(16.55)	(13.31)	
	KO	KO	COST	MKC	
	(9.87)	(9.83)	(9.27)	(12.37)	
	PEP	PEP	KO	CHD	
	(8.59)	(8.61)	(9.13)	(12.18)	
	COST	COST	PEP	EL	
	(6.99)	(6.76)	(7.25)	(11.19)	

Note: The investment universe consists of 32 consumer staples stocks in the S&P 500. Portfolio A is the benchmark portfolio. The benchmark is the market-cap-weighted index of the same 32 stocks. The expected returns and risk are estimated from the economic factor model of Chapter 7. The computation is based on data from January 2016 to December 2020. Expected return and standard deviation (SD) are annualized and in percent. Weights are in percent. Ticker symbols are for the following companies: Walmart (WMT), Procter & Gamble Co. (PG), Coca-Cola (KO), Pepsico (PEP), Costco (COST), McCormick & Company (MKC), Estee Lauder Companies (EL), and Church & Dwight Co. (CHD). In this table we show the weights for the five stocks with the largest weights in each portfolio.

---

[19] Since minimizing squared tracking error is equivalent to minimizing tracking error, we will refer to them interchangeably when disussing the optimization problem.

the same model and data as in Tables 9.1, 9.2, and 9.4. The benchmark is the value-weighted portfolio of 32 stocks in the consumer
staples sector, which is identified as portfolio A in the table. As we
try to obtain higher expected returns, the tracking error increases.
To obtain a 5.29% (6.65% − 1.36%) excess return over the benchmark (portfolio C), the portfolio manager can expect a tracking
error of 1.79%. To obtain a 17.29% excess return over the benchmark (portfolio E), the portfolio manager must accept an expected
tracking error close to 20%.

Minimizing tracking error will force the factor exposures of the
portfolio to be quite close to those of the benchmark, so the first term
in Eq. (9.29) will be less significant than the second term. In fact,
when the portfolio manager has specific desired values for portfolio
factor exposures, the first term can be completely dropped. In this
case the optimization problem is specified simply as minimization
of the variance of error terms subject to the additional constraint
on the portfolio factor exposure. This is a type of *factor tilting*.

Suppose that the portfolio manager wants to tilt the portfolio
toward small growth stocks but in all other respects wants the portfolio's exposures to remain identical to those of the benchmark. He
or she can achieve this by setting the portfolio's exposures to the
size factor and the growth factor higher than the benchmark's
exposures to those factors while keeping its other factor exposures
equal to those of the benchmark. For example, if there are five
factors—market return, log of market capitalization, GDP growth,
unemployment, and consumer sentiment growth—then he or she
can add the following constraints:

$$\mathbf{B}'(\mathbf{w}^P - \mathbf{w}^B) = \mathbf{d} \tag{9.30}$$

where

$$\mathbf{d} = \begin{pmatrix} 0 \\ 0.1 \\ 0.1 \\ 0 \\ 0 \end{pmatrix} \tag{9.31}$$

The zeros in vector $\mathbf{d}$ will make sure that the portfolio's exposures
to the market return, unemployment, and sentiment factors are
identical to the benchmark's exposures to those factors. The value
of 0.1 in vector $\mathbf{d}$ will make sure that the portfolio's exposures to
the size and growth factors will be higher than the benchmark's

exposure to those factors by 0.1. With factor tilting, the optimization problem becomes

$$\min_{\mathbf{w}^P}\left(\mathbf{w}^P - \mathbf{w}^B\right)' V\left(\epsilon\right)\left(\mathbf{w}^P - \mathbf{w}^B\right) \qquad (9.32)$$

subject to Eq. (9.30) and any other constraints.

9.8.3 Ghost Benchmark Tracking

There may be cases in which the portfolio manager does not know the weights of the underlying benchmark's securities or he or she cannot estimate all the benchmark's factor exposures. In this case, the minimization of tracking error involves minimizing the tracking error with respect to the stream of historical returns on the benchmark.

The tracking-error formula must undergo some modification because we do not know the benchmark weights. After some manipulation of the equation, the squared tracking error becomes

$$
\begin{aligned}
TE^2 &= \begin{pmatrix}\mathbf{w}^P\\-1\end{pmatrix}'\begin{pmatrix}\mathbf{B}\\\boldsymbol{\beta}_B\end{pmatrix}V\left(\mathbf{f}\right)\begin{pmatrix}\mathbf{B}\\\boldsymbol{\beta}_B\end{pmatrix}'\begin{pmatrix}\mathbf{w}^P\\-1\end{pmatrix}\\
&+ \begin{pmatrix}\mathbf{w}^P\\-1\end{pmatrix}'\begin{pmatrix}V\left(\epsilon\right) & 0\\0 & V\left(\epsilon_B\right)\end{pmatrix}\begin{pmatrix}\mathbf{w}^P\\-1\end{pmatrix}
\end{aligned}
\qquad (9.33)
$$

In this equation, $\boldsymbol{\beta}_B$ is the benchmark's factor exposure, and ϵ_B is the benchmark's error term. Once the tracking error is defined, the tracking-error minimization can proceed as described earlier.

9.8.4 Risk-Adjusted Tracking Error

In practical situations, the portfolio manager may have some maximum tracking-error constraint, say, 3% per annum. He or she can keep increasing the expected excess return until he or she reaches the tracking-error constraint. This problem is essentially identical to what we discussed so far. The objective function will be the expected return of the portfolio rather than the tracking error, and the constraint will include the tracking error rather than the expected return. Mathematically speaking, given the target tracking error of $\sigma_{x'}$

$$\max_{\mathbf{w}} \mathbf{w}'\boldsymbol{\mu} \quad s.t. \quad V\left(r_P - r_B\right) = \sigma_x^2 \qquad (9.34)$$

and other constraints.

If there is neither a target tracking error nor a target mean, then the problem might be expressed in terms of the tracking-error-adjusted expected return. As we did for the risk-adjusted return, we can adjust the expected return for the tracking risk by subtracting some multiple of the squared tracking error $\mu_p - A\sigma_x^2$. The multiplier A is called the *tracking-error aversion parameter* because a high value of A indicates that the portfolio manager considers the tracking error very costly. Then the problem becomes

$$\max_{\mathbf{w}} \mathbf{w}'\boldsymbol{\mu} - AV\left(r_P - r_B\right) \qquad (9.35)$$

subject to other additional constraints.

Note that there is an important relationship between the two formulations. The set of maximum-return portfolios that we obtain as we vary the target tracking error σ_x is identical to the set of optimal portfolios that we obtain as we vary the tracking-error aversion parameter A. That is, we can always choose the target tracking error σ_x or the tracking-error aversion parameter A so that the two formulations are equivalent. This property can be quite useful in the optimization process. A commercial software package may not support maximizing the expected return subject to a quadratic constraint.[20] In such a case we can maximize the tracking-error-adjusted expected return [i.e., Eq. (9.35)] for a certain value of A. After the maximization, we can check whether the tracking-error constraint is satisfied. If not, we change the value of A and continue this process until we satisfy the tracking-error constraint. The value of A that makes the optimal portfolio satisfy the tracking-error constraint can be found in a small number of iterations using the property that a higher value of A reduces the tracking error of the optimal portfolio. This is the approach we follow in Part V of this book.

9.9 CONCLUSION

In this chapter we showed how to turn the factor model's predictions of stock return and risk into a portfolio through various methods of stock weighting. As we saw, there are a number of very simple ad hoc ways to assign weights in a portfolio that are not measured against a benchmark, but they do not allow the portfolio manager to maintain good control of the risk of the portfolio. For

---

[20] IBM's CPLEX package does provide this functionality. It is discussed in more depth throughout this book, especially in Appendix 9B.

nonbenchmarked portfolios, we instead recommended mean-variance optimization (MVO), which maximizes the portfolio's return and minimizes its risk while also allowing the manager to impose certain constraints on the portfolio's characteristics. More often than not, though, managers try to track a benchmark with their portfolios, so we turned our attention to weighting methods that take into account the relationship between the portfolio and the benchmark. Again, we found that ad hoc methods failed to provide anything more than quick-and-easy but incomplete fixes to the weighting problem. The stratification method was an improvement over ad hoc methods because it offered a very rough risk control mechanism by allowing us to divide stocks into groups and select samples from each group. The factor exposure method also controlled for risk, and it let us "tilt" the portfolio's beta toward the factors that we thought were most important. We saw, however, that the best method of weighting stocks in a bench-marked portfolio is tracking-error minimization because it minimizes the portfolio's tracking error, or risk, without compromising returns (or, conversely, it maximizes the portfolio's return without exceeding a certain tracking error). This method of weighting achieves the highest possible return for the least possible relative risk, works even when the portfolio manager does not know the exact makeup of the benchmark, and allows him or her to place constraints on the portfolio. We have completed the portfolio construction process by showing how to design a portfolio that balances the weights of high-quality stocks in the optimal way. Yet even a well-designed portfolio is always a work in progress. As conditions change, the portfolio needs to be rebalanced, and the transactions costs of rebalancing must be considered. The portfolio also should be refined to operate as best as it can within the tax environment. Many managers fail to counteract the draining effect of taxes, yet there are strategies for fortifying a portfolio against the tax drain. We discuss these sorts of improvements in the next two chapters.

APPENDIX 9A

Quadratic Programming

For most of the portfolio optimization problems that a portfolio manager will encounter, a general quadratic optimization routine will enable him or her to construct the portfolio given his or her objectives.[1] Most commercial softwares packages employ some form of the concepts we will describe below. For portfolio managers who build their own risk models and optimizers, the standard packages have versions of the quadratic programming techniques we will discuss below.[2]

The general quadratic programming problem can be expressed as

$$\min_{x} \frac{1}{2}x'Qx + x'c \quad s.t. \quad Ax \le b \tag{9A.1}$$

where x is the vector of unknowns in the problem, Q is a symmetric positive semidefinite matrix supplying the coefficients on the

---

[1] For those who wish to have more insight into the mathematics of optimization, we recommend two books, Luenberger (1989) and Gill et al. (1981).

[2] For instance, RATS (Regression Analysis of Time Series), produced by Estima Corporation, has a procedure known as LQPROG that performs both linear and quadratic optimizations quite easily. MATLAB, produced by MathWorks Inc., has an optimization toolbox that includes the function QUADPROG, which can handle standard quadratic optimization problems. For a more complete suite of optimization tools that can also be used with other software programs, we recommend IBM's CPLEX software. For quadratic optimizations, this software has functions CPLEXQP, CPLEXMIQP, CPLEXQCP, and CPLEXMIQCP that are useful for advanced optimizations. The open-source programming language R has a function SOLVE.QP that can handle standard quadratic optimizations.

quadratic terms of the optimization problem, **c** is a vector of coefficients related to the linear objective function, **A** is a matrix of coefficients for the equality and inequality constraints, and **b** is a vector of constraint values.[3]

The general quadratic optimization problem works for both quadratic and linear optimization problems. For linear optimization problems, one can make **Q** = **0**, and then the problem becomes a linear programming problem. For quadratic optimizations, one uses the appropriate **Q**. In layperson's terms, the preceding quadratic programming problem says the following: Minimize the function $\frac{1}{2}\mathbf{x'Qx} + \mathbf{x'c}$ by choosing the values of **x** that make it minimized. In addition, make sure that the chosen values of **x** satisfy some other *constraints*, some of which might be equality constraints and some of which might be inequality constraints (i.e., *s.t.* **Ax** $\leq$ **b**, where *s.t.* stands for "subject to"). The objective function and the constraints can be almost anything. In the general optimization problem, these are just mathematical concepts. It is only when we apply these tools to actual real-world problems that they make more sense. We will do this in the next section of this appendix.

Let's consider two special cases of the general quadratic optimization program. In one case, we specify only equality constraints. In the other case, we will allow for inequality as well as equality constraints. The reason we separate these into two categories is that with equality constraints, we actually can solve for the optimal weights with a *closed-form solution*.[4]

9A.1 QUADRATIC PROGRAMMING WITH EQUALITY CONSTRAINTS

With only equality constraints, the quadratic optimization can be solved in closed form. The problem becomes

$$\min_{\mathbf{x}} \frac{1}{2}\mathbf{x'Qx} + \mathbf{x'c} \quad s.t. \quad \mathbf{Ax} = \mathbf{b} \tag{9A.2}$$

---

[3] The matrix **Q** in most portfolio problems actually will be positive definite. The symmetry of the matrix is very important. This refers to a matrix for which entry $a_{i,k} = a_{k,i}$ for all i and k. In layperson's terms, the matrix on either side of the diagonal terms looks like a mirror reflection of the other side.

[4] In mathematics, the term *closed-form solution* refers to an expression for a given function or quantity that can be expressed in terms of known and well-understood quantities. These solutions are preferable because, given a set of variables, you can plug them into an equation and know the optimal solution immediately.

If matrix $\mathbf{A}$ is of full rank and matrix $\mathbf{Q}$ is positive definite, then a unique solution exists for $\mathbf{x}$.[5] By a unique solution, we mean that there is one set of values for $\mathbf{x}$ that creates the minimum value of our objective function. Using the Lagrange method, we can find the first-order optimality conditions to solve the minimization problem.[6] The Lagrangian is

$$\mathscr{L} = \frac{1}{2}\mathbf{x}'\mathbf{Q}\mathbf{x} + \mathbf{x}'\mathbf{c} - \lambda(\mathbf{b} - \mathbf{A}\mathbf{x}) \qquad (9A.3)$$

By taking the partial derivatives with respect to $\mathbf{x}$ and λ, we obtain the Lagrange necessary (or first-order) conditions for a solution:

$$\mathbf{Q}\mathbf{x} + \mathbf{A}'\lambda + \mathbf{c} = 0 \qquad (9A.4)$$

$$\mathbf{A}\mathbf{x} - \mathbf{b} = 0 \qquad (9A.5)$$

The solution for the optimal $\mathbf{x}$ can be found by algebraically manipulating these equations. From the first equation, we have

$$\mathbf{x} = -\mathbf{Q}^{-1}\mathbf{A}'\lambda - \mathbf{Q}^{-1}\mathbf{c} \qquad (9A.6)$$

Substitution of this into the second equation will give us

$$\lambda = -(\mathbf{A}\mathbf{Q}^{-1}\mathbf{A}')^{-1}(\mathbf{A}\mathbf{Q}^{-1}\mathbf{c} + \mathbf{b}) \qquad (9A.7)$$

As a final step, we substitute this value of λ back into the original expression for $\mathbf{x}$ so that we have a closed-form solution for $\mathbf{x}$. The value of $\mathbf{x}$ that minimizes the earlier general minimization problem with equality constraints is

---

[5] A symmetric matrix is called *positive definite* if $\mathbf{x}'\mathbf{Q}\mathbf{x} > 0$ for all $\mathbf{x} \neq 0$. A matrix has *full rank* if it has rank equal to the number of rows or columns, whichever is less. If a nonzero $\mathbf{x}$ for which $\mathbf{A}\mathbf{x} = 0$ exists, then $\mathbf{A}$ is not of full rank. It also means that the columns of $\mathbf{A}$ are linearly dependent. That is, at least one row of $\mathbf{A}$ can be expressed as a simple linear transformation of another. This will lead to nonunique solutions. The reader should consult a book on linear algebra for more details, for example, Anton (1991) or Greene (2002).

[6] The Lagrange method is a method of solving these types of constrained optimization problems. It is a clever method of reducing a constrained optimization problem to an unconstrained optimization problem by introducing *Lagrange multipliers*. It is named after Joseph Louis Lagrange, an Italian-born French mathematician and physicist who was a professor at the University of Turin in 1755. He later succeeded Euler as director of mathematics at the Berlin Academy of Science. He made many contributions to mathematics, including probability theory, number theory, the theory of equations, and the foundations of group theory.

$$\mathbf{x} = -\mathbf{Q}^{-1}[\mathbf{I} - \mathbf{A}'(\mathbf{AQ}^{-1}\mathbf{A}')^{-1}\mathbf{AQ}^{-1}]\mathbf{c}$$
$$+ \mathbf{Q}^{-1}\mathbf{A}'(\mathbf{AQ}^{-1}\mathbf{A}')^{-1}\mathbf{b} \qquad (9A.8)$$

where $\mathbf{I}$ is the identity matrix.[7]

9A.1.1 A Numerical Example

Typically, in a portfolio risk-minimization problem, a portfolio manager would like to choose the weights of his or her stocks so as to minimize the variance of the portfolio for a given expected return level. The portfolio manager typically will have an equality constraint that the weights of the portfolio sum to 1. We can translate this easily into the quadratic optimization problem. The risk of a portfolio of stocks with weights $\mathbf{w}$ is given by

$$\mathbf{w}'\Sigma\mathbf{w} \qquad (9A.9)$$

where Σ is the variance-covariance matrix of the stock returns, and $\mathbf{w}$ is the vector of stock weights. We also would like to express the mean return for any given selection of weights. The mean return of the portfolio will be $\mu_p = \mathbf{w}'\mu$, where $\mathbf{w}$ represents the stock weights and μ is a vector of mean returns for each of the stocks. We also would like to constrain the weights of the portfolio to sum to 1. This can be represented as $\mathbf{w}'\iota = 1$, where ι is just a vector of 1s.

We can see how easily this fits into our quadratic optimization framework. Simply replace $\mathbf{Q}$ with Σ, replace $\mathbf{x}$ with $\mathbf{w}$, and let $\mathbf{c} = \mathbf{0}$. We must be careful how we modify the matrix $\mathbf{A}$ and the vector $\mathbf{b}$. In particular, we want

$$\mathbf{A} = \begin{bmatrix} 1 & 1 & \cdots & 1 \\ \mu_1 & \mu_2 & \cdots & \mu_N \end{bmatrix} \qquad (9A.10)$$

$$\mathbf{b} = \begin{bmatrix} 1 \\ \mu_p \end{bmatrix} \qquad (9A.11)$$

Now we can substitute these values into our standard quadratic optimization problem with equality constraints, and the solution is readily available from Eq. (9A.8). Since $\mathbf{c} = \mathbf{0}$, the solution will be

---

[7] The identity matrix is a diagonal matrix in which every diagonal term is equal to 1, and all other elements in the matrix are equal to 0.

$$\mathbf{w} = \Sigma^{-1}\mathbf{A}'(\mathbf{A}\Sigma^{-1}\mathbf{A}')^{-1}\mathbf{b} \qquad (9A.12)$$

Let's create a simple six stock portfolio to illustrate the application in more detail. Suppose we have six stocks with annualized mean returns of $\mu_1 = 14.4$, $\mu_2 = 10.19$, $\mu_3 = 9.87$, $\mu_4 = 7.52$, $\mu_5 = 20.05$, and $\mu_6 = 2.66$.[8] We also assume that we have an estimate of the annualized variance–covariance matrix of these stock returns. In our example, the matrix is:

$$
\Sigma = \begin{bmatrix}
\sigma_{11} & \sigma_{12} & \sigma_{13} & \sigma_{14} & \sigma_{15} & \sigma_{16} \\
\sigma_{21} & \sigma_{22} & \sigma_{23} & \sigma_{24} & \sigma_{25} & \sigma_{26} \\
\sigma_{31} & \sigma_{32} & \sigma_{33} & \sigma_{34} & \sigma_{35} & \sigma_{36} \\
\sigma_{41} & \sigma_{42} & \sigma_{43} & \sigma_{44} & \sigma_{45} & \sigma_{46} \\
\sigma_{51} & \sigma_{52} & \sigma_{53} & \sigma_{54} & \sigma_{55} & \sigma_{56} \\
\sigma_{61} & \sigma_{62} & \sigma_{63} & \sigma_{64} & \sigma_{65} & \sigma_{66}
\end{bmatrix}
$$

$$
= \begin{bmatrix}
452.33 & 249.33 & 189.23 & 70.75 & 481.14 & 106.50 \\
. & 1094.09 & 356.85 & 93.51 & 1216.91 & 135.05 \\
. & . & 617.57 & 161.82 & 1304.29 & 110.74 \\
. & . & . & 372.35 & 462.57 & 107.52 \\
. & . & . & . & 5658.42 & 425.35 \\
. & . & . & . & . & 244.31
\end{bmatrix}
$$

$$(9A.13)$$

where σ_{ii} is the variance of stock i, and σ_{ij} is the covariance of stock i with stock j. We can see that this matrix is symmetric. The variances and covariances are written in percentage terms. Thus, for stock 1, the annualized variance is 452.33, which is equivalent to a variance of 452% per year (or standard deviation of 21.26% per year). Finally, we must construct the matrix $\mathbf{A}$ and vector $\mathbf{b}$; they are given by

---

[8] In practice, these can be expected future returns, historical mean returns, or returns from one's factor models. The mean returns are expressed in percentage terms; thus, 14.4 represents an annual return of 14.4%.

$$\mathbf{A} = \begin{bmatrix} 1 & 1 & 1 & 1 & 1 & 1 \\ 14.40 & 10.19 & 9.87 & 7.52 & 20.05 & 2.66 \end{bmatrix} \quad \text{(9A.14)}$$

$$\mathbf{b} = \begin{bmatrix} 1 \\ 8 \end{bmatrix} \quad \text{(9A.15)}$$

where we have explicitly chosen the value of μ_p that we want to reflect an 8% annualized return. Thus, we can now use our formula to find the optimal weights of the six stocks that will achieve the lowest risk for obtaining an expected mean return of 8% per annum. The solution is

$$\mathbf{w} = \mathbf{\Sigma}^{-1}\mathbf{A}' \left(\mathbf{A}\mathbf{\Sigma}^{-1}\mathbf{A}' \right)^{-1} \mathbf{b}$$

$$= \begin{bmatrix} 0.305 \\ 0.057 \\ 0.204 \\ 0.274 \\ -0.085 \\ 0.245 \end{bmatrix} \quad \text{(9A.16)}$$

Thus, the optimal solution for a portfolio with capital of $1 is to buy $0.305 of stock 1, buy $0.057 of stock 2, buy $0.204 of stock 3, buy $0.274 of stock 4, short sell −$0.085 of stock 5, and buy $0.245 of stock 6.[9] The short position in stock 5 might not be feasible for many portfolio managers for a variety of reasons. Thus, the portfolio manager might like to add inequality constraints—for instance, that the weight of security 2 should be greater than 0.10, or 10%. In addition, the portfolio manager may wish to have the weights of all the securities be greater than 0. In our preceding optimization, we did not apply these restrictions. We will continue with our present example in the following application adding these restrictions.

9A.2 QUADRATIC PROGRAMMING WITH INEQUALITY CONSTRAINTS

The quadratic optimization problem with inequality constraints cannot be solved with a closed-form solution. The solution is

---

[9] One can compute the transpose of the matrices (i.e., $\mathbf{A}'$) and the inverse of the matrices (i.e., $\mathbf{\Sigma}^{-1}$) using a software program or manually.

obtained through numerical solution methods. Numerical solutions have become much more reliable and feasible owing to the increased power of computers and some advances in linear and quadratic programming. The most typical method that is used is the *active-set method* or *projection method*. Other methods are used as well, including the *interior-point method*.[10] Since most portfolio managers and quantitative researchers will have access to robust optimizers, we will not go into detail on the mathematics of each numerical method.[11]

9A.2.1 A Numerical Example

We will continue the previous numerical example, adding some inequality constraints. We will use the active-set method to solve the problem. The three inequality constraints that we will add are that the weights of each individual stock cannot be less than 0, except for stock 2, which will not be allowed to have a weight of less than 0.10. Thus $\mathbf{w} \geq 0$ and $w_2 \geq 0.10$. These inequality constraints can be added easily to our matrix $\mathbf{A}$.[12] In fact, the new optimization problem with the first two rows of $\mathbf{A}$ representing equality constraints and the last seven rows representing inequality constraints is[13]

$$\min_{\mathbf{w}} \frac{1}{2} \mathbf{w}' \Sigma \mathbf{w} \quad s.t. \quad \mathbf{A}\mathbf{x} \leq \mathbf{b} \qquad (9A.24)$$

where

---

[10] The state-of-the-art quadratic programming algorithms with inequality constraints are two kinds of approaches called the *active-set method* and the *interior-point method*. Both kinds of approaches solve a series of subproblems where there are only equality constraints. The two approaches differ only in how they arrange the order of the subproblems to be solved. In the active-set method, we proceed along the boundary of the feasible set defined by the constraints. In the interior-point method, we proceed within the feasible set.

[11] For a book on the details of the different types of numerical optimization procedures, see Nocedal and Wright (1999). Some software optimizers use a combination of techniques, such as RATS' LQPROG, which uses the active-set method with the conjugate gradient method. MATLAB's QUADPROG uses the interior-point algorithm. IBM's CPLEX suite uses a variety of techniques. See also Sharpe (1987) for an interesting algorithm for portfolio optimization improvement.

[12] Many software applications that have optimizers allow the user to specify upper- and lower-bound weights rather than having to include them in a constraint matrix.

[13] Many quadratic programming optimizers allow the user to specify the equality $\mathbf{A}_{eq}$ and inequality matrices $\mathbf{A}_{ineq}$ as two different matrices rather than one ($\mathbf{A}$).

$$\mathbf{A} = \begin{bmatrix} \mathbf{A}_{eq} \\ \mathbf{A}_{ineq} \end{bmatrix} = \begin{bmatrix} 1 & 1 & 1 & 1 & 1 & 1 \\ 14.40 & 10.19 & 9.87 & 7.52 & 20.05 & 2.66 \\ -1 & 0 & 0 & 0 & 0 & 0 \\ 0 & -1 & 0 & 0 & 0 & 0 \\ 0 & 0 & -1 & 0 & 0 & 0 \\ 0 & 0 & 0 & -1 & 0 & 0 \\ 0 & 0 & 0 & 0 & -1 & 0 \\ 0 & 0 & 0 & 0 & 0 & -1 \\ 1 & 0 & 1 & 1 & 1 & 1 \end{bmatrix} \tag{9A.25}$$

$$\mathbf{b} = \begin{bmatrix} 1 \\ 8 \\ 0 \\ 0 \\ 0 \\ 0 \\ 0 \\ 0 \\ 0.90 \end{bmatrix} \tag{9A.26}$$

Notice that to express the constraint that $w_2 \geq 0.10$, we stated that $w_1 + w_3 + w_4 + w_5 + w_6 \leq 0.90$. Sometimes, depending on the types of programs we use, the most obvious constraints need a bit of reengineering. The solution using a standard optimization routine is[14]

$$\mathbf{w} = \begin{bmatrix} 0.256 \\ 0.100 \\ 0.026 \\ 0.287 \\ 0.000 \\ 0.331 \end{bmatrix} \tag{9A.27}$$

---

[14] Using MATLAB, this optimization took 0.0068 second to reach a solution.

Advanced Techniques for Quadratic Optimization

Most portfolio optimization problems are covered by the basic techniques discussed in this chapter. However, there are many situations in which the portfolio optimization requires an expansion of the basic optimization setup. For example, a portfolio manager may wish to add transactions costs (discussed in the appendix to Chapter 10) or create a market-neutral portfolio with leverage constraints (discussed in the appendix to Chapter 13). There are other situations in which a portfolio manager wishes to have a limitation on the number of stocks in the portfolio, or in which the number of stocks in the portfolio is between some minimum and maximum, or, alternatively, in which the weights of any security are either zero or between a minimum and maximum weight. These and many other conceivable preferences in the optimization will require an expanded optimization framework. In other situations the portfolio optimization problem might require quadratic constraints, which are not part of the typical optimization framework. In this appendix we will discuss the basic building blocks for expanding the optimization framework to deal with these advanced optimization situations.

9B.1 PHANTOM WEIGHTS

In the portfolio optimization problems discussed in Chapter 9, we typically had only N unknowns, which were the portfolio weights. In some nonstandard portfolio problems, it is useful to create what we term "phantom weights." The idea of phantom weights is to create additional weights, in addition to the actual weights of the portfolio, for which the optimizer will also find optimal values. These can be used for a variety of purposes. Perhaps the simplest example is to create a set of buy and sell weights. Suppose the optimization problem has N stocks. In addition to the portfolio weights w_1 to w_N, we create an additional $2N$ weights $w_1^+, \ldots, w_N^+$, and $w_1^-, \ldots, w_N^-$. The new optimization is now more complicated because we have $3N$ weights to choose. These phantom weights offer many benefits in a portfolio optimization. Oftentimes, the phantom weights have a specific relationship to the underlying weights, such as $w_i = w_i^+ - w_i^-$.

9B.2 BINARY WEIGHTS

In addition to creating phantom weights for the portfolio optimization, it may also be useful to create binary variables as optimization weights. These binary weights are very similar to the concept of phantom weights. They are additional weights for the optimizer to select, but the weights are constrained to be binary (i.e., have a value of 0 or 1).

One very practical use of the binary variables is to force the phantom weights to be orthogonal. That is, if the actual weights and phantom weights have the following relationship, $w_i = w_i^+ - w_i^-$, we could have a situation where $w_i > 0$ and both $w_i^+ > 0$ and $w_i^- > 0$. This is a wasteful solution because we have a long position and a short position on the same stock. We can use binary variables to prevent this occurring.

Suppose one creates the following binary variables, v_i^+ and v_i^- for each one of the N stocks. One can then add a constraint of the following form:

$$v_i^+ \kappa_l \leq w_i^+ \leq v_i^+ \kappa_h \tag{9B.1}$$

$$v_i^- \gamma_l \leq w_i^- \leq v_i^- \gamma_h \tag{9B.2}$$

If we set $\kappa_l = \gamma_l = 0$ and $\kappa_h = \gamma_h = 1$ so that we allow the weights to fluctuate between 0 and 1, and add the constraint that $v_i^+ + v_i^- \leq 1$, we will force the phantom weights to be orthogonal. That is, for every stock i, if $w_i^+ > 0$, then $w_i^- = 0$ and vice versa.

Of course, this useful portfolio setup is not without costs. The additional phantom and binary weights and associated constraints make the optimization problem more difficult and complicated to solve.

9B.3 QUADRATIC CONSTRAINTS

Conventional quadratic optimizers typically allow for linear equality and inequality constraints. In some instances, it will be useful to specify quadratic constraints, in addition to a quadratic objective function.[1] The portfolio optimization structure is very similar to the standard one; however, the user typically can also specify constraints of the following form: $l'x + x'Q^*x \leq r$.

9B.4 PRACTICAL EXAMPLES

9B.4.1 Market Neutrality with Leverage Constraints

If we add the following constraints that $w_i = w_i^+ - w_i^-$, $\Sigma_{i=1}^N w_i^+$, $\Sigma_{i=1}^N w_i^-$, and that $\mathbf{w}^+ \geq 0$ and $\mathbf{w}^- \geq 0$, the resulting optimization will create a market-neutral portfolio that is dollar neutral (i.e., the sum of weights of the long stocks equals the sum of weights of the shorted stocks) and such that the leverage of the market-neutral portfolio is limited to 2 (i.e., the portfolio is 100% long and 100% short of the assets under management). If the market-neutral manager wanted more excessive leverage, this could easily be changed by the constraints on the sum of the phantom long and short weights (i.e., $\Sigma_{i=1}^N w_i^+ = l_l$, $\Sigma_{i=1}^N w_i^- = l_s$, where l_l is the long exposure and l_s is the short exposure). For example, a 130–30 long–short portfolio could be constructed by making $l_l = 1.3$ and $l_s = 0.3$. More on the exact portfolio setup will be discussed in Appendix 13A.

9B.4.2 Transactions Costs

Fixed Costs

If we want to rebalance a portfolio and we have to select new target weights while acknowledging our current portfolio weights, the use of phantom weights and binary variables will enable us to find an exact solution to the portfolio optimization problem while

---

[1] For example, IBM's CPLEX optimization system has a function called CPLEXQCP for standard optimization with quadratic constraints and CPLEXMIQCP for mixed-integer quadratic optimizations with quadratic constraints.

considering transactions costs. In particular, we can add the follow-ing constraints $w_i^a = w_i^+ - w_i^- + w_i^b$, where w_i^b represents the current weights of the portfolio, and w_i^a represents the after-rebalancing weights of the portfolio. We can set the same relationship on the binary variables such that $\kappa_l = \gamma_l = 0$ and $\kappa_h = \gamma_h = 1$ so that we allow the weights to fluctuate between 0 and 1 and add the con-straint that $v_i^+ + v_i^- \leq 1$, which will force the phantom weights to be orthogonal. Stocks whose weight is reduced vis-à-vis the prior portfolio will have negative net weights, but their phantom weights (w_i^-) will be positive—thus the transactions cost vector can be multi-plied by their value. Similarly, the stocks for which the portfolio increases the weight will be positive (w_i^+), and these can also be mul-tiplied by the transactions cost vector. The optimized final weights of the portfolio will be w_i. Thus, in the case of transactions costs, the phantom weights simply serve as a mechanism to denote the change to the current weights, storing the positive changes in the positive phantom weights and the negative changes in the negative phantom weights. Since both positive and negative phantom weights are positive, our transactions cost vector can remain positive, and the transactions cost rebalance problem is resolved. More on the exact portfolio setup will be discussed in Appendix 10A.

Market Impact Costs

These techniques along with quadratic optimization with qua-dratic constraints can be used to construct portfolios while accounting for market impact costs from a variety of market impact cost models.[2] More on the exact details will be discussed in Appendix 10C.

9B.4.3 Elimination of Small-Weight Stocks

Sometimes a portfolio manager will wish to reduce the number of securities. That is, the portfolio manager might have a desire to construct an optimized portfolio that forces the weights of individual stocks to be above a minimum or below a maximum weight. The traditional portfolio optimization allows this very easily. One simply adds an inequality constraint that the optimal weights are above and below a given weight, which can differ by stock or be the same for all stocks. The problem with the traditional

---

[2] See Chincarini (2017).

method is that there might be many circumstances with no solution to the optimization because it forces all stocks to be within a given range—which may be far from optimal and will not resolve the initial problem of eliminating many stocks with trivial weights. However, the use of binary variables can create the optimization that forces the optimizer to only find weights between the minimum and maximum or forces the weight of that particular stock to zero. This will result in more successful optimizations and will be more in line with the portfolio manager's thought process. For simplicity, we will focus only on the situation where the portfolio manager would like all stock weights to be between a lower bound (κ_l) and an upper bound (κ_h). This constraint can be implemented on just the long portion of the portfolio or the long and short portions of the portfolio. Here we consider only the long portion of the portfolio. Using the inequality relationship of the binary variables and phantom weights, $v_i^+ \kappa_l \leq w_i^+ \leq v_i^+ \kappa_h$ and $v_i^- \gamma_l \leq w_i^- \leq v_i^- \gamma_h$, once we specify our values for κ_l, γ_l, κ_h, and γ_h, we have effectively accomplished our goal. If the portfolio is just a long portfolio, phantom weights are not needed and the one set of binary variables should be constructed with respect to the actual weights, w_i. Since the binary variables are either 0 or 1, the weights of the portfolio will be chosen to be within the minimum and maximum weights or to equal 0.

A Numerical Example

We will continue the numerical example in Appendix 9A. Thus we will seek a portfolio with an average annualized return of 8%, with no short sales allowed, and the weights of the portfolio must sum to 1. We will then add the constraint that a stock can only have a weight greater than 0.03 (i.e., 3%) or less than 0.30 (i.e., 30%) or else it must have a value of 0.

The quadratic programming problem can be expressed as[3]

$$\min_{x} \frac{1}{2} x' \Sigma x \quad s.t. \quad Ax \leq b \tag{9B.3}$$

where

---

[3] The Q matrix containing the variance–covariance matrix must also be expanded to account for the additional x variables by placing zeros throughout the larger matrix. That is, in this case with the N actual weights and N binary variables,

$$Q = \begin{bmatrix} 2\Sigma_{N \times N} & 0_{N \times N} \\ 0_{N \times N} & 0_{N \times N} \end{bmatrix}. \text{ Also, } x = \begin{bmatrix} w & v^+ \end{bmatrix}'.$$

$$\mathbf{A} = \begin{bmatrix} \mathbf{A}_{eq} \\ \mathbf{A}_{ineq} \end{bmatrix} = \begin{bmatrix}
1 & 1 & 1 & 1 & 1 & 1 & 0 & 0 & 0 & 0 & 0 & 0 \\
14.40 & 10.19 & 9.87 & 7.52 & 20.05 & 2.66 & 0 & 0 & 0 & 0 & 0 & 0 \\
1 & 0 & 0 & 0 & 0 & 0 & -0.3 & 0 & 0 & 0 & 0 & 0 \\
0 & 1 & 0 & 0 & 0 & 0 & 0 & -0.3 & 0 & 0 & 0 & 0 \\
0 & 0 & 1 & 0 & 0 & 0 & 0 & 0 & -0.3 & 0 & 0 & 0 \\
0 & 0 & 0 & 1 & 0 & 0 & 0 & 0 & 0 & -0.3 & 0 & 0 \\
0 & 0 & 0 & 0 & 1 & 0 & 0 & 0 & 0 & 0 & -0.3 & 0 \\
0 & 0 & 0 & 0 & 0 & 1 & 0 & 0 & 0 & 0 & 0 & -0.3 \\
-1 & 0 & 0 & 0 & 0 & 0 & 0.03 & 0 & 0 & 0 & 0 & 0 \\
0 & -1 & 0 & 0 & 0 & 0 & 0 & 0.03 & 0 & 0 & 0 & 0 \\
0 & 0 & -1 & 0 & 0 & 0 & 0 & 0 & 0.03 & 0 & 0 & 0 \\
0 & 0 & 0 & -1 & 0 & 0 & 0 & 0 & 0 & 0.03 & 0 & 0 \\
0 & 0 & 0 & 0 & -1 & 0 & 0 & 0 & 0 & 0 & 0.03 & 0 \\
0 & 0 & 0 & 0 & 0 & -1 & 0 & 0 & 0 & 0 & 0 & 0.03
\end{bmatrix} \tag{9B.4}$$

$$\mathbf{b} = \begin{bmatrix} 1 \\ 8 \\ 0 \\ 0 \\ 0 \\ 0 \\ 0 \\ 0 \\ 0 \\ 0 \\ 0 \\ 0 \\ 0 \\ 0 \end{bmatrix} \tag{9B.5}$$

The first two rows of this $\mathbf{A}$ matrix are the equality constraints that the sum of weights equals 1 and that the target mean is 8%. For the binary weights, a 0 is placed in the matrix since binary weights are not relevant for these constraints. The rest of the rows represent inequality constraints to restrict the weights of every stock between 0.03 and 0.30, or a weight of 0. That is, we chose the values of κ_l and κ_h such that $v_i^+ 0.03 \le w_i \le v_i^+ 0.30$. Since v_i^+ is a binary choice variable, if this variable equals 1, then the weight of stock i will be forced to lie in the range of 0.03 and 0.30; however, if it's more optimal to make its weight 0, then $v_i^+ = 0$ and w_i will also be equal to 0.

With many constraints and more stocks, these matrices can become very large. As a result, we will sometimes represent these matrices as a series of matrices. For example, it is convenient to write matrix $\mathbf{A}$ in Eq. (9B.4) as

$$\mathbf{A} = \begin{bmatrix} \mathbf{A}_{eq} \\ \mathbf{A}_{ineq} \end{bmatrix} = \begin{bmatrix} \boldsymbol{\iota}_{1\times6} & \mathbf{0}_{1\times6} \\ \boldsymbol{\mu}_{1\times6} & \mathbf{0}_{1\times6} \\ \mathbf{I}_{6\times6} & -0.3\cdot\mathbf{I}_{6\times6} \\ -1\cdot\mathbf{I}_{6\times6} & 0.03\cdot\mathbf{I}_{6\times6} \end{bmatrix} \tag{9B.6}$$

$$\mathbf{b} = \begin{bmatrix} 1 \\ 8 \\ \mathbf{0}_{6\times1} \\ \mathbf{0}_{6\times1} \end{bmatrix} \tag{9B.7}$$

where $\boldsymbol{\mu}_{1\times6} = [14.40\ \ 10.19\ \ 9.87\ \ 7.52\ \ 20.05\ \ 2.66]$, $\boldsymbol{\iota}_{1\times6}$ is a row of six ones (that is, the first six entries of matrix $\mathbf{A}$'s row 1 are 1s), $\mathbf{0}_{1\times6}$ is a row of 6 entries of 0, $\mathbf{I}_{6\times6}$ is the identity matrix (that is, a 6×6 matrix with 1s on the diagonal and 0s everywhere else), and so on and so forth.

The solution using an optimization routine with continuous and binary variables is[4]

$$\mathbf{w} = \begin{bmatrix} 0.217 \\ 0.045 \\ 0.137 \\ 0.300 \\ 0.000 \\ 0.300 \end{bmatrix} \tag{9B.8}$$

9B.4.4 Restricting the Number of Stocks

Sometimes portfolio managers will wish to restrict the number of stocks in their portfolio. There could be a variety of reasons for this

---

[4] Using the CPLEX function CPLEXMIQP, available through the CPLEX library in MATLAB, this optimization took 0.0141 second to reach a solution. This technique is better than placing limits on the minimum and maximum value of stocks, which is an easier optimization to set up. The reason is that rather than eliminating small, unnecessary stocks (as in this case, stock 5), the optimizer will be forced to keep them at the minimum weight, which will lead to a higher risk for a given return. For the portfolio constructed here, the standard deviation was 13.51% per year, while the other type of optimization had a standard deviation of 14.77% with the following weights: $w_1 = 0.149$, $w_2 = 0.058$, $w_3 = 0.163$, $w_4 = 0.3$, $w_5 = 0.03$, and $w_6 = 0.3$.

preference. For example, if it's a regularly rebalanced quantitative model, it might be beneficial from a logistical point of view to manage the portfolio with fewer stocks. Whatever the reason, the portfolio optimization can be done such that the portfolio managers can limit the number of stocks within a range of n_l and n_h, where n_l is the smallest number of stocks they want in their portfolio and n_h is the largest number of stocks they want in their portfolio. In this particular example, phantom weights are not needed, unless the managers are doing this for a long–short portfolio. However, if the portfolio managers are simply restricting the number of stocks, they need only use the binary variables. For a long-only portfolio, the managers should create one set of N binary variables, v_i^+. For a long–short portfolio, the managers should create two sets of binary variables, v_i^+ and v_i^-, allowing them to specify the range of stocks in both the long and short portfolios, respectively. For both situations, the portfolio managers should add two inequality constraints. The first is that $\Sigma_{i=1}^{N} v_i^+ \leq n_h$ (i.e., that the number of stocks in the long portfolio is less than n_h) and $n_l \leq \Sigma_{i=1}^{N} v_i^+$ (i.e., that the number of stocks in the long portfolio is greater than n_l). In reality, most optimization frameworks will require a transformation of the second inequality into $-\Sigma_{i=1}^{N} v_i^+ \leq -n_l$. Of course, with a long–short portfolio, the portfolio manager would add similar constraints on the short portfolio with the corresponding binary variables.

A Numerical Example

We will continue the previous numerical example. Thus we will seek a portfolio with an average annualized return of 8%, with no short sales allowed, and the weights of the portfolio summing to 1. We will allow the weights to have any value between 0 and 1; however, we will not allow the portfolio to have more than three stocks (even though there are six stocks available to purchase). The quadratic programming problem can be expressed as[5]

$$\min_{x} \frac{1}{2} x' \Sigma x \quad s.t. \quad \mathbf{A}x \leq \mathbf{b} \tag{9B.9}$$

where

---

[5] The **Q** matrix containing the variance–covariance matrix must also be expanded to account for the additional **x** variables by placing zeros throughout the larger matrix. That is, in this case with the N actual weights and N binary variables,

$$\mathbf{Q} = \begin{bmatrix} 2\Sigma_{N \times N} & 0_{N \times N} \\ 0_{N \times N} & 0_{N \times N} \end{bmatrix} \text{ Also, } x = \begin{bmatrix} \mathbf{w} & \mathbf{v}^+ \end{bmatrix}'.$$

$$A = \begin{bmatrix} \mathbf{A}_{eq} \\ \mathbf{A}_{ineq} \end{bmatrix} = \begin{bmatrix} 1 & 1 & 1 & 1 & 1 & 1 & 0 & 0 & 0 & 0 & 0 & 0 \\ 14.40 & 10.19 & 9.87 & 7.52 & 20.05 & 2.66 & 0 & 0 & 0 & 0 & 0 & 0 \\ 1 & 0 & 0 & 0 & 0 & 0 & 0 & 0 & 0 & 0 & 0 & 0 \\ 0 & 1 & 0 & 0 & 0 & 0 & 0 & 0 & 0 & 0 & 0 & 0 \\ 0 & 0 & 1 & 0 & 0 & 0 & 0 & 0 & 0 & 0 & 0 & 0 \\ 0 & 0 & 0 & 0 & 0 & 0 & 0 & 0 & 0 & 0 & 0 & 0 \\ 0 & 0 & 0 & 0 & 0 & 0 & 0 & 0 & 0 & 0 & 0 & 0 \\ 0 & 0 & 0 & 0 & 0 & 0 & 0 & 0 & 0 & 0 & 0 & 0 \\ -1 & 0 & 0 & 0 & 0 & 0 & 0 & 0 & 0 & 0 & 0 & 0 \\ 0 & -1 & 0 & 0 & 0 & 0 & 0 & 0 & 0 & 0 & 0 & 0 \\ 0 & 0 & -1 & 0 & 0 & 0 & 0 & 0 & 0 & 0 & 0 & 0 \\ 0 & 0 & 0 & -1 & 0 & 0 & 0 & 0 & 0 & 0 & 0 & 0 \\ 0 & 0 & 0 & 0 & -1 & 0 & 0 & 0 & 0 & 0 & 0 & 0 \\ 0 & 0 & 0 & 0 & 0 & -1 & 0 & 0 & 0 & 0 & 0 & 0 \\ 0 & 0 & 0 & 0 & 0 & 0 & 1 & 1 & 1 & 1 & 1 & 1 \\ 0 & 0 & 0 & 0 & 0 & 0 & -1 & -1 & -1 & -1 & -1 & -1 \end{bmatrix} \tag{9B.10}$$

$$b = \begin{bmatrix} \mathbf{b}_{eq} \\ \mathbf{b}_{ineq} \end{bmatrix} = \begin{bmatrix} 1 \\ 8 \\ 1 \\ 1 \\ 1 \\ 1 \\ 1 \\ 1 \\ 0 \\ 0 \\ 0 \\ 0 \\ 0 \\ 0 \\ 3 \\ 0 \end{bmatrix} \tag{9B.11}$$

The first two rows of this **A** matrix are the equality constraints that the sum of weights equals 1 and that the target mean is 8%. For the binary weights, a 0 is placed in the matrix since binary weights are not relevant for these constraints. The rest of the rows represent inequality constraints to restrict the weight of every stock to between 0 and 1. The last two rows represent inequality constraints on the binary variables—in particular, that the sum of the binary variables be between 0 and 3. This is equivalent to constraining the number of stocks to be less than or equal to three.

The solution using an optimization routine with continuous and binary variables is[6]

$$\mathbf{w} = \begin{bmatrix} 0.326 \\ 0.000 \\ 0.000 \\ 0.312 \\ 0.000 \\ 0.362 \end{bmatrix} \tag{9B.12}$$

---

[6] Using MATLAB and CPLEX's CPLEXMIQP function, this optimization took 0.0178 seconds to reach a solution. There are weights for only three stocks, as desired by the portfolio manager.

QUESTIONS

9.1. The solution to the mean-variance optimization problem with no constraints can be expressed as

$$\mathbf{w}^* = \frac{Y\Sigma^{-1}\iota - X\Sigma^{-1}\mu}{YZ - X^2} + \frac{Z\Sigma^{-1}\mu - X\Sigma^{-1}\iota}{YZ - X^2}\mu_P$$

where

$$X = \iota'\Sigma^{-1}\mu$$
$$Y = \mu'\Sigma^{-1}\mu$$
$$Z = \iota'\Sigma^{-1}\iota$$

Show that this can be derived from the general solution to the quadratic optimization solution with equality constraints, that is, $\mathbf{x} = -\mathbf{Q}^{-1}[\mathbf{I} - \mathbf{A}'(\mathbf{A}\mathbf{Q}^{-1}\mathbf{A}')^{-1}\mathbf{A}\mathbf{Q}^{-1}]\mathbf{c} + \mathbf{Q}^{-1}\mathbf{A}'(\mathbf{A}\mathbf{Q}^{-1}\mathbf{A}')^{-1}\mathbf{b}$.

9.2. Explain the circumstances under which shorts sales are not feasible.

9.3. Explain why true diversification may be achieved even when the conventional diversification constraints are violated.

9.4. Some computer software packages require every constraint to the minimization to be in inequality form. Rewrite the following constraints in the inequality form: $\mathbf{w}'\mu = \mu_P$, $\mathbf{w}'\iota = 1$

9.5. Consider the following variance-minimization problem:

$$\min_{\mathbf{w}} \mathbf{w}'\Sigma\mathbf{w} \quad s.t. \quad \mathbf{w}'\mu = \mu_P, \mathbf{w}'\iota = 1$$

(a) Show that this problem is equivalent to minimization of the standard deviation.

(b) In general, we may consider the minimization of a function of the variance; that is,

$$\min_{\mathbf{w}} f(\mathbf{w}'\Sigma\mathbf{w}) \quad s.t. \quad \mathbf{w}'\mu = \mu_P, \mathbf{w}'\iota = 1$$

What is the property of function $f(\cdot)$ that makes the preceding minimization equivalent to the variance minimization?

9.6. Consider the variance minimization

$$\min_{\mathbf{w}} \mathbf{w}'\Sigma\mathbf{w} \quad s.t. \quad \mathbf{w}'\mu = \mu_P, \mathbf{w}'\iota = 1$$

and the expected return maximization

$$\max_{\mathbf{w}} \mathbf{w}'\mu \quad s.t. \quad \mathbf{w}'\Sigma\mathbf{w} = \sigma_P^2, \mathbf{w}'\iota = 1$$

(a) If the two problems produce the same solution **w**, what are the portfolio variance and portfolio expected return?

(b) Can we say that the set of solutions to the variance minimization is identical to the set of solutions to the expected-return maximization as we vary the values of μ_p and σ_p^2?

9.7. Consider the following minimization problem:

$$\min_{\mathbf{w}} \mathbf{w}'\Sigma\mathbf{w} \quad s.t. \quad \mathbf{w}'\boldsymbol{\mu} = \mu_p, \mathbf{w}'\iota = 1$$

The Lagrangian function is defined as

$$\mathcal{L} = \mathbf{w}'\Sigma\mathbf{w} + \lambda(\mu_p - \mathbf{w}'\boldsymbol{\mu}) + \lambda'(1 - \mathbf{w}'\iota)$$

The first-order condition of this minimization problem is identical to the first-order condition for minimizing the Lagrangian with respect to **w**, λ, and λ'. What are the roles of λ and λ' in the first-order condition?

9.8. The portfolio optimization may be expressed as

$$\min_{\mathbf{w}} \mathbf{w}'\Sigma\mathbf{w} + \lambda\mathbf{w}'\boldsymbol{\mu} \quad s.t. \quad \mathbf{w}'\iota = 1$$

(a) Show that given μ_p, there exists λ such that the solution $\mathbf{w}^*$ to this problem satisfies $\mathbf{w}^{*'}\boldsymbol{\mu} = \mu_p$.

(b) Explain why λ may be interpreted as a measure of risk tolerance of the portfolio manager.

9.9. The quality of stratified sampling critically depends on the number of strata and the number of observations drawn from each stratum. Suppose that the portfolio manager wants to select 100 stocks out of a universe of 10,000 stocks. One alternative is to make 5 strata and select 20 stocks from each stratum. The second alternative is to make 10 strata and select 10 stocks from each stratum. Under which conditions would the portfolio manager prefer the first alternative to the second?

9.10. What is factor tilting? Explain when factor tilting is desirable and how to accomplish it.

9.11. Show that minimizing tracking error is equivalent to minimizing the mean squared error defined as

$$\text{MSE}(r_P - r_B) = V(r_P - r_B) + [E(r_P - r_B)]^2$$

9.12. Tracking error can be defined alternatively by looking at the downside deviation only. That is, instead of calculating the standard deviation of $r_P - r_B$, we could calculate the standard deviation of $\min(r_P - r_B, 0)$. Would this alternative definition change the optimal portfolio?

9.13. It is easy to combine the standard risk minimization with tracking-error minimization. Write down the minimization problem of the portfolio manager who wants to minimize the sum of the portfolio risk and the tracking error.

9.14. Suppose that we constructed a portfolio through factor exposure targeting. Then the return of this portfolio can be expressed as follows:

$$r_P = \alpha_P + \boldsymbol{\beta}_B' \, \mathbf{f} + \epsilon_P$$

where $\boldsymbol{\beta}_B$ is the factor exposure of the benchmark.

(a) Express the tracking error of this portfolio in terms of $\mathbf{w}_P$, $\mathbf{w}_B$, and $\boldsymbol{\Sigma}_\epsilon$ (the variance-covariance matrix of the stock-return errors).

(b) Is the size of the tracking error bounded?

9.15. Describe the situation in which the ghost benchmark tracking technique may be used.

9.16. This question concerns phantom weights and binary weights.

(a) What are phantom weights?

(b) What are binary weights?

(c) Why are these weights important in advanced portfolio optimizations? In particular, what problems can they help solve?

CHAPTER 10

Rebalancing and Transactions Costs

Changes aren't permanent, but change is.

—Neil Peart

10.1 INTRODUCTION

In April 2020, Invesco reported a rebalancing error with its Invesco Equally-Weighted S&P 500 Fund. Invesco simply forgot to rebalance the fund on April 24, 2020, which cost Invesco a total of $105 million over 5 days.[1] Even when funds rebalance correctly, transactions costs can severely deteriorate their returns. In 2019, the small-cap growth managers who traded most often had annual trading costs of more than 2.5%, while those who traded more cautiously had trading costs below 1%. This difference in costs and ultimately net returns could be the difference between investment success and failure. While the mistake in rebalancing by Invesco and the story of small-cap growth funds magnifies the rebalancing problem considerably, the lesson applies to all funds: managers cannot afford to ignore the intricacies of rebalancing and transactions costs.

Almost all portfolios need to be adjusted during their lifetimes, so incurring periodic transactions costs is inevitable—it is simply a question of how often and how much. The portfolio manager's

---

[1] Due to volatility in the markets caused by the coronavirus, the S&P Dow Jones index committee made a decision to postpone their rebalancing date to April 24, 2020. Invesco simply forgot to rebalance on April 24, 2020, and did so on April 29, 2020. See Riquier (2020).

decision regarding an adjustment to the portfolio is called the *rebalancing decision*. Three types of events potentially could trigger rebalancing decisions: cash inflows, cash outflows, and changes in the underlying parameters of the stock-return model. Cash inflows and outflows require adjustments to the portfolio's positions, and the simplest way to adjust the portfolio in such cases is to buy or sell stocks using the current portfolio weights. (There are better ways to adjust the portfolio in the face of cash flows, but we will come back to that later.) Changes in the underlying parameters do not automatically require adjustments in the portfolio. The portfolio manager needs to decide whether a parameter change is big enough to warrant incurring transactions costs. Suppose that the transaction cost of making some adjustment to the portfolio is 5 basis points (i.e., 0.05% of the total portfolio value).[2] If, by making the adjustment, the portfolio manager can increase the expected return of the portfolio by only 3 basis points, then he or she has not recovered 2 basis points of transactions costs.

When the portfolio manager does decide to rebalance the portfolio, the transactions cost will affect the composition of the optimal portfolio. We ignored transactions costs in previous chapters partly because we wanted to focus on the main ideas of modeling and portfolio construction and partly because transactions costs do not greatly affect the initial creation of the portfolio. However, after the portfolio is in place and changes must be made midstream, transactions costs take on greater significance.

Transactions costs affect the returns on stocks within the portfolio. Take stock A, which has an exceptionally high transaction cost of 1% owing to thin trading but a relatively high expected return of 12%. Also consider stock B, which has a relatively low transaction cost of 10 basis points and an expected return of 10%. Not including transactions costs, the difference in the expected return between stocks A and B is 2%. However, including transactions costs, $100 invested in stock A will return $10.88, whereas $100 invested in stock B will return $9.89.[3] Thus, after transactions

---

[2] It is more common to discuss transactions costs with respect to the amount traded. However, when comparing transactions costs to the expected returns of the portfolio, it is better to convert this amount into a number that can compare the cost as a fraction of the entire portfolio value.

[3] The transactions costs reduce the $100 invested in stock A to $99, which will earn 12%, or $11.88. So stock A will reach a total value of $110.88. Transactions costs for stock B reduce the $100 to $99.9, which will earn 10%, or $9.99. Stock B therefore will reach a total value of $109.89.

costs, the difference in the expected return between the two securities is less than 1%. This certainly has an impact on the composition of the optimal portfolio.

We begin this chapter with a discussion of the rebalancing decision. Then we discuss how the optimal portfolio changes when we consider transactions costs. In the last section of the chapter we explain ways to control transactions costs.

10.2 THE REBALANCING DECISION

The rebalancing decision involves two questions: when to rebalance the portfolio and how to go about it. From an econometric point of view, the answer to the first question is clear. The factor model we used to pick stocks implies a certain rebalancing period. If we estimated the model on monthly returns, then our optimal portfolio is optimal only for one month. If we estimated the model on quarterly returns, then our optimal portfolio is optimal for one quarter. We must rebalance whenever the optimal portfolio expires, which is the model's periodicity. We discuss model periodicity in the first part of this section. The more challenging rebalancing question is how to change α or other parameters in the model in order to update the portfolio. We will discuss that aspect of rebalancing in the second part of this section.

10.2.1 Rebalancing and Model Periodicity

Financial economists have discovered that models of stock returns do not predict daily returns well. Models approximate patterns that emerge from returns over time, whereas daily returns are heavily influenced by specific news and events that a model often does not take into account. In the extreme case of hourly returns, a model's predictive powers will approach zero. Some financial economists have had moderate success in applying their models to weekly returns. On the whole, though, weekly returns are still too influenced by specific events. For this reason, the majority of financial research is conducted on monthly returns. On the flip side, the danger of trying to apply the model to longer periods is that the parameters may change during the period. For example, to estimate the β of annual returns, one would need a sample spanning at least 20 years. It is unlikely that the β of a firm would stay constant for 20 years. The same problem arises for quarterly returns. Monthly returns are an acceptable middle-of-the-road solution to the tradeoff between predictive power and the risk of unstable parameters.

Whether monthly rebalancing is really the best route depends on market conditions. Markets may be very stable for a month so that nothing fundamental changes. Or markets may fluctuate rapidly, forcing more frequent rebalancing. External restrictions on the portfolio manager, such as large cash inflows and outflows, also alter the rebalancing frequency.

Our suggestion is to "update" the estimation of the models at least once a month if the model uses monthly returns. Updating the estimation does not necessarily lead to rebalancing. The portfolio manager simply should make sure that his or her information is up to date, and from there, he or she can decide whether to rebalance.

10.2.2 Change in α and Other Parameters

Changes in the parameters of a stock-return model can trigger rebalancing. Recall from the previous discussion of the factor model that the stock return can be expressed as

$$r_i = \alpha_i + \beta_{i1} f_1 + \cdots + \beta_{iK} f_K + \epsilon_i \qquad (10.1)$$

If we used an economic factor model to predict stock returns, then we should be on the lookout for changes in α and the factor exposures $(\beta_{i1}, \ldots, \beta_{iK})$. If the model is the fundamental factor model, then we should be concerned about α and the factor premiums $(f_1, \ldots, f_K)$.

Parameters can change at any time. Corporate actions and major changes in the business environment all affect the parameters of a model. If firm A merges with firm B, for instance, the α and other parameters of firm A are bound to change. If the government imposes a new restriction on the activity of firm A, its α and other parameters most likely will change. Even a CEO's retirement can affect a stock's parameters. Then there are changes that do not become public knowledge. If the portfolio manager bases α on private information, α could react to new private information.

Quantitative portfolio managers always should think in terms of the model. If a manager reads a piece of negative news about a stock, it warrants a little time considering whether the news lowers the value of α or another parameter.

When the manager suspects that a parameter has changed, it is time to reestimate the model. Updating the values of the parameters updates the expected return and risk of each stock, and it changes the optimal portfolio. After finding the new optimal portfolio, the manager can decide whether to rebalance the portfolio by comparing the benefit of rebalancing to the transactions costs.

10.3 UNDERSTANDING TRANSACTIONS COSTS

By *transactions costs*, we generally mean the commissions that brokerages charge to execute orders. The commissions vary among brokers and also depend on the trades themselves. The same broker may charge different commissions for trading the same stock depending on the number of shares of the trade or the value of the transaction.

There are also two kinds of hidden transactions costs that portfolio managers should be aware of. These are the *bid–ask spread* and the *price impact*. The bid–ask spread equals the difference between the price at which one can buy the stock (the ask price) and the price at which one can sell the stock (the bid price). The bid–ask spread may reflect the operation cost and profit of a market maker or designated market maker. The lower the liquidity of a stock, the bigger is its bid–ask spread.

Figuring out the bid–ask spread can be tricky.[4] The bid–ask spread is not fixed over time, and, at any given moment, we may be able to observe either the bid price or the ask price. If you compare the ask price from one moment to the bid price from another moment, it is unclear whether the difference between these two numbers reflects the change in the equilibrium price or the bid–ask spread.[5]

Price impact is the effect that large orders have on the observed stock price. A large order will move the stock price, causing the portfolio manager to pay more when buying, or earn less when selling, than the price per share quoted before trading. Price impact increases as the transaction size becomes large relative to the market size or daily trading volume of the stock. For a large order, the entire order may not be executed at the quoted price, so the average transaction price for the trade may be quite different from the quoted price before trading. This difference is one measure of the costs of price impact.

---

[4] See Roll (1984), Glosten (1987), and Glosten and Harris (1988).
[5] It is somewhat helpful that NASDAQ Level II and III allow many users to see the national best bid and offer prices for given volumes at any given point in time.

According to one estimate, the average broker commission is about 4 basis points of the transaction value, while the price impact is about 21 basis points. If one includes the price effect of delayed trades, the transaction cost exceeds 0.4% of the transaction value. As mentioned earlier, trading small-cap stocks costs more than trading large-cap stocks. The average commissions for large-cap stocks and small-cap stocks are 2.4 and 5.9 basis points, respectively. The average price impact is about 21 basis points for large cap and 19.9 basis points for small cap. Including the price effect of delayed trades, the total transaction cost is around 44.6 basis points for small-cap stocks.[6]

In general, it is impossible to anticipate the exact cost of the transaction in advance of its execution. This is especially true of the price impact and the bid–ask spread. One can develop a model and make an educated guess, but that is still far from knowing the exact number.[7]

10.4 MODELING TRANSACTIONS COSTS

Given the complicated and unpredictable nature of transactions costs, it is conventional to model them as a fixed proportion of the total value of the transaction. That is, we choose a constant, perhaps 5 or 10 basis points, to approximate the transaction cost per dollar transaction. Let us call this constant c. If the transaction value is $10, then the transaction cost is $10c$.

The total transaction value (TV) is easy to determine. Let V_t denote the dollar value of the current portfolio. Let $\{w_1^b, \ldots, w_N^b\}$ denote the weights of stocks in the current portfolio and $\{w_1^a, \ldots, w_N^a\}$ denote the weights of stocks in the prospective portfolio. (Superscript b refers to "before," and superscript a refers to "after.") That is, w_i^b is the weight of stock i in the current portfolio, and w_i^a is the weight of stock i in the prospective portfolio. Then $V_t w_i^b$ is the current holding of stock i in dollar terms, and $V_t w_i^a$ is the prospective holding of stock i in dollar terms. If $V_t w_i^a$ is greater than $V_t w_i^b$, it suggests buying stock i. If $V_t w_i^a$ is smaller than $V_t w_i^b$, it suggests selling stock i. In both cases, the difference, $V_t w_i^a - V_t w_i^b$, shows how much to buy or sell, in dollar terms. Therefore, the transaction value is simply the sum of this difference across all stocks:

---

[6] The data were obtained from Abel Noser and reflect one-way transactions costs in 2020. See Table 16.12 in Chapter 16.

[7] Many commercial software providers attempt to supply price impact models to help portfolio managers and traders estimate these costs.

$$TV = \sum_{i=1}^{N} \left| V_t w_i^a - V_t w_i^b \right| \tag{10.2}$$

The transaction cost (*TC*) is a constant fraction of the transaction value; thus

$$TC = cV_t \sum_{i=1}^{N} \left| w_i^a - w_i^b \right| \tag{10.3}$$

Eventually, we want to include the transactions cost formula in our optimization problem. For that purpose, it is useful to write down *TC* as a linear function, that is,

$$TC = V_t \sum_{i=1}^{N} c_i \left(w_i^a - w_i^b \right) \tag{10.4}$$

where

$$c_i = \begin{cases} c & \text{if } w_i^a > w_i^b \\ -c & \text{if } w_i^a < w_i^b \end{cases} \tag{10.5}$$

Once formulated in this way, we can express the transaction cost as a vector product of the weight vector and the transactions cost vector. Let us denote the vector of the current weights as $\mathbf{w}^b$ and the vector of the prospective weights as $\mathbf{w}^a$. That is, $\mathbf{w}^b = \{w_1^b, \ldots, w_N^b\}$, and $\mathbf{w}^a = \{w_1^a, \ldots, w_N^a\}$. Also, we define the vector of transactions costs as $\mathbf{c}$. That is, $\mathbf{c} = \{c_1, \ldots, c_N\}$. Then

$$TC = V_t(\mathbf{w}^a - \mathbf{w}^b)'\mathbf{c} \tag{10.6}$$

Note that the exact value of $\mathbf{c}$ depends on the values of $\mathbf{w}^a$ and $\mathbf{w}^b$. Thus $\mathbf{c}$ is not a constant; rather it is a function of $\mathbf{w}^a$ and $\mathbf{w}^b$ in the mathematical sense [see Eq. (10.5)].

We can generalize our discussion of transactions costs and allow for different stocks to have different transactions costs. Considering the bid–ask spread and, especially, the price impact, one may want to model the transactions cost as proportional to the liquidity of each stock. For example, one might calculate the average trading volume of each stock and assume that the trading cost is inversely proportional to the trading volume. Elements of **c** then would have both different signs and different absolute values.[8]

10.5 PORTFOLIO CONSTRUCTION WITH TRANSACTIONS COSTS

No matter what conditions or costs arise, the principle of portfolio selection always remains the same. Given whatever constraints we may face, we always want the portfolio with the best combination of expected return and risk. (In the case of managing against a benchmark, we always want the best combination of expected excess return and tracking error.) Transactions costs introduce a new variable into the process of determining the optimal portfolio (or the optimal tracking portfolio), but they do not alter the selection principle itself.

10.5.1 The Optimal Portfolio with Transactions Costs

We may formulate the problem of optimizing the portfolio in the face of transactions costs as a problem of minimizing risk given a certain expected return. In the context of our discussion of rebalancing, however, we prefer to use an alternative but equivalent formulation. Specifically, we formulate the optimization problem as one of maximizing the risk-adjusted return on the portfolio, where the risk-adjusted return is defined as the expected return in excess of the variance.

We start by recalculating the expected return of the portfolio, taking into account the transactions costs. If the expected return of the portfolio is μ_p and V_t dollars are invested in it, the value of the portfolio at the end of the holding period equals $V_t(1 + \mu_p)$.

---

[8] If the transactions costs are not a constant fraction of transaction value, then c_i defined in this section becomes a nonlinear function of transaction value. If, for example, the portfolio manager gets charged a flat fee for trades, then c_i is inversely proportional to the transaction value. When c_i is nonlinear, the portfolio optimization problem becomes nonlinear as well. Some commercial software packages have nonlinear programming routines to deal with this, but the reliability of these routines varies. Market impact also can alter the relationship between the trade size and transactions costs. There is a recursive effect because the optimal trade size depends on the transactions costs, which, in turn, depend on the trade size. In Appendix 10B, we describe a method for an exact solution to the optimization problem that resolves most of these problems. In Appendix 10C, we describe a technique that allows the portfolio optimization to deal with a variety of market impact cost models.

However, the portfolio manager needs to spend $(V_t\mathbf{w}^a - V_t\mathbf{w}^b)'\mathbf{c}$ in transactions costs, and the ending value of the portfolio must take this into account. That is, we need to subtract $(V_t\mathbf{w}^a - V_t\mathbf{w}^b)'\mathbf{c}$ $(1 + \mu_p)$ from the ending portfolio value. Similarly, we need to subtract the transactions costs from the expected return. That is,

$$\text{Effective expected return} = \mu_p - (\mathbf{w}^a - \mathbf{w}^b)'\mathbf{c} - (\mathbf{w}^a - \mathbf{w}^b)'\mathbf{c}\mu_p \quad (10.7)$$

The effective expected return has three components. The first component is the gross expected return of the portfolio. The second component, to be subtracted from the gross expected return, is the transactions cost expressed as a fraction of the portfolio value.[9] The last component is the time value of the transactions cost. Since the transactions cost is paid up front rather than at the end of the period, the portfolio manager loses twice, once by paying the cost and once again by not being able to invest and create profit. The second and the third components of the expected return reflect these losses.

For realistic values of the transactions cost and the expected return, the time value of the transactions cost is very small. For example, if the transactions cost is about 0.1% of the transaction value and the expected return is 1%, then the time value of transactions cost is only 0.001% of the transaction value. Therefore, in the discussion that follows, we ignore the time-value term.[10]

To obtain the expression for the risk-adjusted return, let us introduce additional notation. Let $\mu = \{\mu_1, \dots, \mu_N\}$ be the vector of the expected stock returns. That is, μ_i is the expected return of stock i. Let Σ be the variance-covariance matrix of stock returns. That is,

$$\Sigma = \begin{bmatrix} \sigma_1^2 & \sigma_{12} & \cdots & \sigma_{1N} \\ \sigma_{21} & \sigma_2^2 & \cdots & \sigma_{2N} \\ \vdots & & & \\ \sigma_{N1} & \sigma_{N2} & \cdots & \sigma_N^2 \end{bmatrix} \quad (10.8)$$

---

[9] Note that there is no adjustment for how long the portfolio is going to be held. We are assuming that the expected return is expressed for the investment horizon. That is, if the portfolio manager plans to rebalance the portfolio six months later, then μ_p represents the return for six months. As long as the expected return is expressed for the investment horizon, there is no need to adjust the transactions cost $\mathbf{c}$. Some portfolio managers "amortize" the transactions cost to reflect the holding period, but a simpler, equivalent way is to restate μ_p.

[10] If we do not ignore the time-value term, then the optimization problem in the next section becomes rather complicated; the effective expected return becomes quadratic, rather than linear, in weights. Fortunately, the time-value term is small in most cases.

where σ_i^2 denotes the variance of the return of stock i, and σ_{ij} denotes the covariance between the return of stock i and the return of stock j. Thus $\mu_p = \mathbf{w}^{a\prime}\boldsymbol{\mu}$ is the expected return of the prospective portfolio, and $\sigma_p^2 = \mathbf{w}^{a\prime}\Sigma\mathbf{w}^a$ is the variance of the prospective portfolio return. Let us define the *risk-aversion parameter* as A. Given A, we define the risk-adjusted return as $\mu_p - A\sigma_p^2$. Thus $A = 2$ means that the portfolio manager would not mind if the variance goes up by 1% as long as the expected return goes up by 2%.

Using the preceding notation and considering the transactions costs, the risk-adjusted return becomes

Effective risk-adjusted return $= \mu_p - (\mathbf{w}^a - \mathbf{w}^b)^\prime \mathbf{c} - A\mathbf{w}^{a\prime}\Sigma\mathbf{w}^a$

$$= \mathbf{w}^{a\prime}(\boldsymbol{\mu} - \mathbf{c}) + \mathbf{w}^{b\prime}\mathbf{c} - A\mathbf{w}^{a\prime}\Sigma\mathbf{w}^a \quad (10.9)$$

The optimal portfolio can be found by maximizing Eq. (10.9) subject to

$$\mathbf{w}^{a\prime}\boldsymbol{\iota} = 1 \quad\quad\quad\quad (10.10)$$

and any other relevant constraints.

While Eq. (10.9) looks like a typical quadratic equation, in fact, it is highly nonlinear. The transactions cost vector $\mathbf{c}$ depends on the weight vector $\mathbf{w}^a$ [see Eq. (10.5)]. Thus this problem cannot be solved by a conventional quadratic optimization technique. In Appendix 10A we present a simple technique that will produce an approximate solution.

10.5.2 The Tracking Portfolio with Transactions Costs

If the portfolio manager is more concerned about tracking error than overall risk, then he or she should maximize the effective tracking-error-adjusted return rather than the effective risk-adjusted return.

Recall that the tracking error (TE) of the portfolio is defined as the standard deviation of the difference between the portfolio return r_p and the benchmark return r_B:

$$TE^2 = V(r_p) - 2C(r_p, r_B) + V(r_B)$$

$$= \mathbf{w}^\prime \Sigma \mathbf{w} - 2\mathbf{w}^\prime \boldsymbol{\gamma} + V(r_B) \quad (10.11)$$

where

$$\boldsymbol{\gamma} \equiv C(\mathbf{r}, r_B) \quad\quad\quad\quad (10.12)$$

As explained in Chapter 9, the last term does not depend on the weight vector, so only the first two terms will be used in the optimization problem.

The *tracking-error-aversion parameter A* measures the manager's aversion to squared tracking error in the portfolio. The effective tracking-error-adjusted return becomes

$$\text{Effective } TE - \text{adjusted return} = \mathbf{w}^{a\prime}(\boldsymbol{\mu} - \mathbf{c}) + \mathbf{w}^{b\prime}\mathbf{c} - A[\mathbf{w}^{a\prime}\Sigma\mathbf{w}^{a} - 2\mathbf{w}^{a\prime}\boldsymbol{\gamma} + V(r_{B})] \tag{10.13}$$

To find the optimal tracking-error portfolio, we maximize the effective tracking-error-adjusted return with certain constraints. For the purpose of solving this optimization problem, we can ignore the terms that do not include $\mathbf{w}^{a}$ or $\mathbf{c}$. Thus we solve

$$\max_{\mathbf{w}^{a}} \mathbf{w}^{a\prime}(\boldsymbol{\mu} - \mathbf{c} + 2A\boldsymbol{\gamma}) + \mathbf{w}^{b\prime}\mathbf{c} - A\mathbf{w}^{a\prime}\Sigma\mathbf{w}^{a} \tag{10.14}$$

subject to the constraint that the sum of weights should be 1 and any other constraints. This problem cannot be solved by a conventional quadratic optimization technique because $\mathbf{c}$ is a function of $\mathbf{w}$. In Appendix 10A we present a simple technique that will produce an approximate solution and in Appendix 10B we present a more complicated optimization framework that produces an exact solution.

10.6 DEALING WITH CASH FLOWS

As we mentioned in the introduction to this chapter, a manager sometimes has to rebalance the portfolio, or at least make additional investments outside the regular rebalancing schedule. Cash inflows and outflows require this sort of extra rebalancing. In this section we discuss some common methods that the portfolio manager can use to reduce transactions costs in the presence of cash flows. The first method involves investing cash temporarily in index futures or exchange-traded funds (ETFs) until there is a better time (such as the next scheduled rebalancing period) to return it to the portfolio. The second method involves purchasing specific, perhaps more liquid, stocks so as to achieve target portfolio weights through fewer transactions.

10.6.1 Reducing Transactions Costs Using Futures and ETFs

For portfolio managers who have daily cash inflows and outflows, adjusting the portfolio at each cash movement is just not practical.[11] For the typical fund, daily flows are small relative to the fund's assets, and new contributions frequently offset fund redemptions. For such a fund, net inflows can be invested temporarily in cash or money market instruments without adversely affecting the portfolio return. Conversely, the fund's cash buffer can handle small redemptions, avoiding the need to liquidate any stocks. However, for funds with large daily net flows, maintaining a large cash reserve will negatively affect the portfolio return, especially in an environment of low interest rates. If outflows are large, the manager cannot rely on the cash buffer to meet redemptions and may be forced to liquidate part of the portfolio. This, of course, can be particularly problematic if there is low liquidity or if spreads are wide in some of the stocks.

In such cases, the manager might be better off adjusting his or her exposure in one of two ways, either by equitizing cash with index futures or by purchasing an ETF that invests in the same sector as the fund or a sector very correlated with the fund. ETFs became a more feasible solution for many funds when the Securities and Exchange Commission (SEC) lifted some restrictions on ETF ownership in mutual fund portfolios. Even with the wide availability of sector-specific ETFs, however, a manager still might prefer to use futures because futures have three distinct advantages over ETFs: futures are more liquid in normal trading hours, they can be traded after hours on GLOBEX, and they have an added tax benefit in that gains are treated as partly long term and partly short term. On the other hand, if the horizon for using futures is longer than a few days, then the portfolio manager might have to deal with the challenges of rolling over futures contracts.

10.6.2 Rebalancing toward Optimal Target Weights

Whether in a period of cash flows or at the point of conducting regular rebalancing, a portfolio manager can make the necessary trades in such a way that the portfolio maintains an optimal mix of stock weights. Imagine a portfolio that is rebalanced monthly and experiences cash flows at the end of the month. When it comes

---

[11] This section is a brief summary of Chincarini (2004).

time for the monthly rebalancing, the manager can either trade so that he or she maintains the original optimal portfolio weights or so that he or she achieves the new optimal weights determined by updating/reestimating the model. At the end of the month, the manager faces cash flows but can trade in such a way as to redirect the portfolio toward either the original or new optimal target weights. In the following subsections we discuss the algorithm that enables the manager to conduct optimal trades first in the case of regular rebalancing and then in the case of cash flows. In the analysis, we do not include trading costs per se. Rather, we show that by reducing the amount of trading, we can reduce tax costs as well as direct trading costs.

Standard Rebalancing

Standard rebalancing assumes that the portfolio manager has a target set of stock weights to which he or she wants to rebalance the portfolio. If the portfolio tracks a benchmark, then the target weights are those of the benchmark. Unless a new optimal portfolio with new stock weights has been constructed since the last rebalancing date, standard rebalancing involves selling the "winners" and buying the "losers" of the period since the last rebalancing date. You may be wondering why anyone would want to buy the losers. The reason is that the portfolio manager is concerned about the weights of stocks within the portfolio, not about their individual returns during a given period. Stocks that have performed relatively well will have gained weight in the portfolio so that they now exceed their targets; stocks that have done less well will have lost weight so that they now fall short of their targets. Rebalancing means restoring the weights back to their target levels.

Some notation may be useful. Let's call w_i^b the weight of stock i in the portfolio before rebalancing, w_i^a the target weight of each stock i, p_i the price per share of stock i, s_i^b the number of shares owned in stock i of the portfolio, and s_i^a the number of shares implicitly held in the optimal portfolio. The weights of the target portfolio and the current portfolio at any time $t + 1$ are given by

$$w_{i,t+1}^b = \frac{p_{i,t+1}s_{i,t+1}^b}{V_{t+1}} \tag{10.15}$$

$$w_{i,t+1}^a = \frac{p_{i,t+1}s_{i,t+1}^a}{V_{t+1}} \tag{10.16}$$

At any point in time, one can calculate the difference between the target weights and the current portfolio weights and use this difference to rebalance the portfolio. The number of shares of each stock that must be bought or sold at time $t + 1$ is given by

$$x_{i,t+1} = s^a_{i,t+1} - s^b_{i,t+1} = \frac{w^a_{i,t+1}}{p_{i,t+1}}\left(V_{t+1} + C_{t+1}\right) - s^b_{i,t+1} \qquad (10.17)$$

where V_{t+1} is the value of the portfolio at time $t + 1$ before rebalancing, and C_{t+1} is any monetary contribution to (or withdrawal from) the portfolio at time $t + 1$. The excess shares $x_{i,t+1}$ are negative if one needs to sell shares of the stock and positive if one needs to buy more of the stock. One should bear in mind that these formulas do not take into account the bid–ask spreads or the price impact, both of which slightly distort the rebalancing procedure and create costs to the portfolio.

An Example

This example of standard rebalancing involves a portfolio of seven stocks (A through G). Table 10.1 considers the portfolio at times t and $t + 1$. At time t, the portfolio is valued at $100,000; by time $t + 1$, it has increased to $107,986.68. At time t, the portfolio contains the optimal target stock weights, but as stock prices change between times t and $t + 1$, the portfolio drifts out of alignment with

TABLE 10.1

Standard Rebalancing

Date		Stock Holdings						
		A	B	C	D	E	F	G
t	Price per share	$137.45	$30.46	$115	$75	$85	$15	$42.09
	Shares owned	200	200	200	200	200	200	200
	Weight (w^a_i)	0.2749	0.0609	0.2300	0.1500	0.1700	0.0300	0.0842
$t + 1$	Price-per-share	$154.88	$32.53	$125.35	$76.50	$89.47	$15.37	$45.83
	Shares owned	200	200	200	200	200	200	200
	Weight before rebalance (w^b_i)	0.2869	0.0602	0.2322	0.1417	0.1657	0.0285	0.0849
	Rebalance shares	191.66	202.23	198.14	211.73	205.19	210.76	198.34
	Shares to buy/sell	−8.34	2.23	−1.86	11.73	5.19	10.76	−1.66
	Rebalance weight (w^{RB}_i)	0.2749	0.0609	0.2300	0.1500	0.1700	0.0300	0.0842
	Dollar value	$29,686	$6,579	$24,837	$16,198	$18,358	$3,240	$9,090

the targets. The table shows the difference between the weights at times t (optimal target weights) and $t + 1$ (misaligned weights). The "Shares to buy/sell" row of the table gives the results of the formulas that we presented earlier for calculating the number of stock shares to sell or buy in order to return to the optimal scenario.

Using Cash Flows to Rebalance without Selling

Often it is less costly to let a portfolio drift toward the optimal target portfolio rather than make trades that try to match it exactly. There are tax costs associated with rebalancing owing to the selling of securities with capital gains. There is also a transactions cost with each purchase or sale of a security. Thus the manager can choose to not sell any securities but only buy more shares of the securities whose weights have fallen below target. While it does not rebalance the portfolio immediately, this method gives the portfolio a push in the right direction. It is easy to give the portfolio a push by using any cash inflows to add, proportionally to the optimal target weights, to all the portfolio's existing positions. A slightly harder push, investing the cash inflows according to an algorithm, will send the portfolio a bit faster toward the optimal weights.

The easiest method is to divide the cash inflows among all the portfolio's securities in amounts proportional to the target weights. Thus, if one has $\$C_{t+1}$ in cash to inject into the portfolio at time $t + 1$, then one will purchase $x_{i,t+1}$ of each security:

$$x_{i,t+1} = \frac{C_{t+1} w^a_{i,t+1}}{p_{i,t+1}} \tag{10.18}$$

The new weights that result from this process will fall in between the weights before adjustment and the optimal target weights. Their proximity to the target weights will depend on how large C_{t+1} is relative to V_{t+1}.

An Example

We return to the example of stocks A through G. Now, instead of doing the standard rebalancing, let us rebalance by distributing the cash flow C across the entire portfolio in proportion to the target weights.

The cash injection $C_{t+1} = \$2,000$. One can see from Table 10.2 that the weights *slowly* converge to the target weights.

TABLE 10.2

Rebalancing by Purchasing at Target Weights

Date				Stock Holdings				
		A	B	C	D	E	F	G
t	Price per share	$137.45	$30.46	$115	$75	$85	$15	$42.09
	Shares owned	200.00	200.00	200	200	200	200	200
	Weight (w_i^a)	0.2749	0.0609	0.2300	0.1500	0.1700	0.0300	0.0842
$t+1$	Price per share	$154.88	$32.53	$125.35	$76.50	$89.47	$15.37	$45.83
	Shares owned	200.00	200.00	200.00	200.00	200.00	200.00	200.00
	Weight before rebalance (w_i^b)	0.2869	0.0602	0.2322	0.1417	0.1657	0.0285	0.0849
	Shares to buy/sell	3.55	3.75	3.67	3.92	3.80	3.90	3.67
	New shares owned	203.55	203.75	203.67	203.92	203.80	203.90	203.67
	Rebalance weight (w_i^{RB})	0.2866	0.0603	0.2321	0.1418	0.1658	0.0285	0.0849
	Dollar value	$31,527	$6,628	$25,530	$15,601	$18,233	$3,134	$9,335

Another method for helping the portfolio gravitate toward the benchmark weights more quickly is to invest the new cash only in stocks that are below their corresponding target weights. All the stocks in the portfolio are divided into two groups, one in which stocks exceed their target weights (i.e., $\tilde{w}^b > w^a$) and another in which stocks fall short of target weights (i.e., $\tilde{w}^b < w^a$). It is important to calculate these weights *after* the cash has entered the portfolio. We thus use the symbol $\tilde{w}^b$ to represent the weights of the portfolio considering the current value of the portfolio and the cash inflow. The weight of each stock with the cash inflow is

$$\tilde{w}_{i,t+1}^b = \frac{s_{i,t+1}^b p_{i,t+1}}{V_{t+1} + C_{t+1}} \tag{10.19}$$

All these portfolio weights should be compared with their corresponding target weights ($w_{i,t+1}^a$). We must figure out how much of the cash should be allocated to each of the stocks that are below target weight. Suppose that for the first n_u stocks ($i = 1, \ldots, n_u$), the weights are below the target weights. Let us call the cash allocated to stock i, $c_{i,t+1}$. We can determine this amount for each stock:

$$c_{i,t+1} = w_{i,t+1}^a (V_{t+1} + C_{t+1}) - s_{i,t+1}^b p_{i,t+1} \tag{10.20}$$

After the $c_{i,t+1}$ have been calculated,[12] we need to calculate the sum of them: $\sum_{i=1}^{n_u} c_{i,t+1}$. We then take the difference between the

---

[12] The formula for $c_{i,t+1}$ as presented is equivalent to $c_{i,t+1} = (V_{t+1} + C_{t+1})(w_{i,t+1}^a - \tilde{w}_{i,t+1}^b)$, where the portfolio weights are computed including the cash injection C_{t+1}.

sum and C_{t+1}. The difference, which represents the amount of slack funds, equals $C_{t+1} - \sum_{i=1}^{n_u} c_{i,t+1}$. This number always will be less than or equal to zero. It will equal zero when there are enough funds (enough cash) to perfectly rebalance the portfolio. It will be less than zero when there are too few funds (too little cash) to restore deficient stocks to their required weights. In that case, the amount of cash distributed to each stock will have to be scaled down proportionally. Whether the amount of slack funds is zero or negative, the number of shares $x_{i,t+1}$ that need to be purchased of each stock is[13]

$$ x_{i,t+1} = \frac{c_{i,t+1}}{p_{i,t+1}} \frac{C_{t+1}}{\sum_{i'=1}^{n_u} c_{i',t+1}} \tag{10.21} $$

The benefit of this type of "buy" system for rebalancing is that it should make the portfolio converge toward the optimal target weights at a faster rate than if we simply invested in the stocks in proportion to the target weights.

A manager might want to know exactly how much cash he or she would need to rebalance the portfolio using this system of purchasing deficient stocks. There are two steps to figuring this out. The first step is to calculate the ratio of the weight of each stock before rebalancing and *before* new money has been added ($w^b_{i,t+1}$) to the target weight ($w^a_{i,t+1}$) of each stock minus one. That is,

$$ \left(\frac{w^b_{i,t+1}}{w^a_{i,t+1}} - 1 \right) \tag{10.22} $$

The second step is to find the maximum of those values and multiply it by the total value of the portfolio V_{t+1} at time $t + 1$. That is,

$$ \max \left[\frac{w^b_{1,t+1}}{w^a_{1,t+1}} - 1, \frac{w^b_{2,t+1}}{w^a_{2,t+1}} - 1, \dots, \frac{w^b_{N,t+1}}{w^a_{N,t+1}} - 1 \right] \cdot V_{t+1} \tag{10.23} $$

One can easily verify that this number is the minimum amount of cash inflow required to perfectly rebalance the portfolio without selling.

---

[13] When slack funds equal zero, $\dfrac{C_{t+1}}{\sum_{i'=1}^{n_u} c_{i',t+1}} = 1$.

An Example

This example considers the same portfolio as the one in the two preceding examples. In this case, however, the rebalancing method attempts to achieve the desired weights more quickly. The seventh row of Table 10.3 shows the weights of the stocks in the portfolio after new cash arrives. These values are the result of Eq. (10.19). The next row provides the number of shares to purchase of each stock in order to rebalance as much as possible according to Eq. (10.21). Finally, for this example, the second-to-last row of the table computes the new weights of the portfolio given the cash injection. One can see how this method pushes the portfolio toward convergence with the target weights much more quickly than the preceding buy-only method.[14] In this example, $4,697.43 would have been needed to perfectly rebalance without selling.

The process of rebalancing without selling should be used whenever there are net cash inflows into the portfolio. A corresponding symmetric algorithm can be used when there are net

TABLE 10.3

Rebalancing by Purchasing Only Deficient Stocks

Date		Stock Holdings						
		A	B	C	D	E	F	G
t	Price per share	$137.45	$30.46	$115	$75	$85	$15	$42.09
	Shares owned	200.00	200.00	200	200	200	200	200
	Weight (w_i^a)	0.2749	0.0609	0.2300	0.1500	0.1700	0.0300	0.0842
$t+1$	Price per share	$154.88	$32.53	$125.35	$76.50	$89.47	$15.37	$45.83
	Shares owned	200.00	200.00	200.00	200.00	200.00	200.00	200.00
	Weight before rebalance (w_i^b)	0.2869	0.0602	0.2322	0.1417	0.1657	0.0285	0.0849
	Weight after cash flow $(\tilde{w}_i^b)$	0.2816	0.0592	0.2279	0.1391	0.1627	0.0280	0.0833
	Shares to buy/sell	0.00	4.36	1.32	11.42	6.56	10.70	1.47
	New shares owned	200.00	204.36	201.32	211.42	206.56	210.70	201.47
	Rebalance weight (w_i^{RB})	0.2816	0.0604	0.2294	0.1471	0.1680	0.0294	0.0840
	Dollar value	$30,977	$6,648	$25,236	$16,174	$18,480	$3,239	$9,234

---

[14] In this particular example, one can compute the savings in transactions costs and taxes from using the algorithm. Although very small in percentage terms, the algorithm results in about half the costs of standard rebalancing.

withdrawals, in which case the rebalancing would involve only selling (and no buying). The selling, too, can be done optimally while reducing transactions costs and tax costs.

10.7 CONCLUSION

Much of portfolio management theory talks about optimizing portfolios without considering transactions costs. Unfortunately, some of the best portfolio management strategies involve trading stocks that are either illiquid or have high trading costs. Thinking about transactions costs ahead of time therefore can save a portfolio a great deal of money.[15] For a quantitative portfolio manager who closely tracks a benchmark, even a small drag on performance owing to transactions costs can cause significant underperformance of the benchmark. Thus we have discussed methods of factoring transactions costs into the optimization techniques for tracking portfolios. These methods help a manager to steer clear of stocks that seem to have high α's before trading but in fact have low or even negative α's once trading costs are considered.

In this chapter we also discussed some rather rudimentary ways to reduce transactions costs when there are frequent cash flows into or out of the portfolio. These methods, though simple to implement, work quite well at reducing the number of transactions involved in rebalancing owing to cash flows. They also allow the manager to spread trades out over time so as to avoid a sudden, immense price impact on the portfolio.

Portfolio managers can save a great deal of money by being aware of explicit transactions costs. They can save yet more by anticipating the "hidden" costs of capital gains and dividend taxes. We cover the critical issue of tax management in the next chapter.

---

[15] In fact, a Yale University professor approached one of the coauthors about launching a fund based on the professor's "phenomenal" portfolio strategy. Once the professor and the coauthor considered transactions costs, however, they realized that it actually underperformed the major indices.

Approximate Solution to the Optimal Portfolio Problem

Problems specified by Eqs. (10.9) and (10.14) are not quadratic in $\mathbf{w}^a$ and are difficult to solve with conventional quadratic optimizers. The mathematics to solve this more complicated problem are described in Appendix 10B. The current appendix presents a simple approximate solution that works very well for most situations.

Nonlinearity in Eqs. (10.9) and (10.14) arises because we do not know, before solving the problem, which stock to sell and which stock to buy. If we knew, the problem would be quadratic as usual. Thus, to avoid nonlinearity, we need to determine which stocks to buy and which stocks to sell before solving the problems in Eqs. (10.9) and (10.14).

We suggest the following shortcut. First, we can solve the problem ignoring the transactions costs. That is, solve

$$\max_{\mathbf{w}^a} \mathbf{w}^a{}'\boldsymbol{\mu} - A\mathbf{w}^a{}'\Sigma\mathbf{w}^a \tag{10A.1}$$

subject to

$$\mathbf{w}^a{}'\iota = 1 \tag{10A.2}$$

and any other relevant constraints. Call the solution to this problem $\mathbf{w}^* = \{w_1^*, \ldots, w_N^*\}$. Then define the transactions cost vector $\mathbf{c} = \{c_1, \ldots, c_N\}$ using these weights:

$$c_i = \begin{cases} c & \text{if } w_i^* > w_i^b \\ -c & \text{if } w_i^* < w_i^b \end{cases} \tag{10A.3}$$

That is, we determine which stocks to buy and which stocks to sell based on the optimization without considering transactions costs. Once we have determined which stocks to buy and which stocks to sell, we can impose this as a constraint to the optimization problem in Eqs. (10.9) and (10.14). In the case of Eq. (10.9), the problem to be solved becomes

$$\max_{\mathbf{w}^a} \mathbf{w}^{a'}\left(\boldsymbol{\mu} - \mathbf{c}\right) - A\mathbf{w}^{a'}\Sigma\mathbf{w}^a \qquad (10A.4)$$

subject to

$$\mathbf{w}^{a'}\iota = 1 \qquad (10A.5)$$

$$\begin{aligned} w_i^a > w_i^b \text{ for } i \text{ such that } w_i^* > w_i^b \\ w_j^a < w_j^b \text{ for } j \text{ such that } w_j^* < w_j^b \end{aligned} \qquad (10A.6)$$

and any other relevant constraints. Now $\mathbf{c}$ is a fixed constraint and does not depend on the value of $\mathbf{w}^a$ (as long as the additional constraints we imposed are satisfied), and we can solve this problem using a conventional quadratic optimizer.

An Exact Solution to the Optimal Portfolio Problem

Although more complicated, there is a way to construct the portfolio optimization problem so as to consider transactions costs without having to use an approximate method. The minimization problem is similar to our standard one, such that,

$$\min_{x} \frac{1}{2} x'Qx + x'c \quad s.t. \quad Ax \leq b \tag{10B.1}$$

$$lb \leq x \leq ub \tag{10B}$$

where x is the vector of unknowns in the problem, Q is a symmetric positive semi-definite matrix, c is a vector of coefficients, A is a matrix of coefficients for the equality and inequality constraints, b is a vector of constraint values, lb is a lower-bound vector, and ub is an upper-bound vector.[1]

As explained in Chapter 9, in the traditional mean-variance optimization problem, we substitute the following variables: $x = w$, the stock weights; $Q = 2\Sigma$, the variance-covariance matrix of stock returns; $c = 0$; A is chosen typically to have a row of ones and a row of expected returns, and the other constraints. In many software packages, the A matrix is split into two matrices, one for equality constraints and one for inequality constraints.

In order to solve for the optimal weights of the portfolio given a current portfolio and transactions costs, we start by expanding

---

[1]As we discussed in Appendix 9A, you can also place these upper- and lower-bound constraints directly in the A matrix.

the **x** vector to include six types of variables. In addition to the prospective weights of the portfolio (w_i^a), we create phantom positive weights, w_i^+, which represent the ($N \times 1$) "long" positions of the portfolio; then we create the phantom negative weights, w_i^-, which represent the "short" positions of the portfolio; w_i^b, which represent the current weights of the portfolio, and the binary weights v_i^+ and v_i^-. That is, the **x** variable will consist of six types of variables in the following way:

$$\mathbf{x} = \begin{bmatrix} \mathbf{w}_{N\times1} \\ \mathbf{w}^+_{N\times1} \\ \mathbf{w}^-_{N\times1} \\ \mathbf{w}^b_{N\times1} \\ \mathbf{v}^+_{N\times1} \\ \mathbf{v}^-_{N\times1} \end{bmatrix} = \begin{bmatrix} w_1 \\ w_2 \\ \vdots \\ w_N \\ w_1^+ \\ w_2^+ \\ \vdots \\ w_N^+ \\ w_1^- \\ w_2^- \\ \vdots \\ w_N^- \\ w_1^b \\ w_2^b \\ \vdots \\ w_N^b \\ v_1^+ \\ v_2^+ \\ \vdots \\ v_N^+ \\ v_1^- \\ v_2^- \\ \vdots \\ v_N^- \end{bmatrix} \tag{10B.3}$$

That is, rather than just N weights for N stocks, we have $6N$ weights that have specific importance in the optimization. Of course, in the end, the variables of the ultimate importance are the first N weights: the optimal stock weights.

Since we now have $6N$ weights, the Q matrix must also be modified to be ($6N \times 6N$) by adding zeros all around the variance-covariance matrix so that,

$$Q = \begin{bmatrix} 2\Sigma_{N\times N} & 0_{N\times N} & 0_{N\times N} & 0_{N\times N} & 0_{N\times N} & 0_{N\times N} \\ 0_{N\times N} & 0_{N\times N} & 0_{N\times N} & 0_{N\times N} & 0_{N\times N} & 0_{N\times N} \\ 0_{N\times N} & 0_{N\times N} & 0_{N\times N} & 0_{N\times N} & 0_{N\times N} & 0_{N\times N} \\ 0_{N\times N} & 0_{N\times N} & 0_{N\times N} & 0_{N\times N} & 0_{N\times N} & 0_{N\times N} \\ 0_{N\times N} & 0_{N\times N} & 0_{N\times N} & 0_{N\times N} & 0_{N\times N} & 0_{N\times N} \\ 0_{N\times N} & 0_{N\times N} & 0_{N\times N} & 0_{N\times N} & 0_{N\times N} & 0_{N\times N} \end{bmatrix}_{(6N)\times(6N)} \qquad (10B.4)$$

We constrain the prospective weights of the optimized portfolio, w_i^a, to be related to these phantom weights and the prior portfolio weights as follows:

$$w_i^a = w_i^+ - w_i^- + w_i^b \qquad (10B.5)$$

This essentially makes the phantom weights equal to the incremental buy or sell for each stock in the portfolio from the prior portfolio weights. We also need to constrain the phantom weights, w_i^+ and w_i^-, to be positive and orthogonal to each other (i.e., only one of them is positive for any given security in the portfolio). This is needed so that we do not unnecessarily buy and sell the same stock. Thus, we introduce the binary variables v_i^+ and v_i^- for each stock in the portfolio. We introduce the following constraints in order to ensure that the phantom weights are orthogonal:

$$v_i^+ \kappa_l \leq w_i^+ \leq v_i^+ \kappa_h \qquad (10B.6)$$

$$v_i^- \gamma_l \leq w_i^- \leq v_i^- \gamma_h \qquad (10B.7)$$

$$v_i^+ + v_i^- \leq 1 \qquad (10B.8)$$

Since v_i^+ and v_i^- are binary variables, the inequality constraint in Eq. (10B.8) forces only one of them to be 1 and the other 0. This combined with the constraints in Eqs. (10B.6) and (10B.7) force the phantom weights to also be orthogonal to each other. For generality, we used the parameters κ_l, γ_l, κ_h, and γ_h, but later in this section we will assign them values of 0 and 1 to simplify this particular optimization.[2] We then create a vector of transactions costs, $\mathbf{c}$, as before. Now that the general setup is in place, we show how to arrange the matrices (equality and inequality constraints) to complete the optimization. We will show the equality matrix constraints and inequality matrix constraints separately, but you can also combine them into one $\mathbf{A}$ matrix if desired. The equality matrix, $\mathbf{A}_{eq}$, should be a $(2N + 2)$ by $(6N)$ matrix, and the corresponding $\mathbf{b}_{eq}$ vector will be $(2N + 2)$ by (1).

$$
\mathbf{A}_{eq} = \begin{bmatrix}
\boldsymbol{\iota}_{1\times N} & \mathbf{0}_{1\times N} & \mathbf{0}_{1\times N} & \mathbf{0}_{1\times N} & \mathbf{0}_{1\times N} & \mathbf{0}_{1\times N} \\
\boldsymbol{\mu}_{1\times N} & -\mathbf{c}_{1\times N} & -\mathbf{c}_{1\times N} & \mathbf{0}_{1\times N} & \mathbf{0}_{1\times N} & \mathbf{0}_{1\times N} \\
\mathbf{I}_{N\times N} & -1\cdot\mathbf{I}_{N\times N} & \mathbf{I}_{N\times N} & -1\cdot\mathbf{I}_{N\times N} & \mathbf{0}_{N\times N} & \mathbf{0}_{N\times N} \\
\mathbf{0}_{N\times N} & \mathbf{0}_{N\times N} & \mathbf{0}_{N\times N} & \mathbf{I}_{N\times N} & \mathbf{0}_{N\times N} & \mathbf{0}_{N\times N}
\end{bmatrix}_{(2N+2)\times(6N)}
\tag{10B.9}
$$

$$
\mathbf{b}_{eq} = \begin{bmatrix}
1 \\
\mu_P \\
\mathbf{0}_{N\times 1} \\
\mathbf{w}^b_{N\times 1}
\end{bmatrix}_{(2N+2)\times(1)}
\tag{10B.10}
$$

The inequality matrix, $\mathbf{A}_{ineq}$, should be a $(5N)$ by $(6N)$ matrix and the corresponding $\mathbf{b}_{ineq}$ vector will be $(5N)$ by (1).

$$
\mathbf{A}_{ineq} = \begin{bmatrix}
\mathbf{0}_{N\times N} & \mathbf{0}_{N\times N} & \mathbf{0}_{N\times N} & \mathbf{0}_{N\times N} & \mathbf{I}_{N\times N} & \mathbf{I}_{N\times N} \\
\mathbf{0}_{N\times N} & \mathbf{I}_{N\times N} & \mathbf{0}_{N\times N} & \mathbf{0}_{N\times N} & -\kappa_h\cdot\mathbf{I}_{N\times N} & \mathbf{0}_{N\times N} \\
\mathbf{0}_{N\times N} & -1\cdot\mathbf{I}_{N\times N} & \mathbf{0}_{N\times N} & \mathbf{0}_{N\times N} & \kappa_l\cdot\mathbf{I}_{N\times N} & \mathbf{0}_{N\times N} \\
\mathbf{0}_{N\times N} & \mathbf{0}_{N\times N} & \mathbf{I}_{N\times N} & \mathbf{0}_{N\times N} & \mathbf{0}_{N\times N} & -\gamma_h\cdot\mathbf{I}_{N\times N} \\
\mathbf{0}_{N\times N} & \mathbf{0}_{N\times N} & -1\cdot\mathbf{I}_{N\times N} & \mathbf{0}_{N\times N} & \mathbf{0}_{N\times N} & \gamma_l\cdot\mathbf{I}_{N\times N}
\end{bmatrix}_{(5N)\times(6N)}
\tag{10B.11}
$$

---

[2] It is essential that the software package allows for quadratic optimization with binary variables and continuous variables and that the user specifies which variables are binary variables. If the software only allows for integers, then upper and lower bounds of 0 and 1 on the integers will achieve similar results. The CPLEX suite has these and can be used as a library with MATLAB. For users who do not have the option to specify binary variables in a quadratic optimization, we provide an algorithm later in this appendix to solve for this problem with a linear programming integer optimizer.

$$
\mathbf{b}_{ineq} = \begin{bmatrix} \iota_{N\times 1} \\ \mathbf{0}_{N\times 1} \\ \mathbf{0}_{N\times 1} \\ \mathbf{0}_{N\times 1} \\ \mathbf{0}_{N\times 1} \end{bmatrix}_{(5N)\times(1)} \tag{10B.12}
$$

where $\mu_{1\times N}$ is the row vector of the mean returns for each of the N stocks; μ_p is the desired after-tax portfolio return; $\iota_{1\times N}$ is a row of six 1s (that is, the first six entries of matrix $\mathbf{A}$'s row 1 are 1s); $\mathbf{0}_{1\times N}$ is a row of N entries of 0; $\mathbf{I}_{N\times N}$ is the identity matrix (that is, an N by N matrix with 1s on the diagonal and 0s everywhere else); and so on and so forth. In order to aid the reader, we indicate the dimension of every matrix as a subscript.

The transactions costs are incorporated into the optimization via the second row of the equality matrix, which constrains the optimization so that $\mu'\mathbf{w} - \mathbf{c}'\mathbf{w}^+ - \mathbf{c}'\mathbf{w}^- = \mu_p$. Since the phantom weights must be positive and orthogonal, this creates the appropriate after-tax average return.

As stated earlier, you can either put upper- and lower-bound constraints in the inequality, or $\mathbf{A}_{ineq}$, matrix or specify them directly as upper- and lower-bound vectors in many optimization packages. In this example, we chose to specify them directly; thus we constrain weights and phantom weights to be between 0 and 1, as well as the prior portfolio and the binary weights.[3] Thus

$$
\mathbf{lb} = [\mathbf{0}_{1\times N} \quad \mathbf{0}_{1\times N} \quad \mathbf{0}_{1\times N} \quad \mathbf{0}_{1\times N} \quad \mathbf{0}_{1\times N} \quad \mathbf{0}_{1\times N}] \tag{10B.13}
$$

$$
\mathbf{ub} = [\iota_{1\times N} \quad \iota_{1\times N} \quad \iota_{1\times N} \quad \iota_{1\times N} \quad \iota_{1\times N} \quad \iota_{1\times N}] \tag{10B.14}
$$

We can solve this problem with a mixed integer quadratic optimization (MIQO).[4] If you do not have access to a MIQO optimizer,

---

[3] Some of these weight boundaries were implicitly already constrained by prior constraints.

[4] For example, IBM's CPLEX optimization system has a MIQO function called CPLEXMIQP. These are also referred to as mixed integer quadratic programs (MIQPs).

but have access to a mixed integer linear programming optimizer, then you can use an algorithm to find the solution.[5]

10B.1 A NUMERICAL EXAMPLE

We will continue the numerical example in Appendix 9A. Thus we will seek to construct a portfolio with an after-tax average return of 8%, with no short sales allowed, and the weights of

---

[5] For example, MATLAB does not have an MIQP but does have an MILP called INTLINPROG. In order to use an MILP in place of an MIQP, certain adjustments to the matrices must be made and an iterative procedure followed, which converges to the MIQP solution [Kelley (1960)]. Rather than describe all the details for this particular optimization, we will discuss the general concepts and the principal changes required to do a similar transactions cost optimization using the iterative MILP to replicate an MIQP. The steps are as follows. Step 1: Introduce a slack variable called z to represent the quadratic term. The idea is that instead of minimizing $\lambda x'Qx$, you minimize λz s.t. $x'Qx - z \leq 0$ and $z \geq 0$. Then as you iteratively solve the MILP approximations, include new linear constraints, each of which approximates the nonlinear constraint locally near the current point. This is repeated until a satisfactory solution emerges. Practically, the inequality matrix A_{ineq} is altered to include a second column representing z (which can be thought of an extra choice parameter, like the $N + 1$ weight in a standard N-asset problem), with a lower bound of 0 and an upper bound of infinity. Also, you should specify that the v_i are integers and place upper and lower bounds on them of 0 and 1. Step 2: Transform the nonlinear quadratic objective function, which minimizes risk and maximizes return with a tradeoff of λ, into a linear optimization problem with non-linear (e.g., quadratic) constraints. That is, convert the optimization problem

$$\min_{x} \lambda x'Qx - x'r \qquad (10B.15)$$

into this one:

$$\min_{x,z} \lambda z - x'r \quad s.t. \quad x'Qx - z \leq 0, \quad z \geq 0 \qquad (10B.16)$$

where r is a vector of variables to maximize. For example, in the case of transactions costs, it would represent the mean returns of the stocks as well as the negative of the transactions costs for the phantom weights (i.e., it would consist of the second row of A_{eq} and that row would be removed from A_{eq}). Since many linear programming softwares are set to minimize $f'x$, the f for this particular optimization would look something like

$$f = \begin{bmatrix} -\mu_{N\times1} \\ \lambda_{1\times1} \\ c_{N\times1} \\ c_{N\times1} \\ 0_{N\times1} \\ 0_{N\times1} \\ 0_{N\times1} \end{bmatrix}_{(6N+1)\times(1)} \qquad (10B.17)$$

the portfolio must sum to 1. To make things simple, we will assume all stocks cost 1% to trade, except stock 1, which costs 20% to trade. That is, if one trades $100 of stock 1, one will incur a cost of $20, while a $100 trade of any other stock will result in a cost of $1. This will be represented by a **c** vector. Of course, this solution would work with any cost vector. We also use the following prior weights of the portfolio: $\mathbf{w}^b = [0.23\ 0.1\ 0.12\ 0.14\ 0.13\ 0.28]$. We will construct an optimization that minimizes variance subject to a target after-tax return of 8% while considering the prior portfolio weights, w_i^b.

Since our focus is on transactions costs and not particular upper and lower limits to the phantom weights, we can set the parameters $\kappa_l = \gamma_l = 0$ and $\kappa_h = \gamma_h = 1$ so that we allow the weights to fluctuate between 0 and 1, but force them to be orthogonal to each other. The constraint matrices will be[6]

Use a Taylor series expansion of the constraint around x_0, ignoring squared terms and higher, such that

$$x'Qx - z = x_0'Qx_0 - z + 2x_0'Q(x - x) - O(|x - x_0|^2) \tag{10B.18}$$

$$\approx -x_0'Qx_0 - z + 2x_0'Qx \tag{10B.19}$$

Then add the following constraint to the constraint matrix for the next iteration:

$$2x_k'Qx - z \le x_k'Qx_k \tag{10B.20}$$

Using this approximation, in every iteration of the MILP problem you add a new constraint to the inequality constraint matrix of the form above. In particular, add a row to A_{ineq} with the values of $2x_k'Q$ based on the prior optimized value of asset weights x_k, a -1 for the z term, and then 0s for the other decision variables in the optimization problem (e.g., phantom weights, binary variables, etc). You would also add a value to the **b** vector equal to $x_k'Qx_k$.

On every iteration, instead of using the actual value of x_k from the most recent optimization, one could also use a linear combination of the previous solution and the new solution. That is, use $\tilde{x}_k = 0.5x_k + 0.5x_{k-1}$ instead of x_k when adding the constraint. Continue the process with the new constraints and using the MILP. On every iteration, compare the value of z to the value of the quadratic at the solution point (i.e., $z - x_k'Qx_k$). If that is within the tolerance level, stop the process and you have the optimal value of your stock weights. For example, you could choose to stop when $z < x_k'Qx_k (1 - \epsilon)$, where $\epsilon = 0.0005$.

[6] The **Q** matrix containing the variance-covariance matrix must also be expanded to account for the additional five variables with 0s on the diagonals. See Eq. (10B.4).

$$\mathbf{A} = \begin{bmatrix} \mathbf{A}_{eq} \\ \mathbf{A}_{ineq} \end{bmatrix} = \begin{bmatrix} \boldsymbol{\iota}_{1\times6} & \mathbf{0}_{1\times6} & \mathbf{0}_{1\times6} & \mathbf{0}_{1\times6} & \mathbf{0}_{1\times6} & \mathbf{0}_{1\times6} \\ \boldsymbol{\mu}_{1\times6} & -\mathbf{c}_{1\times6} & -\mathbf{c}_{1\times6} & \mathbf{0}_{1\times6} & \mathbf{0}_{1\times6} & \mathbf{0}_{1\times6} \\ \mathbf{I}_{6\times6} & -1\cdot\mathbf{I}_{6\times6} & \mathbf{I}_{6\times6} & -1\cdot\mathbf{I}_{6\times6} & \mathbf{0}_{6\times6} & \mathbf{0}_{6\times6} \\ \mathbf{0}_{6\times6} & \mathbf{0}_{6\times6} & \mathbf{0}_{6\times6} & \mathbf{I}_{6\times6} & \mathbf{0}_{6\times6} & \mathbf{0}_{6\times6} \\ \mathbf{0}_{6\times6} & \mathbf{0}_{6\times6} & \mathbf{0}_{6\times6} & \mathbf{0}_{6\times6} & \mathbf{I}_{6\times6} & \mathbf{I}_{6\times6} \\ \mathbf{0}_{6\times6} & \mathbf{I}_{6\times6} & \mathbf{0}_{6\times6} & \mathbf{0}_{6\times6} & -1\cdot\mathbf{I}_{6\times6} & \mathbf{0}_{6\times6} \\ \mathbf{0}_{6\times6} & -1\cdot\mathbf{I}_{6\times6} & \mathbf{0}_{6\times6} & \mathbf{0}_{6\times6} & \mathbf{0}_{6\times6} & \mathbf{0}_{6\times6} \\ \mathbf{0}_{6\times6} & \mathbf{0}_{6\times6} & \mathbf{I}_{6\times6} & \mathbf{0}_{6\times6} & \mathbf{0}_{6\times6} & -1\cdot\mathbf{I}_{6\times6} \\ \mathbf{0}_{6\times6} & \mathbf{0}_{6\times6} & -1\cdot\mathbf{I}_{6\times6} & \mathbf{0}_{6\times6} & \mathbf{0}_{6\times6} & \mathbf{0}_{6\times6} \end{bmatrix}_{44\times36} \quad (10\text{B}.21)$$

$$\mathbf{b} = \begin{bmatrix} \mathbf{b}_{eq} \\ \mathbf{b}_{ineq} \end{bmatrix} = \begin{bmatrix} 1 \\ 8 \\ \mathbf{0}_{6\times1} \\ \mathbf{w}^{b}_{6\times1} \\ \boldsymbol{\iota}_{6\times1} \\ \mathbf{0}_{6\times1} \\ \mathbf{0}_{6\times1} \\ \mathbf{0}_{6\times1} \\ \mathbf{0}_{6\times1} \end{bmatrix}_{1\times44} \quad (10\text{B}.22)$$

where $\boldsymbol{\mu}_{1\times6} = [14.40\ 10.19\ 9.87\ 7.52\ 20.05\ 2.66]$; $\mathbf{c}_{1\times6} = [20\ 1\ 1\ 1\ 1\ 1]$; $\boldsymbol{\iota}_{1\times6}$ is a row of six 1s (that is, the first six entries of matrix $\mathbf{A}$'s row 1 are 1s); $\mathbf{0}_{1\times6}$ is a row of six entries of 0; $\mathbf{I}_{6\times6}$ is the identity matrix (that is, a 6-by-6 matrix with 1s on the diagonal and 0s everywhere else); and so on and so forth. In order to aid the reader, we indicate the dimension of every matrix as a subscript, including for the large $\mathbf{A}$ and $\mathbf{b}$ matrices.

The economic meaning of these constraints is the following: the first two rows of this $\mathbf{A}$ matrix are the equality constraints that the sum of weights equals 1 and that the target after-tax average return is 8%.

The third row through the eighth row of the equality matrix establishes the links between the actual portfolio weights that are chosen, the phantom weights, and the prior portfolio weights. Rows 9 through 14 constrain the prior portfolio weights to equal $\mathbf{w}^{b}$. Rows 15 through 20 constrain the binary variables to be orthogonal; that is, only one of them can be positive, which consequently constrains the phantom weights to be orthogonal (i.e., we don't buy and sell the same security). In order to do this, we employ the constraints from rows 21 to 44. As discussed earlier, we accomplish this by setting $\kappa_l = \gamma_l = 0$ and $\kappa_h = \gamma_h = 1$.

The solution using an optimization routine with continuous and binary variables is:[7]

$$\mathbf{w} = \begin{bmatrix} 0.230 \\ 0.081 \\ 0.120 \\ 0.309 \\ 0.000 \\ 0.260 \end{bmatrix} \tag{10B.23}$$

Notice that the solution does not adjust the weight of stock 1 at all. This is quite understandable given the high transactions cost that we imposed on stock 1. In the absence of transactions costs, the optimal portfolio weights would have been [0.287 0.016 0.065 0.283 0 0.348].

[7] Using the CPLEX function CPLEXMIQP, available through the CPLEX library in MATLAB, this optimization took 0.0170 seconds to reach a solution.

An Approximate Optimal Portfolio with Market Impact Costs

Estimating market impact costs can be very valuable for a portfolio manager. Unfortunately, there is a nonlinear element to the market impact of trades. The larger your portfolio, the larger the market impact of a trade. As a result, standard portfolio optimization techniques cannot be used because, as the optimal weight of each stock changes, so does the cost of trading. In addition to the optimization dilemma, the portfolio manager also needs a good description of how the size of a trade and market impact are related. This market impact data can either be obtained from a professional organization that has made detailed estimates of transactions costs or from a parametric model of transactions costs. For example, you might specify transactions costs from trading as

$$tc_{it} = C_{it} + \left| \frac{100 s_{it}/2}{p_{it}} \right| + |c_{it}| \qquad (10C.1)$$

where C_{it} is the percentage commission cost from the trade, s_{it} is the bid–ask spread of stock i at time t, p_{it} is the price of stock i at time t, and c_{it} is the percentage market impact costs for stock i at time t based on a market impact model. These transactions costs, tc_{it}, are in price percentage points (i.e., a value of 0.20 would indicate that this particular trade would lead to costs of 0.20%).

Market impact models will vary but might take a form similar to this:

$$c_{it} = a + \psi \left(\frac{n_{it}}{V_{it}} \right)^{\phi} \qquad (10C.2)$$

where n_{it} represents the number of shares of security i that need to be traded, V_{it} is the average daily trading volume of the stock (shares traded, not dollars traded), and a, ϕ, and ψ are parameters that need to be estimated.[1]

As mentioned previously, market impact transactions cost models are difficult to use in a standard optimization framework.[2] In this appendix we are going to introduce an approximation technique to allow for portfolio optimizations when the user has a detailed model of market impact costs as described above. The first step is to apply an approximation method to approximate a variety of transactions cost models.[3] The second step is to formulate the optimization problem so as to solve for market impact.

---

[1] One such model is the structural model estimated from U.S. equity data by Almgren, Thum,

$$\text{Haptmann, and Li (2005) } c_{it} = \frac{I}{2} + \text{sgn}(n_{it})\eta\sigma_{it}\left|\frac{n_{it}}{V_{it}T}\right|^{3/5}, \text{ where } I = \gamma\sigma_{it}\frac{n_{it}}{V_{it}}\left(\frac{N_{it}}{V_{it}}\right)^{1/4},$$

$\gamma = 0.314$, $\eta = 0.142$, σ_{it} is the daily volatility of the returns of stock i at the beginning of month t; N_{it} is the total amount of shares outstanding in the security; V_{it} (a.k.a. ADTV) is the average daily trading volume of the stock (shares traded, not dollars traded); T is the time interval in which the trade takes place in number of days (in the example that follows, we use $T = 1$); and n_{it} represents the number of shares of security i that the portfolio is trading. Another model is the market impact model of Northfield. The model is of the form $c_{it} = B_{it}|n_{it}| + C_{it}|n_{it}|^{0.5}$, where B_{it} and C_{it} are parameters estimated by Northfield, n_{it} is the number of shares to be purchased for security i in month t, and c_{it} is expressed in terms of percentage price movement. To give an example of how the first cost model works, let's look at the data from two stocks in December 2013: AT&T (ticker symbol: T), a very liquid stock, and AGL Resources (ticker symbol: GAS), a less liquid stock. AT&T for this particular period had a market capitalization of $183 billion, a stock price of $35.16, and a 10-day average daily trading volume of 18,930,000 shares. The spread was 1 cent, or a 0.0284% spread. The trading cost in percentage terms for a 1% position in a $500 million portfolio was 0.0232%. That is, a $5 million trade of AT&T representing 142,000 shares would cost the trader $1,160. This does not represent commissions; it is simply the market impact and spread costs. AGL Resources for this particular period had a market capitalization of $5.6 billion, a stock price of $47.23, and a 10-day average daily trading volume of 490,000 shares. The spread was 2 cents, or a 0.0423% spread. The trading cost in percentage terms for a 1% position in a $500 million portfolio was 0.1621%. That is, a $5 million trade of AGL Resources representing 105,865 shares would cost the trader $8,105.

[2] Furthermore, in the case of our example, transactions cost model 1 was not usable as of 2018 even in the leading software provider platforms for portfolio optimization, such as Axioma, Northfield, and BARRA.

[3] This technique was proposed by Chincarini (2017).

10C.1 APPROXIMATION OF TRANSACTIONS COSTS

The first step is to approximate the transactions cost model, which is usually based on the number of shares traded of a particular stock, and other parameters. The larger the trade of a stock, the larger the market impact. Thus, in order to make the market impact model usable in a standard optimization framework, we need to start with a given portfolio size, say $100 million. We then vary the weights of each stock from 0% of the portfolio to a maximum allowable percentage based on the portfolio manager's needs. We can choose increments of 1% or smaller and for each weighting we compute the model's estimated market impact costs. Once these values of market impact (or total transactions costs) are calculated, a series of weights for each stock along with the market impact for each particular stock weight will be known for each period (e.g., monthly).[4] For example, for stock i, we might have a series of weights $\mathbf{w}_{it}$ = [0.0 0.01 0.02 0.03 0.04 0.05 0.06 0.07 0.08 0.09 0.10] along with the corresponding market impact costs $\mathbf{c}_{it} = [c_{it}^{0.00} \ldots c_{it}^{0.10}]$. From this we compute the total transactions cost vector for each stock, which is given by Eq. (10C.1), and multiply this by $\mathbf{w}_{it}$, to obtain a vector $\widetilde{\mathbf{tc}}_{it}$, which is the weight of stock i for every weight level multiplied by the actual transactions costs $\mathbf{tc}_{it}$, given a portfolio of value $\$V_t$.

The second step is to estimate for each stock a regression of the following form:

$$\widetilde{\mathbf{tc}}_{it} = a_{it}\mathbf{w}_{it} + b_{it}\mathbf{w}_{it}^2 \tag{10C.3}$$

where $\widetilde{\mathbf{tc}}_{it}$ is a vector of transactions costs from the transactions cost model multiplied by each stock's vector of incremental weights, and a_{it} and b_{it} are parameters estimated from the linear regression.[5]

---

[4] This is done by computing the dollar amount of a trade for a given weight and portfolio size. Thus, for a 1% position with a portfolio size of $100 million, the trade size would be $1 million. Then, dividing by the price of the stock in that period, we obtain the number of shares required to be traded in that stock. This is used in the transactions cost model to obtain the market impact costs in percentage terms. Most transactions cost models require some sort of number of shares to be traded to estimate the transactions costs.

[5] There is a different a_{it} and b_{it} for every net asset level since the transactions costs of each stock vary with assets under management. $\widetilde{\mathbf{tc}}_{it}$ can also be thought of as net transactions cost as it represents the percentage transactions cost of each stock multiplied by the stock's weight, w_{it}, reflecting the net transactions cost impact of each stock at each weight to the entire portfolio.

This approximation model works extremely well for many transactions cost models.[6] As an example, the actual transactions costs and approximate transactions costs for AT&T for December 2013 were 0.000232% and 0.000257% for a $5 million trade (i.e., 1% position of a $500 million portfolio).[7]

This approximation is key to allowing for market impact in the optimizations since we now have a clear link between weight choice and transactions costs impact. In the next section, we show how to use this approximation in a portfolio optimization problem.

10C.2 LONG-ONLY PORTFOLIO

In order to incorporate our approximate transactions costs into the portfolio optimization problem, we must modify the quadratic optimization program slightly. First, we must use a quadratic optimization routine that can accept quadratic constraints, in addition to linear constraints, as discussed in Appendix 9B.3.[8] Second, we must modify the traditional portfolio optimization setup to work with transactions costs.

The mathematical expression of the quadratic optimization with quadratic constraints is given as

$$\min_{x} \frac{1}{2} x'Qx + x'c \quad s.t. \quad Ax \leq b \tag{10C.4}$$

$$l'x + x'Q^*x \leq r \tag{10C.5}$$

$$lb \leq x \leq ub \tag{10C.6}$$

where x is the vector of unknowns in the problem, Q is a symmetric positive semi-definite matrix, c is a vector of coefficients, A is a matrix of coefficients for the equality and inequality constraints, b is a vector of constraint values, l is a column vector, r is a scalar, Q^* is a symmetric matrix, lb is a lower-bound vector, and ub is an upper-bound vector.

The main difference in this optimization problem is the quadratic constraint in Eq. (10C.5). In the traditional mean-variance

---

[6] The Weierstrass approximation theorem states that every continuous function defined on a closed interval $[a, b]$ can be uniformly approximated as closely as desired by a polynomial function. In the case of many common transactions cost models, a quadratic function is sufficient for a very good approximation. The $\bar{R}^2$ for stocks is typically very close to 1.

[7] The regression estimates for this particular stock in this particular month were $\hat{a} = 0.0206$, $\hat{b} = 0.5096$, and $\bar{R}^2 = 0.9999$.

[8] For example, CPLEX's CPLEXQCP.

optimization problem, we substitute the following variables: $x = w$, the stock weights, $Q = 2\Sigma$, the variance-covariance matrix of stock returns, $c = 0, 1 = 0, r = 0, Q^* = 0$, A is chosen typically to have a row of 1s and a row of expected returns, and the lower and upper bounds are set as desired.

In order to create an optimal portfolio that minimizes the risk of the portfolio and achieves a desired after-transactions cost return, which includes market impact costs, we must set up additional matrices. For this general discussion, we will not create all of the other constraints; we will just assume that the A and b matrices have been set up for the particular optimization of the portfolio manager. We will assume that the optimization has only N choice parameters, that is, that $x = [w_1 \ w_2 \ ... \ w_N]$. Thus, $Q = 2\Sigma$. We will need to specify, $1, Q^*$, and r as follows:

$$Q = \begin{bmatrix} \hat{b}_1 & 0 & ... & 0 \\ 0 & \hat{b}_2 & \cdots & 0 \\ \vdots & \vdots & \vdots & \vdots \\ 0 & 0 & 0 & \hat{b}_N \end{bmatrix} \qquad (10C.7)$$

and $1 = -\tilde{\mu}$, $\tilde{\mu} = \mu - \hat{a}$, $c = 0$, and $r = -\mu_p$, where $\tilde{\mu}$ is a vector of the expected returns of each stock minus the constant estimate in the transactions cost regression $(\hat{a}_i)$; μ is the expected return of each stock; μ_p is the desired target of after-transactions cost expected return for the portfolio to match; and $\hat{b}_i$ is the coefficient estimate from the transactions cost regression for stock i.[9]

---

[9] Under certain circumstances, a portfolio manager may wish to create a portfolio that maximizes after-transactions cost returns while achieving a certain target variance. The market impact optimization for a long-only portfolio can be modified to achieve this. In this particular case, we assume that the portfolio manager has chosen his other constraints for A and b and modifies the remaining matrices to achieve his goal as follows:

$$Q = \begin{bmatrix} \hat{b}_1 & 0 & ... & 0 \\ 0 & \hat{b}_2 & \cdots & 0 \\ \vdots & \vdots & \vdots & \vdots \\ 0 & 0 & 0 & \hat{b}_N \end{bmatrix} \qquad (10C.8)$$

$$Q^* = 2\Sigma \qquad (10C.9)$$

where Σ is the variance-covariance matrix of stock returns; $1 = 0$, $c = -\tilde{\mu}$, $\tilde{\mu} = \mu - \hat{a}$, and $r = \sigma_p$, where $\tilde{\mu}$ is a vector of the expected returns of each stock minus the constant estimate in the transactions cost regression; μ is the expected return of each stock; σ_p is the target volatility for the portfolio to match; and $\hat{b}_i$ is the coefficient estimate from the transactions cost regression for stock i.

10C.3 MARKET-NEUTRAL PORTFOLIO

The market-neutral problem is slightly more complicated. We need to create phantom weights and binary weights. Once again, we will assume the user has set up their desired constraints for the regular weights ($\mathbf{w}$), phantom weights (both $\mathbf{w}^+$ and $\mathbf{w}^-$), and the binary weights (both $\mathbf{v}^+$ and $\mathbf{v}^-$). We will also have to increase the size of the $\mathbf{Q}$ matrix to accommodate the other variables as

$$\mathbf{Q} = \begin{bmatrix} 2\mathbf{\Sigma}_{N\times N} & \mathbf{0}_{N\times N} & \mathbf{0}_{N\times N} & \mathbf{0}_{N\times N} & \mathbf{0}_{N\times N} \\ \mathbf{0}_{N\times N} & \mathbf{0}_{N\times N} & \mathbf{0}_{N\times N} & \mathbf{0}_{N\times N} & \mathbf{0}_{N\times N} \\ \mathbf{0}_{N\times N} & \mathbf{0}_{N\times N} & \mathbf{0}_{N\times N} & \mathbf{0}_{N\times N} & \mathbf{0}_{N\times N} \\ \mathbf{0}_{N\times N} & \mathbf{0}_{N\times N} & \mathbf{0}_{N\times N} & \mathbf{0}_{N\times N} & \mathbf{0}_{N\times N} \\ \mathbf{0}_{N\times N} & \mathbf{0}_{N\times N} & \mathbf{0}_{N\times N} & \mathbf{0}_{N\times N} & \mathbf{0}_{N\times N} \end{bmatrix} \qquad (10C.10)$$

where $\mathbf{\Sigma}$ is the variance-covariance matrix of stock returns [e.g., see Eq. (9A.13)]. We also need to specify, $\mathbf{l}$, $\mathbf{Q}^*$, and r as follows:

$$\mathbf{Q}^* = \begin{bmatrix} \mathbf{0}_{N\times N} & \mathbf{0}_{N\times N} & \mathbf{0}_{N\times N} & \mathbf{0}_{N\times N} & \mathbf{0}_{N\times N} \\ \mathbf{0}_{N\times N} & \mathbf{\Sigma}_{2,N\times N} & \mathbf{0}_{N\times N} & \mathbf{0}_{N\times N} & \mathbf{0}_{N\times N} \\ \mathbf{0}_{N\times N} & \mathbf{0}_{N\times N} & \mathbf{\Sigma}_{2,N\times N} & \mathbf{0}_{N\times N} & \mathbf{0}_{N\times N} \\ \mathbf{0}_{N\times N} & \mathbf{0}_{N\times N} & \mathbf{0}_{N\times N} & \mathbf{0}_{N\times N} & \mathbf{0}_{N\times N} \\ \mathbf{0}_{N\times N} & \mathbf{0}_{N\times N} & \mathbf{0}_{N\times N} & \mathbf{0}_{N\times N} & \mathbf{0}_{N\times N} \end{bmatrix} \qquad (10C.11)$$

where

$$\mathbf{\Sigma}_2 = \begin{bmatrix} \hat{b}_1 & 0 & \cdots & 0 \\ 0 & \hat{b}_2 & \cdots & 0 \\ \vdots & \vdots & \vdots & \vdots \\ 0 & 0 & 0 & \hat{b}_N \end{bmatrix} \qquad (10C.12)$$

$$\mathbf{l} = \begin{bmatrix} -1 \cdot \mathbf{\mu}_{N\times 1} \\ \hat{\mathbf{a}}_{N\times 1} \\ \hat{\mathbf{a}}_{N\times 1} \\ \mathbf{0}_{N\times 1} \\ \mathbf{0}_{N\times 1} \end{bmatrix} \qquad (10C.13)$$

where μ is the expected return of each stock; $\hat{\mathbf{a}}_{N\times 1}$ is the coefficient on w_i in the regression for stock i; $\hat{b}_i$ is the coefficient estimate on w_i^2

from the transactions cost regression for stock i; $c = 0$, μ_p is the desired target of after-transactions cost expected return for the portfolio to match; and $r = -\mu_p$.[10]

10C.4 MARKET IMPACT DURING REBALANCING

In the previous two sections we showed how to use the market impact approximation on a long-only and a market-neutral optimization when building the portfolio from scratch. It may also be of use to model market impact when rebalancing a portfolio. The approach is very similar to the concepts discussed in Appendix 10B. As before, we will assume the user has set up their desired constraints for the regular weights ($\mathbf{w}$), phantom weights (both $\mathbf{w}^+$ and $\mathbf{w}^-$), prior or current portfolio weights ($\mathbf{w}^b$), and the binary weights (both $\mathbf{v}^+$ and $\mathbf{v}^-$) as described in Appendix 10B. Thus, we will need to specify, $\mathbf{l}$, $\mathbf{Q}^*$, and $\mathbf{r}$ as before. We will also have to modify $\mathbf{Q}$ (i.e., expand the variance-covariance matrix).

---

[10] Under certain circumstances, a portfolio manager may wish to create a portfolio that maximizes after-transactions cost returns while achieving a certain target variance. The market impact optimization for a market-neutral portfolio can be modified to achieve this. In this particular case we assume that the portfolio manager has chosen his other constraints for $\mathbf{A}$ and $\mathbf{b}$ and modifies the remaining matrices to achieve his goal as follows:

$$\mathbf{Q}^* = \begin{bmatrix} 2\Sigma_{N\times N} & 0_{N\times N} & 0_{N\times N} & 0_{N\times N} & 0_{N\times N} \\ 0_{N\times N} & 0_{N\times N} & 0_{N\times N} & 0_{N\times N} & 0_{N\times N} \\ 0_{N\times N} & 0_{N\times N} & 0_{N\times N} & 0_{N\times N} & 0_{N\times N} \\ 0_{N\times N} & 0_{N\times N} & 0_{N\times N} & 0_{N\times N} & 0_{N\times N} \\ 0_{N\times N} & 0_{N\times N} & 0_{N\times N} & 0_{N\times N} & 0_{N\times N} \end{bmatrix} \qquad (10C.14)$$

$$\mathbf{Q} = \begin{bmatrix} 0_{N\times N} & 0_{N\times N} & 0_{N\times N} & 0_{N\times N} & 0_{N\times N} \\ 0_{N\times N} & \Sigma_{2,N\times N} & 0_{N\times N} & 0_{N\times N} & 0_{N\times N} \\ 0_{N\times N} & 0_{N\times N} & \Sigma_{2,N\times N} & 0_{N\times N} & 0_{N\times N} \\ 0_{N\times N} & 0_{N\times N} & 0_{N\times N} & 0_{N\times N} & 0_{N\times N} \\ 0_{N\times N} & 0_{N\times N} & 0_{N\times N} & 0_{N\times N} & 0_{N\times N} \end{bmatrix} \qquad (10C.15)$$

where Σ is the variance-covariance matrix of stock returns, Σ_2 is defined in Eq. (10C.12), $\mathbf{l} = 0$, $\mathbf{c} = -\tilde{\mu}$, $\tilde{\mu}' = [\mu_{1\times N} \ -1 \cdot \hat{a}_{1\times N} \ -1 \cdot \hat{a}_{1\times N} \ 0_{1\times N} \ 0_{1\times N}]$, and $\mathbf{r} = -\sigma_p$, where $\tilde{\mu}$ is a $(1 \times 5N)$ vector of the expected returns of each stock, the constant estimates in the transactions cost regression, and zeros, μ is the expected return vector, σ_p is the after-transactions cost risk for the portfolio to match, and $\hat{a}_{1\times N}$ is the vector of coefficients on w_i in the regression for stock i. The main adjustment is that we switch the matrices $\mathbf{Q}$ and $\mathbf{Q}^*$.

For the market-neutral portfolio described in Appendix 10C.3, we add a prior set of portfolio weights as discussed in Appendix 10B. Thus, the only modification we need to make to $\mathbf{Q}$, $\mathbf{Q}^*$, and $\mathbf{l}$ is to add a column of six $\mathbf{0}_{N \times N}$ matrices between the third and fourth columns of $\mathbf{Q}$ and $\mathbf{Q}^*$ in Eqs. (10C.14) and (10C.15), and add $\mathbf{0}_{1 \times N}$ between the third and fourth columns of $\mathbf{l}$. We also need to add the constraints that come with prior weights, as described in Appendix 10B. These modifications will account for the new prior portfolio weights, and the optimization setup is complete.

For the long-only portfolio, which needs to be set up as in Appendix 10B, we need to remove the second rows of $\mathbf{A}_{eq}$ and $\mathbf{b}_{eq}$ that target an after-transactions cost return and instead alter $\mathbf{Q}$, $\mathbf{Q}^*$, and $\mathbf{l}$ very similarly to the way we did them for the market-neutral portfolio that accounts for market impact during rebalancing.

These changes will allow for optimizations that consider market impact during rebalancing.

10C.5 A NUMERICAL EXAMPLE

We will continue the previous numerical example in Appendix 10B. Thus, we will seek a portfolio with an after-tax average return of 8%, with no short sales allowed, and the weights of the portfolio must sum to 1. In this case we will construct transactions costs for every stock based on the actual spread costs (i.e., bid–ask spread) and market impact costs based on a transaction model used in portfolio management. Although not shown here, we first acquired the relevant data to compute the market impact cost for all of our six stocks in a given period in our sample. We then computed the spread costs for this same period. We then computed the market impact costs for various weights for each of our stocks assuming a portfolio size of $500 million and estimated the linear regression to obtain the $\hat{a}_{it}$ and $\hat{b}_{it}$ for every stock. The regression estimates for the stocks were $\hat{\mathbf{a}}'_t = [0.027 \ 0.019 \ 0.354 \ 0.119 \ 3.654 \ 2.844]$ and $\hat{\mathbf{b}}'_t = [0.511 \ 0.377 \ 58.531 \ 12.694 \ 5704.284 \ 3742.573]$. Thus, for stock 1, a 10% position in this stock would represent a position value of $50 million ($0.10 \cdot 500$). Suppose this stock was trading at $101.2, that would mean that buying 10% of this stock in the portfolio would require purchasing 494,071 shares of the stock. This stock is a quite liquid stock and trades about 12,410,000 shares per day, on average. Thus, this trade would represent only 4% of the average daily volume. The transaction cost for this stock is 0.07784%.

That is, to trade \$50 million all at once would result in a cost of \$38,917. The approximation of transaction cost equals 0.07818% $\left(\frac{0.027\cdot0.10+0.511\cdot0.10^2}{0.10}\right)$.[11]

Thus, our constraints are given as

$$\Sigma_2 = \begin{bmatrix} 0.511 & 0 & 0 & 0 & 0 & 0 \\ 0 & 0.377 & 0 & 0 & 0 & 0 \\ 0 & 0 & 58.531 & 0 & 0 & 0 \\ 0 & 0 & 0 & 12.694 & 0 & 0 \\ 0 & 0 & 0 & 0 & 5704.284 & 0 \\ 0 & 0 & 0 & 0 & 0 & 3742.573 \end{bmatrix} \qquad (10C.16)$$

$$\mathbf{l} = \begin{bmatrix} -1\cdot\mu_{N\times1} \\ 0.027 \\ 0.019 \\ 0.354 \\ 0.119 \\ 3.654 \\ 2.844 \\ \hat{\mathbf{a}}_{N\times1} \\ \mathbf{0}_{N\times1} \\ \mathbf{0}_{N\times1} \\ \mathbf{0}_{N\times1} \end{bmatrix} \qquad (10C.17)$$

The solution to this optimization is

$$\mathbf{w} = \begin{bmatrix} 0.298 \\ 0.000 \\ 0.000 \\ 0.339 \\ 0.078 \\ 0.285 \end{bmatrix} \qquad (10C.18)$$

---

[11] We must divide by 0.10 since the formula is for $\widetilde{tc}_i = tc_i \cdot w_i$.

In order to understand these results, remember that based on our estimations, stocks 1 and 2 are the most liquid (lowest transactions costs), stocks 3 and 4 are the next most liquid, and stocks 5 and 6 are relatively illiquid. Compared to the prior portfolio weights for stock 5 and 6 of 13% and 28%, the optimization barely altered the weight of stock 6 and sold only 5.2% of stock 5 as opposed to an optimization that ignored market impact costs—costs that are increasingly larger for less liquid stocks. We did the same optimization without considering market impact costs, and the optimal solution was $\mathbf{w}' = [0.293 \ 0.017 \ 0.067 \ 0.287 \ 0.000 \ 0.336]$.

QUESTIONS

10.1. Describe the events that might trigger a rebalancing of a portfolio.

10.2. "If the portfolio manager needs to sell a fraction of the portfolio to meet the cash outflow demand and if there is no change in any parameters of the model, then the portfolio manager does not have any reason to change the portfolio weights." Is this statement correct?

10.3. Consider a portfolio consisting of 100 stocks with weights given by $w_1, \ldots, w_{100}$.

   (a) If the one-hundredth stock drops out of the portfolio and if the portfolio manager intends to keep the relative weights unchanged for the remaining 99 stocks, what would be the new weights of the remaining stocks?

   (b) If the portfolio manager needs to add one more stock to the portfolio and makes its weight to be w_{101}, what would be the new weights of the original 100 stocks?

10.4. Suppose that we estimated an economic factor model using monthly data.

   (a) From the estimates of the model, it is possible to predict the annual stock returns by multiplying the predicted return by 12. What is the implicit assumption that allows us to make this inference?

   (b) Explain why it is preferable that the model periodicity be identical to the rebalancing frequency.

10.5. Consider an economic factor model

$$r_{it} = \alpha_i + \beta_i f_t + \epsilon_{it}$$

Using the observations from $t = 1$ to $t = T$, we obtained $\hat{\alpha}_i^{(T)}$ and $\hat{\beta}_i^{(T)}$. Using one more observation, i.e., from $t = 1$ to $t = T + 1$, we obtained $\hat{\alpha}_i^{(T+1)}$ and $\hat{\beta}_i^{(T+1)}$. We would like to test whether the parameters changed.

   (a) Can we say that $\hat{\beta}_i^{(T)}$ and $\hat{\beta}_i^{(T+1)}$ are independent?

   (b) What is the covariance between $\hat{\beta}_i^{(T)}$ and $\hat{\beta}_i^{(T+1)}$?

   (c) Find the formula for the t-statistic when the null hypothesis is that β did not change.

10.6. Evaluate the dividend reinvestment plan offered by certain companies in the context of transactions costs.

10.7. What is the bid–ask spread? Why is it difficult to observe the bid–ask spread in reality?

10.8. On the New York Stock Exchange, designated market makers (DMMs) offer their own bid and ask quotes. Explain whether DMMs would increase or decrease their bid–ask spreads in each of the following situations:
(a) Transaction volume is decreasing.
(b) More and more limit orders arrive.
(c) The company is about to announce earnings.

10.9. Explain the various components of transactions costs, including implicit costs as well as explicit costs.

10.10. Explain why transactions costs may be higher for small stocks than for large stocks.

10.11. One simple way to control transactions costs is to determine what percentage of the *average daily trading volume* (ADTV) is acceptable as a weight for any stock in the portfolio. Let's denote the vector of allowable ranges for all stocks as $\mathbf{w}_{ADVT}$. Write down a problem for finding an optimal portfolio considering these critical weights.

10.12. To set up an optimal portfolio problem considering transactions costs, we need to adjust the expected return of stocks and calculate the transactions-cost-adjusted expected return. Suppose that a $1 transaction creates 5 cents in transactions costs.
(a) If stock A's monthly expected return is 1%, what would be the monthly transactions-cost-adjusted expected return?
(b) If stock A's annual expected return is 15%, what would be the annual transactions-cost-adjusted expected return?
(c) Explain why we would subtract the same percentage from the expected return to account for the transactions costs regardless of whether the return is monthly or annual.

10.13. Let w_i^b denote the weight of stock i in the existing portfolio and w_i^a denote the weight of stock i in the new portfolio to be created. Let c_i denote the transactions cost of stock i.
(a) If μ_i is the expected return of stock i, what is the transactions-cost-adjusted expected return of stock i?
(b) What is the marginal effect of w_i^a on the transactions-cost-adjusted expected return? Explain why this marginal effect can be positive.

10.14. If you hold a stock whose transactions cost is high, it is likely that your *future* transactions costs will be high because you will have to sell the stock eventually. This fact implies that accounting for the *current* transactions costs only is not enough. How should the optimal portfolio problem be modified to account for the future transactions costs?

10.15. Explain the advantage of futures and ETFs in controlling transactions costs.

CHAPTER 11

Tax Management

*It is the mark of an educated man to be able to entertain
a thought without accepting it.*

—Aristotle

11.1 INTRODUCTION

A study by James Garland on taxable investing concluded that
"Those who stand to lose the least—to taxes and fees—stand to win
the most when the game's all over."[1] In the game of investing, the
winners are the ones who know not only how to earn a lot but also
how to hold onto what they earn. Many investment managers have
forgotten to apply this seemingly obvious lesson. From 1996 to
2020, the typical mutual fund lost approximately 24% of its gross
return to the government in taxes.[2] The typical fund manager
undoubtedly put plenty of effort into managing his or her fund,
but he or she got to keep only a little over half of what he or she
earned for his or her efforts.

By devising a solid tax management strategy, the typical manager could have kept more earnings in the portfolio and out of Uncle

---

[1] See Garland (1997).

[2] We used the same methodology as the original Garland study, but we changed the
parameters to reflect the 2020 values of the average expense ratio (1.16%), average
turnover rate (67%), and highest value for long-term capital gains (20%) and for
qualified dividends (20%).

TABLE 11.1

Overview of Tax Management Techniques

Category	Name of Technique	Description
Passive	Dividend management	How to create the portfolio to have the right dividend yield desired by the investor
	Tax-lot management	Which tax lots to sell given that a withdrawal of cash is necessary and a specific stock is chosen
	Capital gain/loss management	Which stocks to sell when it is necessary for a cash withdrawal
Active	Loss harvesting	How to rebalance the portfolio when the amount to be withdrawn is zero

Sam's reach. Taxes are by no means a constant in the investment world. A manager's investment decisions can alleviate or exacerbate the tax burden on the portfolio, with dramatic consequences for the investment return. The manager can take advantage of two types of tax management techniques, passive and active. *Passive* techniques focus on minimizing the tax burden when the portfolio manager must generate cash outflows. Three major passive techniques exist: dividend-income management, tax-lot management, and capital gain and loss management. *Active* techniques aim to create extra tax advantages whether the portfolio manager needs to generate cash outflows or not. Table 11.1 provides an overview of tax management techniques.

We start this chapter by describing the principles underlying all tax management techniques. It is necessary to study these principles carefully to understand tax management tools properly. After studying the principles of tax management, we discuss each of the tax management techniques listed in Table 11.1. The techniques are most relevant to U.S.-taxable investors, but investors in international equities and investors not subject to U.S. tax laws still will find the discussion useful because the same basic tax structure exists in many countries, and the principles of tax management apply everywhere.[3]

---

[3] Since we wrote the first edition of *QEPM*, many robo-advisor companies have been created that employ the techniques we discuss in this chapter. These portfolio techniques are not relevant for nontaxable accounts, such as IRAs and 401(k) accounts.

11.2 DIVIDENDS, CAPITAL GAINS, AND CAPITAL LOSSES

To understand the principles of tax management, let us briefly review how investment income is taxed by the Internal Revenue Service (IRS). As far as taxes are concerned, there are three important types of investment income: dividends, long-term capital gains/losses, and short-term capital gains/losses. Capital gains and capital losses are treated asymmetrically, so there are effectively five types of investment income.

Individual taxpayers used to pay taxes on dividends at the ordinary personal income tax rate.[4] This meant that the government essentially double taxed dividends—once through the corporate income tax on the company distributing the dividends and again through the personal income taxes of the people receiving them. Congress tried to rectify the double-taxation problem in 2003.[5] Under the new rule, the majority of dividends that individuals receive (called *qualified dividends*) are taxed at rates lower than their ordinary income tax rates. In 2020, dividend tax rates ranged from 0% to 23.8% depending on the recipient's income level. The new rule reduces the double-taxation effect, but it does not eliminate it completely. Financial economists have warned that corporations still have a tax incentive to retain earnings rather than pay dividends, so investors should watch out for further changes in the dividend tax structure.

Unlike individuals, corporations that receive dividends can deduct some of them from taxable income.[6] For the 2020 tax year, corporations generally could deduct up to 50%, and, in some cases,

---

[4] The tax rates for individuals for capital gains and dividends have changed substantially over time. Overall, the concepts of tax management still remain valid. For a portfolio manager, however, with a diverse array of clients, the decision of which techniques to use for tax management may vary.

[5] Jobs and Growth Tax Relief Reconciliation Act of 2003 and the Tax Cuts and Jobs Act of 2017. The new rules lowered the tax on qualified dividends and also lowered the corporate and individual income tax rates.

[6] Hedge funds that manage equities usually design their legal structure in such a way as to allow for pass-through taxation. That is, the fund itself does not pay taxes; the income, gains, and losses all "pass through" to the investors, who take them directly on their own tax bills. Mutual funds that manage equities are required by the Investment Company Act of 1940 to distribute 98% of their gains and dividends to avoid being taxed as well. Thus investors in the mutual fund ultimately bear the burden of the taxes. In the case of both institutions, tax-managed techniques could greatly improve the welfare of their investors.

up to 65%, of dividends received.[7] The remainder of the dividend is taxed at the corporate income tax rate. Given the average corporate income tax rate of 26% (including state and federal taxes), the effective tax rate on dividends to most corporations is about 13%. The reason for allowing a dividend deduction is to avoid triple taxation of corporate income. Dividend-paying corporations pay corporate income tax, and individuals who receive dividends pay personal income tax. If dividend-receiving corporations—which redistribute the dividends they receive to their own shareholders—had to pay full taxes, then the dividend income would be taxed three times!

An important thing to remember about dividend taxation is that the same taxes are levied whether dividends are reinvested or not. This is one rather unfair element of the dividend tax system. Dividend recipients who immediately reinvest in the same stock end up paying taxes for nothing. If the corporation had not payed the dividend and had instead kept it as retained earnings, the stock would have grown as much, and because no dividend tax would have been owed, investors' after-tax returns would have been higher.

As far as taxes are concerned, individual investors do not gain from dividends. Those who reinvest the dividends pay taxes for nothing. Those who keep the dividends could have generated the same amount of cash without owing dividend taxes simply by selling part of their holdings in the stock. Since any investor can create this sort of "synthetic dividend" when he or she wants cash, he or she really has no need for a dividend payment from the corporation.

When an individual investor sells shares in a stock, he or she avoids dividend taxes but does potentially incur capital gains taxes. Capital gains taxes apply to profit realized from the sale of a stock.[8] Capital gains on paper, or "paper profit," incur no taxes. For example, if an investor bought 100 shares of XYZ stock at $10 per share and still holds the stock at the current price of $20, then the investor has an unrealized capital gain of $1,000 [$= 100 \cdot (\$20 - \$10)$]. This gain is not taxed until the investor sells the stock.

The tax system distinguishes between capital gains that are long term (holdings over a year) and short term (holdings under a year). Short-term capital gains are taxed at the ordinary personal income tax rate. Long-term capital gains receive preferential

---

[7] In order for a corporation to receive the 65% deduction, the corporation must own between 20% and 80% of the distributing corporation.

[8] Capital gain taxes are also due when a short position is closed out and capital gains are realized.

treatment. For the 2020 tax year, the maximum tax rate applicable to long-term capital gains was 20%. For low-income individuals, the rate was 0%. Thus, for individuals who paid 37% in personal income tax, the short-term capital gains tax was almost twice the long-term capital gains tax. Why does the government give preferential treatment to long-term gains? It may be an attempt to discourage "speculative investing" by rewarding investors who leave their money in one place for a while.

Capital losses also affect taxes. Like capital gains, they are classified as long term or short term. If an individual taxpayer has a long-term capital loss, it is deducted first from long-term capital gains and then from any short-term capital gains. If the individual's capital loss is short term, it is deducted first from short-term capital gains and then from any long-term capital gains. All capital losses, whether long term or short term, that remain after these deductions are deducted from other types of income.

Corporations' capital losses are treated similarly except that they cannot be deducted from other types of income even if they exceed capital gains. If capital losses exceed capital gains, then the difference is deducted from past capital gains and then from future capital gains. In all cases, capital losses can be carried into the future to offset future capital gains.

11.3 PRINCIPLES OF TAX MANAGEMENT

An investor who knows all the different places that taxes could hit him or her can figure out ways to lessen the impact of the blows. There are four principles of tax management to keep in mind when devising such strategies:

1. Individual taxpayers should avoid dividend income, but corporations can handle it more easily.
2. It is better to realize a long-term capital gain than a short-term capital gain.
3. It is better to realize a capital loss than a long-term capital gain.
4. All investors should delay the realization of a capital gain and expedite the realization of a capital loss.

The first principle draws on what we know about dividend taxes on individual investors versus corporations. Dividend taxes are especially burdensome to individuals who do not plan to withdraw cash from their portfolios, but even individuals who want the cash could generate it on their own and avoid the taxes. Individual investors therefore should avoid dividend payments. Corporations, on the other hand, should prefer them to capital gains (as long as they need cash). Corporations pay lower taxes on dividends than on capital gains, so dividends provide a relatively cheap stream of cash.

The second principle simply reflects the fact that the long-term capital gains tax rate is lower than the short-term capital gains tax rate. The third principle is based on the fact that no matter whether they are short term or long term, capital gains increase taxable income, whereas capital losses reduce it.

The fourth principle relies on the concept of the time value of money, which is that a dollar today is worth more than a dollar tomorrow. As long as the interest rate is positive, you can invest a dollar today and end up with a dollar plus interest tomorrow. By expediting the realization of a capital loss, you are decreasing your taxes and giving yourself extra dollars to invest today. By delaying the realization of a capital gain, you are postponing your taxes and giving yourself an extra day to invest your dollars.

How much money could an investor save by following the principles of tax management? Table 11.2 shows the potential savings. Realizing a long-term capital gain of $1 rather than a

TABLE 11.2

Savings from the Principles of Tax Management

Investment Income	Taxes	Savings
Short-term capital gain of $1	37 cents	
Long-term capital gain of $1	20 cents	17 cents
Long-term capital gain of $1	20 cents	
Long-term capital loss of $1	−20 cents	40 cents
Long-term capital gain of $1 now	20 cents	
Long-term capital gain of $1 a year from now	18.52 cents	1.48 cents
Long-term capital loss of $1 a year from now	−18.52 cents	
Long-term capital loss of $1 now	−20 cents	1.48 cents

Note: We assumed a personal income taxpayer whose ordinary income is taxed at the rate of 37% and long-term capital gain is taxed at the rate of 20%. We also assumed that the average investment return is approximately 10%. Most of the calculations are straightforward. For the final four rows, recognize that the gains on the accrued earnings also will be taxed, which results in the difference. Taxes on the long-term capital gain of $1 a year from now is the present value of the taxes imposed on the investor if the investor delayed paying taxes on the $1 current capital gain by one year.

short-term gain of $1 saves 17 cents (for an investor in the 37% income tax/20% long-term capital gains tax bracket). Replacing the long-term capital gain of $1 with a long-term capital loss of $1 saves 40 cents.[9] Delaying a $1 long-term capital gain for one year postpones the payment of 20 cents in taxes for one year. At an average investment return of 10%, this equals 2 cents in savings. However, the extra 2 cents also will be taxed at the long-term capital gains rate, thus leaving the investor with only 1.6 of his or her 2 cents. However, this savings is measured in tomorrow's terms. Thus we need to discount this savings to the present day using the after-tax return of 8%. This leaves us with 1.48 cents. Thus, the total savings is really 1.48 cents. Similarly, realizing $1 of capital loss today rather than next year saves about 1.48 cents.[10]

11.4 DIVIDEND MANAGEMENT

The first principle of tax management states that individual investors taxed at personal income tax rates should buy lowdividend stocks. Corporations, on the other hand, should prefer high-dividend stocks rather than stocks with high capital appreciation and low dividends. Creating a portfolio with the right level of dividend yield is called *dividend management* or, sometimes, *yield management*.

As we explained earlier, personal-taxable investors do not benefit at all from dividends. If they need to withdraw cash from a portfolio, they can create synthetic dividends for themselves by selling a part of the portfolio. If they do not need to withdraw cash from the portfolio, then dividends only create an unnecessary tax burden.

Avoiding dividend-paying stocks completely is one approach that a portfolio manager may adopt. To do so, the portfolio manager simply needs to add the "no-dividend constraint" to the optimization problem. Given the dividend rates of stocks $\mathbf{d} = (d_1, \ldots, d_N)$ and the weights of stocks in the portfolio $\mathbf{w} = (w_1, \ldots, w_N)$, the dividend rate of the portfolio is the weighted average of the

---

[9] Of course, it is not easy to replace a long-term capital gain of $1 with a long-term capital loss of $1. This calculation is for the purpose of illustration.

[10] Another way to think about this is that delaying a $1 long-term capital gain for one year generates a capital gain of $1.1 one year later at the (pretax) investment return of 10%. Thus, the tax payment due is 22 cents ($1.1 \cdot 0.2$), and the after-tax income is 88 cents ($1.1 \cdot 0.8$). We can then discount the 88 cents by the after-tax return of 8% to obtain the present value of 81.48 cents. Compare this to the no-delay after-tax income of 80 cents. Thus the total savings is 1.48 cents. Similarly, realizing $1 of capital loss today rather than next year saves about 1.48 cents.

dividend rate of stocks $\Sigma_{i=1}^{N} w_i d_i$ or, in vector notation, $\mathbf{w'd}$. Then the no-dividend constraint can be written as

$$\mathbf{w'd} = 0 \qquad (11.1)$$

Let μ be the vector of the expected stock returns, Σ the variance-covariance matrix of the stock returns, and A the risk aversion parameter. Then, to find an optimal portfolio, we solve

$$\max_{\mathbf{w}} \mathbf{w'}\mu - A\mathbf{w'}\Sigma\mathbf{w} \qquad (11.2)$$

subject to the constraint that the weights should sum to 1, that is,

$$\mathbf{w'}\iota = 1 \qquad (11.3)$$

and the no-dividend constraint in Eq. (11.1) and other constraints.

While finding an optimal portfolio of non-dividend-paying stocks is feasible, it is not the best we can do. We might end up missing stocks that would lead to the true optimal portfolio. For instance, there may be dividend-yielding stocks that the quantitative model predicts will have very high α's. A better approach than excluding dividend-paying stocks is to assign them some penalty. Given the annual dividend rate d_i of stock i, investing \$1 in stock i will generate an annual dividend of d_i. If the dividend tax rate is τ_d, then the tax burden becomes $\tau_d d_i$. If the weight of stock i in the portfolio is w_i, then the portfolio return will be reduced by $\tau_d w_i d_i$. Considering all the stocks, the portfolio return will be reduced by $\Sigma_{i=1}^{N} \tau_d w_i d_i$ or, in vector notation, $\tau_d \mathbf{w'd}$. This reduction in the expected return is the appropriate penalty for including dividend-paying stocks.[11] Thus we may subtract this amount from the risk-adjusted return of the optimization problem in Eq. (11.2):

Effective risk-adjusted return $= \mathbf{w'}\mu - A\mathbf{w'}\Sigma\mathbf{w} - \tau_d \mathbf{w'd}$

$$= \mathbf{w'}(\mu - \tau_d \mathbf{d}) - A\mathbf{w'}\Sigma\mathbf{w} \qquad (11.4)$$

The new optimization problem is to maximize the effective risk-adjusted return in Eq. (11.4) subject to Eq. (11.3).

---

[11] It is easy to adjust the penalty for dividend-paying stocks if one plans to withdraw cash. If the dividend amount exceeds the amount of cash one plans to withdraw, then the penalty is the tax on the excess dividend. If the dividend does not exceed the withdrawal amount, it may not increase the tax burden at all. Nonetheless, if the existence of dividend income makes the other tax management techniques hard to implement, it still might be best to avoid dividend-paying stocks.

Now let us consider corporations, or corporate-taxable investors. Corporate-taxable investors would prefer dividends as long as the dividend income does not exceed the amount of the required cash needs.[12] If no cash withdrawal is required, dividends are actually as bad for corporate-taxable investors as they are for personal-taxable investors. Thus it makes sense to match the dividend-income schedule to the corporation's cash-withdrawal schedule. Suppose that the dividend rate of d_p would create just enough dividends to cover the cash-outflow requirement. Given the dividend rates of stocks $\mathbf{d} = (d_1, \ldots, d_N)$ and the weights of stocks in the portfolio $\mathbf{w} = (w_1, \ldots, w_N)$, the dividend rate of the portfolio is a weighted average of the dividend rate of the stocks $\sum_{i=1}^{N} w_i d_i$ or, in vector notation, $\mathbf{w}'\mathbf{d}$. To achieve the desired dividend rate, we may add the following "target dividend constraint" to the optimization problem in Eq. (11.2):

$$\mathbf{w}'\mathbf{d} = d_p \qquad (11.5)$$

That is, the new optimization problem is to solve Eq. (11.2) subject to Eqs. (11.3) and (11.5).

Depending on the target dividend rate, the preceding problem may not have a solution. If the target dividend rate is too high and the investment universe does not include enough high-yield stocks, then the problem will not have a solution. And even if the problem has a solution, the resulting portfolio may not be truly optimal; we could have created a better portfolio with a different dividend rate. We therefore generalize the target dividend constraint into a penalty for deviating from the target.

If the dividend income is less than the cash-withdrawal requirement, then a part of the portfolio should be sold to generate cash. If the required cash-withdrawal rate is d_p and the portfolio dividend rate is $\mathbf{w}'\mathbf{d}$, then $(d_p - \mathbf{w}'\mathbf{d})$ dollars should be sold for each current dollar. Although we cannot determine the exact tax consequences of this sale, we can make an approximation. If the long-term capital gains tax rate of τ_l applies, then the tax burden will be $\tau_l(d_p - \mathbf{w}'\mathbf{d})$ dollars for each dollar invested now. Given that dividend income is taxed at the rate of τ_d, the deviation from the target dividend rate increases taxes by $(\tau_l - \tau_d)(d_p - \mathbf{w}'\mathbf{d})$ dollars for each

---

[12] Even for a corporation, it is still better to generate cash by selling loser stocks, but in many cases this is less feasible due to ulterior reasons.

dollar invested. This is in fact the reduction in the expected return and can be considered the proper penalty for the deviation from the target dividend. Thus we may subtract this amount from the risk-adjusted return of the optimization problem in Eq. (11.2):

$$\text{Effective risk-adjusted return} = \mathbf{w}'\boldsymbol{\mu} - A\mathbf{w}'\Sigma\mathbf{w} - (\tau_l - \tau_d)$$
$$(d_p - \mathbf{w}'\mathbf{d}) \tag{11.6}$$
$$= \mathbf{w}'[\boldsymbol{\mu} + (\tau_l - \tau_d)\mathbf{d}] - A\mathbf{w}'\Sigma\mathbf{w}$$
$$- (\tau_l - \tau_d)d_p$$

This effective risk-adjusted return is valid only if the dividend rate is less than or equal to the cash-withdrawal rate. Too many dividends are as bad for corporate-taxable investors as they are for personal-taxable investors. Thus we may add the restriction that the portfolio dividend rate $\mathbf{w}'\mathbf{d}$ is less than or equal to the cash-withdrawal rate d_p, that is,

$$\mathbf{w}'\mathbf{d} \le d_p \tag{11.7}$$

The new optimization problem is to maximize the effective risk-adjusted return in Eq. (11.6) subject to Eqs. (11.3) and (11.7).

11.5 TAX-LOT MANAGEMENT

The second and third principles of tax management imply that investors should realize all capital losses before any capital gains, and then they should realize all long-term capital gains before any short-term ones. The method for prioritizing the realization of losses and gains is called *tax-lot management* (or *tax-lot accounting*). For the discussion of tax-lot management, we assume that the portfolio manager already has determined the stocks and quantity of shares to sell from the optimization.

Let's walk through a simple example to understand the mechanics of tax-lot management. Suppose that you purchased 30 shares of XYZ stock on six different occasions, as shown in Table 11.3, and that you want to sell 10 shares of this stock today. Assume that today's date is March 1, 2020, and that the stock currently trades at $20. Does it matter which shares out of the 30 shares you sell? From the IRS's point of view, it does. Different shares came at different purchase prices on different dates. If you sell shares that you bought on June 5, 2018, then you will realize capital gains and incur long-term capital gains taxes. If you sell shares that were

TABLE 11.3

Tax Lots of Stock *XYZ*

Date of Purchase	Number of Shares	Purchase Price	Gain/ Loss	Long Term/ Short Term	Tax Burden
Jan 10, 2018	5	$22	−$2	Long	−$0.40
Jun 5, 2018	5	$18	$2	Long	$0.40
Feb 12, 2019	5	$24	−$4	Long	−$0.80
Mar 16, 2019	5	$23	−$3	Short	−$1.11
Dec 19, 2019	5	$19	$1	Short	$0.37
Jan 24, 2020	5	$21	−$1	Short	−$0.37

Note: The current price is assumed to be $20 and the current date March 1, 2020. For the purpose of calculating the tax burden, we used a 20% long-term capital gains tax rate and a 37% short-term capital gains tax rate.

bought on January 10, 2018, then you will realize long-term capital losses and reduce your taxable income. On other shares, you may realize a short-term capital gain or a short-term capital loss. A different tax bill accompanies each type of gain or loss.

For purposes of calculating the tax bill, each purchase history is called a *tax lot*. You have six tax lots to choose from when you want to sell the 10 shares of *XYZ* stock. There are two rules for minimizing the tax burden[13]:

1. Sell the shares of the tax lot with the maximum loss first. Continue to sell the tax lots in descending order of tax loss until all tax lots with losses are sold.
2. For each of the remaining tax lots, calculate the tax burden by applying the appropriate capital gains tax rate (long term or short term). Sell the shares of the tax lot with the minimum tax burden first.

---

[13] These tax-lot selection rules might not be optimal if we consider the net capital gains and losses of the entire portfolio. With sufficient net short-term realized gains as well as net long-term gains in the rest of the portfolio, it might be wise to consider short-term losses before long-term losses. Of course, this will then affect total net gains and losses, which will affect other stocks' optimal tax-lot selling decisions. Thus, these simple rules should be considered when selling the shares of a particular stock in isolation of the rest of the portfolio. A more general tax-lot selection approach considering net capital gains and losses of the entire portfolio is discussed in Section 11.7.

In Table 11.3 we have calculated the potential tax burden for each tax lot assuming a 20% long-term capital gains tax rate and 37% short-term capital gains tax rate. According to our two rules, we would sell the tax lot of February 12, 2019, and the tax lot of March 16, 2019, in order to sell the 10 shares. If further sales were necessary, we would then proceed to the tax lots of January 10, 2018, January 24, 2020, December 19, 2019, and June 5, 2018.

More and more brokerages practice tax-lot management automatically for clients, so portfolio managers may not have to worry about this too much.[14] Nonetheless, the portfolio manager needs to be aware of it and understand the logic behind it.

11.6 TAX-LOT MATHEMATICS

Delving into the specifics of tax-lot accounting generally requires use of an elaborate mathematical notation. The notation must keep track of three elements: the stock, the time when a tax lot was purchased, and the current time. To avoid triple subscripts, we have developed a new, streamlined notation for tax-lot accounting.

Instead of denoting the current time using a subscript, we distinguish only between the existing portfolio and the new portfolio using a superscript. We use superscript b ("before") to indicate the existing portfolio and superscript a ("after") to indicate the new portfolio. Thus w_i^b is the weight of stock i in the existing portfolio, whereas w_i^a is the weight of stock i in the new portfolio. Similarly, s_i^b is the number of shares of stock i in the existing portfolio, whereas s_i^a is the number of shares of stock i in the new portfolio. V^b indicates the dollar value of the existing portfolio, and V^a indicates the dollar value of the new portfolio. $V^a - V^b$ gives the net cash inflow. V^a and V^b will differ only when there is cash inflow or outflow.

In order to distinguish between tax lots, we refer to each lot by a combination of a stock indicator i and a time indicator t. That is, tax lot (i, t) refers to the shares of stock i purchased at time t. Stock indicator i varies from 1 to N, where N is the total number of stocks in the investment universe. The time indicator t varies from 1 to T, where T denotes the current time.

---

[14] Many brokerages, however, use the IRS's default accounting method of first in, first out, which in many situations produces higher taxes than the simple rules we propose in this chapter.

Quantities of a particular tax lot are now denoted by adding two subscripts. We will also place a tilde ($\sim$) above a letter to clarify that the notation refers to a tax lot. For instance, $\tilde{w}^b_{i,t}$ is the weight of tax lot (i, t) in the existing portfolio, and $\tilde{w}^a_{i,t}$ is the weight of tax lot (i, t) in the new portfolio. $\tilde{s}^b_{i,t}$ is the number of shares in tax lot (i, t) in the existing portfolio, and $\tilde{s}^a_{i,t}$ is the number of shares in tax lot (i, t) in the new portfolio. Time T indicates the current time, so $\tilde{s}^a_{i,T}$ is the number of shares of stock i to buy for the new portfolio, and $\tilde{w}^a_{i,T}$ is the corresponding weight ($\tilde{s}^b_{i,T}$ and $\tilde{w}^b_{i,T}$ should equal zero). Vectors are defined in a similar manner. For example, $\mathbf{w}^a = (w^a_1, ..., w^a_N)$ is the vector of stock weights in the new portfolio, whereas $\tilde{\mathbf{w}}^a = (\tilde{w}^a_{1,1}, ..., \tilde{w}^a_{1,T}, ..., \tilde{w}^a_{N,1}, ..., \tilde{w}^a_{N,T})$ is the vector of tax-lot weights in the new portfolio.

There is a simple relationship between tax-lot quantities and stock quantities. The sum of the tax-lot weights of one stock equals the stock's weight in the portfolio, and the sum of the tax-lot shares of one stock equals the total number of shares of that stock in the portfolio. That is,

$$w^b_i = \sum_{t=1}^{T} \tilde{w}^b_{i,t}, \quad w^a_i = \sum_{t=1}^{T} \tilde{w}^a_{i,t} \tag{11.8}$$

and

$$s^b_i = \sum_{t=1}^{T} \tilde{s}^b_{i,t}, \quad s^a_i = \sum_{t=1}^{T} \tilde{s}^a_{i,t} \tag{11.9}$$

11.7 CAPITAL GAIN AND LOSS MANAGEMENT

The third principle of tax management is the driving force behind capital gain and loss management. Realizing a capital loss reduces the tax burden, whereas realizing a capital gain increases it. Therefore, to minimize the tax burden, the portfolio manager should sell stocks that have experienced the greatest capital losses or the smallest capital gains. Capital gain and loss management is a systematic approach to identifying the stocks to sell.

In a sense, capital gain and loss management generalizes the concept of tax-lot management. In the tax-lot management section, we did not consider which stocks to sell because we assumed that the manager had already chosen them. Capital gain and loss management provides a method for first determining which stocks to sell and then zeroing in on which specific tax lots should go.

To make the problem tractable, we take the portfolio's cash outflows net of dividend income as a given. We also restrict ourselves to selling and do not allow any buying. Using the notation explained in the preceding section, the portfolio manager needs to generate $V^b - V^a$ dollars of cash by selling some of the current holdings. What the portfolio manager can do is to sort the tax lots of all stocks according to potential capital loss and select the tax lots with the highest potential capital loss first until the cash-outflow requirement is met. The potential capital gain of tax lot (i, t) is $\tilde{s}^b_{i,t}$ $(p_{i,T} - p_{i,t})$, where $p_{i,T}$ is the current price of stock i, $p_{i,t}$ is the purchase price, and $\tilde{s}^b_{i,t}$ is the number of shares in the tax lot in the existing portfolio. We can sort all tax lots in descending order of potential capital gains (i_1, t_1), (i_2, t_2), ... so that

$$p_{i_1,T} - p_{i_1,t_1} \leq p_{i_2,T} - p_{i_2,t_2} \leq \cdots \qquad (11.10)$$

Then we choose M tax lots (i_1,t_1), (i_2, t_2), ..., (i_M, t_M) from the beginning of the list until the cash-outflow requirement is met so that

$$\tilde{s}^b_{i_1,t_1} p_{i_1,T} + \cdots + \tilde{s}^b_{i_M,t_M} p_{i_M,T} = V^b - V^a \qquad (11.11)$$

While this approach certainly will minimize the tax gain, the cash outflow will alter the portfolio's risk profile and even may throw the portfolio out of optimal balance. A better approach would be to include the tax consequence as an additional constraint in the optimization problem. To do so, let us calculate the tax burden more explicitly. Suppose that the long-term capital gains tax rate is τ_l and that the short-term capital gains tax rate is τ_s. Suppose also that we sell $\tilde{s}^b_{i,t} - \tilde{s}^a_{i,t}$ shares from tax lot (i, t). Then the tax burden for tax lot (i, t) is calculated as follows:

$$\tau_{i,t}(p_{i,T} - p_{i,t})(\tilde{s}^a_{i,t} - \tilde{s}^b_{i,t}) \qquad (11.12)$$

where $\tau_{i,t} = \tau_l$ if $T - t$ is greater than one year and $\tau_{i,t} = \tau_s$ if $T - t$ is less than one year. We can reformulate the above in terms of the weight as follows:

$$\tau_{i,t}\left(p_{i,T} - p_{i,t}\right)\left(\frac{V^b \tilde{w}^b_{i,t}}{p_{i,T}} - \frac{V^a \tilde{w}^a_{i,t}}{p_{i,T}}\right)$$

$$= \tau_{i,t}\left(\frac{p_{i,T} - p_{i,t}}{p_{i,T}}\right)\left(V^b \tilde{w}^b_{i,t} - V^a \tilde{w}^a_{i,t}\right) \qquad (11.13)$$

In words, this formula shows that the tax burden is the product of the tax rate $(\tau_{i,t})$, the capital appreciation rate $[(p_{i,T} - p_{i,t})/p_{i,T}]$, and the amount of the sale $(V^b \tilde{w}^b_{i,t} - V^a \tilde{w}^a_{i,t})$. The total tax burden is the sum of the tax burden of each tax lot, and the total tax rate is the total tax burden divided by the portfolio value:

$$\text{Total tax rate} = \sum_{i=1}^{N} \sum_{t=1}^{T-1} \tau_{i,t} \left(\frac{p_{i,T} - p_{i,t}}{p_{i,T}} \right) \left(\frac{V^b}{V^a} \tilde{w}^b_{i,t} - \tilde{w}^a_{i,t} \right) \tag{11.14}$$

In vector notation,

$$\text{Total tax rate} = \tau' \left(\frac{V^b}{V^a} \tilde{w}^b - \tilde{w}^a \right) \tag{11.15}$$

where τ, w^a, and w^b are the vectors made of $\tau_{i,t} [(p_{i,T} - p_{i,t})/p_{i,T}]$, $w^a_{i,t}$, and $w^b_{i,t}$, respectively. Given the tax rate for creating the new portfolio, we can include the rate as a penalty in the objective function of the optimization problem in Eq. (11.2). That is, the effective risk-adjusted return can be modified:

$$\text{Effective risk-adjusted return} = \tilde{w}^{a'} \tilde{\mu} - A\tilde{w}^{a'} \tilde{\Sigma} \tilde{w}^a - \tau' \left(\frac{V^b}{V^a} \tilde{w}^b - \tilde{w}^a \right)$$

$$= \tilde{w}^{a'} \left(\tilde{\mu} + \tau \right) - A\tilde{w}^{a'} \tilde{\Sigma} \tilde{w}^a - \frac{V^b}{V^a} \tilde{w}^{b'} \tau \tag{11.16}$$

Note that all the vectors and matrices including $\tilde{\mu}$ and $\tilde{\Sigma}$ are defined with respect to the *tax lots* rather than the stocks. To find an optimal portfolio, we have to maximize Eq. (11.16) with the constraint that the weights should sum to 1, that is,

$$\tilde{w}' \iota = 1 \tag{11.17}$$

and with the constraint that stock purchases are not allowed,[15] that is,

---

[15] The reader might notice that the variance-covariance matrix $\tilde{\Sigma}$ is not of full rank. This may cause a problem in applying the quadratic programming approach. To avoid this problem, we can restate the maximization problem in terms of $\tilde{w}^a$ and w^a and express the variance-covariance matrix in terms of w^a. Then the problem becomes a standard problem that quadratic programming can handle easily. That is, the effective risk-adjusted return in Eq. (11.16) should be modified so that it is minimized with respect to $\tilde{w}^a$, but the variance-covariance term is used as $w^{a'} \Sigma w^a$, with a constraint that specifies the relationship between $\tilde{w}^a$ and w^a.

$$\tilde{\mathbf{w}}^a \le \frac{V^b}{V^a} \tilde{\mathbf{w}}^b \qquad\qquad (11.18)$$

11.8 LOSS HARVESTING

The three tax management methods that we have discussed so far fall into the passive tax management category. The aim of these methods is to protect the portfolio's gains from taxes by minimizing the tax burden. A savvy investor or portfolio manager can go a step further and actually generate added gains from tax management. The active approach for doing this is called *loss harvesting*. It is based on the fourth principle of tax management, that realizing capital losses early produces potential tax savings. Investors should try to "harvest" as many capital losses as soon as possible.

Loss harvesting may generate an extra return for non-tax-related reasons as well. Loss harvesting is a kind of momentum investment strategy. The portfolio manager sells losing stocks and holds onto winning stocks. If stock prices exhibit positive autocorrelation over time, the winning stocks will do well again in the upcoming period, and the portfolio will earn higher returns. There is some empirical evidence that stock prices are positively autocorrelated over time, especially for periods of less than three months.

There are two loss-harvesting approaches that invest the proceeds from the sale of stock differently. Typical loss harvesting involves creating a new optimal portfolio. This method may not work properly if the *wash-sale rule* is in effect. The wash-sale rule prohibits an investor from purchasing a stock that he or she sold within the past 30 days from a tax perspective. The rule therefore would prevent an optimization solution that requires buying back a stock that just was sold. In a more sophisticated approach, which we call *loss harvesting and characteristic matching*, the stocks sold are replaced with similar stocks without solving the optimization problem again. This avoids conflicts with the wash-sale rule and still maintains the portfolio at an approximately optimal level.

11.8.1 Loss Harvesting and Reoptimizing

To simplify the setup, let us suppose that there is no cash-outflow requirement and no cash inflow either. (Or suppose that we have already taken care of cash outflows and inflows.) Then the loss harvesting and reoptimizing strategy can be carried out in the following manner:

1. Sell all tax lots that have capital losses.
2. Reoptimize the portfolio without selling, and reinvest the proceeds of the sale from the first step.

The first step is straightforward. For each tax lot (i, t), compare the purchase price $p_{i,t}$ with the current price $p_{i,T}$. If the purchase price is higher than the current price, then we sell this tax lot. That is, we will set

$$\tilde{w}^a_{i,t} = 0, \quad \text{if } p_{i,t} > p_{i,T} \tag{11.19}$$

where $\tilde{w}^a_{i,t}$ is the weight of tax lot (i, t) in the new portfolio. If we sell all tax lots with capital losses, then the proceeds from the sale will be $V\Sigma_{(i,t):p_{i,t}>p_{i,T}} \ \tilde{w}^b_{i,t}$ dollars, where $\tilde{w}^b_{i,t}$ is the weight of tax lot (i, t) in the original portfolio.

The second step is to reoptimize the portfolio with the proceeds of the sale, $V\Sigma_{(i,t):p_{i,t}>p_{i,T}} \ \tilde{w}^b_{i,t}$ dollars. To avoid reversing the tax consequences, we need to impose a "no sale" restriction. This restriction can be written as

$$\tilde{w}^a_{i,t} = \tilde{w}^b_{i,t'}, \quad \text{if } p_{i,t} \leq p_{i,T} \tag{11.20}$$

Also, to avoid violating the wash-sale rule, we need to make sure not to buy the stocks that were just sold:

$$\tilde{w}^a_{i,T} = 0, \quad \text{if } p_{i,t} > p_{i,T}, \text{ for any } t = 1, \ldots, T-1 \tag{11.21}$$

Two conditions, Eqs. (11.19) and (11.21), together completely determine the weights of the stocks that we sold. The only "free" weights we need to determine at this point are $\tilde{w}_{i,T}$ for which $p_{i,t} \leq p_{i,T}$ for all t.

Now let us express the optimization problem in terms of the stock weights. For those stocks affected by the loss harvesting, we have already determined the weights:

$$w^a_i = \sum_{t:p_{i,t} \leq p_{i,T}} \tilde{w}^a_{i,t} \tag{11.22}$$

For the stocks not affected by the loss harvesting, the only restriction imposed is

$$w^a_i \geq w^b_i \tag{11.23}$$

if no tax lot of stock i has a capital loss. Then, to find the optimal portfolio, we need to solve the optimization problem in Eq. (11.2) subject to Eqs. (11.3), (11.22), and (11.23).

11.8.2 Loss Harvesting and Characteristic Matching

In the preceding approach we reoptimized the portfolio after harvesting losses. However, this reoptimized portfolio may not really be the optimal portfolio because we had to abide by the no-wash-sale and no-realized-gain constraints. We actually may find a better portfolio if we drop the optimization completely and instead use the *characteristic-matching approach*. The characteristic-matching idea plays a role in the creation of factor models when we estimate factor exposures. Characteristic matching is based on the assumption that stocks with similar characteristics, such as size and book-to-market ratio, have similar expected returns and risk levels. If we sell stock *XYZ* to harvest losses and if we cannot buy stock *XYZ* again because of the wash-sale rule, then the best thing we can do is purchase a stock that is similar to *XYZ*.[16]

The loss-harvesting and characteristic-matching strategy can be implemented with the following steps:

1. Sell all tax lots that have capital losses.
2. Reinvest the proceeds of the sale into *similar* stocks.

The first step here is identical to the first step of regular loss harvesting. We sell all tax lots for which the current price $p_{i,T}$ is lower than the purchase price $p_{i,t}$. If stock j is affected by this loss harvesting, then the proceeds from the sale of stock j are

$$\text{Proceeds from the sale of stock } j = \sum_{t:p_{j,T} \leq p_{j,t}} p_{j,T} \tilde{s}_{j,t}^b \qquad (11.24)$$

In the second step, we need to identify stocks similar to the ones we sold. Suppose that we want to find similar firms using L characteristics. We can calculate the Z-score for each of the L characteristics for all stocks. Given the Z-scores of stock i, $\mathbf{z}_i = (z_{i1}, \ldots, z_{iL})$,

---

[16] Ideally, the stock would possess both similar risk characteristics and a similar expected α or expected return.

and stock j, $\mathbf{z}_j = (z_{j1}, ..., z_{jL})$, we can define the "distance" between two stocks by[17]

$$\text{Distance} = \sum_{k=1}^{L} | z_{ik} - z_{jk} | \qquad (11.25)$$

The stock most similar to stock j is the one with the smallest distance from stock j. That is the stock to purchase using the proceeds from the sale of stock j.

11.8.3 Loss Harvesting with a Benchmark

Loss harvesting can be a powerful tool for the benchmark portfolio manager. In the first part of this section we showed how to create optimal portfolios through loss harvesting. The portfolio manager with a benchmark can create his or her tracking portfolio in the same way. He or she can add the two constraints in Eqs. (11.22) and (11.23) to the tracking-error-minimization problem.

Characteristic matching also can be adjusted for the presence of a benchmark. In picking stocks to replace the losers, the benchmark portfolio manager must consider whether characteristic matching would increase the portfolio's tracking error. To prevent the portfolio from straying further from the benchmark, the replacement stocks should have α's and β's as close to the benchmarks α and β as possible.

For each stock we run the regression of the stock return on the benchmark return:

$$r_i = \alpha_i + \beta_i r_B + \epsilon_i \qquad (11.26)$$

The α and β of this equation are the benchmark α and benchmark β defined in Chapter 2. Once we have obtained the benchmark α and benchmark β for each stock, we add them to each stock's Z-score vector. The last two elements of the characteristic vector $\mathbf{z}_i = (z_{i1}, ..., z_{iL})$ are now the benchmarks α and β. We then determine the similarity between any pair of stocks by Eq. (11.25) as before.

This method preserves the relationship between the portfolio and the benchmark reasonably well, although it may not maintain the absolute lowest tracking error.

---

[17] One could also calculate a weighted distance function that weights each factor differently.

11.9 GAINS FROM TAX MANAGEMENT

We ran a simulation based on real data to show just how big the gains from tax management can be.[18] In the simulation we compare two hypothetical investors. We call the first investor, the *naive* investor, and the second, the *t-smart* investor. The naive investor does not manage taxes efficiently; he simply invests in every stock in a sector index. He rebalances the portfolio every month to adjust for index entries and exits. The t-smart investor chooses the same portfolio as the naive investor initially. However, every month, the t-smart investor sells "loser" stocks (i.e., stocks that have capital losses) and replaces them with characteristically matched stocks from outside the index universe to minimize realized capital gains. We tested each investor's results for the investment period from July 1990 to June 2000.[19] We repeated the simulation for each of the 18 different sector indexes.

Table 11.4 reports the before-tax annualized return, the after-tax annualized return, and the effective tax rate for each investor.[20] Each entry in the table is an average across 18 different sector simulations. The effective tax rate for the two investors differs by 4.82%. This means that the t-smart investor gains an extra 4.82% per year in after-tax portfolio return simply by practicing the tax management techniques we have discussed in this chapter.

As a second illustration of the power of tax management, we consider an alternative situation. This time, the two investors

TABLE 11.4

Comparison of Naive and T-Smart Investors

Investor	Pretax Return (%)	After-Tax Return (%)	Effective Tax Rate (%)
Naive investor	11.99	9.93	26.40
T-smart investor	16.68	14.41	21.58

---

[18] This section is based on Chincarini and Kim (2001). Since this study was written, there has been much more interest in tax-managed strategies (see Chaudhuri et al. (2020)).

[19] For the purpose of calculation, the entire portfolio holding was assumed to be liquidated at the end of June 2000. If the portfolio were not liquidated, future tax liabilities would be erroneously ignored in the calculation.

[20] The pretax return is higher for the t-smart investor than for the naive investor. This is due to the momentum in price movement. When there is momentum in price movement, selling loser stocks and buying something else produces superior returns.

TABLE 11.5

Comparison of Naive and T-Smart Investors, Regular Cash Withdrawal

Investor	Pretax Return (%)	After-Tax Return (%)	Effective Tax Rate (%)
Naive investor	13.44	11.33	24.06
T-smart investor	13.79	12.04	19.37

regularly withdraw cash from their portfolios by cashing out dividends. The naive investor is a buy-and-hold investor. He buys a portfolio at the beginning of the simulation period and holds it until the end of the simulation period. Each month, he cashes out dividends and pays taxes on those dividends. The t-smart investor buys the same portfolio as the naive investor at the beginning of the simulation period. Each month, she also withdraws the same amount of cash from her portfolio as the naive investor does. The difference, though, is that the t-smart investor tries to offset dividends with realized capital losses. She does so by selling losers and replacing them with characteristically matched stocks.

Table 11.5 reports the pretax and the after-tax returns, as well as the effective tax rates, for each investor. Each entry in the table is an average across 18 sector simulations with different cash withdrawal rates. The effective tax rates for the two investors differ by 4.69%. The t-smart investor gains 4.69% extra annual investment income from her tax management strategy.

11.10 CONCLUSION

Portfolio managers who do not want to give away the fruits of their labor must practice effective tax management. In this chapter we discussed passive techniques for protecting the after-tax return of the portfolio and active techniques for boosting the return with additional tax-free gains. For passive tax management, we described three very useful methods: dividend management, tax-lot accounting, and capital gains and loss management. On the active management side, we discussed the strategy of loss harvesting. We showed how the portfolio manager can incorporate these strategies directly into the stock-return model without significantly altering the before-tax α of the portfolio.

As we saw from a simulation using real data, intelligently tax-managed portfolios can earn as much as 4% per year more than portfolios that overlook the effect of taxes. Why turn down an extra return of 4%? In the past, the benefits of tax management techniques might not have always justified the costs and difficulties of implementing them. Recent advances in technology, however, have greatly simplified and lowered the costs of implementation. A portfolio stands to gain only from strategies that keep taxes to a minimum.

QUESTIONS

11.1. Explain the concept of double taxation of corporate income.

11.2. You are a research analyst interested in how dividends affect stock prices. Assume that there is only one income tax rate (τ_i) and a capital gains rate (τ_c). Also assume that the owner has held the stock for more than one year already.

    (a) Denoting the price of the stock before and after the ex-dividend date as p^b and p^a, what should be the theoretical drop in the stock price ex-dividend?

    (b) Suppose that you further study the data since 1984 and find that the typical stock drops by 90% of the dividend on the ex-dividend date. Could you profit from this information if you managed a tax-exempt pension fund? How?

11.3. Explain why individual investors may have preferred capital gains to dividends in the U.S. tax system before 2002.

11.4. Behind the principles of tax management is the concept of the time value of money.

    (a) If the economy is experiencing very high inflation, how would the time value of money be affected?

    (b) If the economy is not growing at all, can the time value of money be negative?

11.5. Explain why realizing a capital loss as early as possible may reduce the tax burden.

11.6. If the value effect (value stocks perform better) dominates, should the dividend management technique be modified? Does your answer change if the dividend rate is one of the factors in the stock return model?

11.7. One assumption behind dividend management is that we can *predict* the dividend amount of each stock fairly accurately. Explain why predicting the dividend amount is easier than predicting earnings or the stock price. How would you actually predict the dividend amount?

11.8. A popular tax-lot management technique, called *highest-in, first-out*, entails selling the tax lot with the highest purchase price first. Is this rule consistent with the fact that short-term capital gains are taxed at a higher rate than long-term capital gains? How should this rule be modified?

11.9. Explain why the first-in, first-out rule of tax-lot management may create unnecessary tax burdens.

11.10. Let $\mathbf{w} = (w_1, \ldots, w_N)$ be the portfolio weights of stocks at the beginning of the month and

$$\tilde{\mathbf{w}} = (\tilde{w}_{11}, \ldots, \tilde{w}_{1T}, \ldots, \tilde{w}_{N1}, \ldots, \tilde{w}_{NT})$$

be the portfolio weights of tax lots at the beginning of the month.

   (a) If $\mathbf{r} = (r_1, \ldots, r_N)$ is the stock return of the month, what would be the weights of the stocks at the end of the month? What would be the weights of the tax lots at the end of the month?

   (b) It is useful to construct matrix $\mathbf{D}$ such that $\mathbf{w} = \mathbf{D}\tilde{\mathbf{w}}$. Specify the typical elements of $\mathbf{D}$.

   (c) Answer part (a) again using matrix $\mathbf{D}$ from part (b).

11.11. If the loss-harvesting strategy is followed for many years, the portfolio manager may get into the situation of not having any capital losses to realize. How should the loss-harvesting strategy be modified to avoid such a situation?

11.12. Explain why loss harvesting may have a negative influence on the portfolio return when returns exhibit negative serial correlation.

11.13. Explain why loss harvesting may increase the tracking error of the portfolio.

11.14. What is the wash-sale rule? Explain how to comply with the wash-sale rule in the portfolio optimization problem.

11.15. The characteristic-matching technique introduced in this chapter is based on ideas from the fundamental factor model. In practice, replacing stocks by characteristic matching affects the return and the risk of the portfolio. For the characteristic matching to be perfect, what would the error term in the fundamental factor model have to be?

11.16. 401(k) accounts are not taxable in principle. However, some people withdraw funds from their 401(k) accounts before they retire, and they pay taxes on the withdrawals. Given the possibility of early withdrawal, how would the portfolio manager of a 401(k) account modify the portfolio?

11.17. Suppose that a taxable investor and a nontaxable investor pool money and create one portfolio.

   (a) Which tax management techniques can be adopted? Which techniques should be avoided?

   (b) Does it really make sense to pool funds from these two investors?

α Mojo

The factor model of stock returns gives the quantitative equity portfolio manager a good idea of what he or she can expect his or her portfolio to earn with a particular investment strategy. The manager can depend on the model because of the reliability of the statistical relationship between stock returns and the model's factors. The effectiveness not only of the model but also of quantitative equity portfolio management (QEPM) as a whole depends greatly on the quality of statistical results.

Yet all great investment strategies do not operate strictly within the boundaries of the factor–return relationship. In fact, to focus only on factor exposures and factor premiums is to ignore the model's greater potential. The data-derived factor model says that higher returns come only from more factor exposure or higher factor premiums. But look at the beginning of the model, and you will find α, a deceptively small term that represents the radical possibility of earning much higher returns *without* absorbing much more risk. How can a portfolio manager activate α and boost the returns he or she gets for the same amount of risk? By tapping into "alpha mojo."

Alpha mojo (a.k.a. α *mojo*) produces outsize returns that defy the presumption of some universal, incontrovertible ratio between risk and reward. There are three major sources of α mojo, discussed in the next three chapters: leverage, which multiplies the portfolio's return; the market-neutral strategy, which insulates the portfolio against the volatile winds of market trends and risks; and

Bayesian α, which introduces the portfolio to new sources of return. Alpha mojo generates results that look like pure investment magic, but just as the magician knows the logic behind his or her tricks, the quantitative equity portfolio manager knows that the sources of mojo are actually quantitative methods of investing that exploit the laws of investing to phenomenal effect—while still upholding the tenets of QEPM.

CHAPTER 12

Leverage

Give me a lever long enough and a fulcrum on which to place it, and I shall move the world.

—Archimedes

12.1 INTRODUCTION

Given a benchmark, the portfolio return can be broken down into two parts: the part related to the benchmark and the part not related to the benchmark. The first part is measured by the benchmark β multiplied by the benchmark return, and the second part is measured by α^B plus a random component.[1] That is,

$$r_P = \alpha^B + \beta r_B + \epsilon \tag{12.1}$$

Part of the portfolio's return is beyond the manager's control. To some extent the portfolio goes the way the benchmark goes (represented by βr_B), and occasionally, it does the proverbial "random walk" (represented by ϵ). Yet the portfolio's success or failure is also up to the manager. He or she has the power to boost the β of the overall portfolio. Better yet, he or she has the power to boost the α^B. We call this power α *mojo*. Leverage is a potent source of α mojo and also can be used to boost the β of the overall portfolio.

Leverage is perhaps the ultimate source of α mojo. In physics, a lever multiplies the force that is applied to it; in investing, leverage

---

[1] See Chapter 2 for further explanation of α^B and other variations of α.

multiplies the force of the portfolio. With leverage in the form of borrowed capital, a portfolio manager can invest double, triple, or even
more of the amount of available equity. If he or she has $10 million
and can find a lender to match that amount, he or she will have a
leveraged portfolio of $20 million, and every dollar that the leveraged
portfolio gains will be twice as much as the unleveraged portfolio
would have garnered. Leverage applied in the correct way also can
generate major α mojo and amplify the benchmark return. Leverage
easily alters the risk-return profile of any portfolio. If the portfolio is
managed well but its risk-return ratio does not satisfy the investor's
appetite for risk, leverage will pump up both the expected return and
the risk level. If the risk is too high, leverage through shorting can
decrease the overall return and risk of the portfolio. Investors who
like to time the market also can leverage the portfolio to enhance the
impact of market-timing trades.[2]

The sort of power that leverage confers can be dangerous,
though. A massive leveraged portfolio can earn the unleveraged
portfolio's profits three times over, but it also will get hit three times
as hard by any losses.[3] Borrowed capital increases the portfolio's
exposure to market swings. It opens up the portfolio manager to
margin-call risk, which threatens the portfolio's liquidity by raising
the possibility of having to meet daily margin requirements in
adverse market conditions. It exacerbates market-timing mistakes.
And if it isn't handled carefully, leverage can turn into an evil mojo,
inflicting severe damage on the portfolio manager's α. A number of
hedge funds have gone bankrupt when the portfolio was heavily
leveraged and the α went negative. Long-Term Capital Management
(LTCM) may be the most notorious case, but there have been others,
such as the Niederhoffer Investments Fund.

For those who dare to use it, leverage comes in different
forms. The manager can borrow additional funds to invest more
than the equity capital. He or she can leverage the portfolio through
the margin account, since most equities require only 50% initial
margin. He or she can use financial instruments and derivatives,

---

[2] See Table 12.1 for a list of the advantages and disadvantages of leverage.
[3] Some forms of leverage, such as a long-short portfolio, actually can reduce the market
    risk of the portfolio. Throughout this chapter, when we speak of leverage, we are
    implicitly referring to an increase in exposure or amplification of the underlying
    position. Some people call this net leverage, which is different than gross leverage,
    which considers the absolute sum of all positions divided by equity capital. We
    discuss long-short types of portfolios in Chapter 13.

TABLE 12.1

The Advantages and Disadvantages of Leverage in
Quantitative Equity Portfolio Management (QEPM)

Advantages	Disadvantages
1. Easily alter the risk-return profile of a portfolio	1. May increase overall risk of the portfolio if direction of leverage is the same as underlying exposure and introduces margin risk
2. May increase the overall expected return of the portfolio	2. May reduce the relative contribution of the portfolio manager's overall α to the total return
3. May increase α to $l \cdot \alpha$, where l is the leverage ratio	3. Will magnify negative α's as well as $l \cdot \alpha$
4. Enhances the market returns of market timers	4. May cause huge losses in the portfolios of market timers

such as REPOs, futures, forwards, equity swaps, and option contracts, which require smaller margin requirements than equities and allow for even higher leverage of the portfolio for a given amount of equity capital. Finally, a portfolio manager can achieve leverage by shorting securities. In this chapter we discuss how to leverage skillfully. We explain practical methods for increasing the leverage of a portfolio primarily through the use of index futures and single-stock futures. We cover several portfolio situations, including that of an index portfolio manager and that of an active portfolio manager attempting to leverage an equity portfolio with a positive α. We also discuss issues related to rebalancing a levered portfolio and protecting against unlimited losses.

12.2 CASH AND INDEX FUTURES

The easiest way to leverage an equity portfolio is to use futures contracts on equity indices such as the Standard & Poor's (S&P) 500 futures, the NASDAQ 100 futures, the Russell 2000 futures, and the S&P 400 futures.[4] Table 12.2 shows the relative monthly trading volume of these and other types of futures contracts, which gives a

---

[4] Futures capital gains and losses are treated differently from other investments for individual investors. In particular, all futures gains and losses are treated as 60% long-term gains and 40% short-term gains regardless of the time of purchase and sale. This can amount to quite a bit for short-term trades. For example, a short-term trade with futures would result in a tax burden of 26.8% with futures compared with a tax burden of 37% with stocks for the top marginal tax rate individual using the individual tax rates of 2020.

TABLE 12.2

Commonly Used Domestic Equity Futures Contracts

Futures Name	Ticker	Exchange	Contract Size	Index Value	Initial Margin ($)	Maintenance Margin ($)	Margin (%)	Volume	Relative Liquidity (% of Total)
S&P 500	SP1	CME	250	3,756.07	60,500	55,000	6.44	2,062	0.39
S&P 500 E-mini	ES1	CME	50	3,756.07	12,100	11,000	6.44	993,343	61.00
NASDAQ 100 E-mini	NQ1	CME	20	12,888.28	17,600	16,000	6.83	280,573	28.06
NASDAQ Comp E-mini	NL1	CME	20	12,888.28	17,600	16,000	6.83	0	0.00
S&P 400 Mid-Cap E-mini	FA1	CME	100	2,306.62	14,850	13,500	6.44	16,031	0.72
S&P 600 Small-Cap E-mini	GN1	CME	100	1,118.93	9,350	8,500	8.36	0	0.00
Russell 2000 T.R.	RTB1	CME	10	10,122.27	7,810	7,100	7.72	0	0.00
Russell 2000 E-mini	RTY1	CME	50	1,974.86	7,150	6,500	7.24	144,363	3.52
Russell 1000 T.R.	RTD1	CME	10	12,531.09	8,580	7,800	6.85	0	0.00
Russell 1000 E-mini	RVY1	CME	50	1,349.62	5,170	4,700	7.66	125	0.01
DJIA T.R.	RDR1	CBOT	2	70,778.10	9,900	9,000	6.99	0	0.00
DJIA E-mini	DM1	CBOT	5	30,606.48	9,900	9,000	6.47	81,740	5.76
DJIA Micro E-mini	HWI1	CBOT	0.5	30,606.48	990	900	6.47	81,092	0.37
S&P 500 Growth	SG1	CME	250	2,577.22	38,500	35,000	5.98	0	0.00
S&P 500 Value	SU1	CME	250	1,267.18	22,000	20,000	6.94	0	0.00
S&P 500 Financial SS E-mini	IXA1	CME	250	363.52	8,250	7,500	9.08	144	0.03
S&P 500 Technology SS E-mini	IXT1	CME	100	1,311.92	10,450	9,500	7.97	97	0.02
S&P 500 Communication Services SS E-mini	XAS1	CME	250	353.47	5,500	5,000	6.22	20	0.00
S&P 500 Consumer Discretionary SS E-mini	IXY1	CME	100	1,625.07	10,450	9,500	6.43	105	0.02
S&P 500 Consumer Staples SS E-mini	IXR1	CME	100	681.07	3,850	3,500	5.65	71	0.01
S&P 500 Energy SS E-mini	IXP1	CME	100	397.55	4,400	4,000	11.07	195	0.02
S&P 500 Health Care SS E-mini	IXC1	CME	100	1,148.03	7,810	7,100	6.80	251	0.02
S&P 500 Industrial SS E-mini	IXI1	CME	100	893.21	7,370	6,700	8.25	72	0.02
S&P 500 Materials SS E-mini	IXD1	CME	100	767.22	5,720	5,200	7.46	126	0.01
S&P 500 Real Estate SS E-mini	XAR1	CME	250	178.33	3,575	3,250	8.02	142	0.00
S&P 500 Utilities SS E-mini	IXS1	CME	100	636.17	5,280	4,800	8.30	291	0.01

Note: Margin requirements differ for speculators, for exchange members, and for hedging purposes. We listed the requirements for speculators, which are the highest margin rates as of December 31, 2020. For speculators, initial margin is 1.10 times the maintenance margin at CME. The futures data were obtained from Bloomberg, and all data are as of the close of business on December 31, 2020. The tickers are Bloomberg tickers for the nearest-term generic futures contracts. The relative liquidity measures the percentage of 30-day ADDTV (average daily dollar trading volume) leading up to December 31, 2020 of that particular contract relative to the other contracts in the table. For instance, 61% of the total trading volume of those listed contracts occurred with the S&P 500 E-mini contract. The margin percentage was computed by dividing the initial margin requirements by the size of one contract using closing prices of the index for December 31, 2020. T.R. is for total return and SS is for Select Sector.

sense of their relative degree of liquidity. The S&P 500 futures and the NASDAQ 100 futures are the most liquid futures contracts available.

In this section we discuss leveraging with equity index futures. The discussion applies mainly to managers whose benchmarks are common equity indices with actively traded futures contracts. We first discuss the magnitude of possible leverage and then examine the practical mechanics.

12.2.1 Theoretical Limits of Leverage

The amount of leverage to add to a portfolio varies with the goals of the manager. Leverage is conventionally measured as the total absolute value of all investment positions divided by the equity capital. Thus, if a manager were long \$100 M of futures and short another \$100 M of index futures, the conventional measure of leverage would be 2. In this chapter, we use an alternative definition of leverage which could also be thought of as net dollar exposure. That is, in our definition, the manager in the preceding example would have a leverage or exposure of 0. In this chapter, we use leverage mainly to refer to futures positions that increase the net exposure of the underlying portfolio position. In these cases, our formula for leverage coincides with the conventional formula for leverage. When futures are shorted with an underlying long position, our definition of leverage is no longer the conventional definition of leverage. Thus when considering long positions combined with short positions, our definition of leverage is more commonly known as the net dollar exposure. We will use the symbol l to illustrate the amount of leverage with respect to the underlying equity capital of the portfolio. Leverage at time t will be given by the expression $l = V_t^f / V_t$, where V_t^f is the total notional value of the futures positions, and V_t is the total equity capital. Thus $l = 1$ represents an exposure equal to 100% of the invested capital and hence may be described as "no leverage" (though we write it as the leverage of one), while $l = 2$ represents a 200% exposure to the equity capital.[5]

In the simple case of cash and index futures, leverage affects the portfolio manager's return primarily by increasing its exposure to the benchmark, its benchmark β. To achieve a certain benchmark β for the portfolio, one needs to compute the appropriate number of futures contracts to purchase. The portfolio manager is limited

---

[5] Note that we are not including the cash position in the numerator when we calculate the leverage ratio as described above, which is standard, since cash is not really considered a risky investment.

by the extent of the margin requirements of the underlying contract. Table 12.2 gives a summary of the percentage requirements of some major futures contracts as of December 31, 2020.

Let us use m_f to denote the margin percentage requirement for every dollar of futures positions acquired. Theoretically, the highest leverage that could be obtained is

$$l^{\max} = \frac{1}{m_f} \tag{12.2}$$

The β of the portfolio is simply the β of the futures contract multiplied by the leverage ratio.[6] Thus the highest β that can be achieved is

$$\beta^{\max} = \frac{\dot{\beta}_f}{m_f} \tag{12.3}$$

where β_f is the β of the futures contract.[7]

Suppose that the benchmark is the S&P 500. If the margin requirement on the S&P 500 futures is 5%, then the maximum leverage that can be achieved is 20 ($= 1/m_f$). This is also equal to the maximum β that can be achieved because the S&P 500 futures have a $\beta_f = 1$ when the benchmark is the S&P 500. At that rather high exposure to the S&P 500, if the S&P 500 had a -4% return, the portfolio would lose approximately -80% ($= -4\beta^{\max} = -4l^{\max}$).

12.2.2 Leverage Mechanics

Although very high levels of leverage theoretically can be achieved in an equity portfolio, rarely do portfolio managers maintain a

---

[6] Throughout this chapter, when we refer to β, we are referring to the β of the respective instrument versus the benchmark. For portfolio managers who are more accustomed to using β with respect to the market (i.e., the S&P 500), one simply need interpret all our β's as the β versus the S&P 500. If one does this, in all cases the overall β of the portfolio will be with respect to the S&P 500, irrespective of the benchmark. Of course, if the benchmark is the S&P 500, the resulting β also will mean a similar thing. The key is that all the measured β's are, with respect to one underlying instrument, either a benchmark or a market index.

[7] Since $l \equiv V_f^l/V_t$, the maximum leverage is achieved when all the equity capital is just sufficient to cover the margin requirements, that is, when $mV_f^l = V_t$. Substituting this into the equation results in the maximum leverage ratio. The β of the portfolio is given by $\beta_p = w\beta_f$, where w is the weight on the futures position (i.e., the futures position over the equity capital). Since we want the maximum β, we will create the maximum leverage on that particular futures contract of $1/m_f$, which by substitution leads to the $\beta^{\max}$.

leverage ratio higher than 2 or 3.[8] There are many reasons for this. Higher amounts of leverage put the portfolio at greater risk of vanishing entirely with a significant adverse market movement. For mutual funds and ETFs, the Securities and Exchange Commission (SEC) has to approve the leverage amount in the prospectus, and it may be very uncomfortable with leverage ratios above 2 or 3. For these practical reasons, we will focus on leverage ratios within a moderate range, but the formulas apply to any sort of leverage up to the theoretical maximum.

In order to construct a portfolio of a given β with cash and futures, we can use a formula that describes the β of the overall portfolio:

$$\beta_P = \sum_{i=1}^{N} w_i \beta_i \qquad (12.4)$$

where β_p is the β of the overall portfolio, β_i represents the β of instrument i, and w_i represents the weight of instrument i in the portfolio. The weights are calculated relative to equity capital V so that the sum of the weights of noncash positions is l. The preceding equation just states the relationship that the β of the overall portfolio is a weighted average of component portfolio β's. The β of cash is equal to 0 and drops out of the equation. Since we are using just cash and one futures instrument, we are left with only one term, the product of the weight of the futures contracts and the β of the futures. We denote the β of the futures as β_f.

In order to find the number of contracts that we need to purchase to achieve a given target β, denoted by β^*, we must satisfy the following equation:

$$\begin{aligned} \beta^* &= w_f \beta_f \\ &= \frac{N_f q S_t}{V_t} \beta_f \end{aligned} \qquad (12.5)$$

---

[8] Rydex pioneered the idea of levered mutual funds and ETFs, which was then copied by other institutions. The early days of creating mutual funds of leverage equal to 2 were challenging. At the time, the CFTC wanted to limit the size of futures positions held by mutual funds and did not allow a mutual fund to hold more than 5% of its NAV in initial margin on futures positions. This made a leverage of 2 or higher untenable with futures contracts. In order to get around this margin restriction, these mutual funds sometimes used options and other loopholes to leverage the portfolio to a level of 2 and higher. The CFTC eventually dismantled most of its margin regulations, and leveraging is less complicated today.

where N_f is the number of futures contracts purchased, q is the futures contract multiplier (e.g., $q = 250$ for the S&P 500 futures contract), and S_t is the value of the index underlying the futures contract at time t (e.g., the S&P 500 value).[9] By rearranging this equation, we obtain the standard formula to determine how many futures contracts should be purchased to achieve a given β^*:

$$N_f = \frac{\beta^* V_t}{\beta_f q S_t} \tag{12.6}$$

Suppose that the benchmark is the S&P 500 and that the portfolio manager is purchasing S&P 500 futures. To achieve a portfolio of $\beta^* = 2$, given an S&P 500 trading at 1,000, a multiplier for the large S&P 500 contracts of 250, and a sum of cash equal to $100 million, the appropriate number of futures contracts to purchase would be 800. (The β of the S&P 500 futures with respect to the S&P 500 is 1.)

When the portfolio manager purchases N_f contracts of the futures, it "costs" him or her $q N_f F_t$ dollars, where F_t is the price of a futures contract. Then the portfolio manager needs to keep $(q N_f F_t) m_f$ dollars in a margin balance and hold the rest of the equity capital in cash earning interest. The general formula for the amount of cash held is $V_t - (q N_f F_t) m_f$.

In our example, the margin amount is $10,075,282 (the product of $q = 250$, $N_f = 800$, $F_t = 1{,}007.53$, $m_f = 0.05$), and the cash portion of the portfolio is $89,924,718 (= $100{,}000{,}000 - $10{,}075{,}282$).

12.2.3 Expected Return and Risk

When the leverage ratio is 1, the return of the futures contracts r_f can be expressed as $\alpha_f + \beta_f r_B + \epsilon_f$, where r_B is the benchmark return. Given the leverage ratio of l, the expected return and risk of the total portfolio become

$$E(r_p) = l(\alpha_f + \beta_f \mu_B) \tag{12.7}$$

$$V(r_p) = l^2(\beta_f^2 \sigma_B^2 + \omega_f^2) \tag{12.8}$$

---

[9] For those unfamiliar with trading futures contracts, these terms might look odd. Every futures contract represents the value of an underlying portfolio. Thus, when buying one futures contract, it is contract to buy $1 \cdot q \cdot S_t$ of the underlying index portfolio at a future date. Thus, if one buys N_f contracts, one is agreeing to buy $N_f \cdot q \cdot S_t$ worth of a portfolio with equal composition to the underlying index at a future date.

where ω_f^2 is the residual risk of the futures contract, μ_B is the mean return of the benchmark, and σ_B^2 is the variance of the benchmark return. This clearly shows that although leverage can increase the expected return of the portfolio, it also increases proportionately the risk of the portfolio. In the case of leveraging by purchasing futures contracts on the benchmark itself, $\beta_f = 1$ and $\alpha_f = 0$ (or close to it), and we can ignore the ϵ_f because it will be very small. In this particular case, if we assume that the portfolio and futures returns already have subtracted the risk-free rate, the Sharpe ratio (SR) of the overall portfolio is equal to

$$SR_P = \frac{\mu_B}{\sigma_B} \qquad (12.9)$$

In this particular case, the Sharpe ratio is independent of the degree of leverage, and the β of the total portfolio equals the leverage ratio.[10]

Most portfolio managers also earn interest on the margined amount minus a small "haircut". On the margined sum, one can assume that the manager will receive something like 98% of the short-term interest rate for cash. Throughout this chapter we will use i to denote the interest rate on the cash position and i' to denote the interest rate on the margin. We expect that $i > i'$ owing to the haircut. In all our calculations for the expected return of the portfolio, we shall ignore the cash returns of the position for simplicity. However, cash returns are not trivial, especially when the portfolio manager has a substantial amount of cash in his or her overall portfolio.[11]

Figure 12.1 show how leverage changes the payoff profile of the portfolio. The horizontal axis represents the value of the index,

---

[10] In the case of cash and futures only, $l = V_t^f/V_t$. Thus, to achieve a desired leverage ratio l^*, the portfolio manager solves $l^* = (N_{f,t} qS_t)/V_t$ for the number of contracts to purchase. Thus, $N_{f,t} = (l^* V_t)/qS_t$. This is equivalent to the β^* formula when $\beta_f = 1$. The leverage ratio in this chapter uses the translation of $V_t^f = N_{f,t} qS_t$, which is known as *equal-position matching*. Some investment professionals prefer to define the leverage ratio in terms of *dollar matching*, where the spot price of the underlying contract would be replaced with the actual price of the futures contract.

[11] For those interested, all the expected-return calculations in this chapter can be modified to include the amount held in cash by adding the term $\xi \cdot r_{cash}$, where ξ is the proportion of equity held in cash. In the case of cash and index futures, $\xi = 1$; it changes in other sections of this chapter. Using notation employed later in this chapter and continuous compounding, the additional cash term can be expressed as $\xi\,(I_{t,t+k} - 1)$, where

$$I_{t,t+k} = \left[\frac{m_f qN_{f,t}F_t}{V_t} \left(e^{i'\frac{k}{360}} - e^{i\frac{k}{360}} \right) + e^{i\frac{k}{360}} \right].$$

If there is no haircut on margin or if margin is covered by other means, let $i' = i$ or let $m = 0$.

FIGURE 12.1

Portfolio payoffs with and without leverage.

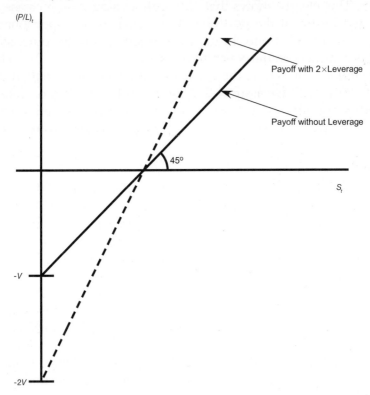

whereas the vertical axis represents profit and loss of the portfolio. If the index were to go to zero, the portfolio would lose the entire value, V. Without leverage, the index value and the payoff move one for one along the 45-degree line. With leverage, the payoff becomes steeper versus the underlying index. This diagram depicts the payoff when the leverage is equal to 2. With leverage equal to 2, if the index drops by 50%, the portfolio would lose more than double its assets, or $2V$.

12.3 STOCKS, CASH, AND INDEX FUTURES

The preceding section dealt with leverage in the case of an index manager. Leverage works somewhat differently for the portfolio manager who does not follow an index and instead selects stocks that he or she believes will outperform the benchmark. This manager will calculate leverage and the number of futures contracts in a similar way, but the underlying portfolio will be a portfolio of stocks with weights that already have been chosen according to the optimization method.[12] In this section we discuss leverage for the portfolio manager who owns a portfolio of stocks that he or she picked. This kind of portfolio most likely will have a β not equal to 1. We will call the β of this portfolio β_s.

12.3.1 Theoretical Limits to Leverage

The portfolio manager may wish to hold cash in addition to stocks. Let's use the term ξ to refer to the percentage of the equity capital that the portfolio manager holds in cash. Thus $1 - \xi$ represents the amount of the portfolio's equity invested in stocks. The maximum l and β the manager can achieve is

$$l^{\max} = \frac{\xi + \left(1 - \xi\right) m_s}{m_f} + \left(1 - \xi\right) \tag{12.10}$$

$$\beta^{\max} = [l^{\max} + (\xi - 1)]\,\beta_f + (1 - \xi)\,\beta_s \tag{12.11}$$

where m_s is the initial margin required on stocks (which is also used in determining the collateral value of stocks), and m_f is the required futures margin.[13] Thus, with $m_f = 0.05$ and $m_s = 0.50$ if the manager wants to hold 50% of the equity in cash ($\xi = 0.50$), the maximum achievable leverage ratio is 15.5. The $\beta^{\max}$, for the case of the S&P 500 assuming that $\beta_f = \beta_s = 1$, is 15.5.

---

[12] This section also applies to the case of a portfolio manager who owns an exchange-traded fund (ETF) as the main portfolio. ETFs are not preferable for index leverage because they cost more than futures. The size of the trade may be too large for the ETF to handle because ETFs are generally less liquid than futures, and ETFs do not trade after market close (futures contracts do, on GLOBEX). Investors in ETFs essentially pay two intermediaries, the broker and the specialist on the exchange, who will most likely hedge the position with futures. ETFs are clearly less efficient, and only certain circumstances call for them. For example, if the index manager is a sector portfolio manager, his or her best bet is to use sector ETFs combined with futures to get some leverage because there are no liquid sector futures contracts. For the best combination of liquid futures to leverage with, see Chincarini (2004).

[13] Since the portfolio manager can use the cash and the equity portfolio as margin for the futures positions, both need to be considered. However, the equity portfolio is worth only m_s, or 50% of cash as collateral. Thus, given that a portion ξ of the equity is held in cash, the amount of cash equivalents available for margining equals $V_t[\xi + (1 - \xi)m_s]$. This should be equal to $m_f V_t^f$ for maximum margin. Rearranging this equation for V_t and plugging it into the equation for leverage results in the equation for maximum leverage when holding a cash-and-equity portfolio. The broker-dealer may require an additional haircut on the equity as margin. Typically, a portfolio management company can have a triparty agreement with its custodian and its broker-dealer such that the custodian sets up a subaccount with securities to be posted for margin for the broker-dealer.

12.3.2 Leverage Mechanics

The portfolio manager may decide to use index futures to alter the overall beta of his or her total portfolio. To achieve the target β^* of the overall portfolio, the manager would have to satisfy

$$\beta^* = w_f \beta_f + (1 - \xi)\beta_s + \xi \underbrace{\beta_{cash}}_{=0}$$

$$= \frac{N_f q S_t}{V_t} \beta_f + (1 - \xi)\beta_s \tag{12.12}$$

By rearranging this equation, we can obtain the number of contracts that the portfolio manager will have to purchase or sell to achieve the desired β^*:

$$N_f = \frac{\left[\beta^* + (\xi - 1)\beta_s\right]V_t}{\beta_f q S_t} \tag{12.13}$$

The portfolio manager can achieve any target β^* provided that $\beta^* \leq \beta^{max}$. The portfolio manager need not hold any cash for most β ranges because the stock portfolio can be used as margin.[14]

Returning to our example from the preceding section, the manager now needs to purchase 600 contracts in order to achieve $\beta^* = 2$ with 50% of the equity in cash and a $\beta_s = 1$. This results in a portfolio that has $(q N_f F_t)$, or \$151,129,500, invested in future contracts when the price of a futures contract F_t is \$1,007.53. The purchase of the contracts requires margin collateral of $(q N_f F_t)m_f$, or \$7,556,462.[15]

12.3.3 Expected Returns and Risk

Given the benchmark return r_B, the return of the stock portfolio can be expressed as

$$r_s = \alpha_s + \beta_s r_B + \epsilon_s \tag{12.14}$$

---

[14] In fact, for $\xi = 0$, $\beta^{max} = 11$ when $m_s = 0.5$, $m_f = 0.05$, and $\beta_s = 1$ as in our example.

[15] In the case of futures, cash, and an underlying stock portfolio, leverage is defined as $l = [V_f^f + (1 - \xi)V_t]/V_t$. One can rearrange this equation in order to find the number of futures contracts required for a given target leverage l^*. It is $N_{f,t} = (V_t/q S_t)\,[l^* + (\xi - 1)]$. For futures indices with $\beta_f = 1$ (e.g., when the benchmark is the S&P 500 and the portfolio manager is using S&P 500 futures), the number of futures contracts required to achieve a certain β^* and l^* is the same.

Similarly, the return of the futures contracts can be written as

$$r_f = \alpha_f + \beta_f r_B + \epsilon_f \tag{12.15}$$

Noting that the weight of the stock portfolio is $(1 - \xi)$ and the weight of the futures contracts is $l + (\xi - 1)$, the return of the overall portfolio is[16]

$$
\begin{aligned}
r_P &= (1 - \xi)r_s + [l - (1 - \xi)]\, r_f \\
&= (1 - \xi)\alpha_s + [l - (1 - \xi)]\, \alpha_f \\
&\quad + \{(1 - \xi)\beta_s + [l - (1 - \xi)]\, \beta_f\}\, r_B + (1 - \xi)\epsilon_s + [l - (1 - \xi)]\, \epsilon_f
\end{aligned}
\tag{12.16}
$$

If the underlying futures index is also the benchmark of the portfolio, then we may assume that $\alpha_f = 0$ and that $\beta_f = 1$. We also will ignore ϵ_f because it is very small. Under these assumptions, the expected return and variance of the overall portfolio are[17]

$$E(r_P) = (1 - \xi)\alpha_s + [(1 - \xi)(\beta_s - 1) + l]\, \mu_B \tag{12.17}$$

$$V(r_P) = [(1 - \xi)(\beta_s - 1) + l]^2\, \sigma_B^2 + (1 - \xi)^2\, \omega_s^2 \tag{12.18}$$

where μ_B and σ_B denote the expected return and the standard deviation of the benchmark, and ω_s denotes the standard deviation of ϵ_s. It is clear that leverage increases the market risk of the portfolio and reduces the relative contribution of stock picking. As leverage moves from $l = 1$ (no leverage) to $l = 2$ (leverage two times equity), the expected return of the total portfolio increases by $E(r_B)$, effectively reducing the value that the portfolio manager adds by stock picking.[18] Depending on the goals of the quantitative manager, this may or may not be a good thing.

Let's assume for a moment that we already have subtracted the risk-free rate from all the return figures; the Sharpe ratio (SR) is defined as the ratio of the expected return to the standard deviation. Thus the squared Sharpe ratio would be

$$SR_P^2 = \frac{\left[(1-\xi)\alpha_s + (1-\xi)(\beta_s-1)\mu_B + l\mu_B\right]^2}{\left[(1-\xi)(\beta_s-1)+l\right]^2 \sigma_B^2 + (1-\xi)^2 \omega_s^2} \tag{12.19}$$

[16] We did not include the cash return in the expected-return calculation; see footnote 10.
[17] The expected return of the portfolio and futures is given by $E(r_s) = \alpha_s + \beta_s E(r_B)$ and $E(r_f) = \alpha_f + \beta_f E(r_B)$.
[18] For example, if $E(r_B) = 0.13$, $\alpha_s = 0.02$, and $\xi = 0$, moving from a leverage ratio of 1 to a leverage ratio of 2 reduces the contribution of α_s as a percentage of the total portfolio return from 13% to 7%.

Rearranging the expression in terms of l, we get

$$SR_P^2 = \frac{\mu_B^2 l^2 + 2\mu_B\left[(1-\xi)\alpha_s+(1-\xi)(\beta_s-1)\mu_B\right]l+\left[(1-\xi)\alpha_s+(1-\xi)(\beta_s-1)\mu_B\right]^2}{\sigma_B^2 l^2 + 2(1-\xi)(\beta_s-1)\sigma_B^2 l+(1-\xi)^2(\beta_s-1)^2\sigma_B^2+(1-\xi)^2\omega_s^2} \quad (12.20)$$

This expression suggests that as the value of l increases, the Sharpe ratio of the overall portfolio approaches the Sharpe ratio of the benchmark.[19] If the Sharpe ratio of the unleveraged portfolio were higher than the Sharpe ratio of the benchmark, then the leverage would reduce the Sharpe ratio eventually.

12.4 STOCKS, CASH, AND SINGLE-STOCK FUTURES

One of the drawbacks to using index futures to leverage a portfolio is that the relative contribution of the α is diminished in the returns of the overall portfolio. We saw in the preceding example that the contribution of stock picking can decrease by as much as 50%. Depending on the goals of QEPM, this may not be a concern, but there is a better way to leverage—through the use of single-stock futures. Leverage created with single-stock futures results in a *leveraged* α rather than just a leveraged portfolio. In other words, it generates α mojo.

Unfortunately, as of December 2020, single-stock futures do not exist in the United States; however, they do exist in other countries, including on Euronext, the European stock exchange.[20] Part of the reason that the U.S. stock futures exchange closed was a lack of investor interest, which subsequently created a set of practical problems for investors wanting to use single-stock futures. First of all, there are typically only a limited number of single-stock futures available for trading.[21] Thus, a manager may not find futures for all the stocks in his or her portfolio.

---

[19] Applying l'Hospital's rule, $\lim_{l\to\infty} SR_P^2 = \mu_B^2/\sigma_B^2 = SR_B^2$

[20] Single-stock futures trading existed from November 2002 to September 2020 in the United States through the exchange OneChicago. OneChicago, LLC, was a joint venture created by the CME, CBOE, and CBOT for the primary purpose of trading single-stock futures (former website: www.onechicago.com). Contract size was 100 shares of the underlying security. Regular trading hours were 8:30 a.m. to 3:00 p.m. Central time. The initial and maintenance margin requirements for single-stock futures were 20% of the cash value of the contract. This was higher than the margin requirement for index futures but still better than buying stocks outright. Also, there was no need to borrow the stock for shorting, nor was there an "uptick" rule.

[21] On January 31, 2005, only 122 individual stock futures were available for trading, although growth in the early years was promising. By April 2006, the number available had grown to 200 securities. Shortly before the exchange closed, on August 7, 2020, there were 1,600 listed securities available for trading, but this also included non-stock securities, such as ETFs. On Euronext, about 350 securities are available as of 2021.

TABLE 12.3

Highest-Volume Single-Stock Futures Contracts

Company Name	Ticker	Volume	Price	Percent of $100 M Portfolio
Itau Unibanco Holding SA ADR	ITUB	5749	4.69	2.696
Ambev SA ADR	ABEV	1685	2.46	0.415
Mosaic Co	MOS	306	17.19	0.526
Gap Inc.	GPS	298	14.08	0.420
Cabot Oil & Gas Corporation	COG	234	20.59	0.482
CME Group Inc	CME	214	167.15	3.577
Walmart Inc	WMT	191	129.98	2.483
Bristol-Myers Squibb Co	BMY	179	61.02	1.092
NRG Energy Inc	NRG	156	34.28	0.535
The AES Corporation	AES	153	17.16	0.263

Note: These statistics were for August 7, 2020. Price data were obtained from Bloomberg, and futures volume data were obtained from www.onechicago.com (now not available). The last column in the table is the percentage of the daily trading volume that would be represented in a $100 million portfolio. For Gap Inc., for example, the daily trading volume would represent less than 0.5% of the portfolio. Thus, if a manager would like a 1% or greater holding of GPS, his or her trade would take up the entire day's trading volume. The formula is percentage $= \dfrac{100 \cdot \text{volume} \cdot \text{price}}{100 \text{ M}}$.

Second, single-stock futures that do exist have less trading liquidity than index futures.[22] Table 12.3 lists some of the major single-stock futures and their volumes on August 7, 2020, shortly before the exchange closed. The table also includes the percentage of a $100 million portfolio that the daily volume represents. Even the third most-traded security has a volume that represents only 2.69% of a $100 million portfolio. For reasonable holdings of around 1% or 2% in a stock, the portfolio manager would have difficulties using single-stock futures contracts to create a leveraged position. This problem becomes more pronounced as one moves down the list of most-traded securities.[23]

12.4.1 Theoretical Limits of Leverage

The theoretical limits to leveraging with single-stock futures are very similar to the limits using index futures. There are three essential differences between the two cases, however. The first is that

---

[22] On August 7, 2020, the total volume of all single-security futures was 11,699 contracts. Furthermore, only 84 contracts had a positive volume on that particular day. The open interest was 149,953.

[23] One method for a portfolio manager to deal with the low trading volume is to place a series of limit orders on individual stock futures and have them executed.

individual stock futures have initial margin requirements that are higher than index futures.[24] The second difference is that single-stock futures allow the manager to increase the maximum β by specifically leveraging higher-β stocks or decrease it by specifically leveraging lower-β stocks. Leveraging single stocks according to their β's is also a sensible way to leverage one's α if one already has chosen the optimal stock weights. A third concern that is unique to leveraging with single-stock futures is that if the futures are not actively traded, then it will be possible to achieve only partial leverage. For the time being, we will assume that the futures are traded actively enough for the portfolio to achieve maximum leverage.

For leveraging a single security, the formulas for the maximum leverage and maximum β for single-stock futures are identical to Eqs. (12.10) and (12.11), but with the single-stock futures margin requirement replacing the index futures margin requirement. For these leverage formulas to be the same for the entire portfolio when leveraging single-stock futures, all stocks must be leveraged in relative proportion to their weights in the portfolio.

12.4.2 Leverage Mechanics

There are numerous ways to weight single-stock futures in order to achieve the desired β level. In this subsection we consider three specific scenarios that a portfolio manager might encounter, each requiring a different weighting scheme.

In one scenario, all single-stock futures contracts are sufficiently liquid to use for leverage. In this case, to achieve his or her target β^* for the overall portfolio, the manager must purchase the following amount of futures contracts[25]:

$$N_i = \frac{\left[\beta^* + (\xi - 1)\beta_s\right]V_t w_i}{\beta_s q_s p_{i,t}} \tag{12.21}$$

In this equation, q_s is the contract multiplier for single-stock futures, which is equal to 100, $p_{i,t}$ is the price of stock i, β_s is the β of the stock portfolio with respect to the benchmark, and w_i is the weight of stock i in the equity portfolio. The preceding formula indicates that

---

[24] Before OneChicago closed, the single-stock futures requirement was 20%. ICE Futures Europe has a margin requirement of 5%–10%, and the Euronext exchange has other margin requirements.

[25] See Appendix 12B for the derivation of these equations.

the portfolio manager may purchase single-stock futures for each stock in proportion to the weight of the stock in the equity portfolio.

The second scenario is that only a subset N_1 of the N stocks in the portfolio is available for single-stock futures trading. The manager therefore uses only the stocks with futures to achieve the desired β. To achieve his or her target β^* for the overall portfolio, he or she must purchase the following amount of futures contracts:

$$N_i = \frac{\left[\beta^* + (\xi - 1)\beta_s\right]V_t \tilde{w}_i}{\tilde{\beta}_s q_s p_{i,t}} \tag{12.22}$$

where $\tilde{w}_i$ is the relative weight of the subset of stocks whose futures contracts are bought from or sold to each other (that is, $\tilde{w}_i = w_i / \Sigma_{j=1}^{N_1} w_j$), $\tilde{\beta}_s$ is the weighted average β of the subset of stocks whose futures contracts are bought and sold (that is, $\tilde{\beta}_s = \Sigma_{j=1}^{N_1} \tilde{w}_i \beta_i$), and all other variables are as defined previously.

In the third scenario, there are futures for some of the stocks in the portfolio, and the manager decides to combine single-stock futures with index futures to achieve the desired leverage. He or she purchases the following amounts of single-stock futures contracts and index futures, respectively:

$$N_i = \frac{\left[\beta^* + (\xi - 1)\beta_s\right]V_t \tilde{w}_i}{q_s p_{i,t}\left[\tilde{\beta}_s + \left(\dfrac{1 - \sum_{i=1}^{N_1} w_i}{\sum_{i=1}^{N_1} w_i}\right)\beta_f\right]} \tag{12.23}$$

$$N_f = \left(\frac{1 - \sum_{i=1}^{N_1} w_i}{\sum_{i=1}^{N_1} w_i}\right)\frac{\sum_{i=1}^{N_1} N_i q_s p_{i,t}}{q S_t} \tag{12.24}$$

An example might help to further illustrate these three scenarios. Suppose that the benchmark is the S&P 500 and that we have a simple five-stock portfolio consisting of the Mosaic Company (MOS), the Gap (GPS), Cabot Oil & Gas (COG), CME Group (CME), and Walmart (WMT). Table 12.4 contains the portfolio and the weights of each stock in the portfolio. Using the preceding formulas, we can compute the number of futures contracts required to achieve our desired β^*. As in previous examples, let's assume that our desired $\beta^* = 2$ and that there is $100 million in equity capital. The actual portfolio β of the five stocks in this example is 0.83, and the β_i for each of the stock's futures contract is listed in the table (we assume that it is the same as the underlying stock's β). The prices of each stock are also listed in the table. For this example, we do not round the futures contracts to the nearest whole number. Of course, in reality, you would have to do this.

Let's walk through the example for each of the three scenarios just outlined. Under the first scenario, in which we can use all the stocks' futures contracts to create leverage, we purchase a total

TABLE 12.4

Example of Single-Stock Leverage in a Simple Portfolio

		Method 1			
Ticker	w_i	β_i	p_i	$N_{f,i}$	$V_{f,i}$
MOS	0.200	1.73	17.19	16,412.71	$28,213,445.19
GPS	0.200	1.56	14.08	20,037.96	$28,213,445.19
COG	0.300	0.27	20.59	20,553.75	$42,320,167.78
CME	0.100	0.30	167.15	843.96	$14,106,722.59
WMT	0.200	0.31	129.98	2,170.60	$28,213,445.19
Total		0.83			$141,067,225.94
		Method 2			
Ticker	$\tilde{w}_i$	β_i	p_i	$N_{f,i}$	$V_{f,i}$
MOS	0.286	1.73	17.19	18,448.72	$31,713,355.02
GPS	0.286	1.56	14.08	22,523.69	$31,713,355.02
COG	0.429	0.27	20.59	23,103.46	$47,570,032.53
CME	0.000	0.30	167.15	0.00	$0.00
WMT	0.000	0.31	129.98	0.00	$0.00
		1.05			$110,996,742.57
		Method 3			
Ticker	$\tilde{w}_i$	β_i	p_i	$N_{f,i}$	$V_{f,i}$
MOS	0.286	1.73	17.19	13,117.15	$22,548,386.65
GPS	0.286	1.56	14.08	16,014.48	$22,548,386.65
COG	0.429	0.27	20.59	16,426.70	$33,822,579.98
CME	0.000	0.30	167.15	0.00	$0.00
WMT	0.000	0.31	129.98	0.00	$0.00
S&P 500		1.00	3351	40.37	$33,822,579.98
Total		1.05			$112,741,933.27

Note: The variables in the table represent attributes of the stocks. $\tilde{w}_i$ represents the stock weight in the underlying equity portfolio; β_i represents the stock's β; p_i represents the stock's actual price as of August 7, 2020; $N_{f,i}$ represents the number of single-stock futures contracts purchased or sold; $V_{f,i}$ represents the notional value of the futures contracts purchased; and $\tilde{w}_i$ represents the relative weight of the subset of securities whose single-stock futures are purchased. The total β's represent the weighted-average β of the subset of stocks whose futures are purchased. In method 1, this corresponds to the β of the underlying stock portfolio.

futures value of \$141,067,225.94 to achieve our desired $\beta^* = 2$. Since the underlying portfolio has a β that is lower than 1 with respect to the benchmark, we need more than an equal amount in dollars to achieve our desired leverage. The number of contracts of each single-stock futures is listed in the table.

Under the second scenario, we assume that some of the single-stock futures—say, CME and WMT—are not liquid enough to trade. Thus we can use only the other three securities' futures to achieve our desired leverage. In this case we purchase a total value of \$110,996,742.57 of futures. This consists of 18,449, 22,524, and 23,103 contracts of MOS, GPS, and COG, respectively. Although in this scenario we have again achieved our desired $\beta^* = 2$, we have leveraged the portfolio disproportionately. The resulting portfolio α is tilted toward the first three stocks.

Under the third scenario, we continue to use the first three single-stock futures, but we also use the index futures of the S&P 500 to achieve the desired β^*. In this case we purchase a total value of \$78,919,353 of the single-stock futures and \$33,822,580 of the index futures (40 contracts). This also achieves our desired goal, but we have diluted the overall α of the portfolio by using index futures.

12.4.3 Expected Returns, Risk, and α Mojo

In the first scenario, the total portfolio is composed of the stock portfolio with the weight of $1 - \xi$ and the portfolio of single-stock futures with the weight of $l - \xi + 1$. Recall that given the benchmark return r_B, the return of the stock portfolio can be expressed as

$$r_s = \alpha_s + \beta_s r_B + \epsilon_s \tag{12.25}$$

The return of the single-stock futures portfolio is essentially identical to the return of the stock portfolio. For simplicity, we assume[26]

$$r_{sf} = \alpha_s + \beta_s r_B + \epsilon_s \tag{12.26}$$

Calculation of the expected return and the variance of the total portfolio is straightforward in this case. Given the weight of the stock portfolio and the single-stock futures portfolio, the total portfolio return is

$$
\begin{aligned}
r_P &= (1 - \xi)r_s + (l - 1 + \xi)r_{sf} \\
&= l\alpha_s + l\beta_s r_B + l\epsilon_s
\end{aligned} \tag{12.27}
$$

---

[26] This assumption is true as long as we ignore basis risk.

The expected return and the variance of the total portfolio are

$$E(r_p) = l\alpha_s + l\beta_s\,\mu_B = lE(r_s) \tag{12.28}$$

$$V(r_p) = l^2\beta_s^2\sigma_B^2 + l^2\omega_s^2 = l^2V(r_s) \tag{12.29}$$

where μ_B and σ_B denote the expected return and the standard deviation of the benchmark, and ω_s denotes the standard deviation of ϵ_s. We can easily calculate the Sharpe ratio (SR) of the total portfolio as well. Assuming that the risk-free rate has been subtracted already, the Sharpe ratio is simply the ratio of $E(r_p)$ to $\sqrt{V(r_p)}$:

$$SR_p = \frac{l\alpha_s + l\beta_s\mu_B}{\sqrt{l^2\beta_s^2\sigma_B^2 + l^2\omega_s^2}} = SR_s \tag{12.30}$$

Thus the Sharpe ratio of the total portfolio is identical to the Sharpe ratio of the stock portfolio, regardless of the leverage. That is, the leverage does not change the Sharpe ratio in the first scenario.

In the second scenario, the total portfolio is again composed of the stock portfolio and the single-stock futures portfolio. The weights of these portfolios are identical to the first scenario. The difference is the composition of the single-stock futures portfolio. The single-stock futures portfolio is N_1 stock futures that are liquid enough. The weights of these futures are given by $\tilde{w}_i = w_i/\sum_{j=1}^{N1} w_j$, $i = 1, ..., N_1$.

It will be useful to think of the stock portfolio as composed of two subportfolios: the portfolio of stocks with liquid futures and the portfolio of stocks without liquid futures. Let us call the first portfolio $s1$ and the second $s2$. Then $s1$ is the portfolio of N_1 stocks with the weights $\tilde{w}_i$ defined earlier. $s2$ is the portfolio of the remaining stocks with the weights $\tilde{w} = w_i/\sum_{j=N_1+1}^{N} w_j$, $i = N_1 + 1, ..., N$. Defining $\psi = \sum_{j=1}^{N_1} w_j$, we may express the return of the stock portfolio as

$$\begin{aligned} r_s &= \psi r_{s1} + (1 - \psi)r_{s2} \\ &= [\psi\alpha_{s1} + (1 - \psi)\alpha_{s2}] + [\psi\beta_{s1} + (1 - \psi)\,\beta_{s2}]r_B \\ &\quad + \psi\epsilon_{s1} + (1 - \psi)\epsilon_{s2} \end{aligned} \tag{12.31}$$

Assuming that the return of the single-stock futures is identical to the return of the underlying stocks, the return of the single-stock futures portfolio is identical to the return of portfolio $s1$.[27] Thus we may express the return of the single-stock futures portfolio as

---

[27] Note that the weights of futures in the futures portfolio are identical to the weights of stocks in portfolio $s1$.

$$r_{sf} = r_{s1} = \alpha_{s1} + \beta_{s1}r_B + \epsilon_{s1} \tag{12.32}$$

Now, calculation of the expected return and the variance of the total portfolio is straightforward. Given the weight of the stock portfolio and the single-stock futures portfolio, the total portfolio return is

$$\begin{aligned}
r_P &= (1 - \xi)r_s + [l - (1 - \xi)]r_{sf} \\
&= [l - (1 - \xi)(1 - \psi)]r_{s1} + (1 - \xi)(1 - \psi)r_{s2} \\
&= [l - (1 - \xi)(1 - \psi)]\alpha_{s1} + (1 - \xi)(1 - \psi)\alpha_{s2} \quad (12.33) \\
&\quad + \{[l - (1 - \xi)(1 - \psi)]\beta_{s1} + (1 - \xi)(1 - \psi)\beta_{s2}\}r_B \\
&\quad + [l - (1 - \xi)(1 - \psi)]\epsilon_{s1} + (1 - \xi)(1 - \psi)\epsilon_{s2}
\end{aligned}$$

The expected return and the variance of the total portfolio are

$$\begin{aligned}
E(r_P) &= [l - (1 - \xi)(1 - \psi)]\alpha_{s1} + (1 - \xi)(1 - \psi)\alpha_{s2} \\
&\quad + \{[l - (1 - \xi)(1 - \psi)]\beta_{s1} + (1 - \xi)(1 - \psi)\beta_{s2}\}\mu_B \quad (12.34)
\end{aligned}$$

$$\begin{aligned}
V(r_P) &= \{[l - (1 - \xi)(1 - \psi)]\beta_{s1} + (1 - \xi)(1 - \psi)\beta_{s2}\}^2\sigma_B^2 \\
&\quad + [l - (1 - \xi)(1 - \psi)]^2\omega_{s1}^2 + [(1 - \xi)(1 - \psi)]^2\omega_{s2}^2 \\
&\quad + 2[l - (1 - \xi)(1 - \psi)][(1 - \xi)(1 - \psi)]\omega_{s12} \quad (12.35)
\end{aligned}$$

where ω_{s12} is the covariance between ϵ_{s1} and ϵ_{s2}.

Assuming that the risk-free rate already has been subtracted, the Sharpe ratio is simply the ratio of $E(r_P)$ to $\sqrt{V(r_P)}$, and the squared Sharpe ratio is the ratio of $E(r_P)^2$ to $V(r_P)$. Expressing the squared Sharpe ratio as a function of the leverage l, one can find the relationship:

$$SR_P^2 \rightarrow \frac{\left(\alpha_{s1} + \beta_{s1}\mu_B\right)^2}{\beta_{s1}^2\sigma_B^2 + \omega_{s1}^2} = SR_{s1}^2 \tag{12.36}$$

as the leverage becomes large.[28] That is, as the leverage gets larger, the risk-return relationship of the total portfolio becomes very similar to that of portfolio s1, the portfolio of stocks with liquid futures.

In the third scenario, the total portfolio is composed of the stock portfolio with weight $1 - \xi$, the index future with weight $(1 - \psi)(l - 1 + \xi)$, and the single-stock futures portfolio with weight

---

[28] Use L'Hospital's rule to show this.

$\psi(l - 1 + \xi)$. The single-stock futures portfolio is the same as the one in the second scenario, that is, the portfolio of $N1$ stock futures that are liquid enough, with weights $\tilde{w}_i = w_i/\sum_{j=1}^{N1} w_j$, $i = 1, ..., N_1$. We will assume that the futures index return is identical to the benchmark return[29] (i.e., $r_f = r_B$). The returns for the stock portfolio and for the single-stock futures portfolio are identical to those of the second scenario, as described in Eqs. (12.31) and (12.32).

The return of the total portfolio can be calculated using the weights of the three subportfolios:

$$
\begin{aligned}
r_P &= (1 - \xi)r_s + (1 - \psi)(l - 1 + \xi)r_f + \psi\,(l - 1 + \xi)r_{sf} \\
&= \psi l r_{s1} + (1 - \xi)(1 - \psi)r_{s2} + (1 - \psi)\,(l - 1 + \xi)r_B \\
&= \psi l \alpha_{s1} + (1 - \xi)(1 - \psi)\alpha_{s2} \qquad\qquad (12.37) \\
&\quad + [\psi l \beta_{s1} + (1 - \xi)(1 - \psi)\beta_{s2} + (1 - \psi)(l - 1 + \xi)]r_B \\
&\quad + \psi l \epsilon_{s1} + (1 - \xi)(1 - \psi)\epsilon_{s2}
\end{aligned}
$$

The expected return and the variance of the total portfolio are

$$
\begin{aligned}
E(r_P) &= \psi l \alpha_{s1} + (1 - \xi)(1 - \psi)\alpha_{s2} \\
&\quad [\psi l \beta_{s1} + (1 - \xi)(1 - \psi)\beta_{s2} + (1 - \psi)(l - 1 + \xi)]\mu_B \quad (12.38)
\end{aligned}
$$

$$
\begin{aligned}
V(r_P) &= [\psi l \beta_{s1} + (1 - \xi)(1 - \psi)\beta_{s2} + (1 - \psi)(l - 1 + \xi)]^2\sigma_B^2 \\
&\quad + \psi^2 l^2 \omega_{s1}^2 + (1 - \xi)^2\,(1 - \psi)^2\omega_{s2}^2 \\
&\quad + 2\psi l(1 - \xi)(1 - \psi)\omega_{s12} \qquad\qquad (12.39)
\end{aligned}
$$

where ω_{s12} is the covariance between ϵ_{s1} and ϵ_{s2} as defined before.

Assuming that the risk-free rate already has been subtracted, the squared Sharpe ratio is the ratio of $E(r_P)^2$ to $V(r_P)$. Expressing the squared Sharpe ratio as a function of the leverage l, one can find the following relationship:

$$
SR_P^2 \rightarrow \frac{\left\{\psi\alpha_{s1} + \left[\psi\beta_{s1} + (1-\psi)\right]\mu_B\right\}^2}{\left[\psi\beta_{s1} + (1-\psi)\right]^2\sigma_B^2 + \psi^2\omega_{s1}^2} \qquad (12.40)
$$

as the leverage increases. Note that the right-hand side of this equation can be interpreted as the Sharpe ratio of a portfolio made of $s1$ (the portfolio of stocks for which liquid futures are available) and the benchmark, with the respective weights of ψ and $1 - \psi$. That is, the Sharpe ratio of the total portfolio approaches the

---

[29] We are assuming that the underlying security of the futures contract is the benchmark and that there is no basis risk.

Sharpe ratio of $\psi r_{s1} + (1 - \psi)r_B$ as the leverage increases. This is not surprising. As the leverage increases, the portfolio is dominated by the stocks with liquid futures available and the benchmark.

From these formulas, we find that the portfolio's α gets the biggest boost from leverage that uses all single-stock futures (scenario 1). When futures are available for all the portfolio's stocks and all the futures have enough trading liquidity, the best approach is to leverage only with single-stock futures. It is the ultimate form of α mojo. Leveraging with a subset of futures provides the next-best α boost, but it may be suboptimal.

12.5 STOCKS, CASH, INDIVIDUAL STOCKS, AND SINGLE-STOCK AND BASKET SWAPS

A portfolio manager who produces positive α may wish to leverage his or her portfolio for a variety of reasons. As we have seen, one of the drawbacks to using index futures for leverage is that it saps the relative α contribution. Although single-stock futures would resolve this problem, they may not have enough breadth or liquidity to serve as a realistic solution. In this section we discuss two more related alternatives to leveraging. The first alternative is to buy individual stocks on margin; the second is to create a series of individual stock swap contracts with a broker-dealer.

12.5.1 Margining Individual Stocks

Buying stocks on margin requires an initial margin of m_s, which according to Regulation T is currently 50%.[30] A manager technically could purchase his or her entire basket of securities on margin, effectively creating a leveraged position as high as $l = 2$. Thus, margining securities allows for any amount of leverage between $l = 1$ and $l = 2$. The benefit of this approach is that the leverage does not diminish the relative α contribution—in fact, margining securities leverages the α of the portfolio manager. The drawback of this form of leverage is that it is more costly than leveraging with index futures. The broker-dealer charges the broker call rate as interest on the margined loans, a rate that is typically higher than

---

[30] Regulation T is the rule established by the Federal Reserve Board that limits the amount that an investor can borrow to establish a new position in a security.

the futures carry rate (i.e., the implied repo rate).[31] Thus, for an index manager who wants to leverage the portfolio, index futures are clearly the better choice. However, a manager who creates α by picking stocks should weigh the extra interest costs of the margin against the strength of his or her α.

12.5.2 Single-Stock and Basket Swaps

In common parlance, a *swap* is an exchange of one thing for another. In financial markets, a swap is an agreement between two parties to exchange payments with each other. The most common swaps are interest-rate and currency swaps. With interest-rate swaps, it is usually the case that one party pays fixed interest and the other party pays floating interest. With currency swaps, one party makes payment in one currency, and the other party makes payment in another.[32]

Equity swaps are usually set up so that one party pays the return of an equity index, whereas the other party pays fixed or floating interest on the notional principal. Equity swaps are a convenient way for portfolio managers to increase or decrease their exposure to the equity index without actually buying or selling equities. For example, a typical equity swap might have a broker-dealer pay fund X the total return on the S&P 500 in exchange for fund X paying the broker-dealer some reference interest rate (say, the 6-month LIBOR rate plus a spread).[33] The swap can be customized many different ways.

Equity swaps can be structured for equity indices or for individual equity securities.[34] The portfolio manager can construct a customized swap with the broker-dealer for a basket of securities (Fig. 12.2.) This basket or portfolio of securities in the swap is the same as the basket of securities that the portfolio manager believes will outperform the market. The broker-dealer will pay the portfolio

---

[31] The cost of carry for a futures contract is the implied rate in the *fair-value equation*,
$$F_t = S_t e^{r(T-t)}.$$

[32] For a more detailed discussion of swaps, the reader is referred to Hull (2005), Cox and Rubenstein (1985), Wilmott et al. (1993), and McDonald (2003).

[33] LIBOR is the London Inter-Bank Offer Rate, the short-term interest rate at which many international banks borrow from each other. Due to the highly publicized LIBOR scandal that broke in 2012, it might be more common to see the new overnight benchmark called the Secured Overnight Financing Rate (SOFR) being used.

[34] Many broker-dealers, including Goldman Sachs, Citibank, and Credit Suisse, structure such equity products. Jefferies, Thomas Weisel Partners, and Raymond James are better for mid-cap or small-cap securities.

FIGURE 12.2

Example of flows from an equity basket swap.

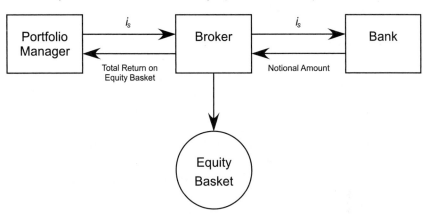

manager the return of the basket of securities during the swap period, whereas the manager will pay the broker-dealer some interest rate i_s typically specified as LIBOR $+ x$. (Alternatively, it might be SOFR $+ x$.) The broker-dealer also will charge the portfolio manager some additional fees for setting up the trades because he or she must hedge his or her position. The broker-dealer typically will hedge the position by buying the actual equity basket of securities and taking on a little risk or by buying a futures contract in proportion to the equity basket and taking on slightly more risk. Collateral for such a trade can be arranged through the custodian of the portfolio manager or directly through the broker-dealer.

The swap periods should match the portfolio's rebalancing frequency. If a portfolio manager rebalances his or her portfolio monthly, the swap should be reset monthly. With a monthly swap, the broker-dealer will pay the portfolio manager the return of the basket at the end of the month, and the portfolio manager will pay the interest cost i_s. The portfolio manager then will reconstruct his or her optimal portfolio, send a new basket list to the broker-dealer, and construct a new swap for the following month. In this arrangement, the portfolio manager can invest directly in the equities and construct a swap for leverage, or he or she just can hold cash and leverage the entire position with individual stock or basket swaps.

Equity swaps have several advantages over other means of leveraging a portfolio. With swaps on a basket of securities, the portfolio manager can alter his or her α directly by choosing a basket of his or her actual optimal portfolio of securities. This is another kind of α mojo that index futures do not provide. Also, leveraging with equity swaps is usually cheaper than margining stocks, and it is an alternative for securities that do not have liquid single-stock futures contracts.

12.6 STOCKS, CASH, AND OPTIONS

A manager who has built a portfolio may wish to leverage the portfolio yet another way. Rather than using index futures to increase the market exposure of the entire portfolio, the manager may wish to leverage the portfolio with index options. The reason to do this is twofold. First of all, options have the potential for a nonlinear payoff. They can leverage returns on the upside without leveraging them on the downside. The second reason is that options offer a greater magnitude of leverage than do index futures. This kind of flexibility comes at a cost, though, because options are pricey.

Figure 12.3 shows how the payoff is altered with a call option on an underlying portfolio. The payoff of the overall portfolio is

FIGURE 12.3

Portfolio payoffs with and without leverage using call options.

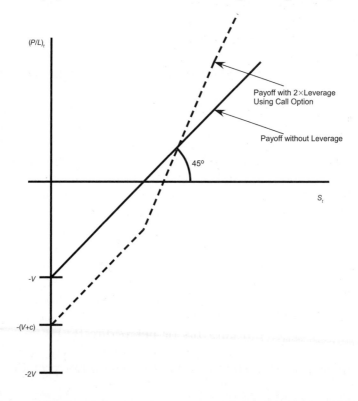

leveraged two times for upward movements in the index but continues to be unlevered for downward movements.

The number of call option contracts required on a given index to achieve a given level of β^* for the entire portfolio given a current β_s for the stock portion of the portfolio will be given by

$$N_O = \frac{\left[\beta^* + (\xi - 1)\beta_s\right]V_t}{\beta_O q_O S_t}$$

$$= \frac{\left[\beta^* + (\xi - 1)\beta_s\right]V_t}{\Delta_O \beta_I q_O S_t}$$

(12.41)

where N_O represents the number of call option contracts to purchase, q_O represents the option contract multiplier, β^* equals the desired level of exposure, β_s is the β of the stock portfolio, Δ_O is the delta of the call option, β_I is the β of the underlying index with respect to the benchmark, and $\beta_O = \Delta_O \beta_I$ is just the delta approximation for the β of the option contract.[35]

For example, suppose that we use the same numbers as in the preceding example. Thus the S&P 500 is trading at 1,000, the portfolio manager would like to hold 50% cash, and the desired $\beta^* = 2$. Normally, a portfolio manager simply will look up the prices of traded call options and either use a standard Black-Scholes Δ or compute his or her own. Suppose that the price of an at-the-money call option (i.e., $K = 1,000$) was $c = 43.58$. Suppose that the Δ of this call equaled 0.55.[36] Using our formula, we find that we should have

$$N_O = \frac{\left[2 + (0.5 - 1) \cdot 1\right]100 \, M}{0.55 \cdot 1 \cdot 100 \cdot 1,000} = 1819.05$$

(12.42)

Thus the portfolio manager should purchase 1,819 calls on the S&P 500. This will provide the desired leverage of 2.

Leveraging through options offers the major advantage of magnifying only the upside. The chief danger of leverage, as explained at the outset of this chapter, is that it creates the possibility of a very hard fall when the portfolio runs into negative returns.

---

[35] Index option contracts are 100 times the actual index. Thus $q_O = 100$. All the major index options are European-style options, except the S&P 100, which is an American-style option. For more details, please consult the Chicago Board Options Exchange (www.cboe.com) and/or a derivatives textbook.

[36] In reality, it will be very unlikely to find a call option that is perfectly at the money (i.e., strike price equal to index value); thus a portfolio manager will have to find the option with the closest moneyness.

With options leverage, though, the portfolio loses only what it would lose anyway. Perhaps this sounds too good to be true. Indeed, the cost of this kind of insurance is steep. The options in this example have a three-month duration. They would cost a total of $100 \cdot 1,819 \cdot 43.58 = \$7,927,202$. Leverage with downside protection costs $8 million dollars for a $100 million portfolio. This is clearly an expensive method of leveraging, feasible only in specific cases in which the risk of the portfolio calls for downside protection.

12.7 REBALANCING

The portfolio manager has to rebalance the portfolio regularly to maintain the desired leverage position. The frequency of the rebalancing depends on how closely and how long he or she wants to track the β^* level. If he or she is leveraging only over the short term, he or she may just close the position at the end of his or her short-term time horizon without rebalancing. Portfolio managers offering the leveraged portfolio to clients through a mutual fund, however, may wish to rebalance daily.[37] Other portfolio managers may believe that leverage will offer higher long-run returns and might choose to rebalance monthly. In this section we describe methods for rebalancing at intervals between t and $t + k$, where k can be any period the portfolio manager chooses from $k = 1$ (1 day) to $k = 20$ (1 month, in business days) or longer.

12.7.1 Cash and Futures

For the simplest case of using cash and futures, we know that the β_p of the portfolio at time t will be

$$\beta_{P,t} = \frac{N_{f,t}qS_t}{V_t}\beta_f \qquad (12.43)$$

where subscript t indicates the time period t of each variable. At $t + k$, some of the variables will have changed. In particular, the total portfolio value V_{t+k} and the value of the index underlying the futures S_{t+k} will have changed.

---

[37] Since we wrote the first edition of this book, many mutual fund and ETF companies offering daily leverage were sued due to a discrepancy between what investors may have expected and the actual returns of the levered portfolios. For more info, see Cheng and Madhaven (2009), Avellaneda and Zhang (2010), Shum and Kang (2012), Tang amd Zu (2013), and Bruno et al. (2014).

On day $t + k$, the portfolio manager will have to compute the desired number of futures contracts required to maintain his or her desired exposure. To satisfy

$$\beta^* = \frac{N_{f,t+k} q S_{t+k}}{V_{t+k}} \beta_f \qquad (12.44)$$

the number of future contracts required is

$$N_{f,t+k} = \frac{\beta^* V_{t+k}}{\beta_f q S_{t+k}} \qquad (12.45)$$

The portfolio manager needs to purchase $N_{f,t+k} - N_{f,t}$ contracts, which can be expressed as

$$
\begin{aligned}
N_{f,t+k} - N_{f,t} &= \frac{\beta^* V_{t+k}}{\beta_f q S_{t+k}} - \frac{\beta^* V_t}{\beta_f q S_t} \\
&= \frac{\beta^*}{\beta_f q} \left(\frac{V_{t+k}}{S_{t+k}} - \frac{V_t}{S_t} \right) \\
&= \frac{\beta^*}{\beta_f q} \frac{V_t}{S_{t+k}} \left(\frac{V_{t+k} - V_t}{V_t} - \frac{S_{t+k} - S_t}{S_t} \right)
\end{aligned}
\qquad (12.46)
$$

This equation says that whether the portfolio manager will have to purchase or sell futures contracts (i.e., whether $N_{f,t+k}$ $N_{f,t}$ is positive or negative) depends on the total return of the portfolio $(V_{t+k} - V_t)/V_t$ and the return of the underlying futures index $(S_{t+k} - S_t)/S_t$. The value of the total portfolio at time $t + k$ is given as

$$V_{t+k} = N_{f,t} q (F_{t+k} - F_t) + I_{t,t+k} V_t \qquad (12.47)$$

where F_{t+k} is the price of the futures contract at time $t + k$, F_t is the price of the futures contract at time t, and $I_{t,t+k} V_t$ represents the interest earned on the margin cash and the other cash of the portfolio at rates i' and i, respectively.[38] Thus the return on the total portfolio is given as

$$\frac{V_{t+k} - V_t}{V_t} = \frac{N_{f,t} q S_t}{V_t} \frac{F_{t+k} - F_t}{S_t} + \left(I_{t,t+k} - 1 \right) \qquad (12.48)$$

---

[38] The actual formula for $I_{t,t+k}$ is $I_{t,t+k} = \left[\left(\frac{m_f q N_{f,t} F_t}{V_t} \right) \left(e^{i' \frac{k}{360}} - e^{i \frac{k}{360}} \right) + e^{i \frac{k}{360}} \right]$. This is simply 1 plus the continuously compounded interest from both the cash position and the margin position, where margin interest i' is typically lower than cash interest i.

The first part of the right-hand side ($N_{f,t}\, qS_t/V_t$) is simply the leverage ratio. Assuming no basis risk, we know that $[(F_{t+k} - F_t)/S_t] = [(S_{t+k} - S_t)/S_t]$, and we can make this substitution into our equation.[39] Thus

$$\frac{V_{t+k} - V_t}{V_t} = l\frac{S_{t+k} - S_t}{S_t} + \left(I_{t,t+k} - 1\right) \tag{12.49}$$

Now we may rewrite Eq. (12.46) as follows[40]:

$$N_{f,t+k} - N_{f,t} = \frac{\beta^*}{\beta_f q}\frac{V_t}{S_{t+k}}\left[(l-1)\frac{S_{t+k} - S_t}{S_t} + \left(I_{t,t+k} - 1\right)\right] \tag{12.50}$$

From Eq. (12.50) we can make the following general statement: For a leveraged position ($l > 1$) and a positive return on the index $[(S_{t+k} - S_t)/S_t > 0]$, the portfolio manager must purchase more futures contracts to maintain β^* or the desired leverage. On the other hand, the portfolio manager will have to sell futures contracts if the index return is sufficiently negative. Since we have a leveraged position, any time the target β^* is greater than the β of the futures contract, we may state the following: If the target β^* is greater than the β of the futures contract, a positive return on the index will lower β over time, and the portfolio manager will have to purchase more futures contracts. A negative index return will increase β over time, and the portfolio manager will have to sell futures contracts. Table 12.5 illustrates the various general rules.

TABLE 12.5

Rebalancing Actions to Achieve Desired β^*

	$r_{t,t+k} > 0$	$r_{t,t+k} < 0$
$\beta^* > \beta_t$	Buy futures	Sell futures
$\beta^* < \beta_t$	Sell futures	Buy futures

---

[39] Basis risk is the risk that the basis will change over time. The *basis* is defined as the futures rate of the index minus the spot rate of the index. That is, $B_t = F_t - S_t$. If the futures are held to expiration, the futures price will converge to the spot price, and there is no basis risk. However, at any time prior to futures expiration, the basis can change, and this introduces basis risk because the futures movement and spot movement do not offset each other. This can be an issue for hedgers or investors who use leverage. Basis risk can also affect the effectiveness of rolling over a hedge. In reality, the basis moves even if just by a little bit owing to contraction of the time until maturity, but this is very insignificant. When the basis risk is 0, it implies that $r^f_{t,t+k} = r_{t,t+k}$.

[40] Since we are dealing with only cash and futures, the leverage ratio reduces to just l.

Suppose that there is a portfolio manager whose benchmark is the S&P 500 and who would like to use S&P 500 futures to leverage his or her portfolio. The following conditions exist: $\beta_f = 1$ for the S&P 500 futures contracts; the multiplier for the contracts is $q = 250$; the beta the manager would like to achieve is $\beta^* = 2$; the value of the equity capital is \$100 million; the S&P 500 and the futures contract are trading at 1,000 and 1,007.53, respectively, on day t; and the continuously compounded annual interest rates on margin and cash are $i' = 0.02$ and $i = 0.03$, respectively. To achieve the desired β of the total portfolio on day t, the manager must purchase exactly $N_{f,t} = \beta^* V_t / \beta_f q S_t = 2 \cdot 100{,}000{,}000 / (1 \cdot 250 \cdot 1{,}000) = 800$ contracts. This will create a portfolio with a $\beta_p = 2$ and a leverage of 2 as well.

Suppose that one day has passed; it is now day $t + 1$. The S&P 500 and futures values have increased by 5% in one day, so the β exposure has changed. The manager wants to readjust it back to 2. Using our formula, we know that the portfolio manager would have to purchase a net amount of futures contracts. This value is given by

$$N_{f,t+k} - N_{f,t} = \frac{\beta^*}{\beta_f q}\left(\frac{V_{t+k}}{S_{t+k}} - \frac{V_t}{S_t}\right)$$

$$= \frac{2}{1 \cdot 250}\left(\frac{110{,}083{,}335.75}{1{,}050} - \frac{100{,}000{,}000}{1{,}000}\right) = 38.73 \qquad (12.51)$$

Now, in reality, the portfolio manager will have to buy either 38 or 39 contracts, unless he or she uses S&P 500 E-minis to fine-tune the purchase. It is better to round to the nearest integer, so he or she probably will purchase 39 contracts.

12.7.2 Stocks, Cash, and Futures

A very similar change in the β of the overall portfolio will occur with the portfolio of stocks, cash, and futures.[41] At $t + k$, the futures prices and portfolio values will have changed. In this case, the portfolio manager actually may change the composition of the underlying portfolio; thus β_s may change from time t to $t + k$. The net change in futures contracts becomes

---

[41] The analysis in this subsection follows also for a portfolio manager who invests in ETFs, cash, and futures.

$$N_{f,t+k} - N_{f,t} = \frac{\beta^*}{\beta_f q}\left(\frac{V_{t+k}}{S_{t+k}} - \frac{V_t}{S_t}\right) + \frac{1}{\beta_f q}\left(\frac{(\xi_{t+k}-1)\beta_{s,t+k}V_{t+k}}{S_{t+k}} - \frac{(\xi_t-1)\beta_{s,t}V_t}{S_t}\right) \quad (12.52)$$

where $\beta_{s,t}$ and $\beta_{s,t+k}$ are the stock portfolio β at times t and $t + k$, respectively. This is more complicated to analyze. However, if we assume that the stock portfolio β is the same or similar between time t and time $t + k$ and that the percentage held in cash is the same, then the net purchases of futures contracts simplifies to

$$N_{f,t+k} - N_{f,t} = \frac{\beta^* + (\xi_{t+k}-1)\beta_s}{\beta_f q}\left(\frac{V_{t+k}}{S_{t+k}} - \frac{V_t}{S_t}\right) \quad (12.53)$$

In this case, the conditions that determine whether there are net purchases or net sales are exactly the same as they were in the preceding subsection with only cash and futures.

12.8 LIQUIDITY BUFFERING

Leveraging a portfolio increases the risk of the portfolio. In fact, except in the case of index options that amplify only gains, leveraging itself can create unrecoverable losses—ones that run in excess of the equity in the portfolio. In order to maintain the portfolio's liquidity, a manager must purchase some form of portfolio insurance. Although there are various ways to achieve this downside protection, we shall focus on how to use *out-of-the-money put options* to prevent the levered portfolio's losses from exceeding the amount of equity in the portfolio. This method is simple to implement.

First, we need to compute the index loss that would exactly use up the equity value of the portfolio. Once we know this value, we can purchase the appropriate put options in terms of strike price and quantity. Liquidity buffering is applicable to all the leveraging methods discussed in this chapter, but we will focus on applying it to the cash and futures leverage case.

When we create leverage with cash and futures, we know that in a period of time between t and $t + k$, the value of the portfolio's equity equals

$$\begin{aligned}
V_{t+k} &= N_{f,t}q(F_{t+k} - F_t) + I_{t,t+k}V_t \\
&= N_{f,t}qS_t r^f_{t,t+k} + I_{t,t+k}V_t \\
&= \left(\frac{\beta^* V_t}{\beta_f qS_t}\right)qS_t r^f_{t,t+k} + I_{t,t+k}V_t
\end{aligned} \quad (12.54)$$

where $r^f_{t,t+k} \equiv (F_{t+k} - F_t)/S_t$, and all other variables have been defined previously. The goal is to find the strike price of the put options at which all the portfolio's equity would be consumed. This is the point at which closing the futures position would wipe out the portfolio's equity. By purchasing put options at this strike price, any further deterioration in the returns of the index and futures would be completely offset by the put options. There would be no further loss in portfolio value, making the leveraged portfolio feasible.

Assuming for simplicity that there is no basis risk (i.e., that we can substitute $r_{t,t+k}$ for $r^f_{t,t+k}$, since they are equal), we must find the index return at which all the account equity would be dissolved.[42] This would be the value that equates the loss on the futures position with the current account equity multiplied by the interest factor, that is,

$$\left(\frac{\beta^* V_t}{\beta_f q S_t}\right) q S_t r_{t,t+k} = -I_{t,t+k} V_t \tag{12.55}$$

which implies

$$r^*_{t,t+k} = \frac{-\beta_f I_{t,t+k}}{\beta^*} \tag{12.56}$$

Let us return to the example we used in the preceding subsection. Suppose that the portfolio manager's target $\beta^* = 2$, $\beta_f = 1$, the index value on day t is 1,000, and the futures' value on day t is 1,007.53. We also will assume for simplicity that interest rates are 0 or that $I_{t,t+k} \approx 1$. The return that would consume the account equity over the k-period horizon would be -0.5, or a negative return of 50%.

We have derived this return on day t, so we need to find the actual strike price of the put options to purchase. In particular, if the index is trading at S_t, then we will want to purchase options with a strike price $K = (1 + r^*_{t,t+k})S_t$. Thus, in our particular example, we would purchase options with a strike price of 500 (or the closest value to that).

The final step is determining how many options contracts to purchase. The simplest method is to use a dollar hedge adjusted

---

[42] With no basis risk, $F_{t+k} - F_t = S_{t+k} - S_t$; thus $(S_{t+k} - S_t)/S_t = (F_{t+k} - F_t)/S_t$. The former is the return on the underlying equity index, which we call $r_{t,t+k}$, and is what we are interested in because the options depend on the value of the underlying index, not the futures. Some people might wish to define the return on the futures contracts as $(F_{t+k} - F_t)/F_t$, but it really does not matter for this analysis. We are merely transforming the equation into the item we are interested in.

for β. Thus we compute the number of options contracts to purchase, given the β of the underlying index. Thus

$$N_O = \frac{\beta^* V_t}{\beta_I q_O S_t} \tag{12.57}$$

where β_I is the β of the underlying index with respect to the benchmark, q_O is the contract multiplier, and N_O is the number of option contracts to purchase.[43] Thus, in our previous example with $\beta^* = 2$, $\beta_I = 1$, $S_t = 1{,}000$, and $F_t = 1{,}007.53$, q_O for the S&P 500 being equal to 100, the number of options contracts to purchase is 2,000.

An illustration of the overall payoff to the portfolio when out-of-the-money options are used to limit the losses of the portfolio to the equity capital is shown in Fig. 12.4. The resulting portfolio looks similar to an in-the-money call option purchased at strike price K and purchased so as to have a twofold exposure to the index in this particular case.

We have closed the matter for day t. We have created a leveraged portfolio and purchased out-of-the-money put options to protect the liquidity of the account. We should note that these options are extremely out of the money, and index options are not typically available extremely out of the money. It is rare, even on a major index, to find any active trading in options even 20% out of the money. When it does happen, the bid–ask spreads are very wide.

Therefore, practically speaking, creating this type of leverage requires the portfolio manager to form some kind of over-the-counter (OTC) trade with one of the major broker-dealers. The portfolio manager can have the structured desk of a broker-dealer create these, or the broker-dealer can create them with *flex options*. Flex options (flexible options) are customized equity or index options contracts available on a number of exchanges, including the Chicago Board Options Exchange (CBOE). The flexible elements of the options include the strike price, contracts terms, exercise styles,

---

[43] In the daily risk management of option contracts, the β of the option contract is actually not the same as the underlying index. That is, $N_O = \frac{\beta^* V_t}{\beta_O q_O S_t}$, where $\beta_O = \beta_I |\Delta|$, and Δ is the option's Δ. In order to determine the number of options to purchase, we use β_I, since our purpose for creating this option is not for daily risk management but rather to protect against the catastrophic scenario of a huge negative return. In that scenario, the Δ of the option will converge to -1 very quickly; thus, for the purposes of liquidity protection, we assume that it is -1 from the onset.

FIGURE 12.4

Portfolio payoffs with and without leverage and liquidity buffering.

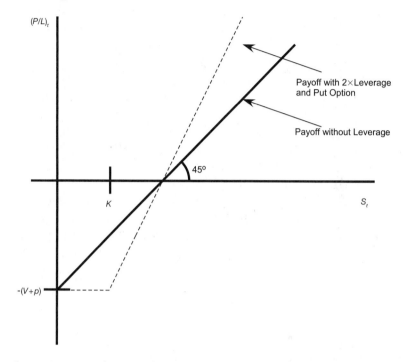

and expiration dates. Flex options eliminate counterparty risk because they are guaranteed by the Options Clearing Corporation, and they offer more liquidity than a typical OTC contract because they trade on a secondary market. They can be traded in size, expanding or even canceling entire positions.

These options might cost slightly more than the Black-Scholes or standard option-pricing model would predict, but being extremely out of the money, they still would be very cheap.[44]

Continuing with the preceding example, we need to purchase 2,000 put option contracts at a strike price of 500. Using the Black-Scholes formula with an interest rate of 3%, a volatility of the S&P 500 of 20%, and a time to maturity of three months, the Black-Scholes price for one option is $1.16 \cdot 10^{-11}$. The cost of 2,000 contracts is thus $2.32 \cdot 10^{-6}$. As a percentage of the equity capital, this

---

[44] The theoretical Black-Scholes price of these options is infinitesimal, but the broker-dealer typically charges more because, at "fair value," he or she earns next to nothing for taking on a risk.

is $2.32 \cdot 10^{-14}\%$. Clearly, the cost of this insurance, at least theoretically, is insignificant. In reality, the broker-dealer might charge as much as 5 cents per options contract.

To absolutely protect the equity value of the portfolio, one would need to rebalance these options daily. Some mutual funds require daily rebalancing. From a practical perspective, though, these out-of-the-money options contracts could be set up for a three-month duration and not rebalanced until they expire. Rebalancing would take place every three months for the entire portfolio. The risk of losing the entire equity value of the portfolio is minute, especially considering the fact that all exchanges implement trading halts during severe declines in equity.[45] Halts in trading give the portfolio manager time to reposition his or her portfolio if his or her downside potential is not perfectly hedged.

We have just illustrated liquidity buffering in the case of cash and futures. Liquidity buffering works just as well for a portfolio of stocks, cash, and futures. In that case, as long as the portfolio beta is well estimated and the portfolio well diversified, the manager can be comfortable that using index options as buffers will prevent catastrophe.

12.9 LEVERAGED SHORT

So far we have discussed the idea of levering a long-only portfolio. What if the portfolio manager has a negative view of the market as a whole? There is no reason that the manager cannot apply these leveraging concepts to short positions as well, whether he or she is an index manager or a stock picker. There are just some minor differences in technique for leveraging a short portfolio.

When an index manager shorts the market, he or she can bypass trading individual stocks altogether, keep his or her equity capital in cash to serve as margin, and short index futures contracts. Shorting is a little more complicated for a portfolio manager who picks stocks to outperform the market. He or she must selectively short low-α stocks. We discuss some of the issues related to shorting individual stocks in the next chapter on market-neutral portfolios. For now, we can say that the stock-picking portfolio

---

[45] The New York Stock Exchange (NYSE) halts trading for 15 minutes if the S&P 500 declines by more than 7% on a given day, for another 15 minutes if it declines by 13%, and for the entire day if it drops by 20% or more. For more information, see www.nyse.com.

manager can short stocks a number of ways: by shorting the stocks combined with shorting index futures, by shorting the stocks combined with single-stock or basket swap contracts (in which, as opposed to the long-position swaps, the portfolio manager pays the stock returns), or by shorting the stocks and/or shorting single-stock futures. The concepts involved are very similar to those that govern the long side; they just operate in reverse.

Consider the case of the index portfolio manager who wishes to short the entire index. We already showed how to find, for the long portfolio, the number of contracts to buy to reach a desired overall portfolio β. With shorting, the only difference is that rather than *buying* the futures, the manager will *short* them. The equations for long-only portfolios apply to short-only portfolios, the only difference being that the number of contracts will be negative (reflecting the fact that the β^* is negative).

Given an S&P 500 trading at 1,000, a multiplier for the large S&P 500 contracts of 250, a sum of cash equal to $100 million, and a $\beta^* = -2$, the appropriate number of futures contracts to sell would be 800. (Remember that $\beta_f = 1$ when the benchmark is the S&P 500.) The portfolio manager should sell the 800 futures contracts at a cost of $(qN_fF_t)m_f$ in margin balance. The remainder is held in cash, earning the interest rate.

As for rebalancing the position, the same concepts apply that apply to long-only portfolios. The triggers for rebalancing simply change. A market rally, for instance, would be cause to short futures contracts. A market decline would call for the purchase of futures contracts.

As for liquidity buffering, the portfolio manager also should follow the guidelines of liquidity buffering for long-only portfolios, except that now he or she should buy out-of-the-money call options rather than out-of-the-money put options.

12.10 CONCLUSION

Leverage is powerful. It introduces plenty of risk into the portfolio and has caused the collapse of entire funds. Yet it is the ultimate source of α mojo, and it can boost the portfolio's overall return. In this chapter we explained leveraging for index managers and stock pickers for long-only portfolios and ones that are short on the market. We looked at leveraging with equity index futures, single-stock futures, equity swaps, and options. We explained methods of fine-tuning the amount of leverage in a portfolio so as to control the amount of associated risk. These methods included calculating the appropriate number of futures contracts to achieve any desired β or leverage level, rebalancing the portfolio back to the desired leverage ratio, and creating buffers to ensure that the portfolio does not lose more than its equity capital. We have seen α mojo at work in the leveraged portfolio. In the next chapter we find it again in the market-neutral portfolio.

APPENDIX 12A

Fair-Value Computations

Fair value is a concept used commonly in futures markets. Since a futures contract trades on the basis of an underlying spot security, there should be some relationship between the underlying security price and the futures price. This theoretical price of the futures contract is known as *fair value*.

There is no perfect formula for computing the fair value of the futures contract. It will depend on the dividends paid by the underlying index, the timing of those dividends, the available interest rates in the market, the number of days until the expiration of the futures contract, and the current index level. Different banks have different ways of computing fair value; however, all fair values are based on a similar fundamental concept known as *present discounted value*. If one is using a continuously compounded interest rate to compute fair value, then the fair-value formula is expressed as

$$F_t = S_t e^{(i-q)(T-t)} \qquad (12\text{A}.1)$$

where F_t is the fair-value futures price, S_t is the current value of the underlying index, i is the prevailing interest rate over the time until expiration of the futures contract, q is the continuously compounded dividend yield of the index, and $T - t$ is the time until the futures contract expires.

Most people in the market do not deal with continuous compounded interest; thus the more popular formula is a formula that involves money market interest conventions. Thus

$$F_t = (S_t - d_t)\left(1 + i\frac{k}{360}\right) \qquad (12A.2)$$

where i is the money market interest rate, k is the number of days until the futures contract expires, and d_t is the present discounted value of dividend payments occurring on the index during the life of the futures contract. Ideally, one should know in advance the payment of all dividends and discount each one appropriately; unfortunately, this is not an easy task. Thus most people who compute fair value just use some estimated value of dividends to be paid on the index and present discount value them by some average time in which they are expected to be received. It really does not have a large effect on the fair value unless the dividend yield of the index is high and/or a lot of dividends are expected to be paid out shortly.

An example might help to illustrate the point. Suppose that the S&P 500 is trading at 1,000, that a 90-day futures contract exists, that the S&P 500 will pay 5 points of dividends at the end of the first month, and that the money market interest rate is 4%. The fair value of the futures contract using Eq. (12A.2) will be

$$\left[1{,}000 - \frac{5}{\left(1 + 0.04 \cdot \dfrac{30}{360}\right)}\right]\left(1 + 0.04 \cdot \frac{90}{360}\right) = 1{,}004.97 \qquad (12A.3)$$

Derivation of Equations (12.21), (12.22), and (12.23)

The derivation of Eq. (12.21) is as follows:

$$\beta^* = \sum_{i=1}^{N}\left(\frac{N_i q_s p_{i,t}}{V_t}\right)\beta_i + (1-\xi)\beta_s \qquad (12B.1)$$

where q_s is the contract multiplier for single-stock futures, which is equal to 100, and $p_{i,t}$ is the price of stock i. For Eq. (12.21), we assumed that the portfolio manager purchases single-stock futures contracts in proportion to the weighting of the underlying equity portfolio. Thus $w_i = N_i q_s p_{i,t} / \sum_{j=1}^{N} N_j q_s p_{j,t}$. Thus we substitute in the preceding expression and obtain

$$\beta^* = \sum_{i=1}^{N}\left(\frac{w_i \sum_{j=1}^{N} N_j q_s p_{j,t}}{V_t}\right)\beta_i + (1-\xi)\beta_s$$

$$= \left(\frac{\sum_{j=1}^{N} N_j q_s p_{j,t}}{V_t}\right)\sum_{i=1}^{N} w_i \beta_i + (1-\xi)\beta_s \qquad (12B.2)$$

$$= \left(\frac{N_i q_s p_{i,t}}{w_i V_t}\right)\beta_s + (1-\xi)\beta_s$$

Rearranging the last term, we obtain

$$N_i = \frac{\left[\beta^* + (\xi-1)\beta_s\right]V_t w_i}{\beta_s q_s p_{i,t}} \qquad (12B.3)$$

The derivation of Eq. (12.22) is very similar to the preceding derivation. However, we make the assumptions that $\tilde{w}_i = N_i q_s p_{i,t}/\sum_{i=1}^{N_1} N_i q_s p_{i,t}$ and that all the arguments are similar to those above, except that we replace w_i with $\tilde{w}_i$ and replace β_s with $\tilde{\beta}_{s'}$ where $\tilde{\beta}_s = \sum_{i=1}^{N_1} \tilde{w}_i \beta_i$. This leads to the expression $N_i = \{[\beta^* + (\xi - 1)\beta_s] V_t \tilde{w}_i\}/\tilde{\beta}_s q_s p_{i,t}$.

The derivation of Eq. (12.23) is also similar to the preceding derivation. However, we need to make an additional assumption about the relative weight of the index futures and the single-stock futures. In particular, we assume that $(1 - \sum_{i=1}^{N_1} w_i)/\sum_{i=1}^{N_1} w_i = N_f q S_t/\sum_{i=1}^{N_1} N_i q_s p_{i,t}$. Thus

$$
\begin{aligned}
\beta^* &= \sum_{i=1}^{N_1} \frac{N_i q_s p_{i,t}}{V_t} \beta_i + \frac{N_f q S_t}{V_t} \beta_f + (1-\xi)\beta_s \\
&= \sum_{i=1}^{N_1} \frac{N_i q_s p_{i,t}}{V_t} \beta_i + \left(\frac{1-\sum_{i=1}^{N_1} w_i}{\sum_{i=1}^{N_1} w_i} \right) \left(\sum_{i=1}^{N_1} N_i q_s p_{i,t} \right) \frac{\beta_f}{V_t} + (1-\xi)\beta_s \\
&= \sum_{i=1}^{N_1} \frac{\tilde{w}_i \left(\sum_{j=1}^{N_1} N_j q_s p_{j,t} \right)}{V_t} \beta_i + \left(\frac{1-\sum_{i=1}^{N_1} w_i}{\sum_{i=1}^{N_1} w_i} \right) \left(\sum_{i=1}^{N_1} N_i q_s p_{i,t} \right) \frac{\beta_f}{V_t} + (1-\xi)\beta_s \\
&= \left(\sum_{i=1}^{N_1} N_i q_s p_{i,t} \right) \left[\frac{\tilde{\beta}_s}{V_t} + \left(\frac{1-\sum_{i=1}^{N_1} w_i}{\sum_{i=1}^{N_1} w_i} \right) \frac{\beta_f}{V_t} \right] + (1-\xi)\beta_s
\end{aligned}
\tag{12B.4}
$$

Rearranging the last term, we obtain

$$
N_i = \frac{\left[\beta^* + (\xi - 1)\beta_s \right] V_t \tilde{w}_i}{q_s p_{i,t} \left[\tilde{\beta}_s + \left(\dfrac{1-\sum_{i=1}^{N_1} w_i}{\sum_{i=1}^{N_1} w_i} \right) \beta_f \right]}
\tag{12B.5}
$$

Once this is known, we already have the relationship between the index futures and the single-stock futures; thus $N_f = [(1 - \sum_{i=1}^{N_1} w_i)/\sum_{i=1}^{N_1} w_i] (\sum_{i=1}^{N_1} N_i q_s p_{i,t}/q S_t)$.

Tables of Futures Leverage Multipliers Needed to Achieve Various Degrees of Leverage

In this appendix we compiled a series of tables with various baseline β_s values of a portfolio manager and the *futures leverage multiplier* $\{[\beta^* + (\xi - 1) \beta_s]/\beta_f \, q\}$ which when multiplied by the ratio of the portfolio's value to the index's value will determine the number of appropriate futures contracts to purchase to alter the β of the total portfolio to the desired level. For these tables, we used S&P 500 E-mini and NASDAQ 100 E-mini futures because they are the most liquid. In both cases we assumed that the benchmark for the portfolio manager was the S&P 500; hence all β's are with respect to the S&P 500. However, the leverage ratio, l, is always with respect to the actual portfolio. As we stated earlier, our measure of leverage is not the conventional measure of leverage. However, they are the same when the futures positions are taken to enhance the exposure of the portfolio. Thus, in the tables, anytime the futures leverage multiplier is positive, the leverage ratio, l, will coincide with the conventional measure of leverage. However, when the futures leverage multiplier is negative (indicating to sell futures), the leverage ratio, l, will not coincide with the conventional measure of leverage. To obtain the conventional measure of leverage when the futures multiplier is negative, use the formula $l^c = (1 - l) + 1$, where l^c is the symbol for the conventional leverage measure. Our leverage ratio can also be interpreted as the net dollar exposure of the entire position. We also assume that the portfolio manager does not hold cash ($\xi = 0$).

Table 12C.1 presents the S&P 500 E-mini leverage multiplier assuming $\beta_f = 1$. Table 12C.2 presents the NASDAQ 100 E-mini

TABLE 12C.1

S&P 500 E-mini Futures' Leverage Multipliers to Obtain Desired β* or Leverage (*l*)

β_s	\(\beta^*\) 0.2	0.4	0.6	0.8	1	1.2	1.4	1.6	1.8	2	3	4
0.20	0.0000 / 1.00	0.0040 / 1.20	0.0080 / 1.40	0.0120 / 1.60	0.0160 / 1.80	0.0200 / 2.00	0.0240 / 2.20	0.0280 / 2.40	0.0320 / 2.60	0.0360 / 2.80	0.0560 / 3.80	0.0760 / 4.80
0.40	−0.0040 / 0.80	0.0000 / 1.00	0.0040 / 1.20	0.0080 / 1.40	0.0120 / 1.60	0.0160 / 1.80	0.0200 / 2.00	0.0240 / 2.20	0.0280 / 2.40	0.0320 / 2.60	0.0520 / 3.60	0.0720 / 4.60
0.60	−0.0080 / 0.60	−0.0040 / 0.80	0.0000 / 1.00	0.0040 / 1.20	0.0080 / 1.40	0.0120 / 1.60	0.0160 / 1.80	0.0200 / 2.00	0.0240 / 2.20	0.0280 / 2.40	0.0480 / 3.40	0.0680 / 4.40
0.80	−0.0120 / 0.40	−0.0080 / 0.60	−0.0040 / 0.80	0.0000 / 1.00	0.0040 / 1.20	0.0080 / 1.40	0.0120 / 1.60	0.0160 / 1.80	0.0200 / 2.00	0.0240 / 2.20	0.0440 / 3.20	0.0640 / 4.20
1.00	−0.0160 / 0.20	−0.0120 / 0.40	−0.0080 / 0.60	−0.0040 / 0.80	0.0000 / 1.00	0.0040 / 1.20	0.0080 / 1.40	0.0120 / 1.60	0.0160 / 1.80	0.0200 / 2.00	0.0400 / 3.00	0.0600 / 4.00
1.20	−0.0200 / 0.00	−0.0160 / 0.20	−0.0120 / 0.40	−0.0080 / 0.60	−0.0040 / 0.80	0.0000 / 1.00	0.0040 / 1.20	0.0080 / 1.40	0.0120 / 1.60	0.0160 / 1.80	0.0360 / 2.80	0.0560 / 3.80
1.40	−0.0240 / −0.20	−0.0200 / 0.00	−0.0160 / 0.20	−0.0120 / 0.40	−0.0080 / 0.60	−0.0040 / 0.80	0.0000 / 1.00	0.0040 / 1.20	0.0080 / 1.40	0.0120 / 1.60	0.0320 / 2.60	0.0520 / 3.60
1.60	−0.0280 / −0.40	−0.0240 / −0.20	−0.0200 / 0.00	−0.0160 / 0.20	−0.0120 / 0.40	−0.0080 / 0.60	−0.0040 / 0.80	0.0000 / 1.00	0.0040 / 1.20	0.0080 / 1.40	0.0280 / 2.40	0.0480 / 3.40
1.80	−0.0320 / −0.60	−0.0280 / −0.40	−0.0240 / −0.20	−0.0200 / 0.00	−0.0160 / 0.20	−0.0120 / 0.40	−0.0080 / 0.60	−0.0040 / 0.80	0.0000 / 1.00	0.0040 / 1.20	0.0240 / 2.20	0.0440 / 3.20
2.00	−0.0360 / −0.80	−0.0320 / −0.60	−0.0280 / −0.40	−0.0240 / −0.20	−0.0200 / 0.00	−0.0160 / 0.20	−0.0120 / 0.40	−0.0080 / 0.60	−0.0040 / 0.80	0.0000 / 1.00	0.0200 / 2.00	0.0400 / 3.00
3.00	−0.0560 / −1.80	−0.0520 / −1.60	−0.0480 / −1.40	−0.0440 / −1.20	−0.0400 / −1.00	−0.0360 / −0.80	−0.0320 / −0.60	−0.0280 / −0.40	−0.0240 / −0.20	−0.0200 / 0.00	0.0000 / 1.00	0.0200 / 2.00
4.00	−0.0760 / −2.80	−0.0720 / −2.60	−0.0680 / −2.40	−0.0640 / −2.20	−0.0600 / −2.00	−0.0560 / −1.80	−0.0520 / −1.60	−0.0480 / −1.40	−0.0440 / −1.20	−0.0400 / −1.00	−0.0200 / 0.00	0.0000 / 1.00

Note: For these examples, we use $\beta_f = 1$, $q = 50$, and $\xi_t = 0$. The first number is the futures leverage multiplier $\dfrac{[\beta^* + (\xi - 1)\beta_s]}{\beta_f \, q}$, and the number below it is the effective leverage *l* of the portfolio from this action. Our leverage ratio is not always equal to the conventional leverage ratio. The text describes how to convert our leverage ratio (a.k.a. net leverage) to the conventional leverage ratio (a.k.a. gross leverage). The futures multiplier is rounded to four decimal places.

TABLE 12C.2

NASDAQ 100 E-mini Futures' Leverage Multipliers to Obtain Desired β^* or Leverage (l)

β_s	β^* 0.20	0.40	0.60	0.80	1.00	1.20	1.40	1.60	1.80	2.00	3.00	4.00
0.20	0.0000	0.0091	0.0182	0.0273	0.0364	0.0455	0.0545	0.0636	0.0727	0.0818	0.1273	0.1727
	1.00	1.18	1.36	1.55	1.73	1.91	2.09	2.27	2.45	2.64	3.55	4.45
0.40	−0.0091	0.0000	0.0091	0.0182	0.0273	0.0364	0.0455	0.0545	0.0636	0.0727	0.1182	0.1636
	0.82	1.00	1.18	1.36	1.55	1.73	1.91	2.09	2.27	2.45	3.36	4.27
0.60	−0.0182	−0.0091	0.0000	0.0091	0.0182	0.0273	0.0364	0.0455	0.0545	0.0636	0.1091	0.1545
	0.64	0.82	1.00	1.18	1.36	1.55	1.73	1.91	2.09	2.27	3.18	4.09
0.80	−0.0273	−0.0182	−0.0091	0.0000	0.0091	0.0182	0.0273	0.0364	0.0455	0.0545	0.1000	0.1455
	0.45	0.64	0.82	1.00	1.18	1.36	1.55	1.73	1.91	2.09	3.00	3.91
1.00	−0.0364	−0.0273	−0.0182	−0.0091	0.0000	0.0091	0.0182	0.0273	0.0364	0.0455	0.0909	0.1364
	0.27	0.45	0.64	0.82	1.00	1.18	1.36	1.55	1.73	1.91	2.82	3.73
1.20	−0.0455	−0.0364	−0.0273	−0.0182	−0.0091	0.0000	0.0091	0.0182	0.0273	0.0364	0.0818	0.1273
	0.09	0.27	0.45	0.64	0.82	1.00	1.18	1.36	1.55	1.73	2.64	3.55
1.40	−0.0545	−0.0455	−0.0364	−0.0273	−0.0182	−0.0091	0.0000	0.0091	0.0182	0.0273	0.0727	0.1182
	−0.09	0.09	0.27	0.45	0.64	0.82	1.00	1.18	1.36	1.55	2.45	3.36
1.60	−0.0636	−0.0545	−0.0455	−0.0364	−0.0273	−0.0182	−0.0091	0.0000	0.0091	0.0182	0.0636	0.1091
	−0.27	−0.09	0.09	0.27	0.45	0.64	0.82	1.00	1.18	1.36	2.27	3.18
1.80	−0.0727	−0.0636	−0.0545	−0.0455	−0.0364	−0.0273	−0.0182	−0.0091	0.0000	0.0091	0.0545	0.1000
	−0.45	−0.27	−0.09	0.09	0.27	0.45	0.64	0.82	1.00	1.18	2.09	3.00
2.00	−0.0818	−0.0727	−0.0636	−0.0545	−0.0455	−0.0364	−0.0273	−0.0182	−0.0091	0.0000	0.0455	0.0909
	−0.64	−0.45	−0.27	−0.09	0.09	0.27	0.45	0.64	0.82	1.00	1.91	2.82
3.00	−0.1273	−0.1182	−0.1091	−0.1000	−0.0909	−0.0818	−0.0727	−0.0636	−0.0545	−0.0455	0.0000	0.0455
	−1.55	−1.36	−1.18	−1.00	−0.82	−0.64	−0.45	−0.27	−0.09	0.09	1.00	1.91
4.00	−0.1727	−0.1636	−0.1545	−0.1455	−0.1364	−0.1273	−0.1182	−0.1091	−0.1000	−0.0909	−0.0455	0.0000
	−2.45	−2.27	−2.09	−1.91	−1.73	−1.55	−1.36	−1.18	−1.00	−0.82	0.09	1.00

Note: For these examples, we use $\beta_f = 1.10$, $q = 20$, and $\xi_t = 0$. The first number is the futures leverage multiplier $\dfrac{[\beta^* + (\xi_t - 1)\beta_s]}{\beta_f\, q}$, and the number below it is the effective leverage l of the portfolio from this action. Our leverage ratio is not always equal to the conventional leverage ratio. The text describes how to convert our leverage ratio (a.k.a. net leverage) to the conventional leverage ratio (a.k.a. gross leverage). The futures multiplier is rounded to four decimal places.

leverage multiplier needed to achieve the desired β^* for a given portfolio β_s. For the NASDAQ 100 E-mini, we used $\beta_f = 1.10$ (since the benchmark is the S&P 500). The portfolio manager can use these tables as rough guides to adjust either the β of the portfolio or the overall leverage of the portfolio.

Thus suppose that a portfolio manager is managing a portfolio with a $\beta_s = 1.6$ with respect to the benchmark, which we have assumed is the S&P 500, and he or she would like to increase the overall β of the portfolio to 3. His or her portfolio has a value of $100 million, and the current level of the S&P 500 is 3,756. In Table 12C.1, we find the 1.6 value under the β_s column and then slide over until we reach the column under $\beta^* = 3$, which tells the portfolio manager that the futures leverage multiplier is 0.0280. The ratio of the portfolio's value to the index's value is 26,624.07 ($100 M/3,756). Thus, the appropriate number of futures contracts to purchase to achieve the desired position is 745.47 ($= 0.0280 \cdot$ 26,624.07). Thus, in practice, we would round to the nearest integer and actually purchase 745 futures contracts. This will achieve his or her desired β^* and a leverage ratio of 2.4 (the number below the futures multiplier in the table). To accomplish the same sort of β^* with respect to the benchmark using NASDAQ 100 futures would require purchasing 493.48 ($= 0.0636 \cdot 7,759.16$) futures contracts but result in a lowered leveraged position of 2.27 owing to the higher β of the NASDAQ 100 versus the benchmark (for this example we assumed the NASDAQ was at 12,888). In practice, we would round to the nearest integer and purchase 493 NASDAQ 100 futures contracts.

In the two preceding examples, our leverage ratio, l, is equal to the conventional measure of leverage. Suppose instead, we wish to use S&P 500 futures to reduce our overall β to 1. In this particular case we find the value of 1.6 under the β_s column and slide over until we reach the column under $\beta^* = 1$, which tells the portfolio manager that the futures leverage multiplier is -0.0120. The appropriate number of futures to short will be 319.49 ($= -0.0120 \cdot$ 26,624.07). This will achieve the desired β^* and a leverage ratio or net dollar exposure of 0.40. The conventional leverage measure in this example would be $1.6[(1 - 0.4) + 1]$. If we were instead to use NASDAQ 100 futures to achieve the same position, we would sell 211.83 ($= -0.0273 \cdot 7,759.16$) futures contracts resulting in a leverage ratio or net dollar exposure of 0.60. The conventional leverage measure in this example would be $1.4[(1 - 0.6) + 1]$.

QUESTIONS

12.1. Name four ways an equity manager can leverage a portfolio.

12.2. Name three advantages of using leverage in QEPM.

12.3. Name three disadvantages of using leverage in QEPM.

12.4. What type of portfolio manager is most likely to use leverage with only cash and index futures?

12.5. In the case of a portfolio manager using only cash and S&P 500 futures, what is theoretically the largest leverage he or she could achieve? The largest portfolio β he or she could achieve? Assume that the margin futures requirement is 6.5% and that the β of the S&P 500 futures is 1.

12.6. Which of the equity index futures contracts that portfolio managers use are the most liquid? What evidence supports your answer?

12.7. Suppose that you are a portfolio manager with $150 million in cash. You would like to create a portfolio with an exposure to the S&P 500 of 2. Use the index values in Table 12.2 for each futures contract.
   (a) How many contracts of the S&P 500 futures must you purchase?
   (b) How many contracts of the S&P 500 E-mini futures would you have to purchase?
   (c) Which one would you probably use and why?

12.8. Suppose that you are a portfolio manager with $50 million in cash. You are interested in using futures to obtain an overall β exposure of 2 to the S&P 500. Use the index values in Table 12.2 for each futures contract.
   (a) How many futures contracts would you need if you used S&P 500 futures to achieve this exposure?
   (b) How many futures contracts would you need if you used Russell 2000 E-mini futures to do this (assume the Russell 2000 futures have a $\beta_f = 1.25$ versus the S&P 500)?
   (c) Which futures contract probably would be the better one to use and why?

12.9. Suppose that a portfolio manager has $10 million in cash and $90 million in a portfolio of equities with $\beta_s = 0.8$. Suppose that the portfolio manager would like to use the S&P 500 futures contracts for leverage (that is, $\beta_f = 1$).
   (a) What is the largest leverage he can achieve?
   (b) What is the largest overall portfolio β he can achieve theoretically?

PART III: α Mojo

12.10. Suppose that a small-cap quantitative equity portfolio manager wishes to leverage his underlying stock portfolio using index futures. Which index futures contract would you probably recommend and why?

12.11. Suppose that a mid-cap quantitative equity portfolio manager wishes to leverage her underlying stock portfolio using index futures. She uses S&P 400 Mid-Cap E-mini contracts. How many futures contracts will she be required to purchase?

12.12. Suppose that the portfolio manager holds no cash and a portfolio of equities with an exposure versus the benchmark of $\beta_s = 0.9$. The α_s of the portfolio is 2% per annum, the expected return of the benchmark is 10%, the benchmark risk or standard deviation is 16%, and the residual risk of the portfolio versus the benchmark is 4%. The leverage of the portfolio is 2 (that is, $l = 2$) using future contracts on the underlying benchmark.

    (a) What is the expected return and risk of the overall portfolio?

    (b) How does it compare with that of the benchmark?

12.13. Name an advantage and a disadvantage of using single-stock futures versus index futures for leverage.

12.14. Is the theoretical maximum leverage larger or smaller using single-stock futures versus index futures? Why?

12.15. Suppose that a portfolio manager has the following $10 million portfolio. He has three stocks A, B, and C. Each stock has a weight of 0.30, 0.40, and 0.30, respectively. The price of each stock is $20, $50, and $100, respectively. The β of each stock with respect to the benchmark is 0.5, 0.7, and 0.9, respectively.

    (a) What is the overall β of the portfolio β_s?

    (b) How many futures contracts would have to be purchased if the portfolio manager would like to increase the overall portfolio β to 2.5? (Specify for N_A, N_B, and N_C.) Assume that all single-stock futures are available and liquid and that the portfolio manager uses scenario 1 in the text.

12.16. True or false: leveraging with index futures has no effect on the Sharpe ratio.

12.17. Using the relative contribution of the α^B to the overall expected portfolio return, show whether index leverage or single-stock leverage results in better leverage for a portfolio manager who is good at stock picking. Show your work.

12.18. Suppose that a portfolio manager has a stock portfolio and cash and wants to use single-stock futures and index futures to increase her leverage to a value of $l = 2$ using scenario 3. Given the following parameters: $\xi = 0.3$, $\psi = 0.60$, $\alpha_{s1} = 0.02$, $\alpha_{s2} = 0.015$, $\beta_{s1} = 0.95$, $\beta_{s2} = 0.95$, $\beta_f = 1$, $\mu_B = 0.15$, $\sigma_B = 0.40$, $\omega_{s1} = 0.10$, $\omega_{s2} = 0.05$, and $\omega_{s1's2} = 0.02$.
  (a) What is the expected return of the portfolio?
  (b) What is the expected risk?

12.19. What could a quantitative equity portfolio manager use to boost his α^B in the absence of liquid single-stock futures contracts?

12.20. What are the advantages of using options to leverage? What is the practical disadvantage?

12.21. Suppose that a portfolio manager started with a portfolio of stocks and cash. She used index futures to leverage the portfolio. The original stock portfolio had a $\beta_s = 1.2$, the futures $\beta_f = 2$ with respect to the benchmark, and the value of the portfolio was $100 million at date t, of which $40 million was in cash ($\xi = 0.40$). The target β^* versus the benchmark was set to be 3. The contract multiplier of the futures contract is 20. After 15 days, the market collapses, with the market going down by 15%. In particular, the underlying index of the futures contract has dropped from $S_t = 1{,}240$ to $S_{t+k} = 1{,}054$. The value of the overall portfolio has dropped from $V_t = 100$ million to $V_{t+k} = 77.5$ million. [*Note:* For simplicity, assume that the return on cash over this period is negligible (that is, $I_{t,t+k} = 1$)].
  (a) How many futures contracts does the portfolio manager need to purchase on date t to establish $\beta^* = 3$ for the portfolio?
  (b) What was the return on the underlying benchmark over the period t to $t + k$? (*Hint:* The benchmark is not the same as the index underlying the futures contract.)
  (c) What was the return on the overall leveraged portfolio?
  (d) Considering your answer in part (b), what does this say about leverage?
  (e) What is the number of futures contracts the portfolio should purchase to reestablish an overall $\beta^* = 3$ at time $t + k$?

12.22. Suppose that we assume that there is no basis risk, and there is a portfolio manager who uses only cash and index futures to manager his equity exposure. He uses S&P 500 futures, not the E-minis. His benchmark is the S&P 500. Suppose that from time t to time $t + k$, the S&P 500 moves from 3,584 to 4,480. Suppose also that over the period the interest on cash is a total of 1% (that is, $I_{t,t+k} = 1.01$). The portfolio manager's original $\beta^* = 1.50$, and the original value of the portfolio is $500 million.

    (a) Does the portfolio manager need to purchase or sell futures contracts to reestablish the original β^*?

    (b) How many futures contracts does he need to buy or sell? (*Hint:* You need to determine the contract multiplier associated with this contract and the original leverage l.)

12.23. Explain what is meant by *liquidity buffering*? Why is it important?

12.24. Is leveraging short any different from leveraging long? If so, how?

CHAPTER 13

Market Neutral

Not being able to govern events, I govern myself.

—Michel de Montaigne

13.1 INTRODUCTION

Market-neutral strategies have gained popularity over the last few years. From 2000 to 2020, the equity market-neutral strategy declined from 2.57% of the hedge-fund universe to 1.51%.[1] The first known hedge fund was market neutral. It was founded in 1949 by Alfred W. Jones, an Australian-born Harvard graduate who believed that he had an ability to predict individual stock returns but no ability to time the market or predict its general direction. Jones realized that if he could, in the right proportion, short the securities that he thought would lose value and buy the securities that he thought would gain value, he would effectively eliminate the impact of the overall market return on his portfolio. His portfolio's return would equal the difference in returns between the winners and losers, reflecting only his ability to pick the stocks. Jones's track record was quite impressive. In fact, a 1966 *Fortune* article entitled, "The Jones That Nobody Can Keep Up With," reported that his fund beat the best-performing mutual fund of that year by 44%.

---

[1] *Source*: BarclayHedge. The actual assets under management grew from $5.5 billion to $57.8 billion. The broader category of long-short funds and market-neutral funds declined from 19.45% to 6.07% over the same period.

Jones's market-neutral strategy took hold in the investment community, and although people today apply a variety of techniques and designs to it, the goal remains the same: to reduce the sensitivity of the portfolio to market movements by taking long and short positions in individual securities or market indices that offset the effects of the market. One of those effects is market risk. Table 13.1 shows that over the last 25 years, a market-neutral portfolio would have earned a return a little less than half of the Standard & Poor's (S&P) 500 but with about half of the volatility. In fact, the market-neutral portfolio had less risk than any other major index except for the money market index. By taking a big slice of risk out of the portfolio, market-neutral strategies clear the path for a manager who is good at stock picking to focus on his or her strength. This can boost α above the α of the traditional long portfolio. In other words, market neutral is a good source of α mojo.

Market-neutral strategies can work for index managers too. Combined with a long exposure to the equity index, buying favorable stocks and shorting unfavorable ones adds the α from stock picking to the benchmark return. Market-neutral portfolios also can help to diversify an investor's overall portfolio because they have very low correlations with the market. Table 13.1 shows that

TABLE 13.1

Statistics of a Market-Neutral Portfolio versus Other Major Indices

Index	Average Return (%)	SD (%)	Correlation with Market Neutral
Market neutral	4.49	9.08	1
S&P 500	11.19	15.09	0.28
NASDAQ 100	16.43	24.58	0.23
Government bond	8.27	10.22	−0.24
Commodity	2.19	22.53	0.27
Money market	2.41	0.65	0.14
Real estate	10.91	19.08	0.35

Note: All index statistics were measured over the period 12/31/1994 to 12/31/2020 using monthly return data. Market neutral is the Credit Suisse Equity Market Neutral Index; the S&P 500 represents S&P 500 total returns; NASDAQ 100 represents the NASDAQ 100 price returns; the government bond index is the Bloomberg U.S. Government Bond Index; the commodity index is the total return S&P GSCI Commodity Index; the money market index is the S&P Treasury Bill Total Return Index; and the real estate index is the Dow Jones U.S. Real Estate Total Return Index. Data were obtained from Bloomberg. Average return and standard deviation (SD) have been annualized.

the correlations between the market-neutral portfolio and various indices are all less than 0.36.[2]

In this chapter we discuss the basics of equity market-neutral strategies of portfolio management. We show the various methods for constructing a market-neutral portfolio, go over the basic mathematics, and discuss the advantages of the strategy.

13.2 MARKET-NEUTRAL CONSTRUCTION

The market-neutral concept applies to a variety of investment strategies, including convertible arbitrage, fixed-income arbitrage, and risk arbitrage. Here we focus on applying it to an equity portfolio run by a stock-picking manager.

A manager can construct a market-neutral position by purchasing stocks that he or she thinks are "buys" and shorting ones that he or she thinks are "sells." He or she can separate the buys from the sells with an aggregate Z-score model, a fundamental factor model, or an economic factor model—any of these will help to rank the stocks by expected return. He or she also can sort these stocks using other methods, including directly through an optimization. Then, to achieve market neutrality, the manager must use some mechanism for controlling risk so that the entire portfolio has *zero net exposure* to the market even as it captures the excess return from stock picking. Risk-control mechanisms run the gamut from very simple to quite complex. We discuss a number of them in this section.

13.2.1 Security Selection

In order to construct the portfolio, the manager must identify the buys and sells. With a quantitative model, he or she can estimate the expected returns or α's of the stocks in his or her investment universe. Stocks with low expected returns or α's go in the "sell" pile; the rest are "buys." We will assume that the manager already has forecasted the expected returns of stocks, or their α's, from either an aggregate Z-score model or a factor model.

---

[2] For more details, see Patton (2004). He uses various definitions of market neutrality and finds that while some market-neutral funds do not behave neutrally with respect to the market, most do. He also finds that market-neutral funds are clearly less affected by the market than are other types of hedge funds.

13.2.2 Dollar Neutrality

The simplest market-neutral strategy is *dollar neutrality*, which means that the dollar amount of the long positions equals the dollar amount of the short positions. Suppose that the portfolio manager has identified 10 stocks that are buys and 10 stocks that are sells and that he or she has $100 million with which to trade. He or she can weight the group of buys and sells in any manner he or she chooses as long as the ratio of the weights of the longs to the weights of the shorts is 1:1. The short positions also will require margin collateral from the broker, but we take up this issue in a later section. If V_L represents the notional amount invested in the long positions and V_S represents the notional amount invested in the short positions, then dollar neutrality implies that

$$V_L = V_S \qquad (13.1)$$

The weights of the long and short stocks each total 1. Thus $\sum_{i=1}^{N_L} w_i^L = 1$ and $\sum_{i=1}^{N_S} w_i^S = 1$, where w_i^L represents the relative weights of stocks in the long portfolio and w_i^S represents the relative weights of stocks in the short portfolio prior to shorting, and N_L and N_S represent the number of stocks in the long and short portfolios, respectively. It is convenient to think of the short portfolio as simply a long portfolio in which the stocks are sold in certain proportions rather than purchased.[3]

Suppose that we have an equity value of $90 million. In Table 13.2 we identify 10 stocks we would like to buy and 10 stocks that we would like to short.

The weights in each portfolio were chosen according to some relative Z-score weighting. The sum of the weights in both portfolios equals 1. The β's are reported with respect to the S&P 500. The weighted-average β for the long portfolio is 1.78, whereas the weighted-average β of the short portfolio is 2.36. The number of shares to go long and short, also listed in the table, are a function of the value of the portfolio and the current price of the stocks. This is a dollar-neutral portfolio, but it is not neutral to market risk. In fact, the β of the overall portfolio is roughly

---

[3] In terms of writing a computer program, however, it may be more convenient to remove the short-sale constraint in the optimization and treat the weights of stocks in the short portfolio as the stocks that produce negative weights. An additional constraint can be added that the negative weights sum to -1 and the positive weights sum to positive 1 to maintain the dollar neutrality.

TABLE 13.2

Example of a Dollar-Neutral Portfolio

Good/Long Portfolio					
Ticker	w_i^L	β_i	**Dollar Amount**	**Share Price**	**Shares**
TSLA	0.264	2.18	$23,715,735.07	705.67	33,607
ETSY	0.107	1.66	$9,616,896.10	177.91	54,055
NVDA	0.102	1.46	$9,161,536.05	522.2	17,544
PYPL	0.094	1.12	$8,482,215.28	234.2	36,218
LB	0.092	1.66	$8,300,605.96	37.19	223,195
ALB	0.087	1.60	$7,861,523.59	147.52	53,291
AMD	0.087	2.28	$7,790,410.83	91.71	84,946
FCX	0.084	2.28	$7,603,621.21	26.02	292,222
CDNS	0.083	1.05	$7,467,455.90	136.43	54,735
NOW	0.080	1.14	$7,195,380.82	550.43	13,072
Total	1.000	1.78	$90,000,000.00		
Bad/Short Portfolio					
Ticker	w_i^S	β_i	**Dollar Amount**	**Share Price**	**Shares**
SLB	0.089	2.28	$7,982,029.72	21.83	365,645
AAL	0.091	1.82	$8,161,269.58	15.77	517,519
NOV	0.091	2.22	$8,171,115.07	13.73	595,129
FANG	0.093	2.59	$8,376,817.73	48.4	173,075
HFC	0.094	1.83	$8,464,580.37	25.85	327,450
MRO	0.102	3.36	$9,172,852.41	6.67	1,375,240
UAL	0.103	1.62	$9,268,717.94	43.25	214,306
OXY	0.112	2.35	$10,060,697.52	17.31	581,207
FTI	0.112	2.50	$10,060,713.91	9.4	1,070,289
NCLH	0.114	2.86	$10,281,205.74	25.43	404,294
Total	1.000	2.36	$90,000,000.00		

Note: The data are from December 2020. The total portfolio β represents the weighted average of the β's of each portfolio (long and short) independent of the other. The weights presented in the table may not add up to 1 due to rounding.

$$\beta_P = \beta_L + (-1)\beta_S = 1.78 - 2.36 = -0.58 \qquad (13.2)$$

A portfolio neutral to market risk would display a β_P of 0. This dollar-neutral portfolio's β of -0.58 exhibits some market risk.

13.2.3 Beta Neutrality (a.k.a. Risk-Factor Neutrality)

The dollar-neutral portfolio is relatively uncorrelated with the market. Whenever one side of the portfolio (long or short) rises, the other side drops. However, dollar neutrality does not guarantee that the overall portfolio is neutral with respect to many of the risk factors in the economy. A dollar-neutral portfolio may have very low exposure to risk factors, but there is no guarantee that the exposure will be zero. Generally, it could even be quite high or negative. Thus it is better to create a market-neutral portfolio that is not only dollar neutral but also neutral with respect to market risk factors according to some risk model of equities.

The market-neutral portfolio should be, at the very minimum, both dollar neutral and neutral to market risk. For the portfolio to be neutral to market risk, the weighted-average capital asset pricing model (CAPM) β of its long and short sides must equal 0.[4] Thus

$$\sum_{i=1}^{N_L} w_i^L \beta_i = \sum_{i=1}^{N_S} w_i^s \beta_i \qquad (13.3)$$

where N_L and N_S represent the number of stocks in the long and short portfolios, respectively, and β_i is the β of stock i with respect to the market index return.[5] One should remember that in the short portfolio, the stocks will be shorted; thus the actual exposure will be the negative of the overall β of the short portfolio.

With this method, the manager achieves a simple yet effective market-neutral portfolio. Some managers may want to make the portfolio neutral to many more factors—perhaps all the factors—contained in some risk model. This can be done by building the entire portfolio with a constraint that sets all the factor exposures to zero. More generally, the optimization would be run such that

$$\sum_{i=1}^{N_L} w_i^L \beta_{i,k} = \sum_{i=1}^{N_S} w_i^s \beta_{i,k}, \quad \text{for all } k \qquad (13.4)$$

where k represents the kth factor. With no exposure to any of the risk factors, the portfolio theoretically should return the risk-free rate and have an α of 0. However, to the extent that markets are not efficient, the portfolio may have a positive α.

---

[4] To leave some exposure to market risk, the portfolio can be set with a β not exactly equal to 0. Even if β_p is not exactly equal to 0, it is sometimes possible to achieve β neutrality with a futures overlay. At this point, though, we are not considering the use of futures.

[5] Of course, the portfolio manager can construct the market-neutral portfolio to be neutral with respect to the market index of his or her choice (e.g., S&P 500, Russell 1000, and NASDAQ 100).

TABLE 13.3

Example of a Dollar-Neutral and β-Neutral Portfolio

Good/Long Portfolio					
Ticker	w_i^L	β_i	Dollar Amount	Share Price	Shares
TSLA	0.186	2.18	$16,758,853.37	540.73	30,993
ETSY	0.089	1.66	$8,013,791.20	305.34	26,245
NVDA	0.057	1.46	$5,129,344.51	1386.71	3,699
PYPL	0.019	1.12	$1,736,408.45	472.27	3,677
LB	0.090	1.66	$8,059,242.39	269.05	29,954
ALB	0.083	1.60	$7,435,420.35	582.94	12,755
AMD	0.000	2.28	$0	92.85	−
FCX	0.455	2.28	$40,912,457.48	117.4	348,488
CDNS	0.000	1.05	$0	195.18	−
NOW	0.022	1.14	$1,954,572.25	387.83	5,040
Total	1.000	2.00	$90,000,000.00		
Bad/Short Portfolio					
Ticker	w_i^L	β_i	Dollar Amount	Share Price	Shares
SLB	0.030	2.28	$2,716,195.44	570.56	4,761
AAL	0.009	1.82	$822,773.14	384.33	2,141
NOV	0.027	2.22	$2,465,736.48	168.4	14,642
FANG	0.045	2.59	$4,008,451.59	143.5	27,933
HFC	0.009	1.83	$842,532.27	258.91	3,254
MRO	0.094	3.36	$8,456,794.48	88.65	95,395
UAL	0.655	1.62	$58,937,517.68	141.77	415,726
OXY	0.034	2.35	$3,016,089.98	721.54	4,180
FTI	0.040	2.50	$3,610,344.11	379.85	9,505
NCLH	0.057	2.86	$5,123,564.84	92.48	55,402
Total	1.000	2.00	$90,000,000.00		

Note: The data are from December 2020. The total portfolio β represents the weighted average of the β's of each portfolio (long and short) independent of the other. The weights presented in the table may not add up to 1 due to rounding.

Continuing with our example from the preceding section, we use an optimizer[6] to construct a dollar-neutral and β-neutral portfolio. Table 13.3 contains the portfolios, which are both dollar neutral and β neutral. Notice that we have allowed a relatively high β of 2.0 for the long and short portfolios because if we had tried to keep their β's lower, it would have been difficult to achieve a β-neutral portfolio without excluding many stocks. Even with such a high β, on the long side we end up having to altogether forgo purchasing two of our preferred stocks, AMD and CDNS. On

---

[6] We discuss optimizers in Chapter 9.

the short side, in order to achieve the high β, we have to assign a 65.5% weight to UAL. This means shorting \$59 million of UAL. Here we run into some practical limitations of the optimization. Shorting so much of one stock might not be feasible from a liquidity point of view, and it would reduce the overall diversification of the portfolio. We will discuss these sorts of practical issues in more detail in the last part of this book (Chapters 16 and 17), which covers empirical examples of quantitative equity portfolio management (QEPM). In this case, a better way to achieve the β neutrality might have been to relax the dollar-neutrality constraint.

13.2.4 Market-Neutral Portfolio Out of a Long-Only Portfolio

An alternative way to create a dollar-neutral portfolio or a β-neutral portfolio is to create one out of two existing portfolios. A dollar-neutral portfolio can be created easily as long as we have two portfolios with different expected returns. Suppose that we have two portfolios, A and B. Portfolio A's expected return is higher than portfolio B's expected return. A simple way to create a dollar-neutral portfolio with a positive return is to take a long position in portfolio A and a short position of the same size in portfolio B.

For a β-neutral portfolio, we need two portfolios with identical factor exposures.[7] Suppose that portfolio A has factor exposures identical to benchmark B's factor exposures. The portfolio manager could have constructed portfolio A using the technique of factor exposure targeting described in Chapter 9. Then, taking a long position in portfolio A and a short position of the same size in benchmark B results in a β-neutral portfolio. If the benchmark is also traded as a futures contract, this market neutrality can be achieved easily by shorting the futures contract.[8]

13.3 MARKET NEUTRAL'S MOJO

Suppose that a portfolio manager creates a market-neutral portfolio hedged against all risk factors. It is then possible to compute the expected return of this strategy. Assuming that stock returns are

---

[7] In general, we can create a β-neutral portfolio if we have two portfolios whose factor exposure profiles are a multiple of one another.

[8] In Part V of this book we implement this technique as well as the more direct construction of market-neutral portfolios, as explained earlier.

driven by some multifactor model, the excess return of stock i can be represented as

$$r_i = \alpha_i + \beta_{i,1}f_1 + \cdots + \beta_{i,K}f_K + \epsilon_i \qquad (13.5)$$

where there are K factors representing security returns, $\beta_{i,k}$ is the sensitivity of stock i to factor k, f_k is the factor excess return, and ϵ_i is the residual return of security i. The excess return to a market-neutral portfolio when all risk factors are set to be neutral is

$$
\begin{aligned}
r_P &= \sum_{i=1}^{N_L} w_i^L r_i^L - \sum_{j=1}^{N_S} w_j^S r_j^S \\
&= \sum_{i=1}^{N_L} w_i^L \alpha_i - \sum_{j=1}^{N_S} w_j^S \alpha_j + \sum_{i=1}^{N_L} w_i^L \epsilon_i - \sum_{j=1}^{N_S} w_j^S \epsilon_j \\
&\equiv \alpha_L - \alpha_S + \epsilon_L - \epsilon_S
\end{aligned}
\qquad (13.6)
$$

Thus the expected excess return of the market-neutral portfolio is

$$E(r_P) = \sum_{i=1}^{N_L} w_i^L \alpha_i - \sum_{j=1}^{N_S} w_j^S \alpha_j \qquad (13.7)$$

According to the arbitrage pricing theory (APT), the market-neutral portfolio should have no expected excess return, but we are assuming that the market is not completely efficient and/or that the portfolio manager is good at picking outperforming and underperforming stocks. If you make a further assumption that $\alpha_L = -\alpha_S = \alpha$ (i.e., that the long portfolio's α and the short portfolio's α have the same absolute value but opposite signs), then the market-neutral portfolio achieves its 2α, that is,

$$E(r_P) = 2\alpha \qquad (13.8)$$

This is the market-neutral strategy's hidden source of α mojo. It is one of the advantages of the market-neutral portfolio over a long-only portfolio, which can achieve only 1α. It is important to point out, though, that this α mojo comes purely from the leverage in the market-neutral portfolio, in which the full capital is invested both on the long side and on the short side.[9] Without the leverage,

---

[9] We will see in the margin section of this chapter that in practice the maximum α mojo that can be achieved is 1.8 owing to additional cash requirements by the brokers. Theoretically, though, a market-neutral portfolio can achieve two times the α of a long-only portfolio. Hedge funds that use prime brokers can increase their leverage beyond a leverage of two, depending on the relationship with the prime broker.

the α would be no greater than the long-only portfolio's α unless very big, unexploited opportunities existed on the short side.

In addition to the expected return, it is possible to calculate the variance of the market-neutral portfolio:

$$\begin{aligned} V(r_p) &= V(\alpha_L - \alpha_S + \epsilon_L - \epsilon_S) \\ &= V(\epsilon_L - \epsilon_S) \\ &= V(\epsilon_L) + V(\epsilon_S) - 2C(\epsilon_L, \epsilon_S) \end{aligned} \quad (13.9)$$

If we make the assumption that $V(\epsilon_L) = V(\epsilon_S) = \omega^2$, then the variance of the market-neutral portfolio reduces to

$$V(r_p) = 2\omega^2(1 - \rho) \quad (13.10)$$

where ρ is the correlation coefficient between ϵ_L and ϵ_S.

Though α mojo is by itself a benefit, extra α comes at a price, and this should matter to the portfolio manager. The manager should be concerned with attaining a higher *information ratio* than the long-only portfolio.[10] The information ratio (*IR*) of a long-only portfolio is

$$IR_L = \frac{\alpha}{\sqrt{\omega^2}} \quad (13.11)$$

whereas the information ratio of the market-neutral portfolio we considered earlier is

$$IR_N = \frac{2\alpha}{\sqrt{2\omega^2 (1 - \rho)}} \quad (13.12)$$

Thus the ratio of information ratios of a market-neutral to a long-only portfolio is

$$\begin{aligned} \frac{IR_N}{IR_L} &= \frac{\dfrac{2\alpha}{\sqrt{2\omega^2 (1 - \rho)}}}{\dfrac{\alpha}{\sqrt{\omega^2}}} \\ &= \sqrt{\frac{2}{1 - \rho}} \end{aligned} \quad (13.13)$$

---

[10] The information ratio is a common performance-measurement criterion for active managers. It is the ratio of active return to active risk. A higher ratio implies a better portfolio manager, one who achieves more return for the same amount of risk. This is described in more detail in Chapter 15 on performance measurement.

One can immediately see the benefits of a market-neutral strategy in the information ratio. Since the correlation between ϵ_L and ϵ_S is always less than or equal to 1, the market-neutral strategy improves on the long-only portfolio. In the extreme case of perfect correlation, the ratio of information ratios tends toward infinity.[11] In this case, the long and short portfolios (after shorting) move in opposite directions, reducing the overall portfolio variance.

Market neutral's advantage, however, does not come only from the correlation between the long and short portfolios. The mere ability to short securities itself offers a distinct advantage. A long-only manager cannot take any particular action on a stock that he or she expects will crash; all he or she can do is not buy it. These constraints may actually cause greater mispricings and make $\alpha^S > \alpha^L$. With a long-short portfolio, the portfolio manager can have an outright negative weight on the stock and take advantage of this.

13.4 THE MECHANICS OF MARKET NEUTRAL

This section guides you through the mechanics of creating long and short positions in the securities markets.

13.4.1 Margin and Shorting

Equity securities in the United States can be purchased on margin. This allows an investor to invest more in securities than he or she has in cash. The Federal Reserve Board regulates margin and margin requirements through Regulation T.[12] For some time now, Regulation T has required that a customer deposit at least 50% of the current market value (CMV) of a marginable security. This is known as the *initial margin*, which is the margin required on first purchase of the equity security. For example, if a portfolio manager purchases 20,000 shares at $10 per share, the customer technically could borrow up to $100,000 from the broker for this $200,000

---

[11] These arguments were presented in Michaud (1993). Michaud argues, however, that additional costs associated with the short side of the strategy actually may reduce this efficiency of the portfolio. He also worries about the true ability to perfectly hedge all the additional risk factors. It should be mentioned that the ratio in Eq. (13.13) holds even without any additional leverage in the market-neutral over the long-only portfolio.

[12] The Securities Exchange Act of 1934 granted the Federal Reserve Board this authority.

purchase of securities. Of course, the broker-dealer will charge interest on the margin, often the broker *call rate* (the rate the bank charges the broker-dealer) plus some markup. We will call this margin rate i_M.[13] There is margin for both going long and shorting stocks. However, because of the interest cost of trading on margin, the portfolio manager should trade on margin only with a specific objective in mind.

Suppose that a portfolio manager buys 200 shares of ABC at a price per share of $50 and on 50% margin. This would be $10,000 of security ABC. His or her CMV is $10,000, his or her debit balance D is $5,000, and his or her equity E is $5,000 ($E = \text{CMV} - D$). These are broker-dealer terms. Clearly, as each day passes and the brokerage firm marks to market, the CMV, and hence the equity, will change. Marking to market means the broker-dealer obtains the current value of the security each day and monitors whether the funds deposited by the portfolio manager are sufficient to cover the risks of a margined position. For example, if the price of ABC drops to $30 the next day, the account equity will drop to $1,000. This is worrisome because the manager has only $1,000 in equity and a loan of $5,000. To address this sort of problem, the Financial Industry Regulatory Authority (FINRA) and the stock exchanges have established rules that require a *minimum maintenance margin*. If a customer's equity value falls below some threshold, the broker-dealer makes a *margin call* that requires the customer to deposit extra securities or cash. The current threshold value is 25% of the CMV.[14] If a customer receives a margin call, he or she must deposit enough funds to reach the minimum maintenance margin, or the broker-dealer may sell securities to achieve this minimum.

When a portfolio manager shorts a stock, he or she is effectively borrowing the stock from someone (the broker-dealer arranges this) and then selling it. Since this is like trading on margin, the manager must deposit margin for the stock. Regulation T therefore applies to short sales of equity securities as well. With a short

---

[13] Broker-dealers make a large amount of their profits from margin lending.

[14] There are other rules as well. The customer must have a minimum equity of $2,000. (This is mostly a concern for individual investors, not usually for managers who run portfolios with millions of dollars in assets.) Some firms also have higher maintenance margins than the minimum requirement. For example, during the internet bubble of 2000, many brokerages placed especially high maintenance margins on certain internet stocks.

account, the initial margin is also 50%, but the minimum mainte-nance margin is 30%.[15] Accounting for a short position differs slight-ly from accounting for long margin trades, but the concepts are basically the same. On shorting the security, the broker-dealer receives the value of the short sale in cash plus additional cash (or some other deposit) representing the 50% margin. We call this initial cash balance C. The CMV of the securities is computed daily. The equity E of the account is equal to the cash deposit less the CMV, that is, $C - CMV$. For example, to short 200 shares of a stock at a price per share of $50, using a 50% margin, the portfolio manager deposits $5,000 as cash. The proceeds from the short sale are $10,000. The cash in the account is therefore $15,000. The CMV is $10,000, so the equity in the account is $5,000. As with long positions, if the stock price rises, the broker-dealer may require additional deposits as the minimum maintenance margin is reached.[16]

When a portfolio manager has both long positions and short positions with a broker-dealer, the broker-dealer computes the margin requirements of the long and short accounts separately and then nets them to determine the total equity in the account.

13.4.2 The Margin and Market Neutral

With Regulation T in mind, a market-neutral portfolio manager with $V in capital can invest $V in a long portfolio and then short $V of the short portfolio. A margin account will be required for every security sold short in the short portfolio, so the manager will have to post margin. In this case, though, the long positions can be used as margin collateral. Given the 50% margin requirement, the portfolio manager either could deposit $V/2 in cash with the bro-ker to cover the shorts or could just deposit $V of long securities.[17] Theoretically, the portfolio manager could purchase $V of the long portfolio and short $V of the short portfolio and satisfy the Regulation T margin requirements.

In practice, however, a broker or prime broker usually requires an additional *liquidity buffer* to meet mark to markets on the short

---

[15] The minimum maintenance margin is only 5%, though, if the portfolio manager shorts against the box (i.e., shorts the same security that he or she is long).

[16] The value of the stock position that will result in a margin call can be figured out by dividing the cash balance by $(1 + m_{MM})$, where m_{MM} is the minimum maintenance margin requirement.

[17] Unmargined securities are worth half the equity of cash. Many hedge funds achieve greater leverage than described here due to their relationships with prime brokers.

FIGURE 13.1

Flows in creating a market-neutral portfolio.

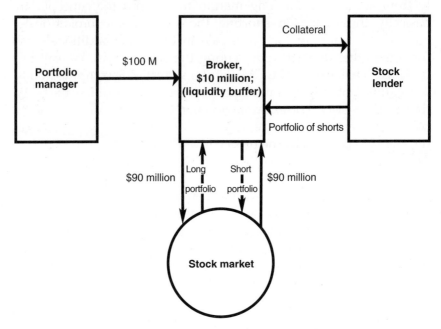

portfolio and to satisfy dividend payments on the short portfolio.[18] Thus the broker may require an additional 10% of the value of the capital. In our example, this would be an additional 0.10V. Let's call this extra liquidity buffer requirement m_{lb}. For any amount of capital V, the maximum that can be invested on one side in a fully leveraged market-neutral portfolio is $V^* = V(1-m_{lb})$. Thus the total maximum amount invested would be $2V^*$. Of course, the portfolio manager can choose to leverage to a lesser degree. He or she could invest $V/2$ in the long portfolio and $V/2$ in the short portfolio, and this would achieve the same degree of gross leverage as a long-only portfolio, but zero net leverage.[19]

13.4.3 Sources of the Return

Suppose that a portfolio manager has identified a basket of securities to go long and a basket of securities to sell short. Call these

---

[18] When someone shorts a stock, all dividend payments from the shorted stocks must be paid to the stock's owner.

[19] In Chapter 12, we defined leverage to be net leverage or leverage with respect to market exposure. Gross leverage is also used by practitioners and is the sum of the absolute positions of a trade or portfolio divided by equity capital.

portfolios L and S. A quantitative model has predicted excess returns for the long portfolio and negative or relatively lower excess returns for the short portfolio. The manager's equity capital is V, and the additional margin required by the broker is 10% ($m_{lb} = 0.10$). Let's assume that the manager has $100 million in equity capital ($V = \$100$ million). Given the margin requirement, he or she will purchase $90 million of the long portfolio and sell short $90 million of the short portfolio. Thus the portfolio manager has chosen to fully leverage the market-neutral portfolio (i.e., V^* invested in the long and short sides). He or she also has chosen to be dollar neutral. Figure 13.1 illustrates the pattern of flows to create this market-neutral portfolio.

Ignoring any margin calls, we can dissect the returns that will accrue to the market-neutral portfolio. The first source of return is the difference in total return between the long portfolio and the short portfolio, $r_L - r_S$, where r_S is the return *before shorting*, the actual return of the weighted short portfolio.[20] The expected α of the overall portfolio, if the hedging is done perfectly, equals $\alpha_L - \alpha_S$. In practice, it may differ slightly from this value, but it can be measured exactly.

The second source of return is the interest on the proceeds of the short sale that are used as collateral. It usually will be a haircut to competitive short-term investment opportunities available in the marketplace. One should expect to receive, over a period of k days and using continuous compounding, $V^*(e^{i\frac{k}{360}} - 1)$.[21]

The third source of return is the interest paid by the broker on the liquidity buffer. We shall assume that the liquidity buffer rate is i'. Thus, over a period of k days, one would receive $m_{lb}V(e^{i'\frac{k}{360}} - 1)$.

The value of the portfolio after k days (assuming we close all positions) would be[22]

---

[20] While the differences in dividend payments for stocks in the long portfolio and the short portfolio can be considered as a source of return as well, this is already reflected in the return formula.

[21] Interest rates from the broker are not continuously compounded rates, but they can be converted to continuously compounded rates, and this makes the math more presentable. Also, one may wish to alter the day count convention from $k/360$ to something else. For a discussion on conversions between rates and general conventions, see Steiner (1998).

[22] For the actual computation of historical returns of a market-neutral portfolio, we briefly discuss these calculations in Chapter 15 on performance measurement. The formula is $r_P = r_L - r_S + r_{cash}$.

TABLE 13.4

Sources of Return from Example Market-Neutral Portfolio

Number Source	Rate of Return (%)	Formula	P/L ($)
1. Total return from long portfolio	7	$r_L V_t^*$	6,300,000
2. Total return from short portfolio	−4	$-r_S V_t^*$	3,600,000
3. Interest on collateral	2	$V_t^* (e^{i \frac{k}{360}} - 1)$	150,125.07
4. Interest on liquidity buffer	2	$V_t m_{lb} (e^{i' \frac{k}{360}} - 1)$	16,680.56
5. Total portfolio	10.07	Sum rows 1–4	10,066,805.63

Note: The total return for the long and short portfolios includes dividends. Of the $100 million equity capital, only $90 million is invested long and $90 million is invested short owing to the liquidity buffer needed on the shorts by the broker-dealer equal to $10 million.

$$V_{t+k} = V_t + V_t^* r_L - V_t^* r_S + \left(V_t - V_t^*\right)\left(e^{i \frac{k}{360}} - 1\right) + V_t^* \left(e^{i \frac{k}{360}} - 1\right)$$
$$= V_t \left(1 - m_{lb}\right) + V_t \left(1 - m_{lb}\right)\left(r_L - r_S\right) + V_t m_{lb} \left(e^{i \frac{k}{360}}\right) + V_t \left(1 - m_{lb}\right)\left(e^{i \frac{k}{360}} - 1\right) \qquad (13.14)$$

Suppose that we hold the market-neutral portfolio for one month ($k=30$). Portfolio L increases by 7%, whereas portfolio S decreases by 4%. Suppose that the interest on the collateral and liquidity buffer is 2% per annum at a continuously compounded rate. In our example, the new value of the portfolio would be $110,066,805.63. This is composed of the long P/L of $6,300,000.00 plus the short P/L of $3,600,000.00 plus the interest on the collateral of $150,125.07 and finally the interest on the liquidity buffer of $16,680.56. The return is 10.07% for the one-month period. This calculation is summarized in Table 13.4.

13.5 THE BENEFITS AND DRAWBACKS OF MARKET NEUTRAL

Market-neutral portfolios offer a host of benefits for quantitative portfolio managers who wish to select specific stocks with their quantitative models. They allow the portfolio manager to focus his or her ability on stock selection with few disruptions from movements of the overall market. There are also some minor drawbacks to a market-neutral portfolio, including, of course, the transactions costs of creating it. Table 13.5 lists more of the benefits and drawbacks.

TABLE 13.5

Benefits and Drawbacks of a Market-Neutral Portfolio

Benefits	Drawbacks
1. There may be more inefficiencies on the *short* side of the market. Analysts tend to be biased toward buys, there are institutional constraints on short selling, and several behavioral biases (e.g., "It's un-American to short") also prevent it.	Shorting stocks is subject to the *uptick rule* given certain market conditions. Borrowing certain stocks is sometimes difficult.
2. Bad stocks can be weighted less than 0%, whereas 0% is the minimum weight in long-only portfolios.	The short side of the portfolio requires an extra liquidity buffer of cash, which handles the short margin maintenance. The rebalancing of the short side can be costly, especially for large upside moves in the marketplace.
3. A truly market-neutral portfolio has no benchmark and hence has fewer weight constraints than a long-only portfolio, allowing for more opportunity to exploit inefficiencies.	The interest on the proceeds from the short sale of securities is up to the discretion of the broker. There is usually a haircut from available interest rates in the market for institutional investors, while retail investors usually receive zero interest.
4. There are extra benefits of diversification to the extent that the short portfolio and long portfolio are less than perfectly correlated. The information ratio may be higher for a market-neutral portfolio (see Section 13.3).	Even if scaled down appropriately, a short position theoretically has the potential for unlimited losses, especially for concentrated portfolios.*
5. The portfolio is generally uncorrelated with stock market movements and thus may be a suitable equity investment for those not interested in having market exposure. An investor can have positive returns whether the market goes up or down.	The market-neutral portfolio generally will have lower performance than a long-only portfolio in a strong bull market.
6. It allows the portfolio manager to focus on stock picking and not worry about market timing.	A bad quantitative model to predict will be amplified.

* Leverage risk is often cited as a drawback to the market-neutral portfolio. However, this is not entirely correct. A market-neutral portfolio manager does not have to create a fully leveraged portfolio. He or she can create a portfolio with 50% of the capital invested in the long portfolio and 50% of the capital invested in the short portfolio that would have a leverage risk very similar to that of a long-only portfolio. It should be remembered, though, that the market-neutral portfolio still will have slightly higher risk, because a short position theoretically can have an unlimited loss.

Perhaps the most return-enhancing benefit of a market-neutral portfolio is the ability to short stocks. There tends to be a long bias in the market. Many money managers, including mutual fund managers, are restricted to long-only positions by institutional rules, and a majority of investors are either not aware of or just plain wary of shorting strategies. A wide variety of stocks may be overpriced owing to the lack of adequate shorting in the market. Thus the very act of shorting may exploit market inefficiencies.

A closely related advantage of a market-neutral portfolio is that in a long-only portfolio the worst view of a stock results in only a 0% weighting of that stock, whereas in a market-neutral portfolio, the manager can express a negative view with an outright negative weighting.

A third benefit is that the market-neutral portfolio is more flexible than the long-only portfolio. The long-only portfolio cannot stray too far from the benchmark owing to risk constraints, so it's stock weightings must match more closely those of the benchmark. The market-neutral portfolio is not bound to the benchmark, so its stock weightings can follow many different patterns.

Extra diversification is another big benefit of the market-neutral portfolio when the stocks in the long and short portfolios are not very correlated. We know from basic portfolio theory that combining two securities with less than perfect correlation results in diversification. That is, by combining the two securities, the portfolio manager obtains a portfolio with returns similar to but with risk less than what either security in isolation would achieve. Since most stocks tend to be somewhat positively correlated, a long-only manager can get only so much of this diversification kick. However, since the stocks in the short portfolio are sold short, the manager effectively creates a negative correlation between the short and long portfolios. Depending on the extent of this negative correlation, the market-neutral portfolio can achieve greater diversification than can the long-only portfolio.

The benefit of diversification is truly amazing. Consider Table 13.6, which describes two portfolios if they are both held long. One is the "good" portfolio because its expected return is high, and the other is the "bad" portfolio because its expected return is low. Both portfolios have similar risk.

Now consider the possible ways of owning the two portfolios. For an overall portfolio that is long only, the weightings of the long and short portfolios must sum to 1. That is, we could own 100% of

TABLE 13.6

Return and Risk Characteristics of Good and
Bad Stock Portfolios

	μ	σ
Good portfolio	0.20	0.30
Bad portfolio	0.06	0.32
$\rho=0.5$		

Note: μ is the expected return of each portfolio, σ is the standard deviation or risk of each
portfolio, and ρ is the correlation between the good and bad portfolios (before shorting).

the good portfolio and 0% of the bad portfolio or 0% of the good
portfolio and 100% of the bad portfolio or some combination in
between those two extremes. From the perspective of diversification, it is better to own a bit of both portfolios. Figure 13.2 illustrates
the idea. As we move from the point at which 100% is invested in
the bad portfolio to the point at which 55% is invested in the good

FIGURE 13.2

Diversification enhancement from a long-short portfolio.

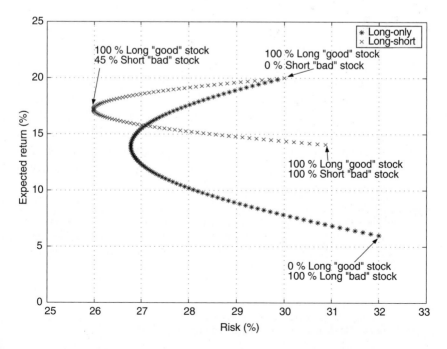

and 45% in the bad, we improve our risk-return combination. The frontier between 100% in the good portfolio and 55%–45% represents the efficient portfolios for a long-only manager, and we would pick an investment point along this frontier.

However, if we could short stocks, we could do better. By allowing for shorting the bad portfolio, the efficient frontier actually moves to the left. There is a whole area, ranging from 100% long the good portfolio to 100% long the good portfolio and 71% short the bad portfolio, where we actually achieve lower risk for the same return that we could earn with the long-only portfolio. This risk reduction demonstrates the power of market-neutral investing.

In addition to the low correlation between the long and short sides of the portfolio, the market-neutral portfolio is relatively uncorrelated with market movements. This offers a benefit to investors who wish to invest in equities but do not wish to be exposed to overall market risk.

A final benefit of market-neutral portfolios is that they allow the portfolio manager to focus on stock picking without having to worry about market timing or exposure to a poorly performing market. During the internet bubble, a market-neutral manager would not have been outright long internet stocks. He or she would have been long certain stocks while shorting others so that his or her portfolio probably would have fared well even when the bubble burst.

Most of the drawbacks of the market-neutral portfolio are not terribly detrimental. Shorting stocks is subject to certain restrictions that make shorting stocks sometimes difficult.[23] This means that one cannot always short quite as easily as one can go long. Interest rates on the proceeds from the short sale may be less than current market rates, causing a slight loss in potential return. Prime brokers typically require an additional cash liquidity buffer to handle the short portfolio for things such as dividend payments and margin

---

[23] For many years, stocks were subject to the uptick rule, which stated that a listed security could only be sold short at a price above the price of the preceding sale (plus tick) or at the last sales price if higher than the previous sale. Short sales were not permitted on minus ticks or zero-minus ticks. Since many practitioners believed these rules did very little for markets, they were removed in 2007. However, in 2010, after the great financial crisis of 2008, the SEC modified the rule, which is now known as the *alternative uptick rule* or the *short-sale restriction*. The rule only prohibits the execution of a short sale order at a price that is less than or equal to the current national best bid if the price of that covered security decreases by 10% from the prior day. This prohibition stays in effect the rest of that trading day plus the next trading day.

calls. This takes some of the portfolio out of the market, but it is not a big problem because the market-neutral portfolio is usually leveraged anyway.[24] In a bull market, market-neutral portfolios will usually underperform all equity portfolios. This is the price of avoiding market collapses. Finally, a market-neutral portfolio focuses the returns on stock picking. Thus, while it aids a manager who is good at stock picking, it only magnifies the losses of a manager who, either for lack of a good model or simply because of bad luck, does not pick stocks well. There is no market-neutral strategy to disguise a poor model.

13.6 REBALANCING

Market-neutral portfolios need to be rebalanced as time passes to maintain market neutrality. At the same time, the market-neutral portfolio must meet margin requirements. We shall briefly discuss these two rebalancing needs.

Let's start with the case of dollar neutrality. Suppose that we create a dollar-neutral portfolio at time t. At time $t + 1$, the weights of the long portfolio and short portfolio will have changed. In particular, dollar neutrality at time t implies that

$$\frac{V_t^L}{V_t^S} = \frac{\sum_{i=1}^{N_L} w_{i,t}^L V_t^L}{\sum_{j=1}^{N_S} w_{j,t}^S V_t^S} = 1 \tag{13.15}$$

At time $t + 1$, this will no longer be true because

$$\frac{V_{t+1}^L}{V_{t+1}^S} = \frac{\sum_{i=1}^{N_L} w_{i,t}^L \left(1 + r_{i,t+1}\right) V_t^L}{\sum_{j=1}^{N_S} w_{j,t}^S \left(1 + r_{j,t+1}\right) V_t^S} \neq 1 \tag{13.16}$$

Only if the long portfolio and short portfolio had performed identically during the period would the overall portfolio have remained perfectly balanced. In all but the rarest of cases, therefore, the dollar neutrality must be reestablished. If the long portfolio has grown larger than the short portfolio, then selling stocks (in amounts proportional to their weights) from the long portfolio and keeping the

---

[24] Many investors believe that market-neutral portfolios must be leveraged. This is not true. Leverage is the choice of the portfolio manager. One can create a market-neutral portfolio that has the same leverage as a long-only portfolio.

funds in cash will reestablish the dollar neutrality. If the short port-folio has grown larger than the long portfolio, then buying back or covering some of the shorts will reestablish the dollar neutrality.

For the case of β neutrality, at time t, we have

$$\frac{\beta_t^L}{\beta_t^S} = \frac{\sum_{i=1}^{N_L} w_{i,t}^L \beta_i}{\sum_{j=1}^{N_S} w_{j,t}^S \beta_j} = 1 \qquad (13.17)$$

However, at time $t + 1$, we have

$$\frac{\beta_{t+1}^L}{\beta_{t+1}^S} = \frac{\sum_{j=1}^{N_S} w_{i,t}^S \left(1 + r_{j,t+1}\right)}{\sum_{i=1}^{N_L} w_{i,t}^L \left(1 + r_{i,t+1}\right)} \frac{\sum_{i=1}^{N_L} w_{i,t}^L \left(1 + r_{i,t+1}\right)\beta_i}{\sum_{j=1}^{N_S} w_{j,t}^S \left(1 + r_{j,t+1}\right)\beta_j} \neq 1 \qquad (13.18)$$

At time $t + 1$, rebalancing reestablishes β neutrality. The rebalancing process is simpler for β neutrality than it is for dollar neutrality. You can restore β neutrality by reducing the dollar value of the portfolio that now has the larger β, as in the case of dollar neutrality. You also can adjust the weights of the stocks within one of the portfolios, either the long or the short, so that the average weighted β is the same as it was originally. Or, in lieu of either of these methods, the portfolio manager simply can use index futures to alter the entire portfolio β. If the overall β has become slightly positive (or slightly negative), the portfolio man-ager can use concepts from Chapter 12 on leverage to reduce (or increase) the β to 0.[25]

13.7 GENERAL LONG-SHORT

This chapter has focused on the construction of market-neutral portfolios in which the securities that the portfolio manager goes long exactly offset the securities that he or she shorts. Some portfo-lio managers bias the portfolio toward either the long or short sides either by design or as a consequence of their investment processes. This style of managing the portfolio not to be perfectly market neu-tral is known as *long-short*. In this section we discuss the general concept of partially hedging the portfolio this way. We also discuss the concept of *equitization*, or using index futures contracts to alter

---

[25] In addition to rebalancing needs for dollar and β neutrality, there are also rebalancing needs owing to the management of short positions.

the portfolio's exposure to the overall market. Finally, we discuss *pair trading*, which is a bit like market neutrality on a pair of stocks.

13.7.1 Long-Short

Up to this point in the chapter we have looked at market-neutral portfolios that are either dollar neutral or risk factor neutral. Some portfolio managers want to construct their portfolios so that they are not entirely market neutral but retain some bias toward either the long or the short side. All of the concepts that we have explored thus far still apply, except that in the *long-short* portfolio there is some difference between either the dollar values or the risk exposures of the long and short sides. For example, the portfolio may have an overall β of 0.4 with respect to the market portfolio. It is not really market neutral, although it certainly has less risk than an all-equity index such as the S&P 500.

Long-short is a common portfolio style. It represents about 5% of the hedge fund world.[26] A long-short manager who is bearish on the equity market might be slightly short, whereas another who is optimistic might be slightly long. Along with the additional risk, the long-short strategy lets a manager benefit from overall market movements and α mojo.

13.7.2 Equitization

Equitization is the process of converting cash into a synthetic equity position with equity futures, forwards, or options. Through equitization, a portfolio manager with a market-neutral portfolio can keep his or her α and also have full exposure to the equity market. To alter the portfolio's exposure to the market, the manager can use equity index futures to go long the index an amount equal to 100% of the equity capital.[27] The return on the new portfolio will equal the return from the market-neutral side plus the return on the index futures. The market risk of the portfolio will be 1 (that is, $\beta_p = 1$). The portfolio will have all the attributes of a long-only portfolio, as well as the advantages of a market-neutral portfolio.

---

[26] *Source*: BarclayHedge and author's calculations.
[27] This example assumes that the β of the market-neutral portfolio is equal to 0. While there will be a requirement by the futures broker for margin on the index futures, this amount can be supplied through the liquidity buffer used for the short positions. Since the long futures contract will implicitly hedge the short positions, less is required on both sides of the deal to meet margin requirements.

Equitization is especially useful to a portfolio manager who must maintain a significant exposure to a specific equity benchmark but has views on the relative performance of stocks. To take one example, if the manager feels that certain sectors of the economy are the most mispriced, he or she can focus on making many trades in those sectors. If he or she finds great opportunities in, say, the consumer staples sector, he or she can create a market-neutral position within consumer staples, leaving other sector exposures long-only, as dictated by the long index futures position. The resulting portfolio will still behave very much like the benchmark, but benefit from the hidden α of the market-neutral position in consumer staples.

13.7.3 Portable α

Equitization can be taken a step further via the concept of *portable* α.[28] Portable α is α that can be transported from the portfolio to another asset class or subclass entirely. This allows plan sponsors, financial advisors, pension fund managers, and other investors the flexibility to separate decisions relating to α from the asset-allocation decision. For portfolio managers, portable α makes it possible to separate the α from the β of the portfolio. The construction of portable α combines concepts from leverage (Chapter 12) and market neutrality (this chapter).

For example, suppose that a portfolio manager is very good at managing small-cap stocks but thinks that large-cap stocks will outperform small-cap stocks. He or she always has had a positive α^B when it comes to managing small-cap stocks against a small-cap benchmark such as the Russell 2000. He or she believes that his or her success is due to many inefficiencies in the small-cap universe that he or she is able to exploit with quantitative models. His or her models are less successful in the large-cap universe, perhaps because there are fewer inefficiencies there. He or she tends to manage mainly small-cap stocks, but given that his or her benchmark is the S&P 500 (not the Russell 2000), he or she realizes that if he or she is correct about large-cap stocks performing better than small-cap stocks, this will hurt his or her relative performance tremendously. This is a perfect situation for the manager to transport his or her small-cap α. The manager can continue to manage his or

---

[28] Some people refer to this as α *transport*.

her portfolio as he or she wishes, choosing small-cap stocks that he or she feels are relatively mispriced, but he or she also should short the Russell 2000 futures in order to achieve β neutrality vis-à-vis the Russell 2000 and purchase S&P 500 futures so as to achieve a β equal to 1 versus the S&P 500. This leaves the manager with a portfolio that has the overall market risk of the S&P 500 plus the α^B of his or her portfolio over the Russell 2000.[29]

Below we describe the steps of transporting α in this example and the resulting overall portfolio:

Step 1: Find the β of the small-cap portfolio versus the Russell 2000: $\tilde{r}_P = \alpha_{P,R} + \beta_{P,R}\tilde{r}_R + \epsilon_{P,R}$.[30]

Step 2: Short the required amount of Russell 2000 futures to achieve a $\beta^* = 0$ for the overall portfolio. Then the excess return of the new portfolio becomes $\tilde{r}_P - \hat{\beta}_{P,R}\tilde{r}_R$.

Step 3: Find the β of the new portfolio versus the S&P 500. This is done by regressing $\tilde{r}_P - \hat{\beta}_{P,R}\tilde{r}_R$ against the excess returns of the S&P 500 ($\tilde{r}_S$). The new beta estimate will be given by $\dfrac{\hat{C}[\ \tilde{r}_P - \hat{\beta}_{PR}\tilde{r}_R, \tilde{r}_S]}{\hat{V}(\tilde{r}_S)} = \dfrac{\hat{C}[\tilde{r}_P, \tilde{r}_S]}{\hat{V}(\tilde{r}_S)}$ $- \hat{\beta}_{PR}\dfrac{\hat{C}[\tilde{r}_R, \tilde{r}_S]}{\hat{V}(\tilde{r}_S)} = \hat{\beta}_{P,S} - \hat{\beta}_{P,R}\hat{\beta}_{R,S}$. The constant term, or alpha intercept, will be given as $E[\tilde{r}_P - \hat{\beta}_{P,R}] - (\hat{\beta}_{P,S} - \hat{\beta}_{P,R}\hat{\beta}_{R,S})\ E[\tilde{r}_S] = \hat{\alpha}_{P,R} - (\hat{\beta}_{P,S} - \hat{\beta}_{P,R}\hat{\beta}_{R,S})\ \bar{\tilde{r}}_S$.

Step 4: Go long the required amount of S&P 500 futures to achieve a $\beta^* = 1$ (i.e., $1 - [\hat{\beta}_{P,S} - \hat{\beta}_{P,R}\hat{\beta}_{R,S}]$). The new excess return of the portfolio will be $\tilde{r}_P - \hat{\beta}_{P,R}\tilde{r}_R + (1 - \hat{\beta}_{P,S} + \hat{\beta}_{P,R}\hat{\beta}_{R,S})\tilde{r}_S$.

Step 5: The α of the new portfolio with respect to the S&P 500 is $E[\tilde{r}_P - \hat{\beta}_{P,R}\tilde{r}_S - (\hat{\beta}_{P,S} - \hat{\beta}_{P,R}\hat{\beta}_{R,S})\tilde{r}_S] = \hat{\alpha}_{P,R} - (\hat{\beta}_{P,S} - \hat{\beta}_{P,R}\ \hat{\beta}_{R,S})\ \bar{\tilde{r}}_S$. Thus, this method gives the

---

[29] The portfolio manager will achieve perfect α transport only under certain conditions discussed in the detailed steps to create portable α.

[30] We use double subscripts (P,R) to indicate the regression of the portfolio excess return ("P") on the Russell 2000 excess return ("R"), where $\tilde{r}_P = r_P - r_f$, and $\tilde{r}_R = r_R - r_f$ (i.e., the excess return of the portfolio or of the Russell 2000 over the risk-free rate). We also use ("S") to represent the S&P 500. The user can do the entire analysis with or without the risk-free rate. A bar over a variable indicates the in-sample average of the variable. For example, $\bar{\tilde{r}}_S$ is the average return of the S&P 500 minus the risk-free rate over the estimation period.

portfolio manager a β exposure of 1 to the S&P 500 with an α of $\hat{\alpha}_{P,R} - (\hat{\beta}_{P,S} - \hat{\beta}_{P,R}\hat{\beta}_{R,S})\bar{r}_S$. This means that the portfolio manager achieves a perfect α transport when $\hat{\beta}_{P,S} = \hat{\beta}_{P,R}\hat{\beta}_{R,S}$. Depending on other values, his transported α might be larger or smaller than his original Russell 2000 α.

Portable α creates a host of possibilities for transporting α in the manager's portfolio. Given that there is no strict mandate on the portfolio's base exposure, the manager even could transport α from an equity universe to a bond universe. For example, the portfolio manager in the preceding example has a positive α versus the Russell 2000 equity benchmark by managing a portfolio of small-cap stocks. He or she could short the Russell 2000 futures in the same proportion so as to neutralize his or her overall β. He or she then could use the proceeds to invest in either 10-year bond futures or bond exchange-traded funds (ETFs) to acquire a market exposure to the bond markets.

The concept of portable α is quite useful, although there are some problems associated with it. First, derivatives, swaps, and even liquid futures do cost money to buy and sell. Second, index futures may not perfectly track the underlying portfolio, even if the β versus the index has been measured. The resulting residual risk may be larger than the α that the portfolio manager is trying to transport. Third, futures may not exist for a particular portfolio or asset class. In other cases, the futures may exist but be insufficiently liquid. For example, there are some futures for certain sector indices, but they are extremely illiquid and thus not practical. Fourth, while quantitative portfolio managers have the expertise to transport α, many pension fund committees and other investors simply do not have the expertise to handle α mojo. Fifth, margin may need to be posted for the futures trading, so a slightly lower interest rate is received than with alternative investment vehicles. Sixth, index futures have roll-over risk and basis risk, and swaps have counterparty risk. For the most part, these risks are small.

Despite the minor problems associated with portable α, it is a low-cost mechanism to use capital efficiently and separate the α from the β of the portfolio so as to achieve the best of both worlds for the investor.

13.7.4 Pair Trading

Pair trading means creating a market-neutral balance between two securities that are similar except that one is undervalued and one is overvalued (according to a quantitative model of stock returns). The pair trade involves buying the undervalued security and shorting the overvalued security. Just as a market-neutral portfolio removes exposure to market risk and solidifies the connection between the portfolio's return and its α, a pair trade removes market risks from the pair and brings out the α's of the individual securities. Pair trades can be very useful for quantitative portfolio managers for a variety of reasons. They allow the portfolio manager to make trades that focus on α without the complications of market or industry risk. Second, they expand the investment universe to stocks in otherwise overlooked sectors. Even if the manager considers the consumer discretionary sector extremely overvalued as a whole, he or she may find good picks within that sector. Pair trading takes advantage of picking these stocks while still avoiding exposure to the overvalued sector. A long-only portfolio simply would avoid the sector altogether. Another useful aspect of pair trading is that it uses equity capital efficiently. The pair trade involves using margin on the short side, so every dollar invested in the pair trade is equivalent to $2 invested in a long-only portfolio without leverage. This is the same efficient use of capital that a leveraged long-only portfolio would provide.

A pair trade can occur when the portfolio manager believes that there is a difference between either the *absolute values* or the *relative values* of the two securities. It could be that the securities are both expected to have a positive α, but one of them is expected to have a much higher α. In this case, buying the security with the higher α and shorting the one with the lower α is still a reasonable pair trade because there is a difference in the relative expected movements of the securities. Or it could be the case that a portfolio manager finds two securities that are similar, but one is expected to have a negative α and the other a positive α. This is an absolute pair trade, the ideal case.

The first step in pair trading is to identify similar stocks, and *similar* has more than one meaning. One is that the stocks are in the same industry. The manager can apply his or her quantitative model to stocks within an industry and then rank them by aggregate Z-score, or α, or expected return. The pair could be two stocks at opposite ends of the ranked list.

Similar stocks also can be found with *characteristic matching*, as discussed in Chapter 7. The manager looks for stocks with close fundamental ratios. One should be careful to look at fundamental ratios that are not factors in the quantitative model of stock returns because those factors already drive the expected α's.

Statistical analysis can help to identify stocks that have behaved similarly over time. One test is take the historical returns of stocks and estimate their correlations with each other (their β coefficients).[31] Two stocks whose returns are highly correlated, or whose β with respect to one another is close to 1 and statistically significant, have behaved very similarly in the past and may tend to in the future. The problem with this sort of analysis is that it applies a relationship gleaned from past data to future expected returns. The value of the analysis, though, comes from the fact that the daily relative volatility of a pair of stocks will be under control if the stocks are highly correlated.

Another way to find similar stocks is to run a regression of stock A's returns against stock B's returns using daily data for a period of one year. The manager runs a series of regressions for every month of the past year and stores the α's of the regression. He or she looks for pairs in which the β is close to 1 and the α of one stock versus the other is significant and related over time. This kind of similarity would show up in the autoregressive behavior of the α of two stocks relative to each other. If the pattern appears, there is a potential pair trade. The risk of one stock offsets the risk of the other, but one stock has an excess return over the other that seems to persist.

It is also possible to take a contrarian view of pair trades. Historical statistical data show whether or not two stocks that are similar have diverged in return movement. If they have, one might believe that they eventually must converge. In the contrarian pair trade, one would short the stock that has had the higher return over some period and purchase the one that has had the lower return.

Many portfolio managers spend a lot of time researching the fundamentals of the companies before enacting the pair trade. A quantitative portfolio manager, however, relies on his or her quantitative models and statistical techniques. Once a pair-trade candidate has been identified, the next step is to determine how much to trade. There are a number of methods for this, as well. Some managers want to be a bit long or a bit short on one side of a pair trade. We will focus on the case in which the portfolio manager wants to eliminate

---

[31] One also could use a multifactor model to infer the implied correlations among stocks.

as much risk as possible and focus on the relative α's of the stocks. As with a market-neutral portfolio, this sort of pair trade can be dollar-neutral or risk-factor-neutral—although, unlike the market-neutral portfolio, it cannot be both at once. Dollar-neutral pair trades are common, although they may be flawed if one stock is much more volatile than the other. Dollar neutrality implies that $w_A = w_B$, where the same dollar amount is placed in stock A and stock B. Risk-factor neutrality adjusts for the risk-factor β. The β of each stock is measured against some index, $w_B = w_A(\beta_A/\beta_B)$, where β_A and β_B are the measured β's of each stock over the same time horizon with respect to some industry index or the market index. You can use $w_A = 1$ and get the appropriate risk-adjusted weight for stock B for the pair trade. Since a pair trade is ever undiversified, a portfolio manager may wish to use volatility instead of β to determine the relative sizes of the stock trades. In this case, the weights would be determined as $w_B = w_A(\sigma_A/\sigma_B)$.

Suppose that a quantitative portfolio manager ran his or her quantitative model on the pharmaceutical industry. From the model, he or she has determined that Johnson & Johnson is relatively more attractive than Merck. Since the companies are similar in that they come from the same industry and specialize in drug manufacturing, the manager wants to make a pair trade on these two stocks from January 2021 onward.

The manager already has completed the first step of identifying the stocks to pair trade. The next step is to determine the weights to hold in each security. Using historical data from December 31, 2014, to December 31, 2020, the portfolio manager estimates $\beta_{JNJ} = 0.717$ and $\beta_{MRK} = 0.513$ versus the S&P 500. For β neutrality, he or she will short $1.40 times Merck for every $1.00 exposure to Johnson & Johnson. Another way of saying this is that the relative normalized weights (weights that sum to 1) should be 0.417 and 0.582 for JNJ and MRK, respectively. If, instead, the portfolio manager wants to be dollar neutral, he or she should short $1 of Merck for every $1 of Johnson & Johnson so that the relative weights are 0.50 and 0.50.

The performance of such a pair trade from December 31, 2020, to August 31, 2021, appears in Table 13.7. From this table we can see that owning JNJ outright would have provided a decent return over the period of 10.01%, but with an annualized volatility of 10.79%. Shorting Merck also would have produced a positive 2.19% return but with higher annualized volatility of 17.42%. Together, though, the dollar-neutral pair trade produced an unleveraged return of 6.10% with a lower volatility of 9.77%. Thus, for an average return

TABLE 13.7

Example of a Pair Trade

	Holding Period Return (%)	SD (%)	Correlation with S&P 500
JNJ	10.01	10.79	−0.38
MRK	−2.19	17.42	0.23
Pair (dollar-neutral)	6.10	9.77	−0.41
Pair (beta-neutral)	5.45	9.59	−0.43

Note: Data were obtained from Bloomberg. The holding-period returns and other statistics were computed, over the period of December 31, 2020, to August 31, 2021. The position initiated on December 31, 2020, was either β neutral or dollar neutral and not rebalanced for the entire duration of the trade.

similar to that of either trade on its own, the pair trade produced a volatility that was less than the volatility of either of the individual securities. The correlation with the S&P 500 was −0.41 compared to −0.38 and 0.23. The β-neutral pair trade did not perform quite as well as the dollar-neutral one, but both accomplished the desired goal of maintaining return while reducing risk.

13.8 CONCLUSION

Where leverage multiplies a portfolio's exposure to the market, the market-neutral strategy insulates the portfolio from market winds. Market-neutral strategies reduce or eliminate an investor's exposure to the volatility of the marketplace while still producing substantial returns. In fact, these strategies even can boost the relative contribution of a portfolio's α and be used to transport α across asset classes. In this chapter we discussed the two main variants of market neutrality: dollar neutrality, in which the long and short positions equal each other in dollar value, and β neutrality, in which the long and short positions have similar β's with respect to certain risk factors. We showed that market-neutral investing is a great source of α mojo because, by letting the portfolio manager sell bad stocks short, it boosts α and the information ratio. We also discussed cousins of the market-neutral strategy, including long-short strategies, equitization of a market-neutral strategy, portable α, and pair trading.

We have not exhausted the wellsprings of α mojo quite yet. In the next chapter we uncover the third major source of investing mojo, a rigorous statistical theory that boosts the value of α by quantifying qualitative information.

Market-Neutral Portfolio Construction Techniques

As discussed in Appendix 9B, phantom weights and binary variables can be used to construct a market-neutral portfolio optimization that allows for more general portfolios, including leverage constraints, number of long and short positions, and other possibilities. In this appendix, we will review the ideas in Appendix 9B and illustrate an example of constraining leverage.

In order to constrain the total leverage of the portfolio, we will want the sum of the long weights plus the sum of the short weights to equal some amount, say l_p. For example, if we want a portfolio with a leverage of 2, we would specify that $l_p = 2$. If we want a portfolio of leverage 4, we would specify that $l_p = 4$, and so on. Some investors might want to constrain leverage further, such that the long and short leverages are different. In this case, the user might specify that the sum of the long weights equals l_l (long exposure) and the sum of the short weights equal l_s (short exposure). For example, if a user wanted to create a 130–30 portfolio, then $l_l = 1.30$ and $l_s = 0.30$. When using phantom weights and binary variables, these constraints are quite easy to add to the market-neutral optimization.

We start by expanding the $\mathbf{x}$ vector to include five types of variables. They include the N actual portfolio weights, w_i; the phantom positive weights w_i^+, which represent the N "long" positions of the portfolio; the phantom negative weights, w_i^-, which represent the N "short" positions of the portfolio; and the binary variables v_i^+ and v_i^- for each stock in the portfolio. We then introduce the following constraints in order to ensure that the phantom weights are orthogonal to each other and are also related to the actual weights (w_i) of the portfolio:

$$w_i = w_i^+ - w_i^- \qquad (13A.1)$$

and

$$v_i^+ \kappa_l \leq w_i^+ \leq v_i^+ \kappa_h \qquad (13A.2)$$

$$v_i^- \gamma_l \leq w_i^- \leq v_i^- \gamma_h \qquad (13A.3)$$

$$v_i^+ + v_i^- \leq 1 \qquad (13A.4)$$

Since v_i^+ and v_i^- are binary variables, the inequality constraint in Eq. (13A.4) forces only one of them to be 1 and the other 0. This constraint combined with the constraints in Eq. (13A.2) and (13A.3) forces the phantom weights to also be orthogonal to each other. For generality, we used the parameters κ_l, γ_l, κ_h, and γ_h, but in most market-neutral applications, it will be sufficient to set these equal to 0 and 1. When constructing the optimization, it is important to specify that v_i^+ and v_i^- are binary variables.[1]

The minimization problem is similar to our standard one:

$$\min_x \frac{1}{2} x'Qx + x'c \quad s.t. \quad Ax \leq b \qquad (13A.5)$$

$$lb \leq x \leq ub \qquad (13A.6)$$

where x is the vector of unknowns in the problem, Q is a symmetric positive semi-definite matrix, c is a vector of coefficients, A is a matrix of coefficients for the equality and inequality constraints, b is a vector of constraint values, lb is a lower-bound vector, and ub is an upper-bound vector.[2]

We will show the equality matrix constraints and inequality matrix constraints separately, but you can also combine them into one A matrix if desired. The equality matrix, A_{eq}, will be an $(N + 4)$ by $(5N)$ matrix and the b_{eq} vector will be $(N + 4)$ by (1).

$$A_{eq} = \begin{bmatrix} \boldsymbol{\iota}_{1 \times N} & \mathbf{0}_{1 \times N} & \mathbf{0}_{1 \times N} & \mathbf{0}_{1 \times N} & \mathbf{0}_{1 \times N} \\ \boldsymbol{\mu}_{1 \times N} & \mathbf{0}_{1 \times N} & \mathbf{0}_{1 \times N} & \mathbf{0}_{1 \times N} & \mathbf{0}_{1 \times N} \\ \mathbf{I}_{N \times N} & -1 \cdot \mathbf{I}_{N \times N} & \mathbf{I}_{N \times N} & \mathbf{0}_{N \times N} & \mathbf{0}_{N \times N} \\ \mathbf{0}_{1 \times N} & \boldsymbol{\iota}_{1 \times N} & \mathbf{0}_{1 \times N} & \mathbf{0}_{1 \times N} & \mathbf{0}_{1 \times N} \\ \mathbf{0}_{1 \times N} & \mathbf{0}_{1 \times N} & \boldsymbol{\iota}_{1 \times N} & \mathbf{0}_{1 \times N} & \mathbf{0}_{1 \times N} \end{bmatrix}_{(N+4) \times (5N)} \qquad (13A.7)$$

---

[1] It is essential that the software package allows for quadratic optimization with binary variables and continuous variables. The CPLEX suite has these and can be used through the CPLEX library in MATLAB. For users who do not have this option, we provide an algorithm in Appendix 10B that can be adapted for a market-neutral portfolio optimization.

[2] As we discussed in Appendix 9A, one can also place these upper- and lower-bound constraints directly in the A matrix.

$$\mathbf{b}_{eq} = \begin{bmatrix} 0 \\ \mu_p \\ \mathbf{0}_{N \times 1} \\ l_l \\ l_s \end{bmatrix}_{(N+4) \times (1)}$$ (13A.8)

The inequality matrix, $\mathbf{A}_{ineq}$, would be set up as follows:

$$\mathbf{A}_{ineq} = \begin{bmatrix} \mathbf{0}_{N \times N} & \mathbf{0}_{N \times N} & \mathbf{0}_{N \times N} & \mathbf{I}_{N \times N} & \mathbf{I}_{N \times N} \\ \mathbf{0}_{N \times N} & \mathbf{I}_{N \times N} & \mathbf{0}_{N \times N} & -1 \cdot \mathbf{I}_{N \times N} & \mathbf{0}_{N \times N} \\ \mathbf{0}_{N \times N} & -1 \cdot \mathbf{I}_{N \times N} & \mathbf{0}_{N \times N} & \mathbf{0}_{N \times N} & \mathbf{0}_{N \times N} \\ \mathbf{0}_{N \times N} & \mathbf{0}_{N \times N} & \mathbf{I}_{N \times N} & \mathbf{0}_{N \times N} & -1 \cdot \mathbf{I}_{N \times N} \\ \mathbf{0}_{N \times N} & \mathbf{0}_{N \times N} & -1 \cdot \mathbf{I}_{N \times N} & \mathbf{0}_{N \times N} & \mathbf{0}_{N \times N} \end{bmatrix}_{(5N) \times (5N)}$$ (13A.9)

$$\mathbf{b} = \begin{bmatrix} \iota_{N \times 1} \\ \mathbf{0}_{N \times 1} \\ \mathbf{0}_{N \times 1} \\ \mathbf{0}_{N \times 1} \\ \mathbf{0}_{N \times 1} \end{bmatrix}_{(5N) \times (1)}$$ (13A.10)

where $\mu_{1 \times N}$ is the row vector of the mean returns for each of the N stocks, μ_p is the desired annualized portfolio return, $\iota_{1 \times N}$ is a row of six 1s (that is, the first six entries of matrix $\mathbf{A}$'s row 1 are 1s), $\mathbf{0}_{1 \times N}$ is a row of N entries of zero, $\mathbf{I}_{N \times N}$ is the identity matrix (that is, an N-by-N matrix with 1s on the diagonal and 0s everywhere else), and so on and so forth. In order to aid the reader, we indicate the dimension of every matrix as a subscript.

As stated earlier, you can either put upper- and lower-bound constraints in the inequality, or $\mathbf{A}_{ineq}$ matrix, or specify them directly as upper- and lower-bound vectors in many optimization packages. In this example, we chose to specify them directly; thus we constrain weights, phantom weights, and binary weights to be between 0 and 1.[3] Thus,

$$\mathbf{lb} = \begin{bmatrix} \mathbf{0}_{1 \times N} & \mathbf{0}_{1 \times N} & \mathbf{0}_{1 \times N} & \mathbf{0}_{1 \times N} & \mathbf{0}_{1 \times N} & \mathbf{0}_{1 \times N} \end{bmatrix}$$ (13A.11)

$$\mathbf{ub} = \begin{bmatrix} \iota_{1 \times N} & \iota_{1 \times N} & \iota_{1 \times N} & \iota_{1 \times N} & \iota_{1 \times N} & \iota_{1 \times N} \end{bmatrix}$$ (13A.12)

---

[3] Some of these weight boundaries were implicitly already constrained by prior constraints.

The **x** solution variables are

$$
\mathbf{x} = \begin{bmatrix} \mathbf{w}_{N\times1} \\ \mathbf{w}^+_{N\times1} \\ \mathbf{w}^-_{N\times1} \\ \mathbf{v}^+_{N\times1} \\ \mathbf{v}^-_{N\times1} \end{bmatrix} = \begin{bmatrix} w_1 \\ w_2 \\ \vdots \\ w_N \\ w^+_1 \\ w^+_2 \\ \vdots \\ w^+_N \\ w^-_1 \\ w^-_2 \\ \vdots \\ w^-_N \\ v^+_1 \\ v^+_2 \\ \vdots \\ v^+_N \\ v^-_1 \\ v^-_2 \\ \vdots \\ v^-_N \end{bmatrix}
\tag{13A.13}
$$

We can solve this problem with a mixed integer quadratic programming (MIQP) optimizer.[4] If an MIQP optimizer is not available, but a mixed integer linear programming (MILP) optimizer is, then use an algorithm similar to the one discussed in Appendix 10B to find the solution.

---

[4] For example, IBM's CPLEX optimization software has a MIQP function called CPLEXMIQP.

13A.1 A NUMERICAL EXAMPLE

We will continue the numerical example in Appendix 9A. However, we will change the target return. Typically, with market-neutral portfolios, a lower return target should be sought, since the net position of the portfolio is zero. For this example, we chose a target return of 2% and the leverage of the long and short portfolios equal to 1 (i.e., a total leverage of 2, where $l_l = l_s = 1$).

The quadratic programming problem can be expressed as

$$\min_{\mathbf{x}} \frac{1}{2} \mathbf{x}' \Sigma \mathbf{x} \quad s.t. \quad \mathbf{A}\mathbf{x} \le \mathbf{b} \tag{13A.14}$$

where

$$\mathbf{A} = \begin{bmatrix} \mathbf{A}_{eq} \\ \mathbf{A}_{ineq} \end{bmatrix} = \begin{bmatrix} \boldsymbol{\iota}_{1\times6} & \mathbf{0}_{1\times6} & \mathbf{0}_{1\times6} & \mathbf{0}_{1\times6} & \mathbf{0}_{1\times6} \\ \boldsymbol{\mu}_{1\times6} & \mathbf{0}_{1\times6} & \mathbf{0}_{1\times6} & \mathbf{0}_{1\times6} & \mathbf{0}_{1\times6} \\ \mathbf{I}_{6\times6} & -1\cdot\mathbf{I}_{6\times6} & \mathbf{I}_{6\times6} & \mathbf{0}_{6\times6} & \mathbf{0}_{6\times6} \\ \mathbf{0}_{1\times6} & \boldsymbol{\iota}_{1\times6} & \mathbf{0}_{1\times6} & \mathbf{0}_{1\times6} & \mathbf{0}_{1\times6} \\ \mathbf{0}_{1\times6} & \mathbf{0}_{1\times6} & \boldsymbol{\iota}_{1\times6} & \mathbf{0}_{1\times6} & \mathbf{0}_{1\times6} \\ \mathbf{0}_{6\times6} & \mathbf{0}_{6\times6} & \mathbf{0}_{6\times6} & \mathbf{I}_{6\times6} & \mathbf{I}_{6\times6} \\ \mathbf{0}_{6\times6} & \mathbf{I}_{6\times6} & \mathbf{0}_{6\times6} & -1\cdot\mathbf{I}_{6\times6} & \mathbf{0}_{6\times6} \\ \mathbf{0}_{6\times6} & -1\cdot\mathbf{I}_{6\times6} & \mathbf{0}_{6\times6} & \mathbf{0}_{6\times6} & \mathbf{0}_{6\times6} \\ \mathbf{0}_{6\times6} & \mathbf{0}_{6\times6} & \mathbf{I}_{6\times6} & \mathbf{0}_{6\times6} & -1\cdot\mathbf{I}_{6\times6} \\ \mathbf{0}_{6\times6} & \mathbf{0}_{6\times6} & -1\cdot\mathbf{I}_{6\times6} & \mathbf{0}_{6\times6} & \mathbf{0}_{6\times6} \end{bmatrix}_{40\times30} \tag{13A.15}$$

$$\mathbf{b} = \begin{bmatrix} \mathbf{b}_{eq} \\ \mathbf{b}_{ineq} \end{bmatrix} = \begin{bmatrix} 0 \\ 2 \\ \mathbf{0}_{6\times1} \\ 1 \\ 1 \\ \boldsymbol{\iota}_{6\times1} \\ \mathbf{0}_{6\times1} \\ \mathbf{0}_{6\times1} \\ \mathbf{0}_{6\times1} \\ \mathbf{0}_{6\times1} \end{bmatrix}_{40\times1} \tag{13A.16}$$

where $\boldsymbol{\mu}_{1\times6} = [14.40 \quad 10.19 \quad 9.87 \quad 7.52 \quad 20.05 \quad 2.66]$, $\boldsymbol{\iota}_{1\times6}$ is a row of six 1s (that is, the first six entries of matrix $\mathbf{A}$'s row 1 are 1s),

$\mathbf{0}_{1\times6}$ is a row of 6 entries of 0, $\mathbf{I}_{6\times6}$ is the identity matrix (that is, a 6-by-6 matrix with 1s on the diagonal and 0s everywhere else), and so on and so forth, and $\mathbf{x} = [\mathbf{w}_{1\times6} \quad \mathbf{w}_{1\times6}^+ \quad \mathbf{w}_{1\times6}^- \quad \mathbf{v}_{1\times6}^+ \quad \mathbf{v}_{1\times6}^-]'$. In order to aid the reader, we indicate the dimension of every matrix as a subscript, including for the large $\mathbf{A}$ and $\mathbf{b}$ matrices.

The economic meaning of these constraints is the following. The first five rows of this $\mathbf{A}$ matrix are the equality constraints that the sum of weights equals 0, that the average return of the portfolio equals 2%, that $w_i = w_i^+ - w_i^-$, that the sum of the long weights equals 1 ($\Sigma_{i-1}^N w_i^+ = 1$), and that the sum of the short weights equals 1 ($\Sigma_{i=1}^N w_i^- = 1$). For the binary weights, a zero is placed in the matrix since they are not relevant for these constraints. The sixth row in the matrix (which is really the 11th row through the 16th row) constrains the binary variables to be orthogonal—that is, only one of them can be positive—which consequently constrains the phantom weights to be orthogonal (i.e., we don't buy and sell the same security). To establish this, we need the last four rows of constraints (which are really rows 17 to 40).

The solution using an optimization routine with continuous and binary variables is[5]:

$$\mathbf{w} = \begin{bmatrix} -0.213 \\ 0.198 \\ 0.357 \\ 0.445 \\ -0.099 \\ -0.687 \end{bmatrix} \qquad (13A.17)$$

You will notice that the sum of the portfolio weights equals 0 (i.e., a dollar-neutral portfolio) and that stocks 1, 5, and 6 are sold short and stocks 2, 3, and 4 are held long. If you check the results for w_i^+ and w_i^-, you will note that they have the same value as the actual solution (i.e., there is no buying or selling of the same stock). The mean return of this portfolio is 2% with a standard deviation of 14.62%.

---

[5] Using the CPLEX function CPLEXMIQP, available through the CPLEX library in MATLAB, this optimization took 0.0484 seconds to reach a solution.

QUESTIONS

13.1. Who is said to have formed the first market-neutral portfolio? In what year was it formed?

13.2. True or false: Market-neutral portfolios provide a useful addition to an investor's portfolio because they have a low correlation with other asset classes.

13.3. Is there a combination of the risk-free asset and the S&P 500 that also would achieve a low correlation with the market (i.e., the S&P 500)? What about a low β?

13.4. (a) What is dollar neutrality?

    (b) Suppose that we take a simple two-stock portfolio. The portfolio manager shorts $1 million of T with a $\beta = 0.70$ and goes long $1 million of MGM with a $\beta = 2.42$. Is the portfolio market neutral?

13.5. (a) What is beta neutrality?

    (b) What is the minimum level of neutrality that a market-neutral portfolio should have?

13.6. Suppose that a portfolio manager would like to construct a market-neutral portfolio from the four stocks below. He already has identified TGT and BA as stocks for the short portfolio and WYNN and POOL as stocks for the long portfolio. Also suppose that the sum of the weights in the long portfolio must equal 1.

Stock	Ticker	β_i	w_i
1	POOL	0.72	
2	BA	1.65	
3	TGT	0.97	0.670
4	WYNN	2.38	

    (a) Suppose that he wishes to build a dollar-neutral portfolio. What are the weights of the other securities?

    (b) Suppose that he wishes to build a dollar-neutral and beta-neutral portfolio. What are the weights of the other stocks in the portfolio?

13.7. Suppose that a portfolio manager wants to construct a market-neutral portfolio from the four stocks below. She already has identified FIS and KO as stocks for the short portfolio and MMM and ABC as stocks for the long portfolio. She has found the factor exposures of the stocks to two factors that she believes drive stock returns. Also, suppose that the sum of the weights in the long and short portfolios must equal 1.

Stock	Ticker	$\beta_{i,1}$	$\beta_{i,2}$
1	MMM	0.93	-0.49
2	FIS	0.81	-0.68
3	KO	0.58	0.71
4	ABC	0.57	-0.46

(a) Suppose that she wishes to build a dollar-neutral portfolio. What should be the weights of the securities in the portfolio?
(b) Suppose that she wishes to build a portfolio that is dollar neutral and beta neutral to all factors. What should be the weights of the stocks in the portfolio? (*Note*: Round to two decimal places.)

13.8. Suppose that we construct a simple market-neutral portfolio. For each value of ρ below (ρ being the correlation between the residual returns of the long portfolio and the short portfolio), what is the ratio of the information ratio of the market-neutral portfolio to that of the long-only portfolio? (*Note*: Assume that the market-neutral portfolio is fully leveraged.)
(a) $\rho = 0$
(b) $\rho = 0.5$
(c) $\rho = 1$

13.9. Suppose that a portfolio manager shorts 1,000 shares at a price of $50 of stock ZZZ. The initial margin is 50%, and the maintenance margin is 25%. He deposits enough to satisfy the initial margin. At what price will the portfolio manager receive a margin call? (*Note*: Assume unrealistically that the portfolio manager does not have other collateral to satisfy the margin account credit balance.)

13.10. Shortly after it became public that Martha Stewart was being investigated for insider trading, the stock of her company (MSO) dropped from $19.40 in May 2002 to $7.00 by September 2002. A portfolio manager believed that the stock price would not continue to decrease. Thus she wanted to buy the maximum number of shares possible using her margin account.

(a) Given that initial margin is 50%, how many shares could she buy if she deposited $125,000 into her brokerage account?

(b) If the maintenance margin of her account is 25%, what price can the stock reach before she will receive a margin call?

13.11. True or false: To create a market-neutral portfolio, a portfolio manager needs to use cash as collateral on the shorts.

13.12. In a typical market-neutral portfolio, what are the four sources of return when a liquidity buffer is required?

13.13. Suppose that a performance analyst has access to the returns of a market-neutral portfolio. He knows the returns were 2.4% for the month of April 2020. He also knows that the interest rate on both the collateral and liquidity buffer is 5% per annum (that is, $i = i' = 0.05$). The liquidity buffer is 6% (that is, $m_{lb} = 0.06$). The total value of the portfolio is $100 million. Assume that he is fully leveraged up to a liquidity buffer.

(a) What must have been the return difference between the long and short portfolios?

(b) Does the market-neutral manager know how to separate "good" stocks from "bad" stocks?

13.14. Name four advantages of a market-neutral portfolio over a long-only portfolio.

13.15. Name four disadvantages of a market-neutral portfolio over a long-only portfolio.

13.16. Why is rebalancing necessary when managing a market-neutral portfolio?

13.17. Briefly describe each of the following portfolio techniques and their relation to the market-neutral strategy.
(a) Long-short
(b) Equitization
(c) Portable α
(d) Pair trading

13.18. A quantitative portfolio manager is very good at managing against the Russell 2000. In fact, she is expected to achieve an α^B of 0.5% per month. Unfortunately, her benchmark is the S&P 500. She thus shorts the required amount of Russell 2000 futures and purchases an equivalent amount of S&P 500 futures contracts. Suppose that the S&P 500 is expected to have a return of 6% in the next month.

(a) What would be the expected return of her new portfolio?

(b) Would the realized return be similar? Explain.

13.19. In 1999, many stocks were believed to be overvalued by quantitative portfolio managers. One of those stocks was Amazon (AMZN). This stock was particularly overvalued relative to other companies in the same line of business, such as Barnes & Noble (BKS). Suppose that a portfolio manager wanted to construct a pair trade consisting of AMZN and BKS. Use the table below to answer the questions. [*Note*: The β and σ for each stock were measured using monthly historical data from May 1997 to April 1999. The σ is presented in annualized percentage terms. Assume that the long and short weights (before shorting) sum to 1.]

Ticker	β_i	σ_i
AMZN	0.07	120
BKS	0.28	50

(a) How would you weight each stock if you wanted a dollar-neutral pair trade?

(b) How would you weight each stock if you wanted a beta-neutral pair trade?

(c) How would you weight each stock if you wanted a volatility-neutral pair trade?

(d) Which of the three methods above would you actually use, and why?

(e) Below are the results from the three types of pair trades from April 1999 to December 2001. Did the pair trade work for all three types of constructions? Which one worked the best? [*Note*: The standard deviations (SD) are annualized.]

	Holding Period Return (%)	SD (%)
AMZN	−87	88
BKS	−15	58
Pair (dollar-neutral)	36	63
Pair (beta-neutral)	67	78
Pair (volatility-neutral)	15	53

(f) Does risk make sense in this setting? Does β?

13.20. If a portfolio manager constructs a portfolio consisting of 50 pair trades, has he created a market-neutral portfolio? Explain.

13.21. A good friend of yours is a portfolio manager at a leading bank and is very good at creating a positive α^B versus the NASDAQ 100. Unfortunately, her benchmark is the S&P 500, which she is not very good at beating. Thus year after year she has received bad bonuses. What would you advise her to do?

CHAPTER 14

Bayesian α

Fool me once, shame on you. Fool me twice . . . well the point is we can't get fooled again.

— George W. Bush

14.1 INTRODUCTION

Whether from a qualitative research report or from knowledge passed along by word of mouth, portfolio managers usually have useful investing information that does not originate in a data set. Managers often attempt to build such information into an existing quantitative factor model by transforming it into the constant term α, but these attempts can be awkward. Assigning values to qualitative ideas can be somewhat arbitrary, and the new information may not combine efficiently with the estimation in the model. In such cases, *Bayesian theory* is extremely helpful. The theory, which provides a rigorous way to combine heterogeneous sets of information, is a good guide for how best to combine extra qualitative information with the estimation from a factor model.

We start this chapter with a quick review of Bayesian theory and define what we call the *Bayesian* α. We lay out the two stages of Bayesian analysis, determining the prior and determining the posterior. We walk through a number of typical examples to illustrate how to determine the prior, which summarizes all the extra qualitative information that the manager wants to add to the model. We then discuss the posterior, which combines the extra information with the standard estimation from the factor model. At the end of the chapter we warn managers to avoid mistakes in applying the theory that violate the information criterion.[1]

14.2 THE BASICS OF BAYESIAN THEORY

Bayesian theory is a systematic application of a statistical theorem called *Bayes' rule*. To lay the foundation for Bayes' rule, let us review the concept of conditional probability. Conditional probability is the probability of an event (b) happening when we know that another event (a) will happen. For example, event a is, "It will rain tomorrow," and event b is, "The temperature will be below 100 degrees tomorrow." We may ask, "What is the probability of the temperature being below 100 degrees tomorrow if it rains tomorrow?" We can express the question as a conditional probability $P(b \mid a)$. If the answer to this question is 99% (i.e., when it rains, the temperature is unlikely to reach 100 degrees), it is the same as saying that the probability of b conditional on a is 99%, or $P(b \mid a) = 99\%$.

Bayes' rule relates probabilities to each other. It says that the probability of b conditional on a, $P(b \mid a)$, is proportional to two probabilities: the probability of a conditional on b, $P(a \mid b)$, and the probability of b, $P(b)$. Mathematically, we may write

$$P(b \mid a) \propto P(a \mid b)P(b) \qquad (14.1)$$

where $\propto$ means "is proportional to." Continuing the example, if rain is more likely when the temperature is below 100 degrees, then a temperature below 100 degrees is more likely when it rains. In other words, when $P(a \mid b)$ has a high value, $P(b \mid a)$ has a better chance of having a high value as well. Also, if a temperature below 100 degrees is likely whether it rains or not, then it is more likely to be under 100 degrees if it rains. Expressed in terms of probabilities, the idea is that if $P(b)$ has a high value, then $P(b \mid a)$ probably also will be quite high.

We can interpret Bayes' rule in Eq. (14.1) in a more general way. That is, we can take a and b to be random variables rather than events and $P(\cdot)$ to be the probability density of a random variable rather than the probability of an event. *Random* variables are any

---

[1] See Chapter 2 for a discussion of the information criterion.

variables (such as stock returns) that can take on different values, with different levels of likelihood for each potential value. We can revise our example about tomorrow's weather so that we are discussing random variables rather than events. Suppose now that b is a random variable that equals the temperature at noon tomorrow, and a is a random variable that equals the amount of rainfall tomorrow. For discreet random variables (i.e., variables with only a limited set of potential values), probability is the same thing as probability density. For continuous random variables, the probability of attaining a certain value must be recovered by integrating the probability density over an interval. For example, if b is the temperature at noon tomorrow, then the probability that the temperature will be between 90 and 100 degrees can be found by integrating $P(b)$ over b between 90 and 100. Whether it is for a discrete variable or for a continuous variable, the conditional probability density is the probability density of a random variable conditional on a specific value of another random variable. If a is the amount of rainfall tomorrow and b is the temperature at noon tomorrow, then $P(b\,|\,a)$ is the probability density of temperature b given a specific amount of rainfall a.

Let us apply Bayes' rule to a specific kind of conditional probability density, the probability density of parameters conditional on data. We will indicate parameters as $\boldsymbol{\theta}$ (potentially a vector) and data as $\mathbf{x}$ (probably a very long vector). For factor models, the coefficients on explanatory variables and the error variances are the parameters. In the fundamental factor model, the factor premiums and the error variances are the parameters, whereas in the economic factor model, the factor exposures and the error variances are the parameters. For both factor models, the values of dependent and explanatory variables are data.

To apply Bayes' rule to the probability density of parameters conditional on data, we simply can replace b and a in Eq. (14.1) with $\boldsymbol{\theta}$ and $\mathbf{x}$:

$$p(\boldsymbol{\theta}\,|\,\mathbf{x}) \propto p(\mathbf{x}\,|\,\boldsymbol{\theta})p(\boldsymbol{\theta}) \qquad (14.2)$$

This formula takes the central place in Bayesian theory, and each term deserves an explanation. The last term, $p(\boldsymbol{\theta})$, is called the *prior*.[2] This is the probability density of the parameters *prior to* data

---

[2] It is also common to use $f(\cdot)$ to denote probability density functions instead of $p(\cdot)$. $P(\cdot)$ is used to denote the actual probability of a specific event.

analysis. The prior may be based on qualitative or nondata information, intuition, or logic.

The probability density of the data conditional on the parameters, $p(\mathbf{x}|\boldsymbol{\theta})$, is called the *likelihood function*, or the *likelihood* for short. It shows how *likely* it is that the data are drawn from the given parameters. For example, if the data are -100 and -101, then we know that they are very unlikely to be from the normal distribution with a mean of 0 and a variance of 1. On the other hand, if the data are -0.1 and 0.1, then we can say that they are quite likely to be from the normal distribution with a mean of 0 and a variance of 1. The likelihood function expresses this. To put it another way, the likelihood function measures the distance between the data and the parameters.

The probability density of the parameters conditional on the data $p(\boldsymbol{\theta}|\mathbf{x})$ is called the *posterior*. It is the probability density of the parameters *after* we analyze the data. The posterior combines the information we had before analyzing the data (the prior) and the information we obtained from the data (the likelihood). Thus the posterior summarizes all we know about the parameters. The formula in Eq. (14.2) is a simple way to combine nondata or qualitative information about the parameters into the data analysis. We simply need to multiply the prior and the likelihood. Not only is it simple, but it turns out to be the best way of adding nondata information to the data analysis.

Since Bayesian theory seems quite straightforward, one might wonder why it deserves to be called a theory. Although it is indeed straightforward mathematically, Bayesian theory represents a huge philosophical jump from "classical" statistical theories. In classical theory, there is a clear distinction between what is a random variable and what is not a random variable. The parameters of a model are not considered random variables. While we do not know the true values of the parameters, the classical thinking goes, true values must be somewhere "out there," so we cannot treat them as random variables. Thus the parameters cannot have probability distributions, and we can think neither of the prior nor of the posterior. Bayesian theory, on the other hand, makes no distinction between random and nonrandom variables. Even if we do not know the exact value of a variable, we still can assign a probability to each possible value and treat the variable as random. Another important feature of Bayesian theory is that the probabilities do not have to be objective. In fact, the prior is a subjective probability of the parameters. If you have special information, the prior you calculate will be different from the prior another person calculates. In classical theory, the probability of a value is taken almost as a law of nature, and there is no room to add one's subjective opinion to it.

While the philosophical difference between Bayesian and classical is great, the practical differences should not be exaggerated. When both the classical theory and the Bayesian theory are applicable, their conclusions are identical more often than not. In this chapter we are mostly interested in situations in which only the Bayesian theory is applicable. Classical theory has only limited use (or almost no use) when one attempts to combine qualitative information with data analysis. In such cases, we do not have any choice but to adopt Bayesian theory.

14.3 BAYESIAN α MOJO

Instead of adopting the Bayesian approach from beginning to end, we will focus on where Bayesian theory clearly adds value to quantitative equity portfolio management (QEPM), which is in incorporating qualitative information on α into the QEPM process in a systematic way. Portfolio managers often have nondata information on individual stocks, and this information is often qualitative rather than quantitative. Maybe a research report appears saying that stock XYZ has an exceptionally positive outlook but that its current stock price does not reflect the positive outlook. Maybe an analyst, who has information not available to the portfolio manager, comes up with a selection or a ranking of stocks, and the portfolio manager would like to incorporate that into the analysis. Or perhaps the manager has a data set that he or she finds informative but not suitable as the basis for a factor model.

In such cases, a portfolio manager typically attempts to set the value of α in the factor model in some ad hoc way that reflects the extra information. The portfolio manager may use the following economic factor model to estimate the return of stock i, r_i:

$$r_i = \alpha_i + \beta_{i1}f_1 + \cdots + \beta_{iK}f_K + \epsilon_i \qquad (14.3)$$

where $f_1, \ldots, f_K$ are factor premiums, $\beta_{i1}, \ldots, \beta_{iK}$ are factor exposures of stock i, and ϵ_i is the error component of stock i's return. The alpha of stock i, α_i, is the part of the average stock return that the model cannot explain. The portfolio manager bases the factor premiums and factor exposure on his or her original data set. Since this data-based model cannot explain α_i, the manager attempts to set the value of α_i according to his or her nondata information. However, since the nondata information is qualitative, assigning values could be arbitrary.

Bayesian theory becomes very useful at this stage. Rather than setting the value of α in an arbitrary way, the portfolio manager can adopt the Bayesian approach and assign a distribution to the α that is consistent with the nondata information. This assigned distribution is what Bayesian theorists call the *prior*. Once the prior is assigned, the portfolio manager can follow the standard procedure of the Bayesian approach to obtain the best estimates of Eq. (14.3) that reflect not only the information in the data but also the useful nondata information. Calculating the *Bayesian* α, as we call it, is consistent with the information criterion that we introduced in Chapter 2. Attempts to incorporate nondata information into the model without calculating the Bayesian α most likely will fail to exploit the information completely and violate the information criterion, seriously distorting the portfolio. The Bayesian α, on the other hand, is entirely a gain to the portfolio manager and another strong source of α mojo.

14.4 QUANTIFYING QUALITATIVE INFORMATION

The first step of Bayesian analysis is to decide on the prior of the α from the nondata information, a somewhat challenging step because nondata information is often qualitative. In this section we will go through three relatively simple but commonly faced situations involving calculating the prior. More complicated cases will be dealt with in the next two sections. First, we will start with the situation in which the portfolio manager receives a list of stocks screened by other analysts. Then we will consider the case in which the portfolio manager receives a ranking of selected stocks. Lastly, we will consider the case in which the portfolio manager wants to incorporate buy and sell recommendations for selected stocks.

14.4.1 Quantifying a Stock Screen

Suppose that we have many lists of analyst-recommended stocks, each list made by an analyst through some screening process. How can we convert these lists into the prior for the α of each stock? When a stock is included in a list, it means that an analyst believes that the stock is likely to outperform the stocks not included in the list. That is, a listed stock is likely to have a higher α than that of an unlisted stock. If stock A is included in a list but stock B is not, we can say that

$$P(\alpha_A > \alpha_B) > 0.5 \qquad (14.4)$$

If stock A is included in many analysts' lists and stock B in none, then we can be more confident that α_A is greater than α_B because more analysts agree on the superiority of stock A. Specifically, if we consider each list (or analyst) equally reliable, then we can say that

$$P\left(\alpha_A > \alpha_B\right) = \frac{\text{number of lists including stock } A}{\text{number of all lists}} \qquad (14.5)$$

That is, if half the analysts say that α_A is greater than α_B, then we may be 50% sure that α_A is greater than α_B. If every analyst says that α_A is greater than α_B, then we may be (almost) 100% sure that α_A is greater than α_B.

If stock B is not included in any of the lists, the lists do not say anything about stock B. Thus, as far as α_B is concerned, we do not need to do anything special. We can estimate α_B in the usual way and obtain the estimate $\hat{\alpha}_B$ and its standard error $S(\hat{\alpha}_B)$. From the Bayesian perspective, $\hat{\alpha}_B$ and its standard error are considered to be the mean and the standard deviation of α_B. That is, assuming a normal distribution, we can write

$$\alpha_B \sim N[\hat{\alpha}_B, S(\hat{\alpha}_B)^2] \qquad (14.6)$$

Once Eqs. (14.5) and (14.6) are obtained, it is straightforward to find the prior distribution for α_A. The inclusion of stock A into the list does not imply anything about the relative amount of uncertainty regarding α_A and α_B. Thus it is reasonable to take $S(\hat{\alpha}_B)$ as the standard deviation of α_A as well. Now we only have to determine the mean of α_A. Let μ_A be the mean of α_A. Assume that α_A has a normal distribution and is independent of α_B (which is reasonable given that we do not have any information indicating otherwise). Then

$$\alpha_A - \alpha_B \sim N[\mu_A - \hat{\alpha}_B, 2S(\hat{\alpha}_B)^2] \qquad (14.7)$$

It follows immediately that

$$p_A \equiv P\left(\alpha_A - \alpha_B > 0\right) = 1 - \Phi\left[\frac{\hat{\alpha}_B - \mu_A}{\sqrt{2}S(\hat{\alpha}_B)}\right] \tag{14.8}$$

where Φ is the standard normal cumulative distribution function. Considering Eqs. (14.5) and (14.8),

$$\mu_A = \hat{\alpha}_B - 2\,S(\hat{\alpha}_B)\Phi^{-1}(1 - p_A) \tag{14.9}$$

where Φ^{-1} is the inverse standard normal cumulative distribution function that takes a probability as the argument. Thus we have determined the prior distribution for α_A. We can generalize this analysis in a number of directions. First of all, we can find the distribution of α_B using all the stocks that are not included in any of the lists. If we cannot find such stocks, then we can use an arbitrary set of stocks and modify Eq. (14.5). Also, if different analysts are not equally reliable, then we may assign different weights to different analysts and lists.

A more important generalization of the analysis is the case in which there is only one list of stocks. It may be that all analysts work as a team and produce a single list, or it may even be the case that the portfolio manager is the one who produces the list. For one stock list, the preceding analysis is still valid except for Eq. (14.5). For Eq. (14.5), the portfolio manager himself or herself must decide on the probability that α_A is greater than α_B. While this may seem quite subjective, this is not necessarily a problem. The prior distribution is meant to represent subjective opinion. Unless the portfolio manager chooses different probabilities for different stocks, Eq. (14.9) is common for all stocks included in the list. That is, all stocks in the list have the same mean as expressed in Eq. (14.9).

14.4.2 Quantifying a Stock Ranking

Suppose that instead of having a simple list of stocks, we have analyst-prepared rankings of stocks. We can easily extend the idea developed in the preceding subsection to this case. If stock A is ranked higher than stock B, it means that an analyst believes that the α of stock A is higher than the α of stock B. The probability of the α of stock A being higher than the α of stock B can be computed by comparing the number of analysts who believe this to be true to the total number of analysts who do not. That is,

$$P\left(\alpha_A > \alpha_B\right) = \frac{\text{number of analysts ranking stock } A \text{ higher than stock } B}{\text{number of all analysts}} \tag{14.10}$$

Note that Eq. (14.10) is essentially identical to Eq. (14.5). Thus we can follow the same procedure for dealing with stock screens.

Once stock B is chosen, this same stock should be compared with all the other stocks to exploit all the information in the ranking. One possibility is to choose for stock B a stock that is ranked most frequently at the bottom of ranked lists, and for each of the remaining stocks, calculate Eq. (14.10) relative to stock B. In any case, how stock B is selected does not really matter as long as it is compared with all other stocks. The procedure is identical whether all stocks are ranked by every analyst or different stocks are ranked by different analysts. If there is only one ranking (perhaps made by the portfolio manager himself or herself), then the portfolio manager assigns a number to $P(\alpha_A > \alpha_B)$ in Eq. (14.10) and follows the same procedure.

14.4.3 Quantifying the Buy and Sell Recommendations

Qualitative information also may be in the form of analysts' buy and sell recommendations. Instead of a simple "buy" or "sell," analysts often give stocks one of five recommendations: strong buy, buy, neutral, sell, and strong sell. These recommendations can be converted easily into the probability of one stock having a higher α than another stock. One way to do this is to use the *buy ratio*, which is the number of buy recommendations divided by the total number of buy and sell recommendations. Once the buy ratio is calculated for every stock, we can find the probability of the α of stock A being greater than the α of stock B by subtracting the buy ratio of stock B from the buy ratio of stock A. That is,

$$
P(\alpha_A > \alpha_B) = \frac{\text{number of buy recommendations for } A}{\left(\begin{array}{l}\text{number of buy recommendations for } A \\ + \text{ number of sell recommendations for } A\end{array}\right)}
$$
$$
- \frac{\text{number of buy recommendations for } B}{\left(\begin{array}{l}\text{number of buy recommendations for } B \\ + \text{ number of sell recommendations for } B\end{array}\right)}
$$
(14.11)

The buy ratio of stock A shows what fraction of analysts believes that stock A is superior, and the buy ratio of stock B shows the fraction of analysts that believes that stock B is superior. The difference between the two buy ratios shows the fraction of analysts that believes that stock A is superior to stock B. This is exactly true if the same analysts make recommendations for stocks A and B and approximately true in other cases. After Eq. (14.11) is determined, we can proceed as we did in the previous cases.

14.5 THE Z-SCORE-BASED PRIOR

The Z-score approach explained in Chapter 5 produces rankings of stocks based on certain factors. It is therefore possible to generate the prior of the α from the Z-score and then estimate a factor model using other unused information. This approach is superior to using the Z-score alone because it employs all the information available in the data. Suppose that we have L factors and a calculated Z-score for each stock. If we have not aggregated the Z-score, then the Z-score for each stock is a vector of L numbers. Let $\mathbf{z}_i = (z_{i1}, \ldots, z_{iL})$ be the Z-score of stock i. The Z-score for each factor implies a certain ranking of stocks. Since there are L factors, we have L implied rankings of stocks. Once we interpret the Z-score as the ranking of stocks, the prior of the α can be generated according to the method for stock rankings described earlier. That is, given stock A and stock B, the probability that the α of stock A is greater than the α of stock B is

$$P\left(\alpha_A > \alpha_B\right) = \frac{\sum_{l=1}^{L} I\left(z_{Al} > z_{Bl}\right)}{L} \tag{14.12}$$

where $I(\cdot)$ is an indicator function returning the value 1 if the expression inside the parentheses is true and 0 if not.

The preceding formula is based on the idea that each factor is equally informative. However, as we discussed in Chapter 5, we may have reason to assign different weights to different factors. Suppose that for factor l we want to assign weight v_l so that $v_1 + \ldots + v_l = 1$. Then the probability that the α of stock A is greater than the α of stock B changes to

$$p_A = P\left(\alpha_A > \alpha_B\right) = \sum_{l=1}^{L} v_l I\left(z_{Al} > z_{Bl}\right) \tag{14.13}$$

After the probability is calculated, we can easily determine the prior of the α of stock A as explained in the preceding section. We choose an arbitrary stock B and obtain the estimate $\hat{\alpha}_B$ and its standard error $S(\hat{\alpha}_B)$ from a factor model. Then the prior for the α of stock A becomes

$$\alpha_A \sim N[\mu_A, S(\hat{\alpha}_B)^2] \qquad (14.14)$$

where

$$\mu_A = \hat{\alpha}_B - \sqrt{2}S(\hat{\alpha}_B)\Phi^{-1}(1 - p_A) \qquad (14.15)$$

The derivation of this formula is the same as the derivation explained in the preceding section. That is, p_A is calculated from Eq. (14.8), and we can substitute p_A into Eq. (14.15).

14.6 SCENARIO-BASED PRIORS

The prior of the α can be generated systematically from what is known as *scenario analysis*. Scenario analysis is suitable when the portfolio manager has strong opinions about how individual stocks will perform under specific situations. Different variables in the economic or natural environments present opportunities for scenario analysis. For instance, investors use scenario analysis before presidential elections to guess how different election outcomes will affect stocks. Investors in the agricultural and certain manufacturing industries use it to try to anticipate the effect of weather patterns on future stock returns. The portfolio manager can systematically incorporate his or her views about stock returns under different conditions into the prior of the α through scenario analysis. For each scenario, the portfolio manager determines—whether based on his or her own beliefs or on some outside evidence—two quantities: the probability of the scenario being realized and the α of the stock when the scenario is realized. Given the probability of each scenario and the value of the α, he or she can construct a distribution for the stock's α, which becomes the prior of the α.

The first step in scenario analysis is to identify all possible scenarios. Typically, this can be done with an *event tree*. Suppose that the portfolio manager has certain beliefs about future stock returns, which are conditional on the following events: high or low inflation, high or low unemployment, high or low productivity growth, and high or low oil prices. An event tree organizes these events, as illustrated in Figure 14.1, producing 16 possible scenarios. In general, if E pairs of events are considered, then 2^E scenarios are possible.

FIGURE 14.1

Scenario analysis event tree.

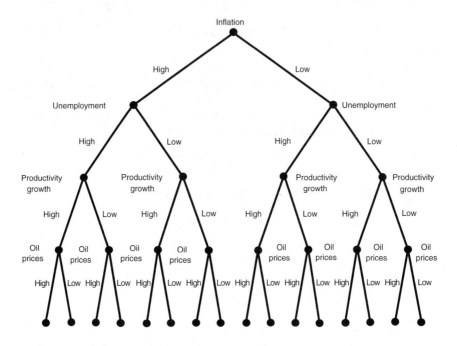

The second step in scenario analysis is to assign probabilities to each scenario. If each pair of events is independent of the others, then the probability of a scenario is simply the product of the probabilities of the events that happen in the scenario. For example, the probability of scenario 1 is given by[3]

---

[3] The probability of each event can be found in various ways. For example, suppose that a portfolio manager is interested in the effect on certain stocks of a Federal Reserve (Fed) easing. Prior to 2008, the probability of a Fed easing (or tightening) could be derived from Fed fund futures. This probability could be used in an event tree dependent on Federal Open Market Committee (FOMC) actions. After 2008, the Fed switched to an upper and lower Fed funds target rate to allow flexibility in managing the Fed funds rate. Thus, in order to estimate the probability of a Fed change in rates, the portfolio manager needs to estimate the effective daily funds rate before and after the FOMC meeting. Although not exact, the portfolio manager can make the assumption that the effective funds rate will be at the midpoint of the upper and lower Fed funds target rate. Thus, the probability of a Fed move can be expressed as $p = \dfrac{i_t^f - i_t^{pre}}{\left(i_t^{post} - i_t^{pre}\right)\frac{d_2}{B}}$, where i^f is the futures rate implied by the relevant

P(high inflation, high unemployment, high productivity growth, high oil price) = P(high inflation) · P(high unemployment) · P(high productivity growth) · P(high oil price)   (14.16)

However, if each pair of events is not independent, this formula does not work, and the probability of each scenario must be found individually through, for instance, the forecasting methods discussed in Chapter 8.

The third step is to determine the α of each stock. There are two approaches to this, the subjective approach and the event-study approach. The subjective approach draws on the portfolio manager's personal beliefs. The event-study approach assigns the α based on historical data. To determine α through the event-study approach, we need first to define the event exactly. For example, we may define high unemployment as an unemployment rate of above 5% and low unemployment as an unemployment rate of below 5%. Then we need to find the average abnormal return for each event. During the period from January 2011 to December 2020, 72 months can be categorized as high-unemployment months, and the remaining 48 months can be categorized as low-unemployment months. The abnormal return can be calculated in various ways, but the simplest method is to calculate the excess return of each stock over the market return. Table 14.1 shows the average abnormal returns as well as the standard deviation of selected stocks for low- and high-unemployment months. These average abnormal

---

contract, i^{pre} is the midpoint of the upper and lower target Fed Funds rate prevailing before the FOMC meeting, i^{post} is the midpoint of the upper and lower target rate that the investor expects to prevail after the FOMC meeting, d_2 is the number of days between the FOMC meeting and the current month's end, and B is the number of days in the month. This formulation assumes no Fed funds changes between meetings and that the midpoint of the upper and lower target Fed funds rate is a reasonable proxy for the actual effective Fed funds rate over the period before and after the FOMC meeting—although this is often not true. For example, if the Fed funds futures (i_f^f) is 2.06% (100 − 97.94), the midpoint of current target rates (i_f^{pre}) is 2.125, and the expected lower range is from 1.75 to 2 with a midpoint (i_f^{post}) of 1.875, and given that the FOMC meeting takes place on the 18th day of the month, then there is a 65% probability that the Fed will lower its target range from 2-to-2.25 to 1.75-to-2. There are other methods of making this calculation, including using the most recent average effective funds rate for the value of i_f^{pre}. In this particular example, using this value would give a 75% probability of a Fed reduction in target rates. A negative probability implies that the market expects the Fed to do the opposite of what the investor believes; thus he or she should change expected change to its opposite and recalculate.

TABLE 14.1

Average Abnormal Returns of Selected Stocks in the High-/ Low-Unemployment Scenario

Scenario	AAPL	AMZN	JNJ	MSFT	WMT
Low unemployment	19.49	16.34	1.54	23.02	11.73
	(21.84)	(21.62)	(13.55)	(12.07)	(19.19)
High unemployment	13.31	22.62	−1.01	3.96	−8.58
	(23.78)	(25.22)	(11.71)	(18.55)	(17.90)

Note: The numbers represent the annualized return of each stock in excess of the market return averaged across the months following a month whose unemployment rate is below 5% (N = 48) or above 5% (N = 72) between January 2011 and December 2020. The figures in the parentheses are standard errors.

returns can be used as α's. When applying the event-study approach, one should be careful not to base the prior on the data that eventually will be used to estimate the stock return model. This issue will be discussed further toward the end of this chapter.

Suppose that we defined S scenarios. Let $P(s)$ be the probability of scenario s and $\alpha_i(s)$ be the α of stock i in scenario s. Then the profile of the probability and the α {$[\alpha_i(1), P(1)]$, ..., $[\alpha_i(S), P(S)]$} completely determine the distribution of the α. We certainly could stop here as far as the prior is concerned. However, approximating the prior distribution as a normal distribution reduces the computational burden significantly at a later stage of the analysis. The approximate normal distribution is given as follows:

$$\alpha_i \sim N(\mu_i, \sigma_i^2) \tag{14.17}$$

where

$$\mu_i = \sum_{s=1}^{S} P(s)\alpha_i(s) \tag{14.18}$$

and

$$\sigma_i^2 = \sum_{s=1}^{S} P(s)\left[\alpha_i(s) - \mu_i\right]^2 \tag{14.19}$$

14.7 POSTERIOR COMPUTATION

Once the prior is determined, the posterior can be computed from Bayes' rule. While the formula for the posterior may look complicated, the computation itself is straightforward. This is especially true when the prior is a normal distribution. When the prior is a normal distribution, the posterior is also a normal distribution, and we only have to determine the mean and the variance of the posterior. In this section we focus on the interpretation of the posterior formula.[4]

Suppose that the portfolio manager uses the following factor model to estimate the return of individual stocks:

$$r_i = \alpha_i + \beta_{i1}f_1 + \cdots + \beta_{iK}f_K + \epsilon_i \qquad (14.20)$$

where r_i is the return of stock i, $f_1, \ldots, f_K$ are factor premiums, $\beta_{i1}, \cdots, \beta_{iK}$ are factor exposures of stock i, and ϵ_i is the error component of stock i's return. α_i is the α of stock i for which the portfolio manager defined the following prior using one of the approaches described in the preceding section:

$$\alpha_i \sim N(\mu_{\alpha_i}, \sigma^2_{\alpha_i}) \qquad (14.21)$$

We assume that the portfolio manager did not define the prior for $\beta_{i1}, \ldots, \beta_{iK}$. The computation is in fact easier if the prior for $\beta_{i1}, \ldots, \beta_{iK}$ is defined as well, but we will focus on the more typical situation in which it is not.[5]

Since the posterior combines the information in the prior and the information in the data [which is summarized in the ordinary least squares (OLS) estimate], for α_i, the posterior mean is the weighted average of the prior mean and the OLS estimate. The weights are the inverse of the respective variances. For the prior mean, the weight is the inverse of the prior variance, and for the OLS estimate, the weight is the inverse of the OLS variance of the estimate (i.e., the squared standard error of the estimate). The inverse of the variance shows how precise the quantity is. If the variance is large, the quantity is less precise, and if the variance is small, the quantity is more precise. For this reason, the inverse of the variance is called the *precision* of the estimate. It is often said that the posterior mean is the *precision-weighted average* of the prior mean and the OLS estimate. The posterior mean of α_i is given as follows:

---

[4] The derivation is presented in Appendix 14A, which can be found at https://ludwigbc. com/books/qepm/exclusive_qepm_content_2020/ or at www.ludwigbc.com and look for QEPM Exclusive Content.

[5] See Appendix 14A at www.ludwigbc.com and look for QEPM Exclusive Content for the posterior when the prior for $\beta_{i1}, \ldots, \beta_{iK}$ is defined.

$$\mu_{\alpha_i}^* = \left(\frac{1}{\sigma_{\alpha_i}^2} + \frac{1}{\sigma_{\epsilon_i}^2}\iota'\mathbf{M}\iota\right)^{-1}\frac{1}{\sigma_{\alpha_i}^2}\mu_{\alpha_i}$$

$$+ \left(\frac{1}{\sigma_{\alpha_i}^2} + \frac{1}{\sigma_{\epsilon_i}^2}\iota'\mathbf{M}\iota\right)^{-1}\left(\frac{1}{\sigma_{\epsilon_i}^2}\iota'\mathbf{M}\iota\right)\hat{\alpha}$$

$$(14.22)$$

where ι is a T-dimensional vector of 1s and T is the number of observations in the estimation, and $\mathbf{M}$ is the residual matrix (defined in Appendix 14A). As explained earlier, the posterior mean is the weighted average of the prior mean (μ_{α_i}) and the OLS estimate ($\hat{\alpha}$). The average is taken using the prior precision ($1/\sigma_{\alpha_i}^2$) and the OLS precision $[(1/\sigma_{\epsilon_i}^2)\iota'\mathbf{M}\iota]$ as the weights. The "denominator" (in the matrix sense), $(1/\sigma_{\alpha_i}^2) + (1/\sigma_{\epsilon_i}^2)\iota'\mathbf{M}\iota$, is simply the sum of the prior precision and the OLS precision. By "dividing" each weight by this quantity, the sum of the weights equals 1.

The posterior variance of α_i is the inverse of the sum of the prior precision and the OLS precision. That is, the posterior precision is the sum of the prior precision and the OLS precision. The precision shows how much confidence we have in a given quantity. If we have great confidence in our prior (there is high prior precision), then we still will have great confidence after the estimation (high posterior precision). Even if we have little confidence in our prior, if the OLS produces reliable results (there is high OLS precision), then our confidence level will go up (high posterior precision). Thus it makes sense to add the prior precision and the OLS precision to get the posterior precision.

The posterior variance of α_i is given as

$$\left(\sigma_{\alpha_i}^*\right)^2 = \left(\frac{1}{\sigma_{\alpha_i}^2} + \frac{1}{\sigma_{\epsilon_i}^2}\iota'\mathbf{M}\iota\right)^{-1}$$

$$(14.23)$$

It is the inverse of the sum of the prior precision ($1/\sigma_{\alpha_i}^2$) and the OLS precision $[(1/\sigma_{\epsilon_i}^2)\iota'\mathbf{M}\iota]$.

The formulas for the posterior mean and the variance of $\beta_{i1}, ..., \beta_{iK}$ (together with other useful quantities) are presented in Appendix 14A.[6] Here we only note that while the prior is defined

---

[6] Appendix 14A can be found under Chapter Appendices at https://ludwigbc.com/books/qepm/exclusive_qepm_content_2020/.

only for α_i, the estimates of β_{i1}, ..., β_{iK} will be affected by the prior as well. This is so because there is a correlation between the estimate of α_i and the estimates of β_{i1}, ..., β_{iK}. Since the prior influences the estimate of α_i, it also will indirectly affect the estimates of β_{i1}, ..., β_{iK}, even though there is no prior for β_{i1}, ..., β_{iK}.

14.8 THE INFORMATION CRITERION AND BAYESIAN α

The Bayesian approach is an extremely powerful tool for combining two sets of information, typically data information and nondata information. Data information is summarized by the factor model (i.e., the likelihood), and nondata information is summarized by the prior. The two sets of information are optimally combined in the posterior. While the Bayesian approach is quite useful, it is easy to make certain mistakes in applying it, especially (though not only) when the prior is determined from data information. If the prior is determined from data information and if the data are not properly *excluded* from the model estimation, one will end up double counting certain information. The following are examples of possible *mistakes* that portfolio managers might be tempted to make:

- Screen stocks based on the price-to-earnings ratio, develop the prior for the alpha based on the screen, and use the price-to-earnings ratio again as a factor in the estimation of the factor model.
- Rank stocks based on momentum or some other factor, develop the prior for the alpha based on the ranking, and use momentum again as a factor in the estimation of the factor model.
- Generate the prior based on analyst recommendations, and when estimating the factor model, use the analyst factor again based on the same information.
- Base the prior on the Z-score of certain factors, and use some of these factors again when estimating the factor model.
- Do the scenario analysis based on the past stock performance when inflation was high or low, and use the same inflation data as a factor in the factor model.

The list of possible mistakes is infinite, but the general idea is the same: Information should not be used twice. If a piece of information was used to make the prior, it should not be used in estimating the model. The information criterion we developed in Chapter 2 encapsulates this rule. In Chapter 2 we emphasized that information should not be wasted and that all information should be combined in the most efficient way. Using the same information twice is inefficient. In fact, it violates all the fundamental assumptions of statistical inference. Thus the standard errors will be wrong if the same information is used twice.

14.9 CONCLUSION

Bayesian theory represents a major step forward from classical statistical theory because it allows us to treat any variable as a random variable and assign subjective probabilities, based on qualitative or nondata information, to the variable's potential values. Bayesian theory opens up the possibility of encapsulating such extra information in a Bayesian α that amplifies the QEPM model of stock returns. In this chapter we first showed how to calculate the Bayesian α's prior, which summarizes and quantifies extra information that does not originate in the data set with which the factor model was estimated. This extra information can come from stock screens and rankings, buy/sell recommendations, Z-scores, or scenario analysis. We then discussed how to calculate the Bayesian α's posterior, which summarizes all the available information by combining the prior and the factor model estimation. Having calculated the posterior, we can fully describe the distribution of Bayesian α. As long as all pieces of extra information contained in the α are distinct from the data used to estimate the factor model, adding Bayesian α to the model upholds the information criterion. Bayesian α, with its ability to widen the scope of a purely data-based factor model into diverse kinds of information, is our third source of α mojo.

QUESTIONS

14.1. Prostate cancer affects roughly 12.5% of the male population. A prostate-specific antigen (PSA) test is able to detect
whether men might have the disease. The test has a type I
error of 70% (when the person does not have cancer, there is
a 70% chance that the test will conclude that he does) and a
type II error of 20% (when the person does have cancer,
there is a 20% chance that the test will conclude that he does
not). In a recent testing at UCSF Medical Center, a person
tested positive for prostate cancer.
  (a) What is the probability that the person has prostate
       cancer?
  (b) A company called Grail has a blood cancer screening
       test called Galleri. Its false-positive rate is 0.5% and its
       false-negative rate is 0.6%. If 100,000 men took the new
       test over the old test, how many more people with
       cancer would be alerted early? How many more people
       without prostate cancer would avoid the psychological
       stress and physical inconvenience of a biopsy? (*Note*:
       The false-positive and false-negative rates were
       obtained from a study by Grail; however, they are for
       detecting all cancers and not specifically prostate can-
       cer. The prostate-specific cancer numbers were not
       available).

14.2. The probabilities for events A and B are given as follows:
$P(A) = \frac{1}{2}$, $P(B) = \frac{1}{3}$, $P(A \cap B) = \frac{1}{6}$. Find the probability of
event A happening conditional on event B happening, that
is, $P(A|B)$.

14.3. Suppose that the stock return r has the following conditional
distribution: $r|\mu \sim N(\mu, 1)$. μ has the following distribution:
$\mu \sim N(\alpha, \beta)$.
  (a) What is the expected value of r?
  (b) What is the variance of r?
  (c) What is the marginal distribution of r?

14.4. What is the prior? Explain the possible role of the prior in
quantitative equity portfolio management (QEPM).

14.5. Explain the difference between the Bayesian approach and
the classical approach to estimation.

14.6. One criticism of the Bayesian approach is that different
analysts may come to different conclusions. Explain how a
Bayesian statistician would respond to such criticism.

14.7. In the Bayesian framework, the OLS estimation is a special case of Bayesian analysis. Describe the prior distribution under which Bayesian analysis and an OLS estimation would produce identical results.

14.8. Suppose that the stock return r has the following conditional distribution:

$$r \mid \mu \sim U[\mu - 1, \mu + 1]$$

where μ may take a value of 0 or 1 with equal probability, and U indicates a uniform distribution. That is, the probability density function of r is

$$f(r) = \begin{cases} \frac{1}{2} & \text{if } \mu - 1 \le r \le \mu + 1 \\ 0 & \text{otherwise} \end{cases}$$

(a) If you observe the value of r to be 1.9, what do you conclude the value of μ to be?

(b) If you observe the value of r to be -0.5, what would do conclude the value of μ to be?

(c) Find the posterior distribution of r in each of the above cases.

14.9. The capital asset pricing model (CAPM) is a special case of the economic factor model. Suppose that we estimated the CAPM in the following form:

$$r_i = \alpha_i + \beta_i r_M + \epsilon_i$$

Using the OLS method, we obtained the following estimates:

$$\hat{\alpha}_i = 0.5 \ (0.3) \quad \hat{\beta}_i = 0.9 \ (0.4)$$

The numbers inside the parentheses are standard errors.

(a) One implication of the CAPM is that the true value of α is 0. If you believe the CAPM 100%, what would be the posterior distribution of α_i?

(b) If you are convinced that the CAPM is not true, but if you do not have any other prior opinion about the value of α, what would be the posterior distribution of α_i?

(c) If you believe that there is a 50% chance that the CAPM is correct and that there is a 50% chance that the CAPM is incorrect, what would be your posterior distribution of α_i?

14.10. The return of stock A is known to have the normal distribution with mean 10 and variance 25, that is,

$$r_A \sim N(10, 25)$$

The return of stock B is known to have a normal distribution with a variance of 25, but the mean μ of the distribution is not known, that is,

$$r_B \sim N(\mu, 25)$$

Assume that r_A and r_B are independent.

(a) A poll of 100 analysts indicates that 50 of 100 analysts believe that stock B will outperform stock A, whereas the remaining 50 analysts believe that the opposite will happen. Considering the poll, what is your best guess at the value μ?

(b) Suppose that 70 of 100 analysts believe that stock B will outperform stock A. Find the value of μ that is consistent with the poll.

(c) If the variance of r_B is not known, how would you change your answers to parts (a) and (b)?

(d) If r_A and r_B are not independent, how would you change your answers to parts (a) and (b)?

(e) If the distribution of r_A is not known, how would you change your answers to parts (a) and (b)?

14.11. An event tree is useful in identifying different scenarios. Draw an event tree for a scenario in which the stock return depends on the following two outcomes: (a) which party (Republican, Democratic, or Green) wins in the next U.S. presidential election and (b) whether NASA's spaceship lands on Venus.

14.12. The return of stock A heavily depends on the oil price. The return of stock $A(r_A)$ conditional on the oil price (G) is given as follows:

$$\text{If} \quad G < 30, \qquad\qquad \text{then} \quad r_A \sim U[-10, 0]$$

$$\text{If} \quad 30 \leq G < 40, \quad \text{then} \quad r_A \sim U[0, 10]$$

$$\text{If} \quad 40 \leq G < 50, \quad \text{then} \quad r_A \sim U[10, 20]$$

$$\text{If} \quad G \geq 50, \qquad\qquad \text{then} \quad r_A \sim U[20, 30]$$

(a) Suppose that the probability of each of the four scenarios happening is 25%. Describe the distribution of r_A.

(b) Estimation of an economic factor model suggests that

$$r_A \sim N(10, 25)$$

Treating the distribution given in part (a) as a prior, describe the posterior distribution of r_A.

14.13. The posterior mean is the weighted average of the prior mean and the OLS estimate, where the weights are the precisions. Explain the similarity between this formula and the formula for the optimal portfolio weights in Chapter 9. Is the similarity a coincidence?

14.14. The posterior computation can be carried out using a pseudo-random-number generator. This exercise outlines the steps.

(a) Show that if x is a random draw from the uniform distribution $U[0, 1]$, then $y = \Phi^{-1}(x)$ may be considered a random draw from the standard normal distribution $N(0, 1)$.

(b) Show that if y is a random draw from $N(0, 1)$, then $z = \mu + \sigma y$ is a random draw from $N(\mu, \sigma^2)$.

(c) Let $z^1, \ldots, z^J$ be random draws from $N(\mu, \sigma^2)$. Show that the expected value of a function of z, $f(z)$, can be approximated as

$$E[f(z)] \approx \frac{1}{J}\sum_{j=1}^{J} f(z^j)$$

(d) Let $p(\theta)$ be the prior and $l(\theta)$ be the likelihood. Show that

$$P(a < \theta < b) = \frac{\int \theta l(\theta) p(\theta) d\theta}{\int l(\theta) p(\theta) d\theta}$$

(e) Let $\theta^1, \ldots, \theta^J$ be the random draws from the prior. Show that the probability in part (d) can be approximated by

$$\frac{\frac{1}{J}\sum_{j=1}^{J} \theta^j l(\theta^j) p(\theta^j)}{\frac{1}{J}\sum_{j=1}^{J} l(\theta^j) p(\theta^j)}$$

14.15. The Bayesian approach can be very powerful in combining qualitative information with quantitative data. However, when two sets of quantitative data are to be combined, there is a danger of double counting the same piece of data in the prior and in the estimation. What would be the consequence of such double counting?

Performance Analysis

We have revealed the three sources of α mojo—leverage, the concept of market neutral, and Bayesian α. Portfolio managers ought to try their hand at harnessing the power of α mojo by applying these strategies to the portfolio or testing them on hypothetical portfolios. The true test of any strategy or model is the performance of the portfolio that is based on it. Personal investors and professional managers alike can learn a great deal by measuring and examining the performance of a portfolio at the end of every investment period.

We cannot overstate the importance of learning from past outcomes. Portfolio managers should strive to both *earn* and *learn* from their investment strategies. Understanding the portfolio's results, whether good or bad, is the key to managing the portfolio masterfully. This is why performance measurement and attribution, which we describe in the next chapter, are just as much a part of quantitative equity portfolio management (QEPM) as the construction of the portfolio itself.

Performance Analysis

CHAPTER 15

Performance Measurement and Attribution

There are two ways to spread light: to be the candle or the mirror that reflects it.

—Abraham Lincoln

15.1 INTRODUCTION

Performance measurement and attribution are extremely important to the quantitative equity portfolio management (QEPM) process. Measurement of a portfolio's return shows how much value the portfolio manager has added to the investment process overall. Performance attribution dissects the return in order to pinpoint the exact sources of value. QEPM is an ongoing process of analysis, implementation, and further analysis. An in-depth review of the portfolio's performance at regular intervals is essential to honing the investment strategy. Yet portfolio management shops often fail to do this either because they focus exclusively on the bottom line (asking only, "Did our return beat the benchmark return?") or because they put so much effort into building portfolios that little time or resources are left for performance analysis. Sometimes performance analysis, which is hardly the highest-paying job in a QEPM department, fails to attract the best talent.

Performance measurement, however, is a fundamental activity in portfolio management. It ensures that the returns of the portfolio are understood accurately, according to an accepted standard. This reason may be quite obvious to many portfolio managers, but one cannot forget the scandal surrounding the *Beardstown ladies* in the late 1990s. The Beardstown ladies were a group of elderly women from the central Illinois town of Beardstown who created an investment club that, according to them, had generated returns of 23.4% from 1983 to 1993, beating the Standard & Poor's (S&P) 500 by 8% per year, on average. They sold over 800,000 books on their investment technique and spoke publicly about their investing acumen. In 1998, Price Waterhouse performed an audit of the Beardstown ladies' portfolio that revealed that their actual return over the 10-year period was a market-lagging 9.1%. It turned out that whenever there were inflows into their investment portfolio (e.g., when new money was invested in the portfolio), the ladies counted the inflows as part of the ultimate return.[1,2] A professional manager would be unlikely to make this sort of accounting error unwittingly, but the Beardstown ladies' blunder serves as a reminder that accurate calculations of portfolio results are an important demonstration of transparency on the part of whoever manages the portfolio.

Another important function of performance measurement is to determine whether the portfolio manager outperformed or underperformed the benchmark and whether the difference was due to skill or luck. (We will see, though, that this unfortunately requires a substantial amount of data, and the time it takes to amass those data does not usually fit into the time period in which bonuses are awarded.) Another significant piece of information that comes from performance measurement is the risk of a portfolio. The risk levels of multiple portfolios can be aggregated into a general level of risk for an entire firm. Performance measurement lays out the portfolio's results for marketing and eventually for the general public so that comparisons can be made between portfolios and managers.

---

[1] *Source*: Karen Hube. "How to Sidestep a 'Beardstown Blunder' When Calculating Portfolio Performance," *Wall Street Journal*, March 25, 1998.

[2] For example, suppose that a portfolio began with $10,000 in it and that over one year the true portfolio return on the investment was about 8%. Then the ending value would be $10,800. Suppose that just prior to the last day of the year, a new investor placed $10,000 in the portfolio. The end-of-year value of the portfolio would be $20,800. If you did not account for this cash inflow appropriately, you might be led to compute the performance of the portfolio as $(20,800/10,000) - 1 = 108\%$. Clearly, this would be an incorrect measurement of performance because the new investor's money should not be part of the portfolio's return.

Performance attribution is a vital follow-up to performance measurement. Attribution means taking the overall results and breaking them down into their underlying causes. This allows a portfolio manager to understand why the portfolio over- or under-performed the benchmark. If my portfolio performance was 10% and the benchmark's performance was 8%, what was the primary cause for my extra 2% return? Was it that I picked stocks well over-all, or was it that I chose to overweight certain industries? Was it primarily that I bought stocks with substantial earnings revisions, or was it that I bought stocks with low analyst coverage? Answering these kinds of questions about the sources of excess returns is key to understanding how well and efficiently the factor model and all other parts of the investing strategy are working.

We begin this chapter by discussing performance measurement, including the basics of return and risk calculations. We explain risk-adjusted measures of performance, including the Sharpe ratio, Jensen's α, and the information ratio. Then we dig a bit deeper into stock returns with standard performance attribution. Finally, we highlight issues of performance measurement and attribution related specifically to the quantitative portfolio manager.[3]

15.2 MEASURING RETURNS

Accurately calculated returns are the clearest measure of the success of an actual portfolio or a yet-to-be implemented portfolio strategy. The return of the actual, managed portfolio is the manager's grade for the quarter or the year. The return of a *paper portfolio*, or *hypothetical portfolio*, gives an idea of how the manager might do. Hypothetical returns are useful for backtesting a strategy on historical data, setting up factor portfolios going forward, or creating a model portfolio in real time. The techniques used to compute the performance of a paper or hypothetical portfolio differ slightly from the computation of real portfolio performance because they usually involve computing the weights and returns of each stock in the portfolio. For calculating the return on the actual portfolio, most firms typically have some kind of accounting system that keeps track of the market value of all the securities and the entire portfolio on a daily basis. The computational techniques we

---

[3] For a discussion of performance presentation standards in the industry, please see the Global Performance Investment Standards (GIPS), which can be found at www.gipsstandards.org.

describe may apply to either actual or hypothetical portfolios, although some are applied more commonly to one or the other.

15.2.1 No Cash Flows

Measuring the return of a portfolio is usually simple, but sometimes it can get "weird." Consider an equity portfolio with only stocks. Suppose that the portfolio holds N securities such that the weight of each security is given by $w_{i,t}$, where the weights sum to 1 (that is, $\Sigma_{i=1}^{N} w_{i,t} = 1$). We are interested in measuring the return of the portfolio over some period, and our smallest interval of time is one day. We probably do not need to know the performance over an increment smaller than one day. (Tracking stock movements hour by hour is for day traders.) We can denote the return from day t to day $t+1$ as $r_{t,t+1}$. The return from day t to day $t+k$, where k can be many days (e.g., 10, 100, 250, etc.), will be denoted by $r_{t,t+k}$.

To determine the return of the entire portfolio, we first must determine the returns of each of the stocks within the portfolio. Most portfolio managers subscribe to databases that provide stock return data. To calculate the return on a stock over some period, we take the closing price[4] of the stock on day $t + k$ divided by its closing price on day t to obtain the *gross price return*. We then subtract 1 from the gross price return to obtain the price return. Thus

$$r_{i,t,t+k} = \frac{p_{i,t+k}}{p_{i,t}} - 1 \qquad (15.1)$$

The individual stocks in the portfolio might pay dividends during the return measurement period. Dividends have the effect of decreasing the stock price by the amount of the dividend. Thus, if dividends are paid during the return measurement period, one should modify the preceding formula to add the dividend back into the *price return*. The total return is the return that accounts for dividends:

$$r_{i,t,t+k} = \frac{p_{i,t+k} + d_{i,t,t+k}}{p_{i,t}} - 1 \qquad (15.2)$$

Most data providers compute *total returns*.[5] For a performance analyst who does not rely on preadjusted data and instead calculates

---

[4] Closing prices are the most commonly available data on stock prices.

[5] Even finance.yahoo.com allows the user to download "adjusted prices" for stocks, which are prices that include the dividend. The adjusted prices let you compute the return in the normal way.

his or her own dividend-adjusted returns, there is the issue of when to add the dividend to the stock price. If the analyst uses monthly data (i.e., month-end closing prices and monthly dividends), there is not much of a choice. The dividend should be added to the ending price of the stock, and the monthly return should be computed using the formula for total returns. This is equivalent to assuming that the portfolio manager kept the dividend under the mattress until reinvesting it in the stock at the end-of-month closing price. When the dividend yield is small, this technique does not distort returns very much. Remember, the cash held by the portfolio manager normally would earn interest.

If the analyst uses *daily data*, there are more choices of how to treat the dividend. The databases that he or she uses should tell him or her various things about the dividend, including the *payable date*, the day the dividend is paid out to owners of the security, and the *ex-dividend date*, the date before which one must buy the stock in order to receive the dividend. As long as the portfolio owned the security prior to the ex-dividend date, the dividend can be included in the return calculation.

With daily data, the portfolio analyst could compute the daily return of the stock including the dividend on the payable date. This would assume that the portfolio manager invested the dividend back into the stock at the closing price of that day.

An alternative is to assume that the portfolio manager waited until the end of the month to reinvest dividends (which is likely in practice). Until the last day of the month, the performance analyst could increase the cash in the portfolio by the dividend amount and accurately record interest on these dividends.

Yet another method is to compute the return including the dividend on the ex-dividend date. The idea is that, on this day, the price of the stock would have dropped by the amount of the dividend. Thus, adding the dividend amount back to the stock price removes distortion from the daily stock returns. Of course, this assumes that the manager reinvested the dividend on the ex-dividend date, which is unlikely in practice. These issues are primarily concerns for back-testing or for paper performance calculations. For the actual portfolio returns, the performance analyst will have accurate market values of the entire portfolio on a daily basis.

For most stocks, the price return and total return formulas are all that are needed to compute the performance of individual stocks, but there are some *corporate actions* that occasionally make the return calculation more difficult. A company could go into bankruptcy, be acquired by another company, or have a stock split during the performance period. We leave discussions of the treatment of these sorts of events to other books. Analysts and portfolio managers should make sure that their data providers have adjusted stock return data to account for the effects of these events.

Once the returns of the individual stocks have been computed, it is possible to compute the return of the entire portfolio. The return of the entire portfolio will be given by a weighted sum of the returns of the individual stocks, where the weights are as of the beginning of the return measurement period. Thus

$$r_{P,t,t+k} = \sum_{i=1}^{N} w_{i,t}^{P} r_{i,t,t+k} \tag{15.3}$$

where $w_{i,t}^{P}$ is the weight of security i in the portfolio at the close of business on day t.[6]

The weights of each stock in the portfolio will change over time as prices change. Thus, to compute the performance of the portfolio for a subsequent period, the portfolio weights must be updated. The update formula is

$$w_{i,t+k}^{P} = \frac{w_{i,t}^{P}\left(1+r_{i,t,t+k}\right)}{\sum_{j=1}^{N} w_{j,t}^{P}\left(1+r_{j,t,t+k}\right)} \tag{15.4}$$

Most of these steps are required for computing the performance of a hypothetical portfolio. To compute the returns of an actual portfolio, however, the performance analyst typically obtains individual securities' weights by dividing closing market values for all securities in the portfolio by the sum of the market values of all securities in the portfolio. Similarly, the returns for the entire portfolio can be computed more easily just by dividing today's closing market value by yesterday's closing market value. That is, the return of the actual portfolio also can be calculated as the market value of the portfolio at time $t + k$ divided by the market value of the portfolio at time t [that is, $r_{P,t,t+k} = (V_{t+k}/V_t) - 1$].

---

[6] The formulas are easiest for equal-weighted and value-weighted portfolios. For an equal-weighted portfolio, the formula is $r_{P,t,t+k} = \frac{1}{N}\sum_{i=1}^{N} r_{i,t,t+k}$ For a value-weighted portfolio, the formula is $r_{P,t,t+k} = \sum_{i=1}^{N}(V_{i,t}/V_t) r_{i,t,t+k}$ or $(\sum_{i=1}^{N}(V_{i,t+k}/V_t)) - 1$, where $V_{i,t+k}$ and $V_{i,t}$ are the market value of security i at $t + k$ and t, respectively, and V_t is the market value of the portfolio at time t.

If the portfolio in question had no cash flows during the performance period, the foregoing calculations are enough to give an accurate measurement of the portfolio's returns. The formulas assume that there are no buys or sells during the performance measurement period. This is fine for a paper portfolio, which is just a model without real customers. Actual portfolios, though, most likely will have experienced customer withdrawals or investments or other cash flows during any given period. As the Beardstown ladies' mistake made embarrassingly clear, the effects of cash flows have to be removed from the calculations before a portfolio manager can claim some return figure as evidence of his or her superior stock-picking skills.

15.2.2 Inflows and Outflows

Movements of cash into or out of the portfolio complicate the calculations of actual returns. Cash inflows in particular demand a decision about how to allocate new money—whether to keep it in cash reserves, purchase additional shares of the portfolio's stocks in proportion to their weights, or equitize the cash with futures. No matter how the manager decides to use the new cash, the inflows will distort return calculations performed on daily market values of the portfolio. This is a problem that the performance analyst cannot ignore. To tackle the problem, he or she can draw from the portfolio management system's store of information, which typically records cash flows and end-of-day market values of the portfolio.

Simple calculations of return can distort performance quite severely. Consider portfolio X, which had a market value of $100,000 on day $t − 1$. On day t, some time after the market opened, a customer transferred $30,000 into the portfolio. As soon as the money came in, the portfolio manager invested the money in each of the portfolio's stocks in proportion to its weight in the portfolio. Suppose that the weighted return, the true return, of all the stocks in the portfolio for day t was 5% and that the portfolio ended the day at a market value of $136,269.23. If a performance analyst were to use the typical calculation of return—the market value at the close of day t divided by the market value at the close of day $t−1$—he or she would calculate a return of $r_{t-1,t} = (V_t/V_{t-1})$ $−1 = 0.3627$, or 36.27%. This is clearly way off the 5% mark.

When there are cash flows into or out of the portfolio, the analyst must calculate the portfolio's *time-weighted return* (TWR). The

TWR reduces the influence of cash flows on the calculated return so that the return reflects the return on the investments themselves. Ideally, the TWR would be calculated after every inflow or outflow, although the fact that some assets are priced only once a day often prevents exact intraday calculations. Other formulas, most popularly the Dietz method, must be used to approximate the actual TWR.[7] The Dietz method computes daily performance as

$$r_{t,t+1}^{\text{Dietz}} = \frac{V_{t+1} - V_t - C_{t+1}}{V_t + 0.5C_{t+1}} \tag{15.5}$$

where V_t and V_{t+1} measure the portfolio value at the close of day t and day $t + 1$, respectively, and C_{t+1} represents the net cash flows in the portfolio on day $t + 1$.

In the case of portfolio X, the Dietz method computes a daily return of 0.0545, or 5.45%, much closer to the 5% one-day return than the inflated 36.27% suggested by the simple return calculation. Analysts should be aware that the Dietz and other approximations of the TWR grow imprecise when the daily return is very large and when the cash flow represents a very high percentage of the underlying value of the portfolio prior to the flows.[8] The Dietz method should be adequate for portfolio management firms that price their portfolios daily because the daily flows and returns are probably not large enough to distort performance. Firms that value their portfolios less frequently, say, monthly, and that have flows throughout the month should use the more accurate *modified Dietz* method.[9]

---

[7] The Dietz method is named after Peter Dietz. See Dietz (1966). Another method very similar to Dietz is known as the ICAA method. ICAA stands for the Investment Council Association of America.

[8] This is a more significant issue for separate account platforms, in which advisors or investors tend to move a substantial amount of assets from one portfolio to another over the course of a day. Modified Dietz and other TWR approximations mitigate the effect of these sorts of large flows.

[9] The modified Dietz method weights the cash flows at the times they actually occurred during the performance period rather than at the midpoint of the period, as the normal Dietz method does. For portfolios priced on a monthly basis, this distinction greatly improves the approximation. Each movement of cash is weighted in proportion to the number of days in the portfolio. The formula for multiple cash flows in a month is given by $r^{MD} = \dfrac{V_{t+1} - V_t - \sum_{i=1}^{n_{cf}} CF_i}{V_t + \sum_{i=1}^{n_{cf}} CF_i W_i}$, where $W_i = \dfrac{N - n_i}{N}$ is the modified Dietz weight, with n_i being the number of days between the beginning of the period and the timing of cash flow i, and N being the number of days in the whole performance measurement period. CF_i represents the net cash flow i during the period, and n_{cf} is the number of cash flows. For more details, see Dietz and Kirschman (1983).

After calculating accurate daily returns, the performance analyst can compute returns for longer periods by *geometrically linking* the daily returns. The analyst gathers all the daily returns from a particular month (or year) and computes the one-month (or one-year) return as

$$r_{t,t+k} = \prod_{s=0}^{k-1}\left(1+r_{t+s,t+1+s}\right)-1 \tag{15.6}$$

where k is the total number of daily periods in the month (or year or whatever time period the analyst has chosen to look at), $\prod$ is the product sign indicating to multiply a group of variables, and $r_{t,t+k}$ is the return of the portfolio over the k measured days of returns within the month (or year, etc.).

When it comes time to draft marketing reports or meet with clients, the general convention is to present *annualized* returns. It is fine to stick to this convention as long as the portfolio actually has existed—or has been monitored, in the case of a hypothetical portfolio—for at least a year.[10] To annualize the return, first calculate the preceding formula for geometrically linking daily returns, setting the value of k equal to the total number of daily returns on record for the entire lifetime of the portfolio. Second, take that geometrically linked return and compute the annualized return as follows:

$$r^{\text{annualized}} = \left(1+r_{t,t+k}\right)^{\frac{\bar{D}}{k}}-1 \tag{15.7}$$

where k is the number of calender days for which the portfolio has existed, $r_{t,t+k}$ is the geometrically linked return over the entire life of the portfolio, and $\bar{D}$ equals the average number of days in a typical year. $\bar{D}$ can be computed by dividing the total number of days that the portfolio has existed by the number of years it has existed.

Suppose that a performance analyst obtained the daily returns of a portfolio that has existed for 2 years and 10 days. He or she computes the geometrically linked return as 26% (that is, $r_{t,t+k} = 0.26$). Suppose that the portfolio has existed for 740 days ($k = 740$) and that the average number of days in a year is 365 ($\bar{D} = 365$). The annualized return will be: $r^{\text{annualized}} = (1.26)^{(365/740)} - 1 = 0.1207$, or 12.07%.

---

[10] For returns of less than 1 year, the convention is to not annualize the returns.

15.2.3 Measuring Returns for Market-Neutral and Leveraged Portfolios

So far we have only shown how to assess the performance of a plain vanilla portfolio. Since we spent an entire section of this book extolling the benefits of α mojo, we assume that many managers will try something a little more daring than straight buying and selling. If a manager uses leverage or a market-neutral strategy, for instance, how will he or she be able to tell that the α mojo is working? This section explains how to accurately measure the results of leveraged and market-neutral portfolios. We focus on certain basic scenarios, but the techniques can be applied to more complicated versions of leverage and market neutrality as well.

The Leveraged Returns

We discussed many forms of leverage in Chapter 12, but here we focus on how to compute the return on a stock-and-cash portfolio that was leveraged with index futures.[11] We assume that this portfolio manager rebalances his or her portfolio every k days to achieve the desired β^* of the portfolio. The value of his or her overall equity at time $t + k$ is given by

$$V_{t+k} = (1-\xi_t)V_t(1+r_{s,t,t+k}) + \xi_t V_t I_{t,t+k} + N_{f,t}q(F_{t+k}-F_t) \quad (15.8)$$

where ξ_t is the percentage of equity held in cash at time t, V_t is the value of the portfolio equity at time t, $r_{s,t,t+k}$ is the return of the underlying stock portfolio from time t to time $t+k$, $N_{f,t}$ is the number of futures contracts purchased or sold at time t, q is the contract multiplier, and F_{t+k} and F_t represent the futures price at the two respective times.[12] Since we have assumed that the quantitative manager rebalanced his or her portfolio at every rebalancing period to achieve the desired overall β of the portfolio β^*, we can substitute the equation for $N_{f,t} = \{[\beta^*+(\xi_t-1)\beta_{s,t}]/(\beta_{f,t}qS_t)\}V_t$. Thus, making this substitution into Eq. (15.8) with some minor rearrangement of variables gives us the formula for the returns of the leveraged portfolio. Formally,

$$r_{P,t,t+k} = (1-\xi_t)r_{s,t,t+k} + \xi_t(I_{t,t+k}-1) + \left[\frac{\beta^*+(\xi_t-1)\beta_{s,t}}{\beta_{f,t}S_t}\right](F_{t+k}-F_t) \quad (15.9)$$

---

[11] In our formulas we will ignore issues related to the rollover of the futures contracts. We also assume that margin requirements can be settled through use of the underlying stock portfolio.

[12] All this notation is described in more detail in Chapter 12.

where S_t is the value of the futures contract index.[13] Thus, given a set of historical data, a quantitative analyst easily can compute the historical returns of a leveraged portfolio with rebalancing at a k-period interval by obtaining the underlying returns of the stock portfolio every period, the desired overall β, the percentage of equity held in cash each period, the value of the underlying index each period, the β of the underlying portfolio with respect to the underlying index, and the price of the index futures at each rebalancing point.[14]

The Market-Neutral Returns

For a general market-neutral or long-short portfolio, the value of the account equity at time $t + k$ can be expressed as

$$V_{t+k} = V_t^L \left(1 + r_{L,t,t+k}\right) - V_t^S r_{S,t,t+k} + V_t^S \left(e^{i'\frac{k}{360}} - 1\right)$$
$$+ m_{lb} V_t e^{i'\frac{k}{360}} + \left(V_t - V_t^L - m_{lb} V_t\right) e^{i\frac{k}{360}}$$

$$(15.10)$$

where V_t^L and V_t^S are the notional amounts of the long and short portfolios, respectively, $r_{L,t,t+k}$ and $r_{S,t,t+k}$ are the returns of the long-only part of the portfolio and the short-only part of the portfolio before shorting, respectively, m_{lb} is the additional liquidity buffer required on the short position (or total position) as a fraction of the total equity (which may take on any value including zero in certain cases depending on the positions taken), and $e^{i'k/360}$ and $e^{ik/360}$ represent the continuous compounded gross return on the margin deposit and the other cash in the portfolio including the proceeds from the short sale, respectively. We can simplify the notation by calling r_{lb} and r_{cash} the return on the margin deposit $(e^{i'k/360} - 1)$ and the return on the other cash $(e^{ik/360} - 1)$. Let's also express the long-only part of the position as $\kappa_t^L = V_t^L / V_t$ and the short-only part of the position as $\kappa_t^S = V_t^S / V_t$. These terms just represent the notional amounts of the long-only and short-only parts of the portfolio as fractions of the original equity.

---

[13] This formula simplifies for many backtests. If the index futures are on the underlying benchmark, β_f will be equal to 1 and can be removed from the equation. Also, if $\xi = 0$ and $I_{t,t+k} = 1$, then the formula reduces to $r_{s,t,t+k} + [(\beta^* - \beta_{s,t})/S_t] (F_{t+k} - F_t)$.

[14] Of course, this formula is not exact because it assumes that the portfolio manager can purchase fractional amounts of the futures contract, which is not possible in practice. Nevertheless, this computation will be quite close and satisfactory for historical backtests.

We can express the return of the overall market-neutral or long-short portfolio as

$$r_{P,t,t+k} = \left(1 - \kappa_t^L\right) r_{cash} + \kappa_t^L r_{L,t,t+k} - \kappa_t^S r_{S,t,t+k} + \kappa_t^S r_{cash} + m_{lb}\left(r_{lb} - r_{cash}\right) \quad (15.11)$$

This is a comprehensive formula for computing the returns of a market-neutral or long-short portfolio using historical or real-time data. One can simplify the equation for common situations. Suppose that the market-neutral portfolio manager is dollar-neutral (that is, $V_t^L = V_t^S$) and the return on the liquidity buffer equals the return on the cash (that is, $r_{lb} = r_{cash}$). Then

$$r_{P,t,t+k} = r_{cash} + \kappa_t^L\left(r_{L,t,t+k} - r_{S,t,t+k}\right) \quad (15.12)$$

Thus, given a set of historical data, one can compute the returns of a hypothetical market-neutral (specifically, dollar-neutral) portfolio by computing the returns of the long-only part of the portfolio each period, the returns of the short-only portfolio each period (before shorting), the return on any cash (which is paid to the short proceeds, the liquidity buffer, and other cash), and the proportion of the original equity that is invested in the long-only and short-only parts of the portfolio.[15]

15.3 MEASURING RISK

We have measured the return of portfolios, but return is only half the story. Risk matters, too. Perhaps some portfolio boasts an outstanding one-year return. The savvy investor will greet the return figure with a bit of skepticism because he or she knows that if the portfolio is very volatile, last year's great returns easily could be followed by next year's losses. The portfolio manager ought to be concerned with risk as well. A portfolio that goes through boom-and-bust cycles will scare away clients. The manager must strike some balance between the potential rewards of risk taking and the security of risk minimization.

There are a number of risk measurements: the standard deviation (or variance) of portfolio returns, the semivariance of returns, the tracking error of returns, the VaR (value at risk) of returns, the correlation and covariance of the portfolio, and the β of the

---

[15] In the case of a maximum leveraged dollar-neutral portfolio, $\kappa^L = \kappa^S = (1 - m_{lb})$.

portfolio. These are not measures of all types of investment risk but of the risks inherent in market price fluctuations.[16]

15.3.1 Standard Deviation

The standard deviation measures how much the returns of a portfolio move around the average return. The standard deviation grows as returns move further above or further below the average. As a measurement of risk, most investors only care about the standard deviation of a stock in one direction, above or below the mean. Investors who are long stocks do not want returns to dip below the mean, but they certainly would be happy with returns that exceed it. If the returns of the portfolio are normally distributed, then the standard deviation is a valid measure of returns that are below the mean. If returns are not normal but skewed, then the standard deviation is less meaningful—but we will talk about that in the next section.

A performance analyst would like to know the portfolio's true future standard deviation. Unfortunately, this is not possible; he or she must estimate the standard deviation using past data.[17] To estimate the standard deviation of a series of portfolio returns, the performance analyst computes

$$\hat{\sigma}_P = \sqrt{\hat{V}(r_P)} = \sqrt{\frac{\sum_{t=1}^{T}(r_{P,t} - \bar{r}_P)^2}{T-1}} \tag{15.13}$$

where $r_{P,t}$ represents the portfolio return for period t, $\bar{r}_P$ represents the average return of all the portfolio returns, $\hat{V}$ represents the sample variance, and T represents the number of portfolio returns.

---

[16] A nonfinancial friend of ours once asked us, "Why should I care about the variance if in the long run the stock market goes up?" It was a good question, but then we realized it was based on an investor fallacy in thinking, which is that the stock market always goes up over the long run. Variance of returns means that there is the probability, however small, that the market potentially could go down over the long run. This probability is the basis for the portfolio insurance business. If you wish to insure your portfolio even over many years, it usually costs anywhere from 5% to 10% of your investment. Someone else once criticized portfolio insurance as "ridiculous—since we know stocks always go up over the long term, this insurance should be free." A few months later, the internet bubble burst and, along with it, his portfolio, which fell by 80%. This may have been an unfortunate lesson in the fact that depending on what years you look at, the stock market sometimes may decline over a longer time frame.

[17] Implied volatilities from the option prices of stocks are also used to forecast future volatility.

This formula can be estimated using daily, monthly, or annual data. The performance analyst should be sure to have enough data.

15.3.2 Semi-Standard Deviation

When stock or portfolio returns are not normally distributed, the standard deviation of returns does not really measure risk the way that investors think of risk.[18] A better measure of risk as most investors define it—the chance of losing money—is one that only reflects the likelihood of poor returns.

For example, suppose that our distribution of returns or excess returns is log normal.[19] This distribution is not symmetric. It is *skewed* to the right. If we chose to find investments with low variances or standard deviations in this distribution, we actually would reduce disproportionately the upside of the distribution.[20]

---

[18] A performance analyst may wish to test for the normality of the distribution of portfolio returns. A popular test, known as the *Jarque-Bera test*, is based on two central moments of the distribution of stocks returns, called *skewness* and *kurtosis*. The test is based on the sample skewness and kurtosis of stock returns. The Jarque-Bera test statistic is given by $JB = T\left[\dfrac{\text{Skew}^2}{6} + \dfrac{(\text{Kurt} - 3)^2}{24}\right] \sim \chi_2^2$, where χ_2^2 is the chi-square distribution with 2 degrees of freedom,

$$\text{Skew} = \frac{\hat{m}_3}{(\hat{m}_2)^{\frac{3}{2}}},$$

$$\text{Kurt} = \frac{\hat{m}_4}{(\hat{m}_2)^2},$$

$$\hat{m}_k = \frac{1}{T}\sum_{t=1}^{T}(r_{p,t} - \bar{r}_p)^k,$$

and

$$\bar{r}_p = \frac{1}{T}\sum_{t=1}^{T}r_{p,t}.$$

Most popular software packages have some variant of this test built directly into their software. For example, in STATA, you can use the function SUMMARIZE to get skewness and kurtosis and then compute the Jarque-Bera (JB) statistic or use the command VECNORM to conduct the Jarque-Bera Test. You can also conduct the JB test in R, using the function JARQUE.BERA.TEST; in MATLAB, using the function JBTEST; and in RATS, using the function STATISTICS.

[19] When a random variable, X, has a normal distribution, then $Y = e^X$ has a log-normal distribution. If μ and σ are the mean and standard deviation of X, then the probability density function for Y is

$$f(y) = \frac{1}{\sqrt{2\pi}\,\sigma y}e^{-[(\log y - \mu)^2]/2\sigma^2}, \quad y \geq 0$$

[20] Now, had the distribution been negatively skewed, or skewed left, the variance/standard deviation analysis would have placed too little weight on the downside risk.

We would be better off by reducing the downside risk, which is measured by the *semivariance or semi-standard deviation.*

The general measure for downside risk is given by

$$\hat{\sigma}_P^{DR} = \sqrt{\frac{1}{T-1}\sum_{t=1}^{T}[\min(r_{P,t}-k),0]^2} \qquad (15.14)$$

where k is an arbitrary constant.[21] When $k = \bar{r}_p$, then the measure is known as semi-standard deviation because it is measuring the deviations from the average return on the downside.

Although downside risk, or semi-standard deviation, is one of the most robust measures of risk, it presents computational difficulties that deter many practitioners. It does not work well, for instance, with standard quadratic optimization.[22] In any case, performance analysis software these days can easily compute the ex-post downside risk of any actual portfolio or model portfolio.

15.3.3 Tracking Error

Tracking error is a familiar concept to quantitative portfolio managers, index portfolio managers, and qualitative portfolio managers alike. Tracking error measures the deviation of a portfolio's return from the return of the benchmark, be it a target asset class or a major index. The "perfect" index manager has a tracking error (*TE*) of 0. Real index managers do not track the benchmark perfectly owing to transactions costs, reinvestment of dividends, and sampling methods of replicating the benchmark, but they do try to get as close as possible. Quantitative portfolio managers, on the other hand, are not trying to eliminate tracking error. They purposefully choose stocks and/or weights so as to achieve a higher return than the benchmark. The point is to keep the tracking error stable. The portfolio manager typically has to operate under some sort of constraint, such as that the ex-ante tracking error cannot exceed 5%. This controls the risk of the portfolio versus the benchmark.

By *ex-ante tracking error,* we mean the tracking error that the portfolio manager attempts to build into the portfolio initially. The derivation of ex-ante tracking error was shown in Chapter 9. There is also *ex-post tracking error,* which is the actual or realized tracking

---

[21] There are alternative methods of computing this, including dividing by the total number of downside observations rather than the total number of observations.

[22] See Chapter 9.

error over a given period. Performance measurement is mainly concerned with measuring the ex-post tracking error of the portfolio, but it also might involve measuring the difference between the ex-post and ex-ante tracking errors. Ex-post tracking error typically is defined as the standard deviation of the difference in returns of the portfolio and the benchmark (in other words, of the excess return). The formula is

$$TE = \hat{\sigma}_x = \sqrt{\hat{\sigma}_x^2} = \sqrt{\frac{1}{T-1}\sum_{t=1}^{T}(x_t - \bar{x})^2} \qquad (15.15)$$

where $x_t = r_{P,t} - r_{B,t}$ and $\bar{x} = \frac{1}{T}\Sigma_{t=1}^{T} x_t$. Tracking error typically is annualized. If the tracking error is measured using any particular interval of data, the performance analyst can annualize it by multiplying by the square root of the number of intervals required to make the measurement period a full year. Thus, if the tracking error has been computed using monthly data, one can annualize it by multiplying it by $\sqrt{12}$.

15.3.4 CAPM β

Modern portfolio theory and the capital asset pricing model (CAPM) gave birth to β. The β of the portfolio measures the risk of the portfolio in relation to the overall market, which is usually considered to be the S&P 500. A β of 1 indicates that the portfolio's returns move one for one with the market returns. A β greater than 1 indicates that the portfolio amplifies the market's return in both the positive and negative directions. A β of less than 1 represents a portfolio in which market swings are to some degree muted. A β of 0 means that the portfolio is not correlated with the market.

A performance analyst can find β either by taking the weighted average of the β's of each stock in the portfolio or by running a linear regression of the portfolio's returns against the market's returns. For the first method, the performance analyst needs to estimate the β of each individual stock. In Appendix 15E we discuss one method, but here we will just say that stock β's are available from most data providers.[23] The β of the overall portfolio is computed from the individual stock data as follows:

---

[23] Appendix 15E can be found under Chapter Appendices at https://ludwigbc.com/books/qepm/exclusive_qepm_content_2020/ or at www.ludwigbc.com under QEPM Exclusive Content.

$$\beta_{P,t} = \sum_{i=1}^{N} w_{i,t}^{P} \beta_{i,t} \qquad (15.16)$$

where N is the number of stocks in the portfolio, $w_{i,t}^{P}$ is the weight of stock i in the portfolio at time t, and $\beta_{i,t}$ is the β of stock i at time t.

The second way to find β_P is to run the following regression:

$$r_{P,t} - r_{f,t} = \alpha + \beta_P \left(r_{M,t} - r_{f,t} \right) + \epsilon_t \qquad (15.17)$$

where $r_{f,t}$ represents the risk-free rate, which can be monthly returns of the three-month Treasury bill, and $r_{M,t}$ represents the monthly market return, with the S&P 500 typically used as a proxy for the market.

Here are some practical comments about β measurement: (1) The greater the number of stocks in the portfolio when estimating β, the more stable β is over time. Stability in the β estimate means that the analyst can rely on it as an accurate description of the portfolio's relative market risk in the future. (2) Extreme β's tend to regress toward the mean of 1. This had led many practitioners to construct an *adjusted* β, which is a function of both the measured β and the market β. Thus $\beta_{adj} = a\beta + (1 - a)1$. The parameter a is flexible. (3) Most data providers furnish similar stock β's. (4) The β's of individual companies usually are measured using monthly data over a three- or five-year horizon. Most data providers do not publish β's for stocks that have less than three years' worth of data. In Appendix 15E, we show one method of computing individual stock β's when the data are limited. (5) If the performance analyst plots the measured β's of individual stocks against the subsequent returns of the stocks and the market, he or she will find that the slope of the line is smaller than theory would predict.[24] Increases in β do not increase returns as much as the regression equation predicts, and decreases in β do not decrease returns as much as the regression equation predicts. This is, in part, related to observation (2). (6) Many practitioners have found that β does not adequately explain stock returns.

---

[24] See Friend and Blume (1970), Black, Jensen, and Scholes (1972), and Stambaugh (1982). Chincarini et al. (2020) found that the relationship is much stronger if one accounts for the ages of firms.

15.3.5 Value-at-Risk

Value-at-risk (VaR) is a concept that is mainly used to control the possibility for potential losses of an entire bank's investment positions or to control the risk of an individual trading position. It is more of a short-term risk concept. VaR is defined as the maximum expected loss over a target horizon within a given confidence interval. There are many specialized techniques to compute VaR, but if the returns of the portfolio are normally distributed, then the calculation of VaR is straightforward.[25]

Once the standard deviation and expected return of the portfolio have been estimated, then one uses the standard normal table to determine the critical value of the VaR calculation for the desired significance. For example, for a 95% significance, the critical value is 1.65. For 97.5%, 99%, and 99.5%, the critical values are 1.96, 2.33, and 2.58, respectively. Thus, if the estimated mean of the portfolio is $\hat{\mu}_p$, the estimated standard deviation of the portfolio is given by $\hat{\sigma}_p$, and the confidence level critical value is given by k, then the VaR is

$$\text{VaR}_t = V_t \, (\hat{\mu}_p - k\hat{\sigma}_p) \tag{15.18}$$

where V_t is the value of the portfolio at time t.

Suppose that our \$100 million portfolio has an annualized mean of 10% and a standard deviation of 20%. Suppose, also, that we wish to have a confidence interval of 97.5%. Then the VaR of our portfolio is

$$\text{VaR}_t = 100,000,000(0.10 - 1.96 \cdot 0.20) = -29,200,000$$

We can be 97.5% confident that, in a given year, the worst loss that the portfolio could suffer is \$29,200,000. Users of VaR often prefer to have a VaR measure over a shorter period of time, such as one day or one week, so that they can understand a bank's exposure over a short period of time. The VaR calculation for any subperiod using annualized data is simply

$$\text{VaR}_t = V_t(\hat{\mu}_p s - k\hat{\sigma}_p \sqrt{s}) \tag{15.19}$$

where s is measured in fractions of a year. Thus, for a one-month VaR, $s = 1/12$. In our earlier example, using $s = 1/24$, we find that the VaR over a two-week period for the portfolio would be \$7,584,999.

---

[25] For more details on VaR, see Jorion (1997) or Dowd (1998).

15.3.6 Covariance and Correlation

The covariance or correlation ρ of a portfolio with a major index indicates the risk of the portfolio with respect to the index. It also indicates the diversification benefits from combining the portfolio with other portfolios. The covariance of a portfolio ex ante or ex post can be constructed from the individual securities that make up the portfolio. We showed how to do this in Chapters 6 and 7. Here we show how to take a set of portfolio returns and compute the covariance and correlation.

The covariance of the portfolio with any other index is computed by gathering the returns of the portfolio and the index and computing the following:

$$\hat{C}\left(r_P, r_I\right) = \frac{1}{T} \sum_{t=1}^{T} \left(r_{P,t} - \overline{r}_P\right)\left(r_{I,t} - \overline{r}_I\right) \tag{15.20}$$

The correlation between the portfolio and the index can be computed as follows:

$$\hat{\rho}\left(r_P, r_I\right) = \frac{\hat{C}\left(r_P, r_I\right)}{\hat{\sigma}_P \hat{\sigma}_I} \tag{15.21}$$

where $\hat{\sigma}_P$ and $\hat{\sigma}_I$ are the standard deviations of the portfolio and the index over the sample period. The correlation is more pleasant to deal with than the covariance because it always must be between -1 and 1. A correlation of 1 represents two return streams that always move together. A correlation of -1 represents the other extreme, two return streams that move in opposite directions.

15.4 RISK-ADJUSTED PERFORMANCE MEASUREMENT

Many personal investors focus with tunnel vision on raw returns. This is why, each year, most mutual fund investments flow into the funds that had the best performances or highest returns in the previous year. It is absolutely a mistake, though, to look at returns out of the context of risk. Consider Figure 15.1.

Looking only at returns, one would conclude that portfolio manager C is the best. Manager C has the highest return over the

FIGURE 15.1

Risk return of three portfolios.

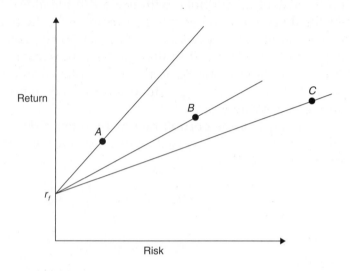

period, manager B has the second highest, and manager A has the lowest return over the period. Portfolio manager A would be considered the worst manager. One notices, though, that portfolio manager C is taking on a lot more risk than portfolio managers A and B. If we borrowed—using the risk-free asset of a margin account—at some given interest rate r_f, we could increase the returns and the risk of portfolio manager A. If we borrowed enough, we could increase his or her risk until it was equal to the risk of portfolio manager C. At that same risk level, portfolio manager A's return actually would be much higher than portfolio manager C's.[26] The most accurate comparison of portfolio managers, therefore, is a comparison not of returns but of risk-adjusted returns. One of the most important measures of risk-adjusted returns is the Sharpe ratio.

---

[26] Mathematically, one can observe that if the expected leveraged return of portfolio A is $E[r_{Al}] = (1+\alpha)\mu_A - \alpha r_f$, and the risk of the leveraged portfolio A is $\sigma_{Al} = (1+\alpha)\sigma_A$, then a leveraged portfolio A with the same risk as portfolio C always will have a higher expected return if $(\mu_A - r_f)/\sigma_A > (\mu_C - r_f)/\sigma_C$. This condition is that the slope of the line through the risk-free rate and portfolio A is greater than the slope of the line through the risk-free rate and portfolio C.

15.4.1 The Sharpe Ratio

William F. Sharpe won the Nobel Prize in Economic Sciences for his development of the CAPM.[27] Among the many things that came out of this work is a measurement for risk-adjusted returns that is appropriately called the *Sharpe ratio*. The Sharpe ratio (SR) measures the portfolio's excess return above the risk-free rate per unit of risk. It is given by

$$SR = \frac{\bar{r}_p - \bar{r}_f}{\hat{\sigma}_p} \tag{15.22}$$

where SR is the Sharpe ratio measured over the sample period, $\bar{r}_p$ is the average portfolio return, $\bar{r}_f$ is the average risk-free rate, and $\hat{\sigma}_p$ is the estimated standard deviation of the portfolio returns.[28] In practice, this ratio is computed as follows: Suppose that one has the monthly returns of a portfolio. One should take the arithmetic average of those returns. Thus, if one has 25 months of monthly portfolio returns, one should compute the average as $\bar{r}_p = \frac{1}{25} \Sigma_{t=1}^{25} r_{p,t}$. For the risk-free rate, the exact value actually does not matter for comparison purposes, as long as some consistent rate is chosen. Many people use the average monthly return on 1-month or 3-month United States Treasury bills as $\bar{r}_f$.[29] Finally, one needs to compute the portfolio risk over the period by taking the monthly returns and computing the standard deviation of the monthly returns. One can use the basic formula: $\hat{\sigma}_p = \sqrt{\sum_{t=1}^{T} (r_{p,t} - \bar{r}_p)^2 / (T-1)}$

The Sharpe ratio provides a basis for comparing portfolios. In isolation, it does not mean much. Even when managers speak of "good" and "bad" Sharpe ratios, they are speaking only in relative

---

[27] Jan Mossin, John Linter, and Jack Treynor also did work at the same time as Sharpe to develop the CAPM. Some people refer to this as the Linter-Mossin-Sharpe-Treynor CAPM. Harry Markowitz told us that the most elegant paper to read on the topic was written by Mossin (1966).

[28] When returns are non-normal, it is better to divide the numerator by the semi-standard deviation. This modified Sharpe ratio is also known as the *Sortino ratio*. Risk-adjusted hedge fund returns are sometimes measured with the Sterling and Calmar ratios, which are ratios of the annualized returns of the portfolio over some period divided by a type of downside risk measure known as drawdown. *Drawdown* measures the absolute value of the return loss from the peak to trough of the portfolio value. The peak and trough are recognized, once a new peak is reached by the portfolio. The Calmar ratio uses the absolute maximum drawdown over the measurement period, while the Sterling ratio uses the absolute average drawdown minus some constant.

[29] When total returns are not available for Treasury bills, some people just use the time-series average of the Treasury yields as a proxy for the Treasury bill return.

terms.[30] If portfolio manager A has the highest Sharpe ratio of several managers, you can say that he or she has the highest risk-adjusted return of the managers for the period. If you actually believe that there is something inherently stable about portfolio manager A's performance, then you could leverage portfolio manager A and achieve the return of any other manager with lower risk. Of course, there is no guarantee that the same risk-adjusted return will continue in the next period.

15.4.2 The Information Ratio

The information ratio (IR) measures the risk-adjusted performance of portfolio managers who manage to a benchmark. It is the ratio of the benchmark α they produced to the residual risk they took on with respect to the benchmark.[31] An index manager should have an IR of 0 because his or her α theoretically should be 0, and his or her residual risk theoretically should be 0. An active portfolio manager intentionally deviates from the benchmark weightings to outperform the

---

[30] For example, some portfolio managers say that a Sharpe ratio above 0.5 is really good. What they are really saying is, "Of all the portfolios I've seen managed, I haven't seen a Sharpe ratio above 0.5 too often."

[31] The ex-ante information ratio is used to described the expected portfolio information ratio, while the ex-post information ratio is used to measure actual risk-adjusted performance. Some portfolio managers measure the ex-post information ratio as

$IR^\star = \dfrac{\bar{r}_P - \bar{r}_B}{\hat{\sigma}_x}$, where $\bar{r}_P$ is the average return of the portfolio, and $\bar{r}_B$ is the average

return of the benchmark over the measurement period. $\hat{\sigma}_x$ is the tracking error (i.e., the standard deviation of the difference in returns between the portfolio and the benchmark). Portfolio managers often use this measure as it is easier to compute. However, this measure can lead to misleading conclusions about the respective information ratios of different managers with different exposures to the benchmark

(i.e., their β). To understand this, note that $IR^\star = \dfrac{\bar{r}_P - \bar{r}_B}{\hat{\sigma}_x} = \dfrac{\hat{\alpha} + (\hat{\beta} - 1)\bar{r}_B}{\sqrt{(\hat{\beta} - 1)^2 \hat{\sigma}_B^2 + \hat{\omega}^2}}$, where

$\hat{\omega}^2$ is the residual variance of the portfolio. Thus, the two measures of information ratio, $IR^\star$ and $IR^\star$, are only equal when the measured β of the portfolio versus the benchmark is equal to 1; otherwise, they are different. If you take the derivative of

$IR^\star$ with respect to β, you will find that $\dfrac{\partial IR^\star}{\partial \beta} = \left[\bar{r}_B \hat{\omega}^2 - (\hat{\beta} - 1)\hat{\sigma}_B^2 \hat{\alpha}\right] \Big/ \left[(\hat{\beta} - 1)\hat{\sigma}_B^2 + \hat{\omega}^2\right]^{3/2}$.

Thus, $\dfrac{\partial IR^\star}{\partial \beta} > 0$, whenever $\bar{r}_B > 0$, $\hat{\alpha} > 0$, and $\hat{\beta} < 1$. Thus, for upward-drifting markets ($\bar{r}_B > 0$), among portfolio managers with a similar positive α, a less aggressive portfolio manager (smaller β, $\beta < 1$) will look worse (i.e., lower $IR^\star$). Whenever $\bar{r}_B < 0$, $\hat{\alpha} > 0$, and $\hat{\beta} > 1$, the higher manager will have a lower $IR^\star$. In both of these cases, the $IR^\star$ measure leads to erroneous interpretation of the managers, while IR does not. In fact, in both of these cases, the IR of the managers is the same.

benchmark. This creates his or her α and also generates residual risk versus the benchmark. Thus the information ratio is defined as

$$IR = \frac{\hat{\alpha}^B}{\hat{\omega}} \qquad (15.23)$$

where $\hat{\alpha}^B$ is the estimate of α from the regression of the portfolio returns on the benchmark returns for the measurement period, and $\hat{\omega}$ is the estimate of the residual standard deviation of the regression.[32]

As with the Sharpe ratio, the higher the value of the IR, the better the portfolio manager performed on a risk-adjusted basis. As with the Sharpe ratio, the correct IR is easy to compute over a period. All one needs is the returns of the portfolio and the returns of the benchmark.

The information ratio typically is computed by running a regression of the portfolio returns against the benchmark returns. The idea is that the portfolio manager is being measured against the benchmark, so we should consider his or her excess risk-adjusted return over the benchmark divided by his or her excess (residual) risk. A regression similar to the CAPM α (see subsection 15.4.3) is run over the relevant performance measurement period. The estimated α, $\hat{\alpha}$, is stored, as well as the residual standard deviation, which is given by $\hat{\omega} = \sqrt{\hat{V}(\hat{\epsilon}_t)}$, where $\hat{\epsilon}_t = (r_{P,t} - r_{f,t}) - \hat{\beta}(r_{B,t} - r_{f,t})$. All the ingredients to measure the information ratio come directly from the CAPM α regression, with the benchmark replacing the market return.

15.4.3 The CAPM α and the Benchmark α

In Chapter 2 we discussed the various types of α relevant to quantitative equity portfolio management (QEPM). We also briefly discussed the distinction between ex-ante and ex-post α. When we measure the risk-adjusted performance of a portfolio, we are always measuring the ex-post α. We now discuss the CAPM α (α^{CAPM}) and the benchmark α (α^B) in this light. The CAPM implies the following relationship between the portfolio return and the market index return:

$$r_{P,t} - r_{f,t} = \alpha + \beta(r_{M,t} - r_{f,t}) + \epsilon_t \qquad (15.24)$$

---

[32] Some practitioners use the notation $\hat{\sigma}_\epsilon$ instead of $\hat{\omega}$.

While the theory itself says that the value of α should be 0, practitioners nonetheless estimate α and use it as a measure of risk-adjusted return. If α is positive, then the portfolio manager has provided an extra return over the market portfolio that is not explained by the extra risk he or she is taking. If the α is negative, then the portfolio manager is losing value versus the market portfolio.

The CAPM α is a very popular method for measuring portfolio managers' performance and for ranking portfolio managers. CAPM α is also called *Jensen's* α after a paper that Michael Jensen wrote in 1968 that introduced a new method of determining whether mutual fund portfolio managers outperformed the market. Jensen was essentially trying to determine whether portfolio managers had positive α's. Owing to the large number of mutual funds he studied, he could not determine the benchmark of each one. Instead, he used the market return as a proxy for each benchmark.

Given the popularity of the CAPM, it is not surprising that the CAPM equation or single-index model has been used for many other indices and benchmarks. When we estimate the CAPM equation replacing the market portfolio with the benchmark, we call the resulting α the *benchmark* α. The benchmark α is obtained from the following regression[33]:

$$r_{P,t} - r_{f,t} = \alpha + \beta(r_{B,t} - r_{f,t}) + \epsilon_t \qquad (15.25)$$

If the α from this regression is positive, it is an indication that the portfolio manager is outperforming the respective index on a risk-adjusted basis, whereas if the value of α is negative, this is a sign that the portfolio manager is underperforming the index on a risk-adjusted basis. Both for CAPM α and for benchmark α, not only is the sign of the α important, but the analyst also must determine whether the α is statistically significant. Most regression analyses will supply the *t-statistic* of the estimate of α.[34] Generally, for a large enough sample (e.g., 40), a t-statistic greater than 2 will be sufficient for a 95% confidence level and 2.7 for a 99% confidence level.[35] These regressions can be corrected for heteroscedasticity and autocorrelation in the residuals if needed.

---

[33] Some practitioners estimate this regression without subtracting the risk-free rate.
[34] The *t*-statistic is discussed in Section 15.4.5.
[35] The critical *t*-statistic can be found for any specific situation after determining the degrees of freedom. However, for most circumstances, this rule of thumb is sufficient.

15.4.4 The Multifactor α

Many studies have shown that the CAPM fails to explain security returns adequately. Thus multifactor models of stock returns have become more popular, especially in performance measurement.[36] In academic circles, two models have gained popularity. One is a three-factor model, which includes the market, the small-cap premium, and the book-to-market premium. The other is a four-factor model, which includes all the variables in the aforementioned three-factor model in addition to a momentum term.

To compute the multifactor α (α^{MF}), one needs to know the returns on the factors that are believed to represent security returns and the portfolio's returns over time. The multifactor α is usually calculated by regressing the monthly or quarterly returns of the portfolio against the return on the market index or benchmark and other factors. The most commonly used multifactor models accepted by academics and many practitioners are the two written below[37]:

$$r_{P,t} - r_{f,t} = \alpha + \beta_1(r_{M,t} - r_{f,t}) + \beta_2 SMB_t + \beta_3 HML_t + \epsilon_t \quad (15.26)$$

$$r_{P,t} - r_{f,t} = \alpha + \beta_1(r_{M,t} - r_{f,t}) + \beta_2 SMB_t + \beta_3 HML_t \\ + \beta_4 RMW_t + \beta_5 CMA_t + \beta_6 MOM_t + \epsilon_t \quad (15.27)$$

where β_i are the coefficients of each of the factor returns or factor exposures, $(r_{M,t} - r_{f,t})$ represents the stock market return minus the risk-free rate of return,[38] and SMB_t, HML_t, RMW_t, CMA_t, MOM_t are the value-weighted, zero-investment, factor-mimicking portfolios for market capitalization, book-to-market, profitability, investment, and momentum. These six factors can be constructed in a variety of ways. We discuss the most common academic constructions of these variables. SMB_t is the size or market capitalization factor,

---

[36] See Fama and French (1993) and Carhart (1997).
[37] When we published the first edition of this book, the most commonly used academic model was the three-factor Fama-French model plus momentum. In recent years, many researchers have extended the three-factor model into a five- or six-factor model, including Eugene Fama and Kenneth French. Thus, we present the Fama-French six-factor model or five-factor model plus momentum. That there has been so much change over the years in the accepted factor models and the growing literature on data mining of factors (which always concerned Fischer Black) remind us how difficult it is to precisely quantify the behavior of asset prices.
[38] Academics typically use a value-weighted portfolio of New York Stock Exchange (NYSE), American Stock Exchange (AMEX), and National Association of Securities Dealers Automated Quotations (NASDAQ) stocks to proxy for the market.

which is constructed by subtracting a portfolio of equal-weighted small-cap stocks from a portfolio of equal-weighted large-cap stocks. HML_t is the value factor, which is constructed by subtracting a portfolio of high B/M (book-to-market) stocks from a portfolio with low B/M stocks. RMW_t is the profitability factor, which is constructed by subtracting a portfolio of high operating profitability stocks from a portfolio of low-profitability stocks. CMA_t is the investment factor, which is constructed by subtracting a portfolio of smaller asset growth (conservative) stocks from a portfolio with higher asset growth (aggressive) stocks. MOM_t is a portfolio of high-return stocks minus a portfolio of low-return stocks, where momentum is defined as the previous eleven-month returns lagged by one month (i.e., the returns from the month $t - 12$ to the end of month $t - 2$ when the ranking date is the end of month $t - 1$ for a portfolio in month t) and is updated monthly.[39]

If α is positive, then the portfolio manager has provided an extra return that is not explained by the extra risk he or she is

[39] Fama and French construct it as $SMB_t = \frac{1}{3}(Small\ Value + Small\ Neutral + Small\ Growth) - \frac{1}{3}(Big\ Value + Big\ Neutral + Big\ Growth)$, where the six portfolios in the equation are constructed by dividing the NYSE, AMEX, and NASDAQ stocks into two buckets on either side of the median market capitalization of the NYSE stocks. The small and big buckets are further divided into three buckets based upon the 70% and 30% breakpoints of book-to-market ratios of NYSE stocks. These six portfolios then correspond to the names listed prior, with value being high B/M and growth being low B/M. To construct the HML_t factor, Fama-French use $HML_t = \frac{1}{2}(Small\ Value + Big\ Value) - \frac{1}{2}(Small\ Growth + Big\ Growth)$. The first factor weights the portfolios so that both the small portfolio and big portfolio have about the same average B/M ratio. The second factor weights the portfolios so that the high B/M portfolio and low B/M portfolio have the same weighted-average size, to remove the size effect. The profitability (RMW_t) and investment (CMA_t) factors are constructed similarly to the value factor. Thus, once sorts are complete, $RMW_t = \frac{1}{2}(Small\ Robust + Big\ Robust) - \frac{1}{2}(Small\ Weak + Big\ Weak)$, where Robust is for high operating profitability and Weak is for low operating profitability. $CMA_t = \frac{1}{2}(Small\ Conservative + Big\ Conservative) - \frac{1}{2}(Small\ Aggressive + Big\ Aggressive)$. Operating profitability is defined as annual revenues minus COGS minus interest expense minus SGA divided by book equity. Investments are defined as change in total assets divided by total assets. Robust profitability firms are firms with higher profitability, and Conservative firms are the firms with the lowest change in investments. The momentum (MOM_t) factor is also constructed similarly to the value factor. Thus, once sorts are complete, $MOM_t = \frac{1}{2}(Small\ High + Big\ High) - \frac{1}{2}(Small\ Low + Big\ Low)$, where the high and low return portfolios are separated by the previous eleven-month cumulative returns lagged by one month (i.e., $t - 12$ to $t - 2$). For MOM_t, portfolios are formed monthly rather than annually. For more details, see Fama and French (1993, 2015). The portfolio manager can create his own factor portfolios using similar concepts. There is no need to follow the Fama-French methodology.

taking, which is encapsulated by the β's. If α is negative, then the portfolio manager is losing value. However, not only is the sign of the α important, but the analyst must determine whether the α is statistically significant. Most regression analyses will supply the t-statistic of the estimate of α.

When the multifactor α is used to judge the performance of a portfolio manager, it tends to rate him or her less favorably than CAPM α would because it considers additional risk factors. In fact, it is very common to find a negative value for multifactor α. However, there is still a debate over whether it is appropriate to use a multifactor α model to judge a portfolio manager's performance. Some academics believe that the additional risk factors are not truly risk factors in the economy. They argue that the decision to load up on those factors is a decision that should in fact be rewarded. Other academics claim that a multifactor risk model is more appropriate as a surrogate for overall risks in the economy; although the typical Fama-French factors are not real economy-wide risks, they can act as proxies for them. One also could argue that since almost every commercial risk model is a multifactor model, it is inconsistent not to count these factors as risk factors for performance measurement yet include them in the risk model for managing the portfolio. A portfolio manager can outperform the benchmark by loading up on factors that have positive risk premiums or through individual stock picking. Loading up on factors that have a positive premium is a mechanical strategy that could be replicated by a machine.[40] Should bonuses be awarded for this? If you think so, then use a CAPM version for measuring α. If you believe that portfolio managers should be rewarded for their ability to pick individual stocks that have positive α's after accounting for the multifactor risk in their portfolios, then use a multifactor model to measure α. Either way, the debate is sure to continue between defenders of the CAPM and proponents of the multifactor model.[41]

---

[40] In fact, since we wrote the first edition of this book, many practitioners have created what are known as *smart-beta strategies*. These factor strategies are based on a formula and are offered to investors in the form of a mutual fund or ETF or separate account.

[41] The joke we make to our students is that if you're a portfolio manager, you want to convince the performance measurement department to use a CAPM-based or Jensen's α measurement. If you're the CIO, you want to use the multifactor model.

15.4.5 Practical Issues with Risk-Adjusted Measures

Fund-of-fund managers and financial advisors look for good portfolio managers to include in their asset allocations, and CIOs look for good portfolio managers to hire. But what is the measure of a "good" portfolio manager? For an index manager, good means adequately tracking the benchmark; the closer the returns are to the benchmark, the better. For an enhanced index manager or an active manager, good generally means tracking the benchmark but consistently earning a higher return than the benchmark. Even if we know what we are looking for in a good manager, two obstacles get in the way of finding it. The first is that assessing a manager's performance over an investment period requires a significant amount of data, which may not be available. The second is that we have to assume that past performance is somewhat indicative of future performance. We cannot resolve these problems, but we can look for the signs of a good manager.

Let's start with benchmark α (i.e., Jensen's α). The t-statistic generally is used to determine whether the α (or any other coefficient in a regression for that matter) of a manager is statistically different from a given value or not. The t-statistic is given by $t = (\hat{\alpha} - \alpha_0)/\hat{S}(\hat{\alpha})$, where $\hat{S}(\hat{\alpha})$ is the standard error of the estimate of α. This formulation is for testing whether the portfolio manager's α is significantly different from the given value α_0. Typically, as performance analysts, we care whether or not a positive or negative α is significantly different from 0 rather than being concerned with some other value. Thus our t-statistics are simplified to $t = \hat{\alpha}/\hat{S}(\hat{\alpha})$. Fortunately, most software programs that portfolio managers use produce all the values from a simple linear regression, including $\hat{\alpha}$, $\hat{S}(\hat{\alpha})$, and the actual t-statistic. Thus this calculation is simple to perform. The performance analyst simply compares the calculated value of t with the t_c or critical t-statistic in the t-statistic table and determines whether the portfolio manager's α is significant at the desired significance level. As we already stated, for most cases, this is a value greater than 2.

In the special case in which all the classical assumptions of linear regression apply, the t-statistic becomes[42]

---

[42] The reader should be aware that this formulation for the standard error of $\hat{\alpha}$ does not apply when standard errors are corrected for heteroscedasticity, autocorrelation, or other effects.

$$t = \frac{\hat{\alpha}}{\hat{\omega}\sqrt{\dfrac{1}{T} + \dfrac{\bar{r}_B^{*2}}{\sum_{t=1}^{T}\left(r_{B,t}^* - \bar{r}_B^*\right)^2}}}$$

$$= \frac{IR}{\sqrt{\dfrac{1}{T} + \dfrac{\bar{r}_B^{*2}}{\sum_{t=1}^{T}\left(r_{B,t}^* - \bar{r}_B^*\right)^2}}} \tag{15.28}$$

where T is the number of measurement periods (e.g., monthly returns for the portfolio manager and benchmark), $\bar{r}_B^*$ is the average of the benchmark returns minus the risk-free rate, IR is the measured information ratio, and other variables are as defined previously.

With some minor manipulation, one will notice that the second term in the denominator is similar to the squared Sharpe ratio of the benchmark. That is,

$$SR_B^2 = \left[\frac{\bar{r}_B^*}{\hat{S}\left(r_B^*\right)}\right]^2 = \frac{\bar{r}_B^{*2}\left(T-1\right)}{\sum_{t=1}^{T}\left(r_{B,t}^* - \bar{r}_B^*\right)^2} \tag{15.29}$$

Substituting this into Eq. (15.28), we obtain

$$t = IR\frac{1}{\sqrt{\dfrac{1}{T} + \dfrac{SR_B^2}{T-1}}} \tag{15.30}$$

We can use this equation to tell us how many monthly returns we need for a given significance level and a given information ratio to obtain a significant estimate of α (and hence of the manager's information ratio). Let us choose a value for the IR of our hypothetical manager and the SR of the benchmark. Then t_c will depend on the number of monthly returns.[43] The t value shown in Eq. (15.30) will also depend on the number of monthly returns. We can then choose the minimum number of time periods, T^*, such that $t > t_c$. Table 15.1 shows the minimum number of time periods, T^*, for

---

[43] To construct the number of monthly returns, we had to consider the relationship between IR, SR, and the t-statistic as well as the relationship between t_c and T. To make this exercise meaningful, we are assuming that IR and SR do not change as we vary the number of months. Also, it should be remembered that the number of months minus 2 is the appropriate degrees of freedom.

a manager's empirical α to be statistically significant for various portfolio manager information ratios and benchmark Sharpe ratios. Assuming a benchmark such as the S&P 500, one could estimate the Sharpe ratio at about 0.25. Thus, for a portfolio manager with an information ratio of 0.5, it takes at least 22 monthly returns to determine whether or not he or she had a significantly positive α or not. The number of months needed becomes less stringent as the IR of the portfolio manager increases. However, for most reasonable IR ranges, one can see the problem that a CIO faces. Bonuses typically are given biannually or annually. Clearly, for most portfolio managers, there will not be a sufficient amount of data available when it comes time to determine whether a bonus should be given or not.

Although we used the more exact formula, some practitioners have become more familiar with the approximation that $t \approx IR\sqrt{T}$. This comes from assuming that the SR_B^2 term is small and can be neglected. For those who are more familiar with this formula, you should just observe the column in Table 15.1 where $SR = 0$. However, for large values of the SR for the benchmark, the number of monthly returns needed is much greater than the approximation would suggest.

In addition to the risk-adjusted measures we have mentioned, there are others. Which ones should an analyst use? We suggest using the ones that we have mentioned, but we realize that even among these the ranking of portfolios will not always be similar. The Sharpe ratio is equal to $\hat{\alpha}_p/\hat{\sigma}_p + \hat{\rho}SR_M$.[44] That is, the Sharpe ratio

TABLE 15.1

Months Required to Verify a Portfolio Manager's α and Information Ratio

	Benchmark's Sharpe Ratio (SR_B)						
IR	0	0.1	0.25	0.5	0.75	0.9	1
0.25	64	65	68	80	99	115	126
0.5	18	19	19	22	27	31	34
0.6	14	14	15	17	20	23	25
0.7	11	11	12	13	16	18	19
0.8	9	9	10	11	13	14	16
0.9	8	8	8	9	11	12	13
1	7	7	8	8	10	11	11

Note: IR signifies the portfolio manager's information ratio, SR is the benchmark's Sharpe ratio.

---

[44] This can be derived by starting with the CAPM equation and making a substitution of variables.

of a portfolio is equal to the sum of (1) the α of the portfolio divided by the portfolio's standard deviation and (2) the correlation of the portfolio's returns with the market multiplied by the Sharpe ratio of the market. Thus, depending on the various values, the ranking of portfolios by Jensen's α and by the Sharpe ratio may differ. One might even ask a different question. Suppose that we begin with a portfolio that is perfectly indexed to the market, but then we alter it slightly so as to create a positive α. Will our new portfolio also have a higher Sharpe ratio than the market? It depends. Because $SR_P - SR_M = (\hat{\alpha}_P/\hat{\sigma}_P) + (\hat{\rho} - 1)SR_M$, it depends on whether the correlation with the market drops significantly from 1, and if it does, it also depends on the magnitude of the drop compared with the increase in α.

15.5 PERFORMANCE ATTRIBUTION

Performance attribution dissects a portfolio's return into its components, yielding a valuable insight into the exact sources of gains and the effectiveness of the stock selection process. Performance attribution must be tailored to the specific investment process of a portfolio manager's department. Not all processes fit the same department. Although many simple attribution systems exist for traditional qualitative equity portfolio managers, it is much more difficult to build a suitable system for a quantitative equity portfolio manager. We begin this section by discussing traditional attribution systems and then suggest methods that might be used to determine the sources of a quantitative manager's performance.

15.5.1 Classical Attribution

Brinson, Beebower, and Hood (1986) showed how portfolio returns could be decomposed into various categories. Classical categories include the *security-selection effect* and the *sector-allocation effect*. The security-selection effect is the part of the excess return over the benchmark that is attributable to stocking-picking skill, whereas the sector-allocation effect reflects how well the manager allocated his or her equity portfolio among different stock sectors.

The first step of classical attribution is to compute the return of the portfolio and the return of the benchmark over the measurement period from the individual stock weights and returns. Thus

$$r_P = \sum_{i=1}^{N} w_i^P r_i \qquad (15.31)$$

$$r_B = \sum_{i=1}^{N} w_i^B r_i \qquad (15.32)$$

The second step is to decide the relevant sector breakdown. If there are 10 sectors in the investment universe, for instance, stocks in the benchmark and the portfolio should be divided into these sector buckets. The performance analyst then should compute the overall weight of the benchmark and portfolio in each of the sectors. Thus

$$w_j^P = \sum_{i \in S_j} w_{i,j}^P \qquad (15.33)$$

$$w_j^B = \sum_{i \in S_j} w_{i,j}^B \qquad (15.34)$$

where $w_{i,j}^B$ and $w_{i,j}^P$ are the weights of stock i in sector j of the benchmark and the portfolio, respectively, and S_j is the set of stocks in sector j. The performance analyst also should compute the contribution of return from each sector for the benchmark and the portfolio. Thus

$$r_{P,j} = \frac{1}{w_j^P} \sum_{i \in S_j} w_{i,j}^P r_i \qquad (15.35)$$

$$r_{B,j} = \frac{1}{w_j^B} \sum_{i \in S_j} w_{i,j}^B r_i \qquad (15.36)$$

This calculation simply computes the overall return of each sector from the benchmark and the portfolio. Thus it is the return as if the entire portfolio or benchmark was invested in only that sector.

With this information, we can perform the third step. The allocation effect (AE) then can be computed as

$$AE = \sum_j w_j^P r_{B,j} - r_B \qquad (15.37)$$

where AE is the allocation effect. One can see that it makes sense intuitively. The allocation effect is computed by using the *sector returns* of the benchmark—this accepts the returns attributable to the sector—but assigning them the weights given to sectors in the portfolio. This value minus the value of the overall benchmark return r_B represents the excess return of the portfolio owing to sector allocation.

The fourth step is to compute the security-selection effect (*SSE*). It is computed as

$$SSE = r_P - \sum_j w_j^P r_{B,j} \qquad (15.38)$$

where *SSE* represents the security-selection effect. One can see that this also makes sense intuitively. The difference between the actual portfolio return r_P and the return of the portfolio with benchmark returns in every sector (with exactly the same weighting in every sector as the actual portfolio) will be due to the differential returns in each sector between the benchmark and the portfolio. But this differential can only be due to the difference between the individual stock selections and weights within each sector. Thus it represents the portion of the excess returns attributable to the *stock-selection effect*.

As a final check on this type of attribution scheme, we make sure that all the components add up. The excess return of the portfolio over the benchmark should be explained fully by the sector-allocation effect and the security-selection effect. In fact, it is. After canceling terms, $r_P - r_B = AE + SSE$. This classical attribution can be done in a variety of ways, but it helps us understand the source of the portfolio manager's excess returns over the benchmark. What portion of the returns was due to efficient sector allocation, and what portion was due to security selection within the sectors? If the portfolio manager uses a model to predict all stock returns with no restriction on sector weights and finds that the sector-allocation bets are not performing well, he or she might want to consider running his or her quantitative stock-picking model while completely eliminating sector deviations from the benchmark. It thus helps the portfolio manager to uncover shortcomings in the investment process.

Suppose, for example, that we divide the stock universe into three sectors: technology, financial, and other. Suppose that we have already computed the weights and returns of the portfolio and benchmark in each sector as listed in Table 15.2.

TABLE 15.2

Performance of Portfolio and Benchmark in Selected Sectors

	Portfolio		Benchmark	
Sector	w_j^P	r_j^P	w_j^B	r_j^B
Financial	20	25	40	20
Technology	60	8	50	10
Other	20	28	10	12
	100		100	

Note: All variables are expressed in percentage terms. For example, 40 is for 40%.

From this table we can compute the return of the portfolio r_P = 15.4%, the benchmark return r_B = 14.2%, the excess returns of the portfolio over the benchmark $r_P - r_B$ = 1.2%, the allocation effect AE = −1.8%, and the security-selection effect SSE = 3%. From this simple example we can state that over the measurement period, the portfolio manager's models did well at selecting individual securities within sectors but did not do so well at selecting sectors. If this type of bias continues in future attribution reports, the portfolio manager might consider optimizing his or her portfolio with the constraint that portfolio sector weights equal the benchmark sector weights.

15.5.2 Multifactor QEPM Attribution

Quantitative portfolio managers usually build the kind of stock models we described in Chapters 5, 6, and 7. In Chapter 9 we discussed the importance of creating a model that generates security returns in order to produce risk estimates of the portfolio and optimize the portfolio against a benchmark. These concepts are used to construct the ex-ante optimal portfolio, which is optimized with a tracking-error constraint.

These same concepts can be used in turn to produce the ex-post performance attribution of the portfolio. In multifactor performance attribution, we use our multifactor risk model to understand the sources that generated the excess returns of our portfolio for the performance measurement period, whether it be a month, a quarter, or a year. Typically, performance attribution is performed monthly. In this subsection we revisit some of the basic concepts and illustrate some of the typical multifactor attribution reports that could be produced for quantitative portfolios.

We begin with our model for security returns used in the risk model. It is of the form

$$r_i = \alpha_i + \beta_{i1} f_1 + \cdots + \beta_{iK} f_K + \epsilon_i \tag{15.39}$$

When we use this model to construct the portfolio, we must estimate or forecast various components of the equation, as discussed in previous chapters. For performance attribution, we will have realized values of these variables. For the fundamental factor model, we can measure the factor premiums with a cross-sectional regression over all the stocks for the past month of performance. For the factor exposures of each stock, we already know the beginning-period values of those. For the economic factor model, we will have realized values of the factor premiums for the month, and we will use previously estimated factor exposures for each stock. In both cases we have the realized values for the month of attribution that we are concerned with. The α of each stock can be determined as $\hat{\alpha}_i = r_i - \beta_{i1} f_1 + \cdots + \beta_{iK} f_K$ in the case of the fundamental factor model, and $\hat{\alpha}_i = r_i - \hat{\beta}_{i1} f_1 + \cdots + \hat{\beta}_{iK} f_K$ in the case of the economic factor model. That is, for attribution purposes, whatever is not explained by the stock return model in the month we leave as α. Thus this completes the circle for return attribution. At this point, we can perform multifactor attribution. We are concerned with the sources of excess returns over the benchmark. Thus, for a given return period, t, using the notation for the economic factor model,[45]

$$
\begin{aligned}
x &= r_P - r_B \\
&= \sum_{i=1}^{N} \left(w_i^P - w_i^B \right) r_i \\
&= \sum_{i=1}^{N} \left(w_i^P - w_i^B \right) \left(\hat{\alpha}_i + \hat{\beta}_{i1} f_1 + \cdots + \hat{\beta}_{iK} f_K \right) \\
&= \sum_{i=1}^{N} \tilde{w}_i \hat{\alpha}_i + \sum_{i=1}^{N} \tilde{w}_i \hat{\beta}_{i1} f_1 + \cdots + \sum_{i=1}^{N} \tilde{w}_i \hat{\beta}_{iK} f_K
\end{aligned}
\tag{15.40}
$$

where $\tilde{w}_i = w_i^P - w_i^B$. Depending on which model we are using, either the fundamental or economic factor model, we will have the

---

[45] The derivations work for the fundamental factor model as well, only instead of "estimation hats" over the β's, there are hats over the factor premiums, f.

TABLE 15.3

The Multifactor Attribution of the Portfolio

Return Decomposition	
Source	**Value**
$\hat{\alpha}_p$	$\sum_{i=1}^{N} \tilde{w}_i \hat{\alpha}_i$
Name of factor 1	$\sum_{i=1}^{N} \tilde{w}_i \hat{\beta}_{i1} f_1$
Name of factor 2	$\sum_{i=1}^{N} \tilde{w}_i \hat{\beta}_{i2} f_2$
...	...
Name of factor K	$\sum_{i=1}^{N} \tilde{w}_i \hat{\beta}_{iK} f_K$

Risk Decomposition	
Source	**Value**
Name of factor 1	$\left(\sum_{i=1}^{N} \tilde{w}_i \hat{\beta}_{i1}\right)^2 \hat{V}(f_1)$
Name of factor 2	$\left(\sum_{i=1}^{N} \tilde{w}_i \hat{\beta}_{i2}\right)^2 \hat{V}(f_2)$
...	...
Name of factor K	$\left(\sum_{i=1}^{N} \tilde{w}_i \hat{\beta}_{iK}\right)^2 \hat{V}(f_K)$
$\hat{\omega}_p$	$\left(\sum_{i=1}^{N} \tilde{w}_i\right)^2 \hat{V}(\epsilon_i)$
Adjustment for factor correlation	$2\sum_{k=1}^{K} \sum_{l=k+1}^{K} \left(\sum_i \tilde{w}_i \hat{\beta}_{ik}\right)\left(\sum_j \tilde{w}_j \hat{\beta}_{jl}\right) \hat{C}(f_k, f_l)$

Note: The symbols in this table are those for the economic factor model. $\tilde{w}_i$ is the difference in the weight of the portfolio and the benchmark for security i, $\hat{\alpha}_i$ represents the derived α for each stock based on what was not explained by the stock return model in the attribution period, $\hat{\beta}_{ik}$ is the estimated factor exposure of stock i to factor k at the beginning of the attribution period, f_k represents the realized factor premium for the performance attribution period for factor k, $\hat{V}(f_k)$ is the estimated variance of the factor premium, and ϵ_i is the error term for stock i. To obtain the total excess return of the portfolio for any particular month, just sum the elements in the return decomposition part of the table.

corresponding realized values of the appropriate variable during the month of attribution. Each component in this reduced equation makes up our performance attribution of various components as measured by our risk model. The performance attribution report can be presented in a table such as Table 15.3.

In this attribution report, one also will notice a risk decomposition of the variance of the portfolio. Some portfolio managers may wish to view this in their attribution report as well. Technically, though, this report is not a risk attribution report because in a period of one month, there is only one observable factor realization in that particular month for each factor. The factor variances and covariances, as well as the variance of the residuals, typically are estimated from historical data.[46] Thus this risk decomposition is really an ex-ante decomposition rather than a risk attribution analysis.[47] The reader also will notice that in the risk decomposition, we use only the variance of each factor multiplied by the squared active exposure of the portfolio over the benchmark to explain the risk contributed to the tracking error by that particular factor exposure. Technically, this is not the entire story; we are leaving out the cross correlation among factor premiums. Some portfolio managers would choose to have the cross correlations of each factor added to the overall contribution of the risk attributable to that factor (especially when the correlation among factor returns is quite high), whereas other portfolio managers may choose not to have it added (especially when the correlation among factor returns is quite low). We chose to separate it out in a distinct area called "Adjustment for factor correlation" that appears at the bottom of the table. This represents all the cross-correlation effects of the factor returns. Unfortunately, there is no absolutely correct method to decompose this part of the overall risk.

The performance analyst may wish to provide portfolio managers with an individual stock report as well. A report listing multiple securities would be quite long, but it could follow the format of Table 15.4. In this table, r_i represents the return of the security for

TABLE 15.4

Inside a Portfolio

						Exposure on		
Ticker	r_i	w_i^P	w_i^B	x_i	$\hat{\alpha}_i^{MF}$	Name of Factor 1	...	Name of Factor K
ABC								

Note: x_i is the excess return of the portfolio attributable to the individual stock, which can be written as $x_i = (w_i^P - w_i^B) \, r_i = \tilde{w}_i r_i$.

---

[46] With an economic factor model, the factor variance and covariances (or correlations) can be estimated as well as the variance of the error terms on a time series. With the fundamental factor model, the historical variances and covariances (or correlations) of the factors can be estimated with a series of cross-sectional regressions on historical data.

[47] One method to get a risk attribution analysis would be to estimate the daily factor premiums and then compute the daily variances and covariances (or correlations) of the factor premiums during the month and multiply these by 20 to get an estimate of the volatility and correlations of the factors for the month. Although this would be closer to an actual attribution of the portfolio for the particular month, more biases may creep in owing to the noise associated with measurements of daily volatility and issues of non-normality in the data that may arise. For more information, see DiBartolomeo (2003).

the given performance measurement period, w_i^P represents the portfolio weight of the security at the beginning of the performance period, w_i^B represents the benchmark weight of the particular security at the beginning of the performance period, x_i represents the excess return contributed by that particular security, which is equal to $(w_i^P - w_i^B) \, r_i$ or $\tilde{w}_i r_i$, $\hat{\alpha}^{MF}$ is the estimated multifactor of the historical stock return model, and the exposures on each factor represent the excess exposure to each factor given by the portfolio weights (that is, $\tilde{w}_i \hat{\beta}_i$).

A complementary report might be organized like Table 15.5. In this table, many of the variables are similar, except that the $\hat{\alpha}$ represents the individual stock attribution α that is the part of return not explained in the performance period by the multifactor model; the contributions of factor exposure returns are also in this table, describing how each factor contributed to the excess return of the portfolio from the weight differential in that particular stock (that is, $\tilde{w}_i \hat{\beta}_{1i} f_1$ for security i, where f_1 is the period realization of factor 1); and the marginal risk is given by the effect on risk of increasing that particular security's weight by a small amount. If the tracking error (TE) is given by

$$TE = \left[\left(\mathbf{w}^P - \mathbf{w}^B \right)' \mathbf{B} V(\mathbf{f}) \mathbf{B}' \left(\mathbf{w}^P - \mathbf{w}^B \right) + \left(\mathbf{w}^P - \mathbf{w}^B \right)' V(\epsilon) \left(\mathbf{w}^P - \mathbf{w}^B \right) \right]^{\frac{1}{2}}$$

$$= \left[\tilde{\mathbf{w}}' \mathbf{B} V(\mathbf{f}) \mathbf{B}' \tilde{\mathbf{w}} + \tilde{\mathbf{w}}' V(\epsilon) \tilde{\mathbf{w}} \right]^{\frac{1}{2}} \qquad (15.41)$$

then the marginal contribution of risk to the total portfolio tracking risk is given by

$$\frac{1}{TE} \left[\mathbf{B} V(\mathbf{f}) \mathbf{B}' \tilde{\mathbf{w}} + V(\epsilon) \tilde{\mathbf{w}} \right] \qquad (15.42)$$

TABLE 15.5

The Multifactor Attribution of a Portfolio's Individual Stocks

Ticker	r_i	w_i^P	w_i^B	x_i	$\hat{\alpha}_i$	Return on Name of Factor 1	...	Return on Name of Factor K	MR
ABC									

Note: x_i is the excess return of the portfolio attributable to the individual stock, which can be written as $x_i = (w_i^P - w_i^B) r_i = \tilde{w}_i r_i$. $\hat{\alpha}$ is the attribution α, which is the sum of the constant estimate and realized residual. *MR* indicates the marginal risk.

There are some conceptual details that the performance analyst may wish to think about. First of all, this type of multifactor attribution usually is done with the risk model of the commercial software or the in-house risk model. Although the risk model presumably encompasses and explains security returns quite well, is such a decomposition very meaningful to the quantitative portfolio manager? A manager might be more interested in obtaining the performance attribution with respect to his or her α factor model, whether it be an aggregate Z-score model, an economic factor model, or a fundamental factor model. When the risk model is already built and used for the creation of optimized portfolios, this makes it simpler to use the risk model for multifactor attribution. For portfolio managers who use commercial software, there really is no other choice. However, a performance analyst might consider taking the quantitative factors used to forecast α by the portfolio manager and use those to construct some type of risk model that runs parallel to the firm's risk model. Thus, for performance attribution, the performance analyst can present attribution with respect to the factors that the quantitative manager actually uses to pick his or her stocks.

15.6 CONCLUSION

In this chapter we examined various techniques used in performance measurement and attribution. Conceptually, these techniques are straightforward. When they are actually applied to the real world, though, numerous complications arise. There are many answers even to seemingly simple questions such as, "What was the portfolio's return?" When the question becomes, "What was the portfolio's risk (and risk-adjusted return)?" almost every analyst can come up with a different solution. The proliferation of methods for measuring "good" performance simply means that a performance analyst must be careful to pick the technique that best fits the particulars of the situation and states the portfolio's performance clearly and honestly.

Style Analysis

Style analysis is a technique for determining the exposure of a mutual fund, hedge fund, or any equity portfolio to various asset classes. The performance analyst may not know the holdings of a portfolio or the exact types of stocks that its manager tends to buy, but with style analysis, he or she can obtain a pretty clear idea of the portfolio's exposures. Style analysis is less useful for the portfolio manager or a portfolio management shop and more useful for financial advisors, fund-of-fund managers, and other investors in deciding whether to include a particular portfolio or fund manager in their asset allocations.

Style analysis is a powerful technique that was developed by William Sharpe (1988) to analyze the investment styles of portfolio managers. Rather than analyzing individual portfolio holdings, this method looks at how a portfolio's historical returns are related to various investment styles. An investment style can be thought of as a method of investing or even as a kind of benchmark. For example, a portfolio manager who invested primarily in small-cap growth stocks would be said to follow a small-cap growth investment style. Other investment styles include large-cap value style or a government bond investment style.[1] Naturally, a portfolio may be a combination of many styles. For instance, the Fidelity

---

[1] Even though we are concerned with equity managers, certain equity portfolios behave very much like a portfolio of government bonds; thus we can ironically describe an equity manager as having a bond investment style.

Magellan Fund was once classified as 53% large-cap growth, 34% large-cap value, 10% small-cap growth, and 3% foreign stocks. Style analysis can be used to determine whether a portfolio or fund's strategy has deviated from its stated investment objectives. Style analysis measures performance versus the "true" benchmark rather than an arbitrary benchmark such as the S&P 500. Finally, style analysis can be used to understand the true exposures of a portfolio and how it will best fit with an investor's overall asset allocation. Style analysis is a statistical method of decomposing the portfolio's returns into a set of style-specific benchmarks. The choice of benchmark styles can vary from study to study and from one performance analyst to another. Typical benchmarks include cash (a Treasury bill index), a government bond index, a corporate bond index, a foreign bond index, a large-cap value index, a large-cap growth index, a small-cap value index, a small-cap growth index, and a foreign stock index. Once the relevant indices have been chosen, one uses a quadratic optimization technique on the past returns of the portfolio and the relevant indices to find the "style" of the portfolio.

Thus, suppose that we could represent the return of a portfolio or fund as a linear combination of other major asset classes (e.g., large-cap equity, value equity, fixed income, etc.). Thus

$$r_{P,t} = w_1 r_{1,t} + w_2 r_{2,t} + \cdots + w_N r_{N,t} + \epsilon_t \qquad (15A.1)$$

where $r_{P,t}$ represents the monthly returns of the portfolio, $r_{i,t}$ represents the monthly returns for the particular style index, i, w_i represents the style weight for benchmark i, and ϵ_t represents an error term. We can rearrange this equation in terms of ϵ_t, and the goal of style analysis is to minimize the variance of the error term subject to certain constraints.[2] Thus, formally, style analysis involves finding the weights on the style benchmarks w_i such that

$$\min_{\mathbf{w}} \left[\hat{V} \left(\epsilon_t \right) \right] = \min_{\mathbf{w}} \left[\hat{V} \left(r_{P,t} - w_1 r_{1,t} - w_2 r_{2,t} - \cdots - w_N r_{N,t} \right) \right]$$

$$s.t. \quad \sum_{i=1}^{N} w_i = 1 \quad \text{and} \quad 0 \le w_i \le 1, \quad i = 1, \cdots, N \qquad (15A.2)$$

The optimal weights w_i^* multiplied by the returns of the respective benchmark returns can be thought of as the "mimicking"

---

[2] This is very similar to minimizing the tracking error of the portfolio with respect to the linear combination of style benchmarks.

fund for that portfolio or fund. That is, the w_i^* weights are the weights that one would invest in the style benchmarks to achieve the closest tracking error to the actual portfolio. Hence the style benchmark is all the benchmarks with their estimated w_i^* exposure.[3]

Thus, to find the *style weights* in style analysis, one can either use a linear regression with constraints and renormalize the weights or one can use our tools of quadratic programming from Appendix 9A. The inputs for the quadratic optimization must be computed.[4] The matrix $\mathbf{Q}$ is the variance-covariance matrix returns of the style benchmarks and the portfolio. This variance-covariance matrix is computed from historical data. The x's are the weights on the various style benchmarks (i.e., the w's) and the weight on the portfolio. The weights on the asset classes will be determined by the optimization. Thus the vector of weights x will be an $(N + 1) \times 1$ matrix consisting of the N style weights and the portfolio weight. The constraints will be that all asset weights are between 0 and 1, except for the portfolio weight, which will be constrained to be -1.[5] Thus the matrix setup is as follows:

$$\mathbf{x} = \begin{bmatrix} w_1 \\ w_2 \\ \cdots \\ w_N \\ w^P \end{bmatrix} \tag{15A.3}$$

$$\mathbf{Q} = \begin{bmatrix} \hat{\sigma}_1^2 & \hat{\sigma}_{1,2} & \cdots & \hat{\sigma}_{1,N} & \hat{\sigma}_{1,P} \\ \hat{\sigma}_{2,1} & \hat{\sigma}_2^2 & \cdots & \hat{\sigma}_{2,N} & \hat{\sigma}_{2,P} \\ \cdots & \cdots & \cdots & \cdots & \cdots \\ \hat{\sigma}_{N,1} & \hat{\sigma}_{N,2} & \cdots & \hat{\sigma}_N^2 & \hat{\sigma}_{N,P} \\ \hat{\sigma}_{P,1} & \hat{\sigma}_{P,2} & \cdots & \hat{\sigma}_{P,N} & \hat{\sigma}_P^2 \end{bmatrix} \tag{15A.4}$$

$$\mathbf{A}_{eq} = \begin{bmatrix} 1 & 1 & \cdots & 1 & 0 \\ 0 & 0 & \cdots & 0 & 1 \end{bmatrix} \tag{15A.5}$$

---

[3] Some practitioners estimate a portfolio's style by estimating a regression with the constraints that the estimated coefficients sum to 1 and are between 0 and 1.

[4] The optimization will be an optimization with inequality constraints, which can be done quickly by any standard quadratic optimizer.

[5] Some practitioners may take this further and place constraints on the excess return of the portfolio versus the style benchmark. This is a simple addition to the constraints.

$$\mathbf{b}_{eq} = \begin{bmatrix} 1 \\ -1 \end{bmatrix} \tag{15A.6}$$

$$\mathbf{A}_{ineq} = \begin{bmatrix} 1 & 0 & \cdots & 0 & 0 \\ 0 & 1 & \cdots & 0 & 0 \\ & & \ddots & & \\ 0 & 0 & \cdots & 1 & 0 \\ -1 & 0 & \cdots & 0 & 0 \\ 0 & -1 & \cdots & 0 & 0 \\ & & \ddots & & \\ 0 & 0 & \cdots & -1 & 0 \end{bmatrix} \tag{15A.7}$$

$$\mathbf{b}_{ineq} = \begin{bmatrix} 1 \\ \vdots \\ 1 \\ 0 \\ \vdots \\ 0 \end{bmatrix} \tag{15A.8}$$

where $\mathbf{A}_{eq}$ and $\mathbf{b}_{eq}$ are a set of equality constraints and $\mathbf{A}_{ineq}$ and $\mathbf{b}_{ineq}$ are a set of inequality constraints.

Another important aspect of style analysis is to compute the so-called $\bar{R}^2$ of the regression. This measures to what degree the style benchmarks really represent the underlying portfolio. Just as in regression analysis, an $\bar{R}^2$ close to 1 means that the style benchmark accurately represents the return behavior of the portfolio, whereas an $\bar{R}^2$ close to 0 means that the style benchmark does a very poor job at representing the portfolio. Owing to the restrictions on the $w_i s$, and since some people will use the quadratic optimization technique to solve for the optimal weights, we need to construct an $\bar{R}^2$. One way to do this is simply to take the optimal parameters from the quadratic optimization and then create the time series of the style benchmark and subtract it from the portfolio returns. Thus the $\bar{R}^2$ can be computed as

$$\bar{R}^2 = \frac{\hat{V}(\epsilon_t)}{\hat{V}(r_{P,t})} \tag{15A.9}$$

A simple example might be useful. We took three quantitative portfolios that we knew relatively very little about and performed

TABLE 15A.1

Selected Quantitative Portfolios Using Style Analysis

Portfolio Name	Stock Style Benchmarks					Bond Style Benchmarks				R^2
	LCV	LCG	SCV	SCG	World Ex-USA	T Bills	U.S. Govt.	U.S. Corp.	Non-U.S.	
Utilities portfolio	40	0	0	0	1	59	0	0	0	13
Opportunity portfolio	27	58	0	0	1	1	0	0	13	89
Latin America portfolio	30	45	11	11	4	0	0	0	0	56

Note: All variables are expressed in percentage terms. Thus 40 is for 40%. We chose to use these various style benchmarks for our example. LCV stands for large-cap value (Russell 1000 Value), LCG stands for large-cap growth (Russell 1000 Growth), SCV stands for small-cap value (Russell 2000 Value), SCG stands for small-cap growth (Russell 2000 Growth), World Ex-USA is for non-U.S. stock exposure (MSCI EAFE), T bills represent a U.S. Treasury bill index, U.S. Govt. represents a U.S. government bond index, U.S. Corp. represents a U.S. corporate bond index, non-U.S. represents an index of foreign bonds.

a style analysis using nine style benchmarks. The results are presented in Table 15A.1. The three hypothetical portfolios that we chose to study by various portfolio managers were a utilities sector portfolio, an opportunities portfolio, and a Latin America portfolio. The style analysis results help us to understand the portfolio construction a bit better. First, the $\bar{R}^2$ of the utilities portfolio is much too low to make any important inference about it. It does suggest that the utilities portfolio has a strong sensitivity to interest rates given the large bond index exposure. The opportunity portfolio has a decent $\bar{R}^2$. From the style analysis, we can infer that this portfolio behaves as if it were invested in 27% large-cap value, 58% large-cap growth, and 13% in non-U.S. dollar bonds. Thus this portfolio is pretty much a large-cap equity portfolio. For an investor deciding how to allocate this quantatative portfolio to his or her asset allocation, he or she can treat it as a large-cap portfolio or, to be more specific, as a portfolio that is roughly 85% large cap. The Latin America portfolio behaves mainly like a portfolio of U.S. large-cap stocks (75%) but also has a significant exposure to U.S. small-cap stocks (22%). Oddly enough, the returns of this portfolio behave more like U.S. stocks than foreign stocks (4%). This is one of the beautiful aspects of style analysis. Normally, we would consider a portfolio of Latin American stocks to be foreign stocks, but this analysis shows that this particular portfolio's returns behave much like a portfolio of U.S. stocks. Of course, the $\bar{R}^2$ of 56 may warrant further analysis before a firm conclusion is made.

We conclude our discussion on style analysis by mentioning some other issues. First, when computing the style of a portfolio, it is important to consider how much historical data to use. We call this the *time period* or *measurement period*. It should be short enough to capture the style changes of a portfolio but long enough to not be measuring noise. A practitioner will have to gauge what that amount of data is. Typically, three years of monthly data will work well. Second, some practitioners will estimate the style of the portfolio dynamically. That is, they will estimate the style using three-year windows and then roll the window along. This is what is meant by the term *rolling window*. They then plot the style changes of the portfolio. This is known as *style drift*, that is, that the portfolio is changing style over time. Third, using style analysis for portfolio managers of hedge funds may become tricky because these portfolio managers use leverage, derivatives, and other fancy tools. Thus Fung and Hsieh (1998) have suggested how to modify style analysis to measure more complicated managers, such as trend-following commodity trading advisors (CTAs).[6]

Finally, although mutual fund managers are required to report their portfolio holdings only quarterly and there is a lag in this publication, we believe that a clever analyst could combine style analysis with the original stock weightings and holdings to unveil the actual holdings of the mutual fund manager using daily fund returns for mutual funds with low turnover. This might be an area of research for an ambitious performance analyst.

---

[6] For an application to hedge funds, see Chincarini (2014) and Chincarini and Nakao (2011).

Measures of Opportunity

At a monthly investment meeting, portfolio managers typically look at the performance of their portfolios over the month or the quarter. They usually look at classic attribution or risk-model attribution. They may look at which stocks did well and which stocks did not do so well. One question that might be asked in such a meeting is what was the *opportunity* in the investment universe. By opportunity, we mean the possibility to create excess returns through quantitative management. There are many measures of opportunity. For example, the cross-sectional standard deviation of the returns of the stocks in the universe for the given performance period is a measure of opportunity. A larger standard deviation indicates that there was a greater opportunity to pick outperforming stocks. Another measure of opportunity might be the performance of the top decile stocks for the period equally weighted minus the bottom decile of stocks equally weighted. The higher this value, the greater was the opportunity in the universe for that performance period. Although these measures certainly signify some amount of opportunity in the universe for the period, they are more useful for comparisons across time (i.e., the same universe over different measurement periods) or across different sections of the universe (e.g., the opportunity of each sector in the universe for a given sample period). These measures are less useful in the monthly investment meeting relative to the performance of the actual portfolio manager. What might be useful, however, although it involves a bit of work, is creating a series of measures corresponding to portfolio managers with varying levels of skill ex post. There may be many methods to do this, but we describe one possible method here.

The method that we describe consists of taking the ex-post returns of the stocks and using this information to create a series of portfolios based upon the various levels of forecasting skills from 50% to 100%. The portfolios are constructed using the same optimization with constraints that the actual portfolio manager used to create his portfolio. The average returns of many simulated portfolios can then be compared against the portfolio manager's returns. Since they were created in the same fashion, with the exception of the forecasting skill, they give a more accurate assessment of opportunities really available to the particular portfolio manager. We discuss the steps the performance analyst should take to create these portfolios below.

Step 1: The performance analyst should decide the levels of simulated skill he or she would like to produce. For example, a reasonable dispersion of skill might be 50%, 60%, 70%, 80%, 90%, and 100%.

Step 2: For each skill level, use a random number generator to generate random values from a uniform distribution from [0, 1].

Step 3: The critical point on the random draws will be determined by the skill level. For instance, if the skill level is 60%, then every value that is generated from 0 to 0.6 should reflect a correct foresight of the realized return of one stock in the entire universe. If the draw is from 0.6 to 1 (or generally from the critical value to 1), then this should reflect an incorrect forecast of the expected return of one of the universe stocks.

Step 4: Begin by generating N randomly generated uniform draws. The number of draws less than the critical value is n_g, and the number of draws greater than the critical value is n_b. These stand for the number of good and bad predictions, respectively.

Step 5: The performance analyst should begin with the good draws. First, each stock in the universe of N stocks should be given a number 1 to N. For each of the n_g values, another random uniform draw should be made, where one normalizes the uniform distribution by multiplying by N.[1] Thus the number that is drawn is the stock for which the forecaster forecasted the realized return correctly. Remove this stock along with its expected return and repeat the experiment, with $N - 1, N - 2$, and so on.

Step 6: Once the n_g stocks have been removed, the remaining stocks can be assigned randomly the remaining returns. That is, every one of the n_b stocks has a realized return for the period. Rather than using their actual realized returns, randomly distribute these returns to the stocks. This can be done by creating a new uniform draw for every stock and then ordering the stocks by random number and attaching the ranked realized returns to the ordered list. This will maintain the actual realized returns of all stocks for the period but randomly assign them among the bad forecasted stocks.

Step 7: The performance analyst then should compute the mean return vector of the stocks along with the variance-covariance matrix of the stock returns. These should be used in conjunction with the same constraints that were used at the time of the original portfolio construction to construct the "look-ahead" portfolio. The portfolio that emerges with appropriate portfolio weights becomes the forecaster's portfolio with skill level p, where p represents the ranges chosen earlier.

Step 8: The paper performance of this portfolio should be computed.

Step 9: The performance analyst should repeat this 100 times for each skill level and store the results, including the average returns and the SD of the returns.

Step 10: A table should be compiled comparing the different forecasting skill levels' average returns, excess returns, and information ratio to the actual portfolio returns of the portfolio manager.

This methodology is time-consuming, although with an in-house risk optimizer system and the computer speed of today, it is

---

[1] That is, the number drawn will be $N \cdot$ uniform$(0, 1)$.

feasible. This is a method of comparing the true opportunity in the manager's universe because it not only varies the forecasting accuracy of the portfolio manager but also constructs portfolios against the same benchmark and constraints the actual portfolio manager had to face. It is one method of measuring true opportunity for the portfolio manager.

APPENDIX 15C

Short Returns

When a portfolio manager, either in an actual portfolio or a model portfolio, has short positions, the performance analyst will have to compute the return to the short positions (which we will call "short returns") before computing the overall performance of the portfolio. Although this is not a complicated task, it requires some thought for the beginner.

The performance analyst may calculate the *approximate* short returns as the minus of the returns for the corresponding long position. Suppose, for example, that the portfolio has a short position in stock A from period t to $t + k$. Let $r_{t,t+1}, \ldots, r_{t+k-1,t+k}$ be the daily returns of stock A. The approximate short returns would then be given by $r^S_{t,t+1} = -r_{t,t+1}, \ldots, r^S_{t+k-1,t+k} = -r_{t+k-1,t+k}$.

One indication that these short returns are only approximate is the fact that, with these short returns, you cannot use geometric linking as is done with long positions. That is,

$$r^S_{t,t+k} \neq \prod_{i=1}^{k}\left(1 + r^S_{t+i-1,t+i}\right) - 1 \tag{15C.1}$$

To calculate the exact short returns, you need to carefully account for the changes in the portfolio value. If we short \$1 of stock A at the end of day 0 and the day 1 return of stock A is $r_{0,1}$, then the portfolio value at the end of day 1 becomes $1 - r_{0,1}$. If the day 2 return of stock A is $r_{1,2}$, then the portfolio value at the end of day 2 becomes $1 - [(1 + r_{0,1})(1 + r_{1,2}) - 1]$ since the cumulative loss is $(1 + r_{0,1})(1 + r_{1,2}) - 1$.[1] Thus, the short return for day 2 is not $-r_{1,2}$, but $\{1 - [(1 + r_{0,1})(1 + r_{1,2}) - 1]\}/(1 - r_{0,1}) - 1$. Applying this logic, the day i short return is given by $r^{S*}_{i-1,i} = (1 - r_{0,i})/(1 - r_{0,i-1}) - 1$, where $r_{0,i} = \Pi^i_{j=1}(1 + r_{j-1,j}) - 1$.

You can easily verify that geometric linking works with the exact short returns. That is,

$$r^{S*}_{t,t+k} = \prod_{i=1}^{k}\left(1 + r^{S*}_{t+i-1,t+i}\right) - 1 \qquad (15C.2)$$

The difference between the approximate short return $r^{S}_{t,t+k}$ and the exact short return $r^{S*}_{t,t+k}$ is likely to be small when k is small. However, when k becomes large, the use of $r^{S}_{t,t+k}$ may lead to significant underestimation of return volatility as well as the absolute value of returns.

15C.1 A NUMERICAL EXAMPLE

We take a small short portfolio of four stocks, stocks A to D. Each stock starts at a price of $100 and the portfolio manager shorts each stock with a quarter of his portfolio wealth.[2] Table 15C.1 shows the changes in prices from period t to period $t + 6$, along with the period returns of each stock and the weights in each stock based on a long-only portfolio. These weights are used to construct the period portfolio returns (r^L_P), and the short portfolio returns are just given as minus the long portfolio returns. The long portfolio cumulative return over the six periods is 20.10% with a volatility of 2.95% per period. The negative of this would also be the cumulative return for the short portfolio. Thus, the short portfolio's cumulative return over the period is -20.10%. For illustration purposes, we also compounded the short returns, and you can see that they erroneously compound to -17.59%. Table 15C.1 uses the approximate method for computing short returns.

In Table 15C.2 we present the calculations for the exact short portfolio returns. Notice that now the typical equations can be used for computing the short portfolio returns in every period, and the cumulative returns can be computed as normal. Also, the period

---

[1] If the loss is negative, it's actually a gain for the short position.
[2] We do not explicitly consider collateral issues and transactions costs and keep position leverage at 1.

Performance Measurement with a Short Portfolio Using the Approximate Method

Period	A	B	C	D	r_A	r_B	r_C	r_D	w_A^L	w_B^L	w_C^L	w_D^L	r_P^L	r_P^S
t	100.00	100.00	100.00	100.00	—	—	—	—	0.250	0.250	0.250	0.250	—	—
$t+1$	103.09	105.35	105.13	97.52	3.09	5.35	5.13	−2.48	0.251	0.256	0.256	0.237	2.77	−2.77
$t+2$	104.47	105.68	106.02	105.72	1.33	0.31	0.85	8.41	0.248	0.250	0.251	0.251	2.63	−2.63
$t+3$	112.62	107.68	109.43	97.89	7.81	1.89	3.21	−7.40	0.263	0.252	0.256	0.229	1.36	−1.36
$t+4$	118.68	121.27	124.18	101.51	5.38	12.62	13.49	3.69	0.255	0.260	0.267	0.218	8.89	−8.89
$t+5$	125.82	118.00	126.83	97.55	6.02	−2.70	2.14	−3.89	0.269	0.252	0.271	0.208	0.55	−0.55
$t+6$	127.17	111.43	133.03	108.76	1.07	−5.57	4.89	11.49	0.265	0.232	0.277	0.226	2.60	−2.60
Cumulative return					27.17	11.43	33.03	8.76					20.10	−17.59
Volatility					2.72	6.42	4.49	7.43					2.95	2.95

Note: The long-period returns for stocks A through D are given by r_A, r_B, r_C, and r_D. The long weights for each stock are given by w_A^L, w_B^L, w_C^L, and w_D^L. The return of the long portfolio in every period is given by r_P^L, and the negative of this return is the return for the short portfolio r_P^S

TABLE 15C.2

Performance Measurement with a Short Portfolio Using Exact Method

Period	A	B	C	D	r_A^S	r_B^S	r_C^S	r_D^S	w_A^S	w_B^S	w_C^S	w_D^S	r_P^L	r_P^S
t	100.00	100.00	100.00	100.00	—	—	—	—	0.250	0.250	0.250	0.250	—	—
$t+1$	103.09	105.35	105.13	97.52	−3.09	−5.35	−5.13	2.48	0.249	0.243	0.244	0.264	2.77	−2.77
$t+2$	104.47	105.68	106.02	105.72	−1.42	−0.35	−0.94	−8.00	0.253	0.249	0.249	0.249	2.63	−2.78
$t+3$	112.62	107.68	109.43	97.89	−8.54	−2.12	−3.62	8.30	0.235	0.248	0.243	0.274	1.36	−1.52
$t+4$	118.68	121.27	124.18	101.51	−6.93	−14.72	−16.29	−3.54	0.243	0.235	0.227	0.295	8.89	−10.21
$t+5$	125.82	118.00	126.83	97.55	−8.78	4.16	−3.50	4.01	0.224	0.247	0.221	0.309	0.55	−0.77
$t+6$	127.17	111.43	133.03	108.76	−1.82	8.01	−8.47	−10.94	0.228	0.277	0.210	0.285	2.60	−3.67
Cumulative return					−27.17	−11.43	−33.03	−8.76					20.10	−20.10
Volatility					3.38	7.92	5.47	7.45					2.95	3.39

Note: The short-period returns for stocks A through D are given by r_A^S, r_B^S, r_C^S, and r_D^S. The short weights for each stock are given by w_A^S, w_B^S, w_C^S, and w_D^S. The return of the long portfolio in every period is given by r_P^L. The return of the short portfolio in every period using the exact method is given by r_P^S.

short returns are now different than the negative of the long-period returns. Despite this, the short-return portfolio over the period t to $t + k$ is equal to the negative of the long-return portfolio over the period. You will also notice the slightly higher volatility over this period when the short returns are computed exactly, rather than approximately.

APPENDIX 15D

Measuring Market Timing Ability

Although market timing is not usually the forte of the quantitative portfolio manager, there are performance measurement techniques to discover whether the portfolio manager has market *timing ability* as opposed to just general stock-picking ability. Traditionally, these two components have been separated by running either of the following regressions:

$$r_{P,t} - r_{f,t} = \alpha + \beta(r_{M,t} - r_{f,t}) + \gamma(r_{M,t} - r_{f,t})^2 + \epsilon_t \qquad (15D.1)$$

$$r_{P,t} - r_{f,t} = \alpha + \beta(r_{M,t} - r_{f,t}) + \gamma \max[0, -(r_{M,t} - r_{f,t})] + \epsilon_t \quad (15D.2)$$

The α continues to measure portfolio selectivity performance, β continues to represent the market exposure of the portfolio, and a positive γ indicates market timing ability. The first measure is due to Treynor and Mazuy (1966), and the second measure is due to Henrikkson and Merton (1981). In Eq. (15D.2), a perfect market timer should have a $\beta = 1$ and a $\gamma = 1$. This is true for a timer who shorts or goes long 100% the market depending on which does better. Most portfolio managers are not so extreme and will fall somewhere in between, even with perfect ability. There have been squabbles about the potential bias of this measure of market timing [Grinblatt and Titman (1989), Jaganathan and Korajczyk (1986), and Chance and Hemler (2001)]. The reason for this is that one is using the proxy of a monthly put as a market timer measure; however, the portfolio manager may trade daily. Thus one is estimating a misspecified equation. This problem is magnified as the distance between the decision horizon and the evaluation horizon grows (i.e., it is worse for measuring the timing ability of a portfolio manager who makes daily trading decisions using quarterly data). Given the difficulty of access to daily return data, Goetzmann et al. (2000) propose an alternative estimation:

$$r_{P,t} - r_{f,t} = \alpha + \beta\left(r_{M,t} - r_{f,t}\right) + \gamma\left(\left\{\left[\prod_{det}\max\left(1 + r_{M,d}, 1 + r_{f,d}\right)\right] - 1\right\} - r_{M,t}\right) + \epsilon_t \quad (15\text{D}.3)$$

where d is a counter to represent the subperiods within the investment horizon, and the new term is the instrument that simulates a daily market timer's performance over the month. It is correlated with daily put values on the equity market index without the cost of the put premium. When working with a monthly horizon, d indexes the number of days in the month. Thus, in this case, the term after the γ is the product of the maximum of the function related to daily return values during the month. This creates an expression for each period t, which can be used in the regression. Simulations have shown that this measure is able to correct the bias when the portfolio manager trades on a more frequent basis than the measurement horizon.[1]

---

[1] For an application of measuring market timing across multiple factors, see Chincarini and Nakao (2011).

QUESTIONS

15.1. What's the difference between performance attribution and performance measurement? Which should be used to determine bonuses?

15.2. Why is it especially difficult to compute the returns of an actual portfolio when there are cash flows in and out of the portfolio?

15.3. (a) Why do the Global Investment Performance Standards (GIPS) and other associations' guidelines require time-weighted return measurement as the method of computing the performance of actual portfolios?

(b) When measuring the returns of separate accounts, clients typically get confused about time-weighted returns and ask to have internal rate-of-return (IRR) calculations produced instead. Why?

15.4. What is the modified Dietz method?

15.5. Suppose that portfolio X has a closing value of $50 million on day 1. On day 2 there are withdrawals from the portfolio during the day totaling $45 million. The end-of-day value of the portfolio, as measured by the accounting department, is $6 million. Using the Dietz method, what would the performance analyst compute as the daily return of this portfolio? Does the number make sense?

15.6. (a) Which is a better measure of risk, standard deviation or semi-standard deviation?

(b) Under what conditions would standard deviation and semi-standard deviation be equally good measures of risk?

(c) Which one is used more in practice? Why is that?

15.7. Refer to the following table with monthly return data on a portfolio and the benchmark.

(a) What are the standard deviations of the portfolio and the benchmark?

(b) What is the monthly tracking error of the portfolio? The annualized tracking error?

(c) Why might it worry you that practitioners use tracking error as a measurement of risk versus the benchmark?

Date	Portfolio	Benchmark
Nov-18	0.95	0.86
Dec-18	2.01	1.90
Jan-19	3.14	2.94
Feb-19	5.34	5.10
Mar-19	6.11	5.80
Apr-19	6.35	6.02
May-19	6.83	6.50
Jun-19	8.01	7.57
Jul-19	9.30	8.82
Aug-19	10.56	10.00
Sep-19	11.42	10.83
Oct-19	12.96	12.35
Nov-19	0.86	0.85
Dec-19	1.88	1.80
Jan-20	2.08	2.00
Feb-20	0.98	0.90
Mar-20	1.35	1.23
Apr-20	1.33	1.22
May-20	1.51	1.38
Jun-20	1.70	1.53

15.8. Which method would likely be most accurate in reporting the β_p of a portfolio versus a benchmark: taking the weighted average of the individual β's of all the stocks in the portfolio or taking the historical portfolio returns and running a regression of those returns against the benchmark to find β_p? Why?

15.9. Suppose that you are running a complicated hedge fund. One of the founding principles of this hedge fund is to invest in a variety of n strategies. Any pair of these strategies has a correlation of ρ (you also can think of this as the average correlation across strategies), and each strategy has a similar variance of σ^2 and a mean return of μ_i.

(a) Write the formula for the expected return and variance of the entire portfolio when every strategy is equally weighted.

(b) Write down the expected return and risk formula when the portfolio is leveraged in every strategy, proportionally, by an amount l. (*Hint*: Leverage is accomplished by borrowing at the risk-free rate r_f.)

15.10. In the preceding problem, suppose that $n = 50$, $\rho = 0$, $\mu_i = \mu = 0.0057$, $\sigma = 0.04$, $r_f = 0.0048$, and the confidence interval is 95% (that is, $k = 1.65$). These are all monthly return figures and not expressed in percentage terms. Suppose also that the portfolio is valued at $4.1 billion.

    (a) What is the VaR per month given a leveraged value of 1 (that is, $l = 1$)?

    (b) If the leverage is 30 times, what is the VaR of the portfolio in any given month?

    (c) Suppose that the quantitative portfolio manager mis-measured the correlation between strategies and it turned out to be much higher ex post, say, $\rho = 0.2$. How much would the VaR on the $4.1 billion be now?

    (d) What does this illustrate about the dangers of using VaR?

    (e) What's a simple fix the risk analyst could do to measure VaR more accurately?

15.11. Does a correlation of 1 imply a β of 1?

15.12. Which measure of ex-post α is reported most frequently to the quantitative portfolio manager? Which ex-post α might be the most accurate at describing whether the portfolio manager has had excess performance?

15.13. A QEPM department is about to hire a new portfolio manager. A candidate for the job claims that his previous tenure as a portfolio manager was quite successful. The performance analyst of the QEPM department decides to study this claim. She obtains the historical monthly returns of the candidate's portfolio, the benchmark, and the risk-free rate.

    (a) Using these data, compute the Sharpe ratio of the benchmark and the portfolio. Compute the ex-post α^B of the portfolio and its corresponding t-statistic.

    (b) Compute the information ratio of the portfolio using the common but less accurate method and using the more accurate method.

    (c) What do you conclude about this portfolio manager and his claim?

    (d) Would you expect the portfolio manager to perform the same if he were hired by your firm?

Date	r_P	r_B	r_f
Jan-18	2.04	0.85	0.69
Feb-18	2.56	2.43	0.70
Mar-18	−2.54	−2.69	0.70
Apr-18	8.94	9.20	0.71
May-18	0.47	−0.89	0.69
Jun-18	−1.15	−0.52	0.70
Jul-18	−9.81	−9.43	0.67
Aug-18	−6.30	−5.12	0.67
Sep-18	−1.27	−0.67	0.69
Oct-18	7.58	5.99	0.67
Nov-18	3.07	2.48	0.73
Dec-18	6.98	4.15	0.64
Jan-19	8.70	6.73	0.58
Feb-19	3.40	2.22	0.58
Mar-19	0.39	0.03	0.53
Apr-19	5.66	3.86	0.50
May-19	−5.87	−4.79	0.50
Jun-19	6.24	4.49	0.51
Jul-19	3.06	1.96	0.49
Aug-19	−0.39	−1.91	0.47
Sep-19	1.35	1.18	0.45
Oct-19	−4.94	−4.39	0.43
Nov-19	11.87	11.16	0.40
Dec-19	0.03	−1.99	0.39
Jan-20	2.04	0.96	0.35
Feb-20	−2.71	−2.18	0.35
Mar-20	1.49	2.79	0.35
Apr-20	0.95	0.10	0.33
May-20	−1.78	−1.74	0.33
Jun-20	2.80	3.94	0.33
Jul-20	−2.15	−2.40	0.28

Note: All monthly returns are in percentage terms.

15.14. A performance analyst collected the following monthly portfolio returns and the returns of three popular factors for use with a multifactor performance measurement. Use the data to construct a linear regression to assess the performance of this portfolio.

(a) What can you conclude about the portfolio manager's performance over the period?

(b) What type of portfolio is the portfolio manager most likely managing?

Date	$r_P - r_f$	$r_M - r_f$	SMB_t	HML_t
Jan-18	−0.52	2.82	0.85	1.24
Feb-18	0.24	−2.52	2.55	−1.46
Mar-18	−0.24	−4.72	−0.74	1.3
Apr-18	0.25	0.69	−1.51	1.91
May-18	−0.11	0.59	−1.54	0.8
Jun-18	0.7	−3.03	0.12	2.66
Jul-18	−1	2.75	−1.57	1.1
Aug-18	−0.99	4.05	1.66	−3.17
Sep-18	−0.94	−2.33	2.85	−2.23
Oct-18	−0.37	1.29	−2.33	−1.86
Nov-18	−0.3	−4.06	−0.23	0.25
Dec-18	1.27	0.9	0.31	−0.85
Jan-19	0.47	1.72	−2.74	3.24
Feb-19	0.94	3.74	−0.32	0
Mar-19	2.92	2.18	−0.2	−2.86
Apr-19	2.27	2.19	−0.14	1.44
May-19	0.41	2.89	−2.55	1.72
Jun-19	1.52	2.63	2.93	−3.23
Jul-19	0.55	3.65	2.37	−3.17
Aug-19	0.68	0.54	1.71	1.58
Sep-19	−0.57	3.29	−1.71	−1.27
Oct-19	0.28	−1.52	−3.93	−0.83
Nov-19	0.29	3.91	−0.83	−0.46
Dec-19	0.81	1.08	0.34	1.01
Jan-20	2.1	2.29	−2.27	0.04
Feb-20	1.59	1.23	2.02	−2.37
Mar-20	1.65	0.79	1.33	1.35
Apr-20	1.29	2.05	5.05	−4.72
May-20	1.14	2.35	2.7	−2.18
Jun-20	0.24	−1	−3.73	2.61
Jul-20	0.6	−5.95	−3.56	4.27

Note: All monthly returns are in percentage terms.

15.15. Suppose that a QEPM department hires a new quantitative equity portfolio manager to manage one of its portfolios. Suppose that the portfolio manager's benchmark is the S&P 500, with a Sharpe ratio of 0.25. After 1 year, the manager has an information ratio (IR) of 0.5. Should the head of the department award him a bonus based on this IR?

15.16. A performance analyst is worried that the quantitative models produced by the portfolio managers are biased toward selecting financial and utility stocks. The portfolio managers have one model for security returns that they apply to a large universe of stocks and then use as an optimizer to control tracking error. The performance analyst decides to investigate by creating three divisions of the universe of stocks—a financial sector, a utilities sector, and all other sectors. After dividing the universe thus, the performance analyst performs classic attribution. She computes the returns of the portfolio and benchmark in these sectors, as well as the aggregate weights. The following table should be used to answer the follow-up questions.

	Portfolio		Benchmark	
Sector	w_i^P	P_i^P	W_i^B	r_i^B
Financial	40	10	30	8
Utilities	30	12	10	10
All other sectors	30	20	60	18
	100		100	

(a) Based on the preceding table, is the performance analyst's gut feeling correct?

(b) Using the table, compute the portfolio and benchmark returns r_P and r_B.

(c) Compute the allocation effect (AE) and the security-selection effect (SSE) for the portfolio manager. What can you infer about the portfolio manager's stock return models?

(d) Given the results of part (b), what suggestion would you make to the portfolio manager and/or the investment committee regarding the investment process?

15.17. Suppose that a portfolio manager is using index futures to increase the leverage of his overall portfolio. He currently manages a portfolio of $100 million with 10% in cash and 90% invested in a portfolio of stocks with a β versus the benchmark of 1.6 (that is, $\beta_s = 1.6$). He uses futures on the underlying benchmark; thus $\beta_f = 1$. His target is $\beta^* = 3$. The index starts at a value of 1,000. Suppose that after one month the futures value moves from 1,005 to 854.25, and the return of the stock portfolio is -24%. What would be the return of the overall portfolio for the period? (*Hint*: Ignore cash returns in this example, or assume that they are close to 1.)

15.18. A performance analyst is faced with computing the historical returns of a market-neutral portfolio in a backtest. Over a period t to $t + k$, she is given the following information: The initial value of the long portfolio is $65 million, the initial value of the short portfolio is $40 million, and $4 million is required as a liquidity buffer. The return on the liquidity buffer is 2%, the return on cash is 2.5%, the return on the long portfolio is 7%, and the return on the short portfolio (before sorting) is 6%.

(a) What's the overall return of the market-neutral portfolio?

(b) Is it really market-neutral? Why or why not?

15.19. A performance analyst is interested in computing the multifactor attribution of a quantitative portfolio for the month of December 2020. The benchmark is an equal-weighted portfolio of 10 stocks. The portfolio manager uses a three-factor model of stock returns. The analyst collects the information in the table below, including the weight of each stock in the portfolio and the benchmark at the beginning of the month, the return of each stock in the benchmark for the month of January, and the factor exposures of each stock in the benchmark at the beginning of January. The analyst also measures the factor premiums or returns for the month of December, which are 0.47%, 0.29%, and 0.46%, respectively, for factors 1, 2, and 3. Compute the multifactor attribution for the month of January for the returns. (*Hint*: Use a table similar to the one in the top half of Table 15.3.)

Ticker	$r_{i,t}$	$w_{i,t}^P$	$w_{i,t}^B$	$\hat{\beta}_{1,i,t}$	$\hat{\beta}_{2,i,t}$	$\hat{\beta}_{3,i,t}$	$\hat{V}(\epsilon_i)$
GE	0.0131	0.15	0.1	1.1996	0.2007	0.4011	0.0049
SCHW	0.0105	0.15	0.1	0.5652	1.1236	−0.0947	0.0040
ISRG	0.0064	0.15	0.1	0.6867	−0.1724	−0.293	0.0049
AXP	0.0104	0.15	0.1	1.0534	0.1915	−0.0311	0.0056
CAT	0.0093	0.1	0.1	0.7238	−0.1142	0.2652	0.0056
LMT	0.0118	0.1	0.1	1.5304	0.2205	0.6386	0.0061
INTU	0.0080	0.1	0.1	1.5077	0.2465	−0.18	0.0058
MMM	0.0012	0.1	0.1	0.7135	−0.6831	−0.2448	0.0050
TD	−0.0028	0	0.1	0.8384	0.7054	0.2591	0.0042
NOW	−0.0045	0	0.1	0.7672	0.2754	0.2401	0.0038

15.20. Continuing with the information provided in the preceding question, suppose that the performance analyst would like to perform a multifactor risk attribution. In particular, the analyst would like to understand the sources of risk from each factor based on the way the portfolio was constructed. The standard deviation of each factor is 4.43%, 2.89%, and 2.59%, respectively. The correlation between factors 1 and 2 is 0.35, between 1 and 3 is −0.37, and between 2 and 3 is 0.10. The variance of the error terms was estimated using historical data and is listed in the table. Construct a table similar to the one in the bottom part of Table 15.3, and decompose the hypothetical risk of the portfolio into the various components. Why might some portfolio managers claim that this is really not risk attribution?

PART V

Practical Application

In Parts II through IV of this book we presented the basic methods of quantitative equity portfolio management (QEPM). In Part V we will put these methods into action. We will create paper portfolios from a fundamental factor model, an economic factor model, and an aggregate Z-score model and then test the portfolios on approximately a decade's worth of data. The test results themselves are illuminating, but the point of the exercise is not just to evaluate the relative merits of the specific strategies. Rather, we will review each step of forming and testing hypothetical portfolios in order to demonstrate the choices, and potential stumbling blocks, that a manager encounters in practice. This review may be an especially helpful road map for those new to QEPM.

The chapter on the portfolios' results serves as a reference for a range of performance analysis statistics and for the style of report to clients that conforms to the Global Investment Performance Standards (GIPS). The GIPS, established in 1999 by the Association for Investment Management and Research (known now as the CFA Institute) and revised for the year 2020, remain the rule for clear, honest reporting of investment outcomes. The GIPS recommend that performance reports include metrics that explain the volatility of portfolio returns, as well as cumulative return figures for both portfolios and benchmarks for the purpose of side-by-side comparisons. Reporting benchmark returns fits naturally with QEPM's focus on benchmarking, whether to measure an active strategy's outperformance or an indexing strategy's accuracy. In either case, a comparison of the portfolio's returns with the benchmark's returns most likely will put a quantitative manager in a favorable light if he or she has followed a sound strategy.

CHAPTER 16

The Backtesting Process

Tell me and I forget, teach me and I remember, involve me and I learn.

—Benjamin Franklin

16.1 INTRODUCTION

In this chapter we use historical data to formulate models of stock returns and test the performance of hypothetical portfolios based on the models. Building and testing models with past data in this way is referred to as *backtesting*. Backtesting is used widely in quantitative equity portfolio management (QEPM) as a first step in evaluating how well a new investment idea might work. The results of a backtest show whether a strategy would have worked over a significant period in the recent past, which might give an indication of how it will work in the near and not-so-near future.

Certain decisions must be made in the course of backtesting. They include

1. The historical data set and software to use.
2. The time period over which the strategy should be tested and the frequency of the data to be used.
3. The investment universe and the benchmark.[1]

---

[1] Typically, the manager will already know his benchmark. The investment universe is the group of stocks from which holdings can be selected for the portfolio.

4. The factors to use in the quantitative model of stock returns.
5. The type of stock return and risk model with which to pick stocks and manage the risk of the portfolio.[2]
6. The rebalancing frequency.
7. The type of portfolio construction.
8. How to present the performance results of the backtest.

These are the main decisions that the portfolio manager must make in order to set up the test and simulate the results of actual past portfolios. In this chapter we cover the first seven issues of backtesting. We will deal with the presentation of performance results in Chapter 17.

16.2 THE DATA AND SOFTWARE

The choice of data for the backtest is largely determined by the factors that the portfolio manager uses in his or her model of stock returns.[3] For our backtest, we collected five major categories of data: fundamental data, prices and returns, analyst forecasts, social-issue data, and macroeconomic indicators. The fundamental data are from Standard & Poors Compustat database, which contains items from the balance sheets, income statements, and cash-flow statements of the companies. Price and return data are from the University of Chicago's Center for Research in Security Prices (CRSP) database. Basic information related to stock prices such as daily prices, shares outstanding, dividends per share, and trading volumes were obtained from the CRSP database. We supplemented the CRSP volume data with odd-lot volume data downloaded from the U.S. Securities and Exchange Commission's website. Analyst forecasts are from the Institutional Broker Estimates System (IBES) database, and the social-issue data are from the Morgan Stanley Capital International–Kinder Lydenberg Domini (MSCI-KLD) database. Macroeconomic data together with index-related data are from Bloomberg.[4]

---

[2] It is preferable to use the same model for both return and risk, although it is possible to use different ones.
[3] See Chapter 4 for a discussion of factors. For information on databases and vendors, see Appendix D under General Appendices at www.ludwigbc.com under QEPM Exclusive Content.
[4] We downloaded the Survey of Professional Forecasters data from the Federal Reserve Bank of Philadelphia and also utilized the risk-free rate series from the website of Professor Kenneth French of Dartmouth College.

For all of the data, we chose to collect data from 1981 (or the earliest year after 1981 for which data were available) through 2020. This period gave us enough historical data with which to test the performance of our strategies over a relatively long investment horizon. Part of the analyst data was available only beginning in 1993, and the social-issue data were available beginning in 1991. Index future data started in 1982. The industrial classification code we use, the Global Industrial Classification System, began in 1994.

Our raw data are of varying frequencies. Price and return data are daily, analyst forecasts data and many of the macro series are monthly, most of the fundamental data are quarterly, and social-issue data and some of macro series are annual. For ease of management, we arranged all of our data in a monthly format. To do so, certain daily items were summed or averaged across days of a month; quarterly and annual items were recorded in the month when the quarter or the year ended. We also lagged data, to adjust for reporting and release lags, in our historical data set.

A total of 14,945 stocks were included in our historical data set. Two main criteria for inclusion in the historical data set were that both the CRSP and Compustat databases contained the stocks and that the stocks belonged to the top 3,000 in terms of market capitalization at some point during the sample period. More specifically, to construct our database, we went through the following steps. First, for each month t, we selected all the common stocks in the CRSP database (SHRCD = 10, 11, or 12).[5] Second, for each stock month (i, t), we determined whether stock i was the primary share class of a company. For many companies, there exists only one share class, in which case no further action was necessary. When there were multiple share classes, we determined the share class with the largest market capitalization as the primary share. We then excluded nonprimary shares for the purpose of determining the inclusion in our historical data set. (We retained information for nonprimary shares; we just did not consider nonprimary shares for inclusion in our historical data set.) Third, for each stock month (i, t), we checked whether basic items such as total assets, total common equity, sales, and net income were available, assuming a reporting gap of three months; that is, if these items were reported for the quarter ending in month $t - 3$, $t - 4$, or $t - 5$, then we considered month t to have valid data. We then excluded each stock month (i, t) without valid

---

[5] This step excluded most of the REITs from our investment universe.

data. Fourth, for each stock month (i, t), we checked whether monthly returns for the current month and the past 11 months could be retrieved. If not, we excluded the stock. Finally, we ordered the remaining stocks by market capitalization from the largest to the smallest for each month t. Stocks belonging to the top 3,000 for any one month were included in our historical data set. For the purpose of computation, we stored the entire data history of each stock that entered the historical data set in any month.

Our next step was to combine all of the data from all of the databases into one database. Stocks can be identified by CUSIP number or exchange ticker, but these identifiers change over time and, worse yet, are often recycled. For this reason, financial databases use their own, permanent, alphanumeric identifiers for stocks. Linking the permanent identifiers, though, can be a bit of a challenge.

For merging the CRSP and Compustat databases, we utilized the mapping between the CRSP ID (PERMNO) and the Compustat ID (GVKEY) provided by the CRSP database. This mapping was carefully created and maintained by CRSP, so we used it. The CRSP database also provides a mapping between the CRSP ID and the IBES ID. This mapping appears to be somewhat less reliable than the CRSP–Compustat mapping, so we manually examined some of the suspicious matches, checking the CUSIP number, ticker, and company names in both databases.[6]

The MSCI-KLD data were matched to the merged database using the CUSIP number and ticker. When the match was not perfect (i.e., when the CUSIP numbers matched but the tickers did not or when the tickers matched but the CUSIP numbers did not), we manually examined the company names and determined whether the match was valid. The SEC data containing odd-lot volume were matched to the merged database using tickers. In all of the matching procedures, the changes in the CUSIP number, ticker, and company name over time were carefully checked so that our matching was not corrupted by recycled IDs.

Coverage varies in the databases. The percentage of the CRSP–Compustat matched to each of the other databases is listed in Table 16.1. For December 2015, CRSP-Compustat data (after applying the "cleaning" criteria described earlier) included 3,920

---

[6] CUSIP (Committee on Uniform Securities Identification Procedures) numbers are nine-digit identifiers assigned to U.S. stocks and bonds and Canadian stocks. The first six digits of the CUSIP number identify the company; the next two digits identify the type of each security.

TABLE 16.1

Number of Companies in the Historical Data Set

Period	Compustat-CRSP	IBES	Percent	MSCI-KLD	Percent	SEC	Percent
Dec 1990	4,714	2,835	60.14	0	0.00	0	0.00
Dec 1995	5,820	4,021	69.09	640	11.00	0	0.00
Dec 2000	5,501	4,084	74.24	636	11.56	0	0.00
Dec 2005	4,566	3,612	79.11	2,814	61.63	0	0.00
Dec 2010	3,999	3,299	82.50	2,804	70.12	0	0.00
Dec 2015	3,920	3,386	86.38	2,218	56.58	3,468	88.47
Dec 2020	3,459	2,870	82.97	0	0.00	3,031	87.63
Entire Period	4,647.92	3,519.46	75.72	1,747.14	37.59	3,342.31	71.91

Note: The Compustat-CRSP column shows the number of stocks in our historical data set, which includes the entire history of all the stocks that belong to the top 3,000 companies by market capitalization at some point in time after applying the data-cleaning procedures described in the text. For other columns, the table describes the number of stocks or the percentage of stocks in our historical data set that were matched with another database. MSCI-KLD refers to the social responsibility data from MSCI, and SEC refers to the odd-lot volume data from the SEC. The entire period represents the average number of stocks we had in the sample period. For example, when we matched our Compustat-CRSP to the IBES data in December 2020, only 2,870 of the 3,459 companies were matched, representing about 82.97% of our original data. MSCI-KLD data were only available until December 2018, and SEC odd-lot data were only available since 2012.

stocks. When we merged CRSP-Compustat with IBES, we found that only 86.38% of the CRSP-Compustat stocks had valid data in IBES. The percentage of matched stocks declined to 56.58% for MSCI-KLD, while it was higher at 88.47% for the SEC odd-lot volume data. Note that MSCI-KLD data were available only up to 2018, and the SEC odd-lot volume data were available only from 2012 through 2020.

In addition to the matching percentages, we gathered statistics on various variables for various months in our historical sample period. These are provided in Table 16.2. The historical data set for December 2020 contains 2,992 firms with valid earnings-to-price ratios. The average earnings-to-price ratio is −0.053. The minimum is −10.499, which is for AMC Entertainment Holdings (AMC), whereas the maximum is 1.479, which is for Xbiotech Inc. (XBIT). Log market capitalization is calculated for 3,000 firms. The average log market capitalization is 7.631, which corresponds to about 2 billion dollars ($=e^{7.631}$ million dollars). The largest company is Apple Inc. (AAPL), with a log market capitalization of 14.629 (2.256 trillion dollars), and the smallest company is Lightpath

TABLE 16.2

Selected Summary Statistics of the Historical Data Set

Factor	Period	Nobs	Average	SD	Min	Max
Earnings-to-	Dec 1990	2,984	−0.016	1.034	−36.686	5.699
price (E/P)	Dec 2000	2,985	0.013	0.317	−9.378	2.986
	Dec 2010	2,992	0.017	0.157	−2.218	2.123
	Dec 2020	2,992	−0.053	0.395	−10.499	1.479
	All	1,071,502	−0.003	0.680	−157.647	50.937
Log of market	Dec 1990	3,000	5.001	1.749	2.541	11.075
capitalization	Dec 2000	3,000	6.755	1.580	4.626	13.071
(LOGSIZE)	Dec 2010	3,000	7.057	1.581	4.669	12.818
	Dec 2020	3,000	7.631	1.823	4.628	14.629
	All	1,083,000	6.822	1.657	2.541	14.629
Inventory	Dec 1990	2,310	16.040	77.889	0.041	2,456.714
turnover (IT)	Dec 2000	2,111	31.086	149.758	0.050	4,550.412
	Dec 2010	2,196	20.960	127.651	0.013	5,268.000
	Dec 2020	2,122	35.232	318.606	0.009	9,095.750
	All	788,702	30.778	555.739	0.000	128,118.000
Net profit	Dec 1990	2,984	−1.319	43.218	−2,177.000	131.882
margin (NPM)	Dec 2000	2,985	−1.239	26.978	−1,114.882	175.189
	Dec 2010	2,992	−1.365	42.813	−2,062.226	571.027
	Dec 2020	2,992	−7.070	99.338	−3,128.667	1,248.432
	All	1,071,502	−3.709	329.731	−1.544e+05	1,562.764
Cash ratio	Dec 1990	2,541	0.953	2.332	0.000	38.331
(CR)	Dec 2000	2,446	1.988	5.267	0.000	139.254
	Dec 2010	2,509	1.442	2.374	0.000	32.779
	Dec 2020	2,423	2.085	4.561	0.000	122.933
	All	885,195	1.486	3.537	0.000	317.675
Debt-to-equity	Dec 1990	2,947	5.043	100.537	0.012	5,432.474
(D/E)	Dec 2000	2,946	3.170	10.364	0.007	361.450
	Dec 2010	2,911	2.782	8.075	0.018	213.031
	Dec 2020	2,856	4.054	15.684	0.013	577.659
	All	1,054,825	4.461	316.179	0.000	166,256.359
Stock	Dec 1990	2,266	−0.014	0.152	−2.066	2.383
buybacks (SB)	Dec 2000	1,935	−0.021	0.220	−3.606	2.992
	Dec 2010	2,564	−0.010	0.097	−1.315	0.917
	Dec 2020	2,668	−0.009	0.092	−1.173	0.931
	All	870,084	−0.009	0.331	−156.782	5.127
Beta (BETA) /	Dec 1990	3,000	1.017	0.672	−2.947	4.986
market (MKT)	Dec 2000	3,000	0.967	0.863	−6.077	6.679
exposure	Dec 2010	3,000	1.325	0.711	−1.227	6.063
	Dec 2020	3,000	1.381	0.818	−5.784	7.487
	All	1,083,000	1.149	0.833	−15.322	23.678

One-month	Dec 1990	3,000	0.035	0.137	−0.500	1.526
momentum (M1M)	Dec 2000	3,000	0.070	0.198	−0.805	1.279
	Dec 2010	3,000	0.091	0.124	−0.262	2.401
	Dec 2020	3,000	0.092	0.233	−0.662	5.286
	All	1,083,000	0.019	0.155	−0.984	15.774
Consumer	Dec 1990	3,000	0.275	0.348	−1.859	2.993
confidence (CCG)	Dec 2000	3,000	0.192	0.912	−7.130	6.519
exposure	Dec 2010	3,000	0.290	0.295	−2.053	5.005
	Dec 2020	3,000	−0.188	0.431	−4.649	3.656
	All	1,083,000	0.128	0.443	−16.261	16.977
Inflation (CPIG)	Dec 1990	3,000	−3.581	8.925	−119.109	68.213
exposure	Dec 2000	3,000	−5.132	17.300	−135.362	66.112
	Dec 2010	3,000	1.145	7.195	−62.137	88.866
	Dec 2020	3,000	−5.905	12.423	−233.881	109.985
	All	1,083,000	−1.876	13.817	−582.035	754.886
Real GDP growth	Dec 1990	3,000	2.945	5.236	−23.859	101.050
(GDPG) exposure	Dec 2000	3,000	2.335	6.846	−28.839	35.148
	Dec 2010	3,000	0.015	3.394	−52.793	28.878
	Dec 2020	3,000	0.267	1.017	−18.857	9.000
	All	1,083,000	−0.546	5.639	−195.803	224.846
Ten-year-three-	Dec 1990	3,000	−0.994	3.548	−84.386	18.690
month term	Dec 2000	3,000	2.264	7.531	−45.354	67.940
premium (TP3M)	Dec 2010	3,000	0.369	1.978	−33.392	19.801
exposure	Dec 2020	3,000	1.712	8.263	−78.448	205.972
	All	1,083,000	0.153	4.500	−252.524	257.746
Standardized	Dec 1990	1,430	−1.989	8.296	−145.950	46.660
unanticipated	Dec 2000	2,175	−1.612	15.614	−570.667	58.000
earnings (SUE)	Dec 2010	2,603	0.926	6.185	−137.750	135.500
	Dec 2020	2,452	2.184	7.488	−92.159	136.133
	All	824,777	0.189	8.138	−1387.076	1006.000
Diversity (DIV)	Mar 1992	605	0.022	0.116	−0.500	0.429
	Dec 2000	563	0.037	0.218	−0.667	0.875
	Dec 2010	2,441	−0.060	0.241	−0.667	0.875
	Dec 2020	N/A	N/A	N/A	N/A	N/A
	All	543,560	−0.048	0.309	−1.000	1.000

Note: These are the cross-sectional statistics for particular time intervals. Nobs stands for the number of observations used to compute the sample statistics, Average is the average value of a factor across all the stocks in the universe at that particular interval, SD is the standard deviation of a factor across all stocks in the universe at that particular interval, and Min and Max represent the greatest and least values of a factor across all stocks in the universe at that particular interval. Detailed descriptions of each factor appear in Appendix 16A. Our socially reponsible data end in December 2018; thus we had no values for DIV for December 2020.

Technologies Inc. (LPTH), with a log market capitalization of 4.628 (102.3 million dollars). The net profit margin is available for 2,992 firms, with an average of -7.070. The minimum net profit margin is $-3,128.7$ for VolitionRX Ltd (VNRX), and the maximum is 1,248.4 for Virnetx Holding Corp (VHC).

For the computations presented in this and the next chapter, we chose to use two software programs. For the data management and model estimation, we used STATA. For the portfolio optimization, transactions costs, tax management, leverage, and market neutrality, we chose to use MATLAB. STATA is superior in data management, especially when the data are not completely numerical, as is the case in our exercise. MATLAB is superior when matrix algebra and optimization are involved.[7]

16.3 THE TIME PERIOD

If a portfolio manager is considering an investment idea to be implemented a number of years down the road, it is possible to do *real-time testing* rather than backtesting. Real-time testing means applying a new strategy to current data and recording how well the strategy works going forward. This kind of testing, a bit like performing a long-range study, involves years of collecting real-time data. It is therefore quite different from backtesting, which is meant to give a more immediate evaluation of a strategy. As we have mentioned, backtesting requires sophisticated commercial databases with cleaned historical data, as well as programming tools.

The backtesting method is flexible to different test structures, and some real-time testing is often appended to it. Typically, a backtest includes three segments of data, as depicted in Figure 16.1. The first two segments cover the time period from T_0, the earliest date for which there are historical data, to T_2, the present. These segments encompass all the historical data on stocks, factors, and other variables needed for the evaluation of the investing strategy. The third segment of data covers the time period from T_2 to T_3, which is some point in the future. The third segment of data therefore is future data that will be collected on a real-time basis.

---

[7] We provide programs, data, and labs to practice QEPM in STATA, MATLAB, or R. These labs can be downloaded from our website with the appropriate password. They can be found under Classroom Labs at https://ludwigbc. com/books/qepm/exclusive_qepm_content_2020/ or at www.ludwigbc.com and look for QEPM Exclusive Content.

FIGURE 16.1

The backtesting data.

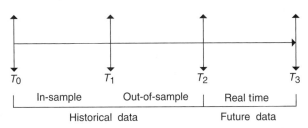

The two historical data segments are the *in-sample* data from T_0 to T_1 and the *out-of-sample* data from T_1 to T_2.[8] A portfolio manager or analyst usually has several competing models of stock returns and performs sequential tests with them, dropping or adding a factor in each test. As we discussed in Chapter 2, though, testing and discarding models until one comes across a "significant" one is a form of data mining. Although the original model may have been based on sound economic theory, the final variation may not be. The analyst therefore should limit the sequential testing to the in-sample data, and then, once he or she finds a satisfactory model, test that one on the out-of-sample data. This mitigates the problem of data mining because, since the out-of-sample data are not used to test the many discarded variations of the model, the degrees of freedom are preserved,[9] and the test statistics can be interpreted normally. If the stock return model performs well on the out-of-sample data, it is a decent indicator that it might work for a real portfolio. Of course, if the model fails on the out-of-sample data, beginning the testing process all over again on the same data will lead to data mining. Everyone in a QEPM research department, manager and analyst alike, needs to be well versed in the correct use of data for backtesting.

Parameter stability, which we discussed in Chapter 2, factors into consideration the time period of the backtest. If relationships

---

[8] A more technically oriented reader may prefer to call the latter period the *pseudo-out-of-sample data*, rather than the out-of-sample data, as they are, technically, both part of our sample. In addition, some readers might be more familiar with the terms *estimation period* and *testing period* or perhaps with the terms *training data* and *validation data*.

[9] *Degrees of freedom* are a measure indicating whether the data set is large enough to run meaningful statistical tests with given the number of parameters in the model. The degrees of freedom are preserved because enough unused data points remain.

between stock returns and factors did not change over time, it would be sufficient to estimate the stock return model once on the in-sample data and then immediately put it to use in the model. Unfortunately, one of the most frustrating parts of being a portfolio manager is that financial market relationships seem to always change. Many relationships between factors and stock returns change. However, it is the goal of QEPM to find relationships that are stable over time [as stated in tenet 6 of QEPM (see Chapter 2)], and this is accomplished with models with stable parameters. If the parameters seem to change over time, the stability of the model can be preserved by using *rolling windows* of data. Rather than estimate the parameters or model on one particular in-sample data period, the analyst should create a *rolling in-sample window* and dynamically reestimate the parameters over time,[10] as depicted in Figure 16.2. For example, suppose that an analyst has five years' worth of data. The in-sample period is January 2010 through December 2010. The out-of-sample period is January 2011 through December of 2015. The rolling in-sample period is one year. The analyst's first step is to estimate the model's parameters on the first year of in-sample data (January 2010 through December 2010), use those parameters to forecast January 2011 returns, and check the model's performance. The next step is to move forward one month in the in-sample data, reestimate the parameters on the year of data from February 2011 through January 2012, and then use those parameters to forecast February 2012 returns and check the model's performance. This process is continued through the December 2015 data, the end of the out-of-sample period. The rolling in-sample window therefore

FIGURE 16.2

Backtesting with rolling in-sample windows. (*Note:* Each horizontal series of dots represents a rolling sample.)

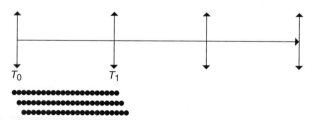

T_0 T_1

---

[10] Some people call this *walk-forward testing.*

ventures into the out-of-sample period, but it does not negate the purpose of the out-of-sample data.

The main difference between this method and the one with a static in-sample period is that the parameters are updated continually to reflect changes in the relationships between factors and stock returns, if there are any. The analyst should be careful to make sure, though, that the reestimations reflect actual changes in the underlying parameters and are not just capturing statistical noise.

For our particular historical backtesting example, we utilize data from 2006 (T_0 = 2006) through 2020 (T_2 = 2020). We treat the first 5 years from 2006 to 2010 as the in-sample period (i.e., T_1 = 2010) and the remaining 10 years from 2011 to 2020 as the out-of-sample period.[11] We believe that 5 years is a reasonable length of time with which to test our factors and to build our stock return models. The remaining 10 years are used for testing our portfolio construction strategies. We used a dynamic rolling in-sample window as described earlier. We discuss more details in Section 16.7 on rebalancing.

We chose a time interval of one month for the data set and obtained end-of-month factors and monthly stock returns to perform our analysis. As we mentioned in the preceding section, any data available only quarterly or annually were recorded to one particular month. To deal with such data we therefore confronted a choice. One way of handling such data is to fill the months that follow with the same piece of data. This leads to some biased relationships, because it joins a static number with varying monthly stock returns. Another way to handle it is to study only the relationships between factors and stock returns at a quarterly or annual interval. This method, though, severely reduces the sample size of the data, making it difficult to infer any statistical relationships between the factor returns and stock returns while also violating our basic decision to use a monthly time interval. For this reason, we chose to fill in quarterly and annual data for the entire period to which they applied. In the end, any potential bias arising from this method was not a concern because none of the quarterly factors was selected for the return model.

---

[11] We constructed the historical database covering the 40-year period from 1981 to 2020. We provide the factor tests for some of the earlier periods in Appendix 16B under Chapter Appendices at https://ludwigbc.com/books/ qepm/exclusive_qepm_ content_2020/ for the curious reader.

16.4 THE INVESTMENT UNIVERSE AND THE BENCHMARK

By delineating an investment universe, the portfolio manager pre-liminarily confines the model and the portfolio to a certain pool of stocks. The investment universe may be defined by some criteria, or it may be shaped via a screening mechanism. The investment universe also may be the portfolio's benchmark, although the port-folio may have a better chance of outperforming the benchmark if stocks can be drawn from a wider selection. The investment uni-verse also might be restricted by the need for trading liquidity. The stock needs to be liquid enough for the manager to make trades whenever necessary. For our backtesting example, the investment universe consisted of the top (in terms of market capitalization) 1,500 stocks in the United States.[12]

The choice of benchmark is motivated by several factors. A good benchmark should be *representative* of the underlying invest-ment universe. Thus, a U.S. equity portfolio manager should choose an index that represents the U.S. equity market. A bench-mark should be *investable and replicable*. That is, the portfolio man-ager should be able to replicate the performance of the benchmark easily, and there should be few securities in the benchmark that either cannot be purchased or are very illiquid. The benchmark should be *accurate and reliable,* and information about it should be *timely* so that performance comparisons and analysis can be done easily. The benchmark should be *transparent*, with known compo-nent securities. The benchmark should have *liquid futures* so that it is possible to use futures contracts for equitization of the portfolio's cash flows. Finally, the benchmark should not experience high *turnover*. This generates high trading costs and causes a drag on the portfolio's returns. Most of the indices that we will discuss meet these basic criteria, although some more than others (see Table 16.3 for the basic criteria).

---

[12] The inclusion in the investment universe was determined separately for each month. Thus, every month the investment universe could potentially change. Our historical data set, as explained earlier, includes every stock that, at one point in time, belonged to the top 3,000 companies ranked by market capitalization. This allows us flexibility in making various calculations and constructing factors. However, this is different than our investment universe, which is the group of stocks that we allow for inclusion in our optimal portfolios.

TABLE 16.3

Important Characteristics of an Equity Benchmark

Characteristic	Explanation
1. Representative	The benchmark should be representative of the style of stocks that the portfolio manager tends to purchase.
2. Investable and replicable	The portfolio manager should be able to purchase all of the stocks in the benchmark according to their weights with relative ease.
3. Accurate and reliable	The reported returns of the index and the quoted prices of stocks in the index should be reliable and accurate.
4. Timely	The index returns should be available at small, regular intervals, ideally once a minute. At worst, they should be available once a day.
5. Transparent	The constituent securities and security weights of the benchmark should be public information and available at all times to the portfolio manager.
6. Liquid futures	The benchmark should have liquid futures contracts for use in cash equitization and leverage.
7. Lower turnover	The benchmark should have relatively low turnover, which minimizes transactions costs and the tax effects of trading as a result of benchmark changes.

16.4.1 U.S. Equity Benchmarks

The major benchmarks for U.S. equity portfolio managers are the S&P 500, S&P 400, S&P 600, and S&P 1500 indices, the Russell 3000, Russell 2000, and Russell 1000 indices, the S&P 500 Barra Value and Growth indices; the Russell Value and Growth indices; the NASDAQ 100; the Dow Jones and the Wilshire 5000. Each of these benchmarks is a paper index created by a committee.

The S&P 500, a large-cap index, is probably the best-known equity benchmark. The S&P 400 is a mid-cap index, and the S&P 600 is a small-cap index. The S&P 1500 is simply a market-cap or float-weighted index consisting of the stocks in the S&P 400, 500, and 600. The stocks in the S&P 400, 500, and 600 are chosen by the Standard & Poors Index Committee, which meets regularly to decide which stocks should be added or dropped from the indices.[13] The committee will consider dropping a stock when

---

[13] For more information on the selection criteria, see https://www.spglobal.com/en/.

stocks are delisted, when there are corporate actions such as mergers, and when basic inclusion criteria are no longer met. Among the
committee's criteria for including a stock in an index are the following: the stock must be a U.S. company; must have positive as-
reported earnings in the most recent quarter, as well as over the
most recent four quarters (summed up); and must have a certain
percentage of its shares freely floating (10% for inclusion in the
S&P 500, 50% for inclusion in the S&P 600 or S&P 400).

The Russell indices, run by the Frank Russell Company, are
also very popular benchmarks for U.S. equity portfolio managers.
The Russell 3000 is an index of the top 3,000 publicly traded stocks
in the United States by market capitalization. The Russell 1000
(a.k.a. Russell Large-Cap) takes the top 1,000 stocks of the Russell
3000, and the Russell 2000 (a.k.a. Russell Small-Cap) takes the bottom 2,000. The criteria for inclusion in the Russell indices are less
subjective than they are for the S&P indices. Once per year, on the
reconstitution date, the Frank Russell Company ranks all the common stocks trading in the United States by market capitalization
and screens certain stocks out of the ranking, including stocks trading below $1.00, pink-sheet or bulletin stocks, non- U.S.-incorporated
stocks, foreign stocks, and American Depository Receipts (ADRs).
Any stocks dropped from the indices during the year in between
reconstitution dates are not replaced until the next reconstitution
date. New shares of stock resulting from spinoffs and other corporate actions are allowed to stay in the index. The Russell indices'
stocks are float-weighted rather than market-cap-weighted. In 2020,
the reconstitution date for these indices was May 8, whereas addi-
tions and deletions were made publicly available in June, and the
new index for the year became effective on June 29.[14]

Standard and Poors created the S&P 500 Value and Growth
indices by ranking companies in the S&P 500 by their growth rank
relative to their value rank. Growth stocks are considered stocks
with high values of growth in earnings-per-share, growth in sales-
per-share, and 12-month price changes, while value stocks are considered stocks with high values of book-to-price, earnings-to-price,
and sales-to-price ratios. Stocks with a high rank in the growth factor compared to the value factor become part of the S&P Growth
Index, while companies with a low rank in the growth factor compared to the value factor become part of the S&P Value Index.

---

[14] For more information, see https://www.ftserussell.com/.

The stocks in the indices are market-capitalization-weighted. These indices are rebalanced annually in December.[15]

The Russell 1000 and Russell 2000 Value and Growth indices are determined by another type of screening. The stocks in the Russell 1000 and Russell 2000 are ranked separately by three variables—the book-to-price (B/P) ratio, the IBES medium-term (2 years) growth forecasts by analysts, and the 5-year historical sales-per-share growth. The stocks are ranked by their scores, and then these scores are combined to determine which stocks become part of the value index and which stocks become part of the growth index. This results in four indices: the Russell 1000 Value, Russell 1000 Growth, Russell 2000 Value, and Russell 2000 Growth. These indices are rebalanced annually along with the rebalancing of the Russell 1000, 2000, and 3000.

The NASDAQ 100 encompasses the largest 100 nonfinancial companies trading on the NASDAQ. Once per year in December, NASDAQ nonfinancial stocks are ranked by market capitalization. The top 75 in the ranking go into the index, while the other 25 are chosen based on preference for companies already in the index that are still ranked in the top 125. New companies that made the top 100 are also considered. The stocks are weighted by a modified-capitalization scheme so that the index is not too skewed toward stocks with high market capitalization. All securities must meet basic eligibility requirements for inclusion.[16] The index is rebalanced quarterly.

The Dow Jones Industrial Average (DJIA) is very popular with personal investors but much less popular as a benchmark for professional portfolio managers. The DJIA contains 30 stocks selected by the Dow Jones Company to represent the U.S. economy.[17] The stocks are price-weighted rather than float-weighted or market-capitalization-weighted, which makes the index susceptible to significant changes from stock splits and other corporate actions that have no bearing on the underlying economics of the index. This is one of the reasons why the DJIA is not a popular benchmark with portfolio managers.

---

[15] For more information on the exact methodology for index construction, see https://www.spglobal.com/en/.

[16] For more information, see https://www.nasdaq.com/nasdaq-100.

[17] The index excludes transportation and utliity stocks. For more information, see https://www.spglobal.com/en/.

The Wilshire 5000 is the index most representative of the U.S. equity market. Despite its name, it does not contain 5,000 stocks.[18] It was created in 1974 to represent the performance of all publicly traded U.S. companies. All companies in the index must be headquartered in the United States. The index is market-capitalization-weighted. The Wilshire 5000 is often referred to as the *total market index*.[19]

16.4.2 A Comparison of the Major U.S. Equity Benchmarks

How do the major domestic equity indices compare with one another in terms of performance? Table 16.4 lists their return statistics from 1995 to 2020.[20] All these statistics include the reinvestment of dividends into the underlying index. The benchmark with the highest geometric return over the period was the NASDAQ 100, with a 14.93% annual return. The S&P 400 (12.14%) and S&P 600 (11.21%) followed closely behind. The Russell 2000 Growth had the lowest annual return for the period (9.04%).

In terms of risk, the NASDAQ 100 had the highest annualized standard deviation (24.58%), and the Russell 2000 Growth had the second highest (22.74%). The benchmark with the lowest annualized standard deviation was the Dow Jones Industrial Average (14.93%).

All the major equity indices exhibit negative skewness. The distributions of their returns are skewed left of the normal distribution, which means that the probability that they have earned less-than-average returns in any given year is less than 50%. All the indices also exhibit positive excess kurtosis. The distributions of their returns have thicker tails than the normal distribution does, so the probability of extreme returns is greater than a normal distribution would predict. The skewness and kurtosis of these indices have been noted in data from other historical periods, not just the rocky period of 1995–2020 covered here. The last column of the table computes a Jarque-Bara test, which is a test for the normality

---

[18] In 2021, it had approximately 3,544 stocks.
[19] Wilshire also has a float-weighted and an equal-weighted version of its index. For more information, see https://www.wilshire.com/.
[20] For the NASDAQ 100, the total return index starts in 1999; thus, from 1995 to 1999, we used the price series and then appended the total return series starting in 1999.

TABLE 16.4

Statistics of Common Benchmarks from 1995–2020

Ticker	Benchmark Name	Arithmetic Mean	SD	Geometric Mean	Median	Max	Min	Skewness	Excess Kurtosis	J-B
SPTR	S&P 500	11.19	15.09	10.52	16.67	12.82	−16.79	−0.64	1.18	39.69
SPTRSVX	S&P 500 Value[a]	10.04	15.75	9.15	16.23	12.88	−17.11	−0.74	1.69	65.73
SPTRSGX	S&P 500 Growth[b]	12.15	15.63	11.48	16.45	14.45	−16.51	−0.54	0.80	23.37
SPTRMDCP	S&P 400	13.11	17.71	12.14	18.38	14.87	−21.74	−0.72	2.34	97.90
SPTRSMCP	S&P 600	12.55	19.22	11.21	19.28	18.17	−22.40	−0.62	1.97	70.00
SPRTR	S&P 1500	11.33	15.21	10.64	17.43	12.89	−17.32	−0.68	1.34	47.19
RU10INTR	Russell 1000	11.41	15.32	10.72	16.57	13.21	−17.46	−0.67	1.36	47.32
RU10VATR	Russell 1000 Value	10.53	15.17	9.78	16.27	13.45	−17.31	−0.77	2.25	96.90
RU10GRTR	Russell 1000 Growth	12.06	17.09	11.11	16.75	14.80	−17.61	−0.63	1.15	37.79
RU20INTR	Russell 2000	11.35	19.95	9.74	20.62	18.43	−21.73	−0.54	1.46	43.11
RU20VATR	Russell 2000 Value	11.25	18.48	9.93	18.01	19.31	−24.67	−0.74	2.78	129.43
RU20GRTR	Russell 2000 Growth	11.31	22.74	9.04	19.13	23.27	−23.08	−0.41	1.08	23.72
RU30INTR	Russell 3000	11.33	15.46	10.61	17.77	13.24	−17.74	−0.70	1.42	51.34
RU30VATR	Russell 3000 Value	10.52	15.24	9.75	16.64	13.80	−17.58	−0.80	2.37	105.97
RU30GRTR	Russell 3000 Growth	11.92	17.26	10.92	17.99	14.80	−17.93	−0.64	1.14	38.16
DWCT	Wilshire 5000	11.37	15.54	10.64	18.92	13.50	−17.61	−0.69	1.38	49.79
DJITR	Dow Jones Industrial Average	11.46	14.93	10.84	14.37	12.14	−14.91	−0.58	1.22	37.13
NDXTR	NASDAQ 100[c]	17.04	24.58	14.93	24.12	24.99	−26.40	−0.33	1.45	32.87

Note: The statistics are for the total returns of the indices during the period from January 1995 through December 2020. The data and tickers were obtained from Bloomberg. Arithmetic returns are annualized by multiplying monthly average return by 12; geometric returns are annualized using the calculation $\left(\frac{V_t}{V_0}\right)^{\frac{12}{N}} - 1$, where N is the number of monthly returns. Max and Min represent the maximum and minimum monthly returns over the sample period; Skewness represents the skewness; Excess Kurtosis refers to the excess kurtosis over the normal distribution; and J-B. is the Jarque-Bera test for normality. The formulas for skewness, kurtosis, and Jarque-Bera are discussed in Chapter 15. All means and standard deviations have been annualized.

[a] Formerly known as the S&P Barra Value Index and the S&P 500 Citibank Value Index.
[b] Formerly known as the S&P Barra Growth Index and the S&P 500 Citibank Growth Index.
[c] The total return of the NASDAQ 100 series started in March 1999. Thus, from 1995 to March 1999, we used the price return series of the NASDAQ 100.

of the return distribution based on the skewness and kurtosis of the returns as compared with a normal distribution. For every benchmark, the test rejects the assumption of normality.[21]

It is often interesting to see how much the returns of different equity benchmarks are related. The correlation of two return series describes how they move in relation to each other. Correlation values range from −1 (the series move in exact opposition to each other) to 1 (the series move in exact unison). Table 16.5 shows the correlations of the returns of the major benchmarks over the period 1995–2020.

It turns out that the S&P 500 is highly correlated with some of the other well-known indices. The S&P 500's correlation with the Russell 1000 is 0.998; with the Russell 3000, 0.994; with the S&P 1500, 0.998; and with the Wilshire 5000, 0.989. The S&P 500 is less correlated with other indices. Its correlation with the NASDAQ 100 is 0.822; with the S&P 400 and S&P 600, 0.906 and 0.826, respectively; and with the Dow Jones Industrial Average, 0.951.

More comparisons are possible by observing some of the indices' fundamental factors or financial ratios. Table 16.6 gives the vital statistics or fundamental ratios of the various indices using data from the end of 2020.[22]

A few patterns stand out. The highest P/S ratio is for growth indices, like the S&P 500 Growth Index and the NASDAQ 100. The highest P/E ratios are from the Russell 2000 Growth and Value indices. The lowest P/E ratio index at the end of 2020 was the Dow Jones Industrial Average with a P/E of 27.12. Not surprisingly, the index with the largest total market capitalization is the Russell 3000, whose stocks trade at a total market cap of $40,930,135 million. The smallest benchmark is the S&P 600, which has a market capitalization of $938,212 million.

16.4.3 The Most Popular Benchmarks and Our Benchmarks

The choice of benchmark is often dictated by a portfolio manager's investment style and by the liquidity of the potential benchmarks'

---

[21] For the 5% significance level, the critical value for the Jarque-Bera test is 5.99.
[22] These ratios are from Bloomberg and may be influenced by missing data and negative-earning companies that are excluded from the P/E calculations for the index.

TABLE 16.5

Correlations of Common Benchmarks from 1995–2020

	SPTR	SPTRSVX	SPTRSGX	SPTRMDCP	SPTRSMCP	SPRTR	RU10INTR	RU10VATR	RU10GRTR
SPTR	1	0.958	0.965	0.906	0.826	0.998	0.998	0.943	0.955
SPTRSVX	0.958	1	0.850	0.902	0.834	0.961	0.956	0.988	0.846
SPTRSGX	0.965	0.850	1	0.844	0.759	0.959	0.963	0.834	0.984
SPTRMDCP	0.906	0.902	0.844	1	0.941	0.929	0.927	0.898	0.866
SPTRSMCP	0.826	0.834	0.759	0.941	1	0.856	0.848	0.821	0.788
SPRTR	0.998	0.961	0.959	0.929	0.856	1	0.999	0.947	0.954
RU10INTR	0.998	0.956	0.963	0.927	0.848	0.999	1	0.941	0.960
RU10VATR	0.943	0.988	0.834	0.898	0.821	0.947	0.941	1	0.811
RU10GRTR	0.955	0.846	0.984	0.866	0.788	0.954	0.960	0.811	1
RU20INTR	0.829	0.822	0.775	0.934	0.984	0.857	0.853	0.804	0.809
RU20VATR	0.804	0.856	0.697	0.912	0.960	0.831	0.820	0.860	0.707
RU20GRTR	0.805	0.755	0.792	0.898	0.939	0.831	0.832	0.722	0.843
RU30INTR	0.994	0.955	0.957	0.940	0.873	0.998	0.999	0.940	0.958
RU30VATR	0.941	0.987	0.831	0.910	0.844	0.947	0.941	0.999	0.810
RU30GRTR	0.953	0.849	0.979	0.882	0.815	0.955	0.960	0.813	0.998
DWCT	0.989	0.945	0.957	0.942	0.882	0.994	0.995	0.927	0.961
DJITR	0.951	0.947	0.886	0.852	0.773	0.948	0.944	0.938	0.866
NDXTR	0.822	0.688	0.885	0.754	0.705	0.823	0.831	0.629	0.925

TABLE 16.5 (Continued)

	RU20INTR	RU20VATR	RU20GRTR	RU30INTR	RU30VATR	RU30GRTR	DWCT	DJITR	NDXTR
SPTR	0.829	0.804	0.805	0.994	0.941	0.953	0.989	0.951	0.822
SPTRSVX	0.822	0.856	0.755	0.955	0.987	0.849	0.945	0.947	0.688
SPTRSGX	0.775	0.697	0.792	0.957	0.831	0.979	0.957	0.886	0.885
SPTRMDCP	0.934	0.912	0.898	0.940	0.910	0.882	0.942	0.852	0.754
SPTRSMCP	0.984	0.960	0.939	0.873	0.844	0.815	0.882	0.773	0.705
SPRTR	0.857	0.831	0.831	0.998	0.947	0.955	0.994	0.948	0.823
RU10INTR	0.853	0.820	0.832	0.999	0.941	0.960	0.995	0.944	0.831
RU10VATR	0.804	0.860	0.722	0.940	0.999	0.813	0.927	0.938	0.629
RU10GRTR	0.809	0.707	0.843	0.958	0.810	0.998	0.961	0.866	0.925
RU20INTR	1	0.949	0.972	0.879	0.827	0.837	0.892	0.764	0.745
RU20VATR	0.949	1	0.851	0.844	0.884	0.731	0.845	0.776	0.585
RU20GRTR	0.972	0.851	1	0.858	0.742	0.871	0.877	0.716	0.823
RU30INTR	0.879	0.844	0.858	1	0.942	0.961	0.998	0.938	0.834
RU30VATR	0.827	0.884	0.742	0.942	1	0.815	0.931	0.934	0.632
RU30GRTR	0.837	0.731	0.871	0.961	0.815	1	0.966	0.863	0.928
DWCT	0.892	0.845	0.877	0.998	0.931	0.966	1	0.929	0.846
DJITR	0.764	0.776	0.716	0.938	0.934	0.863	0.929	1	0.714
NDXTR	0.745	0.585	0.823	0.834	0.632	0.928	0.846	0.714	1

Note: The benchmark statistics are based upon the total returns of the benchmarks during the period from January 1995 through December 2020. The data and tickers were obtained from Bloomberg.

Vital Statistics of Common Benchmarks for December 2020

Bloomberg Ticker	Index Name	S_t	SIZE	DY	P/E	P/B	P/S	P/CF	P/EBITDA	EV/EBITDA	EPS
SPX Index	S&P 500	3756.07	33,166,864	1.57	30.68	4.11	2.81	16.17	16.66	18.96	122.42
MID Index	S&P 400	2306.62	2,162,168	1.47	31.21	2.50	1.63	11.11	13.97	18.87	73.92
SML Index	S&P 600	1118.93	938,212	1.47	57.21	2.05	1.11	9.58	14.70	21.34	19.56
SPR Index	S&P 1500	857.79	36,267,244	1.56	31.08	3.86	2.60	15.49	16.44	19.03	27.60
SVX Index	S&P 500 Value	1267.18	21,543,703	2.46	26.16	2.48	1.83	12.12	12.87	16.20	48.44
SGX Index	S&P 500 Growth	2577.22	22,660,767	0.78	36.24	9.88	5.37	22.98	21.80	22.64	71.12
RAY Index	Russell 3000	2248.44	40,930,135	1.48	34.47	3.90	2.64	16.47	17.40	20.47	65.23
RTY Index	Russell 2000	1974.86	2,938,075	1.19	51.67	2.47	1.43	15.52	23.00	35.30	-3.54
RIY Index	Russell 1000	2120.87	37,992,060	1.50	32.11	4.06	2.81	16.53	17.13	19.75	66.04
RAV Index	Russell 3000 Value	1774.76	26,355,925	2.23	27.86	2.29	1.81	11.86	12.66	16.68	63.71
RAG Index	Russell 3000 Growth	1952.61	26,332,335	0.79	44.25	11.23	4.63	25.79	25.20	26.61	44.12
RLV Index	Russell 1000 Value	1349.62	24,551,133	2.25	26.45	2.38	1.93	12.09	12.59	16.13	51.02
RLG Index	Russell 1000 Growth	2427.77	24,316,644	0.81	40.10	11.93	4.85	25.12	24.46	25.51	60.54
RUJ Index	Russell 2000 Value	1972.38	1,804,792	1.99	118.06	1.50	0.94	9.20	13.79	26.46	16.71
RUO Index	Russell 2000 Growth	1455.25	2,015,691	0.45	143.91	6.06	2.77	42.33	45.71	56.69	-16.49
NDX Index	NASDAQ 100	12888.28	15,083,854	0.76	37.89	8.29	5.21	22.11	21.39	22.24	340.16
W5000 Index	Wilshire 5000	39456.66	N.A.	2.02	N.A.	N.A.	N.A.	N.A.	N.A.	N.A.	N.A.
INDU Index	Dow Jones*	30606.48	9,607,422	2.02	27.12	4.71	2.46	15.47	14.27	17.89	1128.64

Note: The benchmark statistics were computed for December 2020. The data and tickers were obtained from Bloomberg, and the calculations are also from Bloomberg. S_t is the value of the index at the end of 2020. SIZE is the market capitalization (in millions) of each company computed as the end-of-year number of shares outstanding times the end-of-year stock price. DY is the sum of gross dividend-per-share payments over the last 12 months divided by the current stock price. P/E is the relationship between the price of a stock and its earnings per share, calculated as stock price divided by earnings per share. Earnings per share is calculated on a trailing 12-month basis (the most recent four quarters), when data are available. If quarterly figures are not available, the P/E is based on annual earnings or on the earnings of the most recent two semiannual reports. Historically, the P/E ratio field uses the trailing 12-month diluted EPS from continuing operations. P/B is the index value divided by book value per share of the index. P/S is the index value divided by the index sales figure. The index sales figure is calculated by summing the products of the sales per share of the member companies and their stock weights in the index and dividing the total by the index divisor. P/CF is the ratio of a stock's price divided by the cash flow per share. Average shares outstanding are used when calculating cash flow per share. Cash flow per share is calculated on a trailing 12-month basis when data are available. Trailing values are calculated by summing the most recent four quarters. P/EBITDA is price divided by EBITDA per share. EBITDA equals operating income plus depreciation and amortization. EBITDA per share is calculated on a trailing 12-month basis when data are available. Trailing values are calculated by adding the most recent four quarters. EV/EBITDA is the enterprise value of the firm divided by EBITDA. EPS (before extraordinary items) is the composite earnings of the index, calculated by summing the products of the trailing 12-month EPS (before extraordinary items) of the member companies and their shares outstanding and dividing the total by the index divisor.
*The Dow Jones Industrial Index.

underlying futures. Table 16.7 shows that the most popular benchmark is the S&P 500.[23]

The S&P 500 was the first benchmark embraced by investors, and it remained popular because of the liquidity of its securities and futures, because it was more manageable as a benchmark than

TABLE 16.7

Most Popular Benchmarks for Global Equity Managers in 2021

Benchmark	AUM ($ Million)	Percent of Equity Assets	Strategies	Percent of Equity Strategies
S&P 500	7,955,085	29.27	943	14.12
S&P 400	213,429	0.79	43	0.64
S&P 600	104,332	0.38	24	0.36
S&P 1500	60,313	0.22	21	0.31
S&P 500 Value[a]	0	0.00	0	0.00
S&P 500 Growth	51,021	0.19	9	0.13
Russell 3000	519,431	1.91	165	2.47
Russell 2000	558,036	2.05	293	4.39
Russell 1000	629,942	2.32	151	2.26
Russell 3000 Value	99,759	0.37	77	1.15
Russell 3000 Growth	317,674	1.17	59	0.88
Russell 1000 Value	1,563,349	5.75	394	5.90
Russell 1000 Growth	1,847,997	6.80	287	4.30
Russell 2000 Value	373,600	1.37	249	3.73
Russell 2000 Growth	460,027	1.69	195	2.92
NASDAQ 100	269,646	0.99	11	0.16
Wilshire 5000[b]	0	0.00	0	0.00
Dow Jones Industrial Average[c]	0	0.00	0	0.00
MSCI Global with U.S. Benchmarks	4,176,594	15.37	1230	18.42
MSCI Non-U.S. Benchmarks	5,847,813	21.52	1723	25.81
Other	2,127,598	7.83	803	12.03
Total	27,175,646	100	6,677	100

Note: These data were obtained from eVestment, a market-leading database for investment manager information. We screened for benchmarks that had at least $50 billion in AUM managed to them and deleted benchmarks that had very few strategies managed to them to eliminate potentially erroneous data.
[a] The S&P 500 Value had $48 billion in AUM, but because it was lower than our cutoff of $50B, it has a zero in the table.
[b] The Wilshire actually had $72 billion in AUM but was dropped because it had only 2 strategies following it.
[c] The Dow Jones Industrial Average had $91 million in AUM but was dropped because only 3 strategies followed it. These numbers would still make its percentage very close to zero.

---

[23] Since this list contains international benchmarks, like MSCI, if one wants to know the relative use of these benchmarks for U.S.-only benchmarks, one can compute the relative percentage after removing the MSCI component. For example, if one does this, the relative percentage of S&P 500 used as a domestic benchmark is 53% for AUM and 32% for strategies.

indices containing thousands of stocks, and because of its brand recognition, which gave managers the sense that they were measuring themselves against the same benchmark that their peers were. The main drawback to the S&P 500 is that the popularity of the index as a benchmark may create distortions in its returns. If enough index managers make trades that mirror changes in the index, the traded securities' prices will fluctuate simply as a result of being added or dropped from the index.

Like many other portfolio managers, we chose to use the S&P 500 as the benchmark for our backtesting example. Our choice was determined partly by data availability. Having several benchmarks would have allowed us to compare the performance of our portfolios with various types of indices: large-cap, small-cap, value, and growth. The difficulty of obtaining sufficient data for multiple comparisons, however, obliged us to choose only one benchmark. Benchmarking with the S&P 500 made sense for a number of reasons. As the most popular benchmark used by portfolio managers, it is likely quite familiar to our readers. It is also highly correlated with many of the other major equity benchmarks. It has the most liquid futures contracts available for trading, which is useful when we consider leverage. From a practical standpoint, the fact that the Compustat database has a flag to identify each S&P 500 stock in every month of our historical data made it fairly easy for us to construct the benchmark historically for optimizations and other analyses. Finally, although we use the S&P 500 as our benchmark, we allow our investment universe to be any of the top 1,500 stocks in the United States by market capitalization.[24]

---

[24] We considered using the Russell 3000 as our benchmark because it is representative of the larger market. However, our data source does not have a flag indicating every stock included in the Russell 3000 historically, and tickers and CUSIPs are recycled. Even with a list of distinct, historical Russell 3000 tickers, if we searched for these tickers in our data set, we might not find them. Our next natural choice of benchmark was the S&P 1500 Composite, which combines the S&P 500, 400, and 600. For no particular reason, we did not choose this as our benchmark. Alternatively, we could have created a custom benchmark closely related to the Russell 3000. That is, for every year of data, we could have ranked all the stocks in the United States by market capitalization and called that group of stocks our benchmark. We would have rerun this ranking, just as Russell does, for every year of data and created a customized benchmark related to the well-known Russell 3000.

16.5 THE FACTORS

We discussed factor choice at length in Chapter 4. In this section we list factors that we think might be important in explaining stock returns and in generating α^B. We also show statistics on the significance of various factors.

Before testing factors, the data need to be organized and cleaned. All researchers know the immense challenges of data organization and cleaning. There are really three steps in preparing the data for use in testing. The first is to check the general consistency and accuracy of the data. Are all the financial variables for each stock computed correctly, or are there some clear data errors? Errors could include ratios that are glaringly off (e.g., an earnings-to-price ratio of 0.000002) or, harder to detect, ratios computed with erroneous inputs. The second step is to check that the data are recorded as of the correct dates. Some data vendors record earnings per share (EPS) as of the quarter in which they were earned even though they were not reported until a few months after the quarter ended. This creates *look-ahead bias*. Any data recorded this way should be moved to the month in which it actually became available to the public. The third step in preparing the data is the arduous task of *data organization*, which includes anything else necessary to get the data in the right shape to be read into the model and portfolio-building software. One problem encountered at this point is *survivorship bias*. Owing to mergers, acquisitions, delistings, bankruptcies, and other events, some stocks that existed in the past do not exist today. If a backtest uses only data on stocks that exist today, the results of the test will be biased, usually upward. A backtest always should include all the data available on any stock that meets the investment universe criteria on any given date. Some databases, such as CRSP, provide returns of extinct stocks based on their likely selling prices (i.e., the prices at which investors actually would have been able to sell shares back to the company or to creditors). If the portfolio manager does not have access to a database with these sorts of estimated returns, he or she will have to make up his or her own sensible rules for dealing with extinct stocks in the backtest.

To begin the factor testing for our backtest, we considered some of the most important factors that might be related to stock returns. Our initial selection of factors, drawn from the factors described in Chapter 4, was based on theoretical reasoning. In Table 16.8, we name the factors we chose, the reason for choosing

TABLE 16.8

Initial Factor Choices

Factor	Reason	Ex-Ante Sign
Fundamental—Valuation		
1. Dividend Yield (DY)	The rationale is that stocks trading at high dividend yields may have had recent drops in price, which led to overreaction from investors. Also, these stocks are trading at cheaper prices versus valuation criteria.	+
2. EBITDA-to-EV (EBITDAEV)	Same	+
3. Book-to-Price (B/P)	Same	+
4. Cash Flow-to-Price (CF/P)	Same	+
5. Earnings-to-Price (E/P)	Same	+
6. EBITDA-to-Price (EBITDAP)	Same	+
7. E/P times Historical Earnings Growth (IPEGH)	Same	+
8. E/P times Forecasted Earnings Growth (IPEGF)	Same	+
9. E/P times Growth plus Yield (IPEGY)	Same	+
10. Sales-to-Price (S/P)	Same	+
Fundamental—Size		
11. Log of Common Equity (LOGCE)	Smaller firms might offer a premium because they are less followed, hence relatively less efficiently priced relative to larger stocks.	−
12. Equity Growth (LOGCEG)	Growing companies might be good investments.	−
13. Long-Term Equity Growth (LLOGCEG)	Same as (12)	−
14. Log of Market Capitalization (LOGSIZE)	Same as (11)	−
15. Log of Total Assets (LOGTA)	Same as (11)	−
16. Asset Growth (LOGTAG)	Same as (12)	−
17. Long-Term Asset Growth (LLOGTAG)	Same as (12)	−
Fundamental—Operating Efficiency		
18. Cash Conversion Cycle (CCC)	Higher values can be a sign of efficient cash management and power in industry.	−
19. CCC minus Industry Average (CCCX)	Same	−
20. Annual Change in Cash Conversion Cycle (CCCD)	Same	−

TABLE 16.8 *(Continued)*

Fundamental—Operating Efficiency

21. Cost Management Index (CMI)	Higher values can be a sign of less efficient management.	−
22. CMI minus Industry Average (CMIX)	Same	−
23. Cost Management Index (CMI)	Same	−
23. Annual Change in CMI (CMID)	Same	−
24. Equity Turnover (ET)	Higher and rising values can be signs of efficient management of firm's equity.	+
25. ET minus Industry Average (ETX)	Same	+
26. Annual Change in ET (ETD)	Same	+
27. Fixed Asset Turnover (FAT)	A higher ratio might mean more efficient use of assets.	+
28. FAT minus Industry Average (FATX)	Same	+
29. Annual Change in FAT (FATD)	Same	+
30. Inventory Turnover (IT)	A higher ratio means a business is more efficient at distributing goods. Depends on industry, and sometimes, higher isn't better.	+
31. IT minus Industry Average (ITX)	Same	+
32. Annual Change in Inventory Turnover (ITD)	Same	+
33. Receivables Turnover (RT)	May measure the effectiveness of firm's credit policies.	+
34. RT minus Industry Average (RTX)	Same	+
35. Annual Change in Receivables Turnover (RTD)	Same	+
36. Total Asset Turnover (TAT)	Measures how efficiently assets are managed by firm. Filtering of these data may catch firms neglected by others.	+
37. TAT minus Industry Average (TATX)	Same	+
38. Annual Change in TAT (TATD)	Same	+

Fundamental—Operating Profitability

39. Current Accruals (CACC)	We might expect firms with lower accruals and a higher cash-flow component of profits to be more reliable.	−
40. Total Accruals (TACC)	Same	−
41. Cash Flow to Total Assets (CFTA)	Same	+
42. Cash Flow to Total Sales (CFTS)	Same	+
43. Gross Profit Margin (GPM)	Profits ultimately produce returns to investing. Ultimately, we want to identify companies with high current and future profit margins not expected by others.	+

44. Annual Change in GPM (GPMD)	Same	+
45. Gross Profit Growth (GPG)	Same	+
46. Long-Term Gross Profit Growth (LGPG)	Same	+
47. Gross Profit to Total Assets (GPTA)	Same	+
48. Net Profit Margin (NPM)	Same	+
49. Annual Change in NPM (NPMD)	Same	+
50. Net Profit Growth (NPG)	Same	+
51. Long-Term Net Profit Growth (LNPG)	Same	+
52. Net Profit to Total Assets (NPTA)	Same	+
53. Operating Profit Margin (OPM)	Same	+
54. Annual Change in OPM (OPMD)	Same	+
55. Operating Profit Growth (OPG)	Same	+
56. Long-Term Operating Profit Growth (LOPG)	Same	+
57. Operating Profit to Total Assets (OPTA)	Same	+
58. Return on Assets (ROA)	Same	+
59. Return on Common Equity (ROCE)	Same	+
60. Return on Owner's Equity (ROE)	Same	+
61. Return on Total Capital (ROTC)	Same	+
Fundamental—Solvency		
62. Cash-Flow-From-Operations Ratio (CFOR)	Indicator of financial solvency of a firm. Firms with stronger ratios won't blow up during stressful times.	+
63. Annual Change in Cash-Flow-From-Operations Ratio (CFORD)	Companies with improving ratios may be an early indicator of better times ahead.	+
64. Cash Ratio (CR)	Same as (62)	+
65. Annual Change in Cash Ratio (CRD)	Same as (63)	+
66. Current Ratio (CUR)	Same as (62)	+
67. Annual Change in the Current Ratio (CURD)	Same as (63)	+
68. Quick Ratio (QR)	Same as (62)	+
69. Annual Change in the Quick Ratio (QRD)	Same as (63)	+
Fundamental—Financial Risk		
70. Inverse Cash-Flow Coverage Ratio (ICFCR)	Higher cash-flow coverage ratio is better, thus higher inverse CFCR is worse.	−
71. ICFCR minus Industry Average (ICFCRX)	Same	−
72. Annual Change in ICFCR (ICFCRD)	Same	−
73. Debt-to-Equity (D/E)	Higher debt/interest payments pose greater risk to equity holders of firms, and may make it hard for good companies to withstand troubled times.	−
74. DE minus Industry Average (DEX)	Same	−
75. Annual Change in DE (DED)	Same	−
76. Financial Leverage Ratio (FLR)	Same	−
77. FLR minus Industry Average (FLRX)	Same	−

TABLE 16.8 *(Continued)*

Fundamental—Financial Risk		
78. Annual Change in FLR (FLRD)	Same	−
79. Inverse Interest Coverage Ratio (IICR)	Higher interest coverage ratio is better, thus higher inverse ICR is worse.	−
80. IICR minus Industry Average (IICRX)	Same	−
81. Annual Change in IICR (IICRD)	Same	−
82. Total Debt Ratio (TDR)	Higher debt/interest payments pose greater risk to equity holders of firms, and may make it hard for good companies to withstand troubled times.	−
83. TDR minus Industry Average (TDRX)	Same	−
84. Annual Change in TDR (TDRD)	Same	−
Fundamental—Corporate Activity		
85. Stock Buybacks (SB)	Management likes company or is being responsible with its cash.	+
86. R&D to Sales (RNDS)	Might indicate a company that is preparing for future growth, which short-term investors neglect.	+
87. The Change in R&D to Sales (RNDSD)	Same	+
Technical—Liquidity Risk		
88. Amihud Illiquidity (AILIQ)	Illiquidity might pay a premium in equilibrium, but not necessarily. This is a measure of illiquidity.	+
89. Crowding Analysts (CROWDA)	Higher crowding might indicate more risk and lower future returns.	−
90. Crowding Value (CROWDV)	Same as (89)	−
91. Invariance Illiquidity (INVIL)	Higher illiquidity might pay a premium. This is an illiquidity measure.	+
92. Modified Amihud Iliquidity (MAILIQ)	Same	+
93. Pastor and Stambaugh Liquidity (PSL)	This is a macro factor and one must measure a firm's exposure to the factor. Higher exposure is more negative for expected return.	−
94. Trading Turnover (TT)	Higher trading turnover is a sign of a more liquid stock.	−

Technical—Price Based

95. Beta (BETA) / Market (MKT)	Technical indicators may help over a one-month rebalancing horizon, since they have the ability to capture information dispersion faster than fundamental data. Secondly, if enough traders follow these indicators, they may cause a self-fulfilling prophecy in the short run. Beta could be positive (if you believe the CAPM) or negative if you think the CAPM isn't a good enough model of stock returns.	+
96. Bollinger Bands (BB)	Same	−
97. Channel Breakouts (CB)	Same	+
98. One-Month Momentum (M1M)	Same	+
99. Three-Month Momentum (M3M)	Same	+
100. Six-Month Momentum (M6M)	Same	+
101. Nine-Month Momentum (M9M)	Same	+
102. Nine-Month Momentum Lag 1 (M9ML1)	Same	+
103. Twelve-Month Momentum (M12M)	Same	+
104. Moving Average (MA)	Same	+
105. Moving Average Convergence-Divergence Indicator (MACD)	Same	+
106. Price (P)	Same	−
107. Relative Strength Index (RSI)	Same	−
108. Support Resistance (SR)	Same	+
109. Volatility (VOL)	Same	−

Technical—Volume Based

110. Odd-Lot Balance (OLBI)[†]	Same	−
111. On-Balance Volume (OBV)	Same	+
112. Short-Interest Ratio (SIR)	Same	~
113. SIR minus SIR One-Year Average (SIRX)	Same	~
114. Volume Lead (VL)	Same	−

Technical—Overall Market Movement

115. Advance–Decline Ratio (ADR)	A high value of the ADR might indicate an overbought market and a stock with high exposure to this might indicate a sell and vice versa.	−

TABLE 16.8 *(Continued)*

	Technical—Overall Market Movement	
116. Arms Index (ARMS)	Many analysts believe that a value that is less than one (or lower value) is a bullish signal as there is more volume in the average up stock versus the average down stock. A value of greater than one (or higher) is perceived as a bearish signal as there is more volume in the average down stock versus the average up stock.	−
117. Upside–Downside Ratio (UDR)	Same	+
118. Upside–Downside Volume (UDV)	Same	+
	Economic	
119. Consumption Growth (PCG)	Macro variables are the original APT factors and sources of underlying risks to the entire economy. Survey forecast changes may capture information faster than actual economic data. The exposure of stocks to these factors will provide different types of return in equilibrium.	+
120. PC Revision (PCR)	Same as (119)	+
121. Consumer Confidence Growth (CCG)	Same as (119)	+
122. Consumer Sentiment Growth (CSG)	Same as (119)	+
123. Change in Commodity Index (CIG)	Same as (119)	+
124. BBB Spread (BBBS)	Firms that provide hedges against adverse events might be expected to have lower returns in equilibrium.	−
125. Change in BBB Spread (BBBSD)	Same as (124)	−
126. Swap Spread (SS)	Same as (124)	−
127. Change in Swap Spread (SSD)	Same as (124)	−
128. Industrial Production (IPG)	Same as (119)	+
129. IP Revision (IPR)	Same as (119)	+
130. Business Confidence Growth (BCG)	Same as (119)	+
131. Inflation (CPIG)	Same as (119)	+
132. Real GDP Growth (GDPG)	Same as (119)	+
133. Real GDP Revision (GDPR)	Same as (119)	+
134. Real GDP Surprise (GDPS)	Same as (119)	+
135. Ten-Two-Year Term Premium (TP2Y)	Same as (119)	−
136. Ten Year-Three-Month Term Premium (TP3M)	Same as (119)	−

| 137. Unemployment (UR) | Firms that provide hedges against adverse events might be expected to have lower returns in equilibrium. | − |
| 138. Change in Unemployment (URD) | Same as (137) | − |

Alternative—Analysts

139. Analyst Rating—Median Rating (ARMR)	Analysts study companies in detail and their opinions contain valuable information about stock returns.	+
140. Analyst Rating—Percent Buys (ARPB)	Same as (139)	+
141. Analyst Rating—Percent Sells (ARPS)	Same as (139)	−
142. Analyst Rating—SD of Ratings (ARSD)	It's not clear how the divergence of opinions will affect individual stock prices. Some believe divergence will lead to higher ex-post returns on average.	+
143. Analyst Rating—Percent Downgrades (ARPD)	Same as (139)	−
144. Analyst Rating—Percent Upgrades (ARPU)	Same as (139)	+
145. Analyst Rating—Median Change (ARMD)	Same as (139)	+
146. EPS Forecast—Normalized SD (EPSSD)	It's not clear how the divergence of opinions will affect individual stock prices. Some believe divergence will lead to higher ex-post returns on average.	+
147. EPS Revision—Percent Downward (EPSFPD)	Same as (139)	−
148. EPS Revision—Percent Upward (EPSFPU)	Same as (139)	+
149. Number of Analysts (EPSFN)	However, if many analysts follow a stock, this might be an indicator of a very reliable or efficient price.	−
150. Standardized Unanticipated Earnings (SUE)	Earnings surprises may have an effect on future stock returns due to behavioral biases and inattention.	+

Alternative—Socially Responsible

151. Community Contribution (CC)	Some social criteria provide insights into how a company is run. They may also influence short-term stock price due to taste buying or selling.	+
152. CC minus Industry Average (CCX)	Same	+
153. Corporate Governance (CG)	Same	+
154. CG minus Industry Average (CGX)	Same	+

TABLE 16.8 *(Continued)*

Alternative—Socially Responsible		
155. Diversity (DIV)	Same	~
156. DIV minus Industry Average (DIVX)	Same	~
157. Employee Relations (ER)	Same	+
158. ER minus Industry Average (ERX)	Same	+
159. Environment (E)	Same	~
160. E minus Industry Average (EX)	Same	~
161. Human Rights (HR)	Same	~
162. HR minus Industry Average (HRX)	Same	~
163. Product (PRO)	Same	+
164. PRO minus Industry Average (PROX)	Same	+

Note: A "+" indicates that we believe a high value of this variable will increase stock returns. A "−" indicates that we believe a high value of this variable will decrease stock returns. A "~" indicates that we do not have an opinion ex ante about how stock returns will respond to this variable.

them, and our ex-ante belief about how they relate to the cross section of stock returns in the fundamental factor model.[25]

In order to test the factors, we first created programs that computed the historical factor exposures for every stock in our database. We ran these programs at monthly intervals to create a historical series of monthly factor exposures for each stock, all the while being vigilant about look-ahead bias. The historical book-to-price (B/P) ratios, for example, were computed by dividing each company's total common equity by the product of the company's price per share and the number of shares outstanding. For common equity, we allowed for a lag in reporting of three months, so we searched for the book value as reported three months prior to the month for which we created the B/P ratio. For a detailed description of all our factor formulas, see Tables 16A.1 to 16A.13 in Appendix 16A.

For macroeconomic factor exposures, the computation was slightly more complicated. We first collected the premium for all of the macroeconomic factors, again avoiding look-ahead bias by taking into account the appropriate lags in the reporting of indicators.

---

[25] The relationship between factors and returns is easier to describe for the fundamental factor model than for the economic factor model. For the fundamental factor model, we can describe the relationship in terms of the sign of the estimated factor premium; for the economic factor model, the sign of the estimated factor exposure varies from stock to stock. For some factors, we were unsure what the sign should be. These were given an ambiguous signal.

For example, to create the monthly inflation variable for a given month, we divided the consumer price index (CPI) of the previous month by the CPI of two months prior and subtracted 1 from that value. This avoids look-ahead bias by recognizing the one-month delay in CPI releases. This type of logic was applied to all our macroeconomic variables so that we created a time series of macroeconomic factors that would have been available at the end of each month. We then ran individual regressions of each stock's monthly returns against each monthly economic factor up to 60 months and no less than 12 months. We required all the stocks in our investment universe in month t to have at least a 12-month return history. Thus, we were able to calculate factor exposures for all the stocks in our investment universe. To keep the estimates fresh, we constructed the factor exposures on a rolling basis for each month looking back a maximum of four years.

The resulting factor exposures give us a direct relationship between factor values and stock returns. For example, the factor exposure of Boston Beer Company (SAM) to GDP growth each year was mostly negative in recent periods. The estimate for December 2020 was -1.145. If GDP growth for the quarter prior to December 2020 was 1%, then the expected return on the stock would be -1.145% (ignoring the constant term). Similarly, if GDP growth for the prior quarter was -1%, we would expect the stock price to have gone up by 1.145%. The negative exposure fits with the intuition that SAM is a defensive stock. There were some outliers in the factor exposure estimates as well. Some practitioners will carefully remove these outliers; instead we chose not to remove the extreme observations in our backtests.[26] One outlier that sticks out in the data is Eastman Kodak (KODK). The stock has an exposure to GDP growth of -18.857 due to the extreme volatility in July and August of 2020. This volatility was related to the news that the U.S. government wanted the firm to produce pharmaceutical components to fight the pandemic (although they never actually ended up doing this).

Once we created the factor exposures for every stock per month, we wrote programs to perform the factor tests using simple single-factor regressions and testing the returns of unidimensional zero-investment portfolios, as explained in Chapter 4. The results of these factor tests are shown in Table 16.9. Since the out-of-sample time period was 2011–2020, we could use only the years

---

[26] Econometricians say that all the information is in the outliers, anyway.

prior to 2011 to perform our initial factor tests. We chose to concentrate on factor tests for the five-year period from 2006–2010.

The astute reader will notice that out of 164 factors listed in Table 16.9, one factor is missing in Table 16.9. The odd-lot balance factor (numbered 110) is not included for factor testing as the underlying data for this factor were only available beginning in 2012. In Appendix 16B, we report factor tests for different time periods, and in some of those tests we include the odd-lot balance factor.[27]

With the results in Table 16.9, we proceeded to select the factors for our stock return models.[28] We selected two sets of factors, one set to build a fundamental factor model and another set to build an economic factor model. We also constructed a Z-score model, for which we used the same set of factors that we used for the fundamental factor model. Our selection proceeded as follows.

First, we checked whether the return-exposure regression coefficient $\hat{\beta}$ sign (positive or negative) was in accordance with what we expected from theory and whether it was statistically significant. Only when the sign of the coefficient corresponded with our ex-ante theoretical beliefs shown in Table 16.8, and the absolute value of the associated t-statistic was greater than 1.64, did we keep the factor as a candidate for the fundamental factor model. Out of 163 factors (164 factors less the odd-lot balance factor), only the following 19 factors satisfied our requirements: EBITDA-to-EV (EBITDAEV), long-term asset growth (LTAG), annual change in ET (ETD), total asset turnover (TAT), TAT minus industry average (TATX), annual change in TAT (TATD), total accruals (TACC), cash flow to total assets (CFTA), gross profit to total assets (GPTA), return on common equity (ROCE), return on owner's equity (ROE), return on total capital (ROTC), cash-flow-from-operations ratio (CFOR), inverse cash-flow coverage ratio (ICFCR), annual change in D/E (DED), Pastor and Stambaugh liquidity (PSL), Bollinger bands (BB), consumer confidence growth (CCG), business confidence growth (BCG), and standardized unanticipated earnings (SUE). As for an economic factor model, we determined the candidate factors based on the zero-investment portfolio return r_{ZI} and the associated t-statistic. We kept a factor as a

---

[27] Appendix 16B can be found under Chapter Appendices at https://ludwigbc.com/ books/qepm/ exclusive_qepm_content_2020/ or at www.ludwigbc.com and look for QEPM Exclusive Content.

[28] We did not consider the MSCI-KLD socially responsible factors for this exercise, because we only had data through 2018, while our testing period extends through 2020.

TABLE 16.9

Results of Factor Analysis from 2006–2010

Factor	Obs.	Beg. Period	End Period	$\hat{\beta}$	t-stat	r_{ZI}	t-stat
Fundamental—Valuation							
1. Dividend Yield (DY)	60	Jan 2006	Dec 2010	−0.720	−0.202	−0.250	−0.700
2. EBITDA-to-EV (EBITDAEV)	60	Jan 2006	Dec 2010	3.790	2.590	0.877	2.367
3. Book-to-Price (B/P)	60	Jan 2006	Dec 2010	−0.265	−1.251	0.283	0.557
4. Cash Flow-to-Price (CF/P)	60	Jan 2006	Dec 2010	0.344	1.427	0.565	1.345
5. Earnings-to-Price (E/P)	60	Jan 2006	Dec 2010	0.597	1.475	−0.163	−0.451
6. EBITDA-to-Price (EBITDAP)	60	Jan 2006	Dec 2010	−0.211	−0.380	0.558	1.169
7. E/P times Historical Earnings Growth (IPEGH)	60	Jan 2006	Dec 2010	−0.000	−0.606	0.290	0.812
8. E/P times Forecasted Earnings Growth (IPEGF)	60	Jan 2006	Dec 2010	0.037	0.255	0.195	0.529
9. E/P times Growth plus Yield (IPEGY)	60	Jan 2006	Dec 2010	0.004	0.034	0.133	0.346
10. Sales-to-Price (S/P)	60	Jan 2006	Dec 2010	0.070	0.782	0.763	1.291
Fundamental—Size							
11. Log of Common Equity (LOGCE)	60	Jan 2006	Dec 2010	0.005	0.066	0.065	0.222
12. Equity Growth (LOGCEG)	60	Jan 2006	Dec 2010	−0.043	−1.385	−0.347	−1.078
13. Long-Term Equity Growth (LLOGCEG)	60	Jan 2006	Dec 2010	−0.009	−1.521	−0.349	−1.504
14. Log of Market Capitalization (LOGSIZE)	60	Jan 2006	Dec 2010	−0.045	−0.411	−0.086	−0.207
15. Log of Total Assets (LOGTA)	60	Jan 2006	Dec 2010	−0.034	−0.421	−0.172	−0.526
16. Asset Growth (LOGTAG)	60	Jan 2006	Dec 2010	−0.214	−1.504	−0.464	−1.505
17. Long-Term Asset Growth (LLOGTAG)	60	Jan 2006	Dec 2010	−0.024	−1.955	−0.266	−1.203

TABLE 16.9 (Continued)

				Fundamental—Operating Efficiency			
18. Cash Conversion Cycle (CCC)	60	Jan 2006	Dec 2010	0.000	0.902	0.705	2.423
19. CCC minus Industry Average (CCCX)	60	Jan 2006	Dec 2010	-0.000	-1.033	0.261	1.697
20. Annual Change in Cash Conversion Cycle (CCCD)	60	Jan 2006	Dec 2010	-0.000	-1.259	-0.118	-0.456
21. Cost Management Index (CMI)	60	Jan 2006	Dec 2010	0.001	1.826	0.549	1.514
22. CMI minus Industry Average (CMIX)	60	Jan 2006	Dec 2010	0.001	1.428	-0.106	-0.360
23. Annual Change in CMI (CMID)	60	Jan 2006	Dec 2010	0.001	1.365	0.357	0.976
24. Equity Turnover (ET)	60	Jan 2006	Dec 2010	0.018	1.268	0.584	2.093
25. ET minus Industry Average (ETX)	60	Jan 2006	Dec 2010	0.005	0.366	-0.099	-0.541
26. Annual Change in ET (ETD)	60	Jan 2006	Dec 2010	0.041	1.671	0.185	1.051
27. Fixed Asset Turnover (FAT)	60	Jan 2006	Dec 2010	-0.001	-0.323	-0.083	-0.326
28. FAT minus Industry Average (FATX)	60	Jan 2006	Dec 2010	0.000	0.286	0.397	2.112
29. Annual Change in FAT (FATD)	60	Jan 2006	Dec 2010	0.001	0.477	0.012	0.065
30. Inventory Turnover (IT)	60	Jan 2006	Dec 2010	-0.000	-0.489	-0.245	-1.526
31. IT minus Industry Average (ITX)	60	Jan 2006	Dec 2010	0.000	0.245	0.356	1.253
32. Annual Change in Inventory Turnover (ITD)	60	Jan 2006	Dec 2010	0.000	0.184	-0.006	-0.044
33. Receivables Turnover (RT)	60	Jan 2006	Dec 2010	0.001	0.910	0.321	1.433
34. RT minus Industry Average (RTX)	60	Jan 2006	Dec 2010	0.001	0.744	0.048	0.240
35. Annual Change in Receivables Turnover (RTD)	60	Jan 2006	Dec 2010	-0.002	-0.786	-0.068	-0.447
36. Total Asset Turnover (TAT)	60	Jan 2006	Dec 2010	0.296	2.700	0.782	2.959
37. TAT minus Industry Average (TATX)	60	Jan 2006	Dec 2010	0.192	2.020	0.256	1.379
38. Annual Change in TAT (TATD)	60	Jan 2006	Dec 2010	0.491	2.170	0.291	1.663

622

Fundamental—Operating Profitability

#	Metric							
39.	Current Accruals (CACC)	60	Jan 2006	Dec 2010	−1.107	−1.217	−0.287	−1.499
40.	Total Accruals (TACC)	60	Jan 2006	Dec 2010	−0.968	−1.920	−0.174	−0.625
41.	Cash Flow to Total Assets (CFTA)	60	Jan 2006	Dec 2010	1.572	2.190	0.653	2.069
42.	Cash Flow to Total Sales (CFTS)	60	Jan 2006	Dec 2010	0.001	1.135	−0.154	−0.516
43.	Gross Profit Margin (GPM)	60	Jan 2006	Dec 2010	0.002	1.146	−0.107	−0.388
44.	Annual Change in GPM (GPMD)	60	Jan 2006	Dec 2010	−0.002	−0.651	−0.057	−0.232
45.	Gross Profit Growth (GPG)	60	Jan 2006	Dec 2010	0.022	1.312	−0.238	−0.662
46.	Long-Term Gross Profit Growth (LGPG)	60	Jan 2006	Dec 2010	0.001	0.994	0.029	0.086
47.	Gross Profit to Total Assets (GPTA)	60	Jan 2006	Dec 2010	0.884	2.579	0.736	2.706
48.	Net Profit Margin (NPM)	60	Jan 2006	Dec 2010	0.001	0.942	−0.367	−0.786
49.	Annual Change in NPM (NPMD)	60	Jan 2006	Dec 2010	−0.003	−0.745	−0.278	−0.852
50.	Net Profit Growth (NPG)	60	Jan 2006	Dec 2010	0.000	0.028	−0.301	−1.035
51.	Long-Term Net Profit Growth (LNPG)	60	Jan 2006	Dec 2010	0.000	0.121	0.119	0.348
52.	Net Profit to Total Assets (NPTA)	60	Jan 2006	Dec 2010	0.769	1.228	0.047	0.107
53.	Operating Profit Margin (OPM)	60	Jan 2006	Dec 2010	0.001	1.107	−0.294	−0.854
54.	Annual Change in OPM (OPMD)	60	Jan 2006	Dec 2010	−0.002	−0.633	−0.141	−0.434
55.	Operating Profit Growth (OPG)	60	Jan 2006	Dec 2010	−0.042	−1.340	−0.377	−1.020
56.	Long-Term Operating Profit Growth (LOPG)	60	Jan 2006	Dec 2010	−0.000	−0.061	−0.008	−0.022
57.	Operating Profit to Total Assets (OPTA)	60	Jan 2006	Dec 2010	1.000	1.558	0.556	1.637
58.	Return on Assets (ROA)	60	Jan 2006	Dec 2010	0.786	1.240	0.336	1.008
59.	Return on Common Equity (ROCE)	60	Jan 2006	Dec 2010	0.057	1.792	−0.192	−0.507
60.	Return on Owner's Equity (ROE)	60	Jan 2006	Dec 2010	0.081	2.283	−0.179	−0.470
61.	Return on Total Capital (ROTC)	60	Jan 2006	Dec 2010	0.559	1.895	0.210	0.657

TABLE 16.9 (Continued)

Fundamental—Solvency

62. Cash-Flow-From-Operations Ratio (CFOR)	60	Jan 2006	Dec 2010	0.139	1.684	−0.004	−0.015
63. Annual Change in Cash-Flow-From-Operations Ratio (CFORD)	60	Jan 2006	Dec 2010	−0.082	−1.395	−0.158	−1.064
64. Cash Ratio (CR)	60	Jan 2006	Dec 2010	−0.075	−1.675	−0.251	−0.825
65. Annual Change in Cash Ratio (CRD)	60	Jan 2006	Dec 2010	0.026	0.932	0.039	0.342
66. Current Ratio (CUR)	60	Jan 2006	Dec 2010	−0.047	−1.415	−0.086	−0.376
67. Annual Change in the Current Ratio (CURD)	60	Jan 2006	Dec 2010	0.021	0.857	0.046	0.399
68. Quick Ratio (QR)	60	Jan 2006	Dec 2010	−0.063	−1.598	−0.162	−0.586
69. Annual Change in the Quick Ratio (QRD)	60	Jan 2006	Dec 2010	0.022	0.852	0.018	0.158

Fundamental—Financial Risk

70. Inverse Cash-Flow Coverage Ratio (ICFCR)	60	Jan 2006	Dec 2010	−0.002	−1.878	−0.262	−0.797
71. ICFCR minus Industry Average (ICFCRX)	60	Jan 2006	Dec 2010	0.000	0.132	0.262	0.670
72. Annual Change in ICFCR (ICFCRD)	60	Jan 2006	Dec 2010	−0.000	−0.027	0.260	1.463
73. Debt-to-Equity (D/E)	60	Jan 2006	Dec 2010	−0.002	−0.427	−0.300	−0.862
74. D/E minus Industry Average (DEX)	60	Jan 2006	Dec 2010	−0.001	−0.368	−0.027	−0.125
75. Annual Change in D/E (DED)	60	Jan 2006	Dec 2010	−0.006	−2.210	0.193	0.942
76. Financial Leverage Ratio (FLR)	60	Jan 2006	Dec 2010	−0.002	−0.971	−0.297	−0.936
77. FLR minus Industry Average (FLRX)	60	Jan 2006	Dec 2010	−0.001	−0.902	−0.123	−0.655
78. Annual Change in FLR (FLRD)	60	Jan 2006	Dec 2010	−0.001	−1.318	0.098	0.551
79. Inverse Interest Coverage Ratio (IICR)	60	Jan 2006	Dec 2010	0.026	1.580	−0.071	−0.277
80. IICR minus Industry Average (IICRX)	60	Jan 2006	Dec 2010	0.024	1.418	0.095	0.406
81. Annual Change in IICR (IICRD)	60	Jan 2006	Dec 2010	−0.006	−0.827	0.273	1.241
82. Total Debt Ratio (TDR)	60	Jan 2006	Dec 2010	0.074	0.126	0.064	0.206
83. TDR minus Industry Average (TDRX)	60	Jan 2006	Dec 2010	−0.054	−0.089	−0.022	−0.071
84. Annual Change in TDR (TDRD)	60	Jan 2006	Dec 2010	0.763	1.036	0.226	0.977

Fundamental—Corporate Activity

85. Stock Buybacks (SB)	60	Jan 2006	Dec 2010	0.414	0.609	0.130	0.594
86. R&D to Sales (RNDS)	60	Jan 2006	Dec 2010	−0.002	−1.161	−0.093	−0.198
87. Change in R&D to Sales (RNDSD)	60	Jan 2006	Dec 2010	0.007	1.164	0.145	0.740

88. Amihud Illiquidity (AILIQ)	60	Jan 2006	Dec 2010	−0.042	−0.382	0.053	0.160
89. Crowding Analysts (CROWDA)	60	Jan 2006	Dec 2010	0.001	0.803	−0.228	−0.530
90. Crowding Value (CROWDV)	60	Jan 2006	Dec 2010	−0.021	−0.235	−0.381	−1.218
91. Invariance Illiquidity (INVIL)	60	Jan 2006	Dec 2010	−0.449	−0.170	0.073	0.208
92. Modified Amihud Iliquidity (MAILIQ)	60	Jan 2006	Dec 2010	−0.286	−0.466	0.040	0.121
93. Pastor and Stambaugh Liquidity (PSL)	60	Jan 2006	Dec 2010	0.115	1.690	0.612	1.820
94. Trading Turnover (TT)	60	Jan 2006	Dec 2010	−8.612	−0.614	−0.155	−0.418

Technical—Price Based

95. Beta (BETA)/Market (MKT)[a]	60	Jan 2006	Dec 2010	0.638	1.512	0.966	1.413
96. Bollinger Bands (BB)	60	Jan 2006	Dec 2010	−0.508	−2.412	−0.409	−2.008
97. Channel Breakouts (CB)	60	Jan 2006	Dec 2010	−0.255	−0.477	0.004	0.615
98. One-Month Momentum (M1M)	60	Jan 2006	Dec 2010	−1.318	−1.044	0.023	0.053
99. Three-Month Momentum (M3M)	60	Jan 2006	Dec 2010	0.596	0.664	0.183	0.352
100. Six-Month Momentum (M6M)	60	Jan 2006	Dec 2010	−0.467	−0.464	−0.325	−0.472
101. Nine-Month Momentum (M9M)	60	Jan 2006	Dec 2010	−0.510	−0.578	−0.253	−0.345
102. Nine-Month Momentum Lag 1 (M9ML1)	60	Jan 2006	Dec 2010	−0.643	−0.696	−0.257	−0.372
103. Twelve-Month Momentum (M12M)	60	Jan 2006	Dec 2010	−0.656	−0.827	−0.496	−0.647
104. Moving Average (MA)	60	Jan 2006	Dec 2010	−0.089	−0.512	0.040	0.180
105. Moving Average Convergence-Divergence Indicator (MACD)	60	Jan 2006	Dec 2010	0.000	0.495	0.436	0.754
106. Price (P)	60	Jan 2006	Dec 2010	−0.181	−0.656	−0.465	−0.777
107. Relative Strength Index (RSI)	60	Jan 2006	Dec 2010	−0.011	−1.013	−0.161	−0.722
108. Support Resistance (SR)	60	Jan 2006	Dec 2010	−0.611	−2.423	−0.224	−2.209
109. Volatility (VOL)	60	Jan 2006	Dec 2010	−7.438	−0.436	0.250	0.371

Technical—Volume Based

111. On-Balance Volume (OBV)	60	Jan 2006	Dec 2010	−0.172	−1.703	−0.210	−1.230
112. Short-Interest Ratio (SIR)	60	Jan 2006	Dec 2010	0.000	0.421	0.050	0.134
113. SIR minus SIR One Year-Average (SIRX)	60	Jan 2006	Dec 2010	−0.000	−0.865	−0.139	−0.680
114. Volume Lead (VL)	60	Jan 2006	Dec 2010	0.000	0.377	0.166	0.639

TABLE 16.9 (Continued)

	Technical—Overall Market Movement						
115. Advance-Decline Ratio (ADR)	60	Jan 2006	Dec 2010	11.354	1.398	0.745	1.230
116. Arms Index (ARMS)	60	Jan 2006	Dec 2010	-2.215	-1.081	-0.460	-1.281
117. Upside-Downside Ratio (UDR)	60	Jan 2006	Dec 2010	14.494	1.484	0.636	1.100
118. Upside-Downside Volume (UDV)	60	Jan 2006	Dec 2010	29.214	1.444	0.903	1.335
Economic							
119. Consumption Growth (PCG)	60	Jan 2006	Dec 2010	0.082	1.627	0.729	1.416
120. PC Revision (PCR)	60	Jan 2006	Dec 2010	0.139	1.589	0.511	1.557
121. Consumer Confidence (CCG)	60	Jan 2006	Dec 2010	1.370	1.845	0.689	1.484
122. Consumer Sentiment (CSG)	60	Jan 2006	Dec 2010	0.731	1.476	0.561	1.247
123. Change in Commodity Index (CIG)	60	Jan 2006	Dec 2010	0.695	1.283	0.861	1.386
124. BBB Spread (BBBS)	60	Jan 2006	Dec 2010	-0.118	-1.051	-0.574	-1.046
125. Change in BBB Spread (BBBSD)	60	Jan 2006	Dec 2010	-0.034	-1.408	-0.677	-1.071
126. Swap Spread (SS)	60	Jan 2006	Dec 2010	0.014	1.282	0.505	1.753
127. Change in Swap Spread (SSD)	60	Jan 2006	Dec 2010	0.026	1.989	0.753	1.971
128. Industrial Production (IPG)	60	Jan 2006	Dec 2010	0.134	1.474	0.691	1.287
129. IP Revision (IPR)	60	Jul 1961	Sep 1961	0.055	0.600	0.090	0.411
130. Business Confidence (BCG)	60	Jan 2006	Dec 2010	0.045	1.811	0.862	1.524
131. Inflation (CPIG)	60	Jan 2006	Dec 2010	0.036	1.596	0.522	1.721
132. Real GDP Growth (GDPG)	60	Jan 2006	Dec 2010	0.041	0.836	0.237	0.591
133. Real GDP Revision (GDPR)	60	Jan 2006	Dec 2010	0.013	0.483	0.058	0.193
134. Real GDP Surprise (GDPS)	60	Jan 2006	Dec 2010	0.045	0.780	0.208	0.539
135. Ten-Two Year-Term Premium (TP2Y)	60	Jan 2006	Dec 2010	-0.034	-0.759	-0.850	-1.833
136. Ten Year-Three Month Term Premium (TP3M)	60	Jan 2006	Dec 2010	-0.048	-0.699	-0.824	-1.839
137. Unemployment (UR)	60	Jan 2006	Dec 2010	0.002	0.034	-0.298	-0.693
138. Change in Unemployment (URD)	60	Jan 2006	Dec 2010	-0.012	-0.853	-0.361	-0.827

Alternative—Analysts

139. Analyst Rating—Median Rating (ARMR)	60	Jan 2006	Dec 2010	-0.027	-0.145	-0.005	-0.016
140. Analyst Rating—Percent Buys (ARPB)	60	Jan 2006	Dec 2010	0.107	0.213	0.007	0.020
141. Analyst Rating—Percent Sells (ARPS)	60	Jan 2006	Dec 2010	-0.906	-1.287	0.046	0.290
142. Analyst Rating—SD of Ratings (ARSD)	60	Jan 2006	Dec 2010	0.021	0.151	-0.013	-0.132
143. Analyst Rating—Percent Downgrades (ARPD)	60	Jan 2006	Dec 2010	0.146	0.201	-0.004	-0.137
144. Analyst Rating—Percent Upgrades (ARPU)	60	Jan 2006	Dec 2010	0.903	1.459	0.017	0.722
145. Analyst Rating—Median Change (ARMD)	60	Jan 2006	Dec 2010	-0.001	-0.007	-0.003	-0.190
146. EPS Forecast—Normalized SD (EPSSD)	60	Jan 2006	Dec 2010	-0.100	-1.153	-0.003	-0.008
147. EPS Revision—Percent Downward (EPSFPD)	60	Jan 2006	Dec 2010	-0.413	-1.133	-0.255	-0.878
148. EPS Revision—Percent Upward (EPSFPU)	60	Jan 2006	Dec 2010	0.413	1.133	0.255	0.878
149. Number of Analysts (EPSFN)	60	Jan 2006	Dec 2010	0.027	0.240	0.039	0.189
150. Standardized Unanticipated Earnings (SUE)	60	Jan 2006	Dec 2010	0.122	8.923	3.348	9.830

Alternative—Socially Responsible

151. Community Contribution (CC)	60	Jan 2006	Dec 2010	-0.009	-0.017	-0.006	-0.243
152. CC minus Industry Average (CCX)	60	Jan 2006	Dec 2010	0.163	0.412	0.160	0.702
153. Corporate Governance (CG)	60	Jan 2006	Dec 2010	-0.698	-0.880	-0.195	-1.147
154. CG minus Industry Average (CGX)	60	Jan 2006	Dec 2010	-0.274	-0.409	-0.042	-0.223
155. Diversity (DIV)	60	Jan 2006	Dec 2010	-0.372	-1.106	-0.166	-0.989
156. DIV minus Industry Average (DIVX)	60	Jan 2006	Dec 2010	-0.216	-0.868	-0.086	-0.671
157. Employee Relations (ER)	60	Jan 2006	Dec 2010	-0.212	-0.696	-0.147	-1.386
158. ER minus Industry Average (ERX)	60	Jan 2006	Dec 2010	0.012	0.048	-0.044	-0.440
159. Environment (E)	60	Jan 2006	Dec 2010	-0.609	-0.892	-0.028	-0.869
160. E minus Industry Average (EX)	60	Jan 2006	Dec 2010	-0.320	-0.838	-0.390	-1.393
161. Human Rights (HR)	60	Jan 2006	Dec 2010	-0.974	-1.231	-0.014	-1.352
162. HR minus Industry Average (HRX)	60	Jan 2006	Dec 2010	-0.604	-0.844	0.380	0.960
163. Product (PRO)	60	Jan 2006	Dec 2010	0.015	0.029	-0.003	-0.089
164. PRO minus Industry Average (PROX)	60	Jan 2006	Dec 2010	-0.175	-0.426	-0.478	-1.567

Note: The $\hat{\beta}$ represents the coefficient of a regression of the factor as the independent variable and the stock return as the dependent variable. *t*-stat represents the *t*-statistic for the null hypothesis that the coefficient is 0. r_{Zl} represents the difference between the return of a high-factor portfolio and the return of a low-factor portfolio (in percentage terms). The associated *t*-stat is the *t*-statistic for the null hypothesis that the mean return is 0. For more details, please see Chapter 4.
[a]For the BETA/MKT factor, the regression test (*t*-test reported next to $\hat{\beta}$) can be viewed as the standard Fama-MacBeth test of the CAPM, which is equivalent to the test of the efficiency of the market portfolio. The portfolio test (*t*-test reported next to r_{Zl}) can be viewed as the test of the betting against beta idea; this test is based on the returns to a version of the betting-against-beta strategy.

candidate only if the sign of r_{ZI} corresponded with our ex-ante beliefs shown in Table 16.8 and the absolute value of the t-statistic was greater than 1.64. Out of 163 factors, the following 13 factors satisfied our requirements: EBITDAEV, equity turnover (ET), FAT minus industry average (FATX), TAT, TATD, CFTA, GPTA, PSL, BB, inflation (CPIG), ten-two-year term premium (TP2Y), ten year-three-month term premium (TP3M), and SUE.

Second, we made sure that the selected factors were not too similar to one another. Since our factor tests were univariate tests, there was a possibility that some factors were very similar. To check for this possibility, we calculated the correlation and the rank correlation of every pair of factors.[29] Whenever we found a pair of factors that had a correlation higher than 0.75, we excluded the factor that had the smaller t-statistic. This step eliminated ETD from the candidate factors for the fundamental factor model and TATD from the candidate factors for the economic factor model.

Finally, we performed a multivariate analysis. For the fundamental factor model, we regressed the returns on the 18 potential factors and selected the five most significant variables. For the economic factor model we regressed the returns on dummy variables created from the 12 potential factors. The dummy variable had a value of 1 if the stock had a high value of the factor and a value of 0 if the stock had a low value of the factor. This regression is identical to the test of zero-investment portfolio returns created from 12 potential factors. Again, we selected the five most significant variables. The final factors for the fundamental and economic factor models are listed in Table 16.10. For our aggregate Z-score model, we used the same factors as for the fundamental factor model.

---

[29] For the rank correlation, we calculated the Kendall statistic. A Kendall statistic close to 100% implies that two factors rank stocks exactly the same way, whereas a statistic near −100% implies that two factors rank stocks in exactly the opposite way. The Kendall statistic is a ratio. The numerator equals the number of factor pairs that rank two variables the same way minus the number of pairs that rank two variables completely differently. The denominator is the total number of factor pairs. We adjusted the Kendall statistic for the panel structure of the data. That is, we calculated the numerator and the denominator for each period and then aggregated over the entire time period. The same adjustment was made for the correlation calculation.

TABLE 16.10

Final Factors for Stock Return Models

Factor Group	Factors Selected for Fundamental Factor Model	Factors Selected for Economic Factor Model
Fundamental	LLOGTAG	EBITDAEV
	TACC	
	DED	
Technical	BB	PSL
		BB
Macroeconomic		TP3M
Analyst	SUE	SUE

Note: Factor abbreviations are contained in the notation section at the beginning of this book, as well as the formula tables of Appendix 16A.

16.6 THE STOCK RETURN AND RISK MODELS

With the list of factors finalized, it is possible to create the model of stock returns and risk that eventually will lead to the desired portfolio. As we emphasized with the information criterion, it is best to use the same model to both forecast stock returns and calculate risk. We ran our data through three different models—a fundamental factor model, an economic factor model, and an aggregate Z-score model. The fundamental and economic factor models produce both expected returns and risk for all the stocks in the investment universe, but the aggregate Z-score approach does not. We chose to use the version of the aggregate Z-score in which the Z-score becomes the factor exposure. That is,

$$r_{i,t} = \gamma_i + \delta_1 Z_{i,1,t-1} + \cdots + \delta_K Z_{i,K,t-1} + \epsilon_{i,t} \tag{16.1}$$

where γ_i represents a constant term, δ_k is the coefficient that relates the Z-score to the stock returns, and $\epsilon_{i,t}$ is a typical error term.

In order to construct our optimal portfolio for every period of data, we concerned ourselves only with the specific case of an enhanced active portfolio manager. In all cases, we considered our benchmark to be the S&P 500 and maximized our excess return over the benchmark subject to a tracking-error constraint.

We performed a variety of backtests and optimizations, abiding by the following parameters for the optimizations. The tracking-error constraint was 5%, but we also considered tracking errors of 2% and 10% (that is, $TE \leq 2\%$, 5%, or 10%). We did not allow for short selling (that is, $\mathbf{w} \geq 0$) except for the market-neutral strategy. The portfolio had to be fully invested (that is, $\mathbf{w}'\iota = 1$), except for the market-neutral strategy. We applied a diversification constraint that no individual stock weighting be greater than 5% of the portfolio (that is, $\mathbf{w} \leq 0.05$). For the market-neutral strategy, we required the *absolute* value of any stock weight to be less than 5% of the portfolio value. Finally, we imposed a trading liquidity constraint: Assuming that we were managing a $500 million portfolio, we restricted the weight of each security to less than 33% of the average daily dollar trading volume (ADDTV) so that $\mathbf{w}_t \leq \frac{0.33\text{ADDTV}_t}{V_t}$. We computed the updated ADDTV for every stock every month but did not adjust the relevant size of the portfolio.

We also considered further variations in which the sector weightings were identical to those of the benchmark. Another optimization involved matching the factor exposures of the benchmark.[30]

16.7 PARAMETER STABILITY AND THE REBALANCING FREQUENCY

Before building the stock return models, it is useful to test for parameter stability. Tenet 6 of QEPM states that quantitative models should reflect persistent and stable patterns. Testing for parameter stability determines how frequently a stock return model must be re-estimated to ensure that it describes persistent, stable patterns in the data. Recall that in the factor-selection stage, we regressed the return on the factor exposure for each month. By pooling the monthly regressions, we were able to test whether the factor premium was stable over time.

For instance, consider the regression of the return on the long-term asset growth factor:

$$r_{i,t} = \alpha_t + f_t LLOGTA_{i,t} + \epsilon_{i,t} \tag{16.2}$$

In this equation, $LLOGTA_{i,t}$ is the long-term asset growth of firm i at the beginning of month t or end of month $t - 1$, and f_t is the factor

---

[30] This allowed us to focus solely on the extra return from α^{MF} rather than from α^B.

premium of month t. This equation was estimated for each month t from January 2001 through December 2010. At the end of this procedure, we had 120 sets of estimates for α and f, each set corresponding to one month.

By pooling 120 regressions and running them at the same time, we tested whether f was stable over time. Note that in the pooled regression, we did not impose any restriction on f or α; we still estimated 120 f's and 120 α's. The resulting estimates are identical to those we obtained from the month-by-month regressions. The pooled regression made hypothesis testing easier without adding any restrictions.

Once the pooled regression was estimated, we examined whether the factor premium was stable for a quarter. First, we tested whether the f of January 2001, the f of February 2001, and the f of March 2001 were identical. The null hypothesis was that all three f's were identical; the alternative hypothesis was that they were not identical. If the p-value of this sort of test is high, we have more confidence in the null hypothesis. If the p-value is low, the alternative hypothesis is more likely to be true. We used the conventional cutoff value of 5%. With a cutoff value of 5%, if the p-value is higher than 5%, the null hypothesis is accepted. If the p-value is lower than 5%, the null hypothesis is rejected.

We ran this same test for the next quarter (i.e., for the f of April 2001, the f of May 2001, and the f of June 2001), and we repeated it until we had completed all 40 quarters of data from 2001 through 2010.[31] Of the 40 tests performed, we rejected the null hypothesis 22 times, a rejection rate of 55% ($=22/40 \cdot 100$). This rejection rate indicates that the premium of long-term asset growth is more or less stable in a quarter.

The same testing procedure is easily extended to any other length of time. We carried out the analysis for periods of six months, nine months, and one year, in addition to the quarterly periods. Since we did not use overlapping data in the test, we performed the test on 20 six-month periods (Jan 2001–June 2001, Jul 2001–Dec 2001, ..., Jul 2010–Dec 2010); on 12 nine-month periods (Jan 2001–Sep 2001, Oct 2001–Jun 2002, ..., Jan 2010–Sep 2010); and 10 one-year periods (Jan 2001–Dec 2001, ..., Jan 2010–Dec 2010).

---

[31] We did not use data from the same month twice, so there were no overlapping data. If we had, interpretation of the p-value would have been quite complicated.

Table 16.11 summarizes the rejection rate for selected factors. The rates suggest that for the annual change in D/E, the parameters are stable for one year, whereas for the other factors, the parameters change frequently.

Rather high rejection rates for a quarter suggest that it may be advantageous to keep the period between reestimations shorter than a quarter. We thus decided to reestimate all our models at monthly intervals.

For the construction of our portfolios, we adopted the following strategy. At the end of month T, we estimated three models— the fundamental factor model, the aggregate Z-score model, and the economic factor model—using the 60 months of data (i.e., from month $T - 59$ to month T). After the estimation of each model, we collected monthly factor premiums for these 60 months, used them as inputs to a VAR (vector autoregression), and forecast the factor premium for month $T + 1$.[32] We also collected factor exposures for the beginning of month $T + 1$.[33] Finally, we created the portfolio for month $T + 1$ based on these factor premiums and exposures. We repeated the entire procedure at the end of every month of data by rolling the estimation window forward one month.

An example with actual dates illustrates these procedures. Suppose that we are building the portfolio for January 2011. For the fundamental factor model, we use stock return data from January 2006 to December 2010 and factor exposure data (e.g., LLOGTA) for the beginning of each month of this period. We use the version of

TABLE 16.11

Rejection Rate in Parameter Stability Tests for Selected Factors

Hypothesis	Long-Term Asset Growth	Total Accruals	Annual Change in D/E	Bollinger Band	Standardized Unanticipated Earnings
Stability for a Quarter	0.55	0.65	0.20	0.80	0.73
Stability for Two Quarters	0.70	0.80	0.35	1.00	0.95
Stability for Three Quarters	0.92	0.92	0.38	1.00	1.00
Stability for a Year	0.80	1.00	0.40	1.00	1.00

Note: The rejection rate represents the percentage of times that we rejected the hypothesis that the parameters were stable for the selected investment horizon. Numbers are presented in decimal form; thus 0.55 represents a 55% rejection rate.

---

[32] See Chapter 8 for a discussion of VAR.
[33] As mentioned several times before, you can consider this also the value of the factor exposure as of the end of month T.

the fundamental factor model where we allow factor premiums to change month-to-month. We thus obtain monthly factor premiums from January 2006 to December 2010; by running a VAR using these data, we obtain an estimate of the January 2011 factor premium distribution. By combining this estimate with the beginning-of-January-2011 factor exposure, we are able to compute the expected returns, standard deviations, and correlations of all stocks in the universe and build the portfolio for the beginning of January 2011.

For the economic factor model, we used the same stock return data from January 2006 to December 2010. We combined these data with the factor premium data for the same period. We estimated a VAR using these factor premiums and obtained estimates of the January 2011 factor premium distribution. We also estimated the factor exposure of all stocks from the stock-by-stock regression of returns on factor premiums. By combining the factor exposure estimates with the factor premium distribution estimates, we were able to compute the expected returns, standard deviations, and correlations of all stocks in the investment universe and build the portfolio for the beginning of January 2011. The process was then repeated for every subsequent month of data.

We did not choose factors again over our out-of-sample period. Some quantitative portfolio managers might wish to reselect the underlying factors at some regular interval, say, every five years. To simplify our presentation, we did not do this.

16.8 THE VARIOUS TYPES OF CONSTRUCTED PORTFOLIOS

Our baseline portfolio for each of the three models is the maximum-expected-return portfolio with five constraints: a 5%-tracking-error constraint, a no-short-selling constraint, a full-investment constraint, a diversification constraint, and a trading-volume constraint.

We consider 11 variations on this baseline portfolio. For the first two variations, we replace the 5% tracking error with a 2% and 10% tracking error, respectively. For the third variation, we added a sector weight constraint that required the sector weights of the portfolio to be identical to those of the benchmark. We used the Global Industrial Classification System (GICS) to identify 10 major sectors of stocks and then set up our portfolio so that its weights in those 10 sectors matched the benchmark's weights in those sectors. The fourth-variation portfolio included a factor exposure constraint that required the factor exposures of the portfolio to be identical to those of the benchmark. Since we had five factors, the factor exposure constraint amounted to five constraints. For each of the five factors, we made sure that the portfolio's exposure matched the benchmark's exposure. The fifth and the sixth variations of the baseline portfolio used transactions costs management and tax management, respectively. We made tracking portfolios that maximized the expected excess-return accounting for either transactions costs or taxes. All the other features of the baseline portfolios were maintained.

The remaining five variations involve creating leveraged or short positions. We modified the portfolio to purchase futures contracts so as to increase the portfolio beta (variation 7), created a "sector-matched" tracking portfolio and at the same time sold the S&P 500 (variation 8), and bought the "factor-matched" tracking portfolio and at the same time sold the S&P 500 (variation 9). The last two long-short portfolios are comparable to the one created by relaxing the no-short-sale constraint while imposing a sector-neutral constraint (variation 10) or a factor-neutral constraint (variation 11).

16.8.1 Transactions Costs

Portfolio managers often backtest strategies without considering transactions costs, an omission that colors the test results an unrealistically rosy hue. The portfolio strategy that yields the best results in a test without transactions costs may involve high turnover that will chip away at the manager's α^B when put into practice. Ignoring transactions costs also can bias the manager toward selecting smaller-cap stocks despite the fact that small-caps' trading costs actually are typically higher than the costs associated with large-cap stocks in similar lines of business. A fair backtest must deal with transactions costs in some way.

Our backtest period is 1995–2020. Conversations with traders will give a portfolio manager a rough idea about transactions costs, but a more detailed picture emerges when the manager can examine many trades and determine precisely how transactions costs differ depending on the types of trades.

Abel Noser keeps track of institutional trading costs for U.S. equities.[34] The Abel Noser data divide trading costs into

---

[34] We thank Steve Glass of Aber Noser for supplying us with transactions costs data from 2010 to 2020 for the purposes of our backtests. We also thank Wayne Wagner of the former Plexus Group for supplying us with similar data from 1994 to 2004.

several categories, including *commissions, market impact, delay,* and *opportunity cost.* Commissions are the explicit fee paid for brokerage services to enact a trade. Market impact is any change in the market price of a stock owing to supply/demand imbalances caused by placing a trade. Impact is measured as the difference between the price at which the broker receives the order and the execution price. Delay summarizes the inter-day costs of price movements that occur while orders are held over from one day to the next owing to either lack of liquidity or failure to act. A more esoteric component of trade-related costs is opportunity cost, which is defined as the theoretical loss of return associated with not fully completing a trade order. Opportunity cost results from delaying execution to lessen market impact, from not being able to make the execution at all, or from abandoning part of the trade because the market has turned against the strategy. If an investment manager's strategy envisioned the purchase of 100,000 shares, and only 50,000 were actually purchased, the lost potential returns on the remainder represent an opportunity cost.

These transactions costs can add up significantly. For example, in the fourth quarter of 2020, commissions contributed 3.7 basis points, market impact contributed 20.4 basis points, and delay contributed 19.2 basis points to the total trading costs for all stocks. In total, 43.3 basis points per trade were just transactions costs. A model α^B would have to be rather high to counteract such transaction costs! Table 16.12 gives the breakdown of transactions costs for various years.

To run the variation of the baseline portfolio with transactions costs, we had to decide which costs were relevant. For trades of 25,000 shares or more, practitioners suggest that managers define the average transactions costs as commissions plus market impact plus delay, whereas for transactions of 10,000 shares or less, it is sufficient to use commissions plus market impact. To be conservative, we chose to use the more inclusive definition of trading costs. We calculated the overall transactions costs as 80% of the large-cap costs plus 20% of the small-cap costs.[35]

---

[35] This increased the large-cap costs and slightly decreased the small-cap costs. We chose not to define a cutoff point between large-cap and small-cap and use separate costs for each category. Many stocks would have been categorized as either small-cap or large-cap despite being very close to the cutoff point. An alternative would have been to interpolate the costs around the break point dividing large-cap and small-cap stocks.

TABLE 16.12

Transactions Costs for Selected Periods

Year	Large-Cap			Small-Cap		
	Higher Costs	Lower Costs	Commissions	Higher Costs	Lower Costs	Commissions
1994	−86.0	−34.0	−10.0	−148.0	−51.0	−15.0
2000	−108.0	−47.0	−16.0	−157.0	−60.0	−21.0
2004	−58.0	−27.0	−11.0	−101.0	−38.0	−17.0
2010	−34.6	−21.8	−7.7	−53.6	−31.1	−13.3
2011	−28.6	−17.3	−7.0	−48.1	−29.9	−10.9
2012	−26.4	−17.2	−6.1	−44.0	−26.1	−11.0
2013	−34.9	−18.3	−5.8	−37.6	−24.0	−9.5
2014	−26.3	−14.5	−4.9	−33.0	−18.8	−7.8
2015	−24.8	−17.0	−4.5	−39.5	−22.5	−8.1
2016	−27.4	−16.9	−4.8	−42.7	−22.7	−8.2
2017	−22.2	−15.0	−4.3	−38.7	−21.9	−7.2
2018	−25.6	−14.8	−3.1	−39.3	−21.7	−5.8
2019	−23.2	−16.1	−3.0	−41.6	−19.1	−6.0
2020	−43.3	−23.4	−2.4	−44.6	−25.8	−5.9

Note: The data from 1994 to 2004 were obtained from the former Plexus Group; the data from 2010 to 2020 were obtained from Abel Noser and the authors' own calculations. Higher costs represent the delay plus market impact plus commissions; lower costs are market impact plus commissions. Commissions are the commission per trade. All numbers are in basis points. These costs were applied to large-cap stocks and small-cap stocks with market capitalizations defined by Standard and Poor's at the time of portfolio creation, with the exception of the Plexus Group data, which defined large-cap as $5 billion or greater and small-cap less than $5 billion. All costs are for a one-way trade.

16.8.2 Taxes

Backtesting without considering tax consequences also can seriously distort the test results. As we emphasized in Chapter 11, what matters to investors in the end is the after-tax return, and the after-tax return can be quite different from the before-tax return. Taxes create two tasks for portfolio managers. The first is to calculate and report both the before-tax and after-tax returns of the portfolio. The second is to consider actively tax-managed portfolios that generate extra returns through tax savings.

Calculating the after-tax return is simple in principle but can be demanding in practice. Tax rates vary for different investors, so it is not always obvious which tax rates to apply to long-term capital gains, short-term capital gains, and dividends. Keeping track of tax lots requires additional effort. For the purpose of our backtest, we assumed a 15% rate on long-term capital gains and a 37% rate on short-term capital gains. Tax rates on dividend income vary significantly among different types of investors, so we ignored dividend taxes in the backtest. We did keep track of tax lots and applied the tax-lot selection method detailed in Chapter 11 to minimize the tax burden. In this method, the potential tax burden of each tax lot is calculated before trading so that the first trade uses the lot with the lowest potential taxes.

For the actively tax-managed portfolio, we adopted the loss-harvesting approach. Loss harvesting, which involves selling shares that are trading at less than the purchase price, generates capital losses and reduces the overall tax burden of the portfolio. Loss harvesting every single losing share maximizes the tax benefit but has the undesirable effect of increasing the portfolio's tracking error with respect to the benchmark. For our backtesting example, we implemented a more conservative form of loss harvesting. We created the tax-managed portfolio in two steps. In the first step, we decided which stocks to buy and which stocks to sell, without considering taxes. In the second step, we decided how many shares to buy and how many shares to sell using the loss-harvesting technique. This two-step procedure ensured that the loss harvesting did not raise the portfolio's tracking error too much.

More specifically, in the first step, we determined what our baseline tracking portfolio would be without accounting for taxes. A comparison of this tracking portfolio with the current portfolio told us which stocks to buy and which to sell. To make this comparison, we denoted the weight of stock i in the current portfolio before rebalancing by w_i^b and the weight in the optimal tracking portfolio by w_i^*.[36] If the weight of the stock was higher in the optimal tracking portfolio than in the current portfolio (that is, $w_i^* > w_i^b$), we knew we needed to buy more shares of the stock. On the other hand, if the weight of the stock was lower in the optimal tracking portfolio than in the current portfolio (that is, $w_i^* < w_i^b$), we knew we needed to sell shares of it.

In the second step, we decided exactly how many shares to buy and sell from a loss-harvesting perspective. The idea is to move the new portfolio weights closer to the full loss-harvesting weights to increase the tax benefit. To do so, we subtracted the tax

---

[36] The superscript b indicates before the rebalancing. The superscript $*$, as is conventional, indicates that the weights of the portfolio were created from the optimization.

rate from the expected return of stock i if selling stock i realized a loss and added the tax rate to the expected return of stock i if selling stock i realized a gain. The actual procedure was complicated as we needed to distinguish between short-term and long-term losses and also between short-term and long-term gains. Thus, for each stock included in the current portfolio, we identified tax lots with short-term gains, long-term gains, short-term losses, and long-term losses. We denoted by w^{bL} the weight of tax lots with short-term gains. (*Note:* This weight is always smaller than the total weight of the stock. Thus, $w_i^{bL} \le w_i^{b}$.) We denoted by w_i^{bM} the weight of tax lots with short-term gains plus the weight of tax lots with long-term gains. (That is, w_i^{bM} was the sum of w_i^{bL} and the weight of tax lots with long-term gains. Thus, $w_i^{bL} \le w_i^{bM} \le w_i^{b}$.) Finally, we denoted by w^{bH} the weight of tax lots with short-term gains plus the weight of tax lots with long-term gains plus the weight of tax lots with long-term losses. (That is, w_i^{bH} was the sum of w_i^{bM} and the weight of tax lots with long-term losses. Thus, $w_i^{bM} \le w_i^{bH} \le w_i^{b}$.) We then compared the tax-ignorant optimal weight w_i^* to w_i^{bL}, w_i^{bM}, w_i^{bH}, and w_i^{b} and decided on the necessary adjustment of expected return and the additional constraints to impose.

The additional constraints and the necessary modification of the optimization can be summarized as follows: Let w_i^{a} be the new portfolio weight of stock i. Also, let us use w_i^{bL}, w_i^{bM}, w_i^{bH}, w_i^{b}, and w_i^* as defined above. We will indicate the short-term and long-term tax rates by τ_s and τ_l. Then

1. If $w_i^{b} \le w_i^*$, then ($w_i^{b} \le w_i^{a}$) is added as a new constraint.
2. If $w_i^{bH} \le w_i^* \le w_i^{b}$, then ($w_i^{bH} \le w_i^{a} \le w_i^*$) is added as a new constraint, and the expected return μ_i is replaced with $\mu_i - \tau_s$. This will ensure that we realize more short-term losses than indicated by w_i^*.
3. If $w_i^{bM} \le w_i^* \le w_i^{bH}$, then ($w_i^{bM} \le w_i^{a} \le w_i^*$) is added as a new constraint, and the expected return μ_i is replaced with $\mu_i - \tau_l$. This will ensure that we realize all the short-term losses and some long-term losses.
4. If $w_i^{bL} \le w_i^* \le w_i^{bM}$, then ($w_i^* \le w_i^{a} \le w_i^{bM}$) is added as a new constraint, and the expected return μ_i is replaced with $\mu_i + \tau_l$. This will ensure that we realize all the losses but avoid realizing too much of the long-term gains.
5. If $w_i^* \le w_i^{bL}$, then ($w_i^* \le w_i^{a} \le w_i^{bL}$) is added as a new constraint, and the expected return μ_i is replaced with $\mu_i + \tau_s$.

This will ensure that we realize all the losses but avoid realizing too much of the short-term gains.

All the other features of the baseline portfolios remain unaffected in the optimization.

16.8.3 Leverage

For the leveraged portfolio, we combined the baseline tracking portfolio with S&P 500 futures. Given the capital asset pricing model (CAPM) β of the baseline portfolio, we purchased enough S&P 500 futures to boost the portfolio's β to 2 with respect to the S&P 500. The baseline portfolio's β was computed from the β's of the individual stocks in the portfolio.[37] The correct number of futures to purchase for an overall β of 2 was determined from the following formula[38]:

$$N_f = \frac{\left(\beta^* - \beta_S\right)V_t}{qS_t} \quad (16.3)$$

where β^* is the target β (in our case, 2), β_s is the β of the stock portfolio, V_t is the value of the baseline portfolio at time t, S_t is the spot price of the index underlying the futures contract (in our case, the S&P 500), and q is the size of one futures contract (250).

In Chapter 15 we discussed formulas for computing the returns of leveraged portfolios. In our backtest, we used Eq. (15.10) to compute the returns of the leveraged portfolio:

$$r_{P,t,t+k} = \left(1 - \xi_t\right)r_{s,t,t+k} + \xi_t\left(I_{t,t+k} - 1\right) + \left[\frac{\beta^* + \left(\xi_t - 1\right)\beta_{s,t}}{\beta_{f,t}S_t}\right]\left(F_{t+k} - F_t\right) \quad (16.4)$$

With our specific parameters, $\xi = 0$, $\beta_f = 1$, and $\beta^* = 2$, the resulting equation for returns of the leveraged portfolio is

$$r_{P,t,t+k} = r_{s,t,t+k} + \left(\frac{2 - \beta_{s,t}}{S_t}\right)\left(F_{t+k} - F_t\right) \quad (16.5)$$

16.8.4 Market-Neutral

To test the market-neutral strategy, we created a dollar-neutral portfolio that was β-neutral to each of the factors in the economic

---

[37] The portfolio β is simply the weighted average of the β's of individual stocks, where the weights are the portfolio weights.

[38] This comes from Eq. (12.13) in Chapter 12

factor model. Since we already discussed the construction of a factor-exposure-matched tracking portfolio, we simply took a long position in this optimal tracking portfolio and a short position in the benchmark. The resulting portfolio is dollar-neutral because the long position and the short position were the same in dollar amount. The resulting portfolio is also β-neutral because the tracking portfolio and the benchmark portfolio have the same factor exposures.

In addition to this, we also created a dollar-neutral, sector-neutral portfolio from the sector-matched tracking portfolio and the benchmark. We took a long position in the optimal tracking portfolio and a short position in the benchmark. The resulting portfolio was both sector and dollar neutral.

Finally, we created two market-neutral portfolios directly from the optimization. That is, in the optimization we imposed the dollar-neutrality constraint (that weights sum to 0) and either the factor neutrality constraint (that the portfolio exposure to each factor is 0) or the sector neutrality constraint (that the weight of each sector is 0). We dropped the full-investment constraints, the no-short-sale constraint, and the tracking-error constraint. We modified the diversification constraint and the trading-volume constraint so as to put limits on the absolute weights rather than the weights themselves.

16.9 CONCLUSION

In this chapter we set out to demonstrate the process of backtesting using historical U.S. stock data. Quantitative equity portfolio managers often use backtesting to see how well a strategy would have worked in the past. If past and current conditions relevant to the model are expected to continue, more or less, into the future, then a backtest gives an indication of how well the hypothetical portfolio might perform going forward. How a manager decides to set up and run a backtest influences the test results. We used our decision-making processes in this particular chapter to illustrate reasonable approaches to the practical problems generally encountered at each stage of a test. We discussed our decisions about the data and software, the time period and frequency of the data set, the investment universe and benchmark, the factors to include in the stock return model, the type of model to use, the portfolio's rebalancing frequency, and the type of portfolio construction. Procedures that we outlined briefly in this chapter are described more fully in earlier chapters of the book.

Chapter 17 presents the actual performance statistics of the strategies we backtested and implemented in hypothetical portfolios. We tested three different models—a fundamental factor model, an economic factor model, and an aggregate Z-score model. With each of these models, we then built a baseline portfolio and a number of variations on it with different constraints (on stock weights, factor exposures, transactions costs, or taxes) or different characteristics (leveraged, market-neutral). Some of the portfolios' performance statistics are exciting, others lackluster. The goal of our example is not to advocate particular strategies but rather to show how to test, implement, and evaluate them. Thus, we will not be selective in presenting our results. The judgment on whether a certain strategy is worth pursuing is left to the reader.

APPENDIX 16A

Factor Formulas

Fundamental–Valuation Factors

Factor	Formula	Comments
1. Dividend Yield (DY)	$\dfrac{r_t - rx_t}{1 + r_t}$	Where r_t (RET) is the one-month return of the stock and rx_t (RETX) is the one-month return of the stock minus the dividend payment. Alternatively, one can use the more traditional formula that divides the dividend payments by the price level $\left(\dfrac{d_t}{p_t \cdot n_t}\right)$, where d_t (DVC) is the annualized dividend p (PRC) is price, and n (SHROUT) is shares outstanding. Return and price variables are obtained from CRSP rather than Compustat.
2. EBITDA-to-EV (EBITDAEV)	$\dfrac{\sum_{i=1}^{4} EBITDA_{t-3i}}{p_t \cdot n_t + STD_{t-3} + LTD_{t-3}}$	Where $EBITDA$ (OIBDPQ) is earnings before interest, taxes, and depreciation, STD (DLCQ) is short-term debt, and LTD is long-term debt (DLTTQ). This factor is the inverse of the more commonly known EV/EBITDA ratio.
3. Book-to-Price (B/P)	$\dfrac{CE_{t-3}}{p_t \cdot n_t}$	Only if $CE > 0$; CE is total common equity (CEQQ).
4. Cash Flow-to-Price (CF/P)	$\dfrac{\sum_{i=1}^{4} OCF_{t-3i}}{p_t \cdot n_t}$	Only if $OCF > 0$, where OCF is operating activity net cash flow (OANCFY).

Factor	Formula	Comments
5. Earnings-to-Price (E/P)	$\sum_{i=1}^{4} \dfrac{e_{t-3i}}{p_t \cdot n_t}$	Where e (IBQ) is income before extraordinary items.
6. EBITDA-to-Price (EBITDAP)	$\sum_{i=1}^{4} \dfrac{EBITDA_{t-3i}}{p_t \cdot n_t}$	This factor is the inverse of the more commonly known P/EBITDA ratio.
7. E/P times Historical Earnings Growth (IPEGH)	$\sum_{i=1}^{4} \dfrac{e_{t-3i} \cdot g^h}{p_t \cdot n_t}$	Where g^h is the 5-year historical earning per share growth. This factor is the inverse of the more commonly known PEG ratio.
8. E/P times Forecasted Earnings Growth (IPEGF)	$\sum_{i=1}^{4} \dfrac{e_{t-3i} \cdot g^f}{p_t \cdot n_t}$	Where g^f is the mean forecasted growth rate of analysts.
9. E/P times Growth plus Yield (IPEGY)	$\sum_{i=1}^{4} \dfrac{e_{t-3i}}{p_t \cdot n_t} \cdot (g^f + DP_t)$	Where g^f is the mean forecasted growth rate of analysts. This factor is the inverse of the more commonly known PEGY ratio.
10. Sales-to-Price (S/P)	$\sum_{i=1}^{4} \dfrac{s_{t-3i}}{p_t \cdot n_t}$	Only if $s > 0$, where s is net sales (SALEQ).

Note: The table contains formulas for various factors as we computed them. Our primary data sources were Compustat, CRSP, IBES, MSCI-KLD, Bloomberg, and SEC data. The order of the factors follows the order listed in the tables in Appendix 4A, even though sometimes the variable has been inverted. Also these tables contain derivative variables that might not be listed in Appendix 4A. For convenience, we indicate the Compustat data code for the variable in parentheses the first time the variable appears (e.g., SALEQ is the Compustat code for quarterly net sales). We use the quarterly Compustat series, which means for some variables we must sum the last four quarters to get an annual number. Where CRSP data are used instead of Compustat, we provide the CRSP variable in parentheses. In order to have a richer data set, the inverse of many common ratios is used in our empirical analysis (e.g., EV/EBIDTA, P/B, P/CF, P/E, P/EBITDA, PEG, PEGY). It might be of interest to the reader that Compustat stores cash-flow variables as year-to-date. Thus, when dealing with a cash-flow variable (or PRSTKCY and SSTKY), in order to compute the value of last four quarters, one must adjust the formula by fiscal year end as follows. If the 4th quarter ends in month $t-3$, we use X_{t-3} for last four quarters, where X is the variable of interest, if the 3rd quarter ends in month $t-3$, we use $X_{t-3} + X_{t-12} - X_{t-15}$, if the 2nd quarter ends in month $t-3$, we use $X_{t-3} + X_{t-9} - X_{t-15}$, and if the 1st quarter ends in month $t-3$, we use $X_{t-3} + X_{t-6} - X_{t-15}$. This will be true for all tables that have cash-flow variables.

TABLE 16A.2

Fundamental–Size Factors

Factor	Formula	Comments
11. Log of Common Equity (LOGCE)	$\log_e(CE_{t-3})$	Where CE (CEQQ) is common equity.
12. Equity Growth (LOGCEG)	$\dfrac{\log_e(CE_{t-3})}{\log_e(CE_{t-15})} - 1$	
13. Long-Term Equity Growth (LLOGCEG)	$\dfrac{\log_e(CE_{t-3})}{\log_e(CE_{t-63})} - 1$	

TABLE 16A.2 *(Continued)*

Factor	Formula	Comments
14. Log of Market Capitalization (LOGSIZE)	$\log_e(p_t \cdot n_t)$	Where p (PRC) is price, and n (SHROUT) is shares outstanding.
15. Log of Total Assets (LOGTA)	$\log_e(TA_{t-3})$	Where TA (ATQ) equals total assets.
16. Asset Growth (LOGTAG)	$\dfrac{\log_e(TA_{t-3})}{\log_e(TA_{t-15})}-1$	Only if TA is positive.
17. Long-Term Asset Growth (LLOGTAG)	$\dfrac{\log_e(TA_{t-3})}{\log_e(TA_{t-63})}-1$	

Note: See the note to Table 16A.1.

TABLE 16A.3

Fundamental–Operating Efficiency Factors

Factor	Formula	Comments
18. Cash Conversion Cycle (CCC)	$\dfrac{\left(\dfrac{1}{RT_{t-3}}+\dfrac{1}{IT_{t-3}}-\dfrac{1}{APT_{t-3}}\right).}{365}$	Where RT is receivables turnover, IT is inventory turnover, and APT is accounts payable turnover. $APT = \dfrac{2 \cdot \sum_{i=1}^{4} COGS_{t-3i}}{AP_{t-3}+AP_{t-15}}$, where $COGS$ is costs of goods sold (COGSQ) and AP (APQ) is accounts payable.
19. CCC minus Industry Average (CCCX)	$CCC_t - \overline{CCC}_t$	Where CCC is the cash conversion cycle, and $\overline{CCC}$ is the inventory 2-digit GICS sector average.
20. Annual Change in Cash Conversion Cycle (CCCD)	$CCC_t - CCC_{t-12}$	
21. Cost Management Index (CMI)	$\dfrac{\sum_{i=1}^{4}(COGS_{t-3i}+GSA_{t-3i})}{\sum_{i=1}^{4}OI_{t-3i}}$	Only if $COGS$ is positive, where $COGS$ (COGSQ) is cost of goods sold, GSA (XSGAQ) is general and administrative costs, and OI (OIADPQ) is operating income after depreciation.
22. CMI minus Industry Average (CMIX)	$CMI_t - \overline{CMI}_t$	Where CMI is the cost management index, and $\overline{CMI}$ is the CMI 2-digit GICS sector average.
23. Annual Change in CMI (CMID)	$CMI_t - CMI_{t-12}$	
24. Equity Turnover (ET)	$\dfrac{2 \cdot \sum_{i=1}^{4} s_{t-3i}}{SE_{t-3}+SE_{t-15}}$	Where s (SALEQ) is net sales and SE (TEQQ) is total shareholder equity. If TEQQ is missing, we use SEQQ, if SEQQ is missing, we use CEQQ.

Factor	Formula	Comments
25. ET minus Industry Average (ETX)	$ET_t - \overline{ET}_t$	
26. Annual Change in ET (ETD)	$ET_t - ET_{t-12}$	
27. Fixed Asset Turnover (FAT)	$\dfrac{2 \cdot \sum_{i=1}^{4} s_{t-3i}}{(FA_{t-3} + FA_{t-15})}$	Where *FA* (PPENTQ) is fixed assets.
28. FAT minus Industry Average (FATX)	$FAT_t - \overline{FAT}_t$	
29. Annual Change in FAT (FATD)	$FAT_t - FAT_{t-12}$	
30. Inventory Turnover (IT)	$\dfrac{2 \cdot \sum_{i=1}^{4} COGS_{t-3i}}{I_{t-3} + I_{t-15}}$	Only if *COGS* and *I* are positive, where *COGS* (COGSQ) is cost of goods sold and *I* (INVTQ) is total inventory.
31. IT minus Industry Average (ITX)	$IT_t - \overline{IT}_t$	Where *IT* is inventory turnover, and $\overline{IT}$ is the inventory 2-digit GICS sector average.
32. Annual Change in Inventory Turnover (ITD)	$IT_t - IT_{t-12}$	
33. Receivables Turnover (RT)	$\dfrac{2 \cdot \sum_{i=1}^{4} s_{t-3i}}{REC_{t-3} + REC_{t-15}}$	Where *s* (SALEQ) is net sales and *REC* (RECTQ) is total receivables.
34. RT minus Industry Average (RTX)	$RT_t - \overline{RT}_t$	
35. Annual Change in Receivables Turnover (RTD)	$RT_t - RT_{t-12}$	
36. Total Asset Turnover (TAT)	$\dfrac{s_{t-3}}{TA_{t-3}}$	Only if *s* and *TA* are positive, where *TA* (ATQ) equals total assets.
37. TAT minus Industry Average (TATX)	$TAT_t - \overline{TAT}_t$	Where *TAT* equals total asset turnover and $\overline{TAT}$ is the 2-digit GICS sector average.
38. Annual Change in TAT (TATD)	$TAT_t - TAT_{t-12}$	

Note: See the note to Table 16A.1. Although we did not compute the cost management index for banking firms in this book, some users may wish to do this when evaluating banks. One formula is $\dfrac{XNITB_{t-3}}{(TII_{t-3} - TIE_{t-3}) + INITB_{t-3}}$, where *XNITB* is noninterest expenses, *TII* is total interest income, *TIE* is total interest expense, and *INITB* is noninterest income. These are annual Compustat items. This factor is typically used for banking firms with GICS industry code 4010.

T A B L E   1 6 A . 4

Fundamental—Operating Profitability Factors

Factor	Formula	Comments
39. Current Accruals (CACC)	$[(\Delta CA_{t-3} - \Delta CHE_{t-3}) - (\Delta CL_{t-3} - \Delta STD_{t-3} - \Delta TP_{t-3}) - Dep_{t-3}] / ATA$	Where Δ represents the change of the variable over the last four quarters (i.e., from $t-15$ to $t-3$), ΔCA (ACTQ) is the change in current assets, ΔCHE (CHEQ) is the change in cash and short-term investments, ΔCL (LCTQ) is the change in current liabilities, ΔSTD (DLCQ) is the change in debt included in current liabilities, ΔTP (TXPQ) is the change in income taxes payable, Dep (DPQ) is the depreciation and amortization expense, and ATA (ATQ) is the average of total assets $\left(\text{i.e.,} \dfrac{TA_{t-3} + TA_{t-15}}{2}\right)$. Only if CA, CL, and CHE are available; otherwise, set to missing for that stock.
40. Total Accruals (TACC)	$[\Delta TA_{t-3} - \Delta TL_{t-3} - \Delta CH_{t-3} - \Delta PS_{t-3}] / ATA$	Where Δ represents the change of the variable over the last four quarters (i.e., from $t-15$ to $t-3$), ΔTL is change in total liabilities (LTQ), ΔCH is change in cash (CHQ), and ΔPS is change in preferred stock (PSTKQ). Only if TA and TL are available; otherwise, set to missing for that stock.
41. Cash Flow to Total Assets (CFTA)	$\dfrac{\sum_{i=1}^{4} OCF_{t-3i}}{TA_{t-3}}$	Where OCF (OANCFY) is operating cash flow and TA is total assets.
42. Cash Flow to Total Sales (CFTS)	$\dfrac{\sum_{i=1}^{4} OCF_{t-3i}}{\sum_{i=1}^{4} s_{t-3i}}$	Where OCF is operating cash flow and s is net sales (SALEQ).
43. Gross Profit Margin (GPM)	$1 - \dfrac{\sum_{i=1}^{4} COGS_{t-3i}}{\sum_{i=1}^{4} s_{t-3i}}$	
44. Annual Change in GPM (GPMD)	$GPM_t - GPM_{t-12}$	Where GPM is gross profit margin.
45. Gross Profit Growth (GPG)	$\dfrac{\sum_{i=1}^{4} GP_{t-3i}}{\sum_{i=1}^{4} GP_{t-3i-12}} - 1$	Where GP is gross profit (SALESQ − COGSQ).

Factor	Formula	Comments
46. Long-Term Gross Profit Growth (LGPG)	$\dfrac{\sum_{i=1}^{4} GP_{t-3i}}{\sum_{i=1}^{4} GP_{t-3i-60}} - 1$	
47. Gross Profit to Total Assets (GPTA)	$\dfrac{\sum_{i=1}^{4} GP_{t-3i}}{TA_{t-3}}$	Where *GP* is gross profit and *TA* is total assets.
48. Net Profit Margin (NPM)	$\dfrac{\sum_{i=1}^{4} NI_{t-3i}}{\sum_{i=1}^{4} S_{t-3i}}$	Where *NI* (IBQ) is income before extraordinary items.
49. Annual Change in NPM (NPMD)	$NPM_t - NPM_{t-12}$	Where *NPM* is net profit margin.
50. Net Profit Growth (NPG)	$\dfrac{\sum_{i=1}^{4} NI_{t-3i}}{\sum_{i=1}^{4} NI_{t-3i-12}} - 1$	Also could be called net income growth.
51. Long-Term Net Profit Growth (LNPG)	$\dfrac{\sum_{i=1}^{4} NI_{t-3i}}{\sum_{i=1}^{4} NI_{t-3i-60}} - 1$	
52. Net Profit to Total Assets (NPTA)	$\dfrac{\sum_{i=1}^{4} NI_{t-3i}}{TA_{t-3}}$	Also known as return on assets.
53. Operating Profit Margin (OPM)	$\dfrac{\sum_{i=1}^{4} OI_{t-3i}}{\sum_{i=1}^{4} S_{t-3i}}$	Where *OI* (OIBDPY) equals operating income before depreciation.
54. Annual Change in OPM (OPMD)	$OPM_t - OPM_{t-12}$	Where *OPM* is operating profit margin.
55. Operating Profit Growth (OPG)	$\dfrac{\sum_{i=1}^{4} OI_{t-3i}}{\sum_{i=1}^{4} OI_{t-3i-12}} - 1$	
56. Long-Term Operating Profit Growth (LOPG)	$\dfrac{\sum_{i=1}^{4} OI_{t-3i}}{\sum_{i=1}^{4} OI_{t-3i-60}} - 1$	
57. Operating Profit to Total Assets (OPTA)	$\dfrac{\sum_{i=1}^{4} OI_{t-3i}}{TA_{t-3}}$	
58. Return on Assets (ROA)	$\dfrac{\sum_{i=1}^{4} EBIT_{t-3i}}{TA_{t-3}}$	Where *EBIT* is earnings before interest and taxes (OIADPY).
59. Return on Common Equity (ROCE)	$\dfrac{\sum_{i=1}^{4} (NI_{t-3i} - PD_{t-3i})}{CE_{t-3}}$	If negative, its value is set to missing. Where *PD* is for preferred dividends (DVPQ). If *PD* is missing, we set it to 0. If common equity is not available, we use stockholders equity (TEQQ) minus preferred stock (PSTKQ). If TEQQ is missing, we use SEQQ minus PSTKQ. If CEQQ, TEQQ, and SEQQ are unavailable, we set to missing.

TABLE 16A.4 *(Continued)*

Factor	Formula	Comments
60. Return on Owner's Equity (ROE)	$$\dfrac{\sum_{i=1}^{4} NI_{t-3i}}{TEQQ_{t-3}}$$	If negative, its value is set to missing. If TEQQ is missing, we use SEQQ. If both are missing, we set to missing.
61. Return on Total Capital (ROTC)	$$\dfrac{\sum_{i=1}^{4} EBIT_{t-3i}}{STD_{t-3} + LTD_{t-3} + TEQQ_{t-3}}$$	Where STD (DLCQ) is short-term debt, LTD is long-term debt (DLTTQ), and TEQ (TEQQ) is shareholder equity. If TEQQ is missing, we use SEQQ. If SEQQ is missing, we use total common equity (CEQQ). If all are missing, we set to missing.

Note: See the note to Table 16A.1. Our measure of total accruals is a simplified version of the more complicated version $\dfrac{(\Delta WC_{t-3} + \Delta NCO_{t-3} + \Delta FIN_{t-3})}{ATA}$, where Δ represents the change of the variable over the last four quarters (i.e., from $t - 15$ to $t - 3$), $\Delta WC = (\Delta CA - \Delta CH) - (\Delta CL - \Delta DLC)$, where DLC is the debt in current liabilities (DLCQ), $\Delta NCO = (\Delta TA - \Delta CA - \Delta I) - (\Delta TL - \Delta CL - \Delta LTD)$, where I is investments and advances (IVAOQ) and LTD is long-term debt (DLTTQ), and $\Delta FIN = (\Delta STI + \Delta I) - (\Delta LTD + \Delta DLC + \Delta PS)$, where DLC is debt in current liabilities (DLCQ), STI is short-term investments (IVSTQ), I is change in investments and advances (IVAOQ), and PS is preferred stock (PSTKQ). One can also use $\dfrac{\Delta CE_{t-3} - \Delta CH_{t-3}}{ATA}$ for the total accruals measure. The difference between TEQQ and SEQQ is that the latter does not have non redeemable non controlling interest (MIBNQ). Also, prior to 2009, the data for TEQQ are very unreliable.

TABLE 16A.5

Fundamental–Solvency Factors

Factor	Formula	Comments
62. Cash-Flow-From-Operations Ratio (CFOR)	$$\dfrac{\sum_{i=1}^{4} OCF_{t-3i}}{CL_{t-3}}$$	Where OCF is operating activity net cash flow (OANCFY) and CL (LCTQ) is current liabilities.
63. Annual Change in Cash-Flow-From-Operations Ratio (CFORD)	$CFOR_t - CFOR_{t-12}$	
64. Cash Ratio (CR)	$$\dfrac{CHE_{t-3}}{CL_{t-3}}$$	Only if CHE and CL are positive, where CHE (CHEQ) is cash and short-term investments and CL (LCTQ) is current liabilities.
65. Annual Change in Cash Ratio (CRD)	$CR_t - CR_{t-12}$	
66. Current Ratio (CUR)	$$\dfrac{CA_{t-3}}{CL_{t-3}}$$	Only if CA and CL are positive, where CA (ACTQ) represents current assets.

Factor	Formula	Comments
67. Annual Change in the Current Ratio (CURD)	$CUR_t - CUR_{t-12}$	
68. Quick Ratio (QR)	$\dfrac{CHE_{t-3} + REC_{t-3}}{CL_{t-3}}$	Only if *CHE*, *REC*, and *CL* are positive, where *REC* (RECTQ) is total receivables.
69. Annual Change in the Quick Ratio (QRD)	$QR_t - QR_{t-12}$	

Note: See the note to Table 16A.1.

TABLE 16A.6

Fundamental–Financial Risk Factors

Factor	Formula	Comments
70. Inverse Cash Flow Coverage Ratio (ICFCR)	$\dfrac{STD_{t-3} + LTD_{t-3}}{\sum_{i=1}^{4} OCF_{t-3i}}$	Where *STD* (DLCQ) is short-term debt, *LTD* is long-term debt (DLTTQ), and *OCF* (OANCFY) represents operating cash flows.
71. ICFCR minus Industry Average (ICFCRX)	$ICFCR_t - \overline{ICFCR}_t$	Where *ICFCR* is the inverse cash-flow coverage ratio, and $\overline{ICFCR}$ is the inverse cash-flow coverage ratio 2-digit GICS sector average.
72. Annual Change in ICFCR (ICFCRD)	$ICFCR_t - ICFCR_{t-12}$	
73. Debt-to-Equity (D/E)	$\dfrac{TL_{t-3}}{SE_{t-3}}$	Where *TL* (LTQ) is for total liabilities and *SE* (TEQQ) is for stockholders' equity. If TEQQ is missing, we use SEQQ. If SEQQ is missing, we use total common equity (CEQQ). If all are missing, we set to missing.
74. D/E minus Industry Average (DEX)	$D/E_t - \overline{D/E}_t$	Where *D/E* is the debt-to-equity ratio, and $\overline{D/E}$ is the debt-to-equity ratio 2-digit GICS sector average.
75. Annual Change in D/E (DED)	$D/E_t - D/E_{t-12}$	
76. Financial Leverage Ratio (FLR)	$\dfrac{TA_{t-3}}{CEQ_{t-3}}$	If negative, its value is set to missing. Where *TA* (ATQ) is total assets and *CE* (CEQQ) is common equity. If common equity is not available, we use stockholders' equity (TEQQ) minus preferred stock (PSTKQ). If TEQQ is missing, we use SEQQ minus PSTKQ. If CEQQ, TEQQ, and SEQQ are unavailable, we set to missing.

TABLE 16A.6 *(Continued)*

Factor	Formula	Comments
77. FLR minus Industry Average (FLRX)	$FLR_t - \overline{FLR}_t$	Where FLR is the financial leverage ratio and $\overline{FLR}$ is the financial leverage ratio 2-digit GIC sector average.
78. Annual Change in FLR (FLRD)	$FLR_t - FLR_{t-12}$	
79. Inverse Interest Coverage Ratio (IICR)	$\dfrac{IE_{t-3}}{PI_{t-3}}$	Where IE (XINT) is interest expense and PI (PIQ) is pretax income.
80. IICR minus Industry Average (IICRX)	$IICR_t - \overline{IICR}_t$	Where $IICR$ is the inverse interest coverage ratio and $\overline{IICR}$ is the inverse interest coverage 2-digit GIC sector average.
81. Annual Change in IICR (IICRD)	$IICR_t - IICR_{t-12}$	
82. Total Debt Ratio (TDR)	$\dfrac{STD_{t-3} + LTD_{t-3}}{TA_{t-3}}$	Where STD (DLCQ) is short-term debt, LTD is long-term debt (DLTTQ), and TA (ATQ) is total assets.
83. TDR minus Industry Average (TDRX)	$TDR_t - \overline{TDR}_t$	Where TDR is the total debt ratio and $\overline{TDR}$ is the total debt ratio 2-digit GICS sector average.
84. Annual Change in TDR (TDRD)	$TDR_t - TDR_{t-12}$	

Note: See the note to Table 16A.1. In order to have a richer data set, the inverses of many common ratios are used as our factors. The difference between TEQQ and SEQQ is that the latter does not have non redeemable non controlling interest (MIBNQ). Also, prior to 2009, the data for TEQQ are very unreliable.

TABLE 16A.7

Fundamental–Corporate Activity Factors

Factor	Formula	Comments
85. Stock Buybacks (SB)	$\dfrac{\sum_{i=1}^{4}(SP_{t-3i} - SI_{t-3i})}{SIZE_{t-3}}$	Where SP_{t-3} is all stock purchases (PRSTKCY), SI_{t-3} is all stock issuance (SSTKY), and $SIZE$ [p_t (PRC) $\cdot$ n_t (SHROUT)] is the market capitalization of the company. Prior to 1989, we compute stock buybacks as $\dfrac{T_{t-3} - T_{t-6}}{SIZE_{t-3}}$, where T (TSTKQ) is total treasury stock (common and preferred).
86. R&D to Sales (RNDS)	$\dfrac{\sum_{i=1}^{4} rnd_{t-3i}}{\sum_{i=1}^{4} s_{t-3i}}$	Only if rnd and s are positive, where rnd (XRDQ) is net expenses on research and development.
87. The Change in R&D to Sales (RNDSD)	$RNDS_t - RNDS_{t-12}$	

Note: See the note to Table 16A.1. For the stock buyback factor, PRSTKCY and SSTKY are cash-flow variables; thus we sum them using the methodology described in Table 16A.1.

TABLE 16A.8

Technical–Liquidity Risk Factors

Factor	Formula	Comments
88. Amihud Illiquidity (AILIQ)	$\dfrac{1}{D_y}\sum_{d=1}^{D_y}\dfrac{|r_d|}{DVOL_d}$	Where r_d (RET and DLRET) is the daily return of the stock from the previous close to day d's close, $DVOL_d$ represents the dollar trading volume of the stock on day d, and D_y is the number of days in a rolling 12-month year. Returns are obtained from CRSP, rather than Compustat.
89. Crowding Analysts (CROWDA)	$\dfrac{N_{SB}+N_B}{N}\cdot\dfrac{\Delta SIZE_{t,t-12}}{ADDTV_{t,t-3}}$	Where N_{SB}, N_B, and N are the number of analysts with strong buys, buys, and the total number of analyst recommendations on stock i, $\Delta SIZE$ is the change in the market capitalization of the stock in the last year, and $ADDTV_{t,t-3}$ is the average dollar daily trading volume over the last three calendar months.
90. Crowding Value (CROWDV)	$\left[\dfrac{\left(\frac{\bar{B}}{P}\right)_{i,t,t-84}}{\left(\frac{\bar{B}}{P}\right)_{i,t}}\right]\cdot$ $\begin{bmatrix}ADTV_{i,t,t-6}\\ADTV_{m,t,t-5}\\\overline{ADTV_{i,t-6,t-66}}\\ADTV_{m,t-6,t-66}\end{bmatrix}$	Where $ADTV_{i,t,t-6}$ is average monthly trading volume for the last 6 months for stock i and the whole market m, $ADTV_{i,t-6,t-66}$ is the average monthly trading volume over the last 5 years for the stock i and the market m, $\dfrac{\bar{B}}{P_i}$, represents the book-to-price ratio of the company currently and the 7-year average.
91. Invariance Illiquidity (INVIL)	$\left(\dfrac{\sigma_t^2}{ADDTV_{t,t-3}}\right)^{1/3}$	Where σ_t is the standard deviation of the last 90-day stock returns and $ADDTV_{t,t-3}$ is the average daily dollar trading volume of the stock over the last three calendar months.
92. Modified Amihud Iliquidity (MAILIQ)	$\dfrac{1}{D_y}\sum_{d=1}^{D_y}\dfrac{|ocr_d|}{DVOL_d}$	Where ocr_d is the daily return of the stock from the open to the close of day d, $DVOL_d$ represents the dollar trading volume of the stock on day d, and D_y is the number of days in a rolling 12-month year. The measure is exactly like Amihud's original measure except open-to-close returns are used.

TABLE 16A.8 *(Continued)*

Factor	Formula	Comments
93. Pastor and Stambaugh Liquidity (PSL)	L_t	Where L_t is the aggregate liquidity factor for month t. It is computed in the following steps; Step 1: For each stock in the universe, estimate a regression of daily stock returns in each month (provided a minimum of 15 daily returns exist in that month for that stock and do not use days with zero volume) as $r^e_{i,d+1,t} = \theta_{i,t} + \phi_{i,t} r_{i,d,t} + \gamma_{i,t} \text{sign}(r^e_{i,d,t}) DVOL_{i,d,t} + \epsilon_{i,d+1,t}$, where $d = 1, ..., D$ is the total number of days in month t; $r^e_{i,d,t} = r_{i,d,t} - r_{m,d,t}$, where $r_{m,d,t}$ is the CRSP value-weighted market return on day t. sign $(r^e_{i,d,t})$ is 1 if the return is positive and -1 if the return is negative. $DVOL$ is daily volume measured in millions of dollars. Step 2: Take the monthly values of the $\hat{\gamma}_{it}$ from the individual stock regressions in step 1 for all stocks and compute the following cross-sectional average of stocks in each month: $\Delta\hat{\gamma}_t = \left(\dfrac{m_t}{m_1}\right)\dfrac{1}{N_t}\sum_{i=1}^{N_t} (\hat{\gamma}_{it} - \hat{\gamma}_{it-1})$, where m_t is the market value of all N securities in month $t-1$ and m_1 is the market value of all N securities in December 1981. Step 3: Estimate the following regression using the average value of γ: $\Delta\hat{\gamma}_t = a + b\Delta\hat{\gamma}_{t-1} + c\left(\dfrac{m_{t-1}}{m_1}\right)\hat{\gamma}_{t-1} + u_t$ where $\hat{\gamma}_{t-1} = \dfrac{1}{N_t}\sum_{i=1}^{N_t}\hat{\gamma}_{it-1}$. Step 4: Take the fitted residuals from step 3 and compute $L_t = \dfrac{1}{100}\hat{u}_t$.
94. Trading Turnover (TT)	$\dfrac{ADDTV_{t,t-3}}{SIZE_t}$	Where $SIZE_i [p_t(PRC) \cdot n_t(SHROUT)]$ is the market capitalization of stock i, $ADDTV_{t,t-3}$ represents the past three-month average daily dollar trading volume.

Note: See the note to Table 16A.1.

TABLE 16A.9

Technical–Price Based

Factor	Formula	Comments
95. Beta (BETA) / Market (MKT)[a]	$\hat{\beta}_t$	Where $\hat{\beta}_t$ is the estimate from a rolling regression of weekly stock returns over the previous 3 years (provided a minimum of 6 months of historical data exist) as $r_t - r_{f,t} = \alpha + \beta(r_{M,t} - r_{f,t}) + \epsilon_t$, where r_t is the weekly return of a given stock on day t, $r_{M,t}$ is the weekly CRSP value-weighted market return on day t, and $r_{f,t}$ is the Fama-French total return risk-free rate for the week on day t. This factor exposure is known amongst practitioners as *low beta*. The factor premium (MKT) is given by $r_{M,t} - r_{f,t}$
96. Bollinger Bands (BB)	$\Phi(p_t > [\bar{p} + \sigma])$ $- \Phi(p_t < [\bar{p} + \sigma])$	Where Φ is an operator that is 1 if the condition is true and 0 otherwise, $\bar{p}$ is the daily average of the stock price over the month, and σ is the daily standard deviation of stock prices during the month.
97. Channel Breakouts (CB)	$\Phi(p_t > p_C^H) - \Phi(p_t < p_C^L)$	Where Φ is an operator that is 1 if the condition is true and 0 otherwise, p_C^H is the daily stock price high over last three months, and p_C^L is the prior 60-day stock price low once the channel has been established. For a channel to be formed, $p_C^H/p_C^L - 1 < 0.20$. Once a channel is formed, the signal to buy, sell, or no action is formed.
98. One-Month Momentum (M1M)	r_t	Where r_t (RET) is the one-month return of the stock. Returns are obtained from CRSP rather than Compustat.
99. Three-Month Momentum (M3M)	$\prod_{i=0}^{2}(1 + r_{t-i}) - 1$	Where r_t is the one-month return of the stock.
100. Six-Month Momentum (M6M)	$\prod_{i=0}^{5}(1 + r_{t-i}) - 1$	
101. Nine-Month Momentum (M9M)	$\prod_{i=0}^{8}(1 + r_{t-i}) - 1$	
102. Nine-Month Momentum Lag 1 (M9ML1)	$\prod_{i=1}^{8}(1 + r_{t-i}) - 1$	

T A B L E   1 6 A . 9   *(Continued)*

Factor	Formula	Comments
103. Twelve-Month Momentum (M12M)	$\prod_{i=0}^{11}(1+r_{t-i})-1$	
104. Moving Average (MA)	$\Phi(p_t > \bar{p}) - \Phi(p_t < \bar{p})$	Where Φ is an operator that is 1 if the condition is true and 0 otherwise and $\bar{p}$ is the moving average of the stock price over the last three months.
105. Moving Average Convergence–Divergence Indicator (MACD)	$\bar{p}_t^{12} - \bar{p}_t^{26}$	Where $\bar{p}_t^{12}$ is the 12-day exponential moving average of the stock price and $\bar{p}_t^{26}$ is the 26-day exponential moving average of the stock price. $\bar{p}_t^{12} = kp_t + (1-k)\bar{p}_{t-1}^{12}$, where we use $k = \frac{2}{13}$. $\bar{p}_t^{26} = kp_t + (1-k)\bar{p}_{t-1}^{26}$, where we use $k = \frac{2}{27}$. If signal is greater (less) than 0, then buy (sell).
106. Price (P)	$\log_e(p_t)$	This factor is known amongst practitioners as *low price*.
107. Relative Strength Index (RSI)	$100 - \left(\dfrac{100}{1-U/D}\right)$	Where U equals the average of daily price changes when the price change is positive and D equals the average of daily absolute price changes when the price change is negative for the day. The averages are taken over all the days in the month.
108. Support Resistance (SR)	$\Phi(p_t > p^H) - \Phi(p_t < p^L)$	Where Φ is an operator that is 1 if the condition is true and 0 otherwise, p^H is the daily stock price high in the prior month, and p^L is the daily stock price low in the prior month.
109. Volatility (VOL)	$\sqrt{\dfrac{1}{N_d-1}\sum_{t=1}^{N_d}(r_{it}-\bar{r}_i)^2}$	Where r_{it} is the daily return of the stock i, N_d is the number of return days in the last three months of data, and the standard deviation is computed over the daily returns of the last three calendar months to approximate the three-month historical volatility of the stocks. This factor is known amongst practitioners as *low volatility* or *low vol*.

Note: See the note to Table 16A.1.

[a]Because the beta of a stock is derived from regressing returns against the market factor, we also share this space with the market factor (i.e., the return of the market minus the risk-free rate).

TABLE 16A.10

Technical—Volume Based

Factor	Formula	Comments
110. Odd-Lot Balance (OLBI)[a]	$\left(\dfrac{OLV_t}{SVOL_t} - \hat{\alpha} - \hat{\beta}\overline{p}_t\right) \cdot r_t$	Where OLV_t and $SVOL_t$ are the total odd-lot share volume and total share volume of the stock for the month and $\hat{\alpha}, \hat{\beta}$ are the cross-sectional regression estimates of the average monthly stock price of each security on the percentage of odd-lot volume for the month, and r_t is the return of the stock for the month. That is, $\dfrac{OLV_{it}}{V_{it}} = \alpha + \beta p_{it} + \epsilon_{it}$, where this is a cross-sectional regression on monthly average prices of each stock and monthly odd-lot volume to volume for each stock. This measure accounts for the fact that there might be more odd-lot volume when stock prices are higher.
111. On-Balance Volume (OBV)	$\Phi(OBV_t > 1.10\overline{OBV}) - \Phi(OBV_t < 0.90\overline{OBV})$	Where Φ is an operator that is 1 if the condition is true and 0 otherwise. $\overline{OBV}$ is the prior 30-day moving average of the OBV at the end of the month.
112. Short Interest Ratio (SIR)	$\dfrac{SI_t}{ADTV_{t,t-3}}$	Where $ADTV_{t,t-3}$ is the previous 3 month average daily trading volume of the stock and SI is the number of shares short.
113. SIR minus SIR One-Year Average (SIRX)	$SIR_t - \overline{SIR}_t$	Where SIR is the short interest ratio and $\overline{SIR}$ is the 1-year historical average of SIR for that company.
114. Volume Lead (VL)	$-(ADTV_t - \frac{1}{N}\sum_{i=1}^{N} ADTV_{it})r_t$	Where $ADTV_t$ is the average daily volume of shares traded for the month for each stock, r_t is the return (RET) of the stock for that month, N is the number of stocks in the universe with available data.

Note: See the note to Table 16A.1. [a]Typically, OLBI is computed with the ratio of odd-lot sales to odd-lot purchases. Given that we did not have these data, we chose to modify the formula so that it still represented the basic intuition.

TABLE 16A.11

Technical—Overall Market Movement

Factor	Formula	Comments
115. Advance–Decline Ratio (ADR)	$\dfrac{N_a}{N_d}$	Where N_a are the number of stocks in the universe with a positive return in the month and N_d are the number of stocks in the universe with a negative return in the month.
116. Arms Index (ARMS)	$\dfrac{ADR}{UDR}$	Where ADR is the advance–decline ratio and UDR is the upside–downside ratio.
117. Upside–Downside Ratio (UDR)	$\dfrac{\sum_{i=1}^{N_a} ADTV_i}{\sum_{i=1}^{N_d} ADTV_i}$	Where $ADTV_i$ is the average daily trading volume in the month, N_a is the number of stocks that had a positive return in the month, and N_d is the number of stocks that had a negative return in the month.
118. Upside–Downside Volume (UDV)	$\sum_{i=1}^{N_a} ADTV_i - \sum_{i=1}^{N_d} ADTV_i$	Where $ADTV_i$ is the average daily trading volume in the month, N_a is the number of stocks that had a positive return in the month, and N_d is the number of stocks that had a negative return in the month.

Note: See the note to Table 16A.1.

TABLE 16A.12

Economic Factors

Factor	Formula	Comments
119. Consumption Growth (PCG)	$100\left(\dfrac{gdpctot_{t-1}}{gdpctot_{t-4}} - 1\right)$	Economic variables are defined in Table 16A.14. When the given formula returns a missing value, the time index is moved backward until the formula returns a nonmissing value (e.g., replace $t-1$ with $t-2$ and $t-4$ with $t-5$).
120. PC Revision (PCR)	$100\left(\dfrac{rconm0_{t+1}}{rconp1_{t-2}} - 1\right)$	When the given formula returns a missing value, the time index is moved backward until the formula returns a nonmissing value (e.g., replace $t+1$ with t and $t-2$ with $t-3$). $rconm0$ for each quarter is released one month prior to the end of the quarter. For example, $rconm0$ for Jan 2010–Mar 2010, which we record as

Factor	Formula	Comments
		$rconm0_{\text{Mar 2010}}$, is known by the end of Feb 2010. Thus, the given formula will return a nonmissing value if t is Feb, May, Aug, and Nov. If t is Mar, Jun, Sep, and Dec, the time index needs to be moved backward by one month. If t is Jan, Apr, Jul, and Oct, the time index needs to be moved backward by two months.
121. Consumer Confidence Growth (CCG)	$100\left(\dfrac{conconf_t}{concconf_{t-1}}-1\right)$	Same.
122. Consumer Sentiment Growth (CSG)	$100\left(\dfrac{conssent_t}{conssent_{t-1}}-1\right)$	Same.
123. Change in Commodity Index (CIG)	$100\left(\dfrac{crbcmdt_t}{crbcmdt_{t-1}}-1\right)$	Same.
124. BBB Spread (BBBS)	S_{BBB}	Same.
125. Change in BBB Spread (BBBSD)	$S_{BBB,t}-S_{BBB,t-1}$	Same.
126. Swap Spread (SS)	$y_{swap}-y_{c10}$	Same.
127. Change in Swap Spread (SSD)	$y_{swap,t}-y_{swap,t-1}$	Same.
128. Industrial Production (IPG)	$100\left(\dfrac{ip_{t-1}}{ip_{t-2}}-1\right)$	
129. IP Revision (IPR)	$100\left(\dfrac{ipsfm0_{t+1}}{ipsfp1_{t-2}}-1\right)$	See the comment for PCR.
130. Business Confidence Growth (BCG)	$100\left(\dfrac{busconf_{t-1}}{busconf_{t-4}}-1\right)$	Same.
131. Inflation (CPIG)	$100\left(\dfrac{cpi_{t-1}}{cpi_{t-2}}-1\right)$	Same.
132. Real GDP Growth (GDPG)	$100\left(\dfrac{gdpchwg_{t-1}}{gdpchwg_{t-4}}-1\right)$	See the comment for PCG.
133. Real GDP Revision (GDPR)	$100\left(\dfrac{gdpsfqm0_{t+1}}{gdpsfqp1_{t-2}}-1\right)$	See the comment for PCR.
134. Real GDP Surprise (GDPS)	$100\left(\dfrac{gdpcur\$_{t-1}}{gdpsfqm0_{t-1}}-1\right)$	See the comment for PCG.
135. Ten-Two-Year Term Premium (TP2Y)	$y_{c10}-y_{c2}$	Same.
136. Ten Year-Three-Month Term Premium (TP3M)	$y_{c10}-y_{c3m}$	Same.
137. Unemployment (UR)	$usurtot_{t-1}$	Same.
138. Change in Unemployment (URD)	$usurtot_{t-1}-usurtot_{t-2}$	Same.

Note: The table contains formulas for various factors as we computed them. The raw economic variables are described in Table 16A.14.

TABLE 16A.13

Alternative Factors

Factor	Formula	Comments
	Alternative—Analysts	
139. Analyst Rating—Median Rating (ARMR)	$RECM_t$	Where $RECM$ (MEDREC) is the median recommendation of analysts for the month.
140. Analyst Rating—Percent Buys (ARPB)	Percentage of Buys	(PCTBUY)
141. Analyst Rating—Percent Sells (ARPS)	Percentage of Sells	(SELLPCT)
142. Analyst Rating—SD of Ratings (ARSD)		(STDEVREC)
143. Analyst Rating—Percent Downgrades (ARPD)	$\dfrac{N_{ug}}{N_{ug}+N_{dg}}$	Where N_{ug} is the number of analyst upgrades (NUMRECUP) (e.g., from sell to hold or buy to strong buy) and N_{dg} is the number of downgrades (NUMRECDOWN).
144. Analyst Rating—Percent Upgrades (ARPU)	$\dfrac{N_{ug}}{N_{ug}+N_{dg}}$	
145. Analyst Rating—Median Change (ARMD)	$RECM_t - RECM_{t-1}$	Where $RECM$ (MEDREC) is the median recommendation of analysts for the month.
146. EPS Forecast— Normalized SD (EPSSD)	$S(SEP)/(\overline{|EPS|})$	Where $S(EPS)$ is the standard deviation of EPS (STDEV6) normalized by the absolute mean (MEANEST6).
147. EPS Revision—Percent Downward (EPSFPD)	$\dfrac{N_d}{N_u+N_d}$	Where N_u is the number of upward revisions (NUMUP6) and N_d is the number of downward revisions (NUMDOWN6).
148. EPS Revision—Percent Upward (EPSFPU)	$\dfrac{N_u}{N_u+N_d}$	
149. Number of Analysts (EPSFN)	$\log_e(N_{a,t-3})$	Where $N_{a,t-3}$ is the number of analysts (NUMEST6) at time $t-3$ and all analysts data are obtained from quarterly IBES data.
150. Standardized Unanticipated Earnings (SUE)	$\dfrac{EPS^a - \overline{EPS}}{S(EPS)}$	Where EPS^a is the actual earnings-per-share reported in the given month and $\overline{EPS}$ is the mean earnings-per-share estimates by analysts prior to the earnings announcement. We use quarterly earnings forecasts. We also include companies that had earnings releases in the prior 2 months, which makes the SUE measure slightly less timely. Practitioners may wish to use more recent data and exclude companies that had earnings released in the prior 2 months of the sample.

Alternative—Socially Responsible

151. Community Contribution (CC)	$comstr - comcon$	MSCI–KLD creates an index of strengths and concerns of a company in each category. Our variable is the percentage of strength index (*comstr*) minus the percentage of concern index (*comcon*). That is, if the company satisifes 3 of 5 strength categories and 2 of 6 concern categories, our measure is 3/5 − 2/8 = 0.35. If no data are available for a particular strength or concern, we compute this difference with the remaining categories, provided at least one strength category and one concern category have valid data. Community contribution is COM for data provider.
152. CC minus Industry Average (CCX)	$CC - \overline{CC}$	
153. Corporate Governance (CG)	$cgovstr - cgovcon$	Same as above. Corporate governance is CGOV for data provider.
154. CG minus Industry Average (CGX)	$CG - \overline{CG}$	
155. Diversity (DIV)	$divstr - divcon$	Same as above. Diversity is DIV for data provider.
156. DIV minus Industry Average (DIVX)	$DIV - \overline{DIV}$	
157. Employee Relations (ER)	$empstr - empcon$	Same as above. Employee relations is EMP for data provider.
158. ER minus Industry Average (ERX)	$ER - \overline{ER}$	
159. Environment (E)	$envstr - envcon$	Same as above. Environment is ENV for data provider.
160. E minus Industry Average (EX)	$E - \overline{E}$	
161. Human Rights (HR)	$humstr - humcon$	Same as above. Human rights is HUM for data provider.
162. HR minus Industry Average (HRX)	$HR - \overline{HR}$	
163. Product (PRO)	$prostr - procon$	Same as above. Product is PRO for data provider.
164. PRO minus Industry Average (PROX)	$PRO - \overline{PRO}$	

Note: The table contains formulas for various factors as we computed them. Where relevant, we also include the original variable names from the data provider, like MSCI-KLD for socially responsible data and IBES for analyst data.

TABLE 16A.14

Economic Raw Data

Economic Variable	Description	Data Source	Start Date	Frequency	First Release	Bloomberg Ticker
y_{LIBOR}[a]	US LIBOR O/N Rate	Intercontinental Exchange (ICE)	Jan-01	D	Same Day	US000/N Index
y_{g3m}	Generic 3M Bill	Bloomberg	Jun-83	D	Same Day	USGG3M Index
y_{c3m}	Const Mat 3M	FRB St. Louis (FREDII)	Jan-82	D	Same Day	H15T3M Index
y_{g2}	Generic 2Yr Note	Bloomberg	Jan-77	D	Same Day	USGG2YR Index
y_{c2}	Const Mat 2Yr	FRB St. Louis (FREDII)	Jun-76	D	Same Day	H15T2Y Index
y_{g5}	Generic 5Yr Note	Bloomberg	Jan-75	D	Same Day	USGG5YR Index
y_{c5}	Const Mat 5Yr	FRB St. Louis (FREDII)	Jan-75	D	Same Day	H15T5Y Index
y_{g10}	Generic 10Yr Note	Bloomberg	Jan-75	D	Same Day	USGG10YR Index
y_{c10}	Const Mat 10Yr	FRB St. Louis (FREDII)	Jan-75	D	Same Day	H15T10Y Index
FFT	Fed Funds Target	Federal Reserve	Jan-75	D	Same Day	FDFD Index
EFF	Effective Fed Funds Rate	Federal Reserve	Jan-75	D	Same Day	FEDL01 Index
USCRWTIC	Crude Oil Price Index	Bloomberg	May-83	D	Same Day	USCRWTIC Index
CRBCMDT	Commodity Research Board Index	Bloomberg	May-81	D	Same Day	BCOM Index
y_{swap}	10-Year SWAP Rates	Bloomberg	Jan-00	D	Same Day	I05210Y Index
S_{BBB}	BBB Yield minus 10-year Treasury Yield	Bloomberg	Sep-02	D	Same Day	CSI BBB Index

660

Economic Variable	Description	Data Source	Start Date	Frequency	First Release	Bloomberg Ticker
gdpcur	Gross Domestic Product at current $	BEA	Mar-75	Q	Advanced the month after the quarter end, preliminary in the second month after the quarter end, and final in the third month after the quarter end.	GDP CUR$ Index
gdpchwg	Chain-linked Gross Domestic Product.	BEA	Mar-75	Q	See *gdpcur*.	GDP CHWG Index
gdpdefl	GDP Deflator	BEA	Mar-75	Q	See *gdpcur*.	GDP DEFL Index
gnpcur$	Gross National Product at current $	BEA	Mar-75	Q	See *gdpcur*.	GNP CUR$ Index
gdpctot	Personal Consumption Component GDP.	BEA	Mar-75	Q	See *gdpcur*.	GDPCTOT Index
ip	Industrial Production.	FRB St. Louis (FREDII)	Jan-75	M	Mid month for previous month.	IP Index
usurtot	Unemployment (SA)	BLS	Jan-75	M	1st week of month for previous month (e.g., May 6th for April)	USURTOT Index
usurtotn	Unemployment (NSA)	BLS	Jan-75	M	1st week of month for previous month (e.g., 6 May for April)	USURTOTN Index
cpi	Consumer Price Index	BLS	Jan-75	M	3rd week of month for previous month (e.g., May 17th for April)	CPI INDX Index
ppi	Producer Price Index	BLS	Jan-75	M	3rd week of month for previous month (e.g., May 17th for April)	PPI INDX Index

Economic Variable	Description	Data Source	Start Date	Frequency	First Release	Bloomberg Ticker
busconf	OECD Business Confidence Survey for U.S. This is based on the Manufacturing PMI diffusion index published monthly by the U.S. Institute for Supply Management. This survey is based on a sample of enterprises and respondents that are asked about their assessments of the current situation and expectations for the immediate future. The OECD applies several statistical techniques and reports a standardized series.	OECD & ISM	Jan-60	M	Generally, released within the first 10 business days of month for previous month (e.g., May 11 for April).	OEUSDHAO Index
concconf	Consumer confidence index, which consists of current and future consumer attitudes based on a survey with questions that are slightly different from the Univ. of Michigan index.	Conference board	Jan-78	M	Last Tuesday of month for current month.	CONCCONF Index
conssent	Consumer confidence index, which consists of current and future consumer attitudes based on a survey of 500 people.	Univ. of Michigan	Jan-78	M	Generally released last Friday of the month for current month.	CONSSENT Index

Economic Variable	Description	Data Source	Start Date	Frequency	First Release	Bloomberg Ticker
conscurr	Consumer confidence present sentiment is based upon a subcomponent of questions from the Consumer Confidence Index indicating current sentiment.	Univ. of Michigan	Jan-78	M	Generally released last Friday of the month for current month.	CONSCURR Index
consexp	Consumer confidence expectations sentiment is based upon a subcomponent of questions from the Consumer Confidence Index indicating sentiment of the near future.	Univ. of Michigan	Jan-78	M	Generally released last Friday of the month for current month.	CONSEXP Index
gdpsf	Survey of Professional Forecasters Median GDP.	FRB of Philadephia	Jan-68	Q	Contains forecasts of the previous quarter, current quarter, and several quarters ahead.	NA
unempsf	Survey of Professional Forecasters Median UNEMP.	FRB of Philadephia	Jan-68	Q	Contains forecasts of the previous quarter, current quarter, and several quarters ahead.	NA
ipsf	Survey of Professional Forecasters Median IP.	FRB of Philadephia	Jan-68	Q	Contains forecasts of the previous quarter, current quarter, and several quarters ahead.	NA
cpisf	Survey of Professional Forecasters Median CPI.	FRB of Philadephia	Jan-68	Q	Contains forecasts of the previous quarter, current quarter, and several quarters ahead.	NA

TABLE 16A.14 *(Continued)*

Economic Variable	Description	Data Source	Start Date	Frequency	First Release	Bloomberg Ticker
tbillsf	Survey of Professional Forecasters Median TBILL.	FRB of Philadephia	Jan-68	Q	Contains forecasts of the previous quarter, current quarter, and several quarters ahead.	NA
10yrsf	Survey of Professional Forecasters Median 10-YR Yields.	FRB of Philadephia	Jan-68	Q	Contains forecasts of the previous quarter, current quarter, and several quarters ahead.	NA
rconsf	Survey of Professional Forecasters Median Real Consumption.	FRB of Philadephia	Jan-68	Q	Contains forecasts of the previous quarter, current quarter, and several quarters ahead.	NA
rgdpsf	Survey of Professional Forecasters Median Real GDP.	FRB of Philadephia	Jan-68	Q	Contains forecasts of the previous quarter, current quarter, and several quarters ahead.	NA

Note: See the note to Table 16A.1.

[a]After the LIBOR scandal that was publicized in 2012, there has been a push toward a new overnight benchmark called the Secured Overnight Financing Rate (SOFR). Due to its short history, we used the LIBOR rate for this book. Note: BLS = Bureau of Labor and Statistics, BEA = Bureau of Economic Analysis, BIS = Bank for International Settlements, FRB = Federal Reserve Bank, Univ. of Michigan is from the University of Michigan surveys, FRED = Federal Reserve Economic Data, OECD = Organization for Economic Co-operation and Development, D = daily, M = monthly, and Q = quarterly.

QUESTIONS

16.1. What is backtesting?

16.2. What might be some of the problems a research analyst will encounter when creating a historical equity data set of factors?

16.3. (a) What is real-time testing?

(b) As an outsider or CIO to the portfolio management team, which type of testing would you have more confidence in, backtesting or real-time testing?

16.4. (a) How should a quantitative portfolio manager divide a sample of historical data?

(b) Explain the difference between in-sample and out-of-sample data.

(c) What is a rolling in-sample window? When might it be used appropriately?

16.5. Name the seven important considerations in choosing an equity benchmark.

16.6. For each of the benchmarks listed below, indicate how the stocks are chosen for the index, how many stocks are typically in the index, how frequently the stocks are changed, and how the stocks of the index are weighted.

(a) S&P 500

(b) Russell 1000

(c) DJIA

(d) Wilshire 5000

(e) S&P 600

(f) Russell 2000

(g) S&P 500 Value

16.7. According to the benchmark statistics in Table 16.4, what are the riskiest and the least risky benchmarks?

16.8. Which three indices are the most correlated with the S&P 500?

16.9. (a) What is look-ahead bias?

(b) What must a portfolio manager do to avoid it when backtesting strategies?

(c) Does it bias the performance of the strategies upward or downward?

16.10. (a) What is survivorship bias?

(b) Why is it a potential source of bias when the backtesting of portfolio strategies is done?

(c) Does it bias the performance of the strategies upward or downward?

16.11. Table 16.9 contains the results of factor tests from 2006–2010. Consider a quantitative portfolio manager who is looking for factors to include in his fundamental factor model.

(a) If we consider a confidence interval of 90% (i.e., a critical two-sided t-stat of 1.65 with 60 degrees of freedom), which fundamental valuation factors and which fundamental operating efficiency factors would be considered significant?

(b) What if we increased the confidence interval to 95% (i.e., a critical two-sided t-stat of 2)?

(c) What if we increased it to 98% (i.e., a critical two-sided t-stat of 2.39)?

(d) Repeat part (c) with a portfolio manager using an economic factor model and consider only price-based technical and fundamental valuation factors.

16.12. Describe a simple technique to test for parameter stability.

16.13. Should backtests always include transactions costs, especially for high-turnover strategies?

16.14. Many traders will tell you that the cost of trading for most stocks in 2020 was about 2 cents per share. Why might this be misleading when used in a backtest?

16.15. Describe the following costs.

(a) Commissions

(b) Market impact

(c) Delay

(d) Opportunity costs

16.16. This question refers to the tables on factor tests in the chapter and Appendix 16B which can be found under Chapter Appendices at https://ludwigbc.com/books/qepm/exclusive_qepm_content_2020/ or at www.ludwigbc.com and look for QEPM Exclusive Content.

(a) In the years 1996–2000 and 2001–2005, was the analyst upgrades factor a significant factor in explaining cross-sectional stock returns?

(b) In the years 2011–2015 and 2016–2020, did the relationship between this factor and the cross section of stock returns change? If so, in what way?

(c) What external events might have caused this relationship to change?

CHAPTER 17

The Portfolios' Performance

Beneath the good so far—but far above the great.

—Thomas Gray

17.1 INTRODUCTION

In this chapter we present the historical performance results of the selected portfolio strategies that we discussed in Chapter 16. Our baseline strategy was to create an optimized tracking portfolio that maximized the excess expected return of the portfolio subject to a tracking-error constraint of 5%. In addition to the tracking-error constraint, we imposed three additional constraints: a full-investment constraint, a no-short-selling constraint, and a trading-volume constraint. We implemented our baseline strategy using the economic factor model, the fundamental factor model, and the aggregate Z-score model.

In addition to the baseline strategy, we also performed backtests on 11 additional strategies. These alternative strategies that created our portfolios were based on different levels of tracking error, sector weight and factor exposure matching; transactions costs and tax management; leverage; and market neutrality. The performance statistics of the strategies will give readers an idea of the types of statistics that are relevant to quantitative equity portfolio management (QEPM) and how to interpret them properly. Of course, the reader also may be interested in how these specific strategies worked with our particular historical data set. The first section of the chapter discusses the results of the baseline strategy plus the first four variations implemented with the fundamental factor model, the aggregate Z-score model, and the economic factor model. It also includes a detailed performance attribution for one of the portfolios. The remaining four sections of the chapter look at the remaining portfolios.

17.2 THE PERFORMANCE OF THE BASELINE PORTFOLIO AND VARIATIONS

In this section we present the performance statistics of the baseline strategy and four variations that alter either the tracking error, sector weight matching, or factor exposure matching.

17.2.1 The Fundamental Factor Model Performance

Table 17.1 shows the historical performance of the portfolio strategies based on the fundamental factor model. Five portfolios were created at the end of each month between December 2010 and November 2020. The portfolios came from the same model and the same set of factors but were subject to different constraints. The first three portfolios were subject to the tracking-error constraints of 2%, 5%, and 10% per annum, respectively. The fourth portfolio was subject to the tracking-error constraint of 5%; in addition, it was constrained to have the sector weights identical to those of the benchmark.[1] The fifth portfolio was also subject to the tracking-error constraint of 5%; in addition, it was constrained to have the factor exposures identical to those of the benchmark.

The first row in the table shows the average return of each portfolio. Return figures are annualized monthly returns. For example, the portfolio with a target tracking error of 2% per annum has an average monthly return of 1.44975%, which translates to an average annualized monthly return of 17.397%. That is, an investment in this portfolio at the beginning of the investment period would have

---

[1] It is standard practice among many quantitative portfolio managers to add a sector constraint to the portfolio. However, since we are already controlling the ex-ante tracking error of our portfolio versus the benchmark, to the extent that our modeling procedure is reasonable, we should not expect a further reduction in the ex-post tracking error from this additional constraint.

TABLE 17.1

Historical Performance of the Fundamental Factor Model

	Tracking Portfolio			Sector-Matched	Factor-Matched	Benchmark
	$TE = 2$	$TE = 5$	$TE = 10$	$TE = 5$	$TE = 5$	
Average return	17.397	20.881	25.159	19.954	14.382	14.043
SD return	15.309	18.830	23.357	17.598	18.448	13.601
Min return	−12.691	−14.495	−19.827	−16.035	−16.657	−12.093
Max return	13.123	15.355	20.502	13.967	15.771	12.900
Average excess return	3.354	6.839	11.117	5.912	0.340	—
Ex-post TE	5.020	10.275	15.850	8.753	8.711	—
Min excess return	−4.955	−9.723	−14.868	−8.909	−9.153	—
Max excess return	3.377	6.253	11.396	5.470	4.822	—
$\hat{\alpha}^B$	0.206	0.376	0.596	0.346	−0.214	—
$t(\hat{\alpha}^B)$	1.515	1.365	1.411	1.467	−0.945	—
$\hat{\beta}^B$	1.065	1.173	1.294	1.130	1.215	—
IR	0.144	0.130	0.134	0.139	−0.090	—
$\hat{\alpha}^{MF}$	0.497	0.361	0.719	0.338	0.233	0.932
SR	0.317	0.311	0.304	0.318	0.216	0.286

Note: Portfolios were selected to maximize expected returns subject to the following constraints: (i) Short sales were not allowed ($w \geq 0$). (ii) The portfolio was always fully invested at the rebalancing date ($w'\iota = 1$). (iii) No stock in the portfolio was allowed a weight of more than 5% ($w \leq 0.05$). (iv) The portfolio weights were required, at any rebalancing date, to be less than 33% of the average daily trading volume in absolute dollars of each security, assuming a portfolio value of $500 million (i.e., $w \leq 0.33 \cdot$ **ADDTV**/$500,000,000). (v) The tracking error was one of the following: 2%, 5%, or 10%. For the factor-exposure-matched portfolio, the additional requirement was that the weighted-average factor exposure of the portfolio and the benchmark were perfectly matched for every factor in the stock return model. For the sector-weight–matched portfolio, the additional requirement was that the sector weights of the portfolio and the benchmark were perfectly matched. In the table, average return and average excess return are annualized. TE is the annualized tracking error, and SD is the annualized standard deviation of monthly returns over the entire period. Max and Min stand for the maximum and minimum monthly return. Excess returns are portfolio returns in excess of the benchmark returns annualized. $\hat{\alpha}^B$ and $\hat{\beta}^B$ are the ex-post benchmark α and β (i.e., the estimates from the regression of the portfolio returns on the benchmark returns). $\hat{\alpha}^{MF}$ is the ex-post multifactor α (i.e., the estimate from the regression of the portfolio returns on many factors). IR represents the information ratio of monthly returns of the portfolio (to annualize, multiply by $\sqrt{12}$), and SR is the ex-post Sharpe ratio based upon monthly returns and the one-month Treasury bill return from Fama-French. Performance was calculated from the end of December 2010 to the end of December 2020.

provided the investor with an average return of about 17.397% per year. We can see that, as expected, the average return of the portfolio increases when the target tracking error increases because we are taking more risk in constructing the portfolio.

The fifth row shows the average excess return of the various portfolios. In all cases, the average excess return is positive, which is reassuring because our goal was to create portfolios with the highest possible excess return subject to the tracking-error constraint. The minimum average excess return of 0.34% came from the factor-matched portfolio. The other portfolios have an even higher excess return.

The second and the sixth rows show the standard deviation of the portfolio return and the ex-post (i.e., realized) tracking error of the portfolio, respectively. All standard deviations have been annualized. Thus the standard deviation of 15.309% reflects a standard deviation of monthly returns of 4.419% ($15.309/\sqrt{12}$). Roughly speaking, there is less than a 2.5% probability that the annual return of this particular portfolio will be worse than -13.22% ($=17.40 - 2 \times 15.31$). One also will notice that an increasing average return of the portfolio is accompanied by an increasing standard deviation of returns, which confirms the basic idea of financial theory that risk and return are positively related to each other. For quantitative portfolio managers, the most important measure of risk is the risk versus the benchmark, summed up by the tracking error. Although our portfolios had ex-ante tracking errors of 2%, 5%, or 10%, their ex-post tracking errors were 5.020%, 10.275%, and 15.850%, respectively. Although there are discrepancies because the model cannot exactly describe future stock returns, as our ex-ante tracking error increases, so does our ex-post tracking error. We have some degree of control over the ex-post tracking error of our optimized portfolios.[2]

The worst and best monthly returns over the entire backtesting period are also given in the table. These statistics supplement the standard deviation risk measure and can be useful in explaining the amount of risk in the portfolio to nonquantitative investors.

The rows titled $\hat{\alpha}^B$ and $\hat{\beta}^B$ show the estimated α and β of the tracking portfolios with respect to the benchmark. They are the constant (α) and coefficient (β) in a regression of the tracking portfolio returns on the benchmark returns. The key variable for portfolio managers is the α with respect to the benchmark (α^B). Except for the factor-matched portfolio, all the portfolios have positive values of α^B. The portfolio with a 2% tracking error has a β^B close to 1, so most of its excess return over the benchmark is coming from stock picking, not from increased risk vis-à-vis the benchmark. Quantitative managers also focus on the information ratio (IR), which measures the

---

[2] In the 1st Edition of this book, we warned of the problems with ex-ante and ex-post tracking error. Since then, new techniques have been suggested for how to deal with this. See Bruno et al. (2018), Menchero et al. (2012), and Menchero and Ji (2019).

excess return of the portfolio, as measured by α^B divided by the residual risk of the portfolio. The information ratios of all the portfolios, except for the factor-matched portfolio, are very similar, even though their α^B values differ.

There are many sources of a positive benchmark α. One of these is the multifactor α, $\hat{\alpha}^{MF}$, which is the part of the excess return that is not due to any of the pricing factors that the stock return model identified. It is possible that the multifactor α of a portfolio is larger than its benchmark α since factor exposures and factor premiums may have a negative sign.

The last row shows the Sharpe ratio, another measure of the risk-adjusted average return. All our portfolios, except for the factor-matched portfolio, have a higher Sharpe ratio than the benchmark does, which suggests that they are more efficient than the benchmark. The sector-matched portfolio is the most efficient according to the Sharpe ratio.

Overall, the following conclusions can be drawn from the results of our historical backtests:

1. The optimized tracking portfolios achieve positive average excess returns over the benchmark, ranging from 0.3% to 11.1% per annum.
2. Using multifactor stock return models can control the ex-post tracking error to some extent by optimizing the ex-ante target tracking error.
3. Much of the average excess return of the portfolios over the benchmark is attributable to benchmark α.
4. The information ratios of the portfolios can be as high as 0.5 on an annualized basis. Thus, for every 1% additional excess risk per year, the portfolios provide more than 0.5% in additional excess returns.
5. The Sharpe ratios of many of our portfolios are higher than that of the benchmark, indicating that our stock-selection methodology may create portfolios that earn more than the benchmark on a risk-adjusted basis.

17.2.2 The Aggregate Z-Score Model Performance

Table 17.2 shows the historical performance of the portfolio strategy based on the aggregate Z-score model. The format of this

TABLE 17.2

Historical Performance of the Aggregate Z-Score Model

	Tracking Portfolio			Sector-Matched	Factor-Matched	Benchmark
	TE = 2	**TE = 5**	**TE = 10**	**TE = 5**	**TE = 5**	
Average return	17.188	20.646	25.008	20.257	14.324	14.043
SD return	15.221	18.376	22.988	17.465	18.450	13.601
Min return	−12.948	−14.597	−20.035	−17.182	−16.717	−12.093
Max return	13.161	15.200	20.692	14.249	15.759	12.900
Average excess return	3.146	6.603	10.965	6.214	0.281	—
Ex-post *TE*	4.810	9.671	15.522	8.463	8.686	—
Min excess return	−5.063	−9.290	−15.075	−7.413	−9.145	—
Max excess return	3.157	5.907	9.813	5.549	4.782	—
$\hat{\alpha}^B$	0.191	0.371	0.604	0.371	−0.220	—
$t(\hat{\alpha}^B)$	1.463	1.430	1.456	1.627	−0.978	—
$\hat{\beta}^B$	1.064	1.159	1.276	1.131	1.216	—
IR	0.139	0.136	0.138	0.154	−0.093	—
$\hat{\alpha}^{MF}$	0.524	0.499	0.742	0.475	0.224	0.932
SR	0.315	0.315	0.307	0.325	0.215	0.286

Note: Portfolios were selected to maximize expected returns subject to the following constraints: (i) Short sales were not allowed ($\mathbf{w} \geq 0$). (ii) The portfolio was always fully invested at the rebalancing date ($\mathbf{w}'\iota = 1$). (iii) No stock in the portfolio was allowed a weight of more than 5% ($\mathbf{w} \leq 0.05$). (iv) The portfolio weights were required, at any rebalancing date, to be less than 33% of the average daily trading volume in absolute dollars of each security, assuming a portfolio value of $500 million (i.e., $\mathbf{w} \leq 0.33 \cdot$ **ADDTV**/$500,000,000). (v) The tracking error was one of the following: 2%, 5%, or 10%. For the factor-exposure–matched portfolio, the additional requirement was that the weighted-average factor exposure of the portfolio and the benchmark were perfectly matched for every factor in the stock return model. For the sector-weight–matched portfolio, the additional requirement was that the sector weights of the portfolio and the benchmark were perfectly matched. In the table, average return and average excess return are annualized. *TE* is the annualized tracking error, and SD is the annualized standard deviation of monthly returns over the entire period. Max and Min stand for the maximum and minimum monthly return. Excess returns are portfolio returns in excess of the benchmark returns annualized. $\hat{\alpha}^B$ and $\hat{\beta}^B$ are the ex-post benchmark α and β (i.e., the estimates from the regression of the portfolio returns on the benchmark returns). $\hat{\alpha}^{MF}$ is the ex-post multifactor α (i.e., the estimate from the regression of the portfolio returns on many factors). *IR* represents the information ratio of monthly returns of the portfolio (to annualize, multiply by $\sqrt{12}$), and *SR* is the ex-post Sharpe ratio based upon monthly returns and the one-month Treasury bill return from Fama-French. Performance was calculated from the end of December 2010 to the end of December 2020.

table is identical to the preceding table, so we will just comment briefly on the salient results.

In terms of the average return and the average excess return, the portfolios based on the aggregate Z-score model perform similarly to the portfolios based on the fundamental factor model. The average excess return ranges from 14.324% per annum to 25.008%

per annum, which is not very different from what we obtained from the fundamental factor model.

The standard deviation of returns and the ex-post tracking error also remain at about the same level. Given the similarities in average returns and standard deviations, the information ratio and Sharpe ratio are also comparable to those of the fundamental factor model.

While the overall performance of the aggregate Z-score model portfolios is comparable to that of the fundamental factor model portfolios, some differences can be noticed when we look at the individual portfolios more carefully. For example, the sector-matched portfolio has a higher Sharpe ratio in the case of the aggregate Z-score model, whereas the 2% tracking-error portfolio achieves a slightly better risk-return combination in the case of the fundamental factor model.

17.2.3 The Economic Factor Model Performance

Table 17.3 shows the historical performance of the portfolio strategies based on the economic factor model.

Compared with the portfolios built with the fundamental factor model and aggregate Z-score model, the performance of the portfolios based on the economic factor model are somewhat disappointing. Take, for instance, the portfolio with a tracking-error constraint of 2%. Using the economic factor model, this portfolio's average excess return is comparatively small at 1.006% per annum. Its ex-post tracking error, at 4.869%, is not much smaller than it is using the other models. All the economic factor model portfolios' α^B values are close to zero or negative, suggesting that the portfolio strategy actually performed quite poorly at stock picking vis-à-vis the benchmark. The information ratios are all close to zero or negative, and the Sharpe ratios are below that of the benchmark. In summary, our economic factor model portfolios underperformed our benchmark on a risk-adjusted basis over the backtesting period.

17.2.4 Performance Reports for Distribution

In addition to the raw performance results produced for each model in the preceding subsections, portfolio departments may wish to produce other performance reports for internal or external

TABLE 17.3

Historical Performance of the Economic Factor Model

	Tracking Portfolio			Sector-Matched	Factor-Matched	Benchmark
	TE = 2	TE = 5	TE = 10	TE = 5	TE = 5	
Average return	15.049	16.538	17.463	15.975	16.772	14.043
SD return	15.224	18.606	22.605	17.302	18.818	13.601
Min return	−13.980	−15.869	−19.608	−15.784	−15.692	−12.093
Max return	13.578	17.226	23.946	15.755	18.284	12.900
Average excess return	1.006	2.496	3.421	1.932	2.729	—
Ex-post TE	4.869	9.483	13.862	8.204	9.941	—
Min excess return	−4.148	−7.603	−10.506	−6.824	−8.732	—
Max excess return	4.213	7.099	12.895	7.024	7.234	—
$\hat{\alpha}^B$	0.013	−0.009	−0.123	0.017	0.013	—
$t(\hat{\alpha}^B)$	0.099	−0.037	−0.344	0.078	0.048	—
$\hat{\beta}^B$	1.063	1.193	1.363	1.128	1.191	—
IR	0.009	−0.004	−0.033	0.007	0.005	—
$\hat{\alpha}^{MF}$	0.300	0.357	0.767	0.418	0.345	0.932
SR	0.274	0.248	0.216	0.257	0.248	0.286

Note: Portfolios were selected to maximize expected returns subject to the following constraints: (i) Short sales were not allowed ($w \geq 0$). (ii) The portfolio was always fully invested at the rebalancing date ($w'\iota = 1$). (iii) No stock in the portfolio was allowed a weight of more than 5% ($w \leq 0.05$). (iv) The portfolio weights were required, at any rebalancing date, to be less than 33% of the average daily trading volume in absolute dollars of each security, assuming a portfolio value of $500 million (i.e., $w \leq 0.33 \cdot$ **ADDTV**/$500,000,000). (v) The tracking error was one of the following: 2%, 5%, or 10%. For the factor-exposure–matched portfolio, the additional requirement was that the weighted-average factor exposure of the portfolio and the benchmark were perfectly matched for every factor in the stock return model. For the sector-weight-matched portfolio, the additional requirement was that the sector weights of the portfolio and the benchmark were perfectly matched. In the table, average return and average excess return are annualized. TE is the annualized tracking error, and SD is the annualized standard deviation of monthly returns over the entire period. Max and Min stand for the maximum and minimum monthly return. Excess returns are portfolio returns in excess of the benchmark returns annualized. $\hat{\alpha}^B$ and $\hat{\beta}^B$ are the ex-post benchmark α and β (i.e., the estimates from the regression of the portfolio returns on the benchmark returns). $\hat{\alpha}^{MF}$ is the ex-post multifactor α (i.e., the estimate from the regression of the portfolio returns on many factors). IR represents the information ratio of monthly returns of the portfolio (to annualize, multiply by $\sqrt{12}$), and SR is the ex-post Sharpe ratio based upon monthly returns and the one-month Treasury bill return from Fama-French. Performance was calculated from the end of December 2010 to the end of December 2020.

distribution.[3] Below we provide examples of those types of reports for our backtested portfolios. Table 17.4 compares the various period returns and the annual returns together with risk measures for three tracking portfolios with a 5% target tracking error.

The period returns were calculated counting the years of the period backward. Thus the one-year return is the return for the

---

[3] These reports provide information that is suggested by the Association for Investment Management and Research's Global Investment Performance Standards (AIMR-GIPS).

TABLE 17.4

Summary Portfolio Performance

Return (%)	Tracking Portfolio (*TE* = 0.05)			Benchmark
	Fundamental	Z-Score	Economic	Benchmark
1 year	56.569	56.821	62.574	19.423
3 year	29.204	30.447	23.872	14.404
5 year	25.574	25.788	19.571	15.470
10 year	20.871	20.693	15.866	13.945
2020	56.569	56.821	62.574	19.423
2019	41.337	43.038	24.919	31.350
2018	−2.531	−1.044	−6.407	−4.543
2017	36.863	36.200	23.402	22.409
2016	5.776	4.163	4.203	11.996
2015	7.479	7.776	1.647	1.005
2014	13.587	11.969	5.877	13.268
2013	44.984	45.292	47.065	33.044
2012	25.011	21.897	16.464	16.032
2011	−3.662	−2.550	−3.209	1.765
Risk (%)	Fundamental	Z-score	Economic	Benchmark
SD Return	18.830	18.376	18.606	13.601
$\hat{\beta}^B$	1.173	1.159	1.193	—
Ex-post *TE*	10.275	9.671	9.483	—

Note: The period returns reflect the annualized geometric returns over the period. For example, 3 year is the annualized returns for the last three years. SD is the annualized standard deviation of monthly returns over the entire period. β^{CAPM} is the ex-post CAPM β from a regression of portfolio returns against the returns of the S&P 500. Ex-post *TE* is the ex-post annualized tracking error.

year 2020, the three-year return is the return for years 2018 through 2020, and so on. For all selected periods, the returns of the three tracking portfolios are higher than the benchmark return. This is a very significant result. We already learned that all our optimized portfolios provided average excess returns, but what is more impressive is that they consistently obtain higher returns over various return horizons (one-, three-, five-, and ten-year periods). There are some individual years in which the portfolios do not beat the benchmark, but these are the exception rather than the rule. For many years, each of the tracking portfolios outperforms the benchmark. The portfolios based on the fundamental factor model and the Z-score model outperform the benchmark for eight and seven of the 10 years, respectively. The portfolio based on the economic factor model outperforms the benchmark five of nine years.

The last three rows of the table display different measures of risk. In terms of the total risk (measured by the standard deviation of the return) and the tracking error, the fundamental factor model is the riskiest. However, in terms of the systematic risk (represented by $\hat{\beta}^{CAPM}$), the portfolio based on the economic factor model is the riskiest.

Although we have already considered the ex-ante and ex-post tracking error, we provide a table specifically dedicated to examining how well our models controlled the ex-post tracking error (Table 17.5). As stated before, the ex-ante and ex-post tracking errors do not exactly match because the model cannot anticipate returns exactly. The ex-post tracking error is much higher than we expected. Nevertheless, the ex-ante and ex-post values are related, and by lowering the ex-ante tracking error, we also can lower the ex-post tracking error.

Comparing the performance of the three optimized tracking portfolios, we can make the following conclusions:

1. The tracking portfolios achieve a positive average excess return over the benchmark for the period we examined. Also, the tracking portfolios achieve a positive excess return over the benchmark for each of the one-, three-, five-, and 10-year period returns.
2. Most of the positive average excess return is due to benchmark α rather than benchmark β.
3. The tracking portfolios based on the fundamental factor model and the Z-score model perform better than the tracking portfolio based on the economic factor model for the period we examined.

TABLE 17.5

Tracking-Error Analysis

	Fundamental	Z-Score	Economic
Average Excess Return	6.839	6.603	2.496
Ex-post *TE*	10.275	9.671	9.483
Max Excess Return	6.253	5.907	7.099
Min Excess Return	−9.723	−9.290	−7.603

Note: The average excess return and the ex-post tracking error were computed for the baseline portfolios with an ex-ante tracking-error constraint of 5%. The ex-post tracking error was annualized for comparison purposes.

4. The ex-post tracking error is closest to the ex-ante tracking error for the portfolio based on the economic factor model.

5. While the ex-post tracking error is positive, the actual risk faced by the benchmark manager may be lower than the ex-post tracking error suggests because each period's excess return is positive.

17.2.5 Performance Attribution for the Fundamental Factor Model Baseline Portfolio

In this subsection we look in detail at the results of the portfolio based on the fundamental factor model for December 2020, applying performance attribution techniques discussed in Chapter 15. The classical performance attribution, shown in Table 17.6, identifies

TABLE 17.6

Classical Performance Attribution for a December 2020 Portfolio

GICS Sector	Portfolio		Benchmark	
	w_j^P	r_j^P	w_j^B	r_j^B
Energy (10)	0.009	19.23	0.023	4.38
Materials (15)	0.022	4.17	0.027	2.50
Industrial (20)	0.072	8.09	0.087	1.16
Consumer discretionary (25)	0.124	4.52	0.121	2.45
Consumer staples (30)	0.067	4.34	0.077	1.17
Health care (35)	0.193	6.99	0.136	3.98
Financials (40)	0.040	12.56	0.109	6.18
Information technology (45)	0.302	6.45	0.277	5.87
Telecommunication services (50)	0.060	2.88	0.114	2.91
Utilities (55)	0.038	4.70	0.028	0.70
Real estate (60)	0.002	18.02	0.001	9.54
Unclassified	0.071	9.71	0.000	—

$r_P = 6.584$

$r_B = 3.858$

$r_P - r_B = 2.726$

$AE = -0.284$

$SSE = 3.010$

Note: Return variables are expressed in monthly percentage terms. AE stands for allocation effects and SSE stands for security selection effects. The sectors are the two-digit sector classifications of the Standard & Poor's GICS system. GICS codes are in parentheses. The Unclassified sector is the group of stocks that did not have a GICS sector code in our portfolios.

the portfolio return in each economic sector and then breaks down the excess return into its two parts: the part due to the sector weights and the part due to the within-sector security weights. We chose to use the two-digit sector breakdown according to Standard & Poor's Global Industry Classification Standard (GICS).

Looking at the table, we see that in absolute terms the information technology sector has the highest sector weight of 30.2% in our portfolio. Relative to the benchmark, however, the health care sector has the highest active weight (19.3% for the portfolio versus 13.6% for the benchmark). The return of the health care sector in the benchmark was not small, but not much higher than the other sectors' returns, so on first inspection it is unclear whether our overweighting of the health care sector was a good choice. The returns from the particular health care sector stocks in our portfolio are quite high (6.99%) compared with the returns of the health care stocks included in the benchmark (3.98%). This shows that our quantitative model was able to select superior stocks within the health care sector for the month of December 2020. Of course, the tracking portfolio sometimes selects "wrong" sectors and "wrong" stocks. For example, the tracking portfolio gave a higher weight to the underperforming utility sector than the benchmark did. Overall, though, our optimized tracking portfolio outperformed the benchmark in December 2020 by 2.726%. The table also shows the overall asset allocation effect (AE) and the security selection effect (SSE). The former effect, -0.284%, reflects our model's poor performance in terms of selecting good sectors of the stock market, but the latter effect, 3.010%, shows our model to be quite capable of picking good stocks within a sector.

Quantitative equity portfolio managers may be more concerned with multifactor performance attribution than with the classical attribution, as discussed in Chapter 15. In Table 17.7 we present the multifactor performance attribution. The excess total returns of the portfolio over the benchmark for December 2020 are mainly due to a positive *attribution* α. Attribution α is the residual error in that month (i.e., the part of the return that is not explained by the factors).[4] During the month of December 2020, the portfolio achieved an excess return over the benchmark of 2.726%, of which 2.266% was due to attribution α. The remainder is attributed to the

---

[4] Since attribution α is realized errors of the stock return model, we do not define it elsewhere in the book. Some practitioners may prefer to call it the *unexplained excess return*.

TABLE 17.7

Multifactor Performance Attribution of a December 2020 Portfolio

Return Decomposition	
Source	**Value**
EBITDAP	0.426
BB	−0.060
SUE	0.196
PSL	−0.085
TP3M	−0.016
$\hat{\alpha}$	2.266
Risk Decomposition	
Source	**Value**
EBITDAEV	0.490
BB	0.903
SUE	0.343
PSL	0.094
TP3M	0.000
$\hat{\omega}^2$	27.134
Adjustment for factor correlation	−0.537

Note: All numbers are presented in percentage terms. EBITDAP stands for the EBITDA-to-price ratio, BB for Bollinger bands, SUE for standardized unanticipated earnings, PSL for Pastor-Stambaugh liquidity and TP3M for 10 year-three-month term premium. $\hat{\alpha}$ is the attribution α, which is the realized residual. $\hat{\omega}^2$ is the variance of the residual return. The factor premiums for the five factors in December 2020 were −2.26%, 0.09%, 0.87%, −0.92%, 0.84%, respectively.

exposure to five factors. The exposure to EBITDAEV and SUE had a positive contribution to the excess return, while the exposure to BB, PSL, and TP3M had a negative contribution to the portfolio excess return. Most of the overall risk also was attributable to portfolio-specific diversifiable risk rather than to risk caused by exposure to certain factors.

Sometimes quantitative portfolio managers want to be able to attribute the portfolio's performance to the returns of the individual stock holdings. In Tables 17.8 and 17.9 we produce the weights and returns of 10 stocks whose weights are highest compared with the benchmark weights and 10 stocks whose weights are lowest compared to the benchmark weights, all as of December 2020.[5]

---

[5] For the readers who have forgotten the definitions of the components in this table, please refer back to Chapter 15.

TABLE 17.8

Inside a December 2020 Portfolio

Ticker	r_i	w_i^P	w_i^B	x_i	$\hat\alpha^{MF}$	Exposure on				
						EBITDAP	BB	SUE	PSL	TP3M
Most Overweight										
KMB	−2.464	0.036	0.002	−0.086	0.124	−0.005	−0.018	0.002	0.009	−0.001
NEE	4.838	0.021	0.005	0.079	0.201	0.001	−0.003	0.012	0.000	0.001
FRPT	3.733	0.013	0.000	0.050	4.116	0.002	−0.022	0.009	0.005	−0.018
ERIE	9.740	0.013	0.000	0.129	0.859	0.003	−0.012	0.007	−0.003	−0.007
ZM	−29.484	0.013	0.000	−0.378	3.943	−0.006	−0.014	−0.004	0.006	0.092
ABT	1.174	0.017	0.006	0.013	1.193	0.001	−0.005	0.003	0.001	−0.004
NET	1.212	0.010	0.000	0.012	2.330	−0.001	−0.025	0.002	0.010	0.065
FVRR	−2.611	0.010	0.000	−0.026	−0.249	0.002	−0.031	0.010	0.006	0.125
AHCO	25.787	0.009	0.000	0.227	5.083	0.009	−0.031	0.017	0.001	−0.057
APPF	10.501	0.009	0.000	0.092	−0.235	−0.007	−0.034	0.007	0.015	0.005
Most Underweight										
JPM	7.796	0.002	0.012	−0.075	0.945	−0.008	0.022	−0.002	−0.007	0.004
HD	−3.720	0.000	0.010	0.036	1.923	−0.004	0.010	−0.003	−0.003	0.012
UNH	4.636	0.000	0.010	−0.048	−0.020	−0.001	0.008	−0.001	−0.005	−0.018
FB	−1.376	0.011	0.022	0.015	0.805	−0.007	0.015	−0.007	−0.005	0.008
PG	0.194	0.000	0.011	−0.002	1.160	−0.004	0.009	−0.005	−0.000	0.013
V	3.984	0.000	0.012	−0.045	0.550	0.002	0.016	−0.002	−0.007	−0.001
JNJ	8.778	0.000	0.012	−0.109	−0.110	−0.002	0.013	−0.001	−0.001	−0.006
WMT	−5.308	0.000	0.014	0.074	1.109	−0.003	0.009	−0.004	−0.002	0.002
AAPL	11.457	0.050	0.066	−0.181	1.173	−0.009	0.035	−0.021	−0.005	0.037
BRK.B	1.293	0.000	0.017	−0.023	−0.191	−0.006	0.025	−0.003	−0.009	−0.006

Note: Stock return r_i, excess return $x_i = (w_i^P - w_i^B)r_i$, and $\hat\alpha^{MF}$ are presented in percentage terms. Portfolio and benchmark weights, w_i^P and w_i^B, as well as exposures are not in percentage terms. The factor exposures represent the $\tilde{w}_i\hat\beta_{i,j}$ for each company with respect to each factor as described in Chapter 15. The $\hat\alpha^{MF}$ is not multiplied by $\tilde{w}_i$. Company names are as follows (ticker symbols inside brackets): Kimberly-Clark Corp (KMB), Nextera Energy Inc (NEE), Freshpet Inc (FRPT), Erie Indemnity Co (ERIE), Zoom Video Comunications Inc (ZM), Abbott Laboratories (ABT), Cloudflare Inc (NET), Fiverr International Ltd (FVRR), Adapthealth Corp (AHCO), Appfolio Inc (APPF), J.P. Morgan Chase & Co. (JPM), Home Depot Inc (HD), United Health Group Inc (UNH), Facebook Inc (FB), Procter & Gamble Co (PG), Visa Inc (V), Johnson & Johnson (JNJ), Walmart Inc (WMT), Apple Inc (AAPL), and Berkshire Hathaway (BRK.B). The numbers of stocks in the portfolio and benchmark is 1,491 and 467, respectively. The table lists the 10 stocks whose portfolio weights are highest relative to the benchmark weights and the 10 stocks whose portfolio weights are lowest relative to the benchmark weights. Each weight represents the beginning-of-month weight in the stock for the benchmark and the portfolio. The ex-ante tracking error for this portfolio was chosen as 5%.

For example, Kimberly Clark (KMB) has a weight of 0.036 in the tracking portfolio and a weight of 0.002 in the benchmark. Our portfolio's excess weight in KMB is therefore 0.034, or 3.4%. On the other hand, Berkshire Hathaway (BRK.B) has a zero weight in the tracking portfolio and a weight of 0.017 in the benchmark. Thus, the excess weight in BRK.B is −0.017, or −1.7%. Not all

T A B L E   1 7 . 9

The Multifactor Attribution of a December 2020 Portfolio's Individual Stocks

Ticker	r_i	w_i^P	w_i^B	x_i	$\hat{\alpha}_i$	EBITDAP	BB	SUE	PSL	TP3M	MR
					Most Overweight						
KMB	−2.464	0.036	0.002	−0.086	−0.088	0.011	−0.002	0.002	−0.008	−0.001	1.273
NEE	4.838	0.021	0.005	0.079	0.071	−0.002	−0.000	0.010	−0.000	0.000	0.819
FRPT	3.733	0.013	0.000	0.050	0.067	−0.004	−0.002	0.008	−0.005	−0.015	2.550
ERIE	9.740	0.013	0.000	0.129	0.135	−0.008	−0.001	0.006	0.003	−0.006	0.885
ZM	−29.484	0.013	0.000	−0.378	−0.458	0.013	−0.001	−0.003	−0.006	0.078	3.627
ABT	1.174	0.017	0.006	0.013	0.017	−0.001	−0.001	0.003	−0.001	−0.003	0.729
NET	1.212	0.010	0.000	0.012	−0.035	0.002	−0.002	0.001	−0.009	0.055	4.025
FVRR	−2.611	0.010	0.000	−0.026	−0.127	−0.004	−0.003	0.008	−0.006	0.105	4.951
AHCO	25.787	0.009	0.000	0.227	0.285	−0.021	−0.003	0.015	−0.001	−0.048	3.315
APPF	10.501	0.009	0.000	0.092	0.083	0.017	−0.003	0.006	−0.014	0.004	5.337
					Most Underweight						
JPM	7.796	0.002	0.012	−0.075	−0.103	0.019	0.002	−0.002	0.006	0.003	0.144
HD	−3.720	0.000	0.010	0.036	0.015	0.009	0.001	−0.002	0.002	0.010	0.002
UNH	4.636	0.000	0.010	−0.048	−0.040	0.002	0.001	−0.001	0.005	−0.015	0.303
FB	−1.376	0.011	0.022	0.015	−0.007	0.015	0.001	−0.006	0.005	0.007	0.050
PG	0.194	0.000	0.011	−0.002	−0.020	0.010	0.001	−0.005	0.000	0.011	0.162
V	3.984	0.000	0.012	−0.045	−0.045	−0.005	0.001	−0.002	0.006	−0.001	1.239
JNJ	8.778	0.000	0.012	−0.109	−0.109	0.005	0.001	−0.001	0.001	−0.005	0.254
WMT	−5.308	0.000	0.014	0.074	0.067	0.007	0.001	−0.004	0.002	0.001	0.050
AAPL	11.457	0.050	0.066	−0.181	−0.222	0.020	0.003	−0.018	0.004	0.031	0.808
BRK.B	1.293	0.000	0.017	−0.023	−0.039	0.013	0.002	−0.003	0.008	−0.005	0.411

Note: Stock return r_i, excess return $x_i = (w_i^P - w_i^B)r_p$, $\hat{\alpha}$ returns on factors, and marginal risk MR are presented in percentage terms. Portfolio and benchmark weights w_i^P and w_i^B are not in percentage terms. The factor returns represent the $\bar{w}_i\hat{\beta}_{i,j}\hat{f}_j$ for each company with respect to each factor as described in Chapter 15. Company names are as follows (ticker symbols inside parentheses): Kimberly-Clark Corp (KMB), Nextera Energy Inc (NEE), Freshpet Inc (FRPT), Erie Indemnity Co (ERIE), Zoom Video Comunications Inc (ZM), Abbott Laboratories (ABT), Cloudflare Inc (NET), Fiverr International Ltd (FVRR), Adapthealth Corp (AHCO), Appfolio Inc (APPF), J.P. Morgan Chase & Co. (JPM), Home Depot Inc (HD), United Health Group Inc (UNH), Facebook Inc (FB), Procter & Gamble Co (PG), Visa Inc (V), Johnson & Johnson (JNJ), Walmart Inc (WMT), Apple Inc (AAPL), and Berkshire Hathaway (BRK.B). The numbers of stocks in the portfolio and benchmark are 1,491 and 467, respectively. The table lists the 10 stocks whose portfolio weights are highest relative to the benchmark weights and the 10 stocks whose portfolio weights are lowest relative to the benchmark weights. Each weight represents the beginning-of-month weight in the stock for the benchmark and the portfolio. The ex-ante tracking error for this portfolio was chosen as 5%. The factor premiums for the five factors in December 2020 are −2.26%, 0.09%, 0.87%, −0.92%, and 0.84%, respectively.

overweighted stocks contributed to the excess return, as can be seen from the negative values of x_i. Certain picks such as Adapthealth (AHCO) and Erie Indemnity (ERIE) turned out to be good ones, adding 0.227% and 0.129% to the excess return, respectively. In the end, the total gains from the overweighted stocks exceeded the total losses from the underweighted stocks. This confirms what we already showed elsewhere—that, overall, the tracking portfolio managed to assign greater weights to the "right" stocks.

The table also shows the active exposures to the five factors in December 2020.[6] For example, the active position in KMB has a positive exposure to the standardized unanticipated earnings (SUE) and Pastor-Stambaugh liquidity (PSL) factors and a negative exposure to the EBITDA-to-price ratio (EBITDAP), Bollinger bands (BB), and ten year–three-month term premium (TP3M) factors. Table 17.9 shows the returns of the active positions attributable to the five factors for December 2020.[7] We find that the return of the active position in KMB attributable to all of the five factors is 0.011% − 0.002% + 0.002% − 0.008% − 0.001% = 0.002%. The attribution α for KMB is − 0.088% for December 2020. Given the returns and estimates of the factor premiums for December 2020, we might have expected a return for KMB equal to 0.126%, rather than − 0.086%.[8] The reason for the difference is the random nature of financial markets. Thus, in any given month, the fluctuations of the error term in our model, and also the effect of the misspecification of our stock return model, can lead to differences in what is expected ex ante and what might happen in any given month. The realized α for this stock in December 2020 is just the actual return of the stock minus the factor exposures multiplied by the realized factor estimates. That is, $\alpha_i = x_i - \sum_{j=1}^{5} \tilde{w}_i \hat{\beta}_{i,j} \hat{f}_j = -0.086\% - 0.002\% = -0.088\%$.

17.3 THE TRANSACTIONS COST–MANAGED PORTFOLIO PERFORMANCE

The analysis so far has ignored the transactions costs of buying and selling stocks. The incorporation of realistic transactions costs into our analysis changes the performance reports for the portfolios. We rebalanced these portfolios on a monthly basis, so to account for transactions costs, we computed the necessary

---

[6] Remember, the active exposure is given by $\tilde{w}_i \hat{\beta}_{i,j}$ as explained in Chapter 15. To obtain the actual factor exposures of each stock, one can easily divide the active exposures by $\tilde{w}_i$. They will not be exactly the same due to rounding issues, but they will be close. For KMB, the division results in factor exposures of −0.147, −0.529, 0.059, 0.265, and −0.029, while the actual factor exposures are −0.146, −0.529, 0.054, 0.255, and −0.04.

[7] Remember, the returns of the factors are given by $\tilde{w}_i \hat{\beta}_{i,j} \hat{f}_j$, where $\hat{f}_j$ is the realized factor premium during that month, as estimated by a cross-sectional regression. For more information, see Chapter 15.

[8] This is assuming that our ex-ante α for KMB remained the same in December 2020 at 0.124%.

TABLE 17.10

Historical Performance Considering Transactions Costs

	Tracking Portfolio	Transactions Costs Optimized	Benchmark
Average return	18.122	18.602	13.785
SD return	18.798	19.008	13.601
Min return	−14.774	−15.252	−12.095
Max return	15.105	15.155	12.897
Average excess return	4.337	4.817	—
Ex-post TE	10.258	10.318	—
Min excess return	−9.898	−9.756	—
Max excess return	6.051	6.179	—
$\hat{\alpha}^B$	0.174	0.194	—
$t(\hat{\alpha}^B)$	0.632	0.705	—
$\hat{\beta}^B$	1.170	1.188	—
IR	0.060	0.067	—
$\hat{\alpha}^{MF}$	0.158	0.250	0.971
SR	0.270	0.274	0.280

Note: The tracking portfolio does not consider transactions costs when rebalancing but still incurs them. The transactions cost–optimized portfolio attempts to explicitly limit the impact of transactions costs when rebalancing. Transactions costs are based on Table 16.12 in Chapter 16. Portfolios were selected to maximize expected returns subject to the following constraints: (i) Short sales were not allowed ($w \geq 0$). (ii) The portfolio was always fully invested at the rebalancing date ($w'\iota = 1$). (iii) No stock in the portfolio was allowed a weight of more than 5% ($w \leq 0.05$). (iv) The portfolio weights were required, at any rebalancing date, to be less than 33% of the average daily trading volume in absolute dollars of each security, assuming a portfolio value of $500 million (i.e., $w \leq 0.33 \cdot$ ADDTV/$500,000,000$). (v) The tracking error was 5%. In the table, average return and average excess return are annualized. TE is the annualized tracking error, and SD is the annualized standard deviation of monthly returns over the entire period. Max and Min stand for the maximum and minimum monthly return. Excess returns are portfolio returns in excess of the benchmark returns annualized. $\hat{\alpha}^B$ and $\hat{\beta}^B$ are the ex-post benchmark α and β (i.e., the estimates from the regression of the portfolio returns on the benchmark returns). $\hat{\alpha}^{MF}$ is the ex-post multifactor α (i.e., the estimate from the regression of the portfolio returns on many factors). IR represents the information ratio of monthly returns of the portfolio (to annualize, multiply by $\sqrt{12}$), and SR is the ex-post Sharpe ratio based upon monthly returns and the one-month Treasury bill return from Fama-French. Performance was calculated from the end of December 2010 to the end of December 2020.

costs to rebalance our portfolios using the Abel Noser data, as mentioned in Chapter 16. By subtracting these costs from the returns of our portfolios, we obtained the after-transactions-costs returns.

We present the performance statistics that account for transactions costs in Table 17.10. The optimized tracking portfolio is based on the fundamental factor model and has a target tracking error of 5%. The tracking portfolio still outperforms the benchmark after accounting for the transactions costs, but the average excess return is significantly lower at 4.337% per annum compared with the 6.839% per annum when we ignored transactions costs. In terms of the Sharpe ratio, however, the tracking portfolio fails to outperform the benchmark when transactions costs are accounted for.

This table also shows the performance of the portfolio that was optimized for transactions costs. That is, we created this portfolio using the fundamental factor model while explicitly accounting for the effects of transactions costs, as discussed in Chapters 10 and 16. This transactions cost-optimized portfolio increases the average return by about 0.5% per annum, while the standard deviation goes up by about 0.2%. Relative to the benchmark, the transactions cost–optimized portfolio achieves an excess return of about 5% with a realized tracking error of about 10%. However, its *SR* is not higher than that of the benchmark in this period.[9] Practitioners should include transactions costs in their backtests of models; otherwise, the portfolios that implement the models may have too much turnover and fall short of expected results.

17.4 THE TAX-MANAGED PORTFOLIO PERFORMANCE

Table 17.11 presents the after-tax performance statistics of the tracking portfolio and the tax-managed portfolio. We made adjustments for capital gains and losses. We did not make adjustments for the dividend tax because the tax rates vary for different types of investors. We examined trading at the time of reestimation (the end of each month), calculated the realized capital gains and losses that would occur according to the trades we would have to make, computed the tax burden (applying a 15% tax rate on long-term capital gains and a 37% tax rate on short-term capital gains), and subtracted this value from the return.

In Table 17.11 we consider five portfolios. The first portfolio, Tracking FIFO, is the standard fundamental factor model optimized for a 5% tracking error, but accounting for tax effects. Security lots are sold according to the first in, first out (FIFO) method. The second portfolio, Tracking Optimized, rebalances the portfolio

---

[9] Some of the transactions cost-optimized portfolios that we examined (with a different list of factors) and not presented to the reader did achieve a higher *SR* than the benchmark during this period. Nonetheless, the not-so-impressive performance shown in Table 17.10 illustrates the difficulty of beating the benchmark when aggressive transactions costs are applied, as we do in our analysis.

TABLE 17.11

Historical Performance Considering Taxes

| | Tracking | | Tax-Managed | Benchmark | |
	FIFO	Optimized	Optimized	FIFO	Optimized
Average return	15.946	17.507	19.036	13.877	13.966
SD return	16.289	16.343	17.333	13.593	13.588
Min return	−13.084	−12.776	−14.526	−12.055	−12.035
Max return	12.945	13.166	14.624	12.864	12.874
Average excess return	2.069	3.630	5.159	—	0.090
Ex-post TE	8.565	8.547	8.883	—	0.027
Min excess return	−9.267	−8.914	−8.837	—	−0.001
Max excess return	5.530	5.669	6.266	—	0.044
$\hat{\alpha}^B$	0.151	0.275	0.320	—	0.008
$t(\hat{\alpha}^B)$	0.641	1.170	1.324	—	10.554
$\hat{\beta}^B$	1.019	1.025	1.099	—	1.000
IR	0.061	0.111	0.126	—	1.002
$\hat{\alpha}^{MF}$	−0.058	0.082	0.208	0.913	0.925
SR	0.273	0.299	0.308	0.283	0.285

Note: Tracking FIFO is the standard fundamental factor model optimized for a 5% tracking error, but accounting for the tax effects. Security lots are sold according to the first in, first out (FIFO) method. Tracking Optimized rebalances the portfolio according to the tax optimization rules, presented in Chapter 11, on which tax lots to sell. Tax-Managed Optimized uses tax-harvesting techniques to generate losses and reduce the tax burden, as explained in Chapter 16, Section 16.8.2. Benchmark FIFO and Benchmark Optimized are the benchmark portfolios where stocks are bought and sold, using either the FIFO method or the optimized method of selling tax lots as we do for the Tracking Optimized portfolio. Portfolios were selected to maximize expected returns subject to the following constraints: (i) Short sales were not allowed ($\mathbf{w} \geq 0$). (ii) The portfolio was always fully invested at the rebalancing date ($\mathbf{w}'\iota = 1$). (iii) No stock in the portfolio was allowed a weight of more than 5% ($\mathbf{w} \leq 0.05$). (iv) The portfolio weights were required, at any rebalancing date, to be less than 33% of the average daily trading volume in absolute dollars of each security, assuming a portfolio value of $500 million (i.e., $\mathbf{w} \leq 0.33 \cdot$ **ADDTV**/$500,000,000). (v) The tracking error was 5%. In the table, average return and average excess return are annualized. TE is the annualized tracking error, and SD is the annualized standard deviation of monthly returns over the entire period. Max and Min stand for the maximum and minimum monthly return. Excess returns are portfolio returns in excess of the FIFO benchmark returns annualized. $\hat{\alpha}^B$ and $\hat{\beta}^B$ are the ex-post FIFO benchmark α and β (i.e., the estimates from the regression of the portfolio returns on the FIFO benchmark returns). $\hat{\alpha}^{MF}$ is the ex-post multifactor α (i.e., the estimate from the regression of the portfolio returns on many factors). IR represents the information ratio of monthly returns of the portfolio (to annualize, multiply by $\sqrt{12}$), and SR is the ex-post Sharpe ratio based upon monthly returns and the one-month Treasury bill return from Fama-French. Performance was calculated from the end of December 2010 to the end of December 2020.

according to the tax optimization rules presented in Chapter 11 on which tax lots to sell. The third portfolio, Tax-Managed Optimized, uses tax-harvesting techniques to generate losses and reduce the tax burden, as explained in Chapter 11 and Chapter 16, Section 16.8.2. The fourth and fifth portfolios are benchmark portfolios where stocks are bought and sold using either the FIFO method or the optimized method of selling tax lots as we do for the Tracking Optimized portfolio.

The average excess return of the tracking portfolio is reduced almost by 5% per annum when we properly account for the tax burden. That is, when we compare the fundamental factor model with 5% tracking error from Table 17.1 to the Tracking FIFO portfolio in this table, the performance difference is almost 5% (20.881% to 15.946%), reflecting the losses from taxes. The reduction in performance due to taxes is smaller, about 3% (20.881% to 17.507%), if the optimal tax-lot selection technique, Tracking Optimized, is applied. The benchmark is less affected by taxes, since there is less turnover in the benchmark.

When tax-loss-harvesting techniques were applied to the portfolio optimizations, Tax-Managed Optimized, we were able to outperform the benchmark by 5% per annum with a tracking error of 8.883%. That is, our loss-harvesting technique generated almost 2% extra return every year without adding significant tracking error compared to the simple tax strategies. Along with tax harvesting comes an implicit strategy that tends to overweight recent "winners" (stocks whose prices have risen) and tends to underweight recent "losers." To the extent that stock prices exhibit positive autocorrelation, then past winners will outperform past losers, adding to the gains of a loss-harvesting strategy. This aspect of tax-loss-harvesting depends on the rebalancing frequency; if the "wrong" frequency is chosen, the beneficial returns associated with tax loss harvesting may be substantially smaller.

17.5 THE LEVERAGED PORTFOLIO PERFORMANCE

Some quantitative portfolio managers choose to leverage their equity portfolios in order to enhance returns, as we discussed in detail in Chapter 12 and a bit in Chapter 16. To increase the average return, we created leverage by purchasing S&P 500 futures. The amount of futures was determined so that the β with respect to the S&P 500 was exactly 2 at the beginning of every month. Given a high α, increasing the β of the overall portfolio results in an even higher average return, provided that the stock market returns are generally positive.

Table 17.12 shows the performance statistics of the leveraged portfolio, the tracking portfolio, and the benchmark. For this and the following sections, we present the S&P 500 return figures provided by Compustat. These figures are different from our own

TABLE 17.12

Historical Performance of Portfolio Strategies in a Leveraged Form

	Tracking Portfolio	Leveraged Portfolio	S&P 500
Average return	20.908	35.484	13.982
SD return	18.848	33.022	13.542
Min return	−14.510	−27.927	−12.351
Max return	15.364	27.577	12.819
$\hat{\alpha}^B$	0.389	0.644	—
$t(\hat{\alpha}^B)$	1.395	1.290	—
$\hat{\beta}^B$	1.178	2.043	—
IR	0.133	0.123	—
$\hat{\alpha}^{MF}$	0.355	0.834	—
SR	0.312	0.305	0.286

Note: The leveraged portfolio was constructed by computing the β of the optimized portfolio every month, then purchasing the corresponding number of S&P 500 futures contracts to achieve a desired $\beta = 2$. The tracking portfolio has no leverage, while the leveraged portfolio is levered so as to achieve an overall portfolio $\beta = 2$. Portfolios were selected to maximize expected returns subject to the following constraints: (i) Short sales were not allowed ($\mathbf{w} \geq 0$). (ii) The portfolio was always fully invested at the rebalancing date ($\mathbf{w}'\iota = 1$). (iii) No stock in the portfolio was allowed a weight of more than 5% ($\mathbf{w} \leq 0.05$). (iv) The portfolio weights were required, at any rebalancing date, to be less than 33% of the average daily trading volume in absolute dollars of each security, assuming a portfolio value of $500 million (i.e., $\mathbf{w} \leq 0.33 \cdot$ ADDTV/\$500,000,000). (v) The tracking error was 5%. In the table, average return and average excess return are annualized. *TE* is the annualized tracking error, and SD is the annualized standard deviation of monthly returns over the entire period. Max and Min stand for the maximum and minimum monthly return. Excess returns are portfolio returns in excess of the benchmark returns annualized. $\hat{\alpha}^B$ and $\hat{\beta}^B$ are the ex-post benchmark α and β (i.e., the estimates from the regression of the portfolio returns on the benchmark returns). $\hat{\alpha}^{MF}$ is the ex-post multifactor α (i.e., the estimate from the regression of the portfolio returns on many factors). *IR* represents the information ratio of monthly returns of the portfolio (to annualize, multiply by $\sqrt{12}$), and *SR* is the ex-post Sharpe ratio based upon monthly returns and the one-month Treasury bill return from Fama-French. Performance was calculated from the end of December 2010 to the end of December 2020.

S&P 500 benchmark calculations in prior sections due to our exclusion of certain REIT stocks. The average return of the leveraged portfolio is higher than the return of the tracking portfolio by almost 15% per annum. Since the increase in the average return comes from the high β, the risk also increases from 18.8% per annum to 33% per annum. For the same reason, the information ratio and the Sharpe ratio are slightly reduced.

This leveraged portfolio was rebalanced monthly to achieve an ex-ante β of 2. Our ex-post β (calculated with respect to the

S&P 500 total return index) is very near 2 at 2.043.[10] As for the benchmark , we do not control it directly.[11]

17.6 THE MARKET-NEUTRAL PORTFOLIO PERFORMANCE

Table 17.13 presents the performance statistics of the two market-neutral portfolios, along with the returns on cash (1-month Treasury bill returns) and the S&P 500. One of the market-neutral portfolios, the sector-neutral portfolio, is composed of a long position in the sector-weight-matched tracking portfolio and a short position in the benchmark. The factor-neutral portfolio is composed of a long position in the factor-exposure-matched tracking portfolio and a short position in the benchmark.

It is not always clear what the appropriate benchmark for a market-neutral portfolio is. In a sense, it is the risk-free rate of return because we have attempted to eliminate market risk. From another perspective, it is the market return, because we want our portfolio to have a low correlation with the market. We therefore have included both benchmarks in the performance tables. Both the sector-neutral portfolio and the factor-neutral portfolio are dollar-neutral as well, and their returns are calculated as the tracking portfolio return minus the benchmark return plus the risk-free rate. The average returns of these two portfolios are higher than the cash return, which is the risk-free rate. The standard deviation of the returns (SD) is significantly lowered given the low market exposure of the market-neutral portfolios.

The correlation between the market-neutral portfolios and the S&P 500 ρ^B is quite low, which is the aim of market neutrality. Both market-neutral portfolios have a relatively low β^B. We did not impose neutrality with respect to the benchmark β. However, the sector neutrality or multifactor neutrality affects β^B as well.

Table 17.14 presents the performance of two additional market-neutral portfolios. These portfolios were created directly from the

---

[10] The β^B is not exactly 2 because it is calculated from the portfolio return rather than from the β^B of the individual stocks and weights. Also, it is equal to 2 only at the beginning of every month and consequently can diverge throughout the month because we did not rebalance daily.

[11] In a perfect world, the α of the leveraged portfolio would be identical to the α of the tracking portfolio. In reality, the risk-free rate is not completely independent of the S&P 500.

TABLE 17.13

Historical Performance of Portfolio Strategies in Market-Neutral Form

	Sector-Neutral	Factor-Neutral	S&P 500	Cash
Average return	6.572	0.946	13.982	0.547
SD return	8.786	8.730	13.542	0.229
Min return	−8.688	−9.186	−12.351	0.000
Max return	5.425	4.859	12.819	0.210
ρ^B	0.205	0.339	—	—
$\hat{\alpha}^B$	0.351	−0.213	—	—
$t(\hat{\alpha}^B)$	1.482	−0.943	—	—
$\hat{\beta}^B$	0.135	0.220	—	—
IR	0.141	−0.090	—	—
$\hat{\alpha}^{MF}$	−0.559	−0.670	—	—
SR	0.198	0.013	0.286	—

Note: The sector-neutral portfolio is created by taking a long position in the sector-matched tracking portfolio and a short position in the benchmark so that it is dollar-neutral as well. The factor-neutral portfolio is created by taking a long position in the factor-matched tracking portfolio and a short position in the benchmark so that it is dollar-neutral as well. The tracking portfolios were selected to maximize expected returns subject to the following constraints: (i) Short sales were not allowed ($\mathbf{w} \geq 0$). (ii) The portfolio was always fully invested at the rebalancing date ($\mathbf{w}'\iota = 1$). (iii) No stock in the portfolio was allowed a weight of more than 5% ($\mathbf{w} \leq 0.05$). (iv) The portfolio weights were required, at any rebalancing date, to be less than 33% of the average daily trading volume in absolute dollars of each security, assuming a portfolio value of $500 million (i.e., $\mathbf{w} \leq 0.33 \cdot$ **ADDTV**/$500,000,000). (v) The tracking error was 5%. In the table, average return and average excess return are annualized. TE is the annualized tracking error, and SD is the annualized standard deviation of monthly returns over the entire period. Max and Min stand for the maximum and minimum monthly return. Excess returns are portfolio returns in excess of the benchmark returns annualized. ρ^B is the correlation between the portfolio return and the benchmark return. $\hat{\alpha}^B$ and $\hat{\beta}^B$ are the ex-post benchmark α and β (i.e., the estimates from the regression of the portfolio returns on the benchmark returns). $\hat{\alpha}^{MF}$ is the ex-post multifactor α (i.e., the estimate from the regression of the portfolio returns on many factors). IR represents the information ratio of monthly returns of the portfolio (to annualize, multiply by $\sqrt{12}$), and SR is the ex-post Sharpe ratio based upon monthly returns and the one-month Treasury bill return from Fama-French. Performance was calculated from the end of December 2010 to the end of December 2020.

optimization by imposing two new constraints, while maximizing expected excess return. The dollar-neutrality constraint required that all weights in the portfolio sum to 0. The weights of long positions summed to 1, and the weights of short positions summed to 1 as well. The second additional constraint imposed either factor neutrality or sector neutrality. The factor neutrality constraint required the portfolio to have zero exposure to each factor in the model. The sector-neutrality constraint required the portfolio to have a zero weight for each sector. We dropped the full-investment constraint, the no-short-sale constraint, and the tracking-error constraint. We modified the diversification constraint and the trading-volume

TABLE 17.14

Historical Performance of Optimized Market Neutral Portfolios

	Sector-Neutral			Factor-Neutral			S&P 500	Cash
	Long-Short	Long	Short	Long-Short	Long	Short		
Average return	13.057	19.198	6.688	11.202	19.982	9.328	13.982	0.547
SD return	13.086	19.600	17.038	16.028	23.518	16.618	13.542	0.229
Min return	−10.888	−13.908	−13.670	−27.726	−39.198	−12.169	−12.351	0.000
Max return	13.315	21.758	16.762	17.115	24.118	16.270	12.819	0.210
ρ^B	0.081	0.765	0.816	0.179	0.770	0.916	—	—
$\hat{\alpha}^B$	0.955	0.317	−0.638	0.649	0.124	−0.525	—	—
$t(\hat{\alpha}^B)$	2.664	0.912	−2.354	1.495	0.301	−2.850	—	—
$\hat{\beta}^B$	0.078	1.105	1.027	0.213	1.335	1.122	—	—
IR	0.253	0.087	−0.224	0.142	0.029	−0.271	—	—
$\hat{\alpha}^{MF}$	0.055	1.559	1.504	−0.955	0.962	1.917	—	—
SR	0.277	0.275	0.104	0.192	0.238	0.152	0.286	—

Note: The sector-neutral and factor-neutral portfolios are rebalanced monthly using the optimization algorithm. Every month we optimize these portfolios to achieve the highest expected return subject to a dollar-neutrality constraint (i.e., $\sum_{j=1}^{N} w_j = 0$). For the sector-neutral portfolio, we impose an additional sector-neutrality constraint that all the sector weights of the portfolio are zero. For the factor-neutral portfolio, we impose a factor-neutrality constraint that all the betas of the portfolio are zero. Long-Short is the market-neutral portfolio (long portfolio minus short portfolio), Long is the long portfolio within the market-neutral portfolio, and Short is the short portfolio within the market-neutral portfolio. We apply the following two constraints to the portfolio: (i) No stock in the portfolio was allowed an absolute weight of more than 5% (|w| ≤ 0.05). (ii) The portfolio weights were required, for both long and short positions, at any rebalancing date, to be less than 33% of the average daily trading volume in absolute dollars of each security, assuming a portfolio value of $500 million (i.e., |w| ≤ 0.33 · **ADDTV**/$500,000,000). Average return and average excess return are annualized. *TE* is the annualized tracking error, and SD is the annualized standard deviation of monthly returns over the entire period. Max and Min stand for the maximum and minimum monthly return. Excess returns are portfolio returns in excess of the benchmark returns annualized. ρ^B is the correlation between the portfolio return and the benchmark return. $\hat{\alpha}^B$ and $\hat{\beta}^B$ are the ex-post benchmark α and β (i.e., the estimates from the regression of the portfolio returns on the benchmark returns). $\hat{\alpha}^{MF}$ is the ex-post multifactor α (i.e., the estimate from the regression of the portfolio returns on many factors). *IR* represents the information ratio of monthly returns of the portfolio (to annualize, multiply by $\sqrt{12}$), and *SR* is the ex-post Sharpe ratio based upon monthly returns and the one-month Treasury bill return from Fama-French. Performance was calculated from the end of December 2010 to the end of December 2020.

constraint so as to limit absolute weights rather than weights. Once the market-neutral portfolio was created, we separated it into a long portfolio (the stocks with positive weights) and a short portfolio (the stocks with negative weights). The figures for the short portfolio are presented as if the investor had a long position in the short portfolio.

The optimized market-neutral portfolios recorded much higher returns than the two previous market-neutral portfolios where we simply shorted the S&P 500. The short sides of the optimized market-neutral portfolios had relatively small returns of 6.688% and 9.328%. By shorting these low-return positions rather than shorting the high-return S&P 500, the long-short portfolios produced returns as high as 13.057% and 11.202%. These returns are particularly impressive given the low values of ρ^B and β^B. This suggests that the optimization was quite successful at identifying the stocks that would underperform as well as the stocks that would outperform.

17.7 CONCLUSION

In this chapter we examined the results of our backtests of various types of portfolio strategies described throughout this book. From a backtesting point of view, our primary interest was the average excess returns and the ex-post tracking errors of our portfolios. Many quantitative equity portfolio managers focus on these statistics because they manage their portfolios with respect to a benchmark. For the time period we examined, and from the perspective of these two statistics, the portfolio strategy based on the fundamental factor model performed better than did the strategy based on the economic factor model. Of course, this should not be taken as proof of the superiority of the fundamental factor model in general. Our statistics represent the probable results of specific portfolios from 2011 to 2020. Choosing a model requires consideration of various models' theoretical strengths and appropriateness to current and future conditions. Overall, we were quite satisfied with the performance of the models. We achieved a positive excess return over the benchmark while constraining our tracking error to some degree. In most cases, we achieved a positive α^B over the benchmark with a relatively high information ratio.

The analysis of after-transactions-cost performance and after-tax performance showed that a quantitative portfolio manager can do much more for an investor than just pick the right stocks. Managing transactions costs and tax costs quantitatively is also somewhat more predictable than selecting outperforming stocks. Portfolio managers can and should harness the power of cost and tax management. Our tax-managed portfolios performed much better than the basic tracking portfolio, not only in average return but also in terms of risk-adjusted return. The transactions cost-optimized portfolio did not make a noticeable improvement on the regular tracking portfolio in this particular analysis, but in other data periods it most likely would. It generally makes sense to minimize the portfolio's tax giveaways as much as possible.[12]

We found that leveraging an equity portfolio produced much higher returns and higher risk when the market moved upward. We also showed that it is quite practical to create market-neutral portfolios using a variety of strategies that are relatively uncorrelated with the S&P 500 and yet produce a modest excess return over cash. The results of our example strategies hopefully will aid novices in the field and be of comparative interest to experts.

---

[12] Of course, we used one set of transactions costs assumptions. Readers should make assumptions most appropriate to their own trading practices.

QUESTIONS

17.1. (a) How effective were the optimizations at creating portfolios with the desired tracking error?

   (b) What does this suggest about practical methods of risk
control?

17.2. Discuss the following constraints in practical portfolio optimization. In particular, explain what each constraint means
in layperson's terms and why a portfolio manager might
choose to use it.

   (a) $\mathbf{w} > 0$

   (b) $\mathbf{w}'\iota = 1$

   (c) $\mathbf{w} \leq 0.05$

   (d) $\mathbf{w} \leq \frac{0.33 \cdot \mathbf{ADDTV}_t}{V_t}$

17.3. Did the portfolios with a tracking error of 2% for the fundamental, economic, and Z-score models achieve the following
objectives?

   (a) Positive α^B

   (b) A Sharpe ratio higher than the benchmark's

   (c) The desired tracking error

17.4. In the backtests documented in this chapter, which model
exhibited the smallest difference between ex-ante and ex-
post tracking errors?

17.5. Referring to the December 2020 performance attribution
using the fundamental factor model, please respond to the
following statements.

   (a) The portfolio strategy did well at asset allocation.

   (b) The portfolio strategy did well at stock selection.

   (c) The portfolio strategy was better at asset allocation
than at stock selection.

17.6. These questions relate to the tables on multifactor attribution (Tables 17.7, 17.8, and 17.9).

   (a) In Table 17.7, which factor contributed most to the
excess return?

   (b) In Table 17.7, which factor contributed most to the
excess risk? What is the important contributor to risk?

   (c) In Tables 17.8 and 17.9, which stock contributed most to
the excess return, and by how much? What was the
main source of this stock's contribution to the return?

   (d) In Tables 17.8 and 17.9, which stock contributed the least
to the excess return, and by how much? What was the
main source of this stock's contribution to the return?

17.7. In the backtests that explicitly considered transactions costs,
  (a) How much higher was the average return owing to considering the transactions costs directly in the optimization?
  (b) Was the risk any higher as a result?

17.8. The following questions concern the results of the tax-optimized portfolio versus the portfolios that mildly consider taxes.
  (a) What was the difference in average returns between the Tracking Optimized and the simple Tracking FIFO method?
  (b) Did loss harvesting improve the after-tax returns as illustrated by the Tax-Managed Optimized portfolio?
  (c) Based on the evidence in this chapter, is it important to explicitly consider taxes or not? State your answer and support with evidence.
  (d) How would you have done the backtest better?

17.9. The following questions pertain to the leveraged portfolio results.
  (a) Decompose the leveraged portfolio return into three components: α^B, the part attributable to the S&P 500, that is, $\beta^B r_B$, and the part attributable to the error term.
  (b) How much did the leverage increase the return? How much did it increase the risk? How much did it increase the Sharpe ratio of the portfolio?

17.10. What is the most appropriate benchmark for a market-neutral portfolio?

17.11. The following questions pertain to the information contained in Table 17.13 about the market-neutral portfolios.
  (a) Did the sector-neutral portfolio achieve its objective?
  (b) Did the factor-neutral portfolio achieve its objective?
  (c) Using only the information in the table, was there a better portfolio that could have been constructed over this investment period? If so, what was it?

17.12. The following questions pertain to the information contained in Table 17.14 about the market-neutral optimized portfolios.
  (a) Did the market-neutral optimized portfolios achieve their objective?
  (b) Would you have bought these portfolios? Why or why not?
  (c) What was the main cause of the ex-post average returns of the portfolios?

17.13. Respond to the following statements with regard to the empirical results of our backtests.

    (a)   Market-neutral portfolios are pointless. Holding a portfolio of cash and equities is preferable.

    (b)   Tax-management strategies offer no room for the improvement of after-tax returns because the relative gains on the tax side are offset by the relative losses on the investment side.

    (c)   Accounting for transactions costs that consist of commissions, market impact, and delay does not really affect the average returns of a portfolio. Since you are going to have to buy some and sell some, on balance, the costs even out.

    (d)   Leverage is like magic. It boosts the portfolio's average returns.

GLOSSARY

Active portfolio management   The style of portfolio management in which the goal is to outperform a benchmark or to maximize a certain risk-adjusted return.

Aggregate Z-score   The weighted average of Z-scores of a stock when the Z-scores are calculated with respect to multiple factors.

Anomaly   Any pattern in stock returns that is unexpected from the viewpoint of standard financial theories.

Autoregression model   The model of the stock return or other time-series variables in which the current value of the variable is a linear function of the past values of the variable and a random error.

Backtesting   The process of testing an investment strategy using historical data to find out how the strategy likely would have performed in the past.

Bayes' rule   The mathematical theorem specifying the relationship between the probability of event A conditional on event B and the probability of event B conditional on event A.

Bayesian α   The component of the expected stock return that is obtained by transforming qualitative information into a quantitative measure through the application of Bayesian theory.

Bayesian theory   The statistical theory of combining a researcher's subjective opinion with quantitative data to obtain the optimal assessment of risk.

Behavioral finance theory   The theory that investors' psychology and behavioral patterns explain the movements of the stock market.

Benchmark α   The component of the expected stock return that is not correlated with the benchmark return.

Benchmark portfolio   The portfolio of stocks and other investable assets against which the portfolio manager's performance is measured. The portfolio manager may have to abide by constraints regarding how much the portfolio should resemble the benchmark portfolio.

Beta neutrality   The state of a portfolio with zero exposure to the market factor and/or other factors.

Bid–ask spread The difference between the price at which one can purchase a security and the price at which one can sell a security.

Breadth The number of factors or distinct signals that are used to predict stock returns.

Capital asset pricing model (CAPM) The model of stock returns in which the stock return is a random error plus the product of the market portfolio return and the exposure of the stock to the market portfolio return.

Capital gain and loss management The buying and selling of stocks based on their potential capital gains or capital losses in order to minimize the tax burden of the portfolio.

CAPM α The component of the expected stock return that is not correlated with the market portfolio return.

CAPM β The exposure of the stock to the market portfolio. It is proportional to the correlation between the stock return and the market portfolio return.

Characteristic matching The technique of replacing one stock with another that has identical or similar factor exposures.

Conditional expectation The expected value of one random variable given the value of another random variable.

Conditional probability The probability of one event given that another event has occurred.

Cross-sectional data A set of observations of many individual units, such as firms or countries, at one point in time.

Crowding Crowding occurs when many investors enter the same position or strategy, leading to a concentration of exposure that can ultimately make the liquidity in the market very fragile and alter the future return and risk of the position. In extreme crowding, a small catalyst can lead to a collapse in the position as traders react and influence the dynamics of the price.

Data mining The practice of testing a variety of models on historical stock returns and factors until one finds the model that best predicts or explains past stock returns.

Data snooping The practice of using a model or strategy based solely on having read or heard that it works well.

Delay cost The cost to the trader of a broker's inability to process an order immediately, often due to the fact that the order is large.

Diversifiable risk The component of the portfolio's risk that can be reduced through diversification.

Diversification The process of reducing the investment risk while maintaining the same expected return by creating a portfolio composed of a large number of heterogeneous stocks whose prices move in different directions and at different times.

Dividend management The buying and selling of stocks based on their expected dividend payments in order to achieve a desired level of dividends and minimize the tax burden of the portfolio.

Dollar neutrality The state of a portfolio in which the value of the securities owned is completely offset by the value of the securities sold short.

Economic factor Any economic indicator that may help to explain or predict stock returns, such as an indicator of price levels, interest rates, income, or productivity.

Economic factor model The model of stock returns in which the stock return may be determined primarily by economic factors. In this model, the expected stock return equals the product of the factor premiums and the stock's exposure to the factors.

Efficient-market hypothesis The hypothesis that security prices reflect all available information and cannot be predicted.

ESG investing A type of investing that considers nonfinancial factors in assessing companies. These factors are environmental, social, and governance factors. Environmental factors look at the company's relation to the conservation of the natural world, social factors examine the treatment of people both inside and outside the company, and governance factors consider how a company is run. Also known as *socially responsible investing*.

Exchange-traded fund A portfolio of stocks and other investable assets that is traded as a single security on an organized exchange. Trading an exchange-traded fund is similar to trading any other stock listed on the exchange.

Expected return The expected mean value of a stock return or a portfolio return when the return is considered a random variable.

Factor exposure The sensitivity of a stock return or a portfolio return to a factor premium.

Factor exposure targeting The process of adjusting the portfolio's factor exposure to a target level, typically the factor exposure of the benchmark.

Factor premium The amount that investors are willing to pay for a stock's exposure to some factor; the return to a factor in the model of stock returns.

Factor tilting The process of shifting the portfolio's factor exposures in a certain direction, typically by increasing the exposure of the portfolio manager's favorite factor.

Forecasting rule of thumb The mathematical formula that decomposes the expected return conditional on forecasting factors into the information coefficient, volatility of the stock return, and the Z-score.

Fundamental factor Any observable attribute of firms or stocks that may help to explain or predict stock returns, such as an item from the financial statements, from analyst reports, or from other sources.

Fundamental factor model The model of stock returns in which the stock return is determined primarily by fundamental factors. In this model, the expected stock return equals the product of the factor premiums and the stock's exposure to the factors.

Fundamental law The mathematical formula that states that the information ratio equals the product of the information coefficient and the square root of breadth. The formula aids in understanding how the portfolio manager achieves returns in excess of the benchmark.

Generalized least-squares estimation The estimation technique that produces an efficient estimator when it is known that random errors for different observations have different variances or that they are correlated with one another.

Goodness of fit The measure of how well the regression line fits the data.

Information coefficient The average contribution of a forecasting factor or signal to the forecast of stock returns.

Information criterion   The rule that states that in order to create the best possible portfolio, one must use all available information and combine different sets of information without double-counting data.

Information loss   The difference between the Sharpe ratio of the best portfolio one could have created and the Sharpe ratio of the actual portfolio.

Information ratio   The ratio of the benchmark α to the standard deviation of the residual. The ratio is a risk-adjusted measure of the portfolio manager's excess or active return over the benchmark.

Initial margin   The amount of equity that one needs to deposit with a broker before making a short-sale transaction or a futures transaction. The amount is expressed as a fraction of the value of the transaction.

Investment universe   The set of stocks from which the portfolio manager selects stocks for the portfolio.

IQR method   A method of identifying outliers using an interquartile range during quantitative stock selection.

Leverage   The combination of one's own capital and borrowed capital to purchase an asset or create a portfolio. Buying futures contracts to create an investment position greater than the equity capital creates leverage.

Leveraged short   The combination of one's own portfolio of securities with borrowed securities that are sold short. Selling futures contracts can create a leveraged short position.

Liquidity buffer   A curb on downside risk to maintain the liquidity of the portfolio. Purchasing out-of-the-money put options is one way to create a liquidity buffer.

Look-ahead bias   The estimation bias created by inappropriately assuming that certain information was available at some point when it was not in fact yet available.

Loss harvesting   The selling of stocks with potential capital losses in order to minimize the portfolio's tax burden.

Maintenance margin   The minimal amount of equity required in a brokerage account when trading on margin (i.e., borrowing capital).

Market impact   The change in a stock's price that results from placing a large order. Market impact is a transactions cost if the price moves in a direction unfavorable to the trader.

Market neutrality   The state of a portfolio with zero sensitivity to market fluctuations. Market neutrality can be achieved through dollar neutrality or beta neutrality.

Mean-variance optimization   The technique of minimizing the variance of a portfolio for a given expected return or, conversely, maximizing the expected return of a portfolio for a given variance.

Minimum absolute deviation estimation   The estimation technique that minimizes the sum of the distance between the dependent variable and the regression line. The prediction from this estimation identifies the median value of the dependent variable given the value of the explanatory variables.

Model periodicity   The interval at which each variable in the model is measured (e.g., daily, weekly, monthly, quarterly, or annually).

Momentum   A pattern in which stocks with positive past returns have positive future returns; positive serial correlation.

Multifactor α The component of the expected stock return that is not correlated with any of the factors in a multifactor model.

Multifactor model The model of stock returns in which multiple factors are used to explain stock returns.

Multiple regression The estimation technique in which a dependent variable is related to a linear function of multiple explanatory variables.

Multivariate regression The estimation technique in which multiple dependent variables are related to a linear function of multiple explanatory variables.

Nondiversifiable risk The component of the portfolio's risk that cannot be reduced through diversification.

Normal distribution The symmetric, bell-shaped distribution of a random variable, characterized only by the mean and variance.

Omitted-factor bias The estimation bias created by omitting relevant factors from the estimation.

Optimal portfolio The portfolio that is created through either mean-variance optimization or tracking-error minimization. Given a measure of risk, the optimal portfolio achieves the lowest level of risk while satisfying other requirements, such as a certain expected return.

Ordinary least-squares estimation The estimation technique that minimizes the sum of the squared distance between the dependent variable and the regression line. The prediction from this estimation identifies the mean value of the dependent variable given the value of the explanatory variables.

Outlier A data point that is very far from the regression line.

P-hacking The process of testing many ideas until one obtains a "significant" result. P-hacking is based on the idea of finding a variable with a low p-value or a high t statistic. It is also known as *data dredging, data snooping, data fishing,* and *significance chasing*.

Panel data A set of observations of many individual units, such as firms or countries, at many points in time.

Parameter stability The stability of a parameter over the time period of the data used to estimate it. Parameter stability is necessary for a reliable estimate.

Parameter uncertainty The imprecision of the estimate of a parameter, usually reported as the standard error. Parameter uncertainty requires special attention if the parameter estimate is going to serve as the basis for an investment decision.

Passive portfolio management The style of portfolio management whose goal is to replicate a benchmark without attempting to outperform it.

Performance attribution The process of decomposing the portfolio's performance, for purposes of analysis, into its components, such as the returns attributable to each factor in the stock-return model.

Phantom weights Weight-like variables that are added to a standard portfolio optimization problem to represent a complex portfolio optimization problem in the framework of a standard optimization problem are called phantom weights.

Portable α The concept of α as something that can be transferred from a portfolio to another asset class or subasset class. The concept of a portable α allows plan sponsors, pension funds, and other investors the flexibility to separate α from the asset-allocation decision. The concept allows portfolio managers to separate the α from the β of the portfolio.

Portfolio weight   The weight of a stock or security in the portfolio in terms of its relative market value.

Posterior   The distribution of the parameter one obtains after performing a Bayesian analysis.

Predictive distribution   The distribution of a random variable that one can construct after estimating a model. Typically, the plot of the distribution is made after estimating a forecasting model in order to summarize the forecasting result graphically.

Price impact   Another term for market impact. The change in a stock's price that results from placing a large order. Price impact is a transactions cost if the price moves in the direction unfavorable to the trader.

Principal-component analysis   The technique of identifying a small number of factors that explain the fluctuation in a large number of given variables. The identified factors are linear combinations of the given variables.

Prior   The distribution of the parameter that summarizes one's own subjective opinion before any estimation is performed.

Probability density function   The mathematical function relating a potential value of a random variable to α probability density. By integrating the probability density function, one obtains the probability that the random variable will take on a potential value.

Pure arbitrage opportunity   The opportunity to profit from mispricings without taking any risk.

Quadratic programming   The technique of solving an optimization problem in which the objective function is quadratic in control variables and the constraints are linear.

Qualitative portfolio management   The style of portfolio management in which the portfolio is based primarily on nonquantitative research or the portfolio manager's opinion.

Quantitative portfolio management   The style of portfolio management in which the portfolio is based primarily on the quantitative analysis of financial, economic, or other quantifiable data, typically the estimation of a stock-return model from a large amount of data.

Random error   The unobservable, unpredictable part of a random variable that a model cannot explain, typically assumed to be uncorrelated with any of the explanatory variables or factors in the model.

Rebalancing   The trading of stocks in order to alter or restore the composition of a portfolio.

Residual return   The part of the stock return not explained after the estimation is performed. Residual return can be loosely interpreted as a realized value of the random error in the model. Sometimes it includes the estimated value of α or the constant term in the model.

Risk   The unpredictable variation in the value of a security or a portfolio, typically measured by the variance or the standard deviation of the security or portfolio.

Risk-free rate The rate of return to a security whose value is perfectly predictable.

Robustness of estimation The constancy of an estimate that does not change much even when certain features of the estimation, such as data set or specification, change.

Rolling window A succession of overlapping time periods of data used to obtain smooth estimates of a model over time.

Scenario analysis The technique of predicting the distribution of a stock return or any random variable by analyzing the probability of the variable under various scenarios.

Semi–standard deviation The measure of volatility that measures only the downside deviations from the mean.

Semistrong-form efficiency The level of market efficiency at which security prices reflect all publicly available information.

Serial correlation A pattern in which the current value of a random variable is not independent of its previous value.

Sharpe ratio The ratio of the expected return in excess of the risk-free rate to the standard deviation of the return. Named after economist William Sharpe.

Short sale The sale of a borrowed security. The short position is closed by purchasing the security and returning it to the lender.

Smart beta Smart beta involves using quantitative management to make better portfolios. Smart beta is usually transparent and uses rules-based quantitative strategies to offer investors better portfolios that are a mix of active and passive management. Many strategies take advantage of the many anomalies documented in the investing literature and use those to pick stocks and/or adjust the weighting of stocks in the portfolio.

Socially responsible investing A type of investing that considers nonfinancial factors in assessing companies, such as the company's relationship to the environment, community, human relations, and product quality.

Standard error The estimated standard deviation of the estimate. The standard error is a measure of the precision and reliability of the estimate, with a higher standard error indicating less precision.

Statistical arbitrage opportunity The opportunity to profit from mispricings while taking a small, calculated risk.

Stratification The creation of a sample by first categorizing the population and then randomly selecting a predetermined number of observations from each category. In portfolio construction, the investment universe is categorized, and then a predetermined number of stocks is selected for the portfolio from each category.

Strong-form efficiency The level of market efficiency at which security prices reflect all information, public and private.

Survivorship bias The estimation bias caused by estimating a model using only the data on firms that existed for the entire time period of the data set. The bias occurs if these surviving firms differ significantly from nonsurviving firms in ways relevant to the model.

Tax lot All the shares of one stock that were bought at the same time. All shares in the tax lot have the same potential capital gain or capital loss.

Tax-lot management   The selling of tax lots based on their potential capital gains or capital losses in order to minimize the tax burden of the portfolio.

Technical analysis   Analysis aimed at identifying patterns in stock prices, returns, and trading volumes.

Technical factor   Any characteristic of a stock obtained from price, return, or volume data thought to help explain or predict stock returns.

Time-series data   A set of observations of one unit, such as a firm or a country, at many different points in time.

Tracking error   The standard deviation of the difference between the portfolio return and the benchmark return.

Tracking-error minimization   Minimization of the portfolio's tracking error while satisfying other criteria.

Tracking portfolio   A portfolio created through tracking-error minimization.

Transactions costs   The total costs of trading securities, including indirect costs (e.g., market impact) and direct costs (e.g., the commission).

Trimming   The removal of outliers from the data sample in order to prevent them from unduly influencing the estimate.

t-Statistic   The ratio of the estimate to its standard error. If the true parameter value is zero, then the t-statistic has a t-distribution. The t-statistic can be constructed to test other parameter values as well.

Value-at-risk   The portion of the portfolio's value that could be destroyed by unfavorable investment conditions, typically measured as the worst potential loss of the portfolio excluding the worst 5% of situations.

Variance-covariance matrix   The matrix whose diagonal elements are the variances of the given variables and whose off-diagonal elements are the covariances of all the possible pairs of the given variables.

Vector autoregression model   The model of multiple time-series variables in which the current values of the variables are a linear function of the past values of the variables and a set of random errors.

Volatility   The amount of fluctuation in the price or the return or the unpredictability of the fluctuation. Typically measured by the standard deviation or the variance.

Weak-form efficiency   The level of market efficiency at which security prices reflect all the information included in past security prices. Weak-form efficiency prevents profiting from technical analysis.

Winsorization   The replacement of outliers with other values in order to prevent the outliers from unduly influencing the estimate.

Zero-investment portfolio   A portfolio with zero equity capital created by exactly matching the value of the securities owned and the value of the securities sold short.

Z-score   A standardized variable that results from subtracting the mean from the variable's original value and dividing that difference by the standard deviation. In QEPM, the Z-score refers to the Z-score of a factor exposure.

BIBLIOGRAPHY

Abarbanell, Jeffrey S., and Brian J. Bushee. "Abnormal Returns to a Fundamental Analysis Strategy." *Accounting Review*, **v. 73**, 1998, pp. 19–45.

Acharya, Viral V., and Lasse Heje Pedersen. "Asset Pricing with Liquidity Risk." *Journal of Financial Economics*, August 2005, pp. 375–410.

Achelis, Stephen B. *Technical Analysis from A–Z*. New York: McGraw-Hill, 2001.

Alexander, John C., and James S. Ang. "Do Equity Markets Respond to Earnings Paths?" *Financial Analysts Journal*, **v. 54**, July–August 1998, pp. 81–94.

Ali, A., X. Chen, T. Yao, and Tong Yu. "Do Mutual Funds Profit from the Accruals Anomaly?" *Journal of Accounting Research*, March 2008.

Altman, E. "Financial Ratios, Discriminant Analysis, and the Prediction of Corporate Bankruptcy." *Journal of Finance*, **v. 23**, September 1968, pp. 589–609.

Amel-Zadeh, Amir, and George Serafeim. "Why and How Investors Use ESG Information: Evidence from a Global Survey." *Financial Analysts Journal*, **v. 74**, 2018, pp. 87–103.

Amihud, Yakov, and Haim Mendelson. "Asset Pricing and the Bid–Ask Spread." *Journal of Financial Economics*, December 1986, pp. 223–249.

Amihud, Yakov, Haim Mendelson, and Lasse Heje Pedersen. "Liquidity and Asset Prices." *Foundations and Trends in Finance*, 2005, pp. 269–364.

Ang, A., R. J. Hodrick, Y. Xing, and X. Zhang. "The Cross-Section of Volatility and Expected Returns." *Journal of Finance*, February 2006, pp. 607–636.

Amihud, Yakov. "Illiquidity and Stock Returns: Cross-Section and Time-Series Effects." *Journal of Financial Markets*, January 2002, pp. 31–56.

Angel, James J., and Pietra Rivoli. "Does Ethical Investing Impose a Cost on the Firm? A Theoretical Examination." *Journal of Investing*, Winter 1997, pp. 57–61.

Anton, Howard. *Elementary Linear Algebra*. New York: Wiley, 1991.

Arbel, A. "Generic Stocks: An Old Product in a New Package." *Journal of Portfolio Management*, **v. 11**, Summer 1985, pp. 4–13.

Arbel, A., S. Carvell, and P. Strebel. "Giraffes, Institutions, and Neglected Firms." *Financial Analysts Journal*, **v. 39**, May–June 1983, pp. 57–62.

Arbel, A., and P. Strebel. "The Neglected and Small Firm Effects." *Financial Review*, 1982, pp. 201–218.

Arbel, A., and P. Strebel. "Pay Attention to Neglected Firms." *Journal of Portfolio Management*, **v. 9**, Winter 1983, pp. 37–42.

Ariel, R. A. "A Monthly Effect in Stock Returns." *Journal of Financial Economics*, **v. 18**, March 1987, pp. 161–174.

Armitage, P., and M. Parmar. "Some Approaches to the Problem of Multiplicity in Clinical Trials." *Proceedings of the XIIth International Biometrics Conference in Seattle*, 1986.

Arnott, Robert D. "The Use and Misuse of Consensus Earnings." *Journal of Portfolio Management*, **v. 11**, Spring 1985, pp. 18–27.

Arnott, Rob, Noah Beck, and Vitali Kalesnick. "Timing 'Smart Beta' Strategies? Of Course! Buy Low, Sell High!." Research Affiliates Publication, 2016, pp. 1–30.

Arnott, Robert D., Andrew L. Berkin, and Jia Ye. "How Well Have Taxable Investors Been Served in the 1980s and 1990s?" *Journal of Portfolio Management*, **v. 26**, Summer 2000, pp. 84–93.

Arnott, Robert D., Andrew L. Berkin, and Jia Ye. "The Management and Mismanagement of Taxable Assets." *Journal of Investing*, Spring 2001, pp. 15–21.

Arnott, Robert, Harvey Campbell, Kalesnik Vitali, and Juhani Linnainmaa. "Alice's Adventures in Factorland: Three Blunders that Plague Factor Investing." *Journal of Portfolio Management*, **v. 45**, April 2019, pp. 18–36.

Asch, Solomon E. "Opinions and Social Pressure." *Scientific American*, November 1955, pp. 31–35.

Asness, Cliff. "Fight the Fed Model." *Journal of Portfolio Management*, **v. 30**, Fall 2003, pp. 11–24.

Asness, Clifford S., A., Frazzini, and Lasse Heje Pedersen. "Quality Minus Junk." *Review of Accounting Studies*, November 2019, pp. 34–112.

Avanidhar Subrahmanyam. "The Cross-Section of Expected Stock Returns: What Have We Learnt from the Past Twenty-Five Years of Research?" *European Financial Management*, January 2010, pp. 27–42.

Avellaneda, Marco, and Stanley Zhang. "Path Dependence of Leveraged ETF Returns." *SIAM Journal of Financial Mathematics*, 2010, pp. 586–603.

Bachelier, L. "Theory of Speculation." In *The Random Character of Stock Market Prices*. Cambridge, MA: MIT Press, 1964.

Bai, Jushan, and N. G. Serena. "Determining the Number of Factors in Approximate Factor Models." *Econometrica*, **v. 70**, 2003, pp. 191–221.

Baker, M., B. Bradley, and J. Wurgler. "Benchmarks as Limits to Arbitrage: Understanding the Low-Volatility Anomaly." *Financial Analysts Journal*, 2011, pp. 40–54.

Baker, N., and Robert A. Haugen. "Low Risk Stocks Outperform within All Observable Markets of the World." April 2012.

Bacon, F. *The New Organum and Related Writings*. 1620.

Ball, R. "Anomalies in Relationships between Securities' Yields and Yield-Surrogates." *Journal of Financial Economics*, **v. 6**, 1978, pp. 103–126.

Ball, R., J. Gerakos, Juhani T. Linnainmaa, and Valeri V. Nikolaev. "Deflating Profitability." *Journal of Financial Economics*, August 2015, pp. 225–248.

Baltas, Nick. "The Impact of Crowding in Alternative Risk Premia Investing." *Financial Analysts Journal*, July 2017, pp. 89–104.

Banerjee, A., R. L. Lumsdaine, and James Stock. "Recursive and Sequential Tests of the Unit-Root and Trend-Break Hypotheses: Theory and International Evidence." *Journal of Business and Economic Statistics*, **v. 10**, 1992, pp. 271–287.

Banz, R. "The Relationship between Return and Market Value of Common Stocks." *Journal of Financial Economics*, **v. 9**, March 1981, pp. 3–18.

Barardehi, Yashar H., D. Bernhardt, Thomas G. Ruchti, and Marc Weidenmier. "The Night and Day of Amihud's (2002) Liquidity Measure." *Review of Asset Pricing Studies*, November 2020.

Barardehi, Yashar H., D. Bernhardt, and Ryan J. Davies. "Trade-Time Measures of Liquidity." *Review of Financial Studies*, January 2019, pp. 126–179.

Barber, Brad, and Terrance Odean. "All that Glitters: The Effect of Attention and News on the Buying Behavior of Individual and Institutional Investors." University of Berkeley Working Paper, 2005.

Barberis, Nicholas. "Investors Seek Lessons in Thinking." *Financial Times Mastering Investment*, 2002, pp. 246–251.

Barberis, N., and Andrei Shleifer. "Style Investing." *Journal of Financial Economics*, **v. 68**, May 2003, pp. 161–199.

Barillas, Francisco, and Jay Shanken. "Comparing Asset Pricing Models." *Journal of Finance*, **v. 73**, 2018, pp. 715–754.

Barnett, Vic, and Toby Lewis. *Outliers in Statistical Data*. New York: Wiley, 1994.

Barron, Orie E., and Pamela S. Stuerke. "Dispersion of Analysts' Earnings Forecasts as a Measure of Uncertainty." *Journal of Accounting, Auditing, and Finance*, **v. 13**, Summer 1998, pp. 245–270.

Bartov, E., S. Radhakrishnan, and I. Krinsky. "Investor Sophistication and Patterns in Stock Returns after Earnings Announcements." *Accounting Review*, **v. 75**, 2000, pp. 43–63.

Basu, S. "Investment Performance of Common Stocks in Relation to Their Price-Earnings Ratios: A Test of the Efficient Market Hypothesis." *Journal of Finance*, **v. 31**, June, 1977, pp. 663–682.

Basu, S. "The Relationship between Earnings' Yield, Market Value and Return for NYSE Common Stocks: Further Evidence." *Journal of Financial Economics*, **v. 12**, 1983, pp. 129–156.

Bauman, Scott W., Iskander-Datta Sudip, and E. Mai. "Investment Analyst Recommendations: A Test of 'The Announcement Effect' and 'The Valuable Information Effect.'" *Journal of Business Finance and Accounting*, **v. 22**, July 1995, pp. 659–670.

Beard, Craig, and Richard Sias. "Is There a Neglected-Firm Effect?" *Financial Analysts Journal*, **v. 53**, September–October 1997, pp. 19–23.

Bell, David E. "Regret in Decision Making under Uncertainty." *Operations Research*, September–October 1982, pp. 961–981.

Bello, Zakri Y., and Vahan Janjigian. "A Reexamination of the Market-Timing and Security-Selection Performance of Mutual Funds." *Financial Analysts Journal*, **v. 53**, September–October 1997, pp. 24–30.

Berg, Florian, Julian Klbel, and Roberto Rigabon. "Aggregate Confusion: The Divergence of ESG Ratings." Available at SSRN: https://ssrn.com/abstract=3438533, 2020, pp. 1–63.

Berger, James O. *Statistical Decision Theory and Bayesian Analysis.* New York: Springer, 1993.

Berkin, Andrew L., and Jia Ye. "Tax Management, Loss Harvesting, and HIFO Accounting." *Financial Analysts Journal,* **v. 59**, 2003, pp. 91–102.

Bernard, V., and J. Thomas. "Post-Earnings Annoucement Drift: Delayed Price Response or Risk Premium?" *Journal of Accounting Research,* **v. 27**, 1989, pp. 1–36.

Bernstein, Peter L. *Capital Ideas: The Impropable Origins of Modern Wall Street.* New York: Free Press 1992.

Berry, Michael A., Edwin Burmeister, and Marjorie B. McElroy. "Sorting Out Risks Using Known APT Factors." *Financial Analysts Journal,* **v. 44**, March–April 1988, pp. 29–42.

Bhandari, Laxmi Chand. "Debt/Equity Ratio and Expected Common Stock Returns: Empirical Evidence." *Journal of Finance,* **v. 43**, June 1988, pp. 507–528.

Bhojraj, Sanjeev, and Bhaskaran Swaminathan. "How Does the Corporate Bond Market Value Capital Investments and Accruals?." *Review of Accounting Studies,* March 2009.

Bieri, David S., and Ludwig B. Chincarini. "Riding the Yield Curve: A Variety of Strategies." *Journal of Fixed Income,* September 2005.

Black, Fischer, "How We Came Up with the Option Formula." *Journal of Portfolio Management,* **v. 15**, Winter 1989, pp. 4–8.

Black, F., Michael C. Jensen, William H. Meckling, and Myron Scholes. "The Capital Asset Pricing Model: Some Empirical Tests." In M. C. Jensen (ed.), Studies in the Theory of Capital Markets, 1972, pp. 79–121.

Black, Fischer. "Beta and Return." *Journal of Portfolio Management,* 1993, pp. 8–18.

Black, Fischer, Michael C. Jensen, and Myron Scholes. "The Capital Asset Pricing Model: Some Empirical Tests." In *Studies in the Theories of Capital Markets,* 1972, pp. 79–121.

Black, Fischer, and Myron Scholes. "The Pricing of Options and Corporate Liabilities." *Journal of Political Economy,* **v. 81**, May 1973, pp. 637–654.

Blitz, David C., and Pim Van Vliet. "The Volatility Effect: Lower Risk without Lower Return." *Journal of Portfolio Management,* 2007, pp. 102–113.

Blume, M., and R. Stambaugh. "Biases in Computed Returns: An Application of the Size Effect." *Journal of Financial Economics,* **v. 12**, October 1983, pp. 387–404.

Bogle, John C. *Common Sense on Mutual Funds.* New York: Wiley, 1999.

Bolshakov, A., and Ludwig B. Chincarini. "Manager Skill and Portfolio Size with Respect to a Benchmark." *European Financial Management,* 2020, pp. 176–197.

Bordalo P., N. Gennaioli, and Andrei Shleifer. "Salience Theory of Choice under Risk." *Quarterly Journal of Economics,* August 2012, pp. 1243–1285.

Bouchaud, Jean-Philippe, P. Kruger, A. Landier, and David Thesmar. "Sticky Expectations and the Profitability Anomaly." *Journal of Finance,* April 2019, pp. 639–674.

Bouman, S., and Ben Jacobsen. "The Halloween Indicator, 'Sell in May and Go Away': Another Puzzle." *American Economic Review,* **v. 92**, December 2002, pp. 1618–1635.

Bradshaw, Mark T., Scott A. Richardson, and Richard G. Sloan. "Do Analysts and Auditors Use Information in Accruals?" *Journal of Accounting Research,* June 2001.

Braitsch, Raymond J., Jr. "A Computer Comparison of Four Quadratic Programming Algorithms." *Management Science*, v. 18, July 1972, pp. 632–643.

Breen, William, Ravi Jagannathan, and Aharon R. Ofer. "Correcting for Heteroscedasticity in Tests for Market Timing Ability." *Journal of Business*, v. 59, October 1986, pp. 585–598.

Brennanab, Michael J., and Avanidhar Subrahmanyam. "Market Microstructure and Asset Pricing: On the Compensation for Illiquidity in Stock Returns." *Journal of Financial Economics*, July 1996, pp. 441–464.

Briere, Marie, Jonathan Peillex, and Loredana Ureche-Rangau. "Do Social Responsibility Screens Matter When Assessing Mutual Fund Performance?" *Financial Analysts Journal*, v. 73, 2017, pp. 53 66.

Brock, William, Josef Lakonishok, and Blake LeBaron. "Simple Technical Trading Rules and the Stochastic Properties of Stock Returns." *Journal of Finance* v. 47, December 1992, pp. 1731–1764.

Brown, Gregory W., P. Howard, and Christian T. Lundblad. "Crowded Trades and Tail Risk." July 2020.

Brown, Jeffrey H., Douglas K. Crocker, and Foerster Stephen R. "Trading Volume and Stock Investments." *Financial Analysts Journal*, March–April 2009, pp. 67–84.

Brown, Lawrence D., and David M. Chen. "Composite Analyst Earnings Forecasts: The Next Generation." *Journal of Business Forecasting*, v. 9, Summer 1990, pp. 11–15.

Brown, Lawrence D., and David M. Chen. "How Good Is the All-America Research Team in Forecastings Earnings?" *Journal of Business Forecasting*, v. 9, Winter 1990–1991, pp. 14–18.

Brown, Keith C., W. V. Harlow and Laura T. Starks. "Of Tournaments and Temptations: An Analysis of Managerial Incentives in the Mutual Fund Industry." *Journal of Finance*, v. 51, March 1996, pp. 85–110.

Brown, Lawrence D., and Michael S. Rozeff. "Analysts Can Forecast Accurately!" *Journal of Portfolio Management*, v. 6, Spring 1980, pp. 31–34.

Brown, Lawrence D., and Michael S. Rozeff. "The Superiority of Analyst Forecasts as Measures of Expectations: Evidence from Earnings." *Journal of Finance*, March 1978, pp. 1–16.

Bruno, Salvatore, Ludwig B. Chincarini, and Robert F. Whitelaw. "An Alternative Method to Construct Levered Indexes." *Journal of Index Investing*, Fall 2014, pp. 34–47.

Bruno, S., Ludwig B. Chincarini, and Frank Ohara. "Portfolio Construction and Crowding." *Journal of Empirical Finance*, June 2018, pp. 190–206.

Buckle, David. "How to Calculate Breadth: An Evolution of the Fundamental Law of Active Portfolio Management." *Journal of Asset Management*, v. 4, 2004, pp. 393–405.

Buffett, Warren E. "An Owner's Manual." In *Berkshire Hathaway Annual Report*, 1996.

Buffett, Warren E. "Chairman's Letter to Shareholders." In *Berkshire Hathaway Annual Report*, 2003.

Busse, Jeffrey A. "Another Look at Mutual Fund Tournaments." *Journal of Financial and Quantitative Analysis*, v. 36, March 2001, pp. 53–73.

Cahan, R., and Yin Luo. "Standing Out from the Crowd: Measuring Crowding in Quantitative Strategies." *Journal of Portfolio Management*, 2013.

Cakici, N., S. Chatterjee Tang, and Lin Tong Yi. "Alternative Profitability Measures and Cross-Section of Expected Stock Returns: International Evidence." *Review of Quantitative Finance and Accounting*, 2020.

Calluzzo, Paul, Fabio Moneta, and Selim Topaloglu. "When Anomalies Are Publicized Broadly, Do Institutions Trade Accordingly?" *Management Science*, **v. 65**, 2019, pp. 4555–4574.

Campbell, John Y., Andrew W. Lo, and A. Craig MacKinlay. *The Econometrics of Financial Markets*. Princeton, NJ: Princeton University Press, 1997.

Carhart, Mark. "On Persistence in Mutual Fund Performance." *Journal of Finance*, **v. 52**, March 1997, pp. 57–82.

Carter, Richard B., Frederick Dark, and Ajai Singh. "Underwriter Reputation, Initial Returns, and the Long-Run Performance of IPO Stocks." *Journal of Finance*, **v. 53**, February 1998, pp. 285–311.

Chance, Don M., and Michael L. Hemler. "The Performance of Professional Market Timers: Daily Evidence from Executed Strategies." *Journal of Financial Economics*, **v. 62**, November 2001, pp. 377–411.

Chance, Robin B., Susan Hirshman, and Gordon B. Fowler, Jr. "Is Tax-Loss Harvesting Worth It? Greater After-Tax Returns through Active Selection." *Journal of Financial Planning*, November 2003, pp. 78–84.

Chan, Kalok, Allaudeen Hameed, and Wilson Tong. "Profitability of Momentum Strategies in the International Equity Markets." *Journal of Financial & Quantitative Analysis*, **v. 35**, June 2000, pp. 153–172.

Chan, Louis K. C., Jason Karceski, and Josef Lakonishok. "On Portfolio Optimization: Forecasting Covariances and Choosing the Risk Model." *Review of Financial Studies*, **v. 12**, Winter 1999, pp. 937–974.

Chan, Louis K. C., Jegadeesh Narasimhan, and Josef Lakonishok. "Momentum Strategies." *Journal of Finance*, **v. 51**, December 1996, pp. 1681–1713.

Chaudhuri, Shomesh, Terence Burnham, and Andrew Lo. "An Empirical Evaluation of Tax-Loss-Harvesting Alpha." *Financial Analysts Journal*, **v. 76**, Third Quarter 2020, pp. 99–108.

Chen, Nai-Fu, Richard Roll, and Stephen A. Ross. "Economic Forces and the Stock Market." *Journal of Business*, **v. 59**, July 1986, pp. 383–403.

Chen, T., L. Sun, John Wei, and Feixue Xie. "The Profitability Effect: Insights from International Equity Markets." *European Financial Management*, September 2018, pp. 545–580.

Cheng, M., and A. Madhavan. "The Dynamics of Leveraged and Inverse Exchange-Traded Funds." *Journal of Investment Management*, November 2009, pp. 586–603.

Chincarini, Ludwig B. "The Failure of Long-Term Capital Management." Available at SSRN: https://ssrn.com/abstract=952512, October 8, 1998, pp. 1–16.

Chincarini, Ludwig B. "The Crisis of Crowding: Quant Copycats, Ugly Models, and the New Crash Normal." 2012.

Chincarini, Ludwig B. "The Impact of Quantitative Techniques on Hedge Fund Performance." *European Financial Management*, 2014.

Chincarini, Ludwig B. "Transaction Costs and Crowding." *Quantitative Finance*, August 2017, pp. 1389–1410.

Chincarini, Ludwig B. "Managing Cash Flow in Sector Portfolios: A Hedging Approach." *Derivatives Use, Trading, and Regulation*, **v. 10**, March 2004, pp. 27–45.

Chincarini, Ludwig B., and Daehwan Kim. *Quantitative Equity Portfolio Management. An Active Approach to Portfolio Construction and Management*, 1st ed. New York: McGraw-Hill, 2006.

Chincarini, Ludwig B., and Daehwan Kim. "Another Look at the Information Ratio." *Journal of Asset Management*, v. 8, 2007, pp. 284–295.

Chincarini, Ludwig B., and Frank Fabozzi. "Stephen A. Ross: Excellence Beyond Recognition." *Journal of Portfolio Management*, July 2018, pp. 11–25.

Chincarini, Ludwig B., Daehwan Kim, and Fabio Moneta. "Beta and Firm Age." *Journal of Empirical Finance*, v. 58, 2020, pp. 50–74.

Chincarini, Ludwig B., and Daehwan Kim. "The Advantages of Tax-Managed Investing." *Journal of Portfolio Management*, v. 28, Fall 2001, pp. 56–72.

Chincarini, Ludwig B., and Guillermo Llorente. "Volume and Return Information on Individual Stocks." University of Madrid Working Paper, 1999.

Chincarini, Ludwig B., and Alex Nakao. "Measuring Hedge Fund Timing Ability Across Factors." *Journal of Investing*, 2011.

Choi, Dosoung, and Chen Sheng-Syan. "The Differential Information Conveyed by Share Repurchase Tender Offers and Dividend Increases." *Journal of Financial Research*, v. 20, Winter 1997, pp. 529–543.

Chopra, N., J. Lakonishok, and J. Ritter. "Measuring Abnormal Performance: Do Stocks Overreact?" *Journal of Financial Economics*, v. 31, April 1992, pp. 235–268.

Chopra, N., and Vijay Kumar. "Why So Much Error in Analysts' Earnings Forecasts?" *Financial Analysts Journal*, v. 54, November–December 1998, pp. 35–42.

Chordia, Tarun, Avanidhar Subrahmanyam, and V. Ravi Anshuman. "Trading Activity and Expected Stock Returns." *Journal of Financial Economics*, January 2001, pp. 3–32.

Chow, G. "Tests of Equality between Sets of Coefficients in Two Linear Regressions." *Econometrica*, v. 28, July 1960, pp. 591–605.

Chu, C. S. J., K. Hornik, and C. M. Kuan. "The Moving Estimates Test for Parameter Stability." *Econometric Theory*, v. 11, October 1995, pp. 699–720.

Chue, Timothy K. "Omitted Risks or Crowded Strategies: Why Mutual Fund Comovement Predicts Future Performance." December 2015.

Clarke, R., H. De Silva, and S. Thorley. "Portfolio Constraints and the Fundamental Law of Active Management." *Journal of Portfolio Management*, v. 58, 2002, pp. 48–66.

Clarke, Roger, Harindra De Silva, and Steven Thorley. "Minimum-Variance Portfolios in the U.S. Equity Market." *Journal of Portfolio Management*, 2006, pp. 10–24.

Clarke, Roger, Harindra De Silva, and Steven Thorley. "Minimum-Variance Portfolio Composition." *Journal of Portfolio Management*, 2011, pp. 31–35.

Clement, Michael B. "Analyst Forecast Accuracy: Do Ability, Resources, and Portfolio Complexity Matter?" *Journal of Accounting and Economics*, v. 27, June 1999, pp. 285–303.

Cohen, M. A. "Environmental and Financial Performance: Are They Related?" Owen Graduate School of Management Working Paper, 1995.

Collins, Sean, Rochelle Antoniewicz, Sarah Holden, and Judy Steenstra. *2021 Investment Company Factbook: A Review of Trends and Activity in the Investment Company Industry*. Investment Company Institute, 2021.

Connor, Gregory. "The Three Types of Factor Models: A Comparison of Their Explanatory Power." *Financial Analyst Journal*, **v. 51**, May 1995, pp. 42–46.

Connor, Gregory, and Robert Korajczyk. "A Test for the Number of Factors in an Approximate Factor Model." *Journal of Finance*, **v. 48**, September 1993, pp. 1263–1291.

Conrad, J., and G. Kaul. "Long-Term Overreaction or Biases in Computed Returns?" *Journal of Financial Economics*, **v. 48**, March 1993, pp. 39–64.

Conrad, J., M. Cooper, and G. Kaul. "Value versus Glamour." *Journal of Finance*, **v. 58**, October 2003, pp. 1969–1995.

Constantinides, George. "Optimal Stock Trading with Personal Taxes: Implications for Prices and the Abnormal January Returns." *Journal of Financial Economics*, **v. 13**, March 1984, pp. 65–89.

Cook, T., and M. Rozeff. "Size and Earnings-Price Ratio Anomalies: One Effect or Two?" *Journal of Financial and Quantitative Analysis*, **v. 19**, December 1984, pp. 449–466.

Cornell, Bradford, and Wayne R. Landsman. "Security Price Response to Quarterly Earnings Announcements and Analysts' Forecast Revisions." *Accounting Review*, **v. 64**, October 1989, pp. 680–692.

Coughenhour, Jay F., and Lawrence Harris. "Specialist Profits and the Minimum Price Increment." Available from http://ssrn.com/abstract=537785, April 2004.

Cowles, A. "Can Stock Market Forecasters Forecast?" *Econometrica*, **v. 1**, July 1933, pp. 309–324.

Cox, John C., and Mark Rubinstein. *Options Markets*. Englewood Cliffs, NJ: Prentice-Hall, 1985.

Cross, F. "The Behavior of Stock Prices on Fridays and Mondays." *Financial Analysts Journal*, **v. 29**, November–December 1973, pp. 67–69.

Crowder, Robert G. *Principles of Learning and Memory*. New York: Psychology Press, 1976.

Cusatis, Patrick J., James A. Miles, and Randall Woolridge. "Restructuring through Spinoffs: The Stock Market Evidence." *Journal of Financial Economics*, **v. 33**, June 1993, pp. 293–311.

Daniel, K., and S. Titman. "Evidence on the Characteristics of Cross Sectional Variation in Stock Returns." *Journal of Finance*, **v. 52**, March 1997, pp. 1–33.

Daniel, K., D. Hirshleifer, and A. Subrahmanyam. "Investor Psychology and Security Market Underand Overreactions." *Journal of Finance*, **v. 53**, December 1998, pp. 1839–1885.

Datar, Vinay T., Narayan Y. Naik, and Robert Radcliffe. "Liquidity and Stock Returns: An Alternative Test." *Journal of Financial Markets*, 1998, pp. 203–219.

Debondt, W., and R. Thaler. "Does the Stock Market Overreact?" *Journal of Finance*, **v. 40**, July 1985, pp. 793–805.

Debondt, W., and R. Thaler. "Further Evidence on Investor Overreaction and Stock Market Seasonality." *Journal of Finance*, **v. 42**, July 1987, pp. 557–581.

DeGroot, Morris H. *Probability and Statistics*. Reading, MA: Addison-Wesley, 1986.

Derwall, Jeroen, Nadja Guenster, Rob Bauer, and Kees Koedijk. "The Eco-Efficiency Premium Puzzle." *Financial Analysts Journal*, **v. 61**, March–April 1995, pp. 51–63.

Desai, H., and P. Jain. "Firm Performance and Focus: Long-Run Stock Market Performance Following SpinOffs." *Journal of Financial Economics*, **v. 54**, October 1999, pp. 75–101.

Desai, H., and P. Jain. "Long-Run Common Stock Returns Following Stock Splits and Reverse Splits." *Journal of Business*, **v. 70**, July 1997, pp. 409–433.

Desai, H., Shivaram Rajgopal, and Mohan Venkatachalam. "Value-Glamour and Accruals Mispricing: One Anomaly or Two?" *Accounting Review*, **v. 79**, 2004, pp. 355–385.

Dewynne, Jeff, Sam Howison, and Paul Wilmott. *Option Pricing: Mathematical Models, and Computation*. New York: Oxford Financial Press, 1993.

Dharan, Bala, and David Ikenberry. "The Long-Run Negative Drift of Post-Listing Stock Returns." *Journal of Finance*, **v. 50**, December 1995, pp. 1547–1574.

Dhillon, U., and H. Johnson. "Changes in the Standard & Poor's 500 List." *Journal of Business*, **v. 64**, January 1991, pp. 75–85.

DiBartolomeo, Dan. "Just Because We Can Doesn't Mean We Should." *Journal of Performance Measurement*, **v. 7**, Spring 2003.

Dietz, Peter O. "Pension Fund Investment Performance—What Method to Use When." *Financial Analysts Journal*, **v. 22**, January–February 1966, pp. 83–86.

Diltz, J. David. "Does Social Screening Affect Portfolio Performance?" *Journal of Investing*, Spring 1995, pp. 64–69.

Ding, Zhuanxin, and R. Douglas Martin. "The Fundamental Law of Active Management: Redux." *Journal of Empirical Finance*, **v. 43**, September 2017, pp. 91–114.

Donaldson, William H. "Testimony Concerning Investor Protection Issues Regarding the Regulation of the Mutual Fund Industry." Testimony before the U.S. Senate Committee on Banking, Housing and Urban Affairs, April 8 2004.

Doran, David T. "Stock Splits: Tests of the Earnings Signalling and Attention Directing Hypotheses Using Analysts Forecasts and Revisions." *Journal of Accounting, Auditing, and Finance*, **v. 9**, Summer 1994, pp. 411–422.

Dowd, Kevin. *Beyond Value at Risk: The New Science of Risk Management*. New York: Wiley, 1998.

Dowen, Richard J. "The Stock Split and Dividend Effect: Information or Price Pressure?" *Applied Economics*, **v. 22**, July 1990, pp. 927–932.

Dowen, R., and S. Bauman. "The Relative Importance of Size, P/E, and Neglect." *Journal of Portfolio Management*, 1986, pp. 30–34.

Down, R., and S. Bauman. "A Test of the Relative Importance of Popularity and Price-Earnings Ratio in Determining Abnormal Returns." *Journal of the Midwest Finance Association*, 1984, pp. 34–47.

Dreman, David. *Contrarian Investment Strategies: The Next Generation*. New York: Simon & Schuster, 1998.

Dreman, David. *Psychology and the Stock Market: Investment Strategy beyond Random Walk*. New York: AMACOM, 1977.

Dreman, David N., and Michael A. Berry. "Overreaction, Underreaction, and the Low P/E Effect." *Financial Analysts Journal*, **v. 51**, July–August 1995, pp. 21–30.

Drienkoa, Jozef, Tom Smith, and Anna Von Reibnitza. "A Review of the Return-Illiquidity Relationship." *Critical Finance Review*, January 2018.

Dubey, S. D. "Adjustment of p-Values for Multiplicities of Intercorrelating Symptoms." *Proceedings of the VIth International Society for Clinical Biostatisticians in Germany*, 1985.

Ebbinghaus, Hermann. *Grundzüge der Psychologie*. Leipzig: Veit Co., 1902.
Ellsberg, Daniel. "Risk, Ambiguity, and the Savage Axioms." *Quarterly Journal of Economics*, November 1961, pp. 643–669.
Elton, Edwin J., and Martin J. Gruber. "A Multi-Index Risk Model of Japanese Stock Market." *Japan and the World Economy*, **v. 1**, October 1988, pp. 21–44.
Elton, Edwin J., Martin J. Gruber, and Jeffrey A. Busse. "Do Investors Care about Sentiment?" *Journal of Business*, **v. 71**, October 1988, pp. 477–500.
Engerman, Mark. "Using Fundamental and Economic Factors to Explain Stock Returns." *BARRA Newsletter*, Fall 1993.
Ezeokoli, Ogechukwu, China Layne, Mier Statman, and Oswaldo Urdapilleta. "Environmental, Social, and Governance (ESG) Investment Tools: A Review of the Current Field." Summit Consulting, 2017.

Fama, Eugene F. "Efficient Capital Markets: A Review of Theory and Empirical Work." *Journal of Finance*, **v. 25**, May 1970, pp. 383–417.
Fama, Eugene F. "Efficient Capital Markets: II." *Journal of Finance*, **v. 46**, December 1991, pp. 1575–1617.
Fama, Eugene F., and Kenneth R. French. "Common Risk Factors in the Returns on Bonds and Stocks." *Journal of Financial Economics*, **v. 33**, February 1993, pp. 3–53.
Fama, Eugene F., and Kenneth R. French. "The Cross-Section of Expected Stock Returns." *Journal of Finance*, **v. 47**, June 1992, pp. 427–465.
Fama, Eugene F., and Kenneth R. French. "Average Returns, B/M, and Share Issues." *Journal of Finance*, December 2008.
Fama, Eugene F., and Kenneth R. French. "A Five-Factor Asset Pricing Model." *Journal of Financial Economics*, April 2015, pp. 1–22.
Fama, Eugene F., and Kenneth R. French. "Choosing Factors." *Journal of Financial Economics*, May 2018, pp. 234–252.
Ferris, S., R. D'Mello, and C. Y. Hwang. "The Tax-Loss Selling Hypothesis, Market Liquidity, and Price Pressure around the Turn-of-the-Year." *Journal of Financial Markets*, **v. 6**, January 2003, pp. 73–98.
Ferson, W., and C. Harvey. "Conditioning Variables and the Cross-Section of Stock Returns." *Journal of Finance*, **v. 54**, August 1999, pp. 1325–1360.
Fischhoff, B., and Paul Slovic. "A Little Learning . . .: Confidence in Multicue Judgement Tasks." *Defense Advanced Research Projects Agency*, June 1978.
Fischhoff, Baruch. "Perceived Information of Facts." *Journal of Experimental Psychology*, 1977, pp. 349–358.
Fishe, Raymond P. H., and Michael A. Robe. "The Impact of Illegal Insider Trading in Dealer and Specialist Markets." *Journal of Financial Economics*, **v. 71**, March 2004, pp. 461–488.
Fisher, Philip A. *Common Stocks and Uncommon Profits*. New York: Harper & Brothers, 1958.
Fisher, Philip A. *Common Stocks and Uncommon Profits and Other Writings by Philip A. Fisher*. New York: Wiley, 1996.

Fisher, Philip A. *Conservative Investors Sleep Well*. New York: Harper & Row, 1975.

Fisher, Philip A. *Developing an Investment Philosophy*. New York: Business Classics, 1980.

Frazzini, A., and Lasse H. Pedersen. "Betting Against Beta." *Journal of Financial Economics*, 2014.

Friend, Irwin, and Marhsall Blume. "Measurement of Portfolio Performance under Uncertainty." *American Economic Review*, v. 60, September 1970, pp. 561–575.

Fung, William, and David A. Hsieh. "A Risk Neutral Approach to Valuing Trend Following Trading Strategies." Duke University Working Paper, 1998.

Garland, James R. "The Attraction of Tax-Managed Index Funds." *Journal of Investing*, v. 6, Spring 1997, pp. 13–20.

Gervais, Simon, and Terrance Odean. "The Perils for Investors of Human Nature." *Financial Times Mastering Investment*, 2002, pp. 257–260.

Gibbons, R. D. *Statistical Methods for Groundwater Monitoring*. New York: Wiley, 1984.

Gill, P. E., W. Murray, and M. H. Wright. *Practical Optimization*. New York: Academic Press, 1981.

Givoly, Dan, and Josef Lakonishok. "Financial Analysts' Forecast of Earnings: Their Value to Investors." *Journal of Banking and Finance*, v. 4, September 1980, pp. 221–233.

Givoly, D., and A. Ovadia. "Year-End Tax-Induced Sales and Stock Market Seasonality." *Journal of Finance*, v. 38, March 1983, pp. 171–185.

Givoly, Dan, and Dan Palmon. "Insider Trading and Exploitation of Inside Information: Some Empirical Evidence." *Journal of Business*, v. 58, January 1985, pp. 69–87.

Global Quantitative Equity Group. "The Quant Liquidity Crunch." Goldman Sachs Asset Management Paper, August 2007.

Glosten, Lawrence R. "Components of the Bid-Ask Spread and the Statistical Properties of Transaction Prices." *Journal of Finance*, v. 42, December 1987, pp. 1293–1307.

Glosten, Lawrence R., and Lawrence E. Harris. "Estimating the Components of the Bid-Ask Spread." *Journal of Financial Economics*, v. 21, May 1988, pp. 123–142.

Goetzmann, William N., Jonathan Ingersoll, Jr., and Zoran Ivkovic. "Monthly Measurement of Daily Timers." *Journal of Financial and Quantitative Analysis*, v. 35, September 2000, pp. 257–290.

Goetzmann, W. N., and M. Garry. "Does Delisting from the S&P 500 Affect Stock Price?" *Financial Analysts Journal*, v. 42, March–April 1986, pp. 64–69.

Goldman Sachs Asset Management. "The Liquidity Crunch in Quant Equities: Analysis and Implications." *Goldman Sachs Asset Management Presentation*, December 13, 2007.

Goodman, D., and J. Peavy. "The Interaction of Firm Size and Price-Earnings Ratio on Portfolio Performance." *Financial Analysts Journal*, v. 42, January 1986, pp. 9–12.

Graham, Benjamin. *The Intelligent Investor*. New York: Harper Business, 1934.

Granger, Clive, and Paul Newbold. *Forecasting Economic Time Series*. New York: Academic Press, 1986.

Greene, William H. *Econometric Analysis*. Englewood Cliffs, NJ: Prentice-Hall, 2002.

Grinblatt, M., and S. Titman. "Portfolio Performance Evaluation: Old Issues, New Insights." *Review of Financial Studies*, **v. 2**, 1989, pp. 393–421.

Grinold, Richard. "The APT, the CAPM, and the BARRA Model." *BARRA Newsletter*, 1991.

Grinold, R. C. "The Fundamental Law of Active Management." *Journal of Portfolio Management*, **v. 15**, 1989, pp. 30–37.

Grinold, Richard C., and Ronald N. Kahn. *Active Portfolio Management*. New York: McGraw-Hill, 1995.

Grubbs, Frank. "Procedures for Detecting Outlying Observations in Samples." *Technometrics*, **v. 11**, February 1969, pp. 1–21.

Grundy, Bruce, and J. Spencer Martin. "Understanding the Nature of the Risks and the Source of the Rewards to Momentum Investing." *Review of Financial Studies*, **v. 14**, Spring 2001, pp. 29–78.

Guerard, John B., Jr., "Is There a Cost to Being Socially Responsible in Investing? It Costs Nothing to Be Good." *Journal of Forecasting*, **v. 16**, December 1997, pp. 475–490.

Guerard John B., Jr., and Bernell K. Stone. "Social Screening Does Not Harm Performance." *Pensions and Investments*, September 2002.

Hagstrom, Robert G., Jr. *The Warren Buffett Way: Investment Strategies of the World's Greatest Investor*. New York: Wiley, 1994.

Hallerbach, W. G. "On the Expected Performance of Market Timing Strategies." *Journal of Portfolio Management*, **v. 40**, 2014, pp. 42–51.

Hamilton, James Douglas. *Time-Series Analysis*. Princeton, NJ: Princeton University Press, 1994.

Harris, Lawrence. "How to Profit from Intradaily Stock Returns." *Journal of Portfolio Management*, **v. 12**, Winter 1986, pp. 61–64.

Harris, Lawrence. "A Transaction Data Study of Weekly and Intradaily Patterns in Stock Returns." *Journal of Financial Economics*, **v. 16**, May 1986, pp. 99–117.

Harris, Lawrence, and Eitan Gurel. "Price and Volume Effects Associated with Changes in the S&P 500 List: New Evidence for the Existence of Price Pressures." *Journal of Finance*, **v. 41**, September 1986, pp. 815–829.

Harvey, Campbell R. "Presidential Address: The Scientific Outlook in Financial Economics." *Journal of Finance*, **v. 4**, 2017, pp. 1399–1440.

Harvey, Campbell R., Yan Liu, and Heqing Zhu. "... and the Cross-Section of Expected Returns." *Review of Financial Studies*, **v. 29**, 2016, pp. 5–68.

Haugen, Robert, and Philippe Jorion. "The January Effect: Still There after All These Years." *Financial Analysts Journal*, **v. 52**, January–February 1996, pp. 27–31.

Henriksson, Roy D., and Robert C. Merton. "On Market Timing and Investment Performance II: Statistical Procedures for Evaluating Forecasting Skills." *Journal of Business*, **v. 54**, 1981, pp. 513–533.

Hensel, Chris R., and William T. Ziemba. "Investment Results from Exploiting Turn-of-the-Month Effects." *Journal of Portfolio Management*, **v. 22**, Spring 1996, pp. 17–23.

Hirshleifer, D., and T. Shumway. "Good Day Sunshine: Stock Returns and the Weather." *Journal of Finance*, **v. 58**, June 2003, pp. 1009–1032.

Hochberg, Y. "A Sharper Bonferroni Procedure for Multiple Tests of Significance." *Biometrika*, **v. 75**, 1988, pp. 800–802.

Holm, S. "A Simple Sequentially Rejective Multiple Test Procedure." *Scandanavian Journal of Statistics*, **v. 6**, 1979, pp. 65–70.

Hommel, G. "A Stagewise Rejective Multiple Test Procedure Based on a Modified Bonferroni Test." *Biometrika*, **v. 75**, 1988, pp. 383–386.

Hong, Harrison, and Jeremy Stein. "A Unified Theory of Underreaction, Momentum Trading, and Overreaction in Asset Markets." *Journal of Finance*, **v. 54**, December 1999, pp. 2143–2184.

Hong, Heng, and Jeremy Stein. "Bad News Travels Slowly: Size, Analyst Coverage, and the Profitability of Momentum Strategies." *Journal of Finance*, **v. 55**, February 2000, pp. 265–295.

Hong, Xie. "The Mispricing of Abnormal Accrual." *Accounting Review*, July 2001.

Hou, Kewei, Chen Xue, and Lu Xhang. "Replicating Anomalies." *Review of Financial Studies*, **v. 33**, 2020, pp. 2019–2133.

Hou, K., C. Xue, and L. Zhang. "Replicating Anomalies." Fisher College of Business Working Paper Series, 2017.

Hoyo, J., and Guillermo Llorente. "Stability Analysis and Forecasting Implications." *Proceedings of the Fifth Conference in Computational Finance*, 1997.

Hull, John. *Options, Futures, and other Derivative Securities*. Englewood Cliffs, NJ: Prentice-Hall, 2005.

Ibbotson, Roger G., Zhiwu Chen, Daniel Y.-J. Kim, and Wendy Y. Hu. "Liquidity as an Investment Style." *Financial Analysts Journal*, May–June 2013, pp. 30–44.

Iglewicz, B., and D. C. Hoaglin. *How to Detect and Handle Outliers*. New York: American Society of Quality Control, 1993.

Ikenberry, David, Josef Lakonishok, and Theo Vermaelen. "Market Underreaction to Open Market Share Repurchases." *Journal of Financial Economics*, **v. 39**, October 1995, pp. 181–208.

Ikenberry, David L., Graeme Rankine, and Earl K. Stice. "What Do Stock Splits Really Signal?" *Journal of Financial and Quantitative Analysis*, **v. 31**, September 1996, pp. 357–375.

Ingersoll, Jonathan E., Jr. "Some Results in the Theory of Arbitrage Pricing." *Journal of Finance*, **v. 39**, September 1984, 1021–1039.

Irwin, Francis W. "Stated Expectations as Functions of Probability and Desirability of Outcomes." *Journal of Personality*, March 1953, pp. 329–335.

Jacobs, Bruce I., and Kenneth Levy. "Alpha Transport with Derivatives." *Journal of Portfolio Management*, **v. 25**, May 1999, pp. 55–60.

Jacobs, Bruce I., and Kenneth Levy. "The Long and Short of Long-Short." *Journal of Investing*, **v. 6**, 1997, pp. 73–86.

Jacobs, Bruce I., and Kenneth Levy. "20 Myths about Long-Short." *Financial Analysts Journal*, **v. 52**, September 1996, pp. 81–85.

Jacobs, Heiko, and Sebastian Muller. "Anomalies Across the Globe: Once Public, No Longer Existent?" *Journal of Finance*, **v. 135**, 2020, pp. 213–230.

Jaffe, J., and R. Westerfield. "The Week-End Effect in Common Stock Returns: The International Evidence." *Journal of Finance*, **v. 40**, 1985, pp. 433–454.

Jaffe, Jeffrey F. "Special Information and Insider Trading." *Journal of Business*, **v. 47**, July 1974, pp. 410–428.

Jagannathan, Ravi, and Robert A. Korajczyk. "Assessing the Market Timing Performance of Managed Portfolios." *Journal of Business*, **v. 59**, April 1986, pp. 217–235.

Jain, Prem. "The Effect on Stock Price of Inclusions in or Exclusions from the S&P 500." *Financial Analyst Journal*, 1987, pp. 58–65.

Jegadeesh, Narasimhan. "Evidence of Predictable Behavior of Security Returns." *Journal of Finance*, **v. 45**, July 1990, pp. 881–898.

Jegadeesh, Narasimhan, and Sheridan Titman. "Profitability of Momentum Strategies—An Evaluation of Alternative Explanations." *Journal of Finance*, **v. 56**, April 2001, pp. 699–720.

Jegadeesh, Narasimhan, and Sheridan Titman. "Returns to Buying Winners and Selling Losers: Implications for Stock Market Efficiency." *Journal of Finance*, **v. 48**, March 1993, pp. 65–91.

Jensen, Michael C. "The Performance of Mutual Funds in the Period 1945–1964." *Journal of Finance*, **v. 23**, May 1968, pp. 389–416.

Jones, Charles P., Richard J. Rendleman, and Henry A. Latane. "Stock Returns and SUEs during the 1970s." *Journal of Portfolio Management*, **v. 1**, Winter 1984, pp. 18–22.

Jorion, Philippe. *Value at Risk*. Burr Ridge, IL: *Irwin*, 1997.

Kahneman, D., and A. Tversky. "On the Psychology of Prediction." *Psychological Review*, July 1973, pp. 237–251.

Kahneman, D., and A. Tversky. "Prospect Theory: An Analysis of Decision under Risk." *Econometrica*, March 1979, pp. 263–292.

Kamstra, Mark J., Lisa A. Kramer, and Maurice D. Levi. "Losing Sleep at the Market: The Daylight Saving Anomaly." *American Economic Review*, **v. 90**, September 2000, pp. 1005–1011.

Kamstra, Mark J., Lisa A. Kramer, and Maurice D. Levi. "Winter Blues: A SAD Stock Market Cycle." *American Economic Review*, **v. 93**, March 2003, pp. 324–343.

Kanouse, David E. *Language, Labeling, and Attribution*. General Learning Press, 1971.

Keim, D. "Dividend Yields and the January Effect." *Journal of Portfolio Management*, **v. 12**, Winter 1986, pp. 54–60.

Keim, D. "Dividend Yields and Stock Returns: Implications of Abnormal January Returns." *Journal of Financial Economics*, **v. 14**, September 1985, pp. 473–489.

Keim, Marc R. "Size-Related Anomalies and Stock Return Seasonality: Further Empirical Evidence." *Journal of Financial Economics*, **v. 12**, June 1983, pp. 13–32.

Kennedy, Peter. *A Guide to Econometrics*. Boston: Blackwell, 1992.

Keynes, J.M. "The General Theory of Employment, Interest and Money." *Economic Journal*, June 1936, pp. 238–253.

Khandani, Amir E., and Andrew Lo. "What Happened to the Quants in August 2007?: Evidence from Factors and Transaction Data." Available at: http://ssrn.com/abstract=1288988, 2008.

Kim, D., and M. Kim. "A Multifactor Explanation of Post-Earnings Announcement Drift." *Journal of Financial and Quantitative Analysis*, **v. 38**, June 2003, pp. 383–398.

Kim, Moon K., and David A. Burnie. "The Firm Size Effect and the Economic Cycle." *Journal of Financial Research*, **v. 25**, Spring 2002, pp. 111–124.

Kirschman, Jeannette, and Peter Dietz. "Evaluating Portfolio Performance." *Managing Investment Portfolios*, January 1983.

Koop, Gary. *Bayesian Econometrics*. New York: Wiley Interscience, 2003.

Kung, Edward, and Larry Pohlman. "Portable Alpha: Philosophy, Process, and Performance." *Journal of Portfolio Management*, **v. 30**, Spring 2004, pp. 78–87.

Kurtz, Lloyd, and Dan diBartolomeo. "Socially Screened Portfolios: An Attribution Analysis of Relative Performance." *Journal of Investing*, Fall 1996, pp. 35–41.

Kwan, Clarence C. Y. "Portfolio Analysis Using Single-Index, Multi-Index and Constant Correlation Models: A Unified Treatment." *Journal of Finance*, **v. 39**, December 1984, pp. 1469–1483.

Kyle, Albert S., and Anna A. Obizhaeva. "Market Microstructure Invariance: Empirical Hypotheses." *Econometrica*, July 2016, pp. 1345–1404.

Lakonishok, Josef, Andrei Shleifer, and Robert W. Vishny. "Contrarian Investment, Extrapolation, and Risk." *Journal of Finance*, **v. 49**, December 1994, pp. 1541–1578.

Lakonishok, J., and S. Smidt. "Trading Bargains in Small Firms at Year-End." *Journal of Portfolio Management*, **v. 12**, Spring 1986, pp. 24–29.

Lakonishok, J., and S. Smidt. "Volume and Turn-of-the-Year Behavior." *Journal of Financial Economics*, **v. 13**, September 1984, pp. 435–455.

Lamont, Owen A. "The Curious Case of Palm and 3COM." *Financial Times Mastering Investment*, 2002, pp. 261–266.

LaPorta, Rafael. "Expectations and the Cross-Section of Stock Returns." *Journal of Finance*, **v. 51**, December 1996, pp. 1715–1742.

Latane, Henry A., and Charles P. Jones. "Standardized Unexpected Earnings—A Progress Report." *Journal of Finance*, **v. 32**, December 1977, pp. 1457–1465.

Lehmann, Bruce N., and David M. Modest. "The Empirical Foundations of the Arbitrage Pricing Theory." *Journal of Financial Economics*, **v. 21**, September 1988, pp. 213–254.

Lev, B., and Doron Nissim. "The Persistence of the Accruals Anomaly." *Contemporary Accounting Research*, April 2004.

Li, H., R. Novy-Marx, and M. Velikov. "Liquidity Risk and Asset Pricing." *Critical Finance Review*, March 2019.

Li, Jinliang, Robert M. Mooradian, and Wei David Zhang. "Is Illiquidity a Risk Factor? A Critical Look at Commission Costs." *Financial Analysts Journal*, July–August 2007, pp. 28–39.

Linnainmaa, Juhani T., and Michael R. Roberts. "The History of the Cross-Section of Stock Returns." *Review of Financial Studies*, July 2018, pp. 2606–2649.

Lintner, John. "The Valuation of Risky Assets and the Selection of Risky Investments in Stock Portfolios and Capital Budgets." *Review of Economics and Statistics*, **v. 47**, February 1965, pp. 13–37.

Liu, Berlinda, and Gaurav Sinha. "Spiva U.S. Scorecard." *S&P Dow Jones Indices*, 2021.

Liu, Weimin. "A Liquidity-Augmented Capital Asset Pricing Model." *Journal of Financial Economics*, December 2006, pp. 631–671.

Lo, Andrew, and Craig MacKinlay. *A Non-Random Walk Down Wall Street.* Princeton, NJ: Princeton University Press, 1999.

Lo, Andrew, and Craig MacKinlay. "When Are Contrarian Profits Due to Stock Market Overreaction?" *Review of Financial Studies*, v. 3, 1990, pp. 175–205.

Loomes, G., and Robert Sugden. "Regret Theory: An Alternative Theory of Rational Choice Under Uncertainty." *Economic Journal*, December 1982, pp. 805–824.

Lord, Charles G., L. Ross, and Mark R. Lepper. "Biased Assimilation and Attitude Polarization: The Effects of Prior Theories on Subsequently Considered Evidence." *Journal of Personality & Social Psychology*, 1979, pp. 2098–2109.

Loughran, Timothy, and Jay Ritter. "The New Issues Puzzle." *Journal of Finance*, v. 50, March 1995, pp. 23–51.

Luck, Christopher. "Factor Tilting." *BARRA Newsletter*, July–August 1991.

Luenberger, David G. *Linear and Non-Linear Programming.* Reading, MA: Addison-Wesley, 1989.

Lynch, Peter, and John Rothchild. *Beating the Street.* New York: Fireside, 1993.

Lynch, Peter, and John Rothchild. *One Up on Wall Street: How to Use What You Already Know to Make Money in the Market.* New York: Penguin Books, 1989.

Madhavan, Ananth, Aleksander Sobcsyk, and Andrew Ang. "Toward ESG Alpha: Analyzing ESG Exposures Through a Factor Lens." *Financial Analysts Journal*, v. 77, 2020, pp. 69–88.

Markowitz, Harry. "Market Efficiency: A Theoretical Distinction and So What?" *Financial Analysts Journal*, v. 61, September–October 2005, pp. 17–30.

Markowitz, Harry. "Portfolio Selection." *Journal of Finance*, v. 7, March 1952, pp. 77–91.

Markowitz, Harry M., and Andre F. Perold. "Portfolio Analysis with Factors and Scenarios." *Journal of Finance*, v. 36, September 1981, pp. 871–877.

Marks, Rose W. "The Effect of Probability, Desirability, and Privilege on the Stated Expectations of Children." *Journal of Personality*, March 1951, pp. 431–465.

Martinez, Isabelle. "Fundamental and Macroeconomic Valuation for the Security Prices Valuation: The French Case." *Managerial Finance*, 1999, pp. 17–30.

Mazuy, K. K., and Jack L. Treynor. "Can Mutual Funds Outguess the Market?" *Harvard Business Review*, v. 44, 1966, pp. 131–136.

McDonald, Bill D., and Richard R. Mendenhall. "Implementing the Earnings Surprise Strategy." CRSP Seminar on the Analysis of Security Prices, May 1994.

McDonald, Robert L. *Derivatives Markets.* Reading, MA: Addison-Wesley, 2003.

Mclean, David R., and Jeffrey Pontiff. "Does Academic Research Destroy Stock Return Predictability?" *Journal of Finance*, v. 71, 2016, pp. 5–32.

Menchero, Jose, and Lei Ji. "Portfolio Optimization with Noisy Covariance Matrices." *Journal of Investment Management*, 2019, pp. 77–91.

Menchero, Jose, Jun Wang, and D. J. Orr. "Improving Risk Forecasts for Optimized Portfolios." *Financial Analysts Journal*, May–June 2012, pp. 40–50.

Mendenhall, R. "Arbitrage Risk and Post-Earnings-Announcement Drift." *Journal of Business*, v. 77, October 2004, pp. 875–894.

Merton, Robert C. "A Simple Model of Capital Market Equilibrium with Incomplete Information." *Journal of Finance*, **v. 42**, July 1987, pp. 483–510.

Mezrich, Ben. *Bringing Down the House*. New York: Free Press, 2002.

Michaud, Richard O. "Are Long-Short Equity Strategies Superior?" *Financial Analysts Journal*, **v. 49**, December 1993, pp. 44–49.

Miller, Dale T., and Michael Ross. "Self-Serving Biases in the Attribution of Causality: Fact or Fiction?" *Psychological Bulletin*, 1975, pp. 213–225.

Morgenson, Gretchen. *Forbes Great Minds of Business: A Companion to the Public Television Series*. New York: Wiley, 1997.

Moskowitz, Tobias J., and Mark Grinblatt. "Do Industries Explain Momentum?" *Journal of Finance*, **v. 54**, August 1999, pp. 1249–1290.

Mossin, J. "Equilibrium in a Capital Asset Market." *Econometrica*, **v. 34**, October 1966, pp. 768–783.

Muoz, F., M. Vargas, and I. Marco. "Financial Performance and Managerial Abilities." *Journal of Business Ethics*, **v. 124**, 2014, pp. 551–569.

Murphy, John J. *Technical Analysis of Financial Markets*. New York: Prentice-Hall, 1999.

Neff, John, and S. L. Mintz. *John Neff on Investing*. New York: Wiley, 1999.

Nicholas, Joseph G. *Market Neutral Investing. Long-Short Hedge Fund Strategies*. Princeton, NJ: Bloomberg Press, 2000.

Nisbett, R., and Lee Ross. *Human Inference: Strategies and Shortcomings of Social Judgement*. Englewood Cliffs, NJ: Prentice-Hall, 1980.

Nisbett, Richard E., and Timothy Decamp Wilson. "Telling More than We Can Know: Verbal Reports on Mental Processes." *Psychological Review*, May 1977, pp. 231–259.

Nocedal, Jorge, and Stephen Wright. *Numerical Optimization*. Berlin: Springer-Verlag, 1999.

Novy-Marx, Robert. "The Other Side of Value: The Gross Profitability Premium." *Journal of Financial Economics*, April 2018, pp. 1–28.

Odean, Terrance . "Volume, Volatility, Price and Profit: When all Traders Are Above Average." *Journal of Finance*, December 1998, pp. 1887–1934.

O'Neal, Edward S. "Industry Momentum and Sector Mutual Funds." *Financial Analysts Journal*, **v. 56**, July–August 2000, pp. 37–46.

O'Shaughnessy, James P. *What Works on Wall Street: A Guide to the Best-Performing Investment Strategies of All Time*. New York: McGraw-Hill, 1998.

Oskamp, Stuart. "Overconfidence in Case-Study Judgements." *Journal of Consulting Psychology*, 1965, pp. 261–265.

Pastor, Lubos, and Robert F. Stambaugh. "Liquidity Risk and Expected Stock Returns." *Journal of Political Economy*, June 2003, pp. 642–685.

Pastor, Lubos, Robert F. Stambaugh, and Lucian A. Taylor. "Sustainable Investing in Equilibrium." *Journal of Financial Economics*, Forthcoming.

Patel, Nitin R., and Marti G. Subrahmanya. "A Simple Algorithm for Optimal Portfolio Selection with Fixed Transaction Costs." *Management Science*, **v. 28**, March 1982, pp. 303–314.

Patton, Andrew. "Are 'Market-Neutral' Hedge Funds Really Market Neutral?" FMG Discussion Paper 522, 2004.

Perold, Andre. "Large-Scale Portfolio Optimization." *Management Science*, **v. 30**, October 1984, pp. 1143–1160.

Peters, Donald J. "Are Earnings Surprises Predictable?" *Journal of Investing*, Summer 1993, pp. 47–51.

Peters, Donald J. "Valuing a Growth Stock." *Journal of Portfolio Management*, **v. 17**, Spring 1991, pp. 49–51.

Piotroski, Joseph D. "Value Investing: The Use of Historical Financial Statement Information to Separate Winners from Losers." *Journal of Accounting Research*, **v. 38**, December 2000, pp. 1–41.

PlexusGroup. "How Manager Style Influences Cost." Commentary, May 1998.

PlexusGroup. "The Official Icebergs of Transaction Costs." Commentary, January 1998.

PlexusGroup. "Sneaking an Elephant Across a Putting Green: A Transaction Case Study." Commentary, April 2002.

PlexusGroup. "Time of Day Effects on Trading Costs." Commentary, January 2002.

Ploberger, W., W. Kramer, and K. Kontrus. "A New Test for Structural Stability in the Linear Regression Model." *Journal of Econometrics*, **v. 40**, February 1989, pp. 307–318.

Plott, Charles R., and Kathryn Zeiler. "Exchange Asymmetries Incorrectly Interpreted as Evidence of Endowment Effect Theory and Prospect Theory." *American Economic Review*, September 2007, pp. 1449–1474.

Pogue, G. A. "An Extension of the Markowitz Portfolio Selection Model to Include Variable Transactions Costs, Short Sales, Leverage Policies, and Taxes." *Journal of Finance*, **v. 25**, December 1970, pp. 1005–1027.

Preston, Malcolm G., and Philip Baratta. "An Experimental Study of the Auction-Value of an Uncertain Outcome." *American Journal of Psychology*, April 1948, pp. 183–193.

Recht, Peter. "Identifying Non-Active Restriction in Convex Quadratic Programming." *Mathematical Methods of Operations Research*, 2001, pp. 53–61.

Reilly, Frank, and Dominic R. Marshall. "Using P/E/Growth Ratios to Select Stocks." Financial Management Association Meeting, October 1999.

Reinganum, Marc R. "The Anomalous Stock Market Behavior of Small Firms in January: Empirical Tests for Tax-Loss Selling Effects." *Journal of Financial Economics*, **v. 12**, June 1983, pp. 89–104.

Reinganum, M. "Misspecification of Capital Asset Pricing: Empirical Anomalies Based on Earnings' Yields and Market Values." *Journal of Financial Economics*, **v. 9**, March 1981, pp. 19–46.

Reinganum, Marc R. "The Size Effect: Evidence and Potential Explanations." In *AIMR: Investing in Small-Cap and Micro-Cap Securities*, 1997.

Rendleman, Richard J., Charles P. Jones, and Henry A. Latane. "Empirical Anomalies Based on Unexpected Earnings and the Importance of Risk Adjustments." *Journal of Financial Economics*, **v. 10**, November 1982, pp. 269–287.

Richardson, Scott A., Richard G. Sloan, Mark T. Soliman, and Irem Tuna. "The Implications of Accounting Distortions and Growth for Accruals and Profitability." *Accounting Review*, May 2006.

Richardson, Scott A., Richard G. Sloan, Mark T. Soliman, and Irem Tuna. "Accrual Reliability, Earnings Persistence and Stock Prices." *Journal of Accounting and Economics*, September 2005.

Riquier, Andrea. "A Mutual Fund Made a $105 Million Mistake. Here's What Investors Need to Know." *MarketWatch*, July 29, 2020.

Ritter, Jay. "The Buying and Selling Behavior of Investors at the Turn of the Year." *Journal of Finance*, **v. 43**, July 1988, pp. 701–717.

Ritter, Jay R. "The Long-Run Performance of Initial Public Offerings." *Journal of Finance*, **v. 46**, March 1991, pp. 3–27.

Roediger, Henry L., and Robert G. Crowder. "A Serial Position Effect in Recall of United States Presidents." *Bulletin of the Psychonomic Society*, June 1976, pp. 275–278.

Roll, Richard. "A Mean/Variance Analysis of Tracking Error." *Journal of Portfolio Management*, **v. 18**, Summer 1992, pp. 13–22.

Roll, Richard. "A Simple Implicit Measure of the Effective Bid-Ask Spread in an Efficient Market." *Journal of Finance*, **v. 39**, September 1984, pp. 1127–1140.

Roll, Richard. "Vas Ist Das? The Turn-of-the-Year Effect and the Return Premia of Small Firms." *Journal of Portfolio Management*, **v. 9**, Winter 1983, pp. 18–28.

Rosenberg, Barr, Kenneth Raid, and Ronald Lanstein. "Persuasive Evidence of Market Inefficiency." *Journal of Portfolio Management*, **v. 11**, Spring 1985, pp. 9–17.

Ross, Nikki. *Lessons from the Legends of Wall Street: How Warren Buffett, Benjamin Graham, Phil Fisher, T. Rowe Price, and John Templeton Can Help You Grow Rich.* Chicago: Dearborn Financial Publishing, 2000.

Ross, Stephen. "The Arbitrage Theory of Capital Asset Pricing." *Journal of Economic Theory*, **v. 13**, December 1976, pp. 341–360.

Ross, Stephen. "Neoclassical Finance, Alternative Finance, and the Closed End Fund Puzzle." *European Financial Management*, **v. 8**, June 2002, pp. 129–137.

Rothman, Matthew S. "Turbulent Times in Quant Land." Lehman Brothers Equity Research, August 9, 2007.

Rothman, Matthew S. "August Redux/Redo?." Lehman Brothers Equity Research, January 25, 2008.

Rouwenhorst, K. Geert. "International Momentum Strategies." *Journal of Finance*, **v. 53**, February 1998, pp. 267–284.

Roy, A. D. "Safety First and the Holding of Assets." *Econometrica*, **v. 20**, July 1952, pp. 431–449.

Sadka, Ronnie. "Liquidity Risk and the Cross-Section of Hedge-Fund Returns." *Journal of Financial Economics*, July 2009.

Samuelson, Paul. "Proof that Properly Anticipated Prices Fluctuate Randomly." *Industrial Management Review*, **v. 6**, 1965, pp. 41–49.

Sankoh, A. J., M. F. Huque, and S. D. Dubey. "Some Comments on Frequently Used Multiple Endpoint Adjustment Methods in Clinical Trials." *Statistics in Medicine*, **v. 16**, 1997, pp. 2529–2542.

Schimdt, P., and R. Sickles. "Some Further Evidence on the Use of the Chow Test under Heteroskedasticity." *Econometrica*, **v. 45**, July 1977, pp. 1293–1298.

Schultz, Joseph J., Sandra G. Gustavson, and Frank K. Reilly. "Factors Influencing the NYSE Specialists' Price-Setting Behavior: An Experiment." *Journal of Financial Research*, **v. 8**, Summer 1985, pp. 137–144.

Schultz, P. "Personal Income Taxes and the January Effect: Small Firm Stock Returns before the War Revenue Act of 1917: A Note." *Journal of Finance*, **v. 40**, March 1985, pp. 333–343.

Senchack, A., and J. Martin. "The Relative Importance of the PSR and PER Investment Strategies." *Financial Analysts Journal*, **v. 43**, March–April 1987, pp. 46–56.

Seyhun, H. Nejat. "Insiders' Profits, Costs of Trading, and Market Efficiency." *Journal of Financial Economics*, **v. 16**, June 1986, pp. 189–212.

Seyhun, H. Nejat. "The January Effect and Aggregate Insider Trading." *Journal of Finance*, **v. 43**, March 1988, pp. 129–141.

Shahabuddin, Syed. "Why Forecasts Are Wrong?" *Journal of Business Forecasting Methods and Systems*, **v. 6**, Fall 1987, pp. 16–18.

Sharpe, William F. "An Algorithm for Portfolio Improvement." Mathematical Program Sciences, 1987.

Sharpe, William F. "Asset Allocation: Management Style and Performance Measurement." *Journal of Portfolio Management*, **v. 18**, Winter 1992, pp. 7–19.

Sharpe, William F. "Capital Asset Prices: A Theory of Market Equilibrium under Conditions of Risk." *Journal of Finance*, **v. 19**, September 1964, pp. 425–442.

Shefrin, H., and Meir Statman. "The Disposition to Sell Winners Too Early and Ride Losers Too Long: Theory and Evidence." *Journal of Finance*, July 1985, pp. 777–790.

Shi, Linna, and Huai Zhang. "On Alternative Measures of Accruals." *Accounting Horizons*, 2011.

Shi, Qian, Emily S. Pavey, and Rickey E. Carter. "Bonferroni-Based Correction Factor for Multiple Correlated Endpoints." *Pharmaceutical Statistics*, **v. 11**, 2012, pp. 300–309.

Shleifer, Andrei. "Do Demand Curves for Stocks Slope Down?" *Journal of Finance*, **v. 41**, July 1986, pp. 579–590.

Shum, P., and J. Kang. "The Long and Short of Leveraged ETFs: The Financial Crisis and Performance Attribution." *Journal of Investment Management*, June 2012.

Sloan, R. "Do Stock Prices Fully Reflect Information in Accruals and Cash Flows about Future Earnings?" *Accounting Review*, **v. 71**, July 1996, pp. 289–315.

Sloan, Richard G. "Do Stock Prices Fully Reflect Information in Accruals and Cash Flows About Future Earnings?" *Accounting Review*, July 1996.

Smirlock, M., and L. Starks. "Day-of-the-Week and Intraday Effects in Stock Returns." *Journal of Financial Economics*, **v. 17**, September 1986, pp. 197–210.

Smith, Matthew T., and Elizabeth Durham. "U.S. Equity Index Benchmark Usage." Russell Publication, 2005, pp. 1–5.

Smith, Scott. "The Evolving Role of Behavioral Finance in 2020." *Investments & Wealth Research*, 2020.

Sortino, Frank, and Robert Van der Meer. "Downside Risk." *Journal of Portfolio Management*, **v. 17**, July 1991, pp. 27–31.

Spaulding, David. *Measuring Investment Performance: Calculating and Evaluating Investment Risk and Return*. New York: McGraw-Hill, 1997.

Stambaugh, Robert F. "On the Exclusion of Assets from Tests of the Two-Parameter Model: A Sensitivity Analysis." *Journal of Financial Economics*, **v. 10**, November 1982, pp. 237–268.

Staw, Barry M. "Knee-Deep in the Big Muddy: A Study of Escalating Commitment to a Chosen Course of Action." *Organizational Behavior & Human Performance*, 1976, pp. 27–44.

Stein, David M. "Equity Portfolio Structure and Design in the Presence of Taxes." *Journal of Wealth Management*, 2001.

Stein, David M., and Greg McIntire. "Overlay Portfolio Management in a Multi-Manager Account." *Journal of Wealth Management*, Spring 2003.

Stein, David M., and James P. Garland. "Investment Management for Taxable Investors." *Handbook of Portfolio Management*. 1998.

Stein, David M., and Premkumar Naramsimhan. "Of Passive and Active Equity Portfolios in the Presence of Taxes." *Journal of Private Portfolio Management*, 1999.

Stein, Jeremy C. "Presidential Address: Sophisticated Investors and Market Efficiency." *Journal of Finance*, August 2009, pp. 1517–1548.

Steiner, Robert. *Mastering Financial Calculations: A Step-by-Step Guide to the Mathematics of Financial Market Instruments*, London Pitman Publishing, 1998.

Stock, James. "Unit Roots, Structural Breaks, and Trends." *Handbook of Econometrics*. v. 4, Chapter 46, 1994, pp. 2739–2839.

Stone, Bernell K. "A Linear Programming Formulation of the General Portfolio Selection Problem." *Journal of Financial and Quantitative Analysis*, v. 8, September 1973, pp. 621–636.

Studenmund, A. H., and Henry J. Cassidy. *Using Econometrics. A Practical Guide.* New York: HarperCollins, 1987.

Sullivan, R., A. Timmermann, and H. White. "Dangers of Data Mining: The Case of Calender Effects in Stock Returns." *Journal of Econometrics*, v. 105, November 2001, pp. 249–286.

Swinkels, L. "International Industry Momentum." *Journal of Asset Management*, v. 3, September 2002, pp. 124–141.

Tang, H., and X. E. Xu. "Solving the Return Deviation Conundrum of Leveraged Exchange-Traded Funds." *Journal of Financial & Quantitative Analysis*, February 2013, pp. 309–342.

Tanous, Peter J. *Investment Gurus: A Road Map to Wealth from the World's Best Money Managers*. New York: New York Institute of Finance, 1997.

Taylor, Jonathan. "Risk-Taking Behavior in Mutual Fund Tournaments." *Journal of Economic Behavior & Organization*, v. 50, March 2003, pp. 373–383.

Taylor, Shelley E., and Susan T. Fiske. "Point of View and Perceptions of Causality." *Journal of Personality & Social Psychology*, June 1975, pp. 239–245.

Thaler, Richard. "Seasonal Movements in Security Prices: I. The January Effect." *Journal of Economic Perspectives*, v. 1, Summer 1987, pp. 197–201.

Thaler, Richard. "Seasonal Movements in Security Prices: II. Holidays, Turn-of-the-Month, and Intraday Effects." *Journal of Economic Perspectives*, v. 1, Summer 1987, pp. 169–177.

Thaler, Richard. "Toward a Positive Theory of Consumer Choice." *Journal of Economic Behavior & Organization*, 1980, pp. 39–60.

Theil, H., and C. van de Panne. "Quadratic Programming as an Extension of Classical Quadratic Maximization." *Management Science*, v. 7, October 1960, pp. 1–20.

Thomas, Jacob K., and Huai Zhang. "Inventory Changes and Future Returns." *Review of Accounting Studies*, June–September 2002.

Thomas, Ric, and Robert Shapiro. "Managed Volatility: A New Approach to Equity Investing." *Journal of Investing,* 2009.

Thornton, Thomas, Toby Wade, Kenneth Tsu, Haim Israel, Mark Troman, Eli Kobzev, and Kate Pavlovich. "Alternative Data Primer and 10 Thematic Case Studies for Investors." BofA Global Research, 2020.

Toyoda, T. "Use of the Chow Test under Heteroscedasticity." *Econometrica,* **v. 42**, May 1974, pp. 601–608.

Toyoda, T., and K. Ohtani. "Testing Equality between Sets of Coefficients after a Preliminary Test for Equality of Disturbance Variances in Two Linear Regressions." *Journal of Econometrics,* **v. 31**, February 1986, pp. 67–80.

Train, John. *Money Masters of Our Time.* New York: HarperCollins, 2000.

Treynor, Jack. "Toward a Theory of Market Value of Risky Assets." Unpublished manuscript, 1961.

Tukey, J. W., J. L. Ciminera, and J. F. Heyse. "Testing the Statistical Certainty of a Response to Increasing Doses of a Drug." *Biometrics,* **v. 41**, 1985, pp. 295–301.

Tversky, A., and Daniel Kahneman. "A Heuristic for Judging Frequency and Probability." *Cognitive Psychology,* 1973, pp. 207–232.

Tversky, A., and Daniel Kahneman. "The Framing of Decisions and the Psychology of Choice." *Science New Series,* 1981, pp. 453–458.

Van Loon, R. J. M. "Timing versus Sizing Skill in the Investment Process." *Journal of Portfolio Management,* **v. 44**, 2018, pp. 25–32.

Vanderbei, Robert J. *Linear Programming: Foundations and Extensions.* New York: Springer, 2001.

Veronesi, P. "Stock Market Overreaction to Bad News in Good Times: A Rational Expectations Equilibrium Model." *Review of Financial Studies,* **v. 12**, Winter 1999, pp. 975–1007.

Vijh, A. "S&P 500 Trading Strategies and Stock Betas." *Review of Financial Studies,* **v. 7**, Spring 1994, pp. 215–251.

Volpati, V., M. Benzaquen, Z. Eisler, I. Mastromatteo, B. Toth, and Jean-Philippe Bouchaud. "Zooming in on Equity Factor Crowding." January 2020.

Wachtel, Sidney B. "Certain Observations on Seasonal Movements in Stock Prices." *Journal of Business,* **v. 15**, 1942, pp. 184–193.

Wahal, Sunil. "The Profitability and Investment Premium: Pre-1963 Evidence." *Journal of Financial Economics,* February 2019, pp. 362–367.

Wallace, T. Dudley, and J. Lew Silver. *Econometrics: An Introduction.* Reading MA: Addison-Wesley, 1988.

Wang, K., Y. Li, and J. Erickson. "A New Look at the Monday Effect." *Journal of Finance,* **v. 52**, December 1997, pp. 2171–2187.

Wason, P. C. "On the Failure to Eliminate Hypotheses in a Conceptual Task." *Quarterly Journal of Experimental Psychology,* 1960, pp. 129–140.

Whelan, Tensie, Ulrich Atz, Tracy Van Holt, and Casey Clark. "ESG and Financial Performance: Uncovering the Relationship by Aggregating Evidence from 1,000 Plus Studies Published between 2015– 2020." NYU Stern Center for Sustainable Business Publication, 2020.

White, Gerald I., Ashwinpaul C. Sondhi, and Dov Fried. *The Analysis and Use of Financial Statements.* New York: Wiley, 1997.

Womack, Kent L. "Do Brokerage Analysts' Recommendations Have Investment Value?" *Journal of Finance*, **v. 51**, March 1996, pp. 137–167.

Wurgler, J., and E. Zhuravskaya. "Does Arbitrage Flatten Demand Curves for Stocks?" *Journal of Business*, **v. 75**, October 2002, pp. 583–608.

Yan, Phillip. "The Effects of Short Sales and Leverage Constraints on Market Efficiency." 2014.

Ye, J. "How Variation in Signal Quality Affects Performance." *Financial Analysts Journal*, **v. 64**, July–August 2008, pp. 48–61.

Ye, Jia. "Excess Returns, Stock Splits, and Analyst Earnings Forecasts." *Journal of Portfolio Management*, **v. 25**, Winter 1999, pp. 70–76.

Zellner, Arnold. *An Introduction to Bayesian Inference in Econometrics*. New York: Wiley Interscience, 1996.

Zhong, L., Xiaoya (Sara) Ding, and Nicholas S. P. Tay. "The Impact on Stock Returns of Crowding by Mutual Funds." *Journal of Portfolio Management*, 2017, pp. 87–99.

Zhou, G. "On the Fundamental Law of Active Portfolio Management: What Happens If Our Estimates Are Wrong?" *Journal of Portfolio Management*, 2008a, pp. 26–33.

Zhou, G. "On the Fundamental Law of Active Portfolio Management: How to Make Conditional Investments Unconditionally Optimal." *Journal of Portfolio Management*, 2008b, pp. 12–21.

Ludwig B. Chincarini, CFA, PhD, (San Francisco, CA) is professor of finance in the School of Management at the University of San Francisco and advisor to United States Commodity Fund Investments. As a member of the academic council of Index IQ (bought by NY Life), he was instrumental in creating and developing some of the newest alternative ETFs. Chincarini was on the academic council of Future Advisor, one of the early robo-advisor firms, which was bought by Blackrock in 2015. Chincarini also co-developed the S&P 500 equal-weight ETF (RSP) and index and helped build one of the first basket trading brokerages, Folio Investing (bought by Goldman Sachs), with automated procedures to manage hundreds of quant portfolios. He holds a BA from UC Berkeley and a PhD from MIT.

Daehwan Kim, PhD, (Seoul, South Korea) is a professor in the Department of Economics at Konkuk University, South Korea. Previously, he taught at American University in Bulgaria, Ewha Women's University School of Public Policy, Korea University, Aalto University Executive Program, NUCB Business School in Japan, and Nizhny Novgorod State University in Russia. He worked for FOLIO Investing as a financial economist and for First Private Investment Management in Frankfurt as a senior portfolio manager, and he has advised several hedge funds and investment companies based in East Asia. He holds a BA from Seoul National University and a PhD from Harvard.

INDEX